The Enduring Vision

The
Enduring Vision

A HISTORY OF THE AMERICAN PEOPLE
VOLUME TWO: FROM 1865

Concise Fifth Edition

Paul S. Boyer
University of Wisconsin, Madison

Clifford E. Clark, Jr.
Carleton College

Sandra McNair Hawley
San Jacinto College

Joseph F. Kett
University of Virginia

Neal Salisbury
Smith College

Harvard Sitkoff
University of New Hampshire

Nancy Woloch
Barnard College

Houghton Mifflin Company
Boston   New York

Publisher: Charles Hartford
Senior Sponsoring Editor: Sally Constable
Development Editor: Lisa Kalner Williams
Editorial Assistant: Arianne Vanni
Senior Project Editor: Bob Greiner
Editorial Assistant: Robert Woo
Senior Art and Design Coordinator: Jill Haber
Senior Composition Buyer: Sarah Ambrose
Senior Manufacturing Coordinator: Marie Barnes
Senior Marketing Manager: Sandra McGuire
Marketing Assistant: Molly Parke

Cover: *Spring Turning* by Grant Wood, 1936. Oil on canvas.
Reynolda House Museum of American Art, Winston-Salem, NC/Art © Estate of Grant
Wood/Licensed by VAGA, New York, NY.

Text Credits:

p. 339: Reprinted from John Hope Franklin, *Reconstruction After the Civil War* (Chicago:
University of Chicago Press, 1962), 231, with permission; p. 370: Figure from *The
Economic Transformation of America: 1600 to Present,* Second Edition by Robert L.
Heilbroner and Aaron Singer. Copyright © 1984 by Harcourt Brace & Company.
Reproduced by permission of the publisher.

Printed in the U.S.A.

Library of Congress Catalog Number: 2005921390

Complete volume ISBN: 0-618-47382-3
Volume One ISBN: 0-618-47383-1
Volume Two ISBN: 0-618-47384-X

1 2 3 4 5 6 7 8 9-VH-09 08 07 06 05

Contents

19 Immigration, Urbanization, and Everyday Life, 1860–1900   *388*

20 Politics and Expansion in an Industrializing Age, 1877–1900   *412*

Maps

Charts, Graphs and Tables

Preface

Much has changed in America and the world since we first began *The Enduring Vision* more than a decade ago. Some of these developments have been welcome and positive; others have been troubling and unsettling. In this new Concise Fifth Edition, we fully document the scope of these changes, for good or ill. But we have also taken care to stress the continuities that can provide assurance and inspire hope in troubled times.

For this Fifth Edition, we have reorganized sections of the chapter sequence so the narrative flows more smoothly and assures full coverage of recent events. Two chapters on the late nineteenth-century era, "The Transformation of Urban America" and "Daily Life, Popular Culture, and the Arts, 1860–1900," have been combined into one: Chapter 19, "Immigration, Urbanization, and Everyday Life, 1860–1900." Similarly, the two chapters on the 1930s have been consolidated into Chapter 24, "The Great Depression and the New Deal, 1929–1939." This allows us to convey more directly how the economic crisis and the reform energies of the 1930s played out across American society.

We also decided to shift some material among chapters to promote clarity and coherence. We moved the discussion of early twentieth-century foreign relations, including the Open Door notes to China and the building of the Panama Canal, into Chapter 22, "Global Involvements and World War I, 1902–1920," allowing us to trace America's expanding world role in those crucial years. Similarly, the diplomacy of the 1930s, which as the decade wore on focused heavily on the deepening foreign menace in Europe and Asia, formerly included in the chapter on the Great Depression and the New Deal, is now covered at the beginning of Chapter 25, "Americans and a World in Crisis, 1933–1945," which also deals with World War II.

Having restructured and tightened our treatment of earlier time periods, we were able to add a new concluding chapter. We now devote three full chapters to the eventful contemporary era, from Richard Nixon's resignation in 1974 to the present. The energy crises of the 1970s, the ferment and controversies of the Reagan years, the end of the Cold War, new patterns of immigration, the economic transformation associated with the rise of the service economy and the revolution in information processing, the deadly attack on America in September 2001, and even the war in Iraq in 2004 are now treated in full analytic detail.

New Interpretations, Expanded Coverage

The changes we have made in this latest edition of *The Enduring Vision* extend beyond simply a new chapter arrangement. We have been especially attentive to new work in social and cultural history, building on a strength of the book that instructors have long recognized.

As in earlier editions, our extensive coverage of environmental history, the land, and the West is fully integrated into the narrative, not simply mechanically "tacked on" to a traditional account.

This edition of *The Enduring Vision* pays even closer attention to the crucial role of science, technology, medicine, and disease. In addition, there is additional focus on American's emergence as a world power and the evolution of the nation's global role over time.

Learning And Teaching Ancillaries

The program for *The Enduring Vision*, Concise Fifth Edition includes a number of useful learning and teaching aids. These ancillaries are designed to help students get the most from the course and to provide instructors with useful course management and presentation tools.

The **Houghton Mifflin History Companion** is a collection of resources designed to complement the use of *The Enduring Vision*, Concise Fifth Edition. It is organized according to the chapters in the text and has four parts—the **Instructor Companion website**, the **Instructor Companion CD-ROM**, the **Student Study Companion**, and the **Student Research Companion**. The beginning of each chapter will feature an **hc** icon to remind you of these resources.

The **Instructor Companion website** and **Instructor Companion CD-ROM** features the **Instructor's Resource Manual with Test Items** in addition to hundreds of maps, images, audio and video clips, and PowerPoint® slides for classroom presentation. The Instructor Companion CD-ROM offers the same collection of maps and images with additional audio and video clips for classroom use and a computerized version of the Test Items.

The **Student Study Companion** is a free, online study guide to accompany *The Enduring Vision*. The Study Companion contains a variety of tutorial resources including ACE quizzes with feedback, flashcards, annotated links to history sites, and other interactivities. At the end of each chapter, the **hc** ACE Practice Test icon will refer you to the ACE quizzes on the Student Study Companion.

The **Student Research Companion** is a free, online tool with a wealth of interactive maps and primary sources. Students can use the maps for research, classroom assignments, or review of their geography skills. Primary sources provide a real-world introduction to historical evidence. The sources include headnotes that provide pertinent background information and questions that students can answer and e-mail to their instructors. At key sections of each chapter, **hc** Interactive Map and **hc** Primary Source icons will refer you to related interactive maps and primary sources on the Student Research Companion.

Please contact your local Houghton Mifflin sales representative for more information about the History Companion in addition to our other ancillary materials.

Acknowledgments

Any book, and this one in particular, is the result of the hard work of many people. I would particularly like to acknowledge the contributions of Jan Fitter and Margaret Manos on Volume 2 of *The Enduring Vision*, Concise Fifth Edition. As always, the editorial staff at Houghton Mifflin has been outstanding. Particularly deserving of thanks are Sally Constable; Lisa Kalner Williams; Bob Greiner; Jane W. Sherman; and Sandra McGuire. Warm thanks go as well to my colleagues at San Jacinto College for their support and encouragement; to Jim Heil for his help in all matters digital; and to my daughter Lee Anne for her patience and support. The support of Tina Olivier, Maggie Seaton, Judy Wissing, and Ann Williamson has been invaluable, as are the memories of Kathy Heil and Barbara Rossi. I have also profited from working closely with the authors of the full text—again, many thanks for their patience and help.

As always, we couple our gratitude with the disclaimer that any errors are ours alone.

S.M.H

Former slaves in Jacksonville, Florida

The Crises of Reconstruction, 1865–1877

hc This icon will direct you to additional study and research resources at http://college.hmco.com/history/us/boyer/enduring_concise/5e/students/index.html

"We was all walking on golden clouds," said Felix Heywood, describing the day he and his fellow slaves learned of emancipation. "We all felt like heroes. . . . We was free!" Almost no slaves in Texas had known about emancipation until the arrival of a Union army after the war; to this day, "Juneteenth" (June 19, 1865) is still celebrated by African-Americans in Texas.

Heywood, twenty years old at the war's end, had been owned by a rancher in Bexar County, Texas, not too far from the Alamo, Texas's great symbol of freedom. Many of his friends and relatives moved away when freedom came, he recalled. "Right off colored folks started on the move. They seemed to want to get closer to freedom so they'd know what it was." Heywood and his family stayed in Bexar County, where their former owners gave them ranchland

This chapter focuses on five major questions:

▶ How did Radical Republicans gain control of Reconstruction politics?

▶ What impact did federal Reconstruction policy have on the former Confederacy and ex-Confederates?

▶ In what ways did newly freed slaves reshape their lives after emancipation?

▶ What factors contributed to the end of Reconstruction in the 1870s? Which was most significant?

▶ Was Reconstruction a success or a failure? Why?

and cattle. Ultimately he left ranching and moved to San Antonio, where he worked on the waterworks.

In old age, Heywood looked back to remember the arrival of emancipation. "We know'd freedom was on us, but we didn't know what was to come with it," he recalled. "We thought we was goin' to be richer and better off than the white folks. . . . But it didn't turn out like that. We soon found out that freedom could make folks proud but it didn't make 'em rich."

For the nation, as for Felix Heywood and his fellows, the end of the Civil War was a time of uncharted possibilities—and unresolved conflicts. While former slaves exulted over their freedom, their former owners were often as grim as the ravaged southern landscape. Several thousand fled to Brazil, Mexico, or Europe, but most remained.

After most wars victors care little for the mood of the vanquished, but the Civil War was different. The Union had sought not merely victory but the return of national unity. The federal government faced unprecedented questions. How could the Union be restored and the South reintegrated? Who would control the process—Congress or the

president? Should Confederate leaders be tried for treason? Most important, what would happen to the 3.5 million former slaves? The freedmen's future was *the* crucial postwar issue, for emancipation had set in motion the most profound upheaval in the nation's history. Slavery had been both a labor system and a means of racial control; it had determined the South's social, economic, and political structure. The end of the Civil War, in short, posed two huge challenges that had to be addressed simultaneously: readmitting the Confederate states to the Union and defining the status of free blacks in society.

Between 1865 and 1877, the nation faced major and often divisive challenges and crises. Conflict characterized Congressional debates, the former Confederacy, and the industrializing postwar North. These crises of Reconstruction—the restoration of the former Confederate states and the fate of the former slaves—reshaped the legacy of the Civil War.

RECONSTRUCTION POLITICS, 1865–1868

The end of the Civil War offered multiple possibilities for chaos and vengeance. The federal government could have imprisoned Confederate leaders; former rebel troops could have become guerrillas; freed slaves could have waged a racial war against their former masters. None of this happened. Instead, intense *political* conflict dominated the immediate postwar period. The political upheaval, sometimes attended by violence, produced new constitutional amendments, an impeachment crisis, and some of the most ambitious domestic legislation ever enacted by Congress, the Reconstruction Acts of 1867–1868. It culminated in something that few expected, the enfranchisement of African-American men.

In 1865 only a handful of Radical Republicans advocated African-American suffrage. Any plan to restore the Union, Representative Thaddeus Stevens of Pennsylvania proclaimed, would have to "revolutionize Southern institutions, habits, and manners . . . or all our blood and treasure have been spent in vain." In the complex political battles of Reconstruction, the Radicals won broad support for their program, including African-American male enfranchisement. Just as the Civil War had led to emancipation, so Reconstruction led to African-American suffrage.

Lincoln's Plan

Conflict over Reconstruction began even before the war ended. In December 1863 President Lincoln issued the Proclamation of Amnesty and Reconstruction, which allowed southern states to form new governments if at least 10 percent of those who had voted in the 1860 elections swore an oath of allegiance to the Union and accepted emancipation. This plan excluded most Confederate officials and military officers, who would have had to apply for presidential pardons, as well as African-Americans, who had not voted in 1860. Lincoln hoped both to undermine the Confederacy and to build a southern Republican party.

Radical Republicans in Congress wanted a slower readmission process that would exclude even more ex-Confederates from political life. The Wade-Davis bill, passed by Congress in July 1864, provided that a military government would rule each former Confederate state and that at least one-half of the eligible voters would have to swear allegiance before they could choose a convention to repeal secession and abolish slavery. In addition, to qualify as a voter or a delegate, a southerner would have to take the "ironclad" oath, swearing that he had never voluntarily supported the Confederacy. The Wade-Davis bill would have delayed readmission of southern states almost indefinitely.

Lincoln pocket-vetoed* the Wade-Davis bill, and an impasse followed. Arkansas, Louisiana, Tennessee, and parts of Virginia moved toward readmission under variants of Lincoln's plan, but Congress refused to seat their delegates. Lincoln hinted that he might be moving toward a more rigorous policy than his original one, a program that

---

* Pocket-vetoed: failed to sign the bill within ten days of Congress's adjournment.

would include African-American suffrage. But his death foreclosed the possibility that he and Congress might draw closer to agreement, and Radicals now looked with hope to the new president, Andrew Johnson.

Presidential Reconstruction Under Johnson

At first glance, Andrew Johnson seemed a likely ally for the Radicals. The only southern senator to remain in Congress when his state seceded, Johnson had taken a strong anti-Confederate stance and had served as military governor of Tennessee for two years. Self-educated, an ardent Jacksonian, a foe of the planter class, a supporter of emancipation—Johnson carried impeccable credentials. However, as a lifelong Democrat he had his own political agenda, sharply different from that of the Radicals.

In May 1865, with Congress out of session, Johnson shocked Republicans by announcing his own program, A Proclamation of Amnesty and Reconstruction, to bring the southern states still without Reconstruction governments—Alabama, Florida, Georgia, Mississippi, North Carolina, South Carolina, and Texas—back into the Union. Virtually all southerners who took an oath of allegiance would receive pardon and amnesty, and all their property except slaves would be restored to them. Confederate civil and military officers would still be disqualified, as would well-to-do former Confederates (anyone owning taxable property worth $20,000 or more). By purging the plantation aristocracy, Johnson claimed, he would aid "humble men, the peasantry and yeomen of the South, who have been decoyed . . . into rebellion." Oath takers could elect delegates to state conventions, which would call regular elections, proclaim secession illegal, repudiate debts incurred under the Confederacy, and ratify the Thirteenth Amendment, which abolished slavery.

This presidential Reconstruction took effect in summer 1865, with unforeseen results. Johnson handed out pardons liberally (some 13,000) and dropped his plans for the punishment of treason. By the end of 1865 all seven states had created new

King Andrew

This Thomas Nast cartoon, published just before the 1866 congressional elections, conveyed Republican antipathy to Andrew Johnson. The president is depicted as an autocratic tyrant. Radical Republican Thaddeus Stevens, upper right, has his head on the block and is about to lose it. The Republic sits in chains.

civil governments that in effect restored the *status quo ante bellum*. Confederate officers and large planters resumed state offices, and former Confederate congressmen and generals won election to Congress. Because many of these new representatives were former Whigs who had not supported secession, southerners believed that they genuinely had elected "Union" men. Some states refused to repudiate their Confederate debts or to ratify the Thirteenth Amendment.

Most infuriating to the Radicals, every state passed a "black code" intended to ensure a landless, dependent black labor force—to "secure the services of the negroes, teach them their place," in the words of one Alabamian. These codes, which replaced earlier slave codes, guaranteed the freedmen some basic rights—marriage, ownership of property, the right to testify in court against other blacks—but also restricted freedmen's behavior. Some states established segregation, and most prohibited racial intermarriage, jury service by blacks, and court testimony by blacks against whites. Most harmful, black codes included economic restrictions to prevent blacks from leaving the plantation, usually through labor contracts that stipulated anyone who had not signed a labor contract was a vagrant and subject to arrest.

hc Primary Source: Louisiana Black Code

These codes left freedmen no longer slaves but not really liberated. Although many of their provisions never actually took effect—for example, the Union army and the Freedmen's Bureau suspended the enforcement of the racially discriminatory laws—the black codes reflected white southern attitudes and showed what "home rule" would have been like without federal intervention.

To many northerners, both the black codes and the election of former Confederates to high office reeked of southern defiance. "What can be hatched from such an egg but another rebellion?" asked a Boston newspaper. When the Thirty-ninth Congress convened in December 1865, it refused to seat the southern delegates and prepared to dismantle the black codes and to lock ex-Confederates out of power.

Congress Versus Johnson

Southern blacks' status became the major issue in Congress. With Congress split into four blocs—Democrats, and radical, moderate, and conservative Republicans—a politically adroit president could have protected his program. Ineptly, Johnson alienated the moderates and pushed them into the Radicals' arms by vetoing some key moderate measures.

In late 1865 Congress voted to extend the life of the Freedmen's Bureau for three more years. Staffed mainly by army officers, the bureau provided relief, rations, and medical care; built schools for former slaves; put them to work on abandoned or confiscated lands; and tried to protect their rights as laborers. To strengthen the bureau, Congress had voted to allow it to run special military courts that would settle labor disputes and invalidate labor contracts forced on African-Americans under the black codes. In February 1866 Johnson vetoed the bill; the Constitution, he declared, neither sanctioned military trials of civilians in peacetime nor supported a system to care for "indigent persons." Then in March 1866 Congress passed the Civil Rights Act of 1866, which made African-Americans U.S. citizens with the same civil rights as other citizens and authorized federal intervention to ensure African-Americans' rights in court. Johnson vetoed this measure also, arguing that it would "operate in favor of the colored and against the white race." In April Congress overrode his veto, and in July it enacted the Supplementary Freedmen's Bureau Act over another presidential veto.

These vetoes puzzled many Republicans, for the new laws did not undercut the basic structure of presidential Reconstruction. Although the vetoes gained support for Johnson among northern Democrats, they cost him dearly among moderate Republicans, who began to ally with the Radicals. Was Johnson a political incompetent, or was he merely trying, unsuccessfully, to forge a centrist coalition? Whatever the case, he drove moderate and Radical Republicans together toward their next step: the passage of a constitutional amendment to protect the new Civil Rights Act.

The Fourteenth Amendment, 1866

In April 1866 Congress adopted the Fourteenth Amendment, its most ambitious attempt to deal with the problems of Reconstruction and the freed slaves. In the first clause, the amendment proclaimed that all persons born or naturalized in the United States were citizens and that no state could abridge their rights without due process of law or deny them equal protection under the law. Second, the amendment guaranteed that if a state denied suffrage to any male citizen, its representation in Congress would be proportionally reduced. Third, the amendment disqualified from state and national offices *all* prewar officeholders who had supported the Confederacy. Finally, it repudiated the Confederate debt and maintained the validity of the federal debt. In effect, the Fourteenth Amendment nullified the *Dred Scott* decision, threatened southern states that deprived African-American men of the right to vote, and invalidated most of the pardons that President Johnson had ladled out. Beyond demonstrating widespread receptivity to the Radicals' demands, including African-American male suffrage, the Fourteenth Amendment represented the first national effort to limit the states' control of civil and political rights.

Passage of the amendment created a firestorm. Abolitionists said that it did not go far enough to protect African-American voting rights, southerners blasted it as vengeful, and President Johnson denounced it. The president's unwillingness to compromise solidified the new alliance between moderate and Radical Republicans and transformed the congressional elections of 1866 into a referendum on the Fourteenth Amendment.

Over the summer Johnson set off on a whistle-stop train tour compaigning against the amendment. Humorless and defensive, the president made fresh enemies, however, and doomed his hope of creating a new political party, the National Union party, opposed to the amendment. Meanwhile, the moderate and Radical Republicans defended the amendment, condemned President Johnson, and branded the Democratic party "a common sewer . . . into which is emptied every element of treason, North and South."

Republicans carried the congressional elections of 1866 in a landslide, winning nearly two-thirds of the House and three-fourths of the Senate. They had secured a mandate for the Fourteenth Amendment and their own Reconstruction program.

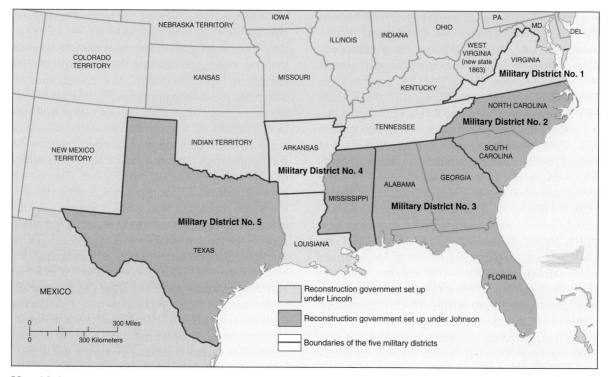

MAP 16.1
The Reconstruction of the South
The Reconstruction Act of 1867 divided the former Confederate states, except Tennessee, into five military districts and set forth the steps by which new state governments could be created. **ℎ𝑐** Interactive Map: The Reconstruction

Congressional Reconstruction, 1866–1867

The congressional debate over reconstructing the South began in December 1866 and lasted three months. Radical leaders, anxious to stifle a resurgence of Confederate power, called for African-American suffrage, federal support for public schools, confiscation of Confederate estates, and extended military occupation of the South. Moderate Republicans accepted part of this plan. The lawmakers debated every ramification of various legislative proposals, and in February 1867, after complex political maneuvers, Congress passed the Reconstruction Act of 1867. Johnson vetoed it, and on March 2 Congress passed the law over his veto. Three more Reconstruction acts, passed in 1867

and 1868 over presidential vetoes, refined and enforced the first act.

The Reconstruction Act of 1867 invalidated the state governments formed under the Lincoln and Johnson plans; only Tennessee, which had already ratified the Fourteenth Amendment and had been readmitted to the Union, escaped further Reconstruction. The new law divided the other ten former Confederate states into five military districts. It provided that voters—all black men, plus whites not disqualified by the Fourteenth Amendment— could elect delegates who would write a new state constitution granting African-American suffrage. After congressional approval of the state constitution, and after the state legislature's ratification of the Fourteenth Amendment, Congress would readmit the state into the Union. The enfranchisement of African-Americans and disfranchisement of so many ex-Confederates made the Reconstruction Act of 1867 far more radical than Johnson's program. Even then, however, it provided only temporary military rule, made no provisions to prosecute Confederate leaders for treason, and neither confiscated nor redistributed property.

Radical Republican leader Thaddeus Stevens had proposed confiscation of large Confederate estates to "humble the proud traitors" and to provide land for the former slaves. He hoped to create a new class of self-sufficient African-American yeomen farmers. Because political independence rested on economic independence, he contended, land grants would be far more valuable to African-Americans than the vote. But moderate Republicans and others backed away from Stevens's proposal. Tampering with property rights in the South might well jeopardize them in the North, they argued, and could endanger the entire Reconstruction program. Thus Congress rejected the most radical parts of the Radical Republican program.

Congressional Reconstruction took effect in spring 1867, but Johnson impeded its implementation by replacing pro-Radical military officers with conservative ones since Reconstruction could not be enforced without military power. Furious and more suspicious than ever of the president, congressional moderates and Radicals again joined forces to block Johnson from further hampering Reconstruction.

The Impeachment Crisis, 1867–1868

In March 1867, responding to Johnson's obstructionist tactics, Republicans in Congress passed two laws to restrict presidential power. The Tenure of Office Act prohibited the president from removing civil officers without Senate consent. Its purpose was to protect Secretary of War Edwin Stanton, a Radical ally needed to enforce the Reconstruction acts. The other law banned the president from issuing military orders except through the commanding general, Ulysses S. Grant, who could not be removed without the Senate's consent. Not sat-

isfied with clipping the president's wings, Radicals also began to look for grounds for impeachment and conviction to remove all possible obstacles to Reconstruction. Intense investigations by the House Judiciary Committee and private detectives turned up no impeachable offenses, but Johnson himself soon provided the charges that his opponents needed.

In August 1867 Johnson suspended Stanton and in February 1868 tried to remove him. The president's defiance of the Tenure of Office Act drove moderate Republicans back into alliance with the Radicals. The House approved eleven charges of impeachment, nine of them based on violation of the Tenure of Office Act and the other two accusing Johnson of being "unmindful of the high duties of the office," of seeking to disgrace Congress, and of not enforcing the Reconstruction acts.

Johnson's trial by the Senate, which began in March 1868, riveted public attention for eleven weeks. Seven congressmen, including leading Radicals, served as prosecutors, or "managers." Johnson's lawyers maintained that he was merely seeking a court test of the Tenure of Office Act, a law that he believed unconstitutional, by violating it. They also contended that the law did not protect Stanton because Lincoln, not Johnson, had appointed him. And they asserted that Johnson was guilty of no crime indictable in a regular court.

The congressional "managers" countered that impeachment was a political process, not a criminal trial, and that Johnson's "abuse of discretionary power" constituted an impeachable offense. Some Senate Republicans wavered, fearful that the removal of a president would destroy the balance of power within the federal government. They also were reluctant to see Benjamin Wade, a Radical Republican who was president pro tempore of the Senate, become president, as the Constitution then provided.

Intense pressure weighed on the wavering Republican senators. Ultimately, seven Republicans risked political suicide by voting with the Democrats against removal, and the Senate failed by one vote to convict Johnson. In so doing, the legislators set two critical precedents: in the future, no president would be impeached on political grounds, nor would he be impeached because two-thirds of Congress disagreed with him. In the short term, nonetheless, the anti-Johnson forces achieved their goals, for Andrew Johnson had no future as president. Republicans in Congress could now pursue their last major Reconstruction objective: guaranteeing African-American male suffrage.

The Fifteenth Amendment and the Question of Woman Suffrage, 1869–1870

African-American suffrage was the linchpin of congressional Reconstruction. Only with the support of African-American voters could Republicans secure control of the southern states. The Reconstruction Act of 1867 had forced southern states to enfranchise black men in order to reenter the Union, but most northern states still refused to grant suffrage to African-Americans. The Fifteenth Amendment, drawn up by Republicans and ap-

proved by Congress in 1869, aimed both to protect black suffrage in the South and to extend it to the northern and border states, on the assumption that newly enfranchised African-Americans would gratefully vote Republican. The amendment prohibited the denial of suffrage by the states to anyone on account of race, color, or previous condition of servitude.

Democrats opposed the amendment on the grounds that it violated states' rights, but they did not control enough states to prevent its ratification. However, to some southerners, the amendment's omissions made it acceptable; as a Richmond newspaper pointed out, it had "loopholes through which a coach and four horses can be driven." Indeed, the new amendment did not guarantee African-American officeholding, nor did it prohibit restrictions on suffrage such as property requirements and literacy tests, both of which might be used to deny African-Americans the vote.

The debate over black suffrage drew new participants into the fray. Women's rights advocates had tried to promote both black suffrage and

The Reconstruction Amendments

Amendment and Date of Congressional Passage	Provisions	Ratification
Thirteenth (January 1865)	Prohibited slavery in the United States.	December 1865
Fourteenth (June 1866)	Defined citizenship to include all persons born or naturalized in the United States.	July 1868, after Congress made ratification a prerequisite for readmission of ex-Confederate states to the Union.
	Provided proportional loss of congressional representation for any state that denied suffrage to any of its male citizens.	
	Disqualified prewar officeholders who supported the Confederacy from state or national office.	
	Repudiated the Confederate debt.	
Fifteenth (February 1869)	Prohibited the denial of suffrage because of race, color, or previous condition of servitude.	March 1870; ratification required of Virginia, Texas, Mississippi, and Georgia for readmission to the Union.

woman suffrage, but Radical Republicans rejected any linkage between the two, preferring to concentrate on black suffrage. Supporters of women's rights were themselves divided. Frederick Douglass argued that black suffrage had to receive priority. "If the elective franchise is not extended to the Negro, he is dead," explained Douglass. "Woman has a thousand ways by which she can attach herself to the ruling power of the land that we have not." Women's rights leaders Elizabeth Cady Stanton and Susan B. Anthony disagreed. If the Fifteenth Amendment did not include women, they emphasized, it would establish an "aristocracy of sex" and increase the disabilities under which women already labored. The argument fractured the old abolition–women's rights coalition and would lead to the development of an independent women's rights movement.

The battle over black suffrage and the Fifteenth Amendment split women's rights advocates into two rival suffrage associations, both founded in 1869. The Boston-based American Woman Suffrage Association sought state-by-state suffrage, while the more radical National Woman Suffrage Association, based in New York and led by Stanton and Anthony, promoted a constitutional amendment for woman suffrage.

Throughout the 1870s the two groups competed for support. Two western states, Wyoming and Utah, extended the vote to women, but the suffrage movement had little to do with it. In 1872 Susan B. Anthony mobilized about seventy women to vote nationwide; she was indicted, convicted, and fined. One of the would-be voters, Virginia Minor, brought suit with her husband against the registrar who had refused to allow her to vote. In *Minor v. Happersett* (1875), the Supreme Court ruled that a state could deny women the right to vote. Woman suffrage advocates braced for a long struggle.

By the time the Fifteenth Amendment was ratified in 1870, Congress could look back on five years of momentous achievement. Three constitutional amendments had broadened the scope of democracy by abolishing slavery, affirming the rights of citizens, and prohibiting the denial of suffrage on the basis of race. Congress had readmitted the former Confederate states into the Union. At the same time, momentum had slowed at the federal level. In 1869 the center of action shifted to the South, where tumultuous change was under way.

RECONSTRUCTION GOVERNMENTS

During the years of presidential Reconstruction, 1865–1867, the southern states faced formidable tasks: creating new governments, reviving war-torn economies, and dealing with the impact of emancipation. Racial tensions flared as freedmen organized political meetings to protest ill treatment and demand equal rights, and deadly race riots erupted in major southern cities. In May 1866 white crowds attacked African-American veterans in Memphis and rampaged through African-American neighborhoods, killing forty-six people. Two months later in New Orleans, whites assaulted black delegates on their way to a political meeting and left forty people dead.

Congressional Reconstruction, supervised by federal troops, began in spring 1867 with the dismantling of existing governments and the formation of new state governments dominated by Republicans. By 1868 most former Confederate states had rejoined the Union, and within two years the process was complete.

But Republican rule did not long endure in the South. Opposition from southern Democrats, the landowning elite, vigilantes, and most white voters proved insurmountable. Nevertheless, these Reconstruction governments were unique because African-American men, including former slaves, participated in them. Slavery had ended in other societies, too, but only in the United States had freedmen gained democratic political rights.

A New Electorate

The Reconstruction laws of 1867–1868 transformed the southern electorate by temporarily disfranchising 15 percent of potential white voters and by enfranchising more than 700,000 freed slaves. Black voters outnumbered whites by

100,000 overall and held voting majorities in five states.

This new electorate provided a base for the Republican party, which had never existed in the South. To scornful Democrats, the Republicans comprised three types of scoundrels: northern "carpetbaggers" who had come south for wealth and power; southern scalawags, poor and ignorant, looking to profit from Republican rule; and hordes of uneducated freedmen, easily manipulated. In fact, the hastily assembled Republican party, crossing racial and class lines, constituted a loose coalition of diverse factions with often contradictory goals.

To northerners who moved south after the war, the former Confederacy was an undeveloped region, ripe with possibilities. The carpetbaggers included many former Union soldiers who hoped to buy land, open factories, build railroads, or simply enjoy the warmer climate. Holding almost one in three state offices, they wielded disproportionate political power.

A handful of scalawags (white southerners who supported the Republicans) were old Whigs, but most were small farmers from the mountain regions of North Carolina, Georgia, Alabama, and Arkansas. Former Unionists who had owned no slaves and who felt no loyalty to the old plantation elite, they wanted to improve their economic position and cared little one way or the other about black suffrage. Scalawags held the most political offices during Reconstruction but proved the least stable element of the Republican coalition. Many drifted back into the Democratic fold.

Freedmen, the backbone of southern Republicanism, provided eight out of ten Republican votes. They sought land, education, civil rights, and political equality and remained loyal Republicans. "We know our friends," an elderly freedman said. Although Reconstruction governments depended on African-American votes, freedmen held at most one in five political offices and constituted a legislative majority only in South Carolina, whose population was more than 60 percent black. No African-Americans won the office of governor, and only two served in the U.S. Senate. A mere 6 percent of south-

ern members of the House were African-American, and almost 50 percent came from South Carolina.

A significant status gap divided high-level African-American officials from African-American voters. Most freedmen cared mainly about their economic future, especially about acquiring land, whereas African-American officeholders concerned themselves far more with attaining equal rights. Still, both groups shared high expectations and prized enfranchisement.

Republican Rule

Large numbers of African-Americans participated in government for the first time in the state constitutional conventions of 1867–1868. The South Carolina convention had an African-American majority, and in Louisiana one-half the delegates were freedmen. In general, these conventions instituted democratic changes such as universal manhood suffrage and public-school systems but failed to provide either integrated schools or land reform. Wherever proposed, plans for the confiscation and redistribution of land failed.

Once civil power shifted to the new state governments, Republican administrations began ambitious public-works programs. They built roads and bridges, promoted railroad development, and funded institutions to care for orphans, the insane, and the disabled. Republican regimes also expanded state government and formed state militia in which African-Americans often were heavily represented. Finally, they created public-school systems, almost nonexistent in the antebellum South.

These reforms cost millions, and state debts and taxes skyrocketed. During the 1860s taxes rose 400 percent. Although northern tax rates still exceeded southern tax rates, southerners, particularly landowners, resented the new levies. In their view, Reconstruction strained the pocketbooks of the properties in order to finance the vast expenditures of Republican legislatures, the "no property herd."

Opponents of Reconstruction viewed Republican rule as wasteful and corrupt, the "most stupendous system of organized robbery in history." Indeed, corruption did permeate some state governments, as in Louisiana and South Carolina. The main profiteers were government officials who accepted bribes and railroad promoters who doled them out. But neither group was exclusively Republican. In fact, corruption increasingly characterized government *nationally* in these years and was both more flagrant and more lucrative in the North. But such a comparison did little to quiet the critics of Republican rule.

Counterattacks

For ex-Confederates, African-American enfranchisement and the "horror of Negro domination" created nightmares. As soon as congressional Reconstruction began, it fell under attack. Democratic newspapers assailed delegates to the North Carolina constitutional convention as an "Ethiopian minstrelsy . . . baboons, monkeys, mules . . . and other jackasses." They demeaned Louisiana's constitution as "the work of ignorant Negroes cooperating with a gang of white adventurers."

But Democrats delayed any political mobilization until the readmission of the southern states was completed. Then they swung into action, often calling themselves Conservatives to attract former Whigs. At first, they pursued African-American votes, but when that initiative failed, they switched tactics. In every southern state the Democrats contested elections, backed dissident Republican factions, elected some Democratic legislators, and lured scalawags away from the Republican party.

Vigilante efforts to reduce black votes bolstered Democratic campaigns to win white ones. Antagonism toward free blacks, long present in southern life, grew increasingly violent. As early as 1865 Freedmen's Bureau agents itemized a variety of outrages against blacks, including shooting, murder, rape, arson, and "severe and inhuman beating." White vigilante groups sprang up in all parts of the former Confederacy, but one organization became dominant. In spring 1866 six young Confederate war veterans in Tennessee formed a social club, the Ku Klux Klan, distinguished by elaborate rituals, hooded costumes, and secret passwords. New Klan dens spread rapidly. By the election of

The Ku Klux Klan
The menacing disguise characterized the Ku Klux Klan's campaign of intimidation during Reconstruction. The Klan strove to end Republican rule, restore white supremacy, and obliterate, in a southern editor's words, "the preposterous and wicked dogma of negro equality."

1868, when African-American suffrage had become a reality, the Klan had become a terrorist movement directed against potential African-American voters.

The Klan sought to suppress black voting, to reestablish white supremacy, and to topple the Reconstruction governments. It targeted Union League officers, Freedmen's Bureau officials, white Republicans, black militia units, economically successful blacks, and African-American voters. Some Democrats denounced Klan members as "cutthroats and riff-raff," but some prominent Confederate leaders, including General Nathan Bedford Forrest, were active Klansmen. Vigilantism united southern whites of different social classes and drew on the energy of many Confederate veterans.

Republican legislatures tried to outlaw vigilantism, but when state militia could not enforce the laws, state officials turned to the federal government for help. In response, between May 1870 and February 1871 Congress passed three Enforcement Acts, each progressively more stringent. The First Enforcement Act protected African-American voters. The Second Enforcement Act provided for federal supervision of southern elections, and the Third Enforcement Act (also known as the Ku Klux Klan Act) authorized the use of federal troops and the suspension of habeas corpus. Although thousands were arrested under the Enforcement Acts, most terrorists escaped conviction.

By 1872 the federal government had effectively suppressed the Klan, but vigilantism had served its purpose. A large military presence in the South could have protected black rights, but instead troop levels fell steadily. Congress allowed the Freedmen's Bureau to die in 1869, and the Enforcement Acts became dead letters. White southerners, a Georgia politician explained in 1871, could not discard "a feeling of bitterness, a feeling that the Negro is a sort of instinctual enemy of ours." The battle over Reconstruction was in essence a battle over the implications of emancipation, and it had begun as soon as the war had ended.

THE IMPACT OF EMANCIPATION

"The master he says we are all free," a South Carolina slave declared in 1865. "But it don't mean we is white. And it don't mean we is equal." Yet despite the daunting handicaps they faced—illiteracy, lack of property, lack of skills—most former slaves found the exhilaration of freedom overwhelming. Emancipation had given them the right to their own labor and a sense of autonomy, and during Reconstruction they asserted their independence by casting off white control and shedding the vestiges of slavery.

Confronting Freedom

For the ex-slaves, mobility was often liberty's first fruit. Some left the slave quarters; others fled the plantation completely. "I have never in my life met with such ingratitude," a South Carolina mistress exclaimed when a former slave ran off.

Emancipation stirred waves of migration within the former Confederacy. Some slaves headed to the Deep South, where desperate planters would pay higher wages for labor, but more moved to towns and cities. Urban African-American populations doubled and tripled after emancipation. The desire to find lost family members drove some migrations. "They had a passion, not so much for wandering as for getting together," explained a Freedmen's Bureau official. Parents sought children who had been sold; husbands and wives who had been separated reunited; and families reclaimed children who were being raised in masters' homes. The Freedmen's Bureau helped former slaves to get information about missing relatives and to travel to find them, and bureau agents also tried to resolve entanglements over the multiple alliances of spouses who had been separated under slavery.

Not all efforts at reunion succeeded. Some fugitive slaves had died during the war or were untraceable. Other ex-slaves had formed new partnerships and could not revive old ones. But the success stories were poignant. "I's hunted an' hunted till I track you up here," one freedman told the wife whom he found twenty years after their separation by sale.

Once reunited, freed blacks quickly legalized unions formed under slavery, sometimes in mass ceremonies of up to seventy couples. Legal marriage had a tangible impact on family life. In 1870 eight out of ten African-American families in the cotton-producing South were two-parent families, about the same proportion as white families. Men asserted themselves as household heads, and their wives and children often withdrew from the work force. Thus severe labor shortages followed immediately after the war because women had made up half of all field workers. However, by Reconstruction's end, many African-American women had rejoined the work force out of economic necessity, either in the fields or as cooks, laundresses, and domestic servants.

Black Institutions

The freed blacks' desire for independence also led to the growth of African-American churches. The African Methodist Episcopal Church, founded by Philadelphia blacks in the 1790s, gained thousands of new southern members. Negro Baptist churches, their roots often in plantation "praise meetings" organized by slaves, sprouted everywhere.

The influence of African-American churches extended far beyond religion. They provided relief, raised funds for schools, and supported Republican policies. African-American ministers assumed leading political roles. Even after southern Democrats excluded most freedmen from political life at Reconstruction's end, ministers remained the main pillars of authority within African-American communities.

Schools, too, played a crucial role for freedmen as the ex-slaves sought literacy for themselves and above all for their children. At emancipation, African-Americans organized their own schools, which the Freedmen's Bureau soon supervised. Northern philanthropic organizations paid the wages of instructors, half of whom were women. In 1869 the bureau reported more than 4,000 African-American schools in the former Confederacy.

The Freedmen's School
Supported by the Freedmen's Bureau, northern freedmen's aid societies, and African-American denominations, freedmen's schools reached about 12 percent of school-age African-American children in the South by 1870. Here, a northern teacher poses with her students at a school in rural North Carolina.

Within three more years each southern state had a public-school system, at least in principle, generally with separate schools for blacks and whites. The Freedmen's Bureau and others also helped to establish Howard, Atlanta, and Fisk Universities in 1866–1867 and Hampton Institute in 1868. Nonetheless, African-American education remained limited. Few rural blacks could reach the schools, and those who tried were sometimes the targets of vigilante attacks. Thus by the end of Reconstruction, more than 80 percent of the African-American population remained illiterate, although literacy was rising among children.

Not only school segregation but also other forms of racial separation were taken for granted. Whether by law or by custom, segregation continued on streetcars and trains as well as in churches, theaters, and restaurants. In 1875 Congress passed the Civil Rights Act, banning segregation except in schools, but in the 1883 *Civil Rights Cases*, the Supreme Court threw the law out. The Fourteenth Amendment did not prohibit discrimination by individuals, the Court ruled, only that perpetrated by the state.

White southerners adamantly rejected the prospect of racial integration, which they insisted would lead to racial amalgamation. "If we have social equality, we shall have intermarriage," contended one white southerner, "and if we have intermarriage, we shall degenerate." Urban blacks occasionally protested segregation, but most freed blacks were less interested in "social equality" than in African-American liberty and community. Moreover, the new black elite—teachers, ministers, and politicians—served African-American constituencies and thus had a vested interest in separate black institutions. Too, rural blacks had little desire to mix with whites; rather, they sought freedom from white control. Above all, they wanted to secure personal independence by acquiring land.

Land, Labor, and Sharecropping

"The sole ambition of the freedman," a New Englander wrote from South Carolina in 1865, "appears to be to become the owner of a little piece of land, there to erect a humble home, and to dwell in peace and security, at his own free will and pleasure." Indeed, to free blacks everywhere, "forty acres and a mule" promised emancipation from plantation labor, white domination, and cotton, the "slave crop." Landownership signified economic independence. "We want to be placed on land until we are able to buy it and make it our own," an African-American minister told General Sherman in Georgia during the war.

But the freedmen's visions of landownership failed to materialize, for large-scale land reform never occurred. A few slaves did obtain land, either through the pooling of resources or through the Southern Homestead Act. In 1866 Congress passed this law, setting aside 44 million acres of land in five southern states for freedmen; but the land was poor, and few slaves had resources to survive until their first harvest. About 4,000 blacks claimed homesteads, though few could establish farms. By the end of Reconstruction, only a fraction of former slaves owned working farms. Without large-scale land reform, barriers to African-American landownership remained overwhelming.

Three obstacles impeded African-American landownership. Freedmen lacked capital to buy land or tools. Furthermore, white southerners generally opposed selling land to blacks. Most important, planters sought to preserve a cheap labor force and forged laws to ensure that black labor would remain available on the plantations.

The black codes written during presidential Reconstruction were designed to preserve a captive labor force. Under labor contracts in effect in 1865–1866, freedmen received wages, housing, food, and clothing in exchange for field work. But cash was scarce, and wages often became a small share of the crop, typically one-eighth or less, to be divided among the entire work force. Freedmen's Bureau agents encouraged African-Americans to sign the contracts, seeing wage labor as a step toward economic independence. "You must begin at the bottom of the ladder and climb up," bureau head O. O. Howard told the freedmen.

Problems arose immediately. Freedmen disliked the new wage system, especially the use of gang labor, which resembled the work pattern under

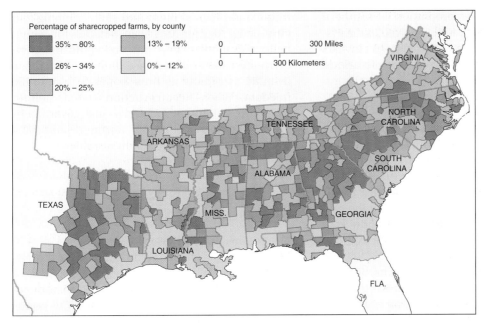

MAP 16.2
Southern Sharecropping, 1880
The depressed economy of the late 1870s caused poverty and debt, increased tenancy among white farmers, and forced many renters, black and white, into sharecropping. By 1880 the sharecropping system pervaded most southern counties, with highest concentrations in the Cotton Belt from South Carolina to eastern Texas. *Source:* U.S. Census Office, Tenth Census, 1880, Report of the Production of Agriculture (Washington, D.C.: Government Printing Office, 1883), Table 5.

slavery. Moreover, postwar planters had to compete for labor even as many scorned African-American workers as lazy or inefficient. One landowner estimated that workers accomplished only "two-fifths of what they did under the old system." As productivity fell, so did land values. Plummeting cotton prices and poor harvests in 1866 and 1867 combined with these other factors to create an impasse: landowners lacked labor, and freedmen lacked land.

Southerners began experimenting with new labor schemes, including the division of plantations into small tenancies. Sharecropping was the most widespread arrangement. Under this system, landowners subdivided large plantations into farms of thirty to fifty acres and rented them to freedmen under annual leases for a share of the crop, usually one-half. Freedmen liked this decentralized system, which let them use the labor of

family members and represented a step toward independence. A half share of the crop far exceeded the fraction that they had received under the black codes. Planters benefited, too, for the leases gave them leverage over their tenants and tenants shared the risk of poor harvests with them. Most important, planters retained control of their land. The most productive land thus remained in the hands of a small group of owners; in effect sharecropping helped to preserve the planter elite.

Although the wage system continued on sugar and rice plantations, by 1870 the plantation tradition had yielded to sharecropping in the cotton South. A severe depression in 1873 drove many blacks and independent white farmers into sharecropping. By 1880 sharecroppers, white and black, farmed 80 percent of the land in cotton-producing states. In fact, white sharecroppers outnumbered black, although a higher proportion of southern blacks, almost 75 percent, were involved in the system. Changes in marketing and finance, meanwhile, made the sharecroppers' lot increasingly precarious.

Toward a Crop-Lien Economy

Before the Civil War planters had depended on factors, or middlemen, who sold them supplies, extended credit, and marketed their crops through urban merchants. Because the high value of slave property had backed these long-distance credit arrangements, this system collapsed with the end of slavery. The postwar South, with its hundreds of thousands of tenant farmers and sharecroppers, needed a local credit system.

Into this gap stepped rural merchants, who advanced supplies to tenants and sharecroppers on credit and sold their crops to wholesalers. Because renters had no property to serve as collateral, merchants secured their loans with a lien, or claim, on each farmer's next crop. Exorbitant interest rates, 50 percent or more, quickly forced many tenants and sharecroppers into a cycle of indebtedness. The sharecropper might well owe part of his crop to the landowner and another part (the rest of his crop, or more) to the merchant. Illiterate tenants who could not keep track of their financial arrangements were at the mercy of sometimes unscrupulous merchants. "A man that didn't know how to count would always lose," an Arkansas freedman explained. Once a tenant's real or alleged debts exceeded the value of his crop, he was tied to the land, to cotton, and to sharecropping.

By the end of Reconstruction, sharecropping and crop liens had bound the South to easily marketable cash crops such as cotton and prevented crop diversification. Soil depletion, land erosion, and outmoded equipment stranded capital-short planters in a cycle of poverty. Postwar changes in southern agriculture left the region with bleak economic prospects.

Trapped in perpetual debt, tenant farmers became the chief victims of the new agricultural order. Cotton remained the only survival route open to poor farmers, regardless of race, but low income

from cotton locked them into sharecropping and crop liens. African-American tenants, for whom neither landownership nor economic independence ever materialized, saw their political rights dwindle as rapidly as their hopes for economic freedom. When Reconstruction ended, neither state governments nor the national government offered them protection, for northern politicians were preoccupied with their own problems.

NEW CONCERNS IN THE NORTH, 1868–1876

The nomination of Ulysses S. Grant for president in 1868 launched a chaotic era in national politics. His eight years in office featured political scandals, a party revolt, a massive depression, and a steady retreat from Reconstruction. By the mid-1870s northern voters cared more about economics, unemployment, labor unrest, and currency problems than the "southern question." Eager to end sectional conflict, Republicans turned their backs on the freedmen.

Grantism

Republicans had good reason to nominate General Grant. A war hero, he was endorsed by veterans, admired throughout the North, and unscathed by the bitter feuds of Reconstruction politics. To oppose Grant, the Democrats nominated Horatio Seymour, arch-critic of the Lincoln administration and an opponent of Reconstruction and greenbacks. Grant ran on his personal popularity more than on issues. Although he carried all but eight states, the popular vote was close; newly enfranchised freedmen provided Grant's margin in the South. When he was inaugurated, Grant pledged to execute all the laws, whether he agreed with them or not, to support sound money, and to follow a humane policy toward the Indians.

Grant's presidential leadership proved as weak as his war leadership had been strong. He had little political skill; his cabinet appointments were at best mediocre, and a string of scandals plagued his administration. In 1869 financier Jay Gould and his partner Jim Fisk attempted to corner the gold market with the help of Grant's brother-in-law. When gold prices tumbled, investors were ruined, and Grant's reputation was tarnished. Near the end of Grant's first term, his vice president, Schuyler Colfax, got caught up in the Crédit Mobilier scandal, an elaborate scheme to skim off the profits of the Union Pacific Railroad. Then in 1875 Grant's personal secretary, Orville Babcock, was found guilty of accepting bribes from the "whiskey ring," distillers who preferred bribery to payment of federal taxes. And in 1876 voters learned that Grant's secretary of war, William E. Belknap, had taken bribes to sell lucrative Indian trading posts in Oklahoma.

Although Grant was not personally involved in the scandals, he did little to restrain such activities, and "Grantism" came to stand for fraud, bribery, and corruption in office. Such evils, however, spread far beyond Washington. The New York City press in 1872 revealed that Democrat boss William M. Tweed led a ring that had looted the city treasury and collected some $200 million in kickbacks and bribes. When Mark Twain and coauthor Charles Dudley Warner published their scathing satire The Gilded Age (1873), readers recognized the novel's speculators, self-promoters, and maniacal opportunists as familiar types in public life.

Grant did enjoy some foreign policy successes. In 1872 his administration engineered the settlement of the Alabama claims with England: an international tribunal ordered Britain to pay $15.5 million to the United States in compensation for damage inflicted by Confederate-owned but British-built raiders. But the administration went astray when it tried to add nonadjacent territory to the Union. In 1867 the Johnson administration had purchased Alaska from Russia at the bargain price of $7.2 million. The purchase had rekindled expansionists' hope, and in 1870 Grant decided to annex the Caribbean island nation of Santo Domingo (the modern Dominican Republic). The president believed that annexation would promote Caribbean trade and provide a haven for persecuted southern blacks. Despite speculators' hopes for windfall profits, the Senate rejected the annexation treaty and further diminished Grant's reputation.

As the election of 1872 approached, dissident Republicans feared that "Grantism" would ruin the party. Former Radicals and other Republicans left out of Grant's "Great Barbecue" formed their own party, the Liberal Republicans.

The Liberals' Revolt

The Liberal Republican revolt split the Republican party and undermined Reconstruction. Liberals demanded civil service reform to bring the "best men" into government. In the South they demanded an end to "bayonet rule" and argued that African-Americans, now enfranchised, could fend for themselves. Corruption in government posed a greater threat than Confederate resurgence, the Liberals claimed, and they demanded that the "best men" in the South, ex-Confederates barred from holding office, be returned to government.

New York Tribune editor Horace Greeley, inconsistently supporting both a stringent Reconstruction policy and leniency toward the ex-Confederates, received the Liberal Republican nomination, and the Democrats endorsed Greeley as well. Republican reformers found themselves allied with the party that they had recently castigated as a "sewer" of treasonable sentiments.

Despite Greeley's arduous campaigning (he literally worked himself to death on the campaign trail and died a few weeks after the election), Grant carried 56 percent of the popular vote and won the electoral vote handily. But his victory had come at a high price: to nullify the Liberals' issues, "regular" Republicans passed an amnesty act allowing all but a few hundred ex-Confederates to resume office. And during Grant's second term Republicans' desire to discard the "southern question" grew as a depression gripped the nation.

The Panic of 1873

The postwar years brought accelerated industrialization, rapid economic expansion, and frantic speculation as investors rushed to take advantage of seemingly unlimited opportunities. Railroads led the speculative boom. The transcontinental line reached completion in 1869 (see Chapter 17), and by 1873 almost 400 railroads crisscrossed the Northeast. But in addition to transforming the northern economy, the railroad boom led entrepreneurs to overspeculate, with drastic results.

In 1869 Philadelphia banker Jay Cooke took over a new transcontinental line, the Northern Pacific. For four years Northern Pacific securities sold briskly, but in 1873 construction costs outran bond sales. In September Cooke, his bank vaults stuffed with unsalable bonds, defaulted on his obligations. His bank, the largest in the nation, shut down. Then the stock market collapsed and smaller banks and other firms followed; and the Panic of 1873 plunged the nation into a devastating five-year depression. Thousands of businesses went bankrupt. By 1878 unemployment had risen to more than 3 million. Labor protests mounted, and industrial violence spread (see Chapter 18). The depression of the 1870s demonstrated ruthlessly that conflicts born of industrialization had replaced sectional divisions.

The depression also fed a dispute over currency that had begun in 1865. During the Civil War Americans had used greenbacks, a paper currency not backed by a specific weight in gold. "Sound-money" supporters demanded the withdrawal of greenbacks from circulation as a means of stabilizing the currency. Their opponents, "easy-money" advocates such as farmers and manufacturers dependent on easy credit, wanted to expand the currency by issuing additional greenbacks. The deepening depression created even more demand for easy money, and the issue split both major parties.

Controversy over the type of currency was compounded by the question of how to repay the federal debt. In wartime the Union government had borrowed astronomical sums through the sale of war bonds. Bond holders wanted repayment in "coin," gold or silver, even though many of them had paid for the bonds in greenbacks. The Public Credit Act of 1869 promised payment in coin.

Senator John Sherman, the author of the Public Credit Act, put together a series of compromises to satisfy both "sound-money" and "easy-money" advocates. Sherman's measures, exchanging Civil War bonds for new ones payable over a longer period of time and defining "coin" as gold only, preserved the public credit, the currency, and Republican unity. His Specie Resumption Act of 1875 promised to put the nation back on the gold standard by 1879.

But Sherman's measures, however ingenious, did not placate the Democrats, who gained control of the House in 1875. Many Democrats, and a few Republicans, were "free-silver" advocates who wanted the silver dollar restored in order to expand the currency and end the depression. The Bland-Allison Act of 1878 partially restored silver coinage by requiring the government to buy and coin several million dollars' worth of silver each month. In 1876 other expansionists formed the Greenback party to keep the paper money in circulation for the sake of debtors, but they enjoyed little success. As the depression receded, the clamor for "easy money" subsided, only to return in the 1890s (see Chapter 20). Although never settled, the controversial "money question" diverted attention away from Reconstruction and thus contributed to its demise.

Reconstruction and the Constitution

During the 1870s the Supreme Court also played a role in weakening northern support for Reconstruction as new constitutional questions surfaced.

Would the Court support laws to protect freedmen's rights? The decision in *Ex Parte* Milligan (1866) had suggested not. In *Milligan,* the Court had ruled that a military commission could not try civilians in areas where civilian courts were functioning, thus dooming the special military courts that had been established to enforce the Supplementary Freedmen's Bureau Act. Would the Court sabotage the congressional Reconstruction plan? In 1869 in *Texas* v. *White,* the Court had let Reconstruction stand, ruling that Congress had the power to ensure each state a republican form of government and to recognize the legitimate government in any state.

However, during the 1870s the Supreme Court backed away from Reconstruction. The process began with the *Slaughterhouse* decision of 1873. In this case the Court ruled that the Fourteenth Amendment protected the rights of *national* citizenship, such as the right to interstate travel, but that it did not protect the civil rights that individuals derived from *state* citizenship. The federal government, in short, did not have to safeguard such rights against violation by the states. The *Slaughterhouse* decision effectively gutted the Fourteenth Amendment, which was intended to secure freedmen's rights against state encroachment.

The Supreme Court retreated even further from Reconstruction in two cases involving the Enforcement Act of 1870. In *U.S.* v. *Reese* (1876), the Court threw out the indictment of Kentucky officials who had barred African-Americans from voting. Another decision that same year, *U.S.* v. *Cruikshank,* again weakened the Fourteenth Amendment. In the *Cruikshank* case, the Court ruled that the amendment barred *states,* but not *individuals,* from encroaching on individual rights.

Continuing this retreat from Reconstruction, the Supreme Court in 1883 invalidated both the Civil Rights Act of 1875 and the Ku Klux Klan Act of 1871. Taken cumulatively, these decisions dismantled Republican Reconstruction and confirmed rising northern sentiment that Reconstruction's egalitarian goals were unenforceable.

Republicans in Retreat

The Republicans gradually disengaged from Reconstruction, beginning with the election of Grant as president in 1868. Grant, like most Americans, hesitated to approve the use of federal authority in state or local affairs.

In the 1870s Republican idealism waned. Instead, commercial and industrial interests dominated both the Liberal and "regular" wings of the party, and few had any taste left for further sectional strife. When Democratic victories in the House of Representatives in 1874 showed that Reconstruction had become a political liability, the Republicans prepared to abandon it.

By 1875, moreover, the Radical Republicans had virtually disappeared. The Radical leaders Chase, Stevens, and Sumner had died, and others

had grown tired of "waving the bloody shirt," or defaming Democratic opponents by reviving wartime animosity. Party leaders reported that voters were "sick of carpet-bag government" and tired of the "southern question" and the "Negro question." It seemed pointless to prop up southern Republican regimes that even President Grant found corrupt. Finally, Republicans generally agreed with southern Democrats that African-Americans were inferior. To insist on black equality, many party members believed, would be a thankless, divisive, and politically suicidal course that would quash any hope of reunion between North and South. The Republican retreat set the stage for Reconstruction's end in 1877.

RECONSTRUCTION ABANDONED, 1876–1877

"We are in a very hot political contest just now," a Mississippi planter wrote his daughter in 1875, "with a good prospect of turning out the carpetbag thieves by whom we have been robbed for the past six to ten years." Indeed, an angry white majority had led a Democratic resurgence throughout the South in the 1870s, and by the end of 1872 four ex-Confederate states had already returned the Democrats to power. By 1876 Republican rule survived in only three southern states. Democratic victories in state elections that year and political bargaining in Washington in 1877 ended what little remained of Reconstruction.

Redeeming the South

After 1872 the Republican collapse in the South accelerated. Congressional amnesty enabled virtually all ex-Confederate officials to regain office, divided Republicans lost their grip on the southern electorate, and attrition diminished Republican ranks. Carpetbaggers returned North or joined the Democrats, and scalawags deserted the Republicans in large numbers. Tired of northern interference and seeing the possibility of "home rule," scalawags decided that staying Republican meant going down with a sinking ship. Unable to win new white votes or retain the old ones, the fragile Republican coalition crumbled.

Meanwhile, the Democrats mobilized formerly apathetic white voters. Although still faction-ridden—businessmen who dreamed of an industrialized "New South" had little in common with the old planter elite, the so-called Bourbons—the Democrats shared one goal: kicking the Republicans out. The Democrats' tactics varied. In several Deep South states Democrats resorted to violence. In Vicksburg in 1874 rampaging whites slaughtered about 300 blacks and terrorized thousands of potential voters. Vigilante groups in several southern states disrupted Republican meetings and threatened blacks who had registered to vote. "The Republicans are paralyzed through fear and will not act," the carpetbag governor of Mississippi wrote his wife. "Why should I fight a hopeless battle?"

Terrorism did not completely squelch black voting, but it did deprive Republicans of enough African-American votes to win state elections. Throughout the South economic pressures rein-forced intimidation; labor contracts included clauses barring attendance at political meetings, and planters threatened to evict sharecroppers who stepped out of line.

Redemption, the word that Democrats used to describe their return to power, introduced sweeping changes. States rewrote constitutions, cut expenses, lowered taxes, eliminated social programs, limited the rights of tenants and sharecroppers, and shaped laws to ensure a stable African-American labor force. Legislatures restored vagrancy laws, strengthened crop-lien statutes, and remade criminal law. New criminal codes directed at African-Americans imposed severe penalties for what formerly were misdemeanors: stealing livestock or wrongly taking part of a crop became grand larceny, punishable by five years at hard labor. By Reconstruction's end, a large African-American convict work force had been leased out to private contractors.

Freedmen whose hopes had been raised by Republicans saw their prospects destroyed by the redeemers. The new laws, Tennessee blacks stated at

The Duration of Republican Rule in the Ex-Confederate State

Former Confederate States	Readmission to the Union Under Congressional Reconstruction	Democrats (Conservatives) Gain Control	Duration of Republican Rule
Alabama	June 25, 1868	November 14, 1874	6 1/2 years
Arkansas	June 22, 1868	November 10, 1874	6 1/2 years
Florida	June 25, 1868	January 2, 1877	8 1/2 years
Georgia	July 15, 1870	November 1, 1871	1 year
Louisiana	June 25, 1868	January 2, 1877	8 1/2 years
Mississippi	February 23, 1870	November 3, 1875	5 1/2 years
North Carolina	June 25, 1868	November 3, 1870	2 years
South Carolina	June 25, 1868	November 12, 1876	8 years
Tennessee	July 24, 1866*	October 4, 1869	3 years
Texas	March 30, 1870	January 14, 1873	3 years
Virginia	January 26, 1870	October 5, 1869†	0 years

*Admitted before the start of Congressional Reconstruction. †Democrats gained control before readmission. *Source:* Reprinted by permission from John Hope Franklin. *Reconstruction After the Civil War* (Chicago: University of Chicago Press, 1962), 231.

an 1875 convention, imposed "a condition of servitude scarcely less degrading than that endured before the late civil war." In the late 1870s an increasingly oppressive political climate gave rise to an "exodus" movement among African-Americans. Nearly 15,000 African-American "exodusters" from the Deep South moved to Kansas and set up homesteads. But scarce resources left most of the freed slaves stranded. Not until the twentieth century would the mass migration of southern blacks to the Midwest and North gain momentum.

The Election of 1876

By autumn 1876, with redemption almost complete, both parties were moving to discard the animosity left by the war and Reconstruction. The Republicans nominated Rutherford B. Hayes, the governor of Ohio, for president. Popular with all factions and untainted by the Grant scandals, Hayes, a "moderate," favored "home rule" in the South and civil and political rights for all—clearly contradictory goals. The Democrats nominated Governor Samuel J. Tilden of New York, a political reformer known for his assaults on the Tweed Ring that had plundered New York's City's treasury. Both candidates were fiscal conservatives, favored sound money, endorsed civil service reform, and decried corruption.

Tilden won the popular vote by a small margin, but the Republicans challenged pro-Tilden electoral votes from South Carolina, Florida, and Louisiana. Giving those nineteen electoral votes to Hayes would make him the winner. The Democrats, for their part, requiring a single electoral vote to put Tilden in the White House, challenged one electoral vote from Oregon. But Southern Republicans managed to throw out enough Democratic ballots in the contested states to proclaim Hayes the winner.

The nation now faced an unprecedented dilemma. Each party claimed victory, and each accused the other of fraud. In fact, both sets of southern votes were fraudulent: Republicans had discarded legitimate Democratic ballots, and Democrats had illegally prevented freedmen from voting. In January 1877 Congress created a special electoral commission to resolve the conflict. The commission originally consisted of seven Republicans, seven Democrats, and one independent, but when the independent resigned, a Republican replaced him. The commission gave the Republican Hayes the election by an 8–7 vote.

Congress now had to certify the new electoral vote. But the Democrats controlled the House, and some planned to forestall approval of the electoral vote. For many southern Democrats, regaining control of their states was far more important than electing a Republican president—*if* the new Republican administration would leave the South alone. Republican leaders, for their part, were willing to bargain, for Hayes wanted not just victory but also southern approval. Informal negotiations followed, with both parties exchanging promises. Ohio Republicans and southern Democrats agreed that if Hayes won the election, he would remove federal troops from all southern states. Other negotiations led to the understanding that southerners would receive federal patronage, federal aid to railroads, and federal support for internal improvements. In

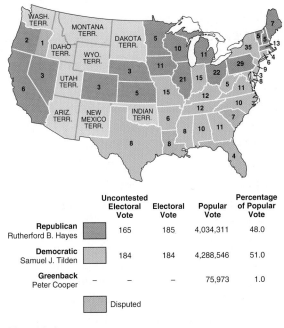

	Uncontested Electoral Vote	Electoral Vote	Popular Vote	Percentage of Popular Vote
Republican Rutherford B. Hayes	165	185	4,034,311	48.0
Democratic Samuel J. Tilden	184	184	4,288,546	51.0
Greenback Peter Cooper	–	–	75,973	1.0
Disputed				

MAP 16.3

The Disputed Election of 1876

Chronology

1863	President Abraham Lincoln issues Proclamation of Amnesty and Reconstruction.
1864	Wade-Davis bill passed by Congress and pocket-vetoed by Lincoln.
1865	Freedmen's Bureau established. Civil War ends. Lincoln assassinated. Andrew Johnson becomes president. Johnson issues Proclamation of Amnesty and Reconstruction. Ex-Confederate states hold constitutional conventions (May–December). Thirteenth Amendment added to the Constitution. Presidential Reconstruction completed.
1866	Congress enacts the Civil Rights Act of 1866 and the Supplementary Freedmen's Bureau Act over Johnson's vetoes. Ku Klux Klan founded in Tennessee. Tennessee admitted to the Union. Race riots in southern cities. Republicans win congressional elections.
1867	Reconstruction Act of 1867. William Seward negotiates the purchase of Alaska. Constitutional conventions meet in the ex-Confederate states. Howard University founded.
1868	President Johnson is impeached, tried, and acquitted. Fourteenth Amendment added to the Constitution. Ulysses S. Grant elected president.
1869	Transcontinental railroad completed.
1870	Congress readmits the four remaining southern states to the Union. Fifteenth Amendment added to the Constitution. Enforcement Act of 1870.
1871	Second Enforcement Act. Ku Klux Klan Act.
1872	Liberal Republican Party formed. Amnesty Act. *Alabama* claims settled. Grant reelected president.
1873	Panic of 1873 begins (September–October), setting off a five-year depression.
1874	Democrats gain control of the House of Representatives.
1875	Civil Rights Act of 1875. Specie Resumption Act.
1876	Disputed presidential election: Rutherford B. Hayes versus Samuel J. Tilden.
1877	Electoral commission decides election in favor of Hayes. The last Republican-controlled state governments fall in Florida, South Carolina, and Louisiana.
1879	"Exodus" movement spreads through several southern states.

turn, southerners promised to accept Hayes as president and to treat the freedmen fairly.

Congress thus ratified Hayes's election. Once in office, Hayes fulfilled many of the agreements made by his colleagues. Republican rule toppled in Louisiana, South Carolina, and Florida. But some of the bargains struck in the so-called Compromise of 1877 fell apart, particularly Democratic promises to treat the freedmen fairly and Hayes's pledges to ensure the freed slaves' rights. "When you turned us loose, you turned us loose to the sky, to the storm, to the whirlwind, and worst of all . . .

to the wrath of our infuriated masters," Frederick Douglass had charged at the 1876 Republican convention. "The question now is, do you mean to make good to us the promises in your Constitution?" By 1877 the answer was clear: "No."

CONCLUSION *hc* ACE Practice Test

Between 1865 and 1877, the United States underwent a series of crises. President Johnson and Congress clashed over his moderate plan for restoring the South. Radicals in Congress impeached the president, and the Radicals took over Reconstruction. Emancipation reshaped black communities as former slaves sought their identity as free people, and transformed the southern economy as a new labor system replaced slavery. The North hurtled headlong into an era of industrial growth, labor unrest, and financial crisis. By the mid-1870s northern politicians were ready to turn their backs on Reconstruction; in the South, Republican regimes toppled and were replaced by Democratic control. Reconstruction's collapse in 1877 reflected not only a waning of northern resolve but also a successful campaign of violence, intimidation, and protest waged by ex-Confederates.

Both political parties were glad to see Reconstruction go. Republicans shed the burden of the "southern question," while Democrats returned to power in the South and would remain entrenched there for more than a century. Reconstruction's end also signified a triumph for nationalism and the spirit of reunion.

Reconstruction's reputation sank. By the early twentieth century it was viewed as a fiasco fashioned by carpetbaggers, scalawags, and Radical Republicans. Historians saw Reconstruction as a failure.

Today historians have a different take on Reconstruction: it was a democratic experiment that did not go far enough. Congress failed to promote freedmen's independence through land reform, leaving southern blacks without the economic power to defend their interests. Additionally, the federal government failed to back reconstruction with military force. Given the choice between protecting blacks' rights at whatever cost or promoting reunion, the government opted for reunion. Thus Reconstruction's failure was essentially the federal government's failure to fulfill its own goals and create a biracial democracy in the South. In many ways the problems of Reconstruction have continued into the twenty-first century.

Reconstruction left a significant legacy in the Fourteenth and Fifteenth amendments, which remain monuments to the democratic zeal that swept Congress in the 1860s. African-Americans created their own monuments in those years in the form of reunited families, newly founded institutions such as schools and churches, and participation, however brief, in government.

But in the 1880s most white Americans left Reconstruction to history and turned their energies to their own economic future—to railroads, factories, and mills, and to the exploitation of the country's bountiful natural resources.

FURTHER READING

David W. Blight, *Race and Reunion: The Civil War in American Memory* (2001). Explores competing views on the significance of the Civil War in the Reconstruction era and in later decades.

Ellen Carol DuBois, *Feminism and Suffrage: The Emergence of an Independent Women's Movement in America, 1848–1869* (1978). Shows how the woman suffrage movement developed in the context of Reconstruction politics.

Eric Foner, *Reconstruction: America's Unfinished Revolution, 1863–1877* (1988). A thorough exploration of Reconstruction that draws on recent scholarship and stresses the centrality of the African-American experience.

Tera W. Hunter, *To 'Joy My Freedom: Southern Black Women's Lives and Labors After the Civil War* (1997). Explores the experience of women workers in Atlanta from Reconstruction into the twentieth century.

Leon Litwack, *Been in the Storm So Long: The Aftermath of Slavery* (1979). A comprehensive study of the African-American response to emancipation in 1865–1866.

Heather Cox Richardson, *The Death of Reconstruction: Race, Labor, and Politics in the Post–Civil War North, 1865–1901* (2004). Explores northern disenchantment with Reconstruction policies and dwindling of northern support for freed blacks in the South.

Kenneth M. Stampp, *The Era of Reconstruction, 1865–1877* (1965). A classic revisionist interpretation of Reconstruction, focusing on the establishment and fall of Republican governments.

Joel Williamson, *The Negro in South Carolina During Reconstruction, 1861–1877* (1965). A pioneer study of African-American life and institutions after emancipation.

17

The Transformation of the Trans-Mississippi West, 1860–1900

CHAPTER OUTLINE

hc This icon will direct you to additional study and research resources at http://college.hmco.com/history/us/boyer/enduring_concise/5e/students/index.html

Red Cloud's Delegation to Washington, c. 1870

In the second half of the nineteenth century, Americans launched one of the greatest migrations in modern history: the exploration and development of half a continent. Lured by tales of the West as a region of free land and rare minerals, miners, farmers, land speculators, and railroad developers flooded onto the fertile prairies of Iowa, Minnesota, and Kansas. Then, aided by the U.S. army, they pushed aside the Indian inhabitants who lived there and swarmed onto the Great Plains and the semiarid regions beyond them. The trans-Mississippi West became a contested terrain as Native peoples fought to preserve their homeland and their freedom to move on the land.

The transformation of the West left a mixed legacy. Although many white families prospered on the High Plains, the heedless pursuit of land and profit proved destructive to Native Americans, to the environment, and often to the settlers themselves. Under the banner of civilization and progress, industrious western entrepreneurs exploited white, Native American, Chinese, and Mexican laborers alike. They slaughtered millions of bison for their hides, skinned the mountainsides in search of minerals, and tore up the prairie sod to build farms even in areas where limited rainfall made farming problematic.

The West's development depended heavily on the federal government. The government sent troops to pacify the Indians, made farm land accessible through the Homestead Act (1862), and subsidized railroad construction. Eastern banks and foreign capitalists provided investment capital and connections with international markets. Yet westerners clung to their ideal of the self-reliant individual who could handle any obstacle. That ideal, though often sorely tested, survived to form the bedrock of western Americans' outlook even today.

NATIVE AMERICANS AND THE TRANS-MISSISSIPPI WEST

No aspect of the transformation of the West was more visible and dramatic than the destruction of the traditional Indian way of life. Even before settlers, ranchers, and miners poured onto the Great Plains at midcentury, Indian life in the trans-Mississippi West was changing. In the Southwest earlier in the century, the Spanish had forcibly incorporated pueblo peoples such as the Hopis and Zuñis into their Mexican trading networks. Other tribes, such as the Navajos, had gradually given up migratory life in favor of settled agriculture. To the north, the Cheyenne and the Lakota Sioux, already expelled from the Great Lakes region by the expansion of white settlement, had moved onto the grasslands of the Great Plains and had seized hunting grounds from their enemies, the Pawnees and the Crows. These and other nomadic warrior tribes, dispersed in small bands and moving from place to place to follow the bison herds, had developed a resilient culture adapted to the harsh environment.

This chapter focuses on five major questions:

▶ How was Indian life on the Great Plains transformed in the second half of the nineteenth century?

▶ What roles did the army and the railroads play in the settlement of the West?

▶ To what extent did the Homestead Act succeed in making free land available to those who settled in the West?

▶ How was the Wild West image of cowboys and Indians created? Why has it remained so popular?

▶ How did some Americans become more aware of the need to conserve natural resources by setting them aside in national parks?

When white pioneers invaded their territory at midcentury, it was the resistance of these nomadic Indians that most captured the public's attention and spurred debate. Caught between a stampede of miners and settlers who took their land and depleted their natural resources and a federal government that sought to force them onto reservations, Native Americans desperately fought back. By the 1890s relocation to distant, often inferior lands had become the fate of almost every Indian nation. Beaten and victimized, resilient Native Americans struggled to preserve their traditions and rebuild their numbers.

The Plains Indians

The Indians of the Great Plains inhabited two major subregions. Several large Siouan-speaking tribes, including the Sioux, Crows, and Assiniboins, dominated the northern Plains from the Dakotas and Montana southward to Nebraska. Mandans, Flatheads, Blackfeet, Cheyennes, and Arapahos also roamed the northern Plains. Some of these were allies, but most were bitter enemies constantly at war. The central and southern Plains were home to the agricultural "Five Civilized Tribes" driven there from the Southeast in the 1830s, to the partially settled Osages and Pawnees, and to the nomadic Comanches, Kiowas, southern Arapahos, and Kiowa Apaches.

Diversity characterized the Plains Indians and sometimes even flourished within divisions of the same tribe. The Dakota Sioux of Minnesota led a semisedentary life of agriculture, maple-sugar harvesting, and deer and bison hunting. In contrast, the Lakota Sioux ranged the High Plains to the west, following the buffalo. Nonetheless, life for all Plains Indians revolved around extended family ties and tribal cooperation. Within the Sioux nation, for example, families and clans joined forces to hunt and farm and reached decisions by consensus.

Religious and harvest celebrations provided the cement for life in Sioux villages and camps. Sioux religion was complex and very different from the Judeo-Christian tradition. Life consisted of a series of circles: family, band, tribe, and Sioux Nation. The Lakota Sioux also believed in plant and animal spirits whose help could be invoked in the Sun Dance. In this ceremony, young men would "sacrifice" themselves by suffering self-torture— stabbing their chests with skewers hung with buffalo skulls, hanging suspended from poles, or cutting pieces of their own flesh to place at the foot of the Sun Dance pole.

On the semiarid High Plains where rainfall averaged less than 20 inches a year, both the bison and the Native peoples adapted to the environment. The huge herds, at their peak numbering an estimated 30 million bison, broke into small groups in the winter and dispersed into river valleys. In the summer, they returned to the High Plains in vast herds. Like the bison, the Indians dispersed across the landscape to minimize their impact on any one place. Hunting the bison not only supplied the Native peoples with food, clothing, and teepee covers, but also created a valuable trading commodity, buffalo robes. This trade led the Indians themselves to dramatically increase their harvest of animals.

The movement of miners and settlers into the eastern High Plains in the 1850s began to erode the bison's habitat and threaten the Native American way of life. The pioneers occupied the river valley sites where the buffalo had wintered and exhausted the tall grasses upon which the animals depended. In the 1860s whites began systematically to hunt the animals, often with Indian help, to supply the eastern market with carriage robes and industrial belting. William F. "Buffalo Bill" Cody killed 4,300 buffalo in only eight months during 1867–1868 to provide food for construction crews for the Union Pacific railroad. Army commanders, seeing the destruction of the buffalo as a way to undermine the resistance of buffalo-dependent tribes, encouraged the slaughter. In the resultant carnage between 1872 and 1875, non-Indian hunters killed 9 million buffalo, taking the skins but leaving the carcasses to rot. By the 1880s the re-

Buffalo Skulls at the Michigan Carbon Works, 1895
Once the vast herds of bison had been decimated, resourceful entrepreneurs, such as those pictured here, collected the skulls and sold them for industrial use. In all, nearly two million tons of bones were processed.

lentless killing had reduced the herds to a few thousand animals, and the Native American way of life dependent on the buffalo had been ruined.

The Destruction of Nomadic Indian Life

By the late 1850s, the Indians who felt pressure from the declining bison herds and deteriorating grasslands faced the onslaught of thousands of pioneers lured by the discovery of gold and silver in the Rocky Mountains. The federal government abandoned the previous position that treated much of the West as a vast Indian reserve and sought to introduce a system of small, separate, bounded areas—tribal reservations—where the Indians were to be concentrated, by force if necessary, and where they were expected to exchange their nomadic ways for a settled agricultural life. To achieve this goal, the army established outposts along well-traveled trails and stationed troops that could be mobilized at a moment's notice.

Some Native Americans, including southwestern Pueblos, the Crows of Montana, and the Hidatsas of North Dakota, accepted this fate. Others, among them the Navajos of Arizona and New Mexico and the Dakota Sioux, opposed the new policy to no avail. However, the remaining Plains Indians, 100,000 strong, resisted. From the 1860s through the 1880s, these tribes—the western Sioux, Cheyennes, Arapahos, Kiowas, Comanches, Nez Percés, Bannocks, and Apaches—faced the U.S. Army in a final battle for the West.

Misunderstandings, unfulfilled promises, brutality, and butchery marked the conflict. A telling example was the eroding relationship between the Cheyennes and Arapahos and the settlers near Sand Creek, Colorado. The Indians, facing starvation because of unfulfilled treaty promises of food, support, and farm equipment, slipped away from the reservation areas to hunt bison and steal livestock from settlers who had swarmed in during a gold rush in the late 1850s. In the spring of 1864, local militia troops attacked Cheyenne and Arapaho camps. The Indians retaliated with a flurry of attacks on travelers. The governor, in a panic, autho-

rized Colorado's white citizenry to seek out and kill all hostile Indians. He then activated a regiment of troops under Colonel John M. Chivington, a Methodist minister. At dawn on November 29, Chivington's troops massacred a peaceful band of Indians, who had camped at Sand Creek believing they would be protected by the nearby fort.

hc Primary Source: Helen Hunt Jackson's Account of Sand Creek

This massacre and others that followed rekindled public debate over federal Indian policy. In response, Congress in 1867 sent a peace commission to end the fighting, and set aside two large districts—one north of Nebraska, the other south of Kansas—where, it was hoped, the nomadic tribes would settle into farming and become Christians. Behind the government's persuasion lay the threat of force. Native Americans who refused to "locate in [the] permanent abodes provided for them," warned the commissioner of Indian affairs, "would be subject wholly to the control and supervision of military authorities, [and] . . . treated as friendly or hostile as circumstances might justify."

At first the plan appeared to work. Representatives of 68,000 southern Plains Indians signed a treaty at Medicine Lodge Creek, Kansas, promising to live on reservations in present-day Oklahoma. The next year, scattered bands of Sioux, 54,000 in number, agreed to move to reservations on the so-called Great Sioux Reserve in the western part of modern South Dakota in return for money and provisions. But Indian dissatisfaction with the treaties ran deep, and many refused to move to, or to remain on, the reservations. A Sioux chief explained, "We do not want to live like the white man. . . . The Great Spirit gave us hunting grounds, gave us the buffalo, the elk, the deer, and the antelope. Our fathers have taught us to hunt and live on the Plains, and we are contented."

In August 1868 war parties of defiant Cheyennes, Arapahos, and Sioux raided frontier settlements in Kansas and Colorado, burning homes and killing whites. In retaliation, army troops attacked Indians, even peaceful ones, who refused confinement. That autumn Lieutenant Colonel George Armstrong Custer's raiding party attacked a sleeping Cheyenne village, killing more than 100 warriors, shooting more than 800 horses, and taking 53 women and children prisoner. Other Cheyennes and Arapahos were pursued, captured, and returned to reservations.

Spurred on by evangelical Christian reformers, Congress in 1869 established the Board of Indian Commissioners to reform the reservation system. But the new, inexperienced Indian agents, drawn from and appointed by the major Protestant denominations, encountered obstacles in trying to implement the board's policies. Lawrie Tatum, a pacifist Quaker, failed to persuade Comanches and Kiowas to cease raiding Texas settlements and to stay on their Oklahoma reservations. Kiowa chiefs Satanta and Big Tree insisted that they could be at peace with the federal government while remaining at war with the Texans. Other agents were unable to restrain scheming whites who fraudulently purchased reservation lands. By the 1880s, the federal government, frustrated with the churches, ignored their nominations for Indian agents and made its own appointments.

Caught in an ambiguous and deceptive federal policy and infuriated by continuing non-Indian settlement of the Plains, Native Americans struck back. In 1874 Kiowa, Comanche, and Cheyenne raids in the Texas panhandle ignited the so-called Red River War. In a fierce winter campaign, regular army troops destroyed Indian supplies, slaughtered one hundred Cheyenne fugitives near the Sappa River in Kansas, and sent more than seventy "ringleaders" to military prison in Florida, ending Native American independence on the southern Plains. In the Southwest, in modern Arizona and New Mexico, Apaches fought a guerrilla war until their leader, Geronimo, surrendered in 1886.

Custer's Last Stand, 1876

Of all the acts of Indian resistance against the reservation policy, none aroused more passion or caused more bloodshed than the conflict between the western Sioux and the U.S. Army in the Dakotas, Montana, and Wyoming. The Treaty of Fort Laramie (1868) had set aside the Great Sioux Reserve "in perpetuity." But not all the Sioux bands had signed the treaty, and some had no intention of moving to the reservation.

Skillfully playing off local officials against the federal government, the Oglala and Brulé bands won permission in 1873 to stay on their traditional lands. To protect these hunting grounds, they raided white settlements, intimidated federal agents, and harassed miners, surveyors, and others who ventured into their territory.

Non-treaty Sioux found a powerful leader in the Hunkpapa Lakota Sioux chief and holy man Sitting Bull. Broad-shouldered and powerfully built, Sitting Bull led by example and had considerable fighting experience. "You are fools," he told the reservation Indians, "to make yourselves slaves to a piece of fat bacon, some hardtack, and a little sugar and coffee."

Pressured by would-be settlers and developers and distressed by the Indian agents' inability to prevent the Sioux from entering and leaving the reservations at will, the federal government took action. In 1874 General William Tecumseh Sherman sent a force under George Armstrong Custer (now a full colonel) into the Black Hills of South Dakota near the Great Sioux Reserve. Thirty-one years old, lean and mustachioed, with shoulder-length red-blond hair, the impetuous Custer had been a celebrity since the Civil War.

Decked out in a fringed buckskin uniform and a crimson scarf, Colonel Custer set out ostensibly to find a location for a new fort and keep an eye on renegade Indians, but his real objective was to confirm rumors about gold deposits in the Black Hills. In a report telegraphed to the *New York World*, Custer described the region as excellent farm country and casually mentioned finding "gold among the roots of the grass." The resulting gold rush gave the army a new justification for proceeding against the Indians. Custer had in fact become part of an army plan to force concessions from the Sioux. The government negotiated to buy the Black Hills but deemed the Indians' asking price too high, and in November 1875, President Ulysses S. Grant and his generals decided to remove all roadblocks to the entry of miners. As of January 31, 1876, the government announced, Indians outside the reservations would be hunted down and taken in by force.

The army mobilized for an assault. In June 1876 Custer led 600 troops of the Seventh Cavalry to the Little Bighorn River area of present-day Montana, a hub of Indian resistance. There, some 1,500 to 5,000 Indians, led by Chief Sitting Bull, were camped along the river. On the morning of June 25 Custer, having underestimated the number of warriors and unwisely divided his force, recklessly led 209 of his men against the Indian encampment. Custer and the outnumbered troops with him were wiped out.

"Custer's Last Stand" shocked Americans. Although the unexpected Indian victory led some pundits to question the wisdom of federal Indian policy, most commentators agreed with the government's determination to crush Native American resistance. "It is inconsistent with our civilization and with common sense," trumpeted the *New York Herald,* "to allow the Indian to roam over a country as fine as that around the Black Hills, preventing its development in order that he may shoot game and scalp his neighbors. . . . This region must be taken from the Indian."

Defeat at Little Bighorn made the army more determined. In Montana troops harassed Sioux bands for more than five years, attacking Indian camps in the dead of winter and destroying all supplies. Sitting Bull, who led his band into Canada to escape the army, held out until 1881, when lack of provisions forced him to give up. Ever resourceful, he joined Buffalo Bill's Wild West Show for a time after his surrender, earning money he used to bring additional supplies to his people.

The army used similar tactics against Chief Joseph and the Nez Percés in Oregon and against the Northern Cheyennes, who had been forcibly transported to Oklahoma after the Battle of Little Bighorn. In September 1878 the Northern Cheyennes' chief, Dull Knife, led 150 surviving men, women, and children north to join the Sioux. The army chased them down and imprisoned them at Fort Robinson, Nebraska. When the army denied their request to stay on a reservation near their traditional lands, the Cheyennes refused to cooperate in being transported. The post commander then withheld all food, water, and fuel. In January 1879 the desperate captives shot their guards and broke

MAP 17.1
Major Indian-White Clashes in the West
Although never recognized as such in the popular press, the battles between Native Americans and the U.S. Army on the Great Plains amounted to a major undeclared war.

for freedom. Startled soldiers gave chase and gunned down half the Indians in the snow, including women, children, and Dull Knife himself. Although some commentators expressed outrage and sporadic attempts to defy white authority continued until the end of the century, such brutal tactics sapped the Indians' ability to resist.

"Saving" the Indians

A growing number of Americans were outraged not only by bloody atrocities like the Fort Robinson massacre but also by the federal government's flagrant violation of the Indian treaties. The Women's National Indian Rights Association, founded in 1883, and other groups took up the cause. Helen

Hunt Jackson, a Massachusetts writer who had recently moved to Colorado, published *A Century of Dishonor* in 1881 to rally public opinion against broken obligations. In the history of government-Indian relations, she wrote, "every page and every year has its dark stain."

Well-intentioned humanitarians concluded that the best way to protect Indian interests would be to break up reservations, end all recognition of the tribes, and propel Native Americans, individually, into mainstream society. They would solve the "Indian problem" by eliminating Indians as a culturally distinct entity. To this end, they threw their support to the Dawes Severalty Act.

The Dawes Act, passed in 1887, aimed to reform the "weaknesses" of Indian life—the absence of private property and the nomadic tradition—by forcing Indians to be farmers and landowners. The law emphasized severalty, the treatment of Indians as individuals instead of as members of tribes, and called for the breakup of reservations. Each head of an Indian family who accepted the law would receive 160 acres of reservation land for farming or 320 acres for grazing. The remaining reservation lands (often the richest) were to be sold to speculators and settlers, and the income thus obtained would go toward purchase of farm tools. To prevent unscrupulous people from gaining control of parcels granted to individual Indians, the government would hold the property of each tribal member in trust for twenty-five years. Indians who at that point had accepted allotments would be declared citizens of the United States.

Speculators who coveted reservation lands and military authorities who wanted to break up reservations lobbied heavily for the Dawes Act. But the bill's strongest support came from such "friends of the Indian" as Helen Hunt Jackson, who believed in the innate superiority of white American culture. Convinced that citizenship would best protect the Indians and full assimilation into society would enable them to get ahead, the reformers tried to "civilize" the Native Americans by weaning them from their traditional culture.

Few land allotments were made until the 1890s, but then the breakup of the reservations accelerated. Ultimately, the Dawes Act proved a boon not to Indians but to speculators, who obtained the best land. By 1934 total Indian acreage had declined by 65 percent, and much of what remained in Indian hands was too dry and gravelly for farming. Ironically, periodic droughts and the High Plains' aridity would push many white farmers back off the land.

Some Native Americans who received land under the Dawes Act became large-scale farmers or ranchers, but countless others languished. Hunting restrictions prevented many from supplementing their land yields, and Indian dependence on federal aid steadily increased. Alcoholism was a continuing problem, worsened by the easy availability of whiskey as a trade item, by boredom resulting from the disruption of traditional pursuits, and by despair at the constraints of reservation life.

The Ghost Dance and the End of Indian Resistance on the Great Plains, 1890

In the late 1880s the Sioux grew desperate. The federal government had reduced their meat rations, and disease had killed one-third of their cattle. In hope of deliverance, they turned to Wovoka, a prophet popular among the Great Basin Indians of Nevada, who promised to restore the Sioux to dominance if they performed the Ghost Dance. In this ritual the dancers, wearing sacred Ghost Shirts decorated to ward off evil, moved in a circle, accelerating until they reached a trance in which they believed they saw visions of the future. Many dancers believed that Ghost Shirts would protect them from harm.

In fall 1890 the spread of the Ghost Dance movement among the Sioux in the Dakota Territory alarmed military authorities. The local reservation agent, Major James McLaughlin, decided to arrest Chief Sitting Bull, whose cabin had become a rallying point for Ghost Dancers. On a freezing December morning, McLaughlin dispatched forty-two Indian policemen to take Sitting Bull into custody. As two policemen pulled the chief from his cabin, his bodyguard shot one of them, and the policeman in turn shot Sitting Bull. Then, in the

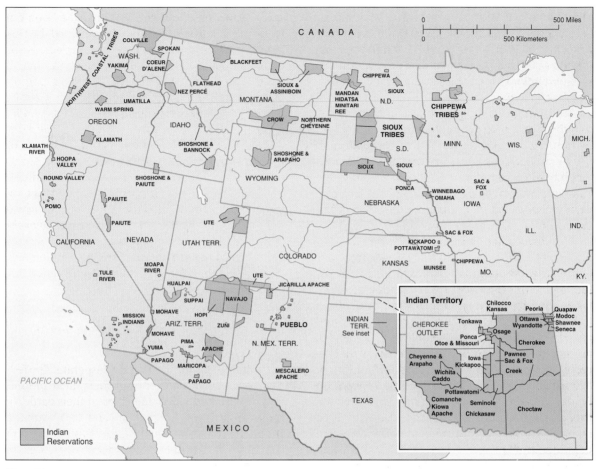

MAP 17.2
Western Indian Reservations, 1890
Native American reservations were almost invariably located on poor-quality lands. Consequently, when the Dawes Severalty Act broke up the reservations into 160-acre farming tracts, many of the semiarid divisions would not support cultivation.

midst of bloody hand-to-hand fighting, Sitting Bull's horse began to perform tricks from its days in the Wild West show. The macabre scene terrified some observers, who concluded that the dead chief's spirit had entered his horse.

Two weeks later, on December 29, 1890, the Seventh Calvary began rounding up 340 starving Sioux at Wounded Knee, South Dakota. One excited Indian fired a gun, and the soldiers retaliated with rapid-fire Hotchkiss cannons. Within a short time 300 Indians, including 7 infants, lay dead.

As the frozen corpses at Wounded Knee were being dumped into mass graves, a generation of Indian-white conflict on the Great Plains shuddered to a close. Some Indians succeeded in adapting to non-Indian ways, but many were devastated at being forced to abandon their religious beliefs and a way of life rooted in hunting, cooperative living, and nomadism. Driven onto reservations, the Plains Indians became almost completely dependent as their cultural traditions, modes of survival, and social organization were crushed. By 1900 the

Wounded Knee
Piled up like cordwood, the frozen bodies of the Sioux slaughtered at Wounded Knee were a grim reminder that the U.S. Army would brook no opposition to its control of Indian reservation life.

Plains Indian population had shrunk from nearly 250,000 to just over 100,000. Nevertheless, after 1900 the population gradually rose. Against overwhelming odds, the pride, group memory, and cultural identity of the Plains Indians survived all efforts to eradicate them.

Unlike the nomadic western Sioux, the more settled Navajos of the Southwest adjusted to the reservation system and preserved traditional ways while incorporating elements of the new order. By 1900 the Navajos had tripled their reservation land, dramatically increased their numbers and their herds, and carved out for themselves a distinct place in Arizona and New Mexico.

By the end of the century, the U.S. government had forced extraordinary changes on Indians. In the name of civilization and progress, civic leaders mixed sincere (if misguided) benevolence, coercion wrapped in an aura of legality, and outbursts of naked violence. Some white Americans felt contempt and hatred toward the Indians, but others sought to uplift, educate, and Christianize them. Government officials and ordinary citizens were equally blind to any inherent value in Native American life and traditions, and both played their part in shattering a proud people and an ancient culture. The Indians' fate would weigh on the American conscience for generations.

SETTLING THE WEST

The Native Americans' defeat opened the way for settlement that would transform the landscape of a vast territory stretching from the Great Plains to the Sierra Nevada and the Cascade Mountains. After 1870, as railroad expansion lessened the time and hazards of the journey west, migration accelerated. In the next three decades, more land was parceled out into farms than in the previous 250 years of American history, and agricultural production doubled.

The First Transcontinental Railroad

Passed in 1862, the Pacific Railroad Act authorized the construction of a new transcontinental link. The act provided grants of land and other subsidies to the railroads for each mile of track laid, which made them the largest landholders in the West. Over the next half-century, nine major routes were built, running from the South or Midwest to the West. More than any other factor, these railroads accelerated the transformation of everyday life west of the Mississippi.

Building the railroads was backbreaking work. Searching for inexpensive labor, the railroads turned to immigrants. The Central Pacific employed Chinese workers, preferred because they worked hard for low wages, did not drink, and furnished their own food and tents. Nearly 12,000 Chinese graded the roadbed, chipping and blasting it from solid rock in the Sierra Nevada, while Irish, Mexican-American, and black workers put down the track.

On May 10, 1869, pealing church bells and booming cannons announced the completion of the first railroad spanning North America. At Promontory Point, Utah, beaming officials drove in a golden spike to link the Union Pacific (stretching west from Omaha, Nebraska) and the Central Pacific (reaching east from Sacramento, California). The nation's vast midsection was now more accessible than it had ever been.

The railroads quickly proved their usefulness. In the battles against Native Americans, the army shipped horses and men west quickly even in winter. The same trains gave hunters easy access to the bison ranges. Once Indian resistance had been broken, the railroads delivered new settlers and their supplies and provided fast shipment of cattle and grain to eastern urban markets.

Settlers and the Railroad

During the decade after the passage of the Pacific Railroad Act, Congress awarded the railroads 170 million acres, worth over half a billion dollars. By 1893 the states of Minnesota and Washington had deeded to railroad companies a quarter of their state lands; Wisconsin, Iowa, Kansas, North Dakota, and Montana had turned over a fifth of their acreage. As mighty landowners, the railroads had a unique opportunity to shape settlement in the region—and to reap enormous profits.

The railroads used several different tactics to attract inhabitants. They created land sales offices and sent agents to the East Coast and Europe to recruit settlers. While the agents glorified the West as a new Garden of Eden, the land bureaus offered prospective buyers long-term loans and free transportation. Acknowledging that life on the Great Plains could be lonely, the promoters advised young men to bring their wives (because "maidens are scarce") and to emigrate as entire families and with friends. Land was available to single women, or "girl homesteaders" as they were known at the time, to establish farms near other family members. In Wyoming single women made up more than 18 percent of the claimants.

In addition to millions of Americans, the railroads helped bring nearly 2.2 million foreign-born settlers to the trans-Mississippi West between 1870 and 1900. Some agents recruited whole villages of Germans and eastern Europeans to relocate to the North Dakota plains. Irish laborers hired to lay track could be found in every town along the rail lines. By 1905 the Santa Fe Railroad alone had transported sixty thousand Russian Mennonites to the fertile Kansas plains where black pioneers called exodusters had preceded them in the 1870s.

The railroads influenced agriculture as well. To ensure quick repayment of the money owed to them, the railroads urged new immigrants to specialize in cash crops—wheat on the northern Plains, corn in Iowa and Kansas, cotton and tobacco in Texas. Although these crops initially brought in high revenues, dependence on a single crop made many farmers vulnerable to fluctuating market forces.

Homesteading on the Great Plains

Liberalized land laws also drew settlers west. Reflecting Republican faith that free land would enable the poor to better themselves, the Homestead Act of 1862 offered 160 acres of free land to any individual who paid a $10 registration fee, lived on the land for five years, and cultivated and improved it. The Homestead Act also attracted immigrants from the British Isles and other areas of Europe where good-quality land was prohibitively expensive.

Although nearly 400,000 families claimed land under the Homestead Act between 1860 and 1900, the law did not function as its authors had intended. Speculators, railroads, and state governments acquired huge portions of land, and only one acre in every nine went to the pioneers for whom it was intended. In addition, the 160-acre limit specified by the Homestead Act was ample for farming rich lands like those of Minnesota or Oregon, but in the West's many drier areas, a farmer needed more land. Congress passed legislation to address this problem: the Timber Culture Act (1873) gave homesteaders an additional 160 acres if they planted trees on 40 acres; the Desert Land Act (1877) made 640 acres available at $1.25 an acre on condition that the owner irrigate part of it within three years; the Timber and Stone Act (1878) permitted the purchase of up to 160 acres of forest land for $2.50 an acre. Speculators, lumber companies, and ranchers abused the laws to amass large holdings. Still, federal laws kept alive the dream of the West as a place for new beginnings.

In addition to practical hardships, almost all settlers faced difficult psychological adjustments to frontier life. The first years of settlement were the most trying. Toiling to build a house and break ground for the first crop, the pioneers put in an average of sixty-eight hours of tedious, backbreaking work a week in severe isolated surroundings that quickly dimmed their shining vision of Edenic farm life. For blacks who emigrated from the South to Kansas and other parts of the Plains after the Civil War, prejudice compounded the burdens of adjusting to a different life.

Many middle-class women found adaptation especially difficult. At least initially, some were enchanted by the haunting landscape, and in letters they described the open Plains as arrestingly beautiful. But far more focused on the "horrible tribes of Mosquitoes;" the violent summer thunderstorms, with hailstones as "big as hen's eggs," and blinding winter blizzards; and the crude sod huts that served as their early homes because timber was so scarce. One young bride, upon first seeing her new sod house, burst into tears and angrily informed her husband that her father had built a better house for his hogs.

Not surprisingly, many newcomers to the Great Plains in these years gave up and moved on. Nearly half of those who staked homestead claims in Kansas between 1862 and 1890 relinquished their rights to the land. However, in places like Minnesota and the Pacific Northwest where Germans, Norwegians, and other immigrants nurtured a tradition of family prosperity tied to continuous landownership, significantly more settlers were likely to stay for a decade or longer.

Many who weathered the lean early years eventually came to identify deeply with the land. Within a decade, the typical Plains family that had "stuck it out" had moved into a new wood-framed house with a proper front parlor. Women worked particularly hard on these farms and took pride in their accomplishments. "Just done the chores," wrote one woman to a friend, "I went fence mending and getting out cattle . . . and came in after sundown. I fed my White Leghorns [chickens] and then sat on the

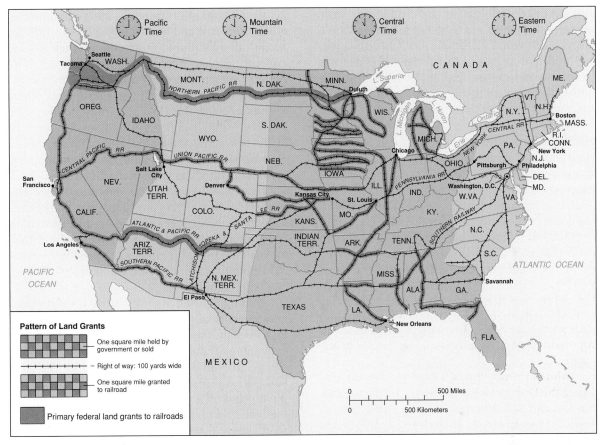

MAP 17.3

Transcontinental Railroads and Federal Land Grants, 1850–1900

Despite the laissez-faire ideology that argued against government interference in business, Congress heavily subsided American railroads and gave them millions of acres of land. As illustrated in the box, belts of land were reserved on either side of a railroad's right of way. Until the railroad claimed the exact one-mile-square sections it chose to possess, all such sections within the belt remained closed to settlement. **hc** Interactive Map: The American West, 1860–1890

step to read over your letter. I forgot my wet feet and shoes full of gravel and giggled joyously."

New Farms, New Markets

Farmers on the Plains took advantage of advances in mechanization and the development of improved strains of wheat and corn. Thanks to efficient steel plows, specially designed wheat planters, and improved threshers and windmills, the Great Plains farmer of the late nineteenth cen-

tury harvested ten times more wheat than his counterpart of 1840. Barbed wire, patented in 1874, allowed farmers to keep roving livestock off their land and touched off violent conflict between farmers and ranchers. Generally, the farmers won, and the "open range" began to vanish.

The invention of labor-saving machinery together with increased demand for wheat, milk, and other farm products created the impression that farming was entering a period of unparalleled prosperity. But few fully understood the sacrifices and perils of agriculture. The cost of the land, horses, machinery, and seed needed to start up a farm could exceed $1,200, far more than the average industrial worker earned. Reliant on cash crops to pay off mortgages, farmers depended on the railroads and were at the mercy of the international grain market's shifting currents.

Western grain growers lost their independence and became players in a world market economy. High demand could bring prosperity, but when overproduction pushed prices down, the heavily indebted farmer faced ruin. These stark realities forced many Plains farmers to abandon their illusions of independence and easy wealth.

On the western Plains, low rainfall, less than twenty inches a year, increased homesteaders' problems. Farmers compensated by "dry farming"—plowing deeply to stimulate the soil's capillary action and harrowing lightly to raise a moisture-protective covering of dirt. They also diverted creeks for irrigation. But a drought that began in the 1870s, together with terrible grasshopper infestations and a national depression between 1873 and 1878, drove many to despair.

Building a Society and Achieving Statehood

Despite the hardships, many remote farm settlements blossomed into thriving communities. Churches and Sunday schools, among the first institutions to appear, became centers of social activity as well as worship. Farmers gathered for barn raisings and group threshings, and families pooled their energies in quilting and husking bees. Cooperation was both a practical necessity and a form of insurance in a rugged environment where everyone was vulnerable to disaster. As settlements mushroomed into towns, their residents eagerly established libraries, lyceums, and Masonic lodges and other social clubs, in part to dispel easterners' images of rural towns as cultural backwaters. Larger communities built fashionable hotels and imported entertainers for their new "opera houses."

To achieve statehood, the residents of a territory had to petition Congress to pass an enabling act establishing the proposed state's boundaries and authorizing an election to select delegates for a state constitutional convention. Once a state constitution had been drawn up and ratified by popular vote, the territory applied to Congress for admission as a state. Under these procedures, Kansas entered the Union in 1861, followed by Nevada in 1864, Nebraska in 1867, and Colorado in 1876. Not until 1889 did North Dakota, South Dakota, Montana, and Washington become states. Wyoming and Idaho entered the Union the following year. Utah, its admission long delayed because of the Mormon practice of polygyny, finally outlawed plural marriages and entered in 1896. With Oklahoma's entry in 1907 and Arizona's and New Mexico's in 1912, the process of creating permanent political institutions in the trans-Mississippi West was complete.

Although socially conservative, the new state governments supported woman suffrage. As territories became states, pioneer women, encouraged by women's rights activists like Susan B. Anthony and Elizabeth Cady Stanton, battled for the vote. Success came first in the Wyoming Territory, where the tiny legislature enfranchised women in 1869 in the belief that having the vote would make them more effective moral caretakers on the rowdy frontier. Utah also supported woman suffrage, and Nebraska and Colorado permitted women to vote in school elections. Still, by 1910 only four states—Idaho, Wyoming, Utah, and Colorado—had granted women full voting rights. Legislators in these new states may have been sensitive to women's important contributions to settlement, but by and large, familiar practices persisted.

THE SOUTHWESTERN FRONTIER

Until 1848, when the Treaty of Guadalupe-Hidalgo ending the Mexican War ceded an immense territory to the United States, Mexicans had controlled the Southwest. They had built their own churches, maintained ranches, and traded with the Indians. Although the peace treaty pledged the United

Santa Fe Plaza, New Mexico, in the 1880s, by Francis X. Grosshenney After the railroad went through in 1878, Santa Fe became a popular tourist attraction known for its historic adobe buildings. Although the town retained a large Spanish-speaking population with their own newspaper, by the 1880s American and German immigrants monopolized most positions in business, government, the professions, and the skilled trades.

States to protect the liberty and property of Mexicans who remained on U.S. soil, over the next three decades aggressive American ranchers and settlers forced the Spanish-speaking population off much of the land. Mexicans who stayed behind adapted to Anglo society with varying degrees of success.

In Texas, where the revolution against Mexico and later the Mexican-American War had left a legacy of bitterness and misunderstanding, Anglos frequently harassed Mexican-Americans and confiscated their lands. Mexican bandits retaliated by raiding American communities. Tensions peaked in 1859 when Juan Cortina, a Mexican rancher, led an attack on Brownsville, Texas, and freed all the prisoners in jail. Cortina slipped back and forth across the U.S.-Mexican border for years until the Mexican government, fearing an American invasion, imprisoned him in 1875.

Similar violence erupted in California in the 1850s and 1860s after a cycle of flood and drought ruined many large ranches owned by the *californios*, Spanish-speaking descendants of the original Spanish and Mexican settlers. The collapse of the ranch economy forced many *californios* to retreat into barrios—socially segregated urban neighborhoods. A rapid increase in Anglo migration left the Mexican-American minorities stranded within the cities, where they survived as low-paid day workers and kept a tenacious hold on their cultural traditions.

In California the pattern of racial discrimination was similar for Mexicans, Native Americans, and Chinese. Anglo newcomers quickly labeled non-Anglo culture and language as inferior, and Anglo legislators passed laws making property ownership difficult for non-Anglos. Relegated to the lowest rung of the labor force, minorities were tagged as shiftless and irresponsible. Yet their labor made possible increased prosperity for the farmers, railroads, and households that hired them.

The adaptation of Spanish-speaking Americans to Anglo society unfolded more smoothly in Arizona and New Mexico, where the original Spanish settlement was sparse and where a small class of wealthy Mexican landowners dominated a poor, illiterate peasantry. As early as the 1820s, wealthy Mexicans in Arizona had educated their children in the United States and formed trading and business partnerships with Americans. Perhaps the most successful was Estevan Ochoa, who with an American partner expanded a freighting business into a lucrative merchandising, mining, and sheep-raising operation. The achievements of Ochoa (who rose to become Tucson's mayor) and other Mexican businessmen helped to moderate Anglo antagonism toward the Mexican-American population. So, too, did popular writers like Bret Harte and Helen Hunt Jackson, who evoked public sympathy with stories portraying an older, gracious Spanish-Mexican past being overwhelmed by the tide of Anglo civilization. Over time, the architecture associated with this romantic past, with its white adobe-style walls and red tile roofs, fused with Anglo building traditions in a distinctive Southwest regional style.

But in the 1880s violence erupted between Mexican-American and Anglo ranchers in Arizona and New Mexico. Organized as *Las Gorras Blancas* (The White Caps) in 1888, Mexican-American ranchers attacked Anglo and Mexican-American settlers who had fenced acreage in northern New Mexico previously used as public grazing land. Still, Anglo-dominated corporate ranching steadily reduced their resources. In the cities Mexican-American businessmen commonly restricted their professional dealings to their own people, and the Spanish-speaking population as a whole became more impoverished. Even in Tucson, where the Mexican-American elite enjoyed considerable prosperity, 80 percent of Mexican-Americans in the work force were laborers by 1880, employed as butchers, barbers, cowboys, and railroad workers.

As increasing numbers of Mexican-American males lost title to their land and became seasonal migrant workers, Mexican-American women held their families and communities together. These women ran their households and created community solidarity by emphasizing traditional customs, kinship, and allegiance to the Catholic church. By raising children, even those of other women, by gardening, and by trading food, soap, and other produce, they maintained stable communities in the face of drought or persecution by Anglos.

During the 1890s, a time of rising racism on the national level, violence and discrimination against the Southwest's Spanish-speaking citizens escalated. Riots flared in the Texas communities of Beeville and Laredo in 1894 and 1899. Anglo anti-Catholicism intensified, as did verbal attacks on Mexican-Americans as violent and lazy. Spanish-speaking citizens' battle for fair treatment and cultural respect would continue into the twentieth century.

EXPLOITING THE WESTERN LANDSCAPE

The domination or removal of those occupying the West opened the way for the transformation and exploitation of the natural environment. White publicists, developers, and boosters had long promoted the region as a place of boundless get-rich-quick opportunities. Between 1860 and 1900, a generation of Americans sought to strike it rich in one of the West's mining, ranching, or farming "bonanzas." In reality, the bonanzas set in motion a boom-and-bust economy in which a few became fabulously rich while many lost their shirts or barely survived. Others were bought out by large-scale enterprises that continue to dominate production today.

The Mining Frontier

Beginning with the California gold rush of 1849, mining booms swept through the West. Prospectors struck gold in British Columbia in 1857. Then in 1858 Henry Comstock stumbled on the rich Comstock Lode of gold and silver along Nevada's Carson River; and a few months later gold and silver seekers found still more precious ore along Clear Creek, Colorado, near present-day Denver. By 1900 California had yielded more than $1 billion in gold, and gold strikes dotted the map from Idaho, Montana, Wyoming, and South Dakota all the way north to the Canadian Klondike bordering Alaska. The strike in the Klondike in 1897 brought thousands of prospectors into the area and eventually enabled Alaska to establish its own territorial government in 1912.

Early discoveries often consisted of "placer" gold, panned from riverbeds and streams. These finds reinforced the myth of the mining country as "a poor man's paradise." In 1860 nearly twenty-five percent of Californians claimed mining as their occupation, and the mining camps had become ethnic melting pots. Although a few prospectors made a fortune, the majority remained poor. Most of the West's mining wealth lay in larger veins of gold and silver ore deep within the earth, and huge amounts of capital were necessary to process these deposits. Large mining companies, backed by eastern and British capital, soon took over the major discoveries. Henry Comstock sold one claim for $11,000 and another for two mules.

Although discoveries such as the Comstock Lode seldom brought great wealth to their discoverers, they did create boom towns. Virginia City, Nevada, was typical. A shantytown in 1859, it had blossomed by 1873 into a metropolis of 20,000 residents, complete with mansions, a six-story hotel, an opera house, 131 saloons, 4 banks, and uncounted brothels. Males outnumbered females three to one. Money quickly earned was even more rapidly lost.

Virginia City's boom-and-bust story replayed again and again across the West between 1870 and 1900. Mark Twain captured the thrill of mining "stampedes" in his book *Roughing It* (1872). "Every few days," he wrote,

> news would come of the discovery of a brand-new mining region; immediately the papers would teem with accounts of its richness, and away the surplus population would scamper to take possession. By the time I was fairly inoculated with the disease, 'Esmeralda' had just had a run and 'Humboldt' was beginning to shriek for attention. 'Humboldt! Humboldt!' was the new cry, and straightway Humboldt, the newest of the new, the richest of the rich, the most marvelous of the marvelous discoveries in silver-land, was occupying two columns of the public prints to 'Esmeralda's' one.

Miners who worked for large corporations typically earned about $2,000 a year (teachers made $450 to $650), but most earned only enough to go elsewhere and try again. Nevertheless, the production of millions of ounces of gold and silver stimulated economic development, lured new foreign investors, and helped usher the United States into the mainstream of the world economy.

Progress came at a price. The long-term cost to the environment to extract these metals was high. Hydraulic mining, which used water cannons to dislodge minerals, polluted rivers and flushed millions of tons of silt into valleys. Mining and smelting operations spewed cyanide, lead, arsenic, and other carcinogenic chemicals over the scarred landscape and into the air. The destruction to the environment is still evident today.

Cowboys and the Cattle Frontier

Just as romanticized accounts of gold strikes fueled the feverish expansion of the mining frontier, romantic tales of hardy cowboys driving longhorns north from Texas sparked the transformation of the cattle industry in these same decades. Businessmen and railroad entrepreneurs promoted cattle herding as the new route to fame and fortune. The cowboy, once scorned as a ne'er-do-well and drifter, was glorified as a man of rough-hewn integrity and self-reliant strength.

In 1868 Joseph G. McCoy, a young cattle dealer from Illinois, combined organizational and promotional skills to revolutionize the cattle industry. Seeing a rich potential in cattle shipping, McCoy had formed a partnership with his brothers in 1867, and he went to Kansas to build a new stockyard in Abilene. By guaranteeing to ship his steers by rail to hungry eastern markets, McCoy gained a $5 kickback on each cattle car. To make the overland drive from Texas easier, he helped to survey and shorten the Chisholm Trail. Finally, in a clever feat of showmanship, he organized the first Wild West show, sending four Texas cowboys to St. Louis and Chicago, where their roping and riding exhibitions attracted exuberant crowds. At the end of McCoy's first year in Abilene, 35,000 steers were trailed north and sold; the following year, the number more than doubled.

The great cattle drives of the 1860s and 1870s became a bonanza for herd owners. Steers purchased in Texas for $9 a head sold for $28 in Abilene. A herd of 2,000 head could generate a tidy $30,000 profit. But cattle ranchers lived at the mercy of high interest rates and unstable markets. During the Panic of 1873, hundreds of cattle drovers fell into bankruptcy.

Little money found its way into the pockets of the cowboys themselves. Cowpunchers who drove herds 800 miles through dirt and dust from Texas to Kansas earned $30 a month, about the same as common laborers. Long hours, low pay, and hazardous work discouraged many older ranch hands from applying. Most cowboys were young men in their teens and twenties who worked for a year or two for quick money and then pursued different livelihoods.

One-fifth of trail riders were black or Mexican. Barred from many other trades, African-American cowboys enjoyed the freedom of life on the trail and distinguished themselves as shrewd and resourceful cowpunchers. Close relationships sometimes developed between black and white cowboys on the trail. One of the best-known African-American cowboys was Nat Love, the son of Tennessee slaves. By his own account, he was "wild, reckless, free" and "afraid of nothing." On July 4, 1876, with the Black Hills gold rush in full swing, Love delivered 3,000 head of cattle and then rode into Deadwood to celebrate. That same day, he won roping and shooting contests and a new title, Deadwood Dick.

At odds with the lonely, dirty, and often boring cowboy life were the exploits of the mythic frontier cowboy, glamorized by the eastern press as early as the 1870s. In 1877 Edward L. Wheeler wrote his first dime novel, *Deadwood Dick, The Prince of the Road: or, the Black Rider of the Black Hills*. Over the next eight years, Wheeler churned out thirty-three Deadwood Dick novels about the adventures of his muscular young hero, who turned his blazing six-shooters on ruthless ruffians and dishonest desperadoes. The fictional character had much in common with the real-life Deadwood Dick except that Wheeler, to appeal to his white readership, made Dick a white man.

The reality was a good deal less picturesque. In Abilene, for example, a brief period of violence and turmoil ended when the town established a police force. City ordinances forbade the carrying of firearms and regulated saloons, gambling, and prostitution. James B. ("Wild Bill") Hickok served as town marshal in 1871, but his tenure was less eventful than legend has it. Dime novelists described him as "a veritable terror to bad men on the border," but Marshal Hickok killed just two men,

one of them by mistake. "Cow towns" like Abilene, Wichita, and Dodge City did not have unusually high homicide rates.

More typical of western conflicts were the "range wars" that pitted ranchers, who thought that the open range should be theirs to exploit, against farmers anxious to fence and plow it. Gaining the upper hand in state legislatures, farm interests tried to cripple the cattlemen with quarantine laws and inspection regulations. Ranchers retaliated first by cutting settlers' barbed wire fences and then by buying and enclosing thousands of acres of their own. Small-scale shooting incidents broke out between farmers and cattle drivers and between rival cattlemen and sheep ranchers.

Peaking during 1880–1885, the bonanza produced more than 4.5 million head of cattle for eastern markets. However, as early as 1882 prices sagged and some ranchers fell into debt. In 1885 President Grover Cleveland, trying to improve federal observance of Indian treaties, ordered cattlemen to remove their stock from the Cheyenne-Arapaho reservation, and 200,000 more cattle crowded onto already overgrazed ranges. In 1885 and 1886 a devil's brew of winter blizzards, searing droughts, and Texas fever destroyed 90 percent of the cattle in some areas of open range and pushed thousands of ranchers into bankruptcy. The cattle industry lived on, but railroad expansion enabled ranchers to ship their steers north. The open range and the great cattle drives were finished.

Bonanza Farms

Like the gold rushes and cattle bonanzas, the wheat boom in the Dakota Territory attracted large capital investments that produced the nation's first "agribusiness." The boom began during the Panic of 1873, when bank failures caused Northern Pacific Railroad bond values to plummet and the railroad exchanged land for the depreciated bonds. Speculators purchased more than 300,000 acres in the fertile Red River valley of North Dakota for between fifty cents and a dollar an acre. Singly or in groups, they established enormous factorylike farms run by hired managers, and they invested heavily in labor and equipment. On the twenty-four-square-mile Cass-Cheney-Dalrymple farm near Fargo, North Dakota, for example, fifty or sixty plows rumbled across the flat landscape on a typical spring day.

The publicity generated by the success of such large investors created an unprecedented wheat boom in the Red River valley. Banking syndicates and small farmers rushed to buy land, North Dakota's population tripled, and wheat production skyrocketed. But the profits soon evaporated, and by 1890 some Red River valley farmers were destitute. Overproduction, high investment costs, erratic rainfall, excessive reliance on one crop, and depressed international grain prices had all contributed to the boom's collapse. Large-scale farmers who had dreamed of getting rich felt lucky simply to survive. By 1889 Oliver Dalrymple, the "king" of the wheat growers, lamented that "it seems as if the time has come when there is no money in wheat raising."

The Oklahoma Land Rush, 1889

Meanwhile, would-be homesteaders greedily eyed the huge Indian Territory (modern Oklahoma). Considering much of the land worthless, the federal government in the 1830s had reserved it for the Five Civilized Tribes. But to punish the tribes for supporting the Confederacy during the Civil War, the government had settled thousands of Indians from *other* tribes in the western part of the territory. In the 1880s land-hungry non-Indians argued that the Civilized Tribes' betrayal of the Union justified further confiscation of their land.

In 1889, over the Native Americans' protests, Congress transferred 2 million acres of unassigned Oklahoma land to the federal public domain. At noon on April 22, 1889, thousands of men, women, and children in buggies and wagons stampeded onto the new lands to stake out homesteads. (Others, the so-called Sooners, had infiltrated the lands illegally and were already plowing fields.) Before nightfall, tent communities had risen at Oklahoma City and Guthrie, near the Santa Fe Railroad. Within two months, 6,000 claims had been filed. As

the Dawes Severalty Act freed up additional land, new torrents of homesteaders poured into the territory.

The land rush demonstrated the continuing power of the frontier myth, which tied "free" land to the ideal of economic opportunity. Most early Oklahoma homesteaders succeeded as farmers because ample rainfall and fertile soil yielded substantial crops. But within two generations, a combination of exploitive farming, poor land management, and drought would turn Oklahoma into the desolate center of the Dust Bowl.

THE WEST OF LIFE AND LEGEND

In 1893, four years after the Oklahoma land rush, the young historian Frederick Jackson Turner delivered a lecture entitled "The Significance of the Frontier in American History." Turner declared that "the frontier has gone, and with its going has closed the first period of American history." Although inaccurate, Turner's linking of economic opportunity to the development of the West caught the popular imagination and created a new school of historians. Today, however, scholars recognize that Turner's ethnocentric omission of Native Americans' claims to the land represented a mythic West that had taken root in the American imagination. Originally the product of nineteenth-century novels, songs, and paintings, the legend would be perpetuated by twentieth-century mass movies and television shows. Its evolution is fascinating, and its influence, far-reaching.

The American Adam and the Dime-Novel Hero

James Fenimore Cooper and other nineteenth-century writers presented the western wilderness as an alternative to society and the frontiersman as an American Adam—simple, virtuous, innocent, and untainted by a corrupt social order. Similarly, an early biographer of Kit Carson portrayed the mountain man as an antidote to refined society, a person of "genuine simplicity . . . truthfulness . . . [and] bravery." And in Mark Twain's *The Adventures of Huckleberry Finn* (1885), Huck heads west "because Aunt Sally she's going to adopt me and sivilize me, and I can't stand it." Themes of adventure, romance, contemplation, and escape from society and its pressures pervaded these works.

An alternative West emerged in the dime novels that blanketed the nation in the 1860s and 1870s. This West featured the image of the frontiersman as a new masculine ideal, the tough guy who fights for truth and honor. In a fictionalized biography of "Buffalo Bill" Cody, Edward Judson (who used the pen name Ned Buntline) made Cody a powerful force for justice and social order as he drives off treacherous Indians and rounds up horse thieves and cattle rustlers. So wildly popular was this new fictional frontiersman that the real Cody started his own Wild West show in 1883. Cody also presented mock "battles" between army scouts and Indians, morality dramas of good versus evil. The Wild West show thus reinforced the dime-novel image of the West as an arena of moral encounter where virtue always triumphed.

Revitalizing the Frontier Legend

Eastern writers and artists eagerly embraced both versions of the myth—the West as a place of escape and as a stage for moral dramas. Three notable members of the eastern establishment, Theodore Roosevelt, Frederic Remington, and Owen Wister, were intensely affected by the time they spent in the West in the 1880s.

The frontier that Roosevelt glorified in *The Winning of the West* (1889–1896) and other works, and that Remington portrayed in his art, was a stark physical and moral environment that tested true character. Roosevelt and Remington painted the disappearing frontier as the proving ground for a new kind of virile manhood and the last outpost of an honest and true social order. This version of the frontier myth reached full flower in Owen Wister's popular novel *The Virginian* (1902). In Wister's tale, the physical and social environment of the Great Plains produced individuals like his un-

named cowboy hero "the Virginian," an honest, strong, compassionate man, quick to help the weak and fight the wicked. The Virginian is one of nature's aristocrats—ill educated and unsophisticated but upright, steady, and deeply moral. For Wister, and for Roosevelt and Remington, too, the cowboy was the Christian knight on the Great Plains, indifferent to material gain as he upheld virtue, pursued justice, and attacked evil.

Western myth was far removed from western realities. The mythical West ignored the hard physical labor of the cattle range and glossed over the ugly underside of frontier expansion—the brutalities of Indian warfare and forced removal, the racist discrimination against blacks and Mexican-Americans, the perils of commercial agriculture and cattle ranching, and the boom-and-bust mentality rooted in the selfish exploitation of natural resources. Further, the myth obscured the complex links between the settlement of the frontier and the emergence of the United States as a major industrial nation tied to a global economy. Indeed, eastern and foreign capital bankrolled mining, ranching, and farming; technology underlay agricultural productivity; and without railroads, western expansion would have been far slower.

Beginning a Conservation Movement

Despite a one-sided, idealistic vision, Wister's celebration of the western experience reinforced a growing recognition that overeager entrepreneurs might well ruin the western landscape. Two important results of the western legend were surging public support for national parks and the beginning of an organized conservation movement.

The natural beauty of the landscape awed the explorers and mappers of the High Plains and Rocky Mountains. Major John Wesley Powell, who charted the Colorado River in 1869, wrote eloquently about the region's towering rock formations and thundering cataracts. Powell's *Report on the Lands of the Arid Regions of the United States* (1878) not only recognized the awesome beauty of the Colorado River basin but also argued that set-

The Grand Canyon of the Yellowstone, by Thomas Moran, 1872
Dazzled by the monumental beauty of the scene, painters strove to portray the western landscape as one of God's wonders. In the process, they stimulated a new popular interest in preserving the spectacular features of the lands.

tlers needed to adjust their expectations about the use of water in the dry western terrain.

At the same time that Powell was exploring the Grand Canyon, General Henry D. Washburn led a party to the Yellowstone River area of Wyoming and Montana. The explorers were stunned. "Amid the canyon and falls, the boiling springs and sulphur mountains, and, above all, the mud volcano and the geysers of the Yellowstone, your memory becomes filled and clogged with objects new in experience, wonderful in extent, and possessing unlimited grandeur and beauty," one member of the party later wrote. The Washburn explorers abandoned their plan to claim this area for the Northern Pacific Railroad and instead petitioned Congress to protect it from settlement, occupancy, and sale. In 1872 Congress created Yellowstone National Park to "provide for the preservation . . . for all time, [of]

mineral deposits, natural curiosities, or wonders within said park . . . in their natural condition."

These steps to conserve the West's natural resources reflected the beginnings of a changed awareness of the environment. George Perkins Marsh, a Vermont architect and politician, used his influential study *Man and Nature* (1864) to attack the view that nature existed to be conquered. He warned Americans to stop their destructive use of the land. "Man," he wrote, "is everywhere a disturbing agent. Wherever he plants his foot, the harmonies of nature are turned to discords."

Marsh's plea for conservation found its most eloquent support in the work of John Muir, a Scottish immigrant who had grown up in Wisconsin. Muir fell in love with the redwood forests of the Yosemite Valley, and for forty years he tramped the rugged mountains of the West. A romantic at heart, he

Chronology

1859	Henry Comstock strikes gold in Nevada.
	Gold discovered at Clear Creek, Colorado.
1861	Kansas becomes a state.
1862	Homestead Act.
	Pacific Railroad Act.
1864	Nevada admitted to the Union.
	Massacre of Cheyennes at Sand Creek, Colorado.
	George Perkins Marsh, *Man and Nature.*
1867	Joseph McCoy organizes cattle drives to Abilene, Kansas.
	New Indian policy of smaller reservations adopted.
	Medicine Lodge Creek Treaty.
1868	Fort Laramie Treaty.
1869	Board of Indian Commissioners established to reform Indian reservation life.
	Wyoming gives women the vote.
1872	Mark Twain, *Roughing It.*
	Yellowstone National Park established.
1873	Panic allows speculators to purchase thousands of acres in the Red River valley of North Dakota cheaply.
	Timber Culture Act.
1874	Invention of barbed wire.
	Gold discovered in the Black Hills of South Dakota.
	Red River War pits the Kiowas, Comanches, and Cheyennes against the U.S. Army.
1876	Colorado admitted to the Union, gives women the right to vote in school elections.
	Massacre of Colonel George Armstrong Custer and his troops at Little Bighorn.

1877	Desert Land Act.
1878	Timber and Stone Act.
	John Wesley Powell, *Report on the Lands of the Arid Regions of the United States.*
1879	Massacre of northern Cheyennes at Fort Robinson, Nebraska.
1881	Helen Hunt Jackson, *A Century of Dishonor.*
1883	William ("Buffalo Bill") Cody organizes Wild West show.
1886	Severe drought on the Plains destroys cattle and grain.
1887	Dawes Severalty Act.
1888	*Las Gorras Blancas* (The White Caps) raid ranchers in northern New Mexico.
1889	Oklahoma Territory opened for settlement.
1889–1896	Theodore Roosevelt, *The Winning of the West.*
1890	Ghost Dance movement spreads to the Black Hills.
	Massacre of Teton Sioux at Wounded Knee, South Dakota.
	Yosemite National Park established.
1892	John Muir organizes the Sierra Club.
1893	Frederick Jackson Turner, "The Significance of the Frontier in American History."
1902	Owen Wister, *The Virginian.*

struggled to experience the wilderness at its most elemental level. Once, caught high in the Rockies during a summer storm, he climbed the tallest pine around and swayed back and forth in the raging wind. Muir became the late nineteenth century's most articulate publicist for wilderness protection. His campaign contributed to the establishment of Yosemite National Park in 1890 and the creation two years later of the Sierra Club, committed to encouraging the enjoyment and protection of the wilderness in the mountain regions of the Pacific coast.

The precedent established by the creation of Yellowstone National Park remained ambiguous well into the twentieth century. Other parks that preserved the high rugged landforms of the West were often chosen because Congress viewed the sites as worthless for other purposes. Awareness of the need for biological conservation would not emerge until later in the twentieth century. Ironically, too, the wilderness-protection movement reaffirmed the image of the West as a unique region whose magnificent landscape produced tough individuals of superior ability. Overlooking the senseless violence and ruthless exploitation of the land, writers, historians, and politicians kept alive the legend of the western frontier as a seedbed of American virtue.

CONCLUSION *hc* ACE Practice Test

Because industrialization, urbanization, and immigration were altering the rest of the nation in unsettling ways, many Americans embraced the legend of the West as an uncomplicated, untainted Eden—what the entire society had once been like (or so Americans chose to believe). But the mythic view of the frontier West obscured the dark side of expansion. Under the banner of economic opportunity and individual achievement, nineteenth-century Americans used the army to drive out the Indians and ruthlessly exploited the region's vast natural resources. Despite the promise of free land under the Homestead Act, much of the best land had been given to railroads, and speculators grabbed other prime locations. In many places, large business enterprises shoved aside the individual prospector and small farmer. The exclusion of blacks, Indians, and Spanish-speaking Americans belied the voiced commitment to an open society.

Nevertheless, the settlement of the vast trans-Mississippi reinforced the popular image of the United States as a land of unprecedented economic opportunity and as a seedbed for democracy. The creation of new towns, states, and their governments and the interaction of different peoples tested these ideas and, with time, forced their rethinking. The willingness to give women the vote in many of the new western states would spread within the next two decades.

Not surprisingly, the remorseless exploitation of the West's extensive natural resources led to the beginnings of the conservation movement and a reassessment of traditional American views of the environment. By the turn of the century, the thriving farms, ranches, mines, and cities of the region would help make the United States one of the world's most prosperous nations.

FURTHER READING

Robert V. Hine and John M. Faragher, *The American West: A New Interpretative History* (2000). An updated and comprehensive summary of the American West's history using the new and provocative scholarship of the last decade.

Andrew Isenberg, *The Destruction of the Bison: An Environmental History, 1750–1900* (2000). A skillful analysis of the grassland environment of the Great Plains and its effect on the bison, Indian life, and the European settlers and the plants, animals, and insects they brought with them.

Peter Iverson, *When Indians Became Cowboys: Native Peoples and Cattle Ranching in the American West* (1994). A useful and important study of the ways in which Native peoples were able to adapt to reservation policies by raising cattle and, at the same time, preserve many of their traditional cultural practices.

Joy S. Kasson, *Buffalo Bill's Wild West: Celebrity, Memory, and Popular History* (2000). An innovative study of Buffalo Bill's Wild West show and its contribution to the mythology of the American West.

Glenda Riley and Richard W. Etulain, eds., *By Grit and Grace: Eleven Women Who Shaped the American West* (1997). Essays on Calamity Jane, Annie Oakley, and other forceful and accomplished western women.

Elliott West, *The Contested Plains: Indians, Goldseekers, and the Rush to Colorado* (1998). The story, with a keen eye for its environmental setting, of the competition among Indians, miners, army volunteers, and settlers on the central Great Plains.

18

The Rise of Industrial America, 1865–1900

CHAPTER OUTLINE

hc This icon will direct you to additional study and research resources at http://college.hmco.com/history/us/boyer/enduring_concise/5e/students/index.html

Night Pageant, the Grand Columbian Carnival, 1893

The industrial transformation of the late nineteenth century both exhilarated and unsettled Americans. At mid-century, the United States had played a minor role in the world economy. Five decades later manufacturing output had expanded fivefold and the United States produced more manufactured goods than England, Germany, and France combined. The hallmark of this prodigious growth was the rise of giant corporations, but important strides also came in countless small industries.

This stunning industrial growth came at a high cost. New manufacturing processes victimized workers and often polluted the environment. The explosive economy, difficult to control, lurched into a crippling depression in 1873 and again in 1893.

THE RISE OF CORPORATE AMERICA

Before the Civil War, the corporate form of business organization had been used to raise capital for costly enterprises like turnpikes and canals. By selling stocks and bonds to raise money, the corporation separated the company's managers, who ran day-to-day operations, from the owners—those who held the stocks and bonds. After the Civil War, American business leaders pioneered new forms of corporate organization to consolidate and manage expanding industrial enterprises. The rise of corporate America in this period is a story of risk-taking and innovation as well as of rapacity and ruthlessness.

The Character of Industrial Change

Six features dominated the birth of modern industrial America: the exploitation of immense coal deposits for cheap energy; rapid technological innovation and the spread of the factory system; pressures to compete tooth and nail; the enormous demand for new workers; a relentless drop in prices; and an inadequate money supply that drove interest rates up and restricted credit.

These six factors were interwoven. The great coal deposits of Pennsylvania, West Virginia, and Kentucky provided cheap energy to fuel railroads, factories, and urban growth. Exploiting these energy sources, new technologies stimulated productivity and ignited explosive industrial expansion. Technology allowed manufacturers to cut costs and to hire cheap unskilled labor. This cost cutting drove firms to undersell each other, destroying weaker competitors and prompting stronger, more efficient, and more ruthless ones to consolidate. Until the mid-1890s, cost reduction, technology, and competition forced prices down. But the depressions of the 1870s and 1890s hit all Americans hard. Above all, business leaders' unflagging drive to maximize efficiency produced colossal fortunes for a handful even as it forced millions to live near the subsistence level.

Out of the new industrial system poured dismal clouds of haze and soot, as well as the first trickle of

This chapter focuses on five major questions:

▶ What innovations in technology and business practice helped launch vast increases in industrial production in the post–Civil War period?

▶ How were Andrew Carnegie, John D. Rockefeller, and other corporate leaders able to dominate their rivals and consolidate control over their industries?

▶ Why did the South's experience with industrialization differ from that of the North and the Midwest?

▶ How did workers respond to the changing nature of work and the growth of national corporations?

▶ In the clash between industry and labor, what tactics enabled corporate executives in the 1890s to undercut labor's bargaining power?

a coming avalanche of consumer goods. In turn, mounting demands for consumer goods stimulated heavy industry's production of capital goods—machines to boost farm and factory output even further. Together with the railroads, the corporations that manufactured capital goods, refined petroleum, and made steel became driving forces in the nation's economic growth.

Railroad Innovations

As the post–Civil War era opened, the aggressive competition that characterized the emergence of industrial America was most intense among the railroads, to many Americans, the symbol of industrial progress. By 1900, 193,000 miles of railroad track crisscrossed the United States—more than in all of Europe, including Russia. Connecting every state in the Union, the railroads opened an immense internal market. Railroad companies pioneered crucial aspects of large-scale corporate enterprise: issuing stock to meet capital needs, separating ownership from management, creating national distribution and marketing systems, and forming new organizational and management structures.

Early railroad entrepreneurs faced huge financial and organizational problems. Laying track, building engines, and buying out competitors were horrendously expensive. Enormous subsidies from federal, state, and local governments helped to provide capital, but the large railroad companies also had to borrow heavily by selling stocks and bonds. By 1900 the combined debt of all U.S. railroads stood at $5.1 billion, five times the federal debt, and the yearly interest payments cut heavily into the railroads' earnings.

Railroads were also innovators in communications and information systems. They relied on the telegraph, invented in 1837, to coordinate the complex flow of cars. Using hierarchical structures and organizing their operations into geographic units, they developed elaborate accounting systems to document costs for each division. With these reports, railroads could set rates and predict profits with unprecedented accuracy. Such management innovations became models for other businesses seeking national markets.

Consolidating the Railroad Industry

The expansion and consolidation of railroading reflected both ingenuity and dishonesty. Although by the 1870s railroads dominated domestic transportation, the industry itself was in a state of chaos. Hundreds of small companies used different rails, track widths, and engine sizes. Financed by large eastern and British banks, entrepreneurs such as Collis P. Huntington, Jay Gould, and others devoured these smaller lines to build large, integrated track networks. In the Northeast four major trunk lines were created. West of the Mississippi five great lines controlled most of the track by 1893.

Contemporaries depicted the larger-than-life railroad leaders as villains and robber barons who manipulated stock markets and company policies to line their own pockets. For example, newspaper publisher Joseph Pulitzer called the short, secretive

Manufacturing Locomotives
In the shop of the Baldwin Locomotive Works, small teams of skilled workers custom built each engine to the specifications of the purchaser.

Jay Gould, president of the Union Pacific, "one of the most sinister figures that have ever flitted bat-like across the vision of the American people." Recent historians, however, have pointed out that although some railroad barons were ironfisted pirates, others were upstanding businessmen who managed their companies with sophistication and startling inventiveness.

The massive trunk systems created by these masterminds became the largest business enterprises in the world, pioneering the most advanced methods of accounting and large-scale organization. The railroads standardized all basic equipment and facilities, from engines to automatic couplers, from air brakes and signal systems to outhouses (now provided in standard one-, two-, and three-hole sizes). In 1883, independently of the federal government, the railroads standardized scheduling by dividing the country into four time zones. In May 1886 all railroads shifted simultaneously to a new standard-gauge track. Finally, with cooperative billing arrangements, railroads could ship cars from other roads at uniform rates nationwide.

But mired in heavy indebtedness, overextended systems, and crooked business practices, railroads competed recklessly with each other for traffic. They cut rates for large shippers, showered free passes on politicians, and granted substantial rebates and kickbacks to favored clients. None of these tactics shored up the railroads' precarious financial position. The continuous push to expand drove some overbuilt lines into bankruptcy.

Caught in the middle of the railroads' tug of war, farmers and small businessmen turned to state governments for help, and in the 1870s many midwestern state legislatures outlawed rate discrimination. In the 1880s, however, the Supreme Court negated such laws by ruling that states could not regulate interstate commerce. In 1887 Congress passed the Interstate Commerce Act, which established the Interstate Commerce Commission (ICC) to oversee interstate railroad practices and banned pooling, rebates, and other monopolistic activity. However, the Supreme Court ruled in favor of railroads over regulators until the Hepburn Act of 1906 strengthened the ICC by empowering it to set rates.

Vicious competition in the rail industry abated only when the national depression that began in 1893 forced several roads into the hands of investment bankers. Supported by major investment houses, J. Pierpont Morgan took over the weakened systems, reorganized them, and refinanced their debts. By 1906, thanks to the bankers' centralized management, seven giant networks controlled two-thirds of the nation's track.

hc Interactive Map: Transcontinental Railroads and Federal Land Grants, 1850–1900

Applying the Lessons of the Railroads to Steel

The career of Andrew Carnegie illustrates the link between railroad expansion and the growth of corporate organization and management. Carnegie was born in Scotland and with his father emigrated to America in 1848 at the age of twelve.

Ambitious and hard-working, Carnegie took a job at $1.20 a week as a bobbin boy in a textile mill. Although he worked 60 hours a week, he also enrolled in a night course to learn bookkeeping. In 1849 the ambitious youth became a Western Union messenger boy, and soon he was Pittsburgh's fastest telegrapher. Decoding messages for the city's business leaders, Carnegie gained an insider's view of their operations.

In 1852 Tom Scott, superintendent of the Pennsylvania Railroad's western division, hired Carnegie as his secretary and personal telegrapher. Seven years later Scott became vice president of the Pennsylvania, and the twenty-four-year-old Carnegie took over Scott's former job. In his six years as western division chief, the daringly innovative Carnegie doubled the road's mileage and quadrupled its traffic. By 1868 his investments in railroads brought him more than $56,000 a year, a substantial fortune.

Carnegie decided in the early 1870s to build his own steel mill, in part because of his connections with the railroad industry, the nation's largest purchaser of steel. His J. Edgar Thompson Mill incorporated the new Bessemer production technology, blasting air through molten iron to burn off carbon and other impurities. Carnegie also used the cost-analysis techniques pioneered by the railroads to cut production costs. His management philosophy was deceptively simple: "Watch the costs, and the profits will take care of themselves." Through rigorous cost accounting and limiting wage increases to his workers, Carnegie was able to price his rails below the competition. And he used his railroad connections to give "commissions" to railroad purchasing agents to ensure huge orders.

As output climbed, Carnegie discovered the benefits of vertical integration—that is, controlling all aspects of manufacturing, from extracting raw materials to selling the finished product. For Carnegie, this control embraced every stage from mining and smelting the ore to selling the steel rails. Carnegie Steel demonstrated how sophisticated technology and innovative management (combined with brutally low wages) might be combined into a mass production system that could slash consumer prices.

Leaving management of daily operations to his close associates, Carnegie was free to pursue philanthropy. Carnegie established foundations and donated more than $300 million for libraries, universities, and international-peace causes. (He also knew that such actions would buttress his popularity.)

By 1900 Carnegie Steel, employing 20,000 people, had become the world's largest industrial corporation. Carnegie's competitors, worried about the wily Scot's domination of the market, decided to buy him out. In 1901 J. Pierpont Morgan, who controlled Federal Steel, asked Charles Schwab, Carnegie Steel's president, to inquire what Carnegie wanted for his share of the corporation. The next day Carnegie gave Schwab a penciled note asking for nearly $500,000,000. "Tell Carnegie I accept his price," Morgan responded. Combining Carnegie's companies with his own Federal Steel, Morgan created the first business capitalized at more than $1 billion. U.S. Steel, with its 200 member companies employing 168,000 people, marked a new scale in industrial enterprise.

Carnegie consistently portrayed his success as the result of discipline and hard work. The full story was more complex. Carnegie had an uncanny

Industrial Consolidation: Iron and Steel Firms, 1870 and 1900

	1870	1900
No. of firms	808	669
No. of employees	78,000	272,000
Output (tons)	3,200,000	29,500,000
Capital invested	$121,000,000	$590,000,000

Source: Robert L. Heilbroner and Aaron Singer, The Economic Transformation of America: 1600 to Present, 2d ed. (San Diego: Harcourt Brace Jovanovich, 1984), 92.

ability to see the larger picture and to hire talented associates; he combined this gift with ingenuity in transferring techniques like cost accounting from railroads to steel, and he callously kept wages as low as possible. To a public little interested in details, Carnegie's success reaffirmed the openness of the American economic system and promised that anyone could rise from rags to riches.

The Trust: Creating New Forms of Corporate Organization

Between 1870 and 1900 rapacious competition also swept the oil, salt, sugar, tobacco, and meatpacking industries. Entrepreneurs raced to reduce costs and pioneered new organizational methods to drive rivals out of the market. For example, Chicago meatpackers Philip Armour and Gustavus Swift introduced multiple efficiencies by using every part of the hog or steer, including bones, which became fertilizer, and hooves, which became gelatin.

The evolution of the oil industry typified this process. After Edwin L. Drake drilled the first successful petroleum well in 1859 near Titusville in northwestern Pennsylvania, competitors rushed into the business of drilling oil and processing it into lubricant and kerosene for lighting. By the 1870s rickety drilling rigs, collection tanks, and ramshackle refineries littered the landscape near Pittsburgh and Cleveland, the sites of the first discoveries. Oil spills were a constant problem.

A young Cleveland merchant, John D. Rockefeller, gradually dominated in this new race for wealth. His methods reflected Carnegie's: cost cutting and efficiency. After founding the Standard Oil Company in 1870, Rockefeller scrutinized the smallest detail of daily operations, insisting that one refinery manager find 750 missing barrel stoppers or that another reduce from 40 to 39 the number of drops of solder used to seal a kerosene can. He recognized that in a mass-production enterprise, small changes could save thousands of dollars.

Like Carnegie, Rockefeller was able to understand the workings of an entire industry and the benefits of vertical integration. Seeing that the firm that controlled the shipment of oil could dominate the industry, Rockefeller purchased his own tanker cars. He wangled a 10 percent rebate from the railroads and a kickback on his competitors' shipments. When new pipeline technology became available, Rockefeller established his own massive interregional pipeline network. And Rockefeller used aggression and deception to force out competitors. He priced his products below cost to strangle rivals, and when they teamed up against him, he set up a

pool—an agreement among several companies—that established production quotas and fixed prices to control the market. By 1879 Rockefeller controlled 90 percent of the nation's oil-refining capacity.

Convinced that competition wasted resources, in 1881 Rockefeller decided to eliminate it by establishing a new form of corporation, the Standard Oil Trust. Instead of the pool, a verbal agreement among companies that lacked legal status, the trust created an umbrella corporation that ran them all. Rockefeller and his associates persuaded stockholders of forty companies to exchange their stock for trust certificates. Stockholders retained their share of the trust's profits while enabling the trust to control production. Within three years, the Standard Oil Trust had consolidated crude-oil buying throughout its member firms and cut the number of refineries by half. In this way Rockefeller integrated the petroleum industry both *vertically,* by controlling every function from production to local retailing, and *horizontally,* by merging competing companies into a single giant system.

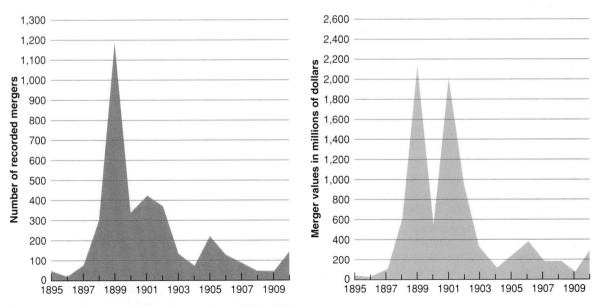

Mergers in Mining and Manufacturing, 1895–1910
A wave of business mergers occurred after the Supreme Court's 1897 and 1898 rulings that any firms concluding price-fixing or market-allocating agreements violated the Sherman Anti-Trust Act. But the merger mania died down when business leaders quickly discovered that companies could remain profitable only through vertical integration.

Success bred imitation, and trusts bloomed in the copper, sugar, whiskey, and lead industries. By limiting the number of competitors, the trusts created an oligopoly, wherein the limited number of sellers can greatly influence price and other market factors. But rapacious tactics, semimonopolistic control, and sky-high earnings provoked a public outcry and led to investigations of the trusts' unscrupulous practices. In 1890 Congress, under the leadership of Ohio senator John Sherman, passed the Sherman Anti-Trust Act, outlawing trusts and any other contracts or combinations in restraint of trade and establishing both fines and jail time as penalties. However, the act never defined clearly either *trust* or *restraint of trade,* and the government prosecuted only a handful of cases before 1904. When Standard Oil was challenged in 1892, it simply reorganized as a holding company. Unlike a trust, which literally owned other businesses, a holding company owned a controlling share of the stock of one or more firms. The nine trustees became the board of directors for Standard Oil of New Jersey, and profits soared.

Supreme Court decisions hamstrung antitrust efforts. In 1895, for example, the federal government brought suit against the sugar trust in *United States* v. *E. C. Knight Company,* arguing that the trust, which controlled more than 90 percent of all U.S. sugar refining, operated in restraint of trade. Asserting that manufacturing was not interstate commerce and ignoring the vast distribution network that enabled the company to dominate the market, the Supreme Court threw out the suit. Thus protected, corporate mergers and consolidations surged ahead. By 1900 mammoth firms controlled nearly 40 percent of all capital investment in manufacturing.

STIMULATING ECONOMIC GROWTH

Although large-scale corporate enterprise contributed significantly to the colossal growth of the U.S. economy in this period, other factors proved equally important, including new inventions, specialty production, and innovations in advertising and marketing. In fact, the resourcefulness of small enterprises in applying these elements enabled many sectors of the economy to grow dramatically.

The Triumph of Technology

New inventions not only streamlined manufacturing but also stimulated consumer demand by creating new product lines. The development of a safe, practical way to generate electricity, for example, made possible a vast number of electrical motors, household appliances, and lighting systems.

Many of the major inventions that stimulated industrial output and underlay mass production remained hidden from public view. Few Americans had heard of the Bessemer process for making steel or of the refrigerated railroad cars that allowed Swift to slaughter beef in Chicago and sell it fresh in New York City. What the public saw were inventions that changed the patterns of everyday life and encouraged consumer demand: the sewing machine, the telephone, the light bulb, and other inventions that eased the drudgery of everyday life and reshaped social interactions. Mass-produced sewing machines replaced hand-sewn with factory-stitched clothing, relieved women of the tedium of hand-making the family apparel, and expanded personal wardrobes. The telephone—patented by Alexander Graham Bell in 1876—not only transformed communications but also undermined the social conventions for polite behavior that had governed face-to-face or written exchanges. The light bulb made it possible to shop after work.

Thomas A. Edison (1847–1931) epitomized the inventive impulse. Largely self-educated, Edison was a born salesman and self-promoter. When he modestly stated that "genius is one percent inspiration and ninety-nine percent perspiration," he was accepting his own image as an inventing "wizard." Like Carnegie, Edison envisioned a large, interconnected industrial system resting on a foundation of technological innovation.

In his early work, Edison concentrated on the telegraph; his first major invention was a stock-quotation printer. His profits enabled him to establish an "invention factory," which he eventually moved in 1876 to Menlo Park, New Jersey, where he

Thomas Edison's Laboratories in Menlo Park, New Jersey, c. 1881
Always a self-promoter, Edison used this depiction of his "invention factory" to suggest that his development of a durable light bulb in 1879 would have an impact on life around the globe.

predicted "a minor invention every ten days, and a big one every six months."

In 1877, buoyed by the success of his invention of the phonograph, Edison set out to develop a practical incandescent light bulb. He perfected a process for generating electricity and discovered a carbon filament that would glow dependably in a vacuum, perfecting the incandescent lamp in 1879. In 1882, backed by J. Pierpont Morgan, the Edison Illuminating Company opened a power plant in New York City's financial district, furnishing lighting for eighty-five buildings.

Others rushed into the electrical field, and Edison sued many of his competitors for patent violations. Embittered by legal battles—defense of his patents cost him more than $2 million—Edison relinquished control of his enterprises in the late 1880s. In 1892, with Morgan's help, his company merged with a competitor to form the General Electric Company. Four years later, GE and Westinghouse agreed to exchange patents under a joint board. Such corporate patent pooling agreements became another way in which to dominate markets.

Edison meanwhile continued to pump out invention after invention, including the mimeograph machine, the microphone, the motion-picture camera and film, and the storage battery. Over his long life, he patented 1,093 inventions and amassed an estate worth more than $6 million.

Perhaps his greatest contribution was his Menlo Park laboratory, a model for industrial research, which demonstrated that the systematic use of science in support of industrial technology paid large dividends. Invention had become big business.

Custom-Made Products

Along with inventors, manufacturers of custom and specialized products dramatically expanded economic output. Using skilled labor, these companies crafted one-of-a-kind or small batches of articles that ranged in size from large steam engines and machine tools to silverware, furniture, and custom-made dresses. Keenly attuned to innovations in technology and design, they constantly created new products tailored to the needs of individual buyers.

Philadelphia's Baldwin Locomotive Works and small dressmaking shops were typical of flexible specialization displayed by small batch processors. Both faced sharp fluctuations in the demand for their products and both employed skilled workers to make small numbers of specialized items. By the 1890s the Baldwin Locomotive Works employed 2,000 workers and produced about 900 engines a year. Although construction was systematized through precision plans, standardization was not possible since no single engine could meet the needs of every railroad.

Until the turn of the twentieth century, when ready-to-wear clothes came to dominate the market, most women's apparel was custom produced in small shops run by women proprietors. Unlike the tenement sweatshops that produced men's shirts and pants, dressmakers paid good wages to highly skilled seamstresses who could shift styles quickly to follow the latest fashions.

Thus, alongside the bureaucratic big businesses like steel and oil in the late nineteenth-century, custom and batch producers also stimulated American productivity, providing a variety of goods that supplemented the bulk-manufactured staples of everyday life.

Advertising and Marketing

As factories spewed out an array of new products, business leaders often discovered that their output exceeded what the market could absorb. This was particularly true for devices for individual use such as sewing machines and farm implements, and for goods such as matches, flour, soap, canned foods, and processed meats. Not surprisingly, these industries were trailblazers in developing advertising and marketing techniques. Strategies for whetting consumer demand and differentiating products represented a critical component of industrial expansion in the post–Civil War era.

The growth of the flour industry illustrates the spread of mass production and the emergence of new marketing concepts. In the 1870s companies installed new machines that processed grain into flour in one continuous, rapid operation. The vastly increased output was more than they could sell. To unload the excess, mills thought up new product lines such as cake flours and breakfast cereals and sold them under easily remembered brand names such as Quaker Oats. Brand names, trademarks, guarantees, slogans, endorsements, and other gimmicks built product demand and consumer loyalty. Americans bought Ivory Soap because of the absurdly overprecise pledge that it was "99 and 44/100s percent pure." The American Tobacco Company used trading cards, circulars, boxtop premiums, prizes, and scientific endorsements to convert Americans to cigarette smoking.

In the 1880s George Eastman invented a paper-based photographic film as an alternative to the bulky, fragile glass plates then in use. Mass-producing a cheap camera, the Kodak, and devising a catchy slogan ("You press the button, we do the rest"), Eastman introduced a system in which customers returned both the one-hundred-exposure film *and* the camera to his Rochester factory. For ten dollars, the company developed and printed the film, reloaded the camera, and shipped everything back to the customer. Eastman had revolutionized an industry and democratized a visual medium once confined to a few.

Economic Growth: Costs and Benefits

By 1900 the chaos of early industrial competition among thousands of companies struggling to enter a national market had given way to the most productive economy in the world, supported by a legion of small, specialized companies and dominated by a few enormous ones. For those that fell behind, the cost was measured in ruined fortunes, bankrupt companies, and shattered dreams. John D. Rockefeller summed up the prevailing atmosphere when he said that in the Standard Oil Trust he wanted "only the big ones, only those who have already proved they can do a big business. As for the others, unfortunately they will have to die."

The cost was high, too, for millions of workers. The new industrial order rested on the backs of laborers who received subsistence wages and could be fired at a moment's notice. Environmental devastation was part of the cost as well. Polluted rivers, smoky skies, and a landscape littered with reeking garbage and toxic by-products bore mute witness to the relentless drive for efficiency and profit.

But industrialization also brought social benefits: labor-saving products, lower prices, and advances in transportation and communication. Benefits and liabilities seemed inextricably interconnected. The sewing machine, for example, created thousands of new jobs, made a wide variety of clothing available, and eased the lives of millions of housewives. However, it also encouraged greedy entrepreneurs to operate sweatshops in crowded,

Industrial Boston
For many Americans, the price of progress was often pollution. Lacking the technology to filter carbon and gases from smoke, factory owners had no choice but to fill the skies with soot.

unsafe tenements where immigrants—often young women—toiled long hours for pitifully low wages.

hc Primary Source: The Impact of the Factory on Worker Health

Whatever the balance sheet of social gains and costs, one thing was clear: the United States had muscled its way onto the world stage as an industrial titan. The ambition of countless inventors, financiers, managerial innovators, and marketing wizards had laid the groundwork for a new social and economic order.

THE NEW SOUTH

The South entered the industrial era far more slowly than the Northeast. As late as 1900, total southern cotton-mill output, for example, remained little more than half that of the mills within a 30-mile radius of Providence, Rhode Island. Moreover, the South's $509 average per capita income was less than half that of northerners.

Many factors hindered the South's progress: the Civil War's physical devastation, the scarcity of towns and cities, lack of capital, illiteracy, northern control of finance, and a low rate of technological innovation. The myth of the Lost Cause—the nostalgic portrayal of the antebellum South as traditional and unchanging—also impeded the region's economic growth.

Obstacles to Economic Development

Much of the South's difficulty in industrializing stemmed from its lack of capital. So many southern banks failed during the Civil War that by 1865 the South, with 25 percent of the nation's population, had only 2 percent of its banks.

Federal policies adopted during the war restricted the expansion of the southern banking system. The Republican-dominated wartime Congress, which created a national currency and banking structure, required anyone wishing to start a bank to have $50,000 in capital. Few southerners could meet this standard.

Country merchants and storekeepers became bankers by default, lending supplies rather than cash to local farmers in return for a lien, or mortgage, on their crops. As farmers sank in debt, they increased their production of cotton and tobacco and became trapped on the land. As a result, the labor needed for industrial expansion remained in short supply. The shift from planting corn to raising cotton and tobacco also made small southern farmers vulnerable to the fluctuations of commercial agriculture. By 1900 the price of cotton in international markets had fallen well below the cost of production, and many southern farmers were desperate.

The South also remained the victim of federal policies designed to aid northern industry. High protective tariffs raised the price of imported machine technology, the demonetization of silver (see Chapter 20), further limited capital, and discriminatory railroad rates hiked shipping prices.

The South's chronic shortage of funds affected the economy indirectly as well by limiting resources available for education. During Reconstruction northern philanthropists together with the Freedmen's Bureau and other relief agencies had begun a modest expansion of public schooling for both whites and blacks, but many southern states operated segregated schools and refused to tax property for school support until 1889. Low school attendance limited the number of educated people available for technical positions in business and industry.

Southern states, like those in the North, often contributed the modest funds they had to veterans' pensions. This practice not only built a white patronage system for Confederate veterans and reinforced the myth of the Lost Cause, but also left little for economic and educational development.

The New South Creed and Southern Industrialization

Despite the obstacles to industrialization, energetic southern newspaper editors championed the doctrine that became known as the New South creed. The South's rich coal and timber resources and cheap labor, they proclaimed in their papers, made it a natural site for industrial development.

During the 1880s, the movement to industrialize the South gained momentum. To attract northern capital, southern states offered tax exemptions for new businesses, set up industrial and agricultural expositions, and leased prison inmates to serve as cheap labor. Florida, Texas, and other states gave huge tracts of lands to railroads, which expanded dramatically throughout the South. Other states sold forest and mineral rights on nearly 6 million acres of federal lands to speculators, mostly from the North, who significantly expanded the production of iron, sulfur, coal, and lumber. Southern iron and steel industries also expanded. Founded in 1871 in the heart of a region blessed with coal, limestone, and iron-ore deposits, by 1900 Birmingham, Alabama, was the nation's largest pig-iron shipper. Chattanooga, Tennessee, housed nine furnaces, seventeen foundries, and numerous machine shops.

Recruiting black workers, southern iron and steel mills contributed to the migration of African-Americans cityward. By 1900, 20 percent of the southern black population was urban. However, southern industry reflected the patterns of racism permeating other aspects of southern life. Tobacco companies used black workers, particularly women, to clean the tobacco leaves while white women ran the machines that made cigarettes. In the iron and steel industry, blacks composed 60 percent of the work force but had no chance of advancement. However, in a rare reversal of usual patterns, black workers in iron and steel on average earned more than white textile workers.

The Southern Mill Economy

Unlike the urban-based southern iron and steel industry, textile mills mushroomed in the southern countryside in the 1880s, often accompanied by the formation of new towns and villages. In southern districts that gradually passed from an agricultural to a mill economy, country ways and values suffused the new industrial workplace.

The cotton-mill economy grew largely in the Piedmont, a beautiful backcountry of rolling hills and rushing rivers stretching from central Virginia to northern Georgia and Alabama. The Piedmont had long been a land of subsistence farming and limited roads. But postwar railroad construction opened the region to outside markets and sparked a period of intense town building and textile-mill expansion. Between 1860 and 1900 cotton-mill capacity shot up 1,400 percent, and by 1920 the South was the nation's leading textile-mill center.

Even sharecroppers and tenant farmers at first hailed the new cotton mills as a way out of rural poverty. But the chief cotton-mill promoters came from the same ranks of merchants, lawyers, doctors, and bankers who had profited from the commercialization of southern agriculture (and from the misfortunes of poor black and white tenant farmers and sharecroppers enmeshed in the new system). R. R. Haynes, from North Carolina's Rutherford County, was typical of the new entrepreneurs. Starting out as a storekeeper, he formed a company in 1884 to finance construction of the Henrietta Mills. By 1913 Haynes owned not only one of the South's largest gingham-producing operations but also banks, railroads, lumber businesses, and general stores.

Mill superintendents drew their workers from poor whites on impoverished nearby farms. Although superintendents promised that textile work would free these families from poverty, mill entrepreneurs shamelessly exploited their workers, paying just 7 to 11 cents an hour, roughly half of comparable wages in New England.

The mills dominated most piedmont textile communities. The mill operator built and owned workers' housing and the company store, supported the village church, financed the local elementary school, and pried into the mill hands' morals and behavior. Mill owners usually kept workers dependent and immobile by paying them only once a month, often in scrip that could buy goods only at the company store. Most families had to buy on credit during the month, overspent, and fell behind in their payments. As charges were deducted from the next month's paycheck, workers fell into a cycle of indebtedness indistinguishable from that of sharecroppers.

Southern mill superintendents hired whole families, including the children. Mothers commonly kept babies in baskets nearby while tending their machines. Little children sometimes operated the machines. Laboring a twelve-hour day together, the mill hands developed strong ties. One employee put it simply, "The mill community was a close bunch of people . . . like one big family. We just loved one another." To help make ends meet, mill workers kept their own gardens and raised chickens and an occasional cow or pig. Southern mill hands thus brought communal farm values into the mills and mill villages. Although they had to adapt to machine-paced work and earned barely enough to live on, the working poor in the mill districts, like their northern counterparts, eased the shift from rural to village-industrial life by clinging to a cooperative country ethic.

The Southern Industrial Lag

Still, with its retarded industrialization, the southern economy remained essentially colonial, subject to control by northern industries and financial syndicates. For example, U.S. Steel controlled the foundries in Birmingham, and it forced southerners to pay higher prices for steel than northerners, even though southern production cost less. Inevitably, environmental damage—polluted streams, blasted forests, grimy coal towns, and soot-blackened cities—accompanied industrialization.

Unfavorable federal banking regulations, scarce capital, staggering debt, and discriminatory business practices by northern-controlled enterprises hampered the South's economic development. Dragged down by a poorly educated and poorly trained population, both white and black, southern industry languished. Limited by outside forces, economic progress in the South occurred in its own distinctly regional way.

FACTORIES AND THE WORK FORCE

Nationally, industrialization proceeded unevenly: during the late nineteenth century most Americans still worked in small shops. But as the century closed, more and more large factories appeared, with armies of workers. Between 1860 and 1900 the number of industrial workers jumped from 885,000 to 3.2 million.

From Workshop to Factory

The changes that led to the factory economy involved a fundamental restructuring of work habits and a new emphasis on workplace discipline. The boot and shoe industry illustrates the impact of these changes. As late as the 1840s, almost every shoe was custom-made, and shoemakers were the aristocrats of labor, working in small, independent shops where they controlled and took pride in the quality of their work. Foreign-born English, German, and Irish shoe workers developed strong ethnic and community pride. They set up ethnic trade organizations; took time off for religious observances, funerals, and holidays; drank sociably together; and helped each other weather accidents or illness.

As early as the 1850s, however, management began to move its growing production staffs into large buildings and broke the manufacturing process into a series of repetitive tasks. Skilled artisans now worked in teams, with each member responsible for a specific task—say, attaching the heel—instead of crafting a pair of shoes from start to finish. Workers lost the freedom to drink on the job or to take time off for special occasions. The working-class culture that had reinforced group solidarity appeared wasteful and inefficient to owners and foremen. Then in the 1880s, as shoe factories became larger and more mechanized, sophisticated machines allowed companies to replace skilled workers with low-paid, unskilled women and children. By 1890 unskilled women made up more than 35 percent of the work force in an industry once dominated by skilled men.

Skilled artisans in other trades also found their responsibilities changing. They no longer participated in the production process *as a whole*. Rather, in new factories specializing in consumer goods, "skilled" workers performed numbingly repetitive tasks. Factory work had become specialized, machine-paced, and deadeningly routine.

The Hardships of Industrial Labor

The expansion of the factory system created an unprecedented demand for unskilled labor. By the 1880s nearly one-third of the workers in the railroad and steel industries were common laborers. In the construction trades, the machine and tool industries, and garment manufacturing, industrialists used the contract system to hire unskilled laborers. Subcontractors hired, managed, and fired these common workers, who were taken on when needed and laid off in slack periods. The steel industry employed them to shovel ore and to move ingots inside the mills. Foremen drove the laborers hard.

Unskilled workers drifted from city to city and from industry to industry. They earned about one-third the wages of skilled artisans. In the late 1870s, bricklayers earned $3.00 a day, but unskilled laborers a mere $1.30. Only southern mill workers, averaging $.84 a day, earned less.

Skilled and unskilled workers alike put in twelve-hour shifts, often under hazardous, unhealthful conditions. An alarming incidence of industrial accidents stemmed from workers' inexperience, dangerous factory conditions, and the rapid pace of production. One steelworker recalled that, on his first day at the mill, "I looked up and a big train carrying a big vessel with fire was making towards me. I stood numb, afraid to move, until a man came to me and led me out of the mill." The accident rate in steel mills was extremely high.

Children as young as eight worked in coal mines and cotton mills. Their attempts to play while on the job made them vulnerable to accidents. In cotton mills, when supervision was lax, child workers would grab the belts that powered the machines and see who could ride closest to the drive shaft in the ceiling before letting go and falling to the floor. In coal mines, child workers sat in a cloud of black dust beneath the breakers that crushed coal, picking out slate and other impurities. Many succumbed to lung disease.

Textile Workers
Young children like this one were often used in the textile mills because their small fingers could tie together broken threads more easily than those of adults.

For adult workers, the railroads presented the greatest peril. In 1889, the first year that reliable statistics were compiled, almost 2,000 railwaymen were killed on the job and more than 20,000 were injured. Disabled workers and widows received minimal aid from employers. Until the 1890s the courts considered employer negligence one of the normal risks borne by the employee. Employers fought the adoption of safety and health standards on the grounds that the costs would be excessive. Workers joined fraternal organizations and ethnic clubs for sickness and accident benefits, but usually the amounts set aside from dues were too low to provide much relief. When a worker was killed or maimed, the family depended on relatives or neighbors for help.

Immigrant Labor

Factory owners turned to unskilled immigrants for the muscle needed in factories, mills, railroads, and heavy construction. In Philadelphia native-born Americans and recent German immigrants domi-nated the highly skilled metal-working trades, and Irish immigrants remained in unskilled occupations until the 1890s, when "new immigrants" from southern and eastern Europe replaced them. On the West Coast, Chinese immigrants performed the dirtiest, most physically demanding jobs in mining, canning, and railroad construction.

In many industries, immigrants disposed to live frugally in a boardinghouse and to work an eighty-four-hour week could save $15.00 a month, far more than they could have earned in their homeland. But rural peasants from southern and eastern Europe found it very difficult to abandon their irregular work habits for the rigid factory schedules. Where sun and season had paced farm routines, factory operations were relentless. When immigrant workers resisted the machines' exhausting tempo, drank on the job, or took unexcused absences, employers used a variety of tactics to enforce discipline. Some sponsored temperance societies and Sunday schools to teach punctuality and sobriety. Others cut wages and put workers on the piecework system, paying them only for the items produced. Sometimes employers provided low-cost housing to gain leverage against work stoppages; if workers went on strike, the boss could simply evict them.

In the case of immigrants from southern Europe, often darker-skinned than northern Europeans, and in the case of fairer-skinned immigrants, whether Irish or Jewish, employers asserted that they were nonwhite and did not deserve the same compensation as native-born Americans. With "whiteness" viewed as the privilege of native birth, rather than a biological trait, the concept of race was thus used to justify the harsh treatment of foreign-born labor.

Women and Work in Industrial America

As with men, marital status, social class, and race shaped women's work experiences. Accepting the image of women as uniquely capable of nurturing families, white married women of all classes tended to remain home rearing children and looking after the household, while men labored in factories and offices. Well-to-do women hired maids and cooks to ease their burdens; working-class married women, in contrast, often had to earn money at home to make ends meet.

Working at home for wages—sewing, button-making, taking in boarders, or doing laundry—predated industrialization. However, in the cities of industrial America, unscrupulous entrepreneurs could exploit the home work force. Cigar manufacturers would buy or lease a tenement and require "their" families to live and work there. Working-class married women and their children often labored long hours in their crowded apartments to finish needlework for the garment industry.

Working-class single women often saw outside work as an opportunity. In 1870 only 13 percent of all women worked outside the home, most often at domestic chores, but that figure had nearly tripled by 1900, when women made up 17 percent of the country's labor force. Many women workers abandoned domestic employment for better-paying, less demeaning jobs in the textile, food-processing,

and garment industries, although discrimination barred black women from following this path. Changes in agriculture prompted countless young farm women to seek employment in the industrial sector, and young immigrant women, too, worked in factories to increase family income. Factory owners welcomed young foreign-born women as a ready source of inexpensive unskilled labor. Young women in the clothing industry earned as little as $5.00 for seventy hours of work but widely relished the independence of working. In fact, however, industrial work enmeshed these women more deeply in families that depended on their earnings.

When the typewriter and the telephone came into general use in the 1890s, women with a high-school education moved into clerical and secretarial positions earlier filled by men. The clean, safe working conditions and relatively good pay attracted them; a first-rate typist could earn $7.00 a week. Even though women were excluded from managerial positions, office jobs carried higher prestige and offered steadier work than employment in factories or shops.

Despite women's growing numbers in the work force, the popular press portrayed their work outside the home as temporary. Few people imagined that women could attain national or even local prominence in the emerging corporate order.

Hard Work and the Gospel of Success

Although women were generally excluded, opinion molders in these years preached that any man could achieve success in the new industrial era. In *Ragged Dick* (1867) and scores of later tales, novelist Horatio Alger recounted the rise of poor but honest lads through ambition, initiative, and self-discipline. In his widely read stories, shoeshine boys stop runaway horses and are rewarded by rich benefactors who give them a start in business. Andrew Carnegie served as proof that the United States remained the land of opportunity and "rags to riches."

Not everyone embraced this belief. Mark Twain, for one, in an 1871 essay, chided the public for its naïveté and suggested that business success was more likely to come to those who lied and cheated. What are the facts? Recent studies reveal that Carnegie was a rare exception and that 95 percent of industrial leaders had middle- and upper-class backgrounds. However, skilled immigrants and native-born working-class Americans had opportunities to rise to the top of small companies. Few reaped immense fortunes, but many attained substantial incomes.

Unskilled workers found far fewer opportunities for advancement. Some did move into semi-skilled and skilled positions. However, most immigrants, especially the Irish, Italians, and Chinese, progressed far more slowly than the sons of middle- and upper-class Americans. Upward mobility for unskilled workers generally meant mobility *within* the working class. Immigrants who got ahead went from rags to respectability, not rags to riches.

Between 1860 and 1900 real wages rose 31 percent for unskilled workers and 74 percent for skilled workers. But injury and unemployment during slack times undercut the gains, especially for unskilled immigrant laborers. Even in a prosperous year such as 1890, one in every five workers was unemployed for at least a month. During the depressions of the 1870s and 1890s, wage cuts, extended layoffs, and unemployment pushed those at the base of the industrial work force to the brink of starvation.

Thus, overall, the question of economic mobility in the late nineteenth century is complex. At the top, the rich amassed enormous fortunes; in 1890 a mere 10 percent of American families owned 73 percent of the nation's wealth. At the bottom, only 45 percent of U.S. industrial laborers took in earnings above the $500 poverty line. Between these extremes, skilled immigrant workers and shopkeepers swelled the middle class. The standard of living rose for millions of Americans, but the gap between rich and poor remained an abyss.

LABOR UNIONS AND INDUSTRIAL CONFLICT

As the rapid growth of large corporations transformed working conditions, millions of American workers sought new forms of support. The expansion into national and world markets gave industrial leaders unprecedented power to control the workplace. To resist this power, labor leaders searched for ways to create broad-based, national organizations. They faced many problems. Ethnic and racial divisions hampered unionizing efforts. Skilled craftworkers felt little kinship with low-paid common laborers. Thus, unionization efforts moved forward slowly, with many setbacks. With unions so weak, labor unrest reached crisis proportions in the 1890s.

Organizing the Workers

The Civil War marked a watershed in the rise of organized labor. Small craft unions, with goals of fighting wage reductions and providing sickness benefits, had existed since the eighteenth century, but after the war labor leaders sought to increase union clout. To many, the answer lay in the formation of a single association that would transcend craft lines and draw a mass membership.

William H. Sylvis, elected president of the Iron Moulders' International Union in 1863, dreamed of creating such a superunion. Strongly built and bearded, with a "face and eyes beaming with intelligence," Sylvis quickly built his union from "a mere pygmy" to a membership of 8,500. In 1866 he called a convention that formed the National Labor Union (NLU). The new organization embraced an eight-hour workday, currency and banking reform, an end to convict labor, a federal department of labor, and restrictions on immigration, particularly of Chinese, to push wage scales higher. Under Sylvis's leadership the NLU also endorsed the cause of working women and elected the head of a union of female laundry workers as one of its national officers. The NLU urged African-American workers to organize as well, although in racially separate unions.

After a strike by Sylvis's own union failed in winter 1866–1867, Sylvis turned to national political reform. In 1868 a number of reformers attended an impressive NLU convention. However, Sylvis's sudden death in 1869 shattered the NLU, which disintegrated by 1873.

The dream of a national labor movement lived on in a new organization, the Noble and Holy Order of the Knights of Labor. Founded in 1869 by Philadelphia tailors as a secret society modeled on the Masonic order, the Knights welcomed all wage earners; they excluded only bankers, physicians, lawyers, stockbrokers, professional gamblers, and liquor dealers. The Knights advocated equal pay for women, an end to child and convict labor, a graduated income tax (at a time when no federal income tax existed), and cooperative employer-employee ownership of factories, mines, and other businesses.

At first the Knights grew slowly, but in the 1880s membership skyrocketed after Terence V. Powderly became the Knights' head. The eloquent Powderly orchestrated successes in a series of labor clashes and brought in thousands of new members.

Ethnic and Racial Hatred
Conservative business owners used racist advertising, such as this trade card stigmatizing Chinese laundry workers, to promote their own products and to associate their company with patriotism.

The Knights of Labor reflected its idealistic origins and Powderly's collaborative vision. Powderly condemned strikes as "a relic of barbarism" and organized producer and consumer cooperatives. He also advocated temperance and offered membership to both African-Americans and women. Recruited by women organizers such as the feisty Mary Harris Jones, known as Mother Jones, by 1886 women made up 10 percent of the Knights' membership.

Powderly and the Knights supported immigration restriction and a total ban on Chinese immigration. Union members feared that immigrants would steal jobs by working too cheaply. Westerners, especially Californians, saw the Chinese as a major threat. In 1877 a San Francisco demonstration for the eight-hour day turned into a riot that destroyed twenty-five Chinese laundries and terrorized the local Chinese population. Five years later Congress passed the Chinese Exclusion Act, placing a ten-year moratorium on Chinese immigration.

Although inspired by Powderly's vision of a harmonious and cooperative future, most rank-and-file members rejected Powderly's antistrike position. In 1883–1884 spontaneous local strikes led by Knights gained only reluctant support from the national leadership. However, in 1885 when Jay Gould tried to drive the Knights out of his Wabash Railroad by firing active union members, Powderly authorized a strike against the Wabash and ordered Knights working for other lines to refuse to handle Wabash cars. With his railroad crippled, Gould, to the nation's amazement, met with Powderly and halted his campaign against the Knights.

Membership soared; by 1886, 6,000 locals served more than 700,000 workers. That fall the Knights entered politics, mounting campaigns in nearly 200 towns and cities, electing several mayors and judges, and helping a dozen congressmen to gain office. In state legislatures they lobbied successfully for laws banning convict labor, and at the national level for legislation against importing foreign contract labor. Conservatives warned darkly that the Knights could cripple the economy and take over the country.

In fact, the Knights' strength soon waned. A series of failed (and unauthorized) strikes in 1886 left members disillusioned. The national reaction to the Haymarket riot, discussed in the next section, also contributed to the union's decline. By the late 1880s, the Knights of Labor was a shadow of its former self. But it had given major impetus to the labor movement and awakened hundreds of thousands of workers to group solidarity and their potential strength.

Even as the Knights became weaker, another labor organization, pursuing more immediate and practical goals, was growing strong. The skilled craft unions had long felt threatened by the Knights' broad base and emphasis on sweeping reform goals. In May 1886 the craft unions left the Knights to form the American Federation of Labor (AFL), which replaced the Knights' grand visions with practical tactics aimed at "bread-and-butter issues."

Samuel Gompers, an English immigrant cigar maker who headed the AFL from its formation until his death in 1924, believed in "trade unionism, pure and simple." Higher wages were necessary to enable working-class families to exist decently, with respect and dignity. Having lost faith in utopian social reforms, Gompers believed that "the poor, the hungry, have not the strength to engage in a conflict even when life is at stake." To stand up to corporations, Gompers argued, labor had to harness the bargaining power of skilled workers, who were not easily replaced, and concentrate on practical goals of raising wages and reducing hours.

A master tactician, Gompers believed that large-scale industrial organization required comparable labor organization. At the same time, he knew that the individual skilled craft unions were committed to controlling their own affairs. Gompers therefore organized the AFL as a *federation* of trade unions, each retaining control of its own members but linked by an executive council to coordinate strategy. Focusing the federation's efforts on short-term improvements in wages and hours, Gompers sidestepped divisive political issues. The AFL advocated an eight-hour workday, employers' liability for workers' injuries, and mine-safety laws. By 1904 the AFL had grown to more than 1.6 million members.

As a whole, however, late-nineteenth-century labor organizations remained weak, enlisting less than 5 percent of the work force. Split between skilled artisans and common laborers, separated along ethnic and religious lines, and divided over tactics, the unions enjoyed only occasional success against the growing power of corporate enterprise. Lacking financial resources, they typically watched from the sidelines as unorganized workers launched wildcat strikes that sometimes turned violent.

Strikes and Labor Violence

Americans had lived with violence from the nation's beginnings and in the nineteenth century witnessed civil war, urban riots, and Indian-white conflict. Terrible labor clashes toward the end of the century were part of this continuing pattern, but they nevertheless shocked and dismayed contemporaries. From 1881 to 1905, close to 37,000 strikes erupted, in which nearly 7 million workers participated.

The Wall Street crash of 1873 triggered a major depression. Businesses collapsed, tramps roamed New York and Chicago streets, and labor unrest mounted. In 1877 a wildcat railroad strike, ignited by a wage reduction on the Baltimore and Ohio Railroad in July, exploded up and down the rail lines and spread quickly from coast to coast. Rioters in Pittsburgh torched Union Depot and the Pennsylvania Railroad roundhouse. By the time newly inaugurated president Rutherford B. Hayes called out federal troops to quell the strike, nearly one hundred people had died and two-thirds of U.S. railroads stood idle.

The strike stunned middle-class America. Hysterical voices proclaimed that "if the club of the policeman, knocking out the brains of the rioter, will answer, then well and good, [but if not] then bullets and bayonets . . . constitute the one remedy." Employers exploited the public hysteria to crack down on labor. Many required workers to sign "yellow dog" contracts, promising not to strike or join a union. Some hired Pinkerton agents to serve as a private police force and, as in the 1877 rail strike, relied on the U.S. Army to suppress unrest.

The 1880s saw more strikes and violence. On May 1, 1886, 340,000 workers walked off their jobs to support the eight-hour workday. Strikers in Cincinnati virtually shut down the city for nearly a month. On May 3, 1886, Chicago police shot and killed four strikers at the McCormick Harvester plant. At a protest rally the next evening in the city's Haymarket Square, someone threw a bomb, killing or fatally wounding seven policemen. In turn, the police fired wildly into the crowd and killed four demonstrators. Business leaders and middle-class citizens lashed out at labor activists, particularly the Haymarket meeting sponsors, most of whom were associated with German anarchism. Eight were arrested. No evidence connected them directly to the bomb, but all were convicted, and four were executed; a fifth committed suicide in prison. Many Americans became convinced that a deadly foreign conspiracy gripped the nation, and animosity toward labor unions intensified.

Confrontations between business and labor continued into the 1890s. National Guard troops were called out to crush strikes by Idaho silver miners at Coeur d'Alene and Carnegie steelworkers at Homestead, Pennsylvania. The most systematic use of troops to smash union action came in an 1894 strike against the Pullman Palace Car Company. George Pullman, a manufacturer of elegant railroad sleeping and dining cars, had constructed a factory and a town called Pullman, south of Chicago. The carefully planned community provided Pullman workers with brick houses, parks, playgrounds, a bank, and a library. However, Pullman policed workers' activities, banned saloons, and insisted that his properties turn a profit.

When the depression of 1893 hit, Pullman slashed wages. But he did not lower rents. Thousands of workers joined the newly formed American Railway Union and went on strike. They were led by a fiery young organizer, Eugene V. Debs, who vowed "to strip the mask of hypocrisy from the pretended philanthropist and show him to the world as an oppressor of labor." Union members working for other railroads refused to switch Pullman cars, paralyzing rail traffic in and out of Chicago, one of the nation's main rail hubs.

In response to the crisis, the General Managers' Association, composed of top railroad executives, decided to break the union. After importing strikebreakers, the organization asked U.S. attorney general Richard Olney, who sat on the board of directors of three major railroads, for a federal injunction against the strikers for allegedly refusing to move rail cars carrying U.S. mail. In fact, however, when union members had volunteered to switch mail cars onto trains that did not carry Pullman cars, the railroads' managers had refused to dispatch trains without the full complement of cars. Olney, supported by President Grover Cleveland, cited the Sherman Anti-Trust Act and secured an injunction against leaders of the American Railway Union for restraint of commerce. When the union refused to order its members back to work, Debs was arrested and federal troops poured in. During the ensuing rioting, 700 freight cars were burned, 13 people died, and 53 were wounded. The strike was crushed.

By exploiting the popular identification of strikers with anarchism and violence, corporate leaders hobbled organized labor's ability to bargain. When the Supreme Court upheld Debs's prison sentence and legalized the use of injunctions against labor unions (*In re Debs*, 1895), business gained a powerful new weapon against labor. In contrast to Great Britain and Germany, where state officials often mediated disputes between labor and capital, federal, state, and local officials often supported employer campaigns to hamstring efforts to build a strong working-class movement. Blocked by officials and frustrated by court decisions, American unions could not expand their base of support. Not until the 1930s would the labor movement shed its negative public image and regain the vitality sapped by post–Civil War turmoil.

Social Thinkers Probe for Alternatives

The widespread industrial turmoil was particularly unsettling when juxtaposed with growing evidence of working-class destitution. Many observers worried about the future of the emerging industrial order. At stake was a critical issue: should government become the mechanism for helping the poor and regulating big business?

Defenders of capitalism preached the laissez-faire ("hands-off") argument that government should never attempt to control business. They cited Scottish economist Adam Smith (1723–1790), who asserted that self-interest acted as an "invisible hand" in the marketplace, automatically balancing the supply of and demand for goods and services. In "The Gospel of Wealth," an influential essay published in 1889, Andrew Carnegie applied British scientist Charles Darwin's evolutionary theories to human society. "The law of competition," Carnegie wrote, "may be sometimes hard for the individual, [but] it is best for the race, because it insures the survival of the fittest in every department." Ignoring the contemporary scramble among businesses to eliminate competition, Carnegie praised unregulated competition as a source of positive long-term social benefits.

Yale professor William Graham Sumner shared Carnegie's disapproval of government interference. In his combative book *What Social Classes Owe to Each Other* (1883), Sumner asserted that unchangeable laws controlled the social order: "a drunkard in the gutter is just where he ought to be. . . . The law of survival of the fittest was not made by man, and it cannot be abrogated by man. We can only, by interfering with it, produce the survival of the unfittest." The state, declared Sumner, owed its citizens only law, order, and basic political rights.

This conservative Social Darwinism (as such ideas came to be called) did not go unchallenged. In *Dynamic Sociology* (1883), geologist Lester Frank Ward argued that human will *could* circumvent the supposed "laws" of nature. Just as scientists had bred superior livestock, government experts could regulate big business, protect society's weaker members, and prevent the reckless exploitation of natural resources.

Henry George, a newspaper editor and economic theorist, proposed in *Progress and Poverty* (1879), that government tax the "unearned increment" that speculators reaped from rising land prices. Funds from this "single tax" could then ameliorate the misery caused by industrialization. Americans could enjoy the benefits of socialism—a state-controlled economic system that distributed resources according to need—without abandoning capitalism or stifling individual initiative. George's program was so popular that he lectured around the country and only narrowly missed being elected mayor of New York in 1886.

Another newspaper editor, Edward Bellamy, turned to fiction to evoke visions of a harmonious industrialized society. In *Looking Backward* (1888), Bellamy's protagonist, Julian West, falls asleep in 1888 and awakens in 2000 to find a nation without poverty or strife, thanks to a centralized, state-run economy. Centralization and a new religion of solidarity have created a society in which everyone works for the common welfare. Bellamy's utopian novel inspired middle-class Americans, fearful of corporate power and working-class violence, to form nearly 500 Nationalist clubs to implement Bellamy's scheme.

Ward, George, and Bellamy did not deny the industrial order's benefits; rather, envisioning a harmonious society whose members all worked together, they sought to humanize it. Marxist socialists advanced a different view. In *Das Kapital* (1867) and other works, German radical Karl Marx argued that the labor required to produce a commodity was the only true measure of that commodity's value. Profit made by a capitalist employer was "surplus value" appropriated from exploited workers. Competition among capitalists would increase, Marx predicted; wages would decline to starvation levels, and finally the impoverished working class would revolt and seize control of the state and the economy. Class struggle would lead to a classless utopia in which the state would "wither away" and exploitation would end. But Marxism had little appeal in late-nineteenth-century America beyond a handful of German-born immigrants. More alarming were the anarchists, mainly immigrants, who rejected Marxist discipline and preached the destruction of capitalism, the violent overthrow of the state, and the immediate introduction of a stateless utopia.

Chronology

1859	First oil well drilled, in Titusville, Pennsylvania.	1886	American Federation of Labor (AFL) formed. Police and demonstrators clash at Haymarket Square in Chicago.
1866	National Labor Union founded.		
1869	Knights of Labor organized.	1887	Interstate Commerce Act establishes the Interstate Commerce Commission.
1870	John D. Rockefeller establishes Standard Oil Company.		
		1888	Edward Bellamy, *Looking Backward*.
1873	Panic of 1873 triggers a depression lasting until 1879.	1889	Andrew Carnegie, "The Gospel of Wealth."
		1890	Sherman Anti-Trust Act.
1876	Alexander Graham Bell invents and patents the telephone. Thomas A. Edison opens research laboratory at Menlo Park, New Jersey.	1892	Standard Oil of New Jersey and General Electric formed. Steelworkers strike at Homestead, Pennsylvania. World's Columbian Exposition opens in Chicago. Miners strike at Coeur d'Alene, Idaho.
1877	Edison invents the phonograph. Railway workers stage the first nationwide strike.	1893	Panic of 1893 triggers a depression lasting until 1897.
1879	Henry George, *Progress and Poverty*. Edison perfects the incandescent lamp.	1894	Pullman Palace Car workers strike, supported by the National Railway Union.
1881	Standard Oil Trust established.		
1882	Edison opens the first electric power station in New York's financial district. Chinese Exclusion Act.	1901	J. Pierpont Morgan organizes United States Steel.
1883	Railroads divide the country into time zones. William Graham Sumner, *What Social Classes Owe to Each Other*. Lester Frank Ward, *Dynamic Sociology*.		

CONCLUSION *hc* ACE Practice Test

By 1900 industrialization had catapulted the United States to world power, lowered the cost of goods, generated thousands of jobs, and made available a wide range of consumer products. But the cost was high. Savage competition, exploited workers, shady business practices, polluted landscapes, and the collapse of an economic order built on craft skills had accompanied the rise of giant corporations. In the South in particular, industrialists adopted a paternalistic, family-oriented approach in the cotton mills and paid exceedingly low wages.

Americans were uncertain about the new industrial order. Enjoying the higher standard of living that industrialization made possible, but fearing capitalist power and social chaos, they tried to keep the material benefits while alleviating the social harm. The Interstate Commerce Act, the Sherman Anti-Trust Act, and the fervor with which many embraced theories like those of utopian Edward Bellamy testify to middle-class qualms. In the Progressive Era of the early twentieth century, Americans would redouble their efforts to create political and social solutions to the changes wrought by the economic transformation.

FURTHER READING

Edward L. Ayers, *The Promise of the New South: Life After Reconstruction* (1992). A comprehensive overview of economic and social change in the post–Civil War South.

David Bain, *Empire Express: Building the First Transcontinental Railroad* (1999). An important study of the early leaders of the railroad industry.

Ron Chernow, *Titan: The Life of John D. Rockefeller, Sr.* (1998). A balanced, insightful examination of the character and business practices of one of the most successful captains of industry.

Wendy Gamber, *The Female Economy: The Millinery and Dressmaking Trades, 1860–1930* (1997). An important study of ways in which women's custom dressmaking businesses provided important entrepreneurial opportunities for women in the late nineteenth century.

Matthew F. Jacobson, *Whiteness of a Different Color: European Immigrants and the Alchemy of Race* (1998). A study of how the concept of race was defined and applied to immigrants in the nineteenth century.

Richard Schneirov, Shelton Stromquist, and Nick Salvatore, eds., *The Pullman Strike and the Crisis of the 1890s: Essays on Labor and Politics* (1999). An important survey of the impact of the Pullman Strike on politics, the role of the state, and the public controversy over governmental regulation of corporate activity.

Philip Scranton, *Endless Novelty: Specialty Production and American Industrialization, 1865–1925* (1997). A useful corrective to the argument that large corporations alone account for American economic growth in the post–Civil War period.

Joel A. Tarr, *The Search for the Ultimate Sink: Urban Pollution in Historical Perspective* (1996). An important study of the environmental problems created by industrialization.

Kim Voss, *The Making of American Exceptionalism: The Knights of Labor and Class Formation in the Nineteenth Century* (1993). A comparative analysis of American labor's attempts to mobilize workers in the face of business opposition.

19

Immigration, Urbanization, and Everyday Life, 1860–1900

hc This icon will direct you to additional study and research resources at http://college.hmco.com/history/us/boyer/enduring_concise/5e/students/index.html

Backyard Baseball, Boston, by Lewis Hine, 1906.

In the early twentieth century the jazzy, syncopated dance music known as ragtime became a national sensation, and Scott Joplin, a young black composer and pianist, became the king of ragtime. Joplin's meteoric rise from unknown saloon pianist to renowned composer reflected not only the commercialization of the entertainment industry but also the class and racial tensions that pervaded popular culture.

Despite Joplin's enormous success, white competitors demeaned his compositions as "coon songs." And Joplin, who dreamed of gaining national recognition for composing opera, found his way blocked by white publishers who refused to accept his work. Opera, after all, was "high art" controlled by the upper class, off-limits to blacks and the lower classes. Racial and class discrimination reinforced each other.

Joplin's thwarted dreams were similar to those of countless others who tried to move up the economic ladder. American society was shifting from a producer economy stressing hard work and thrift to a consumer economy stressing entertainment and possessions, but not everyone would have access to this new world of consumption.

At the same time, Joplin's success as a ragtime composer mirrored the upward mobility of many who profited from the new society. Economic change combined with the proliferation of white-collar jobs to create new expectations for family life and to foster a growing class awareness. The middle and upper classes prospered, while farmers, immigrants, and the urban working class enjoyed only moderate success.

The growth of the consumer economy tended to widen the gulf between the haves and the have-nots while intensifying class consciousness. The very rich lived in a world apart, the middle class embraced its own work code and life-style, and a vigorous working-class culture emerged in the heavily immigrant cities. Despite middle-class efforts to remake working-class ways, the mass lower-class culture ultimately proved most influential in shaping modern America.

EVERYDAY LIFE IN FLUX: THE NEW AMERICAN CITY

Nowhere were the changes in everyday life more visible than in cities. Between 1870 and 1900 New Orleans's population nearly doubled, Buffalo's tripled, and Chicago's increased more than five-fold. By 1900, Philadelphia, New York, and Chicago all had more than a million residents, and 40 percent of all Americans lived in cities.

This spectacular urban growth, fueled by the influx of nearly 11 million immigrants, stimulated economic development. Mushrooming cities created new jobs and markets that in turn dramatically stim-

This chapter focuses on five major questions:

▶ How did the growth of cities and the influx of immigrants create a new awareness of ethnic and class differences? How were racial stereotypes used to reinforce these distinctions?

▶ What was Victorian morality? How did it influence social patterns and daily life?

▶ How did changes in the occupational structure and in education affect women's roles?

▶ How did class conflict reshape attitudes toward leisure and recreation?

▶ Why did Americans become disenchanted with Victorian social and intellectual values?

ulated national economic expansion. Like the frontier, the city symbolized opportunity for all comers.

The city's unprecedented scale and diversity threatened traditional expectations of community life and stability. A medley of immigrant groups contended with each another and with native-born Americans for jobs, power, and influence. Rapid growth strained city services, generating terrible housing and sanitation problems.

Native-born American city-dwellers found the noise, stench, and congestion disturbing. They worried about the newcomers' squalid tenements, fondness for drink, and strange social customs. Reformers who set out to "clean up" the cities aimed not only to improve the physical environment but also to destroy the distinctive customs of the immigrant cultures. The immigrants, resenting attacks on their way of life, fought to protect their traditions. The late nineteenth century thus witnessed an intense struggle among diverse urban constituencies to control the city politically and to benefit from its economic and cultural potential.

Migrants and Immigrants

Since the new industries concentrated in urban settings required thousands of new workers, the promise of good wages and plentiful jobs attracted many rural and small-town dwellers to the cities. So great was the migration from rural areas, especially in New England, that some farm communities vanished from the map.

Young women led the exodus. The growing commercialization and specialization of agriculture had turned much farm labor into male work. Mail-order sales of factory-made goods meanwhile reduced the need for women's work on subsistence tasks. So young farm women flocked to the cities, where they competed with immigrant, African-American, and city-born women for jobs.

From 1860 to 1890, the prospect of a better life also attracted nearly 10 million northern European immigrants to American cities, where they joined the more than 4 million who had settled there in the 1840s and 1850s. Their numbers included 3 million Germans; 2 million English, Scottish, and Welsh; and 1.5 million Irish. Moreover, by 1900 more than 800,000 French-Canadians had migrated southward to work in the New England mills, and nearly 1 million Scandinavians farmed the rich lands of Wisconsin and Minnesota. Then, in the three decades after 1890, more than 18 million "new immigrants" joined these "old immigrants." Predominantly peasants, they came from southern and eastern Europe.

The overwhelming majority of both old and new immigrants settled in cities in the northeastern and north-central states. The numbers were staggering. In 1890 New York City contained twice as many Irish as Dublin, as many Germans as Hamburg, half as many Italians as Naples, and two and a half times the Jewish population of Warsaw. Four out of five people in New York City were immigrants or the children of immigrants.

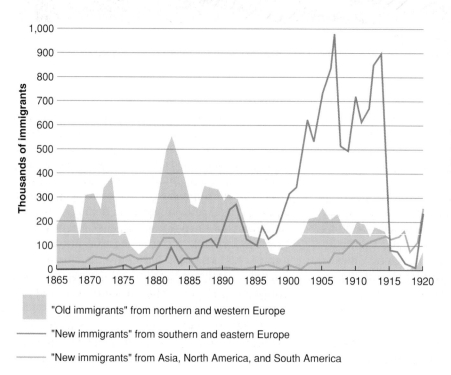

The Changing Face of U.S. Immigration, 1865–1920
Between 1865 and 1895, the majority of newcomers to America hailed from northern and western Europe. But the early twentieth century witnessed a surge of immigration from southern and eastern Europe.
hc Interactive Map: Percentage of Foreign-born Whites and Native Whites of Foreign or Mixed Parentage in Total Populations, 1910

"Old immigrants" from northern and western Europe

"New immigrants" from southern and eastern Europe

"New immigrants" from Asia, North America, and South America

Jakob Mithelstadt and Family, 1905
The Mithelstadts were Russian Germans who arrived in New York City on the S.S. *Pretoria*. The poorest immigrants traveled in steerage, below-deck cargo areas that lacked portholes and originally housed the cables to the ship's rudder.

Overpopulation, crop failure, famine, and industrial depression had driven some of these immigrants from their homelands. At the same time, the promise of high wages lured more than 100,000 Japanese to work on Hawaiian sugar plantations. However, many people, especially single young men, immigrated in the belief that the United States held a better future than their homeland. An eighteen-year-old Norwegian explained his decision: "My father is a schoolteacher and has, besides me, two younger sons, so that it often strains his resources to keep us in school here. . . . I have come to feel that the most sensible thing I can do is to emigrate to America."

The transatlantic journey, cramped and often stormy, featured poor food, little privacy, and rudimentary sanitary facilities. Immigrants arrived tired, fearful, and in some cases very sick. Then customs officials examined them for physical handicaps and contagious diseases. After 1891 those with a "loathsome" infection such as leprosy or a sexually transmitted disease were deported. Immigrants who passed the physical examination had their names recorded. If a customs official had difficulty pronouncing a foreign name, he Anglicized it. One German Jew became flustered when asked for his name and mumbled "Schoyn vergessen [I forget]." The inspector, who did not know Yiddish, wrote, "Sean Ferguson."

In 1892 the federal government established a facility for admitting immigrants on Ellis Island, replacing a nearby facility run by the state of New

York on Castle Garden. Here America's newest residents exchanged foreign currency for U.S. dollars, purchased railroad tickets, and arranged lodgings. Those who arrived with enough cash, including many Germans and Scandinavians, commonly traveled west to Chicago, Milwaukee, and the prairies beyond. But most of the Irish and Italians, largely from poor peasant backgrounds, stayed in eastern cities such as Boston, New York, and Philadelphia, where they filled the lowest-paying jobs. The Irish and Italians who did go west typically made the trip in stages, moving from job to job along the railroad and canal systems.

Adjusting to an Urban Society

Immigrants tended to cluster together to ease the transition to life in a new society. In 1890 a reporter observed that if a map of New York City's streets were colored in by nationality, it "would show more stripes than on the skin of a zebra, and more colors than any rainbow."

Most newcomers preferred to live near others not merely of their own nationality but from their own region or village. New York City held not a single "Little Italy" but dozens of them, inhabited by Neapolitans and Calabrians at Mulberry Bend, Genoese on Baxter Street, northern Italians west of Broadway, and Tyrolese Italians on Sixty-ninth Street near the Hudson River.

In the competition to get ahead, some immigrant groups adjusted more easily than others. Those with skilled trades and familiarity with Anglo-American customs had relatively few problems. Ethnic groups that formed a substantial percentage of a city's population also had a major advantage. The Irish of Boston, New York, and Chicago, as well as the Germans of Milwaukee, dominated local government and church organizations and eased the path for their fellow immigrants.

But the power of the larger immigrant groups sometimes made the adjustment to American society more difficult for members of the smaller groups. The English and Germans who dominated the building trades, for example, limited the numbers of Italians hired. In 1900 only 18 percent of

New York's skilled brick masons were Italians, but 55 percent of its barbers and 97 percent of its poorly paid bootblacks were recent newcomers from Italy.

The smaller immigrant groups sometimes had trouble adjusting to American society, moreover, because many of their members did not intend to stay in the United States. Young Italian males often emigrated to America to earn enough money to return home, where they hoped to buy land or to establish a business. They made little effort to learn English or to understand American customs. Of the Italians who migrated to New York before 1914, nearly 50 percent went back to Italy.

By 1900, whatever the degree of adaptation to the English language and U.S. culture, all immigrant groups faced increasing hostility from native-born Americans, who not only disliked the newcomers' social customs but also feared their growing influence.

Slums and Ghettos

Every major city had run-down, overcrowded slum neighborhoods, created when landlords subdivided old buildings and packed in too many residents. The poorer the renters, the worse the slums. Slums became ghettos when laws, prejudice, and community pressure prevented inhabitants from moving out. During the 1890s, Italians in New York City, African-Americans in Philadelphia and Chicago, Mexicans in Los Angeles, and Chinese in San Francisco increasingly became locked into segregated ghettos.

Life in the slums was particularly difficult for children. Juvenile diseases such as whooping cough, measles, and scarlet fever took a fearful toll, and infant mortality was high. In one immigrant ward in Chicago in 1900, 20 percent of infants died in their first year.

Since tenements often bordered industrial districts, residents had to put up with the noise, pollution, and foul odors of tanneries, foundries, factories, and packing houses. Reliance on coal for steam engines and heating released vast quantities of soot and coal dust to drift over the slums. As smoke tinged the atmosphere a hazy gray, buildings took on a dingy, grimy patina.

Most immigrants stayed in the shabbiest tenements only until they could afford better housing. Blacks, in contrast, were trapped in segregated districts. Driven out of the skilled trades and excluded from most factory work, blacks took menial jobs whose low pay left them little income for housing. Racist city-dwellers used high rents, real-estate covenants (agreements not to rent or sell to blacks), and neighborhood pressure to exclude them from areas inhabited by whites. Because the numbers of northern urban blacks in 1890 remained relatively small—for example, they composed only 1.2 percent of Cleveland's population and 1.3 percent of Chicago's—they could not overcome whites' concerted campaigns to shut them out. Nevertheless, as W. E. B. DuBois, a black sociologist, pointed out in *The Philadelphia Negro* (1899), wealthy black entrepreneurs within these neighborhoods built their own churches, ran successful businesses, and established charitable organizations to help their people.

Fashionable Avenues and Suburbs

The same cities that harbored slums, suffering, and violence also boasted neighborhoods of dazzling opulence. The wealthy built monumental residences on exclusive thoroughfares just outside the downtown, among them Fifth Avenue in New York, Commonwealth Avenue in Boston, and Euclid Avenue in Cleveland.

Middle-class city dwellers followed the wealthy, moving to new suburbs. In the 1890s Chicago developer Samuel Eberly Gross created entire low-cost subdivisions north and west of the city and advertised homes for as little as ten dollars a month. Lawyers, doctors, small businessmen, and other professionals moved farther out along the main thoroughfares served by the street railway and purchased homes with large lots.

A pattern of informal residential segregation by income took shape in the cities and suburbs. Built for families of a particular income level, certain city neighborhoods and suburbs developed remarkably similar internal standards for lot size and house design. Commuters who rode the new street railways out from the city center could identify the changing neighborhoods along the way as readily as a geologist might distinguish different strata on a washed-out riverbank. And with the physical change in American cities came a new awareness of class and cultural disparities.

MIDDLE-CLASS SOCIETY AND CULTURE

Spared the struggle for survival that confronted most Americans, the middle and upper classes faced a different challenge: explaining and rationalizing the material benefits of the emerging consumer society. To justify the achievements of society's wealthiest members, ministers, advice-book writers, and other commentators appealed to Victorian morality, a set of social ideas influential among the privileged classes of England and the United States during the reign (1837–1901) of Britain's Queen Victoria.

Proponents of Victorian morality argued that the success of the middle and upper classes rested on their superior talent, intelligence, morality, and self-control. Women were identified as the driving force for moral improvement. While men engaged in the world's work, women provided the gentle, elevating influence that would lead society in its upward march.

A network of institutions, from elegant department stores to elite colleges and universities, testified to the privileged position of the upper and middle classes.

Manners and Morals

Several fundamental assumptions shaped the Victorian world view. First, human nature was malleable; people could improve themselves. Thus Americans in the Victorian era pursued reform with intense moralism. Second, hard work developed personal self-discipline and also created national progress. Finally, good manners and "culture" in the form of literature and the fine arts were hallmarks of a truly civilized society. Although widely violated in practice, this genteel outlook remained an ideal.

After the Civil War, the middle-class focus on morality and self-discipline degenerated into a preoccupation with manners and social rituals. Behavior as well as income defined social standing. Good manners, including a knowledge of proper etiquette in all social occasions, especially dining and entertaining, became a badge of status. Meals evolved into rituals that differentiated the social classes. They presented occasions for displaying the elaborate silver and china that middle- and upper-class families exclusively possessed, and they provided telltale clues to a family's level of refinement and sophistication.

The Victorian code, with its emphasis on morals, manners, and behavior, heightened class differences and created visible distinctions among social groups. Prominent Victorians might claim their sincere interest in helping others to improve themselves, but more often than not their self-righteous, intensely moralistic outlook simply widened the gap created by income disparities.

The Cult of Domesticity

Victorian views on morality and culture, coupled with rising pressures on consumers to make decisions about a mountain of domestic products, had a subtle but important impact on middle-class expectations about woman's role within the home. From the 1840s onward, the home had been idealized as "the woman's sphere," a protected retreat where she could express her special maternal gifts, including a sensitivity toward children and an aptitude for religion. "The home is the wife's province," asserted one writer; "it is her natural field of labor."

Victorian advocates of the cult of domesticity added a new obligation for women: to foster an artistic environment that would nurture the family's cultural improvement. Houses became statements of cultural aspirations, with rarely used front parlors that were cluttered with ornate furnishings and curios, and elaborately ornamented architectural styles gained popularity. Excluded from the world of business and commerce, women directed their energy to transforming their homes into "a place of repose, a refuge from the excitement and distractions of outside . . . , provided with every attainable means of rest and recreation."

Not all middle-class women pursued this domestic ideal. For some, the drudgery of housework and of running the family overwhelmed any concern for artistic accomplishment. For others, the artistic ideal itself was not to their taste. In the 1880s and 1890s women increasingly sought other outlets for their creative energies.

Department Stores

Although Victorian thought justified the privileges of the well-to-do, many people found it difficult to shake the thriftiness of their early years and accept the new preoccupation with accumulation and display. In the 1880s merchandisers encouraged Americans to loosen their purse strings and enjoy prosperity by emphasizing the high quality and low cost of their goods.

Key to changing attitudes about consumption was the department store. In the final quarter of the nineteenth century, entrepreneurs such as Roland Macy, John Wanamaker, and Marshall Field made the department store an urban institution and transformed the shopping experience for their middle- and upper-class patrons. Merchants such as Macy and Wanamaker overcame middle- and upper-class reluctance to spend by advertising products at "rock-bottom" prices and by waging price wars to validate their claims. End-of-season clearance sales at drastically marked-down prices prevented stock from piling up and attracted the thrifty. Major downtown establishments tried to make shopping an adventure. The stores became more and more ornate, with stained-glass skylights, marble staircases, brilliant chandeliers, and plush carpets.

Department stores lavished care and attention on shoppers, especially women. Richly decorated lounges, elegant restaurants serving modestly

Department Store
Department stores used periodic sales to lure shoppers into their stores. At the special bargain counter at the Siegel Cooper store in New York in 1897, young women mobbed the attendants to purchase inexpensive new products.

priced lunches, and glittering holiday decorations enticed visitors to linger and to buy on impulse. Sales clerks greeted customers at the door, answered questions, and made women feel at home. The large urban department store became a social club and home away from home for affluent women.

The Transformation of Higher Education

At a time when relatively few Americans possessed even a high-school education, colleges and universities represented another stronghold of the business and professional elite and of the moderately well-to-do middle class. Wealthy capitalists gained stature and a measure of immortality by endowing colleges and universities. In 1885 Leland Stanford and his wife launched Stanford University with a bequest of $24 million; in 1891 John D. Rockefeller donated $34 million to the University of Chicago.

Industrialists and businessmen dominated the boards of trustees of many educational institutions, and colleges were viewed as a training ground for future business and professional leaders.

The athletic field as well as the classroom prepared affluent young men for business and the professions. Football, adapted from English rugby in 1869, became an elite sport played by college teams. Some college presidents dismissed football as a dangerous waste of time and money, but alumni and coaches credited the new sport with building character. Because Social Darwinism emphasized struggle, football seemed an ideal arena for improving the strength, courage, and self-discipline of youth. Some defenders of the sport insisted that football could substitute for the frontier experience in an increasingly urban society. By 1900 football had become a popular fall sport, stimulating alumni giving and building goodwill for those elite institutions that otherwise remained far outside the experience of the average American.

Cigar-Box Label, c. 1910
Vassar College, founded in 1865, promoted the new image of womanhood by stressing the interconnections among education, athletics, and ethics.

More than 150 new colleges and universities appeared between 1880 and 1900, and enrollments more than doubled, rising from 1.7 percent of college-age youth in 1870 to 4 percent in 1900. A small but growing number of these newcomers to higher education were women. Wealthy capitalists financed some institutions, but public funds supported the state universities of the Midwest, and religious denominations continued to support many colleges.

Debates about what should be taught and how it should be taught swept through higher education, especially in science and medicine. Antebellum medical education had occupied less than a year of medical students' time, and most received their degrees without ever having visited a hospital or seen a patient. The grim mortality rates of the Civil War, in which twice as many soldiers died from infections as from wounds, graphically illustrated the low state of medical education. In the 1880s and 1890s medical professors, many of whom had studied in France and Germany, began restructuring American medical education, insisting that students be trained in biology, chemistry, and physics. By 1900 the practice of medicine in

America rested on a firm professional foundation. Similar reforms took place in architecture, engineering, and law.

These changes were part of a larger transformation in higher education that produced a new institution, the research university. Unlike antebellum colleges, which taught little beyond classical languages, theology, logic, and mathematics, the new research universities offered courses in a wide variety of subjects, established professional schools, and encouraged faculty members to pursue basic research. For Andrew D. White, the first president of Cornell University (1869), the goal was to create a school "where any person can find instruction in any study." Cornell, the University of Wisconsin, Johns Hopkins, Harvard, and others laid the groundwork for the central role that U.S. universities would play in the intellectual, cultural, and scientific life of the twentieth century. However, higher education remained the privilege of a few as the nineteenth century ended; the age when college attendance would become the norm lay many years ahead.

WORKING-CLASS POLITICS AND REFORM

The contrast between the affluent world of the college-educated middle and upper classes and the gritty lives of the working class was graphically displayed in the nation's growing urban centers, where immigrant newcomers reshaped political and social institutions to meet their needs. If department stores furnished new social spaces for the middle and upper classes, saloons became the poor man's club, and dance halls became single women's home away from home. While the rich and the well-born looked askance at lower-class recreational activities and sought to force the poor to change their ways, working-class Americans, the immigrant newcomers in particular, fought to preserve their own way of life. Indeed, the late nineteenth century witnessed an ongoing battle to eradicate social drinking, reform "boss" politics, and curb lower-class recreational activities.

hc Primary Source: Plunkitt Scorns Reform

Political Bosses and Machine Politics

Earlier in the century the swelling numbers of urban poor had given rise to a new kind of politician, the "boss," who presided over the city's "machine"—an unofficial political organization designed to keep a particular party or faction in office. Whether officially serving as mayor or not, the boss, assisted by local ward or precinct captains, wielded enormous influence in city government. Often a former saloonkeeper or labor leader, the boss knew his constituents well.

For better or worse, the political machine was America's unique contribution to municipal government in an era of pell-mell urban growth. Typified by Tammany Hall, the Democratic organization that dominated New York City politics from the 1830s to the 1930s, machines emerged in a host of cities during the late nineteenth century.

By the turn of the century, many cities had experienced machine rule. Working through the local ward captains to turn out unusually high numbers of voters, the machine rode herd on the tangle of municipal bureaucracies, controlling who was hired for the police and fire departments. It rewarded its friends and punished its enemies through its control of taxes, licenses, and inspections. The machine gave tax breaks to favored contractors in return for large payoffs and slipped them insider information about upcoming street and sewer projects.

At the neighborhood level, the ward boss often acted as a welfare agent, helping the needy and protecting the troubled. Apparent generosity enhanced the bosses' image, at little cost: $10 to pay a tenement dweller's rent meant a lot to the poor but was small change to bosses who raked in millions from public contracts and land deals. While the machine helped alleviate some suffering, it entangled urban social services with corrupt politics and often prevented city government from responding to the real problems of the city's neediest inhabitants.

Under New York City's boss William Marcy Tweed, the Tammany Hall machine sank to new depths of corruption. Between 1869 and 1871,

Tweed dispensed 60,000 patronage positions and pumped up the city's debt by $70 million through graft and inflated contracts. The details of the Tweed ring's massive fraud and corruption were brilliantly satirized in *Harper's Weekly* by German immigrant cartoonist Thomas Nast. In one cartoon Nast portrayed Tweed and his cronies as vultures picking at the city's bones. Tweed bellowed in fury. "I don't care a straw for your newspaper articles—my constituents don't know how to read," he told *Harper's*, "but they can't help seeing them damned pictures." Convicted of fraud and extortion, Tweed

"Let Us Prey," 1871
Cartoonist Thomas Nast hated William Marcy Tweed's ostentatious style. Pictured here as the chief vulture standing over the body of New York City, Boss Tweed wears an enormous diamond, a symbol of his insatiable greed.

was sentenced to jail in 1873, served two years, escaped to Spain, was reapprehended and reincarcerated, and died in jail in 1878.

By the turn of the century the bosses were facing well-organized assaults on their power, led by an urban elite whose members sought to restore "good government." In this atmosphere the bosses increasingly forged alliances with civic organizations and reform leagues. The results, although never entirely satisfactory to any of the parties involved, paved the way for new sewer and transportation systems, expanded parklands, and improved public services—a record of considerable accomplishment, given the magnitude of the problems created by urban growth.

Battling Poverty

In contrast to the bosses' piecemeal attempts to aid the urban poor, middle-class reformers sought comprehensive solutions. Jacob Riis and other reformers believed that immigrants' lack of self-control led to their miseries. Thus reformers often focused on the moral improvement of the poor while ignoring the crippling effect of low wages and dangerous working conditions. Humanitarian campaigns to help the destitute often turned into crusades to Americanize the immigrants and eliminate their "offensive" and "self-destructive" behaviors.

Poverty-relief workers first targeted the young, considered the most malleable. Early Protestant social reformers started charitable societies to help transient youths and street waifs. In 1843 Robert M. Hartley, a former employee of the New York Temperance Society, founded the New York Association for Improving the Condition of the Poor to urge poor families to change their ways. The association also demanded pure-milk laws, public baths, and better housing.

The Young Men's Christian Association (YMCA), founded in England in 1841 and exported to America in 1851, focused on the dislocation and strain experienced by rural Americans who migrated to the cities in the post–Civil War years. The YMCA and later the YWCA (Young Women's Christian Association) provided decent housing and wholesome recreational facilities under close supervision and expelled members for drinking or other forbidden behavior.

By 1900 more than 1,500 YMCAs acted as havens for nearly 250,000 men. But the YMCA and YWCA reached only a small portion of the young adult population. Their moralistic stance repelled some, and others preferred not to ask for help. Narrowly focused, the "Y" strategy could do little to relieve urban problems.

New Approaches to Social Work

The inability of relief organizations to cope with the explosive growth of the urban poor in the 1870s and 1880s convinced many middle-class Americans that urban poverty had reached dangerous proportions. Social reformers began to develop new strategies to fight poverty. One of the earliest and most effective agencies was the Salvation Army. A church established along paramilitary lines in England in 1865 by Methodist minister "General" William Booth, the Salvation Army sent its uniformed volunteers to the United States in 1880 to provide food, shelter, and temporary employment for families. Known for its rousing music and attention-getting street meetings, the group ran soup kitchens and day nurseries and dispatched "slum brigades" to carry the message of morality to the immigrant poor. The army's strategy was simple: attract the poor with marching bands and lively preaching; follow up with offers of food, assistance, and employment; and then teach them the solid, middle-class virtues of temperance, hard work, and self-discipline.

New York's Charity Organization Society (COS), founded in 1882 by Josephine Shaw Lowell, implemented a similar approach, attempting to make the poor more honest and efficient. The society sent "friendly visitors" into the tenements to counsel families on how to improve their lives. Convinced that moral deficiencies lay at the root of poverty, and that the "promiscuous charity" of overlapping welfare agencies undermined the desire to work, the COS tried to foster self-sufficiency in its charges.

Critics justly accused the COS and similar groups of seeking more to control than to help the poor. More often than not, the friendly visitors wore cultural blinders, misunderstanding the real source of the difficulties faced by the poor and expecting to effect change by imposing middle-class standards. One journalist dismissed the typical friendly visitor as "235 pounds of Sunshine." Unable to see slum problems from the vantage point of the poor, the organizations ultimately failed to convert the poor to their own codes of morality and decorum.

The Moral-Purity Campaign

Other reformers pushed for tougher measures against sin and immorality. In 1872 Anthony Comstock, a pious young dry-goods clerk, founded the New York Society for the Suppression of Vice and demanded that municipal authorities close down gambling and lottery operations and censor obscene publications.

Nothing symbolized the contested terrain between middle- and lower-class culture better than the fight over prostitution, socially degenerate to some and a source of recreation to others. The "oldest profession" simultaneously exploited women and offered them good earnings and unbounded personal freedom. Brothels—houses of prostitution—expanded rapidly from the time of the Civil War until the 1880s, when saloons and cabarets, often controlled by political machines, replaced them. Reformers assumed, incorrectly, that immigrant women made up the majority of urban prostitutes.

In 1892 Charles Parkhurst, a Presbyterian minister and New York reformer, founded the City Vigilance League to clean up prostitution, gambling dens, and saloons. Parkhurst blamed the "slimy, oozy soil of Tammany Hall" and the New York City police for the city's rampant evil. In September 1894 a nonpartisan Committee of Seventy elected a new mayor who pressured city officials to enforce the laws against prostitution, gambling, and Sunday liquor sales.

The purity campaign lasted scarcely three years. The reform coalition quickly fell apart. New York's population was too large, and its ethnic constituencies too diverse, for the middle and upper classes to curb all the illegal activities flourishing within the sprawling metropolis.

The Social Gospel

Meanwhile, in the 1870s and 1880s a handful of Protestant ministers explored radical alternatives for aiding impoverished city dwellers. Appalled by slum conditions, they argued that the rich and well-born deserved part of the blame for poverty and thus had a responsibility to do something about it.

William S. Rainsford, the minister of New York City's St. George's Episcopal Church, pioneered the so-called institutional church movement, whereby large downtown churches in once elite districts now overrun by immigrants provided their new neighbors with social services as well as a place to worship. Supported by his wealthy church warden, J. Pierpont Morgan, Rainsford organized a boys' club, built recreational facilities on the Lower East Side, and established an industrial training program.

Another effort within Protestantism to right contemporary wrongs was the Social Gospel movement, launched in the 1870s by Congregational minister Washington Gladden of Columbus, Ohio. Gladden insisted that true Christianity commits men and women to fight social injustice. If Gladden set the tone for the Social Gospel, Walter Rauschenbusch, a minister in New York City's notorious Hell's Kitchen neighborhood, articulated its philosophy. Educated in Germany, Rauschenbusch argued that a truly Christian society would unite all churches, reorganize the industrial system, and work for international peace.

The Social Gospel's fierce attacks on complacent Christian support of the status quo attracted only a handful of Protestants. Their earnest voices, however, blended with a growing chorus of critics bemoaning the nation's urban woes.

The Settlement-House Movement

By the 1880s many concerned citizens had become convinced that reform pressure applied from the top down, however well intentioned, was ineffective and wrong-headed. A new approach to social work was needed. A younger generation of charity workers, led by Jane Addams, developed a new weapon against destitution: the settlement house. Like the Social Gospelers, these reformers recognized that the hardships of slum life were often beyond individuals' control. Stressing the environmental causes of crime and poverty, settlement-house relief workers themselves moved into poor neighborhoods, where, in Addams's words, they could see firsthand "the struggle for existence, which is so much harsher among people near the edge of pauperism."

The youngest daughter of a successful Illinois businessman, Jane Addams purchased a dilapidated mansion in Chicago in 1889. After overseeing extensive repairs, she and her coworkers opened it as Hull House, the first experiment in the settlement-house approach. Drawing on the middle-class ideal of true womanhood as supportive and self-sacrificing, Addams turned Hull House into a social center for recent immigrants. She invited newly arrived Italian immigrants to plays; sponsored art projects; held classes in English, civics, cooking, and dressmaking; and encouraged them to preserve their traditional crafts. She set up a kindergarten, a laundry, an employment bureau, and a day nursery for working mothers. In the hope of upgrading the filthy and overcrowded housing in its environs, Addams and her coworkers made studies of city housing conditions and pressured politicians to enforce sanitation regulations.

By 1895 at least fifty settlement houses had opened around the nation. Their leaders trained a generation of young college students, mostly women, many of whom would later serve as state and local government officials. Through their sympathetic attitudes toward the immigrants and their systematic publication of data about slum conditions, settlement-house workers gave Americans new hope that the cities' problems could be overcome.

Yet settlement houses enjoyed little success in their attempts to bridge the gap between rich and poor and to promote class cooperation and social harmony. Although immigrants appreciated the settlement houses' resources and activity, they widely

Garbage Box, First Ward, Chicago, c. 1900
Lacking space for recreation, immigrant children played atop garbage boxes in crowded alleys. Concerned for their health, Jane Addams wrote that "this slaughter of the innocents, this infliction of suffering on the newborn, is so gratuitous and so unfair, that it is only a question of time until an outraged sense of justice shall be aroused on behalf of these children."

felt that the reformers cared little for increasing immigrant political power. "They're like the rest," complained one immigrant, "a bunch of people planning for us and deciding what is good for us without consulting us or taking us into their confidence."

WORKING-CLASS LEISURE IN THE IMMIGRANT CITY

In colonial America the subject of leisure time had generally arisen only when ministers condemned "idleness" as the first step toward sin. In the rural culture of the early nineteenth century, the unremitting routines of farm labor had left little time for relaxation. Family picnics, horse races, county fairs, revivals, and holidays such as the Fourth of July and Christmas had provided permissible diversion, but even in relaxation earlier generations had guarded against "laziness."

As urban populations and factories multiplied after the Civil War, new patterns of leisure and amusement emerged, especially among the urban working class. After long hours in factories and mills or behind department store counters, working-class Americans craved relaxation and diversion. They thronged the streets, patronized saloons and dance halls, cheered at boxing matches and baseball games, and organized boisterous group picnics and holiday celebrations. Amusement parks, vaudeville theaters, sporting clubs, and racetracks provided further entertainment for workers, and mass leisure became a big business.

As factory work became more routinized and more impersonal, working-class Americans, especially immigrants, cherished their few opportunities for interaction and recreation.

Streets, Saloons, and Boxing Matches

Hours of tedious, highly disciplined, and physically exhausting labor left workers tired but thirsty for excitement and escape from their cramped living quarters. In 1889 a banner carried by a carpenters' union summed up their needs: "eight hours for work, eight hours for rest, and eight hours for what we will."

City streets provided some recreation. Relaxing after a day's work, shop girls and laborers clustered on busy corners, watching shouting pushcart peddlers and listening to organ grinders play familiar melodies. For a penny or a nickel, they could buy a bagel, a baked potato, or a soda. In the summer when the heat and humidity within the tenements reached unbearable levels, the streets became the center of neighborhood life.

The streets beckoned to all, but some leisure institutions drew a male clientele. For example, in cities, such as Baltimore, Milwaukee, and Cincinnati, with a strong German immigrant flavor, gymnastic clubs (*Turnvereine*) and singing societies (*Gesangvereine*) provided men with both companionship and the opportunity to perpetuate Old World traditions.

Saloons offered male companionship, conviviality, and five-cent beer, often with a free lunch thrown in. By 1900 New York City had an estimated 10,000 saloons. As gathering places in ethnic neighborhoods, saloons reinforced group identity and became centers for immigrant politics. Saloonkeepers often doubled as local ward bosses who performed small services for their patrons. With rich mahogany bars, shiny brass rails, and elegant mirrors, saloons provided a taste of luxury for their factory-worker clientele.

What explains the saloons' popularity, and what was their impact? The saloon provided an antidote to the socially isolating routines of factory labor. The saloon scene thus clashed with the increasingly private and family-centered social life of the middle class. But saloons often served as bases for prostitution and criminal activity. Moreover, drinking too much at the saloon frequently led to family violence, and "treating"—buying drinks for friends—cut deeply into already meager paychecks.

For working-class males, bare-knuckles prizefighting also became a popular amusement. Drawing heroes from society's poorer ranks, the boxing rings became an arena where lower-class men could assert their individuality and physical prowess. African-Americans, Irish, and Germans

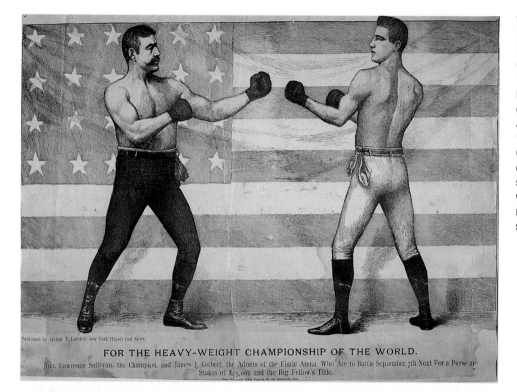

Published by Arthur T. Lumley, New York Illustrated News.

FOR THE HEAVY-WEIGHT CHAMPIONSHIP OF THE WORLD.

John Lawrence Sullivan, the Champion, and James J. Corbett, the Adonis of the Fistic Arena, Who Are to Battle September 7th Next For a Purse and Stakes of $25,000 and the Big Fellow's Title.

World's Heavyweight Boxing Championship, 1892

In dethroning ring champion John L. Sullivan, "Gentleman Jim" Corbett demonstrated that speed and finesse were more than a match for brute strength.

formed their own "sporting clubs" and used athletics to bolster their self-confidence and to reaffirm their racial or ethnic identity.

The Rise of Professional Sports

As an English game called rounders, baseball had existed since the seventeenth century. If Americans did not create baseball, they nevertheless took this informal children's game and turned it into a major professional sport. In 1845 the New York Knickerbockers, the first organized baseball team, was established. In the 1860s rules were codified and the sport assumed its present form, featuring overhand pitching, fielders' gloves, nine-inning games, and bases spaced ninety feet apart. That same decade, promoters organized professional clubs and began to compete for players. In 1869 the Cincinnati Red Stockings, the first team to put its players under contract for the whole season,

toured the country and ended the season with fifty-seven wins and no losses.

Team owners organized the National League in 1876 and took control of the game from the players by forbidding them to play for other teams and limiting each city to a single team. Crowds of 10,000 to 12,000 fans flooded into ballparks each game, creating enormous profits for the owners. By the 1890s baseball was big business. Clubs scheduled double-headers, ran promotions such as ladies' day, and made money by selling beer, peanuts, and hot dogs. The working class particularly took baseball to heart. The most profitable teams came from industrial cities with large working-class populations.

Newspapers thrived on baseball. Joseph Pulitzer introduced the first separate sports page when he bought the *New York World* in 1883, and baseball dominated the paper's sports reporting. Baseball, declared writer Mark Twain, had become "the very symbol . . . and visible expression of the drive and push and rush and struggle of the raging, tearing, booming nineteenth century."

Although no other organized sport attracted as large a following as baseball, horse racing and boxing also drew large crowds of spectators and received wide press coverage. But whereas races such as Louisville's Kentucky Derby became social events for the rich, professional boxing aroused passionate devotion in the working class.

The hero of nineteenth-century professional sports was heavyweight fighter John L. Sullivan. Of Irish-immigrant stock, Sullivan began boxing in 1877 at age nineteen. With his massive physique, handlebar mustache, and arrogant swagger, Sullivan was enormously popular. Barnstorming across the country, he vanquished a succession of local strong men, invariably wearing his trademark green tights with an American flag wrapped around his middle.

Vaudeville, Amusement Parks, and Dance Halls

In contrast to the male preserve of saloons and prizefights, the world of vaudeville shows, amusement parks, and neighborhood dance halls welcomed all comers regardless of gender and proved particularly congenial to working-class women.

Vaudeville, with roots in antebellum minstrel shows that featured white comedians made up as blacks (see Chapter 11), offered a succession of acts designed for mass appeal. The vaudeville show typically opened with an animal act or a dance number, followed by a musical interlude. Then came comic skits ridiculing the trials of urban life, satirizing police and municipal ineptitude, poking fun at the babel of accents in the immigrant city, and mining a rich vein of ethnic humor and stereotypes. After more musical numbers and acts by ventriloquists and magicians, the program ended with a "flash" finale featuring flying-trapeze artists or the like. By the 1880s vaudeville was drawing larger crowds than any other form of theater. It provided an evening of inexpensive, lighthearted entertainment and let immigrants laugh at their own experiences, as translated into slapstick and caricature.

While vaudeville offered psychological release from the stresses of working-class life, amusement parks provided physical escape. The fun houses, thrill rides, and games of New York's Coney Island, opened in 1895 and the prototype of urban amusement parks, sprawled along the Brooklyn waterfront. By 1900 as many as 500,000 people would throng the beach, the boardwalk, and the amusement parks on a summer Saturday. Young couples rode through the dark Tunnel of Love, sped down the dizzying roller coaster, and watched belly dancers in the sideshows, momentarily surrendering to the spirit of exuberant play and forgetting the restrictions and demands of the industrial world.

By the end of the nineteenth century, New York City had well over 300,000 female wage earners, most of them young, unmarried women. The amusement parks with their exhilarating rides and glittering dance pavilions, and the dance halls in the immigrant districts of most cities, exerted a powerful lure. There these women could meet friends, spend time with young men beyond parents' watchful eyes, show off their new dresses, and try out the latest dance steps in a magical release from the drudgery of daily life.

Ragtime

Nothing more vividly illustrates the differences between the cultures of the middle class and the working class than the contrasting styles of popular music that each favored. While the middle class preferred hymns or songs with a moral message, the working class embraced ragtime, the product of African-American musicians in the saloons of the South.

Ragtime developed out of the rich tradition of songs through which black Americans had eased the burdens of their lives. Like spirituals, ragtime used syncopated rhythms and complex harmonies, but it blended them with marching-band musical structures to create a distinctive style. A favorite of "honky-tonk" piano players, ragtime was introduced to the broader public in the 1890s and became a national sensation.

Inventive, playful, and infectiously rhythmic, ragtime had an appealing originality. But part of its popularity also came from its origin in saloons and its association with blacks, whom white Victorians stereotyped as sexual and uninhibited. The "wild" and complex rhythms of ragtime supposedly reflected a freer and more "natural" expression of love and affection. When genteel critics sneered, the new dance music became all the more attractive to the urban working class.

Historians offer conflicting interpretations of the white working-class fascination with ragtime and blackface vaudeville acts. To some, it was a way for the working class to mock upper-class ideals such as thrift and propriety. However, other historians argue that it was a grotesque and demeaning caricature of black Americans that reinforced prejudice and kept blacks confined to lower-class status. Paradoxically, the popularity of black music and blackface vaudeville simultaneously reinforced white solidarity and strengthened the wall separating white from black. Ragtime's popularity proved a mixed blessing for African-Americans. It testified to the achievements of brilliant composers such as Joplin, helped to break down barriers in the music industry, and contributed to a spreading rebellion against Victorian repressiveness. At the same time, it confirmed white stereotypes of blacks as primitive and sensuous, a bias that underlay the racism of the period and helped to justify segregation and discrimination.

CULTURES IN CONFLICT

Class conflict and cultural unrest embroiled the United States in the late nineteenth century, even within the middle class. As 1900 dawned, ethical questions about Victorian morality and new cultural stirrings intensified. At the center of the cultural turbulence stood women, increasingly dissatisfied with the restrictive code of feminine propriety. The growth of women's clubs and women's colleges, and even the bicycle fad of the 1890s, all contributed to the emergence of the "new woman."

At the same time, a widening chasm divided the well-to-do from the mass of immigrant laborers. Perhaps in no period of American history have class conflicts been as open and raw. Nervously eying the noisy culture of city streets, saloons, boxing clubs, dance halls, and amusement parks, middle-class leaders perceived a massive, if unconscious, challenge to their own cultural and social standing. Some middle-class reformers promoted public schools as a means to impose middle-class values on the urban masses, and others battled urban "vice" and "immorality." The genteel mores of the middle class proved particularly vulnerable, so that by 1900 the Victorian social and moral ethos was crumbling.

The Genteel Tradition and Its Critics

In the 1870s and 1880s a group of upper-class writers and editors, led by Charles Eliot Norton of Harvard and E. L. Godkin of *The Nation,* codified standards for writing and design and tried to create a coherent national artistic culture. Joining forces with allies in Boston and New York, these elites lobbied to "improve" American taste in interior furnishings, textiles, ceramics, wallpaper, and books.

Godkin and editors of other "quality" periodicals created an important forum for serious writers in *The Nation* and *The Atlantic Monthly.* Novelist Henry James, who published virtually all of his work in the *Atlantic,* reflected the views of this elite literary establishment. He wrote, "It is art that *makes* life, . . . and I know of no substitute whatever for [its] force and beauty." This art-for-art's-sake movement also influenced architects, jewelers, and interior decorators.

Although these genteel magazines provided an important forum for new authors, their editors' strident elitism and imperialistic desire to control national literary standards bred opposition. Samuel Langhorne Clemens, better known as Mark Twain, spoke for many young writers when he declared as early as 1869 that he was through with "literature and all that bosh." Attacking aristocratic literary conventions, Twain and others who shared his concerns worked to broaden literature's appeal to the general public.

These efforts by a younger generation of writers to chart new directions for American literature rested on sweeping changes within the publishing industry. New magazines such as *Ladies' Home Journal, Cosmopolitan,* and *McClure's* competed with the elite publications. The new magazines slashed their prices and tripled their circulation. Supported by advertising rather than subscriptions, they provided an outlet for younger authors who wanted to write about real people in the "whirlpool of real life."

Some of these writers were labeled regionalists because they captured the distinctive dialects and details of their featured locale, whether New England or the South. Others, among them William Dean Howells, focused on a truthful, if optimistic, depiction of the commonplace. Another group, called naturalists, stressed economic and psychological determinants and often examined the dark underside of life. In *Maggie: A Girl of the Streets* (1893), a bleak story of an innocent girl's exploitation and suicide in an urban slum, Stephen Crane wrote what is generally considered the first naturalist American novel. Labels aside, all these writers shared a skepticism toward literary conventions and an intense desire to understand the society around them.

The careers of Mark Twain and Theodore Dreiser highlight the changes in the publishing industry and the evolution of new forms of writing. Both were products of the Midwest, outsiders to the East Coast literary establishment—Twain from Missouri and Dreiser from Indiana. As young men, both worked as newspaper reporters and traveled widely. Both learned from direct experience about the greed, speculation, and fraud of the era.

Twain and Dreiser called on their own experiences to write about the human impact of the wrenching social changes that surrounded them: the flow of people to the expanding cities and the relentless scramble for power, wealth, and fame. In the *Adventures of Huckleberry Finn* (1884), Twain uses the river journey of two runaways, the rebellious Huck and the slave Jim, to explore the nature of contemporary American society by contrasting the idyllic life on the raft to the tawdry, fraudulent

Mark Twain
Twain not only broke from highbred literary standards but also created a unique personal style through his studied poses and distinctive attire.

world of the small riverfront towns. Dreiser's *Sister Carrie* (1900) traces the journey of Carrie Meeber, an innocent and attractive girl, from her Wisconsin farm home to Chicago. Seduced by a traveling salesman, Carrie moves in with Hurstwood, the married proprietor of a fancy saloon. Driven by her desire for expensive department-store clothes and lavish entertainment, Carrie follows Hurstwood to New York, abandons him when his money runs out, and pursues her own career in the theater.

Twain and Dreiser broke sharply with the genteel tradition's emphasis on manners and decorum. *Century* magazine readers complained that *Huckleberry Finn* was "destitute of a single redeeming quality." The publisher of *Sister Carrie* found the novel so repugnant that he printed only 1,000 copies to fulfill his contract—and then stored them in a warehouse.

Similarly, growing numbers of scholars and critics challenged the elite's self-serving beliefs, including assumptions that moral worth and economic standing were closely linked and that the status quo represented a social order decreed by God and nature alike. Economist Thorstein Veblen's *The Theory of the Leisure Class* (1899) caustically critiqued the life-style of the new capitalist elite. The product of a poor Norwegian farm community in Minnesota, Veblen looked at the captains of industry and their families with a jaundiced eye. He mercilessly documented their "conspicuous consumption" and lamented the widening economic gap between "those who worked without profit" and "those who profited without working."

Within the new discipline of sociology, Annie MacLean exposed the exploitation of department-store clerks, Walter Wyckoff uncovered the hand-to-mouth existence of unskilled laborers, and W. E. B. Du Bois documented the hardships of African-Americans in Philadelphia. The publication of these writings, coupled with the economic depression and seething labor agitation of the 1890s, made it increasingly difficult for turn-of-the-century middle-class Americans to accept the smug, self-satisfied belief in progress and genteel culture that had been a hallmark of the Victorian outlook.

Modernism in Architecture and Painting

The challenge to the genteel tradition also found support among architects and painters. Architects followed the lead of Louis Sullivan, who argued that a building's form should follow its function. In their view, banks, for example, should look like financial institutions, not Greek temples. Rejecting elite pretensions, architects looked to the future— to modernism, a quest for new modes of expression—for inspiration.

Frank Lloyd Wright's "prairie-school" houses, first built in the Chicago suburb of Oak Park in the 1890s, represented a typical modernist break with the past. Wright scorned the bulky Victorian house, with its large attics and basements; his designs, featuring broad, sheltering roofs and low silhouettes harmonious with the flat prairie landscape, used open, interconnecting rooms to create a sense of spaciousness.

Modernism's rejection of Victorian gentility influenced late-nineteenth-century painting as well. Winslow Homer's watercolors pictured nature as brutally tough and unsentimental; in his grim, elemental seascapes, lone men struggle against massive waves that threaten to overwhelm them. Thomas Eakins's canvases of swimmers, boxers, and rowers (such as his well-known *The Champion Single Sculls,* 1871) captured moments of vigorous physical exertion. Obsessed with making his paintings realistic, Eakins studied anatomy at a medical school, did photographic studies and dissection on cadavers in preparation for painting, and used nude models in his drawing classes.

The architects' and painters' revolt symptomized a larger shift in middle-class thought driven by the emergence of a complex social environment. As one minister observed in 1898, the transition from muscle to mechanical power had "separated, as by an impassable gulf, the simple, homespun, individualistic world of the . . . past, from the complex, closely associated life of the present." The increasingly evident gap between the quiet parlors and flickering kerosene lamps of small towns and life in the big, glittering cities of glass and iron made nineteenth-century Americans acutely aware of differences in wealth and upbringing.

Distrusting idealistic Victorian assumptions about social progress, the middle class nevertheless disagreed over how to replace them. Not until the progressive period would social reformers combine new expertise in social research with an enlarged conception of the federal government's regulatory power to break sharply with their Victorian predecessors' social outlook.

From Victorian Lady to New Woman

The role of middle-class women in the revolt against Victorian refinement was complex and ambiguous. Some women's dissatisfaction with the cult of domesticity did not necessarily lead to their open rebellion. Though chafing against the constraints of the genteel code and the assumption that they should limit their activities to the home, many women remained committed to playing a supportive role within the family. In fact, early advocates of a "widened sphere" for women often fused the traditional Victorian ideal of womanhood with a firm commitment to political action.

The career of temperance leader Frances Willard illustrates how the cult of domesticity could evolve into a broader view of women's social and political responsibilities. Willard believed that by nature women were compassionate, nurturing, and sensitive to others; she was equally convinced that drinking encouraged men to squander their earnings and profoundly threatened family life. In 1874 Willard resigned her positions as dean of women and professor of English at Northwestern University to devote her energies completely to the temperance cause. Five years later, she became president of the recently formed Woman's Christian Temperance Union (WCTU).

Willard transformed the cult of domesticity's emphasis on women's unique moral virtues into a rationale for political action. The domestication of politics, she asserted, would protect the family and improve public morality. Choosing as her badge a white ribbon, symbolizing the purity of the home, in 1880 Frances Willard launched a crusade to win women's right to vote so that they could outlaw liquor. Willard also expanded the WCTU's activities to include welfare work, prison reform, labor arbitration, and public health. By 1890 the WCTU, with a membership of 150,000, had become the nation's first mass organization of women. Its members gained experience as lobbyists, organizers, and lecturers, undercutting the assumption of "separate spheres."

An expanding network of women's clubs offered another means by which middle- and upper-class women could hone their skills in civic affairs, public speaking, and intellectual analysis. Club women became involved in social-welfare projects, public-library expansion, and tenement reform. By 1892 the General Federation of Women's Clubs boasted 495 affiliates and 100,000 members.

College education also expanded women's roles. Coeducational colleges and universities in the Midwest enrolled increasing numbers of women, and private universities admitted women to affiliated but separate institutions such as Barnard (1889) and Radcliffe (1894). Between 1880 and 1900 the percentage of colleges admitting women jumped from 30 percent to 71 percent; by the turn of the century, women constituted more than one-third of the total college-student population.

Although the earliest women's colleges had been founded to reinforce prevailing concepts of femininity, participation in college organizations, athletics, and dramatics enabled female students to learn traditionally "masculine" strategies for gaining power. The generation of women educated at female institutions in the late nineteenth century developed the self-confidence to break with the Victorian ideal of passive womanhood and to compete on an equal basis with men by displaying strength, aggressiveness, and intelligence, popularly considered male attributes.

A bicycling vogue that swept urban America at the end of the century further loosened Victorian constraints on women. Fearful of waning vitality, middle- and upper-class Americans sought new means of improving their vigor, ranging from health products such as cod-liver oil and sarsaparilla to enthusiastic participation in basketball. Bicycling, which could be enjoyed individually or in groups, quickly became the most popular sport with those who wished to combine exercise with recreation. The advent in the 1880s of smaller wheels, ball-bearing axles, and air-filled tires helped to make bicycling a national craze, so that by the 1890s more than a million Americans owned bicycles.

Bicycling especially appealed to young women uncomfortable with restrictive Victorian ideas, which included the views that proper young ladies must never sweat, the female body must be fully covered at all times, and physical exertion should take place in private. Pedaling along without corsets or padded clothing, the woman bicyclist implicitly broke with genteel conventions.

Changing attitudes about femininity also found expression in shifting ideas about marriage. Charlotte Perkins Gilman, a suffrage advocate and speaker for women's rights, asserted that women would make an effective contribution to society only when they won economic independence from men through work outside the home. The climbing divorce rate between 1880 and 1900 testified to women's changing relationship to men; in 1880 one in twenty-one marriages ended in divorce, but by 1900 the rate had shot up to one in twelve. Women who sued for divorce increasingly cited their husbands' failure to act responsibly and to respect their autonomy. Accepting such arguments, courts frequently awarded wives alimony, a monetary settlement payable by ex-husbands to support their former spouses.

Women writers generally welcomed the new female commitment to self-sufficiency and independence. Mary Wilkins Freeman's short stories, for example, compare women's expanding role to the frontier ideal of freedom. Her characters fight for their beliefs without concern for society's reaction. Feminist Kate Chopin pushed the debate to the extreme by having the married heroine of her 1899 novel *The Awakening* violate social conventions by falling in love with another man and then taking her life when his ideas about women prove as narrow and traditional as those of her husband.

Nonetheless, attitudes changed slowly. The enlarged concept of women's role in society had its greatest influence on middle-class women who enjoyed the privilege of higher education, possessed some leisure time, and could hope for success in journalism, education, social work, and nursing. For shop girls who worked sixty hours a week to make ends meet, such opportunities remained a distant goal. Although many women sought more independence and control over their own lives, most still viewed the home as their primary responsibility.

Public Education as an Arena of Class Conflict

Controversy over the scope and function of public education engaged Americans of all socioeconomic levels and highlighted class and cultural divisions in late-nineteenth-century society. Viewing public schools as an instrument for indoctrinating and controlling the lower ranks, middle-class educators and civic leaders campaigned to expand and centralize public schooling. These would-be reformers' efforts aroused opposition from ethnic and religious groups whose outlook and interests differed sharply from theirs.

Thanks to the crusade for universal public education started by Horace Mann, most states had public-school systems by the Civil War. More than half the nation's children received some formal education, but most attended only a few years, and few went to high school. In the 1870s middle-class activists, concerned that many Americans lacked sufficient knowledge to participate wisely in public affairs or to function effectively in the labor force, worked to raise the overall educational level and to increase the number of years spent in school.

One such reformer was William Torrey Harris, a Victorian moralist who viewed public schools as a "great instrument to lift all classes of people into . . . civilized life." Harris urged teachers to instill in students a sense of order, decorum, self-discipline, and civic loyalty. Believing that modern industrial society depended on citizens' conforming to the timetables of factory and train, he envisioned schools as models of punctuality and scheduling: "The pupil must have his lesson ready at the appointed time, must rise at the tap of the bell, move to the line, return; in short, go through all the evolutions with equal precision."

To achieve these goals, reform-minded educators such as Harris wrested control of schools from neighborhood leaders and ward politicians by stressing punctuality and order, compulsory-attendance laws, and a tenure system to insulate teachers from political favoritism and parental pressure. By 1900 thirty-one states required all children from eight to fourteen years of age to attend school. But the steamroller methods by Harris and others to systematize public education prompted protests. New York pediatrician Joseph Mayer Rice, after interviewing 1,200 teachers, lashed out at the schools' singsong memorization and prisonlike discipline. In city after city he discovered teachers who drilled students mercilessly and were more concerned about their posture than their learning.

But Rice overlooked real advances; for example, the national illiteracy rate dropped from 17 percent in 1880 to 13 percent by 1900, despite the influx of immigrants. He was on target, however, in assailing many teachers' rigid emphasis on silence, docility, and unquestioning obedience to rules. When a Chicago school inspector found a thirteen-year-old boy huddled in the basement of a stockyard building and ordered him back to school, the weeping boy blurted:

> They hits ye if yer don't learn, and they hits ye if ye whisper, and they hits ye if ye have string in yer pocket, and they hits ye if yer seat squeaks, and they hits ye if ye don't stand up in time, and they hits ye if yer late, and they hits ye if ye ferget the page.

By the 1880s several different groups were opposing the centralized urban public-school bureaucracies. Working-class families that depended on their children's meager wages for survival, for example, resisted attempts to force their sons and daughters to attend school past the elementary grades. Although some immigrant families sacrificed to give their children an education, many withdrew their offspring from school as soon as they had learned the rudiments of reading and writing and sent them to work. Catholic immigrants, moreover, objected to the public schools' overwhelmingly Protestant orientation. The Catholic church thus established separate parochial systems, and it rejected federal aid to public schools as a ploy to "gradually extinguish Catholicity in this country, and to form one homogeneous American people after the New England Evangelical type." At the other end of the social scale from working-class immigrants, upper-class parents,

especially in the Northeast, commonly did not wish to send their children to the immigrant-thronged public schools. Many therefore enrolled their children in private seminaries and academies. Shielding their privileged students from the temptations of urban life while preparing them to go on to college, these institutions reinforced the elite belief that higher education should be the preserve of the well-to-do.

The proliferation of private and parochial schools, along with controversies over compulsory education, public funding, and classroom decorum, reveals the extent to which public education had become entangled in ethnic and class differences. Unlike Germany and Japan, which standardized and centralized their national educational systems in the nineteenth century, the United States created a diverse system of locally run public and private institutions that allowed each segment of society some influence over its schools. Amid the disputes, school enrollments expanded dramatically. In 1870 fewer than 72,000 students attended the nation's 1,026 high schools. By 1900 the number of high schools had jumped to more than 5,000 and the number of students to more than 500,000.

CONCLUSION *hc* ACE Practice Test

By the 1890s class conflict was evident in practically every area of city life, from mealtime manners to entertainment. Ethnic differences were compounded by class differences. Often poor and from peasant or working-class backgrounds, the immigrants took unskilled jobs and worked for subsistence-level wages. Middle- and upper-class Americans often responded by stigmatizing them as nonwhite and therefore racially inferior.

To raise their own standards and to distinguish themselves from these newcomers, native-born Americans adopted a Victorian code of morality that emphasized good manners, decorum, and self-control. These moral standards were reinforced by an emphasis on high school and university education as the path to becoming educators, lawyers, doctors, and other professionals. Middle-

Chronology

1843	Robert M. Hartley founds the New York Association for Improving the Condition of the Poor.	1880	William Booth's followers establish an American branch of the Salvation Army.
1851	The American branch of the Young Men's Christian Association (YMCA) opens.	1882	Josephine Shaw Lowell founds the New York Charity Organization Society (COS).
1865	Vassar College founded.	1884	Mark Twain, *Adventures of Huckleberry Finn*.
1869	Boss William Marcy Tweed gains control of New York City's Tammany Hall political machine.	1889	Jane Addams opens Hull House. Columbia University adds Barnard College as coordinate institution for women.
1871	Thomas Eakins, *The Champion Single Sculls*.	1891	University of Chicago founded.
1872	Anthony Comstock founds the New York Society for the Suppression of Vice.	1895	Coney Island amusement park opens in Brooklyn.
1873	Frances Willard joins the Woman's Christian Temperance Union.	1899	Kate Chopin, *The Awakening*. Thorstein Veblen, *The Theory of the Leisure Class*.
1876	National League of baseball players organized.	1900	Theodore Dreiser, *Sister Carrie*.

and upper-class women, educated in the expanding college and university system, were expected to become the protectors of the home. Discontented with this new role, Jane Addams and other social workers developed the settlement house movement and campaigned for legislation to curb the evils of boss politics and urban blight.

Nowhere was the conflict between the social classes more evident than in the controversy over leisure entertainment. Middle- and upper-class Americans battled "indecent" lower-class pursuits such as gambling, prizefighting, and bawdy boardwalk sideshows. While the elite favored large, impeccably groomed urban parks, models of orderliness and propriety, working people fought for neighborhood parks where they could play ball, drink beer, and escape the stifling heat of tenement apartments.

Although the well-to-do classes often appeared to have the upper hand in these clashes, not all members of the elite agreed. In *Democratic Vistas* (1881), Walt Whitman decried the attempts of "certain portions of the people" to force their cultural standards and moral values on others, who were made to feel "degraded, humiliated, [and] of no account." Charlotte Perkins Gilman criticized middle-class society for its obsession with manners and empty social rituals.

By the end of the century, a series of compromises between the elite and the immigrant working class was emerging. Eroded by dissension within and opposition without, Victorian morality waned, and new standards blended elements of earlier opposing ideas. For example, new rules regulated behavior in boxing and baseball. The elite view of sports as a vehicle for instilling self-discipline faded, and sports became valued as spectacle, entertainment, big business, and an important part of the new consumerism.

Similar patterns of compromise and change took place in other arenas. Vaudeville houses evolved into movie theaters, and ragtime music became jazz. In short, the raffish, raucous, and frequently denounced working-class culture of the immigrant city served as the seedbed of modern mass culture. And everywhere commercial interests came to dominate popular culture, encouraging an increasingly prosperous nation to enjoy—and pay for—goods, leisure, sports, and entertainments.

FURTHER READING

William L. Barney, ed., *A Companion to 19ᵗʰ-Century America* (2001). A useful survey of urbanization, ethnicity, class difference, and other topics in the late nineteenth century.

Martin J. Burke, *The Conundrum of Class: Public Discourse on the Social Order in America* (1995). A pioneering study into the ways in which nineteenth-century Americans tried to understand class difference.

Ruth H. Crocker, *Social Work and Social Order: The Settlement Movement in Two Industrial Cities, 1889–1930* (1992). An important, balanced assessment of the settlement-house movement.

William Cronon, *Nature's Metropolis: Chicago and the Great West* (1991). An innovative study of the link between urban growth and regional economic prosperity in the Midwest.

Elliot Gorn and Warren Goldstein, A *Brief History of American Sports* (1993). A skillful analysis of the impact of urbanization, industrialization, and commercialization on American sports.

Hadassa Kosak, *Cultures of Opposition: Jewish Immigrant Workers, New York City, 1881–1905* (2000). A careful examination of the tensions within an ethnic community and the ways in which a distinctive working-class political culture emerged on New York's Lower East Side.

Martin Melosi, ed., *Pollution and Reform in American Cities, 1870–1930* (1980). A pioneering examination of the environmental impact of U.S. industrial and urban growth.

Carl Smith, *Urban Disorder and the Shape of Belief: The Great Chicago Fire, the Haymarket Bomb, and the Model Town of Pullman* (1995). An innovative study of the ways in which the nineteenth-century responses to urban disorders shaped contemporary perceptions about city life.

Peter Stearns, *Schools and Students in Industrial Society: Japan and the West, 1870–1940* (1998). Stearns's comparative examination of high-school education in Europe, the United States, and Japan highlights the distinctive features of American education.

Virginia Yans-McLaughlin and Marjorie Lightman, *Ellis Island and the Peopling of America* (1997). A broad overview of the process of migration, with useful documents.

Oliver Zunz, *Making America Corporate, 1870–1920* (1990). A pioneering exploration of corporate capitalism's impact on the creation of a consumer culture.

20

Politics and Expansion in an Industrializing Age, 1877–1900

CHAPTER OUTLINE

Party Politics in an Era of Social and Economic Upheaval, 1877–1884

Politics of Privilege, Politics of Exclusion, 1884–1892

The 1890s: Politics in a Depression Decade

The Watershed Election of 1896

Expansionist Stirrings and War with Spain, 1878–1901

hc This icon will direct you to additional study and research resources at http://college.hmco.com/history/us/boyer/enduring_concise/5e/students/index.html

The Politics of Industrialization

James A. Garfield embodied the American dream of the self-made man: born in a log cabin, he had worked his way through college, practiced law, fought in the Civil War, and risen through the political ranks to the presidency in 1880. A decent, well-meaning man, he also embodied a political generation more concerned with the spoils of office than the problems of ordinary people. In Congress Garfield had been tainted by the 1873 Crédit Mobilier scandal and other corruption charges. His nomination was the result of a split in the Republican party between two factions, the Stalwarts and the Half-Breeds, over the power to distribute patronage jobs.

Out of the fog of scandal came Charles Guiteau, a Stalwart disappointed by Garfield's failure to give him a high diplomatic post. The clearly deranged Guiteau saw Garfield's death as a political necessity and expected to be hailed as a hero when he shot the president in July 1881. Instead he was tried for murder, found guilty, and hanged.

The shock of Garfield's assassination built support for civil-service reform, but it would be one of the few political accomplishments of the times. In an age of burgeoning factories, explosive immigration growth, and economic hardship for millions of Americans, the political system seemed paralyzed. Powerful and well-organized groups such as corporate leaders or Union army veterans made themselves heard in Washington, but few others could. On the Great Plains, farm problems led to an agrarian reform movement that challenged but did not change the status quo.

The economic turmoil and social unrest of the 1880s continued into the 1890s, and in 1898 President William McKinley (who would also die of an assassin's bullet), stumbled into a war with Spain, substantially increased U.S. territorial holdings, and established new outposts from which American corporations could gain access to overseas markets.

PARTY POLITICS IN AN ERA OF SOCIAL AND ECONOMIC UPHEAVAL, 1877–1884

Between 1877 and 1894 four presidents squeezed into office by the narrowest of margins; control of the House of Representatives changed hands five times; and seven new western states were admitted into the Union. Amid intense competition, no party could muster a working majority. Republicans, Democrats, and third-party leaders sought desperately to reshape their political organizations to win over and cement the loyalty of their followers. Not until 1896, in the aftermath of a massive depression that hit when their opponents were in office, did the Republicans build a coalition that would control Congress and the presidency for the next fifteen years.

This chapter focuses on four major questions:

▶ How did the Democratic and Republican parties build coalitions of loyal followers out of their diverse ethnic and regional constituencies?

▶ How did environmental factors influence the rise of the Grange and the Farmers' Alliance movements?

▶ Why was the election of 1896 a watershed event? Why did William Jennings Bryan fail to win the presidency?

▶ Why did the United States go to war with Spain and become an imperial power?

Between 1876 and 1896, the intense competition between parties produced an incredible turnout of voters. Although most women did not yet have the vote and blacks were increasingly being disenfranchised, more than 80 percent of eligible white males often voted, and the figure could rise to 95 percent in hard-fought state and local elections. Voter participation a century later would equal scarcely half that level.

At the same time that voter turnout shot up, however, political parties sidestepped many of the issues created by industrialization such as taxation of corporations, support for those injured in factory accidents, and poverty relief. Except for the Interstate Commerce Act of 1887 and the largely symbolic Sherman Anti-Trust Act of 1890, Washington generally ignored the social consequences of industrialization and focused instead on encouraging economic growth.

How can we explain this refusal and, at the same time, account for the enormous popular support for parties? The answer lies in the political ideology of the period and the two major symbolic and economic issues that preoccupied lawmakers nationally: tariffs and civil service reform.

Contested Political Visions

Political parties in the late nineteenth century energized voters not only by appealing to economic self-interest, as in support for industrialization and pensions for Civil War veterans and their widows, but also by linking their programs to deeply held beliefs about the nature of the family and the proper role of government. In its prewar years, the Republican party had enhanced economic opportunities for common people by using governmental authority to expand railroads, increase tariff protection for industry, and provide land subsidies to farmers. It had also espoused a belief in female moral superiority and a willingness to use government as an instrument to protect family life.

After the Civil War, these positions hardened into political ideologies. Republicans justified their support for the tariff and defended their commitment to Union widows' pensions as ways to protect the family home and female wage earners. Men, in particular, associated loyalty to party with a sense of masculinity. Democrats countered, using metaphors of the seduction and rape of white women by external forces and labeling Republican programs as classic examples of the perils of excessive government force. High tariffs imperiled the family and threatened economic disaster.

Despite their differences, neither Republicans nor Democrats believed that the national government had any right to regulate corporations or to protect the social welfare of workers. Members of both parties, particularly among the middle and upper classes, embraced the laissez-faire view that the federal government should promote economic development but not regulate the industries that it subsidized.

Rather than looking to Washington, people turned to local or state authorities. On the Great Plains, angry farmers demanded that their state legislatures regulate railroad rates. In the cities, immigrant groups competed for political power while native-born reformers periodically attempted to oust the political machines. City and state governments vied with each other for control. States often held iron sway over cities. When Chicago wanted to issue permits to street popcorn vendors, for example, the Illinois legislature had to pass a special act.

Both parties, in the North and the South, engaged in election fraud by rigging elections, throwing out opposition votes, and paying for "floaters" who moved from precinct to precinct to vote. Accusations of fraud invigorated party loyalty as members of each party developed moral outrage and a sense of personal grievance at the other's behavior.

By linking economic policy to family values, both national parties encouraged the active role that women played in politics in this period, although most could not vote. Frances Willard and her followers in the Woman's Christian Temperance Union (WCTU), for example, helped create a Prohibition and Home Protection Party in the 1880s. A decade later western women Populists won full suffrage in Colorado, Idaho, and Utah.

Patterns of Party Strength

In the 1870s and 1880s each party had its own ideological appeal and centers of regional strength. The Democrats ruled the South; southern sections of border states like Ohio; and northern cities with large immigrant populations. In the South Democrats viewed Republicans as villains who had devastated their lands and set up fraudulent carpetbag governments. The Democrats campaigned for minimal government expenditures, opposed tariff increases, and attacked "governmental interference in the economy." In addition, Democrats staunchly defended their immigrant followers. On state and local levels, they fiercely opposed attempts to limit alcohol use, and they advocated support for parochial schools and opposed attempts to require English-only schooling.

The Republicans reigned in rural and small-town New England, Pennsylvania, and the upper Midwest and drew support from the Grand Army of the Republic (GAR), a social and political organization of northern Civil War veterans. Republicans often "waved the bloody shirt," invoking the South's responsibility for starting the Civil War as the reason to keep Democrats out of power. The

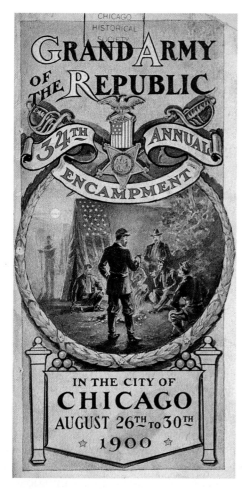

Poster Announcing GAR Encampment, Chicago, 1900
In addition to their nostalgic annual reunions, Union army veterans, organized as the Grand Army of the Republic, were a potent force in Republican party politics, lobbying for pensions and other benefits.

Republicans ran a series of former Union army generals for president and voted generous veterans' benefits.

State and local party leaders managed campaigns. They chose the candidates, raised money, organized rallies, turned out the vote, and—if their candidate won—distributed public jobs to party workers. Although issues of governmental authority dominated on the federal level, family tradition,

ethnic ties, religious affiliation, and local issues often determined an individual's vote. Outside the South, ethnicity and religion were the most reliable predictors of party affiliation. Catholics, especially Irish Catholics, and Americans of German ancestry tended to vote Democratic. Old-stock Protestant northerners and immigrants from northern Europe, in contrast, voted Republican, as did African-Americans, North and South. Although intolerant of racial differences, the Democrats were generally more accepting of religious diversity than were the Republicans. Electoral skirmishes often centered on cultural differences, notably the perennial Republican attempt to force prohibition on Irish whiskey drinkers, German beer drinkers, and Italian wine drinkers.

The Hayes White House: Virtue Restored

In this era of locally based politics and a diminished presidency, the state leaders who controlled both major parties tended to favor appealing but pliable presidential candidates. Rutherford B. Hayes (1877–1881) fit the mold perfectly. Hayes, a Civil War general, had won admiration as an honest Ohio governor, and his major presidential achievement was restoration of respect for the office after the Grant scandals. The benevolent, bearded Hayes brought dignity to the White House. His wife, Lucy, a highly intelligent, college-educated woman of great moral earnestness, actively supported the Woman's Christian Temperance Union (WCTU), and Hayes banished alcohol from the White House. After one presidential dinner, the secretary of state grumbled, "It was a brilliant affair. The water flowed like champagne."

Regulating the Money Supply

In the 1870s, politicians confronted a tough problem of economic policy: how to create a money supply adequate for a growing economy without producing inflation. Americans' almost superstitious reverence for gold and silver added to the difficulty of establishing a coherent monetary policy.

Many believed that the only trustworthy money was gold, silver, or certificates exchangeable for these scarce metals. All antebellum federal currency consisted of gold or silver coins or U.S. Treasury notes redeemable in gold or silver.

There were other issues. Bankers, business leaders, and politicians believed that economic stability required a strictly limited currency supply, which would drive interest rates up and prices down. Debtors, especially southern and western farmers, and manufacturers wanted to expand the money supply, a policy that would help them to pay off their debts. The monetary debate focused on a specific question: Should the Civil War paper "greenbacks" still in circulation be retained, or should they be eliminated to leave a currency backed by gold? The hard times associated with the Panic of 1873 sharpened this dispute.

The Greenback party (founded in 1877) called for an expanded money supply and other measures to benefit workers and farmers. In the 1878 midterm elections, Greenback candidates received more than 1 million votes and won fourteen seats in Congress.

As prosperity returned, the Greenback party faded, but the money issue did not. An even longer-lasting controversy surged over the coinage of silver. In 1873, Congress instructed the U.S. mint to cease making silver coins, thus "demonetizing" silver. But new discoveries in Nevada soon increased the silver supply, and debtor groups now demanded that the government resume coining silver.

Enthusiastically backed by the silver-mine owners, silver forces won a partial victory in 1878, when Congress required the Treasury to buy and mint up to $4 million worth of silver each month. But the Treasury, dominated by monetary conservatives, sabotaged the law's intent by refusing to circulate the silver dollars that it minted.

Frustrated silver advocates tried a new approach in the Sherman Silver Purchase Act of 1890. This measure instructed the Treasury to buy 4.5 million ounces of silver a month, almost exactly the output of the nation's silver mines, and to issue Treasury notes, redeemable in gold or silver, equivalent to the cost of the purchases. The money supply increased slightly, but when world silver prices plummeted af-

ter 1893, the government paid less each month for its purchases and thus issued fewer Treasury notes. The tangled controversy dragged on.

The Spoils System

For decades, successful candidates had rewarded supporters and contributors with jobs ranging from cabinet seats to lowly municipal posts. Defenders called the system rotation in office and claimed that it was a democratic way of filling government positions. Critics, however, dubbed it the spoils system after the old expression "To the victor belong the spoils." Too often, the new officeholders were ill prepared or just incompetent, and once in office they had to continue making campaign contributions to their patrons to keep their jobs.

For years, a small but influential group of reformers had campaigned for a merit-based civil service. Well-bred, well-educated, and well-heeled, these reformers called for a civil service staffed by "gentlemen." They had a point. A professional civil service was needed as the government's functions grew more complex.

Cautiously embracing the civil-service cause, President Hayes in 1877 launched an investigation of the corrupt New York City customs office and demanded the resignations of two officials with strong ties to Conkling, leader of the Stalwarts. When they refused Hayes's order, the president suspended them. Hayes's action won praise from civil-service reformers, but Conkling simply ridiculed "snivel service" and "Rutherfraud B. Hayes."

Civil-Service Reform Succeeds

In 1880 a deadlocked Republican presidential convention turned to dark-horse candidate James A. Garfield of Ohio, who had ties to the Half-Breeds. To soften the blow, the delegates chose Chester A. Arthur—one of the two Conkling loyalists fired by Hayes—as Garfield's running mate. Garfield was healthy, so the choice of the unqualified Arthur on the ticket seemed safe.

Running against both Democratic and Greenback candidates, Garfield won the 1880 election by a razor-thin margin of less than 40,000 votes. Conkling, to protest Garfield's appointment of several of his foes to government posts, resigned from the Senate, confident that the New York legislature would reelect him and thus strengthen his political power. To his surprise, the legislature elected another senator and ended Conkling's political career.

Garfield's assassination in 1881—which brought to the White House Chester A. Arthur, the very symbol of the corrupt patronage system—gave a powerful emotional boost to civil service reform, as reformers painted Garfield as a martyr to the spoils system. In 1883 Congress enacted the Pendleton Civil Service Act, drafted by the Civil Service Reform League that had been created two years earlier. The act created a civil-service commission to establish qualifications for federal jobs and to prepare competitive examinations. Initially, the Pendleton Act covered only 12 percent of federal employees, but it was gradually expanded. The creation of a professional civil service helped bring the federal government in step with the modernizing trends transforming society.

Chester A. Arthur pleasantly surprised those who expected him to be an utter disaster. He supported civil-service reform, and proved quite independent of his former crony Conkling. Nevertheless, in 1882, fed up with feuding Republicans, voters gave Democrats a strong majority in the House of Representatives, and in 1884 they put a Democrat, Grover Cleveland, in the White House for the first time since 1856.

POLITICS OF PRIVILEGE, POLITICS OF EXCLUSION, 1884–1892

Grover Cleveland challenged powerful interests by calling for cuts in the tariff and veterans' pensions. After Cleveland served a single term (1885–1889), one of the most corrupt elections in American history put Republican Benjamin Harrison (1889–1893) in the White House—and restored big business and the veterans' lobby to the driver's seat. Simultaneously, debt-ridden farmers mounted a spirited protest movement. And in the South, the white majority used the machinery of politics to strip black citizens of their basic rights.

1884: Cleveland Victorious

James G. Blaine, the Republican nominee in 1884, typified younger Republicans eager to build a truly national party that would promote economic development and take a greater interest in foreign policy. But Blaine had been sullied in his 1876 senatorial campaign when his opponents had published letters in which he offered political favors to a railroad company in exchange for stock. To civil-service reformers, Blaine epitomized the hated patronage system. He "wallowed in spoils," one reformer said, "like a rhinoceros in an African pool."

Sensing Blaine's vulnerability, the Democrats nominated Grover Cleveland of New York, who had enjoyed a meteoric career—first as Buffalo's mayor and then as New York's governor—as a reformer and opponent of bosses and spoilsmen. Short, rotund, and resembling a bulldog, Cleveland was his own man.

Republican reformers bolted to Cleveland and were promptly nicknamed Mugwumps, an Algonquian term for a renegade chief. Unfortunately, as a young man Cleveland had fathered an illegitimate child. He admitted the indiscretion, but the Republicans still jeered at rallies: "Ma, Ma, where's my pa?" Facing opposition from the New York City Democratic machine that he had fought as governor, Cleveland risked losing his own state. The tide turned in November when Blaine failed to respond to a New York City Protestant clergyman who denounced the Democrats as the party of "Rum, Romanism, and Rebellion." Cleveland carried New York State by 1,200 votes, and with it the election.

Tariffs and Pensions

The corpulent Cleveland settled comfortably into the shadowy role expected of Gilded Age presidents. He had early embraced the belief that government must not meddle in the economy. In Andrew Jackson's day, laissez-faire had been endorsed by ambitious small entrepreneurs; by the 1880s it was the rallying cry of a corporate elite opposed to any public regulation or oversight. Sharing this outlook, Cleveland asserted presidential power mostly through his vetoes and showed little grasp of industrialization's impact. Vetoing a bill that would have provided seeds to drought-stricken farmers in Texas, he warned that people should not expect the government to solve their problems.

One matter did arouse Cleveland: the tariff, an issue entangled in conflicting economic and political interests. A major source of revenue in the era before a federal income tax, tariff duties were really a form of taxation. But which imported goods should be taxed, and how much? Opinions differed radically. Producers of commodities like coal and wool demanded tariff protection against foreign competition, as did many manufacturers, joined by workers in these industries. Other manufacturers, however, while seeking protection for their finished products, wanted low tariffs on the raw materials they required. Most farmers hated all tariffs for inflating farm-equipment prices and making it hard to sell American farm products abroad.

Initially, Cleveland called for tariff reform largely because the high protective tariffs of the era were creating huge federal-budget surpluses. To spend the surpluses, legislators steered federal funds to "pork barrel" projects that benefitted their home districts—and promoted corruption. In his 1887 annual message to Congress, Cleveland argued that lower tariffs not only would cut the federal surplus but also would reduce prices and slow the development of trusts. Although politicians paid little attention, corporate leaders found Cleveland's talk of lower tariffs threatening.

Cleveland stirred up another hornet's nest by opposing the routine payment of veterans' disability pensions. No one opposed pensions for the deserving, but fraudulent claims proliferated; one veteran collected a disability pension for poor eyesight caused, he said, by wartime diarrhea. Cleveland, unlike his predecessors, personally investigated these claims and rejected many. He also vetoed a bill that would have pensioned all disabled veterans and their dependents, whether or not the disability occurred in military service. The pension roll should be an honor roll, he stressed, not a refuge for frauds.

1888: Big Business and the GAR Strike Back

By 1888 some influential groups had concluded that Cleveland had to go. Republican kingmakers nominated Benjamin Harrison, a corporation lawyer and former senator of such personal coldness that some ridiculed him as the human iceberg. In a new style of electioneering, instead of sending the candidate around the country, his managers brought delegations to his Indiana home where he hammered at the tariff issue. They portrayed Cleveland, falsely, as an advocate of "free trade"—the elimination of all tariffs—and warned that only a high tariff could ensure business prosperity, decent wages, and a healthy home market for farmers. Worried business leaders provided $4 million in campaign contributions, which purchased not only advertising but also votes.

In the end, Cleveland received almost 100,000 more votes than Harrison but lost New York, Indiana, and the electoral vote. When Harrison piously observed that Providence had helped the Republican cause, his campaign chairman snorted: "Providence hadn't a damn thing to do with it. . . . [A] number of men . . . approach[ed] the gates of the penitentiary to make him president."

Once in office, Harrison swiftly rewarded his supporters. He appointed a Grand Army of the Republic official as commissioner of pensions. "God help the surplus!" exclaimed the new commissioner who soon expanded the number of pensioners from 676,000 to nearly 1 million. This massive pension system, coupled with medical care through a network of veterans' hospitals, became America's first large public-welfare program. In 1890 the triumphant Republicans also passed the McKinley Tariff, which pushed rates to an all-time high.

Rarely has the federal government been so subservient to entrenched economic interests and so out of touch with the plight of the disadvantaged as during the 1880s. But inaction bred discontent. In 1890 voters ousted the Republicans and put Democrats in control of the House of Representatives. The 1890 election awakened the nation to a tide of political activism in the agrarian South and West spawned by chronic problems in rural America.

The Grange Movement

Plains farming had long been a risky venture. Between 1873 and 1877 terrible grasshopper infestations consumed half the midwestern wheat crop. After 1870 production rose and prices fell. Wheat tumbled from $2.95 a bushel in 1866 to $1.06 in 1880. Farmers who had borrowed to finance their homesteads and machinery went bankrupt or barely survived. In 1874 a struggling Minnesotan wrote to the governor, "We can see nothing but starvation in the future if relief does not come."

When relief did not come, farmers established their own cooperative ventures. In 1867, under the leadership of Oliver H. Kelley, a Department of Agriculture clerk, midwestern farmers formed the Grange, or "Patrons of Husbandry." Membership climbed to more than 1.5 million by the early 1870s. Offering education, emotional support, and fellowship, the Grange maintained a library of information on planting and livestock and organized covered-dish dinners and songfests.

But the central concern was the farmers' economic plight. An 1874 circular defined the Grange's purpose: to help farmers to "buy less and produce more, in order to make our farms more self-sustaining." Grangers shared the Jacksonian belief that the products of the soil formed the basis of all honorable wealth and that the producer classes—people who worked with their hands—formed the true backbone of society. The Grange negotiated discounts from farm-machinery dealers and established "cash-only" cooperative stores and grain elevators to eliminate the "middlemen"—bankers, grain brokers, and merchants who grew rich at the farmers' expense. And the Grangers attacked the railroads, which gave discounts to large shippers, bribed state legislators, and charged higher rates for short runs than for long hauls. Although supposedly nonpolitical, midwestern Grangers lobbied state legislatures for laws setting maximum rates for freight shipments.

The railroads appealed these "Granger laws" to the Supreme Court. But in *Munn* v. *Illinois* (1877), the Court ruled against the railroads and upheld an Illinois law fixing a maximum rate for grain storage. The case of *Wabash* v. *Illinois* (1886), however, prohibited states from regulating *interstate* railroad rates. Then in 1887 Congress passed the Interstate Commerce Act, establishing a new agency, the Interstate Commerce Commission, to investigate and oversee railroad operations. The commission did little to curb the railroads, but it did establish the principle of federal regulation of interstate transportation.

Despite early gains, the Grange movement soon faltered. By 1878, by lobbying at the state level, railroads had won repeal of most state regulations. The cash-only cooperatives failed because few farmers had cash. The Grange ideal of financial independence proved unrealistic because conditions prevailing on the Plains made it impossible to farm without borrowing money.

Was the Grange correct in blaming greedy railroads and middlemen for farm problems? The answer is not simple. From 1873 to 1878, the entire economy was trapped in a depression that stung railroads and farmers alike. Although farm commodity prices fell between 1865 and 1900, so did prices on manufactured goods. Railroads could justify their stiff freight rates in part by the thin pattern of western settlement and the seasonality of grain shipments. Farmers had no control over the prices they received for their crops and were at the mercy of local merchants and farm-equipment dealers who held monopolies. Railroads sometimes transported wheat to only one mill or refused to stop at small towns. These policies left farmers feeling powerless.

When the prices of corn, wheat, and cotton briefly revived after 1878, many farmers deserted the Grange, although it lived on as a social and educational institution. For all its weaknesses, the Grange movement did lay the groundwork for an even more powerful wave of agrarian protest.

Consumer Prices and Farm-Product Prices, 1865–1913

As cycles of drought and debt battered Great Plains wheat growers, a Kansas farmer wrote, "At the age of 52, after a long life of toil, economy, and self-denial, I find myself and family virtually paupers."

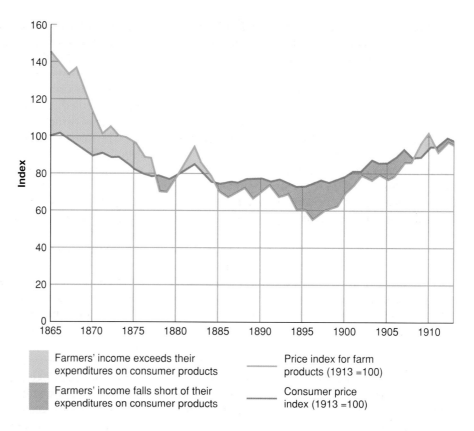

Farmers' income exceeds their expenditures on consumer products

Farmers' income falls short of their expenditures on consumer products

Price index for farm products (1913 =100)

Consumer price index (1913 =100)

The Alliance Movement

The problems that drove midwestern and Great Plains farmers to form the Grange drove southern and western farmers to begin the alliance movement. Southerners found themselves mired in a cycle of debt by the crop-lien system; by 1900 one-third of all southern farmers had become tenants. One historian has called the South of those years "a giant pawnshop."

The Farmers' Alliance movement began in the 1870s when Texas farmers gathered to discuss their problems, and it spread eastward across the lower South. Like Grangers, alliance members initially advocated farmers' cooperatives to purchase equipment and supplies and to market their cotton. And, as had the Grange cooperatives, these generally failed for lack of capital.

In 1887 a farsighted Texan, Charles W. Macune, assumed leadership of the alliance movement. By 1889 Macune had merged several regional groups into the National Farmers' Alliance and Industrial Union, or the Southern Alliance. A parallel organization of black farmers emerged, the National Colored Farmers' Alliance. By 1890 the Southern Alliance boasted 3 million members and its black counterpart another 1.2 million. Alliance members generally comprised the poorest farmers, growers dependent on a single crop, and geographically isolated farmers. Gathering for picnics and rallies, hard-hit farm families realized the political potential of their collective undertaking. As a member wrote in 1889, "Reform never begins with the leaders, it comes from the people." Southern Alliance leaders Tom Watson of Georgia and Leonidas Polk of North Carolina even urged black and white farmers to act together on their common problems. For a while, this message of racial cooperation in the name of reform carried promise.

Meanwhile, alliance fever also hit the Great Plains, where alliances sprang up in Kansas, Nebraska, Iowa, and Minnesota in the drought-plagued years of 1880 and 1881. After renewed rainfall nourished a brief boom, drought returned to rekindle the alliance spirit in 1886–1887. From 1887 to 1897, only two Great Plains wheat crops were worth harvesting. To make matters worse, wheat prices fell as world production increased.

Innumerable midwestern families packed up and returned East. "In God we trusted, in Kansas we busted," some scrawled on their wagons. Western Kansas lost 50 percent of its population between 1888 and 1892. But others hung on, and the Northwestern Alliance, including all the Great Plains states, grew rapidly, although it never approached the Southern Alliance in total size.

In Kansas, meanwhile, Mary E. Lease, a Wichita lawyer, burst on the scene in 1890 as a fiery alliance orator. Other women, veterans of the Granger or prohibition cause, also rallied to the new movement, founding the National Women's Alliance (NWA) in 1891. Declared the NWA, "Put 1,000 women lecturers in the field and revolution is here." In Minnesota activist Ignatius Donnelly's *The Golden Bottle* (1892), a strong feminist strain pervades the portrayal of agrarian reformers.

As the movement swelled, the opposition turned nasty. Jerry Simpson, a Kansas alliance leader, mentioned the silk stockings of a conservative politician in his district and noted that he had no such finery. In response, a hostile newspaper editor labeled him "Sockless Jerry" Simpson, the nickname he carried to his grave. When Mary Lease advised Kansans to "raise less corn and more hell," a conservative newspaper sneered, "[Kansas] has started to raise hell, as Mrs. Lease advised, and [the state] seems to have an overproduction. But that doesn't matter. Kansas never did believe in diversified crops."

From all this came a political agenda. In 1889 the Southern and Northwestern alliances arranged a loose merger and supported candidates who agreed with them. They focused on increasing government action on behalf of farmers and workers and sought tariff reduction, a graduated income tax, public ownership of railroads, federal funding for irrigation research, a prohibition on landownership by aliens, and "the free and unlimited coinage of silver."

The 1890 elections illuminated the depth of agrarian discontent. Alliance-backed candidates won four governorships and controlled eleven legislatures. Three alliance-backed senators and fifty congressmen went to Washington in 1890 as angry winds from the hinterland buffeted the political system.

Northwestern Alliance leaders favored a third party, and by 1892 many Southern Alliance officials had come around to their position. In February 1892 top alliance leaders organized the People's Party of the United States—a name shortened to the Populist party. At their convention that August, delegates nominated for the presidency Iowan James B. Weaver, a Union general in the Civil War and a former Greenback candidate. **hc** Primary Source: Farmers' Alliance Proposes a Cooperative Commonwealth

The Populist platform contained the goals announced by the alliance leaders in 1889 and added a call for the direct popular election of senators and other electoral reforms. Ignatius Donnelly's ringing preamble pronounced the nation "on the verge of moral, political, and material ruin" and proclaimed, "We seek to restore the government of the Republic to the hands of 'the plain people' with which class it originated."

African-Americans After Reconstruction

As populists geared up, a group of citizens with far more profound grievances suffered renewed oppression. The end of Reconstruction in 1877 and the restoration of power to southern white elites spelled bad news for southern blacks. Southern white opinion sought an end to "Negro rule" and tried to suppress the black vote. Initially, whites relied on intimidation, terror, and fraud to limit black voting rights, but in 1890 Mississippi amended its state constitution to exclude most African-American voters, and other southern states followed suit.

The Fifteenth Amendment (1870) had guaranteed all male citizens' right to vote, so local Democratic officials used indirect means such as literacy tests, poll taxes, and property requirements to disfranchise African-Americans. To ensure that these measures excluded only blacks, whites employed such devices as the grandfather clause, which exempted anyone whose ancestor had voted in 1860. African-American disfranchisement proceeded erratically, but by the early twentieth century it was effectively complete.

Disfranchisement was the keystone of an arch of white supremacy that stretched across the South as state after state passed laws strictly segregating many realms of life by race. African-American caterers, barbers, contractors, bricklayers, carpenters, and other artisans lost their white customers. And blacks sent to prison—sometimes for minor offenses—got caught up in the convict-lease system, which allowed cotton planters and others to "lease" prison gangs and to put them to work under degraded conditions.

The convict-lease system not only enforced the racial hierarchy but also played an important economic role. The system provided income to state governments and cheap, easily controlled labor to factories, railroads, and large-scale farms. Thousands died under this brutal system, which survived into the early twentieth century, when it succumbed to humanitarian protests and its own unprofitability.

The lynch rope was the ultimate enforcer of white supremacy. Through the 1880s and 1890s, an average of one hundred African-Americans were lynched annually in the United States, mainly in the South. Rumors and unsubstantiated accusations, frequently of raping a white woman, unleashed this mob violence. ("Attempted rape" could mean a wide range of behavior unacceptable to whites.)

The lynch mob demonstrated whites' absolute power. In a 1995 study of lynchings, historians found that more than 80 percent involved black victims. Lynchings were most common in the Cotton Belt, and they tended to peak when cotton prices were falling and competition between poor whites

and poor blacks was most intense. Not surprisingly, lynching reached its highest point in 1892 as many poor African-Americans joined the agrarian protest and rallied to the Populist party banner.

The relationship between southern agrarian protest and white racism was complex. Some Populists, among them Georgia's Tom Watson, tried to build a genuinely interracial movement and denounced both lynching and the convict-lease system. When an African-American Populist leader pursued by a lynch mob took refuge in Watson's house during the 1892 campaign, he summoned 2,000 armed white Populists to defend the man. But most white Populists, encouraged by such rabble-rousers as "Pitchfork Ben" Tillman of South Carolina, held fast to racism; Watson complained that most poor whites "would joyously hug the chains of . . . wretchedness rather than do any experimenting on [the race] question."

The white ruling elite, eager to drive a wedge in the farm-protest movement, worked to inflame lower-class white racism. Addressing an alliance meeting in 1889, an Atlanta editor warned against division among white southerners; the South's only hope, he said, was "the clear and unmistakable domination of the white race." On balance, the rise of southern agrarian protest deepened racial hatred and worsened blacks' situation. The federal government did nothing. A generation of northern politicians paid lip service to egalitarian principles and failed to apply them to African-Americans.

The Supreme Court similarly abandoned African-Americans to their fates. The Court ripped gaping holes in the Fourteenth Amendment, which guaranteed equal protection of the law, and the Civil Rights Act of 1875, which outlawed racial discrimination. In the *Civil Rights Cases* (1883), the Court threw out the Civil Rights Act of 1875 on the grounds that the Fourteenth Amendment prevented governments, but not individuals, from infringing on civil rights. In *Plessy v. Ferguson* (1896), the Court upheld a Louisiana law requiring segregated railroad cars. Racial segregation was legal, the justices ruled, provided that equal facilities were made available to each race. With the Supreme Court's blessing, the South also segregated its public schools, ignoring the caveat that separate facilities must be equal. White children studied in nicer buildings, used newer equipment, and were taught by better-paid teachers than black children. Not until 1954 would the Court abandon the "separate but equal" doctrine. Rounding out a dismal record, the justices in 1898 upheld the poll tax and literacy tests. Such racist and separatist policies affected blacks nationwide, Mexicans in Texas, and Asians in California among other groups.

Few northerners protested the indignities that underlay the South's white-supremacist society. Until the North condemned lynching, declared aged abolitionist Frederick Douglass in 1892, "it will remain equally involved with the South in this common crime." The restoration of sectional harmony came at a high price: northern acquiescence in the utter debasement of a people whose freedom had cost the lives of thousands of northern men.

Blacks responded in various ways. The nation's foremost African-American leader from the 1890s until his death in 1915 was Booker T. Washington. Born into slavery in Virginia in 1856, the son of a slave woman and her white master, Washington enrolled at a freedman's school in Hampton, Virginia, and in 1881 organized a state vocational school in Tuskegee, Alabama, that became Tuskegee University. Washington attained prominence in 1895 when he gave an address in Atlanta insisting that the first task of African-Americans must be to acquire vocational skills. Once blacks proved their economic value, he predicted, racism would ebb; meanwhile, they must accept their lot. Washington lectured widely, and his autobiography, *Up From Slavery* (1901), recounted his rise from poverty thanks to honesty, hard work, and kindly patrons— themes familiar from Horatio Alger's books.

Black churches provided emotional support, as did black fraternal lodges. And a handful of African-Americans established banks and successful businesses such as insurance companies and barbershops.

Meanwhile, voices of black protest never wholly died out. Frederick Douglas urged African-Americans to press on for full equality, proclaiming, "[Those] who would be free, themselves must strike the first blow." But for some, the solution was to leave the South. In 1879 several thousand moved to Kansas, and 10,000 migrated to Chicago between 1870 and 1890. Blacks who went north, however, discovered that public opinion sanctioned many forms of de facto discrimination. Northern African-American laborers encountered widespread prejudice. Although the Knights of Labor had welcomed blacks, the AFL looked the other way as its member craft unions excluded them.

The rise of the "solid South," firmly established on racist foundations, had profound political implications. For nearly a century, the only important election in most southern states was the Democratic primary. Furthermore, the large bloc of southern Democrats in Congress accumulated seniority and power and helped shape public policy. Finally, the solid South wielded enormous clout in the Democratic party; no national candidate unacceptable to the South stood a chance.

Above all, the rigid caste system of the post-Reconstruction South molded the consciousness of those caught up in it, black and white alike. Describing her girlhood in the turn-of-the-century South, white novelist Lillian Smith wrote: "I learned it is possible to be a gentlewoman and an arrogant callous creature at the same moment; to pray at night and ride a Jim Crow car the next morning; . . . to glow when the word democracy was used, and to practice slavery from morning to night."

THE 1890s: POLITICS IN A DEPRESSION DECADE

In the 1890s smoldering discontent with the major parties and their support for unrestricted business enterprise burst into flames. As banks failed and railroads went bankrupt, the nation slid into a grinding depression. The crises of the 1890s laid bare the paralysis of the federal government—dominated by a business elite—when confronted by the new social realities of factories, urban slums, immigrant workers, and desperate farmers. Through the new Populist party, irate farmers, laborers, and their supporters hoped to change the system.

1892: Populists Challenge the Status Quo

The year 1892 provided evidence of growing discontent. The Populist platform, adopted in July, angrily catalogued agrarian demands. The deaths of thirteen men in a gun battle between strikers and strikebreakers at the Homestead steel mill and the use of federal troops against silver-mine strikers in Idaho seemed to justify the Populists' warning of a nation verging on class warfare.

The 1892 campaign for the White House was a replay of 1888, Harrison versus Cleveland, but this time Cleveland won by more than 360,000 votes, a decisive margin in an age of close elections. A public reaction against labor violence and the McKinley Tariff hurt Harrison. The Populists' strength proved spotty. Their presidential candidate, James B. Weaver, got more than 1 million votes, 8.5 percent of the total, and the Populists elected five senators, ten congressmen, and three governors. But the party made no dent in New England or the urban East and little in the Midwest.

In the South, racism, Democratic loyalty, distaste for the former Union general Weaver, and widespread intimidation and voter fraud kept the Populist tally under 25 percent. The party's failure killed the prospects for interracial agrarian reform. After 1892 southern politicians seeking to appeal to poor whites stayed within the Democratic fold and laced their populism with virulent racism.

The Panic of 1893: Capitalism in Crisis

Cleveland took office and quickly confronted a major crisis: an economic collapse in the railroad industry that quickly spread. Railroads had led the awesome industrial growth of the 1880s, triggering both investment and speculation. In the early 1890s railroad growth slowed, affecting other industries, including iron and steel. The first hint of trouble came in the February 1893 failure of the Philadelphia and Reading Railroad.

This bankruptcy occurred at a moment of weakened confidence in the government's ability to redeem paper money with gold on demand.

Economic problems in London in 1890 had forced British investors to unload millions of dollars in American stocks; $68 million in U.S. gold reserves flowed across the Atlantic to Britain. At the same time, heavy spending on pensions and pork-barrel projects had substantially reduced the federal surplus, while paying for silver purchases under the Sherman Silver Purchase Act was straining the gold reserve. Finally, the election of Democrat Cleveland further eroded confidence in the dollar; although the president endorsed the gold standard, many in his party advocated inflationary policies. From January 1892 to March 1893 (the month Cleveland was inaugurated), the gold reserve fell from $192 million to $100 million. Those who believed that the gold standard offered the only sure evidence of financial stability were alarmed.

With the collapse of the Philadelphia and Reading, fear fed on itself as panicky investors converted their stock holdings to gold. Stock prices plunged, the gold reserve plummeted, and by the end of the year 74 railroads, 600 banks, and 15,000 businesses had failed. Four years of hard times would follow the Panic of 1893.

The Depression of 1893–1897

By 1897 one-third of the nation's railroad mileage was in bankruptcy. The railroad boom had spurred the prosperity of the 1880s, and the railroad collapse of the 1890s battered the economy into a full-scale depression.

In human terms, the depression took a heavy toll. Industrial unemployment ranged from 20 to 25 percent. Millions of factory workers had no money to buy food or to heat their homes, and jobless men tramped the streets looking for work. Unusually harsh winters in 1893 and 1894 aggravated the misery. People were starving to death in New York City as a wealthy New Yorker named Bradley Martin threw a costume ball that cost hundreds of thousands of dollars. Popular outrage at this flaunting of wealth in a prostrate city drove Martin to move abroad.

In rural America, already hard hit by declining agricultural prices, the depression turned trouble into ruin. Farm prices dropped by more than 20 percent: corn plummeted from $.50 to $.21 a bushel and wheat from $.84 to $.51. Cotton fell to $.05 a pound.

Protest swelled among desperate Americans. The populist movement grew stronger. In Massillon, Ohio, self-taught monetary "expert" Jacob Coxey concluded that the answer to unemployment was a $500 million public-works program funded with paper money not backed by gold. Coxey organized a march on Washington in March 1894 to lobby for his scheme. Thousands joined him en route, and several hundred reached Washington in late April. Police arrested Coxey and other leaders for trespassing on Capitol grounds, and his "army" broke up. Though radical in the 1890s, Coxey's proposals anticipated programs that the government would adopt during the depression of the 1930s.

As disquiet intensified, fear and anger clutched middle-class Americans. A church magazine demanded that troops put a "pitiless stop" to outbreaks of unrest. To some, a bloody upheaval seemed imminent.

Business Leaders Hunker Down

In the face of the mass turmoil, Cleveland retreated into a laissez-faire fortress. Boom-and-bust economic cycles were inevitable, he insisted, and government could do nothing. Missing the larger picture, Cleveland focused on a single peripheral issue, the gold standard. In August 1893 he persuaded Congress to repeal the Sherman Silver Purchase Act, which he blamed for the dwindling gold reserve.

But the gold drain continued and the depression deepened. In early 1895, with the gold reserve down to $41 million, Cleveland turned to Wall Street. Bankers J. P. Morgan and August Belmont agreed to lend the government $62 million in exchange for discounted U.S. bonds. The government then purchased gold to replenish the reserve, and Morgan and Belmont resold their bonds for a substantial profit. The deal helped to restore confidence in the government's economic stability. Cleveland had saved the gold standard, but at a high price. His deal with Morgan and Belmont, and the handsome profits they made, seemed to show

more concern for moneyed men than for the average American and confirmed radicals' suspicions of an unholy alliance between Washington and Wall Street.

As the tariff battle made clear, corporate interests held the whip hand. Although Cleveland favored tariff reform, the Democrat-controlled Congress of 1892–1893 generally yielded to lobbyists. The Wilson-Gorman Tariff of 1894 made so many concessions to special interests that a disgusted president allowed it to become law without his signature.

One feature of the Wilson-Gorman Tariff suggested an enlarging vision of government's role in an age of towering fortunes: an income tax of 2 percent on all income over $4,000 (roughly $40,000 in present-day purchasing power). But in 1895 the Supreme Court declared the tax unconstitutional. Thus whether one looked at the executive, the legislature, or the judiciary, Washington's subordination to the corporate elite seemed nearly complete.

The depression also helped reorient social thought. Middle-class charitable workers, long convinced that individual character flaws caused poverty, now realized that even sober, hardworking people could succumb to economic forces beyond their control. As the social work profession took form in the early twentieth century, its members spent less time preaching to the poor and more time investigating the social sources of poverty.

Laissez-faire ideology weakened in the 1890s as depression-worn Americans adopted a broader conception of government's proper role in dealing with the social consequences of industrialization. This new perspective would activate powerful political energies. The depression was thus memorable not only for the suffering it caused but also for the lessons it taught.

THE WATERSHED ELECTION OF 1896

Republican gains in the 1894 midterm elections revealed popular revulsion against Cleveland and the Democrats, whom Americans widely blamed for the hard times. In the 1896 presidential election, the monetary question became the overriding symbolic issue. Conservatives clung to the gold standard, but advocates of "free silver" triumphed at the Democratic convention when a young champion of silver, William Jennings Bryan, secured the nomination. However, his opponent, William McKinley, won the election, and his triumph laid the groundwork for a major political realignment.

1894: Protest Grows Louder

The midterm election of 1894 spelled Democratic disaster. Immigrants, who were battered by the depression, abandoned their traditional Democratic allegiance, and Republicans gained control of Congress and several key states. Populist candidates won nearly 1.5 million votes, 40 percent over their 1892 total. Most Populist gains came in the South.

The serious economic conflict that split Americans focused on a symbolic issue: free silver. Cleveland's rigid defense of the gold standard forced his opponents into an exaggerated obsession with silver, obscuring the genuine issues dividing rich and poor, creditor and debtor, and farmer and city dweller. Conservatives tirelessly upheld the gold standard, and agrarian radicals extolled silver as a universal cure-all. Both sides had a point. Gold advocates recognized the potential disaster of uncontrolled inflation if paper money rested only on the government's ability to run printing presses. Silver advocates knew from personal experience how tight-money, high-interest policies depressed prices and devastated farmers.

Silver Advocates Capture the Democratic Party

At the 1896 Democratic convention in Chicago, western and southern delegates adopted a platform demanding the free and unlimited coinage of silver—in effect, repudiating the Cleveland administration. An ardent advocate of the silver cause captured the party's nomination: William Jennings Bryan of Nebraska. Only thirty-six, the young

lawyer had already served western agrarian interests during two terms in Congress.

Joining Christian imagery with economic analysis, Bryan gave his major convention speech during the debate over the platform. His booming voice carried his rousing words to the highest galleries of the convention hall. Praising farmers as the nation's bedrock, Bryan roared to the cheering delegates, "You shall not press down upon the brow of labor this crown of thorns, you shall not crucify mankind upon a cross of gold."

The silverites' capture of the Democratic party left the Populists with a dilemma. Free silver was only one reform among many that they advocated. If they jumped aboard the Bryan bandwagon, they would abandon their own program. But a separate Populist ticket would siphon votes from Bryan and guarantee a Republican victory. Reluctantly, the Populists endorsed Bryan. Meanwhile, the Republicans nominated former Ohio governor William McKinley on a platform endorsing the high protective tariff and the gold standard.

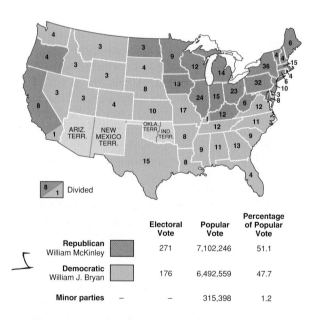

		Electoral Vote	Popular Vote	Percentage of Popular Vote
Republican William McKinley		271	7,102,246	51.1
Democratic William J. Bryan		176	6,492,559	47.7
Minor parties		–	315,398	1.2

MAP 20.1
The Election of 1896

William McKinley's "Front-Porch" Campaign, 1896
McKinley (front row, sixth from left) poses with an Italian-American brass band from Buffalo, New York, in front of his home in Canton, Ohio.

1896: Republicans Triumphant

Bryan did his best to sustain the momentum of the Chicago convention, crisscrossing the country by train to deliver his free-silver campaign speech. One skeptic jeered that Bryan was well nicknamed the "Boy Wonder of the River Platte;" his mouth was just as wide and his mind just as shallow.

Mark Hanna, a Cleveland industrialist, managed the Republican McKinley's campaign. Recognizing that the dignified, somewhat aloof McKinley could not match Bryan's popular touch—one wit noted that McKinley always seemed to be "determinedly looking for his pedestal"—Hanna built the campaign around posters, pamphlets, and editorials that warned of the dangers of free silver, caricatured Bryan as a radical, and portrayed McKinley and the gold standard as twin pillars of prosperity.

Drawing on a war chest possibly as large as $7 million, Hanna spent lavishly. J. P. Morgan and John D. Rockefeller together contributed $500,000 to the McKinley campaign, more than Bryan's total campaign contributions. McKinley himself stayed home in Canton, Ohio, emerging occasionally to read speeches to a stream of visiting delegations, comprising some 750,000 people.

On election day 1896, McKinley swamped Bryan by more than 600,000 votes; the Democrats carried only the South, the Great Plains, and the Rocky Mountains. In nominating Bryan, the Democrats had selected a candidate with little appeal for factory workers, the urban middle class, or immigrants. Furthermore, despite a telling critique of laissez-faire capitalism, the populist vision of returning to a premodern world of independent farmers and entrepreneurs seemed far removed from the new corporate order.

The McKinley administration translated its conservative platform into law. The Dingley Tariff (1897) pushed rates to all-time highs, and the

Currency Act of 1900 committed the United States to the gold standard. Because of returning prosperity, rising farm prices, and the discovery of gold in Alaska, these measures roused little opposition, and McKinley easily defeated Bryan again in 1900.

The elections of 1894 and 1896 produced a Republican majority that, except for Woodrow Wilson's presidency (1913–1921), would dominate national politics until the election of Franklin D. Roosevelt in 1932. Populism collapsed, but an emerging new reform movement, progressivism, would bring many populist reform proposals to fruition.

EXPANSIONIST STIRRINGS AND WAR WITH SPAIN, 1878–1901

Beyond dominating domestic politics, the corporate elite influenced U.S. foreign policy in the late nineteenth century, contributing to surging expansionist pressures. Business leaders, politicians, statesmen, and editorialists insisted that national greatness required America to join Europe in the imperialist theater. Fanned by sensationalistic newspaper coverage of Cuba's struggle for independence from Spain, elite calls for international assertiveness sparked a war between the United States and Spain in 1898.

Roots of Expansionist Sentiment

Since the first European settlers colonized North America's Atlantic coast, the newcomers had been an expansionist people. By the 1840s the push westward had acquired a name: Manifest Destiny. Civil war and industrialization had temporarily damped expansionism, but it revived strongly after 1880 as politicians and opinion molders proclaimed America's global destiny.

European and Japanese imperialism intensified this expansionist sentiment. Great Britain, France, Belgium, Germany, Italy, and Japan were all collecting colonies from North Africa to remote Pacific islands. National greatness, it appeared, demanded

an empire. Corporate leaders held that continued prosperity required overseas markets. With industry and the labor force growing, foreign markets offered a "safety valve" for potentially explosive pressures in the U.S. economy. In 1890 the secretary of state noted that national productivity was outrunning "the demands of the home market" and insisted that American business look abroad.

Proponents of a strong navy contributed to the expansionist mood. In *The Influence of Sea Power upon History* (1890), Alfred Thayer Mahan equated sea power with national greatness and urged a rapid U.S. naval buildup, which required overseas bases. Some religious leaders talked of America's divine mission to spread Christianity, an argument with racist tinges. One minister averred that "God is training the Anglo-Saxon race for its mission"—a mission of bringing Christianity and civilization to the world's "weaker races." Theodore Roosevelt, Henry Cabot Lodge, and diplomat John Hay led a group of Republican expansionists who tirelessly preached imperial greatness and military might. "I should welcome almost any war," Roosevelt declared, "for I think this country needs one." Such advocates of expansionism applied social Darwinist rhetoric of the day to argue that war, as a vehicle for natural selection, would test and refurbish American manhood, honor, and civic commitment. This gendered appeal both counterbalanced concerns about women's political activism and helped forge the disparate arguments for expansionism into a simple, visceral plea that had a broad appeal.

A series of diplomatic skirmishes in the mid-1890s revealed the newly assertive American mood. In the mid-1880s, quarrels between the United States and Great Britain had flared over fishing rights in the North Atlantic and North Pacific, reawakening latent anti-British feelings and the old dream of acquiring Canada. A poem published in the *Detroit News* provided a new nickname for expansionists—jingoists:

> We do not want to fight,
> But, by jingo, if we do,
> We'll scoop in all the fishing grounds
> And the whole dominion too!

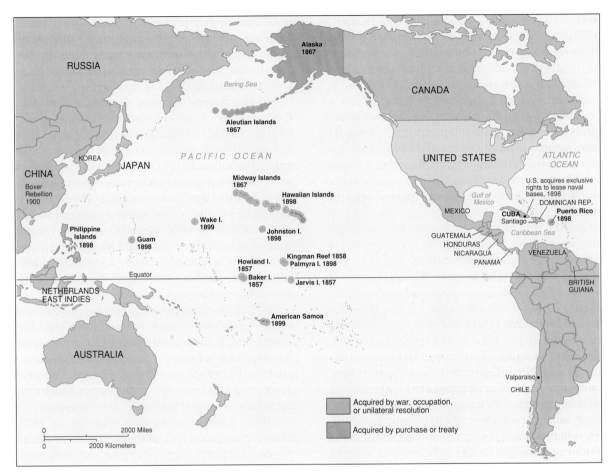

MAP 20.2
U.S. Territorial Expansion in the Late Nineteenth Century
The major period of U.S. territorial expansion abroad came in a short burst of activity in the late 1890s, when newspapers and some politicians beat the drums for empire. *hc* Interactive Map: U.S. Territorial Expansion in the Late 19th Century

In 1898 a compromise settled the fishing-rights dispute, but by then attention had shifted to Latin America. In 1891 tensions had flared between the United States and Chile after a mob in Valparaiso killed two American sailors on shore leave. War fever subsided after Chile apologized and paid an indemnity of $75,000.

Another Latin American conflict arose from a boundary dispute between Venezuela and British Guiana in 1895. When the British rejected a U.S. arbitration offer and condescendingly insisted that

America's revered Monroe Doctrine had no standing in international law, a livid Grover Cleveland asked Congress to set up a commission to settle the dispute even without Britain's approval. As patriotic fervor pulsed through the nation, the British in 1897 accepted the commission's findings.

Pacific Expansion

Meanwhile, the U.S. navy focused on the Samoan Islands in the South Pacific, where it sought the port of Pago Pago as a refueling station. In March 1889 the United States narrowly avoided a naval clash with Germany over the islands when a timely hurricane wrecked both fleets. Ultimately, America established a three-way protectorate over the islands with Germany and Great Britain.

The Hawaiian Islands with their economic and strategic significance also beckoned U.S. imperialists. American missionaries and merchants had been active in the islands since the end of the eighteenth century. American-owned sugar plantations worked by Chinese and Japanese laborers dominated the Hawaiian economy. Under an 1887 treaty, the United States built a naval base at Pearl Harbor, near Honolulu. Then in 1891, angered by American economic domination, islanders welcomed Liliuokalani to the Hawaiian throne. Strong-willed and hostile toward Americans, she became queen amid a crisis set off by a U.S. decision in 1890 to tax Hawaiian sugar. Hawaiian sugar prices plunged 40 percent as a result. Facing ruin, the planters deposed the queen in January 1893, proclaimed the independent Republic of Hawaii, and requested U.S. annexation.

The grab for Hawaii troubled Cleveland, especially when an emissary whom he sent cast doubt on whether the Hawaiians desired annexation. But when McKinley succeeded Cleveland, annexation moved rapidly forward, and in 1898 Congress proclaimed Hawaii an American territory. Sixty-one years later, it joined the Union as the fiftieth state.

Crisis over Cuba

In 1898 American attention shifted to Cuba, where a rebellion against Spanish rule had erupted in 1895. American businessmen had $50 million invested in the island and annually imported $100 million in sugar and other products from Cuba. Revolutionary turmoil would jeopardize these interests. Neither the Cleveland nor the McKinley administration supported the rebellion.

But the rebels won widespread popular backing from Americans, support that increased with revelations that the Spanish commander in Cuba, Valeriano Weyler, was herding vast numbers of Cubans into concentration camps. Malnutrition and disease turned these camps into hellholes in which perhaps 200,000 Cubans died.

Fueling American anger were sensational stories published by two competing New York newspapers, William Randolph Hearst's *Journal* and Joseph Pulitzer's *World*. The *Journal's* color comic strip, "The Yellow Kid," provided a term for Hearst's debased editorial approach: yellow journalism. In the cut-throat battle for readers, both editors exploited the Cuban crisis, turning rumor into fact and detailing "Butcher" Weyler's atrocities. When a young Cuban woman was jailed for resisting a rape attempt by a Spanish officer, a Hearst reporter helped the woman escape and brought her triumphantly to New York.

In 1897 a new, more liberal Spanish government sought a peaceful solution to the Cuban crisis. But Hearst and Pulitzer continued to inflame public opinion. On February 8, 1898, Hearst's *Journal* published a private letter from a Spanish diplomat describing McKinley as "weak" and "a bidder for the admiration of the crowd." Irritation over this incident turned to outrage on February 15, 1898, when an explosion rocked the battleship *Maine* in Havana harbor, killing 226 American crewmen. Newspaper headlines screamed of a Spanish mine. In fact, a 1976 investigation confirmed what experts had thought even in 1898: that an internal explosion in the ammunition storage area had destroyed the battleship. In 1898, however, neither Washington nor the yellow press wanted to see the tragedy as accidental.

Despite further Spanish concessions, on April 11 McKinley sent a war message to Congress, and legislators passed a joint resolution recognizing Cuba's independence and authorizing force to expel the Spanish. An amendment introduced by Senator Henry M. Teller of Colorado declared that the United States had no desire for "sovereignty, jurisdiction, or control" in Cuba and pledged that America would leave the island alone once independence was assured.

The Spanish-American War, 1898

The war with Spain involved only a few days of actual combat. Action began on May 1, 1898, when a U.S. fleet under Admiral George Dewey steamed into Manila Bay in the Philippines and destroyed or captured all ten Spanish ships anchored there, at the cost of 1 American and 381 Spanish lives. In mid-August U.S. troops occupied the capital, Manila.

In Cuba the war's only significant land engagement took place on July 1 when American troops seized two strongly defended Spanish garrisons on El Caney Hill and San Juan Hill overlooking the Spanish military stronghold of Santiago de Cuba. Leading the volunteer "Rough Riders" at San Juan Hill was Theodore Roosevelt, getting his taste of war—and abundant publicity—at last. Two days later, the Spanish fleet at Santiago de Cuba made a gallant but doomed break for the open sea. Blockading American ships sank the seven ancient vessels, killing 474 Spaniards and ending four hundred years of Spanish empire in America.

John Hay thought that it had all been "a splendid little war," but many who served in Cuba found it far from splendid. They went into battle in the tropical midsummer wearing heavy wool uniforms, received abysmal medical care, and died in droves from yellow fever, food poisoning, and malaria. The United States lost more than 5,000 men in Cuba, only 379 of them in combat.

The thousands of black troops who fought in Cuba encountered Jim Crow racism at assembly points in Georgia and their embarkation port in Tampa, Florida. In Tampa, taunted by whites and refused service at restaurants and bars, some black troops exploded in riotous rage on June 6; white troops from Georgia restored order. The transport ships that carried troops to Cuba were segregated, with black troops often confined to the lowest quarters in stifling heat and denied permission to mingle on deck with other units. Despite such encounters with racism, African-American troops served with honor in Cuba, playing key roles in the battles of San Juan Hill and El Caney Hill.

Negotiations in Paris followed a July 17 armistice. On December 10, 1898, the United States and Spain signed the Treaty of Paris. Spain recognized Cuba's independence and, after much pressure and a payment of $20 million, ceded the Philippines, Puerto Rico, and Guam to the United States. Americans possessed an island empire stretching from the Caribbean to the Pacific.

From 1898 to 1902 the U.S. army governed Cuba under the command of General Leonard Wood. Wood's administration improved public health, education, and sanitation but violated the spirit of the 1898 Teller Amendment. The troops eventually withdrew, although the so-called Platt Amendment (1901), requested by the War Department, authorized the withdrawal only after Cuba agreed not to make any treaty with a foreign power limiting its independence and not to borrow beyond its means. The United States also reserved the right to intervene in Cuba and to establish a naval base there (Guantánamo Bay, near Santiago de Cuba, which it still maintains). The Cuban constitutional convention of 1901 accepted the Platt Amendment, which remained in force until 1934. U.S. investments in Cuba, some $50 million in 1898, soared to $500 million by 1920.

Critics of Empire

Some Americans had opposed imperialism for more than a decade, and the victories in Cuba and the Philippines did not bring universal praise. Although few in number, the critics were influential. Some of them, like Carl Schurz and E. L. Godkin, were former Mugwumps. Other anti-imperialists included William Jennings Bryan, settlement-house founder Jane Addams, novelist Mark Twain, and Harvard philosopher William James. Steel king Andrew Carnegie gave thousands of dollars to the cause. In 1898 these critics of empire had formed the Anti-Imperialist League.

For the United States to rule other peoples, the anti-imperialists believed, was to violate the principles of the Declaration of Independence and the Constitution. As one of them wrote, "Dewey took

Manila with the loss of one man—and all our institutions." The military fever that accompanied expansionism also dismayed the anti-imperialists. Some labor leaders feared that imperial expansion would lead to competition from cheap foreign labor and products.

In February 1899 the anti-imperialists failed by one vote to prevent Senate ratification of the expansionist peace treaty with Spain, and McKinley's overwhelming victory in 1900 over anti-imperialist Bryan eroded the cause. Nevertheless, at a time of jingoistic rhetoric and militaristic posturing, the opponents of expansion had upheld an older, finer vision of America.

Guerrilla War in the Philippines, 1898–1902

Events in the Philippines confirmed the anti-imperialists' worst fears. When the Spanish-American War began, few Americans knew what or where the Philippine Islands were. President McKinley confessed that "I could not have told where those darn islands were within 2,000 miles." American business, though, saw them as a steppingstone to the rich China market.

McKinley, reflecting the prevailing mood as always, reasoned that the Filipinos were unready for self-government and would be gobbled up if set adrift in a world of imperial rivalries. He further persuaded himself that American rule would enormously benefit a people he called "our little brown brothers." A devout Methodist, he explained that America's mission was "to educate the Filipinos, and to uplift and civilize and Christianize them, and by God's grace do the very best we could by them." (Most Filipinos were already Christian, a legacy of centuries of Spanish rule.) Having prayerfully reached his decision, McKinley instructed the American peace negotiators in Paris to insist on U.S. acquisition of the Philippines.

"Uplifting" the Philippines proved difficult. In 1896 young Emilio Aguinaldo had organized a Filipino independence movement to drive out the Spanish. In summer 1898, with arms supplied by Admiral Dewey, Aguinaldo's forces captured most of Luzon, the Philippines' main island. Aguinaldo proclaimed Filipino independence and drafted a democratic constitution. In 1899, feeling betrayed by the U.S. decision to take possession of his country, Aguinaldo ordered his troops to fight the occupying American army.

It took the United States four years to crush the Filipino independence movement, which waged a guerrilla war against the U.S. forces. More than 125,000 Americans troops ultimately served in the Philippine jungles, and 4,000 died. As many as 20,000 Filipino independence fighters perished, and untold tens of thousands of civilians died when the Americans implemented the same sort of reconcentration policy that they had denounced in Cuba.

In 1902 a special Senate committee heard testimony from veterans of the Philippines war about executing prisoners, torturing suspects, and burning villages. The humanitarian mood of 1898, when Americans had rushed to save Cuba from the cruel Spaniards, seemed remote indeed. In retrospect, the American troops' attitude toward the Filipinos, while deplorable, is not hard to understand. The cauldron of immigration, imperialism, and the "winning of the West" intermixed racist concerns over "backward" and "useless" peoples with rhetorical pleas for supervision and stewardship. In the process, as was evident in the treatment of American Indians, well-meaning paternalism often degenerated into deadly domination.

The years of expansionism and the subjugation of the Philippines had proclaimed America's debut on the world stage. Nevertheless, most Americans remained ambivalent about the acquisition of territory. While anti-imperialist Mark Twain acidly condemned "the Blessings of Civilization Trust," labor leader Samuel Gompers warned that "an inundation of Mongolians" might steal jobs from white labor. White Americans recoiled from making the "barbarian peoples" of these territories a part of the United States. Not fit to manage their own affairs, Filipinos were placed in a protective status that denied their independence but kept them under U.S. control.

In 1902 Congress passed the Philippine Organic Act, under which a presidentially appointed

Chronology

1877	Rutherford B. Hayes becomes president.
1878	Congress requires U.S. Treasury to purchase silver.
1880	James Garfield elected president.
1881	Assassination of Garfield; Chester A. Arthur becomes president.
1883	Pendleton Civil Service Act.
1884	Grover Cleveland elected president.
1886	*Wabash* v. *Illinois*.
1887	Interstate Commerce Act.
1888	Benjamin Harrison elected president.
1889	National Farmers' Alliance and Industrial Union, or Southern Alliance, formed.
1890	Sherman Silver Purchase Act. Sherman Anti-Trust Act. McKinley Tariff pushes tariffs to all-time high.
1893	Panic of 1893; depression of 1893–1897 begins. Drain of Treasury's gold reserve. Repeal of Sherman Silver Purchase Act. Overthrow of Queen Liliuokalani of Hawaii.
1894	"Coxey's Army" marches on Washington. Wilson-Gorman Tariff.
1895	Supreme Court declares federal income tax unconstitutional. Bankers' loans end drain on gold reserve. United States intervenes in Venezuela–British Guiana boundary dispute.
1896	Free-silver forces capture Democratic party and nominate William Jennings Bryan. William McKinley elected president.
1898	Spanish-American War.
1898–1902	Guerilla uprising in Philippines.
1900	Currency Act officially places United States on gold standard.
1901	Platt Amendment retains U.S. role in Cuba. Assassination of McKinley; Theodore Roosevelt becomes president.
1902	Congress passes the Philippine Organic Act to establish a Philippine government.

governor would rule the islands and a Filipino assembly would be elected. The law also promised eventual self-government. But the Philippines would not become independent until July 4, 1946, nearly half a century after Dewey's guns had boomed across Manila Bay.

CONCLUSION *hc* ACE Practice Test

The Spanish-American War and the subsequent acquisition of far-flung island territories underscored the global reach of U.S. capitalism. But a guerrilla war with Philippine nationalists aroused mounting criticism that highlighted Americans' ambivalence toward expansionism. Left unanswered at the time was the question of how a government designed for a small agrarian nation could meet the needs of an industrialized land of immigrant cities. Clearly, limited laissez-faire government was not the solution.

In the 1890s agrarian discontent underscored major problems and gave rise to the Populist party, which challenged laissez-faire assumptions and demanded that the government play an assertive role in solving social and economic problems. Although the party faded amid Republican ascendancy, its ideas became the basis for the progressive movement, to which we turn in the next chapter.

FURTHER READING

Cesar J. Ayala, *American Sugar Kingdom: The Plantation Economy of the Spanish Caribbean, 1898–1934* (1999). A careful analysis of the consolidation of the sugar industry and its effect on U.S. foreign policy and on the people living in Cuba, Puerto Rico, and the Dominican Republic.

Edward L. Ayers, *The Promise of the New South: Life After Reconstruction* (1992). A richly textured work that explores the complexity of the topic and pays close attention to nonelite men and women.

Richard F. Bensel, *The Political Economy of American Industrialization, 1877–1900* (2000). An astute analysis, based on a close reading of party platforms, of the connections between the tariff, monetary policy, veterans benefits, and industrial expansion.

Robert Cherny, *American Politics in the Gilded Age* (1997). A careful overview of the ethnic and institutional basis of the late nineteenth-century political process.

Rebecca Edwards, *Angels in the Machinery: Gender in American Party Politics from the Civil War to the Progressive Era* (1997). An innovative exploration of women's role in the political process and in the formation of political ideology.

William F. Holmes, ed., *American Populism* (1994). A well-selected set of nineteen scholarly essays interpreting the agrarian reform movement and surveying its varied aspects.

Ari Hoogenboom, *Rutherford B. Hayes: Warrior and President* (1995). A detailed, sympathetic, and balanced assessment of an able and decent public figure constrained by the political realities of his time; a good introduction to the political and economic issues of post-Reconstruction America.

Matthew F. Jacobson, *Barbarian Virtues: The United States Encounters Foreign Peoples at Home and Abroad, 1877–1900* (2000). An innovative study of the interconnections between politics, racism, and American economic development.

Michael Perman, *Struggle for Mastery: Disfranchisement in the South, 1888–1908* (2001). An important examination of the Democratic party's systematic disfranchisement of black voters.

David M. Pletcher, *The Diplomacy of Trade and Investment: American Economic Expansion in the Hemisphere, 1865–1900* (1998). An astute analysis of the direct and indirect governmental support for trade expansionism in the late nineteenth century.

PRICE 25¢

New York Illustrated

The Brooklyn Bridge, c. 1900

21

The Progressive Era, 1900–1917

CHAPTER OUTLINE

Progressives and Their Ideas

State and Local Progressivism

Blacks, Women, and Workers Organize

National Progressivism Phase I:
Roosevelt and Taft, 1901–1913

National Progressivism Phase II:
Woodrow Wilson, 1913–1917

hc This icon will direct you to additional study and research resources at http://college.hmco.com/history/us/boyer/enduring_concise/5e/students/index.html

The new world of corporations, factories, cities, and immigrants brought benefits as well as problems to the United States. For the millions of immigrants in unsafe factories and unhealthful slums, life was a cycle of poverty, exhausting labor, and early death. But at the same time, a new middle class of white-collar workers and urban professionals gained political influence, and women powerfully addressed the social issues of the day. From this volatile social mix pulsed a current of reform that came to be called the progressive movement. In contrast to the

This chapter focuses on five major questions:

▶ How did intellectuals, novelists, and journalists help lay the groundwork for the progressive movement?

▶ What problems of the new urban-industrial order particularly disturbed progressives, and how did they address these problems?

▶ How did progressive reform affect ordinary Americans, including workers, women, immigrants, city dwellers, and African-Americans?

▶ As progressivism emerged as a national movement, which politicians and issues proved most important?

▶ How did progressivism change Americans' view of the proper role of government?

agrarian-based populists, progressives concentrated on the social effects of the new urban-industrial order.

Historians once portrayed this movement rather simplistically as a triumph of "the people" over evil corporations. More recent historians have painted a more complicated picture, noting the role of special-interest groups (including big business) in promoting specific reforms, as well as the movement's darker side (especially with respect to immigration and race), its failures, and, above all, its rich diversity.

Emerging in the 1890s at the city and state levels, a dizzying array of organizations, many led by women, pursued varied reform objectives. At the national level, these reform impulses coalesced into a single movement that turned Washington into a hotbed of activism. By 1917, when reform gave way to war, progressivism had fundamentally altered U.S. government and society.

PROGRESSIVES AND THEIR IDEAS

As the twentieth century dawned, local groups across the nation, from workers to women's clubs to expert investigative commissions, grappled with the problems of the new urban-industrial order. Intellectuals challenged the ideological foundations of a business-dominated social order, and journalists publicized municipal corruption and industrialism's human toll. Reform gained momentum as activists tried to make government more democratic, eradicate dangerous conditions in cities and factories, and curb corporate power.

Although historians group all these efforts under a single label, "progressivism" was in fact never a single movement. It is perhaps best understood as a widespread yearning for reform and an exciting sense of new social possibilities.

The Many Faces of Progressivism

Who were the progressives, and what reforms did they pursue? To answer these questions, we need to look at the pattern of urban growth in the early twentieth century. Along with immigration, a rapidly growing middle class transformed U.S. cities. From the men and women of this class—most of whom were native-born, white, and Protestant—came many of the leaders and foot soldiers of the progressive movement.

From 1900 to 1920, the white-collar work force jumped from 5.1 million to 10.5 million, twice the growth rate for the work force as a whole. This new middle class included such diverse groups as skilled technicians and desk workers, bureaucrats, local business-owners and managers, lawyers, physicians, and teachers. Existing professional societies such as the American Bar Association grew rapidly, and scores of new ones arose, bringing a new emphasis on certification and licensing. Ambitious, well educated, and valuing self-discipline and social stability, members of the new middle class were eager to make their influence felt.

The city posed both opportunity and frustration for middle-class women. Some became public-school teachers, secretaries, clerks, and telephone operators, pushing the number of women in white-collar jobs from 949,000 in 1900 to 3.4 million in 1920. The ranks of college-educated women, although still small, more than tripled in this twenty-year period. But married urban middle-class women, hedged in by the demands of home and children, typically faced isolation and limited opportunity. The divorce rate crept up from one in twelve marriages in 1900 to one in nine by 1916. Many middle-class women mired in domestic routines joined white-collar and college-educated women in a resurgent women's movement, and cultural commentators wrote nervously of the "New Woman."

The progressive reform impulse drew on the energies of this new urban middle class. The initial reform impetus came not from political parties but from women's clubs, settlement houses, and private groups with names like the Playground Asso-

ciation of America and the American League for Civic Improvement. In this era of organizations, the reform movement, too, drew strength from organized interest groups.

Important as it was, the native-born middle class was not the only force behind progressivism. On issues affecting factory workers and slum dwellers, the urban-immigrant political machines—and workers themselves—often took the initiative. Some corporate leaders helped shape regulatory measures in ways to serve their interests.

What, then, was progressivism? At the most basic level, it was a series of political and cultural responses to industrialization and its by-products. In contrast to populism, progressivism's strength lay in the cities. Finally, most progressives were reformers, not radicals. They wished to remedy the social ills of industrial capitalism, not uproot the system itself.

The Gendering of Labor in Corporate America

Male bookkeepers and female "typewriters" at the headquarters of the Metropolitan Life Insurance Company in New York City.

But which parts of the urban-industrial order most needed attention, and what remedies were required? These key questions stirred deep disagreements, and the progressive impulse spawned an array of activities that sometimes overlapped and sometimes diverged. Many reformers wanted stricter regulation of business, from local transit companies to the almighty trusts. Others focused on protecting workers and the urban poor. Still others tried to reform the structure of government, especially at the municipal level. Finally, some reformers fought for immigration restriction or various social-control strategies to combat urban immorality and disorder. All this contributed to the mosaic of progressive reform.

Progressives had a high regard for science and expert knowledge and tended to believe that when channeled through organized effort, such expertise, which had produced the new industrial order, would solve the social problems spawned by industrialism. Progressives marshaled research data, expert opinion, and statistics to support their various causes.

Some historians have portrayed progressivism as an organizational stage that all modernizing societies pass through. This is a useful perspective, provided we remember that it was not an automatic process unfolding independently of human will. Individual reformers and human emotion— whether indignation over child labor, intense moralism, fear of the alien, hatred of unbridled corporate power, or raw political ambition—drove the movement forward.

Intellectuals Offer New Social Views

A group of turn-of-the-century thinkers helped to reorient American social thought and laid the ideological foundation for progressivism. William Graham Summer and other Social Darwinists had argued that "survival of the fittest" justified unrestrained economic competition. Sociologist Lester Ward, utopian novelist Edward Bellamy, and settlement-house and Social Gospel leaders had begun the intellectual attack against these ideas, and the assault intensified in the opening years of the new century.

Economist Thorstein Veblen, a Norwegian-American, was among the sharpest critics of the new business order. In *The Theory of the Leisure Class* (1899), he satirized the life-styles of the captains of industry, charging that their "conspicuous consumption" was a wasteful effort to assert superiority. In later writings he argued that engineers, molded by the stern discipline of the machine, were better fitted than the business class to lead society. Veblen epitomized the era's admiration of efficiency, science, and technical expertise.

Harvard philosopher William James, in an influential 1907 essay called "Pragmatism," argued that truth emerges not from abstract theorizing but from the experience of coping with life. By emphasizing the importance of practical action, James contributed to the progressives' skepticism toward conservative conventional wisdom and to their confidence that intelligent and purposeful effort could better social conditions.

More than anyone else, Herbert Croly embodied the progressive faith in the power of new ideas to transform society. In *The Promise of American Life* (1909), Croly called for an activist federal government that would serve *all* citizens, not just the capitalist class. To build public support for such a conception of government, Croly argued, intellectuals must play a key role. In 1914 he founded *The New Republic* magazine to promote progressive ideas.

Few argued those ideas more effectively than settlement-house leader Jane Addams. In her books *Democracy and Social Ethics* (1902) and *Twenty Years at Hull House* (1910), Addams rejected unrestrained competition as the best path to social progress. Instead, she argued, in a modern industrial society, each individual's well-being depends on the well-being of all. Addams urged privileged middle-class men and women to recognize their common interests with the laboring masses and to demand better conditions in factories and immigrant slums.

With public-school enrollment growing from about 7 million in 1870 to more than 23 million in 1920, philosopher John Dewey saw schools as potent engines of social change. Banishing bolted-down chairs and desks from his model school at the University of Chicago, Dewey encouraged pupils to interact. The ideal school, he said in *Democracy and Education* (1916), would be an "embryonic community" where children would learn to live as members of a social group.

For other thinkers, the key to social change lay in transforming the nation's courts. Instead of citing ancient precedent, according to Oliver Wendell Holmes, Jr., in his influential *The Common Law* (1881), jurists must recognize that law evolves as society changes. "The life of the law has not been logic; it has been experience," he argued. Appointed to the Supreme Court in 1902, Holmes wrote eloquent dissents from the conservative majority. Under the influence of the new social thinking, the courts slowly became more receptive to reform legislation.

Novelists, Journalists, and Artists Spotlight Social Problems

While intellectuals reoriented American social thought, novelists and journalists roused the reform spirit by chronicling corporate wrongdoing, municipal corruption, and slum conditions. Advances in printing and photo reproduction ensured a mass audience and sharpened the emotional impact of the message.

In his popular novel *The Octopus* (1901), the young San Francisco writer Frank Norris portrayed California wheat growers' epic struggle against the state's railroad barons. Theodore Dreiser's novel *The Financier* (1912) featured a hard-driving business tycoon utterly lacking a social conscience. Norris and Dreiser both modeled their stories on actual tycoons. Like Veblen's *Theory of the Leisure Class*, such works aroused sentiment against the industrial elite and in favor of tougher regulation of business.

Mass-circulation magazines such as *McClure's* and *Collier's* published articles exposing urban corruption and corporate wrongdoing. President Theodore Roosevelt criticized the authors as "muckrakers" obsessed with the seamier side of American life, but the name became a badge of honor, and the circulation of *McClure's* and *Collier's* soared. Journalist Lincoln Steffens began the exposé vogue in October 1902 with a *McClure's* article documenting municipal corruption in St. Louis.

The muckrakers emphasized facts rather than abstractions; some actually worked as factory laborers or lived in slum tenements. In a 1903 series, journalist Maria Van Vorst described her experiences working in a Massachusetts shoe factory where women's fingernails rotted away from repeated immersion in caustic dyes. Some magazine exposés later appeared in book form, including Lincoln Steffens's *The Shame of the Cities* (1904), Ida Tarbell's damning *History of the Standard Oil Company* (1904), and David Graham Phillips's *Treason of the Senate* (1906).

Artists and photographers played a role as well. A group of New York painters dubbed the Ashcan School portrayed the harshness of life in the city's crowded slums. The Wisconsin-born photographer Lewis Hine captured images of immigrants and factory laborers. His photos of child workers, with their stunted bodies and worn expressions, helped build support for national laws against child labor.

STATE AND LOCAL PROGRESSIVISM

Middle-class readers also observed firsthand, in their own communities, the problems besetting urban-industrial America. In fact, the progressive movement began with grass-roots campaigns at the local level from New York to San Francisco. Eventually, these state and local movements came together in a powerful national surge of reform.

Reforming the Political Process

Beginning in the 1890s, native-born elites and middle-class reformers battled corrupt city governments. New York City experienced a succession of reform spasms in which Protestant clergy rallied against Tammany Hall, the city's entrenched Democratic organization. In Detroit the reform mayor Hazen Pingree (served 1890–1897) brought honesty to city hall, lowered transit fares, adopted a fairer tax structure, and provided public baths and other services for the poor. Pingree once slapped a health quarantine on a brothel, refusing to let a prominent business leader leave the premises until he promised to back Pingree's reforms.

In San Francisco in 1907, the original prosecutor in a case against the city's corrupt boss, Abe Reuf, was gunned down in court. Attorney Hiram Johnson took over the case, and Reuf and his cronies were convicted. Sternly self-righteous and full of reform zeal—one observer called him "a volcano in perpetual eruption"—Johnson rode his newly won fame to the California governorship and the U.S. Senate. In Toledo, Ohio, the colorful eccentric Samuel M. "Golden Rule" Jones led the reform campaign. A self-made businessman converted to the Social Gospel, Jones introduced profit sharing in his factory; as mayor, he established playgrounds, free kindergartens, lodging houses for tramps, and an open-air church for all faiths.

As the urban reform movement matured, it probed the roots of urban misgovernment, including the uncontrolled private monopolies that ran city water, gas, electricity, and transit systems. Reformers passed laws regulating the rates that utilities could charge, taxing them more equitably, and curbing their political influence. Some advocated public ownership of utilities.

Reflecting the Progressive Era vogue of expertise and efficiency, a number of municipal reformers sought to substitute professional managers and administrators, chosen in citywide elections, for mayors and aldermen elected on a ward-by-ward basis. Supposedly above politics, these experts were to run the city like an efficient business. Natural disasters sometimes spurred this particular reform. Dayton, Ohio, went to a city-manager system after a ruinous flood in 1913.

Different groups supported reforms, depending on the issue. The native-born middle class provided the initial impetus for urban beautification and political reform. Business leaders often supported city-manager systems and citywide elections, which diminished the power of the ward bosses and increased that of the corporate elite. On practical matters such as municipal services, immigrants and even political bosses supported reform.

The movement for electoral reform soon expanded to the state level. By 1910 all states had instituted secret ballots, making it much harder than before to rig elections. Another widely adopted reform was the direct primary, in which party members, rather than leaders, selected candidates for public office. And some western states inaugurated the initiative, referendum, and recall. By an initiative, voters can instruct the legislature to consider a specific bill. In a referendum, they can actually enact a law or, in a *nonbinding* referendum, express their views on a measure. By a recall petition, voters can remove an official from office by gathering enough signatures. The culmination of this flurry of electoral reforms came in 1913 with the ratification of the Seventeenth Amendment to the Constitution, which shifted the election of U.S. senators from state legislatures to the voters at large.

These reforms aimed to restore government by the people and to reduce the power of moneyed interests, but party leaders and interest groups soon learned to manipulate the new electoral machinery. Ironically, the new procedures may have weakened party loyalty and reduced voter interest. Voter-participation rates dropped steeply in these years, while political activity by organized interest groups increased.

Regulating Business, Protecting Workers

The late-nineteenth-century corporate consolidation that produced giants like Carnegie Steel and Standard Oil continued after 1900. Following the United States Steel pattern, J. P. Morgan in 1902 combined six competing companies into the International Harvester Company, which dominated the farm-implement business. The General Motors Company, formed in 1908 by William C. Durant, bought up various independent automobile manufacturers, from the inexpensive Chevrolet to the luxury Cadillac.

Many workers benefited from this corporate growth. Industrial workers' average annual real wages (defined, that is, in terms of actual purchasing power) rose from $532 in the late nineteenth century to $687 by 1915. In railroading and other unionized industries, wages climbed still higher.

But even though the cost of living was far lower than today, such wages could barely support a family.

To survive, entire families went to work. Two-thirds of young immigrant women entered the labor force in the early 1900s, working in factories, laundries or bakeries, or as domestics. Even children worked. In 1910 the nonfarm labor force probably included at least 1.6 million children aged ten to fifteen. One investigator found a girl of five working at night in a South Carolina textile mill.

Most laborers faced long hours and great hazards. Despite the eight-hour movement of the 1880s, in 1900 the average worker still toiled 9 1/2 hours a day. Some southern textile mills required workdays of 12 or 13 hours. In one typical year (1907), 4,534 railroad workers and more than 3,000 miners were killed on the job. Few employers accepted responsibility for work-related accidents and illnesses. Vacations and retirement benefits were rare.

Efficiency experts used time-and-motion studies to increase production and make human workers as predictable as machines. In *Principles of Scientific Management* (1911), Frederick W. Taylor explained how to increase output by standardizing job routines and rewarding the fastest workers. Most workers deeply resented the drive for "efficiency."

For Americans troubled by the social implications of industrialization, the drive to regulate big business, inherited from the populists, became vitally important. Since corporations had benefited from government policies such as high protective tariffs, reformers reasoned, they should also be subject to government supervision.

Of the many states that passed laws regulating railroads, mines, and other businesses, none did so more avidly than Wisconsin under Governor Robert ("Fighting Bob") La Follette. As a Republican congressman, La Follette had feuded with the state's conservative party leadership, and in 1900 he won the governorship as an independent. Challenging the state's long-dominant business interests, La Follette and his administration adopted the direct-primary system, set up a railroad regulatory commission, increased corporate taxes, and limited campaign spending. Reflecting progressivism's faith in experts, La Follette met regularly with reform-minded professors at the University of Wisconsin and set up a legislative reference library so lawmakers would not have to rely on corporate lobbyists for factual information. La Follette's reforms gained national attention as the "Wisconsin Idea."

If electoral reform and corporate regulation represented the brain of progressivism, the impulse to improve conditions in factories and mills represented its heart. This movement, too, began at the local and state level. By 1907, for example, thirty states had outlawed child labor. A 1903 Oregon law limited women in industry to a ten-hour workday.

Campaigns to improve industrial safety and otherwise better conditions for the laboring masses won support from political bosses in cities with large immigrant populations. In 1911, a fire swept through the Triangle Shirtwaist Factory in New York City, leaving 141 dead, mostly young women. Many of the victims, unable to escape the inferno, jumped from windows to their deaths. State senator Robert F. Wagner, a leader of Tammany Hall, headed the committee that investigated the tragedy and documented numerous unsafe conditions in the factory, including exits that were locked shut. In response, New York legislators passed fifty-six worker-protection laws. By 1914, spurred by the Triangle disaster, twenty-five states had passed laws making employers liable for job-related injuries or deaths.

Florence Kelley was a leader in the drive to remedy industrial abuses. The daughter of a conservative Republican congressman, Kelley became a Hull House resident in 1891 and helped secure passage of an Illinois law prohibiting child labor and limiting working hours for women. In 1899 she became general secretary of the National Consumers' League, which mobilized consumer pressure for improved factory conditions. Campaigning for a federal child-labor law, Kelley pointedly asked, "Why are seals, bears, reindeer, fish, wild game in the national parks, buffalo, [and] migratory birds all found suitable for federal protection, but not children?"

Like many progressive reforms, the crusade for workplace safety relied on expert research. Alice Hamilton, for example, a pioneer in the new field of "industrial hygiene," taught bacteriology at

Northwestern University while also working at Hull House. In 1910 she conducted a major study of lead poisoning among industrial workers. Appointed an investigator by the U.S. Bureau of Labor in 1911, Hamilton became an expert on and campaigned against work-related medical hazards.

Workers themselves provided further pressure for reform. For example, when new power drills created a fine dust that granite workers inhaled, the *Granite Cutters' Journal* warned of "stone cutters' consumption" and called the new drills "widow makers." Sure enough, investigators soon linked the dust to a deadly respiratory disease, silicosis—another industrial hazard that worker-safety advocates sought to remedy.

Making Cities More Livable

In the early twentieth century, America became an urban nation. By 1920 the urban population passed the 50 percent mark, and sixty-eight U.S. cities boasted more than a hundred thousand inhabitants. New York City grew by 2.2 million from 1900 to 1920, and Chicago by 1 million.

As manufacturing and businesses grew, a surging tide of immigrants and native-born newcomers engulfed the cities. Overwhelmed by this rapid growth, many cities became dreary, sprawling human warehouses lacking basic civic amenities such as parks, municipal services, and public-health resources. Unsurprisingly, as the progressive movement took shape, urban problems loomed large.

Drawing on the efforts of Frederick Law Olmsted and others, reform-minded men and women campaigned for parks, boulevards, and street lights and proposed laws against billboards and unsightly overhead electrical wires. An influential voice for city planning and beautification was Daniel Burnham, who developed city plans for Washington, D.C., Cleveland, San Francisco, and other cities. Burnham's 1909 Plan of Chicago offered a seductive vision of a city both more efficient and more beautiful. The focal point was a majestic domed city hall and vast civic plaza. Although not all of Burnham's plan was adopted, Chicago spent more than $300 million on projects

Proposed Chicago Civic Center, 1910
In their plan for the growing immigrant city on Lake Michigan, Daniel Burnham and Edward H. Bennett envisioned a soaring new civic center "to be seen and felt by the people as the symbol of civic order and unity."

reflecting his ideas. Many Progressive Era urban planners shared Burnham's faith that beautiful cities and imposing public buildings would ensure a law-abiding and civic-minded urban populace.

Beyond urban beautification, reformers worked for such practical goals as decent housing and better garbage collection and street cleaning. Providing a model for other cities and states, the New York legislature passed laws imposing strict health and safety regulations on tenements in 1911. The discovery in the 1880s that germs cause diseases such as cholera and typhoid fever made municipal hygiene and sanitation high priorities. Progressive reformers called for improved water and sewer systems, regulation of milk suppliers and food handlers, school medical examinations and vaccination programs, and campaigns to spread public-health information to the urban masses.

These efforts bore fruit. From 1900 to 1920, infant mortality (defined as death in the first year of life) dropped from 165 per 1,000 population to around 75, and the tuberculosis death rate fell by nearly half. The municipal health crusades had a social-class dimension. Middle-class reformers set the "sanitary agenda," and the campaigns often targeted immigrants and the poor as the sources of contagion. When Mary Mallon, an Irish-immigrant cook in New York, was found to be a healthy carrier of the typhoid bacillus in 1907, she was confined for years by city health authorities and demonized in the press as "Typhoid Mary."

Urban reformers also shared the heightened environmental consciousness of these years. The battle against air pollution illustrates both the promise and the frustrations of municipal environmentalism. Coal-fueled steam boilers, the major energy source for factories, produced massive amounts of soot and smoke, which by the early 1900s physicians had linked to respiratory problems.

As with other progressive reforms, the resulting antismoke campaign combined expertise with activism. Civil engineers formed the Smoke Prevention Association in 1906, and researchers at the University of Pittsburgh documented the hazards and costs of air pollution. As women's clubs and other civic groups embraced the cause, many cities passed smoke-abatement laws. But coal still provided 70 percent of the nation's energy as late as 1920, and railroads and corporations fought back in the courts and often won. Not until years later, with the shift from coal to other energy sources, did the battle against municipal air pollution make significant headway.

Progressivism and Social Control

Progressives' belief that they could improve society through research, legislation, and aroused public opinion sprang from their confidence that they knew what was best for other people. While municipal corruption, unsafe factories, and corporate abuses captured their attention, so, too, did issues of personal behavior, particularly the behavior of immigrants. The problems they addressed deserved attention, but their self-righteous rhetoric and the remedies they proposed also betrayed an impulse to impose their own moral standards by force of law.

Moral Control in the Cities

Early twentieth-century urban life was more than crowded slums and exhausting labor. For all their problems, cities also offered fun and diversion. Department stores, vaudeville, music halls, and amusement parks continued to flourish. While some vaudeville owners strove for respectability, raucous and bawdy routines full of sexual innuendo, including those of the comedienne Mae West, were popular with working-class audiences. New York City's amusement park, Coney Island, drew more patrons than ever. A subway ride from the city, it attracted as many as a million visitors a day by 1914.

For families, amusement parks provided escape from tenements. For female garment workers or department-store clerks, they provided an opportunity to spend time with friends, meet young men, and show off new outfits. With electrification, simply riding the streetcars or taking an evening stroll on well-lit downtown streets became leisure activities in themselves. News of Orville and Wilbur Wright's successful airplane flight in 1903, and the introduction of Henry Ford's Model T in 1908, which transformed the automobile from a toy of the rich to a vehicle for the masses, heightened the sense of exciting changes ahead, with cities at the heart of the action.

Jaunty popular songs were introduced in the music halls and produced in a district of lower Manhattan called Tin Pan Alley. The blues, rooted in the chants of southern black sharecroppers, reached a broader public with such songs as W. C. Handy's classic "St. Louis Blues" (1914). Ragtime, another import from the black South, enjoyed great popularity.

These years also brought a new medium of mass entertainment—the movies. Five-cent halls called "nickelodeons" appeared in immigrant neighborhoods and at first featured brief comic sequences like *The Sneeze* or *The Kiss*. With *The Great Train Robbery* (1903), the movies began to tell stories, and *A Fool There Was* (1914), with its famous line, "Kiss me, my fool!", made Theda Bara (really Theodosia Goodman of Cincinnati) the first female movie star. The British music-hall performer Charlie Chaplin emigrated to America in 1913 and appeared in some sixty short comedies between 1914 and 1917. Like amusement parks, the movies allowed immigrant youth to briefly escape parental supervision. As a New York garment worker recalled, "The one place I was allowed to go by myself was the movies. My parents wouldn't let me go anywhere else."

Ironically, the diversions that made city life more bearable for the poor struck some middle-class reformers as moral traps. Fearful of immorality and social disorder, reformers campaigned to regulate amusement parks, dance halls, and the movies. The darkened nickelodeons struck many middle-class men and women as potential dens of vice. Warning of "nickel madness," reformers demanded film censorship. Several states and cities set up censorhip boards, and the Supreme Court upheld such measures in 1915.

Building on the moral-purity crusade of the Woman's Christian Temperance Union (WCTU) and other groups in the 1890s, reformers also targeted prostitution, a major urban problem. The paltry wages paid women for factory work or domestic service diverted many to this more-lucrative occupation. One prostitute wrote that she was unwilling "to get up at 6:30 . . . and work in a close stuffy room . . . until dark for $6 or $7 a week" when an afternoon with a man could bring in more.

As prostitution came to symbolize the larger moral dangers of cities, a "white slave" hysteria gripped the nation amid warnings of farm girls' being kidnapped and forced into urban brothels. In the usual progressive fashion, investigators gathered statistics on what they called "the social evil." The American Social Hygiene Association (1914), financed by John D. Rockefeller, Jr., sponsored medical research on sexually transmitted diseases, paid for "vice investigations" in various cities, and drafted model municipal statutes against prostitution. The federal Mann Act (1910) made it illegal to transport a woman across a state line "for immoral purposes." Amid much fanfare, reformers shut

down the red-light districts of New Orleans, Chicago, and other cities.

Racism, anti-immigrant prejudice, fear of the city, and anxieties about changing sexual mores all fueled the antiprostitution crusade. Tipped off by neighbors and angry spouses, authorities employed the new legislation to pry into private sexual behavior. Scam artists entrapped men into Mann Act violations and blackmailed them.

Battling Alcohol and Drugs

Temperance had long been part of the American reform agenda, but reformers' tactics and objectives changed in the Progressive Era. Most earlier campaigns had urged individuals to give up drink. The powerful Anti-Saloon League (ASL), founded in 1895, shifted the emphasis to legislating a ban on the sale of alcoholic beverages, and its presses produced propaganda touting prohibition. As the ASL added its efforts to those of the WCTU and various church bodies, many localities banned the sale of alcoholic beverages and the campaign for national prohibition gained strength.

This was a heavy-drinking era, and alcohol abuse did indeed contribute to domestic abuse, health problems, and work injuries. But like the antiprostitution crusade, the prohibition campaign pitted native-born citizens against new immigrants. The ASL, while it raised legitimate issues, also embodied Protestant America's impulse to control the immigrant city.

These years also saw the first sustained campaign against drug abuse—and for good reason. Many easily obtained medicines contained opium and its derivatives morphine and heroin. Cocaine was widely used as well. Coca-Cola contained cocaine until about 1900.

As reformers focused on the problem, the federal government backed a 1912 treaty aimed at halting the international opium trade. The Narcotics Act of 1914 strictly regulated opiates and cocaine. In their battle against drugs, as in their environmental concerns, the progressives anticipated an issue that would remain important into the twenty-first century. But here, too, racist undertones colored antidrug crusaders' warnings about Chinese "opium dens" and "drug-crazed Negroes" who imperiled white womanhood.

Immigration Restriction and Eugenics

While many of the new city dwellers came from farms and small towns, the main source of urban growth continued to be immigration. More than 17 million newcomers arrived from 1900 to 1917 and most settled in cities. As in the 1890s, the influx came mainly from southern and eastern Europe, but some 200,000 Japanese, 40,000 Chinese, and thousands of Mexicans also arrived between 1900 and 1920. Some immigrants prospered, but many sank into poverty.

The obvious answer to the threats posed by the immigrant city, some reformers concluded, lay in excluding immigrants. The many progressives who supported immigration restriction documented their case with alleged scientific expertise. In 1911 a congressional commission produced a statistical study "proving" the new immigrants' innate degeneracy. In 1914 the progressive sociologist Edward A. Ross described recent immigrants as "hirsute, low-browed, big-faced persons of obviously low mentality." In 1896, 1913, and 1915, Congress passed literacy-test bills aimed at slowing immigration, but they fell victim to veto by a succession of presidents. In 1917, however, such a bill became law over President Wilson's veto. This, too, was part of progressivism's ambiguous legacy.

Immigration to the United States, 1870–1930

With the end of the depression of the 1890s, immigrants from southern and eastern Europe poured into America's cities, spurring an immigration-restriction movement, urban moral-control campaigns, and efforts to improve the physical and social conditions of immigrant life.

Sources: *Statistical History of the United States from Colonial Times to the Present* (Stamford, Conn.: Fairfield Publishers, 1965); and report presented by Senator William P. Dillingham, Senate document 742, 61st Congress, 3rd session, December 5, 1910: Abstracts of Reports to the Immigration Commission.

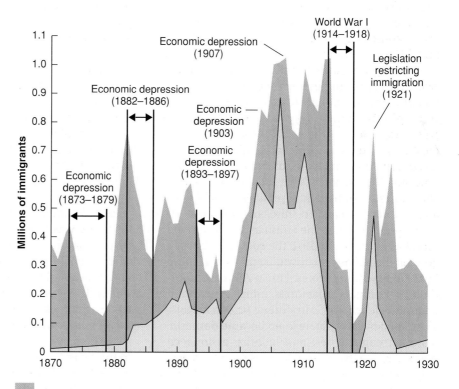

Total number of immigrants

Southern and eastern European immigrants

Anti-immigrant fears helped fuel the eugenics movement. Eugenics is the control of reproduction to alter a plant or animal species, which some U.S. eugenicists believed could be used to improve human society. A leading eugenicist, the zoologist Charles B. Davenport, urged immigration restriction to keep America from pollution by "inferior" genetic stock.

In *The Passing of the Great Race* (1916), Madison Grant, a prominent progressive and eugenics advocate, used bogus data to denounce immigrants from southern and eastern Europe, especially Jews. He also viewed African-Americans as inferior. Anticipating the program of Adolf Hitler in the 1930s, Grant called for racial segregation, immigration restriction, and the forced sterilization of the "unfit," including "worthless race types." The vogue of eugenics gave "scientific" respectability to anti-immigrant sentiment, as well as the racism that pervaded white America in these years. Inspired by eugenics, many states legalized the sterilization of criminals, sex offenders, and persons adjudged mentally deficient. In the 1927 case *Buck* v. *Bell,* the Supreme Court upheld such laws.

Racism and Progressivism

Progressivism arose at a time of significant changes in African-American life—and also one of intense racism in white America. These racial realities are crucial to a full understanding of the movement.

In 1900 more than two-thirds of the nation's 10 million blacks lived in the South as sharecroppers and tenant farmers. By 1910 the cotton boll weevil and ruinous floods had driven 20 percent of these southern blacks into cities. Urban African-American men took jobs in factories, mines, docks, and railroads or became carpenters or bricklayers, while African-American women became domestic servants, seamstresses, and laundry or tobacco workers. By 1910, 54 percent of America's black women worked.

Across the South, legally enforced racism peaked in the early twentieth century. Local "Jim Crow" laws segregated streetcars, schools, parks, and even cemeteries. The facilities for blacks, including the schools, were invariably inferior. Many southern cities imposed residential segregation by law until the Supreme Court restricted it in 1917. Most labor unions excluded black workers. Disfranchised and trapped in a cycle of poverty, poor education, and discrimination, southern blacks faced bleak prospects.

Fleeing poverty and racism and drawn by job opportunities, two hundred thousand African-Americans migrated north between 1890 and 1910. World War I drew still more, and by 1920, 1.4 million African-Americans lived in the North. Northern blacks encountered conditions similar to those in the South. Racism had deepened after 1890 as depression and immigration heightened social tensions. Segregation, although not legally imposed, existed everywhere, supported by social pressure and occasional violence. Blacks lived in run-down "colored districts," attended dilapidated schools, and took the low-paying jobs. Although African-Americans voted, their allegiance to the Republican party gave them little influence. Even the newest mass medium, the movies, reinforced racism. D. W. Griffith's 1915 film classic *The Birth of a Nation* glorified the Ku Klux Klan and vilified and ridiculed African-Americans.

Smoldering racism sometimes exploded in violence. Antiblack rioters in Atlanta in 1906 murdered twenty-five blacks and burned many black homes. Lynchings continued, an average of about seventy-five yearly from 1900 to 1920, often as reprisal for assertive behavior or economic aspirations that angered whites. Some lynchings involved incredible sadism: with large crowds on hand, the victim's body was mutilated and graphic postcards were sold later. Authorities rarely intervened. At a 1916 lynching in Texas, the mayor warned the mob not to damage the hanging tree, since it was on city property.

In the face of adversity, African-Americans developed strong social institutions and a vigorous culture. Black religious life, centered in the African Methodist Episcopal church, provided a bulwark of support for many. Black colleges and universities, among them Fisk in Nashville and Howard in Washington, D.C., survived against heavy odds.

The urban African-American community included black-owned insurance companies and banks and boasted a small elite of entrepreneurs, teachers, ministers, and sports figures, including Texan Jack Johnson, who won the heavyweight boxing championship in 1908. Although major-league baseball excluded blacks, a thriving Negro League attracted many black fans.

In this racist age, progressives compiled a mixed record on racial issues. Muckraker Ray Stannard Baker documented racism in his 1908 book, *Following the Color Line*. Settlement-house worker Mary White Ovington helped found the National Association for the Advancement of Colored People in 1909 and wrote *Half a Man* (1911) about the emotional scars of racism.

But most progressives kept silent as blacks' rights were trampled, viewing blacks as inferior and prone to immorality and social disorder. White progressives generally supported segregation and the strict moral oversight of African-American communities, occasionally advocating, at best, paternalistic efforts to "uplift" this supposedly backward and childlike people. Viciously racist southern politicians like Governor James K. Vardaman of Mississippi and Senator Ben Tillman of South Carolina also supported progressive reforms. Southern woman-suffrage leaders argued that granting women the vote would strengthen white supremacy.

BLACKS, WOMEN, AND WORKERS ORGANIZE

The organizational impulse so important to progressivism generally also proved a useful strategy for groups that found themselves discriminated against or exploited, such as African-Americans, middle-class women, and wage workers. All three groups organized to address their grievances in these years.

African-American Leaders Organize Against Racism

With racism on the rise, Booker T. Washington's accommodationist message (see Chapter 20) seemed increasingly unrealistic, particularly to educated northern blacks. In 1902 one editor of a black newspaper called Washington's go-slow policies "a fatal blow . . . to the Negro's political rights and liberty." Another opponent was black journalist Ida Wells-Barnett, who mounted a national antilynching campaign in contrast to Washington's public silence on the subject.

Washington's most potent challenger was W. E. B. Du Bois (1868–1963). After earning a Ph.D. in history from Harvard in 1895, Du Bois taught at Atlanta University. Openly criticizing Washington in *The Souls of Black Folk* (1903), he rejected Washington's emphasis on patience and manual skills. Instead, Du Bois demanded full racial equality and called on blacks to resist all forms of racism.

Du Bois's militancy signaled a new era of African-American activism. Beginning in 1905 in Niagara Falls, under his leadership, blacks who favored vigorous resistance to racism held annual conferences for the next few years. In 1909 a group of white reformers who also rejected Washington's cautiousness joined Du Bois and other blacks from the Niagara Movement to form the National Association for the Advancement of Colored People (NAACP). This new organization called for vigorous activism, including legal challenges, to achieve political equality for blacks and full integration into American life. Attracting the urban black middle class, by 1914 the NAACP had six thousand members in fifty branches.

Revival of the Woman-Suffrage Movement

By 1910, following six failed state referenda on woman suffrage in 1896, women could vote in only four thinly populated western states: Wyoming, Utah, Colorado, and Idaho. But the progressive reform movement, and women's prominence in it, gave the cause fresh vitality. That recently arrived immigrant men could vote and they could not especially galled middle-class women. A vigorous suffrage movement in Great Britain reverberated in America as well. Like progressivism itself, the revived U.S. campaign started at the grass roots.

The suffrage campaign in California, as recounted by historian Gayle Gullett, underscored the movement's new momentum and illustrates both its strengths and its limitations. By the early 1900s California's women's clubs had evolved into a potent statewide organization active in municipal reform and public-school issues. This activism convinced many members that full citizenship meant the right to vote. A state woman-suffrage referendum lost in 1896. The leaders bounced back to form alliances with labor leaders and male progressives, built on a shared commitment to "good government." But while joining forces with male reformers, these woman-suffrage strategists insisted on the unique role of "organized womanhood" in building a better society. Success came in 1911 when California voters approved woman suffrage.

"Organized womanhood" had its limits. The California campaign was led by elite and middle-class women, mainly based in Los Angeles and San Francisco. Working-class and farm women played little part; African-American, Mexican-American, and Asian-American women were almost totally excluded.

New leaders built the momentum in California and other states into a revitalized national movement. When Susan B. Anthony retired from the presidency of the National American Woman Suffrage Association (NAWSA) in 1900, Carrie Chapman Catt of Iowa succeeded her. Under Catt's shrewd direction, NAWSA adopted the so-called Winning Plan: grass-roots organization with tight central coordination.

Suffragists shrewdly deployed techniques drawn from the new urban consumer culture. They not only lobbied legislators, but they also organized parades in open cars, held photo opportunities, and devised catchy slogans that they used in newspaper ads and posters; they distributed fans, playing cards, and other items emblazoned with the suffrage message. Gradually, state after state fell into the suffrage column. A key victory came in 1917 when New York voters approved a woman-suffrage referendum.

Parading for Woman Suffrage

Suffrage leaders built support for the cause by using modern advertising and publicity techniques, including automobiles festooned with flags, banners, and—in this case—smiling little girls.

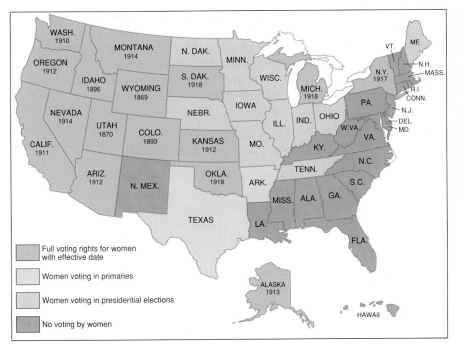

MAP 21.1

Woman Suffrage Before the Nineteenth Amendment

Beginning with Wyoming in 1869, woman suffrage made steady gains in western states before 1920. Farther east, key victories came in New York (1917) and Michigan (1918). But much of the East remained an anti-woman suffrage bastion throughout the period.

hc Interactive Map: Woman Suffrage Before 1920

Full voting rights for women with effective date

Women voting in primaries

Women voting in presidential elections

No voting by women

As in California (and like progressive organizations generally), NAWSA's membership remained largely white, native born, and middle class. Some upper-class women opposed the reform. The leader of the "Antis," wealthy Josephine Dodge of New York, argued that women already had behind-the-scenes influence, and that to invade the male realm of electoral politics would tarnish their moral and spiritual role.

Not all suffragists accepted Catt's strategy. Alice Paul, who had observed the British suffragists' militant tactics while studying in England, grew impatient with NAWSA's state-by-state approach. In 1913 Paul founded the Congressional Union for Woman Suffrage, renamed the National Woman's party in 1917, to pressure Congress for a woman-suffrage amendment. Paul and her followers picketed the White House round the clock in the war year of 1917. Several protesters were jailed and, when they went on a hunger strike, force-fed. At both the state and federal levels, the momentum of the organized woman-suffrage movement had become well-nigh irresistible.

Enlarging "Woman's Sphere"

The suffrage movement did not exhaust American women's talents or organizational energies. Women's club members, settlement-house leaders, and individual female activists joined in various campaigns: to bring playgrounds and day nurseries to the slums, to abolish child labor, to improve conditions for women workers, and to ban unsafe foods and quack remedies.

Cultural assumptions about "woman's sphere" crumbled as women became active on many fronts. Katherine Bement Davis served as the innovative superintendent of a woman's reformatory before becoming New York City's commissioner of corrections. Anarchist Emma Goldman crisscrossed the country delivering riveting lectures on politics, feminism, and modern drama while coediting a radical monthly, *Mother Earth*. A vanguard of pioneering women in higher education included Marion Talbot, first dean of women at the University of Chicago.

In *Women and Economics (1898)* and other works, feminist intellectual Charlotte Perkins

Gilman explored the historical and cultural roots of female subordination and linked women's inferior status to their economic dependence on men. Confining women to the domestic sphere, Gilman argued, was an evolutionary throwback that had become outdated and inefficient. She advocated economic independence for women through equality in the workplace; the collectivization of domestic chores; and state-run day-care centers.

No Progressive Era reform raised the issue of women's rights more directly than the campaign challenging federal and state laws banning the distribution of contraceptives and birth-control information. Although countless women, particularly the poor, suffered health problems from frequent pregnancies, artificial contraception was widely denounced as immoral. In 1914 Margaret Sanger of New York, a practical nurse and socialist whose mother had died after bearing eleven children, began her crusade for birth control, a term she coined. When the authorities proscribed her journal *The Woman Rebel* on obscenity charges, Sanger fled to England. She returned in 1916 to open the nation's first birth-control clinic in Brooklyn. In 1918 she founded a new journal, the *Birth Control Review*, and three years later she founded the American Birth Control League, the ancestor of today's Planned Parenthood Federation.

Meanwhile, another New Yorker, Mary Ware Dennett, a feminist and activist, had also emerged as an advocate of birth control and sex education. Her 1919 pamphlet for youth, *The Sex Side of Life*, discussing human reproduction in clear, straightforward terms, was long banned as obscene. Dennett founded the National Birth Control League (later the Voluntary Parenthood League) in 1915. While Sanger championed direct action, Dennett urged lobbying efforts to amend obscenity laws. More importantly, while Sanger insisted that only physicians should supply contraceptives, Dennett argued that they should be freely available. Sanger's inability to tolerate any other leaders in the movement made for bad relations between the two women.

In retrospect, the emergence of the birth-control movement stands as one of progressivism's most important and little-recognized legacies. At the time, however, it stirred bitter resistance among conservatives and many religious leaders. Indeed, not until 1965 did the Supreme Court fully legalize the dissemination of contraceptive materials and information.

Workers Organize; Socialism Advances

In this age of organization, labor unions continued to expand. The American Federation of Labor (AFL) grew from less than half a million members in 1897 to 4 million by 1920—but this was only 20 percent of the nonfarm labor force. With immigrants hungry for jobs, union activities could be risky; bosses could easily fire an "agitator" and hire a newcomer. Judicial hostility also plagued the labor movement. In the 1908 *Danbury Hatters* case, a unanimous Supreme Court ruled that boycotts in support of strikes violated the Sherman Anti-Trust Act. The AFL's strength remained in the skilled trades, not in the factories and mills where most immigrants and women worked.

A few unions did try to reach these laborers. In 1900 immigrants in New York City founded the International Ladies' Garment Workers' Union (ILGWU), which conducted successful strikes in 1909 and 1911. The women on the picket lines found these strikes both exhilarating and frightening. Some were beaten by police; others fired. But workers gained better wages and improved working conditions.

The Industrial Workers of the World (IWW), or Wobblies, founded in Chicago in 1905, also targeted the most exploited workers. Led by the colorful and compelling William D. "Big Bill" Haywood, the IWW was never large and was torn by dissent. It peaked at around 30,000 members, mainly western miners, lumbermen, fruit pickers, and itinerant laborers. But it captured the imagination of young rebels in New York City's Greenwich Village, where Haywood often visited.

The IWW led some mass strikes of miners and timber workers, but its greatest success came in 1912 when it won a rancorous textile strike in

Lawrence, Massachusetts. The victory owed much to Elizabeth Gurley Flynn, a fervent Irish-American orator, and Margaret Sanger, who publicized the cause by sending strikers' children to New York sympathizers for temporary care.

The Wobblies had a reputation, much exaggerated, for violence and sabotage, and they faced unremitting government harassment, especially during World War I. By 1920 the IWW's strength was broken.

Others appalled by capitalism's human toll, including some in the middle class, turned to socialism. Socialists advocated an end to capitalism and demanded public ownership of factories, utilities, railroads, and communications systems. But American workers generally rejected the revolutionary ideology of German social theorist Karl Marx in favor of democratic socialism achieved at the ballot box. In 1900 democratic socialists formed the Socialist Party of America (SPA). Eugene V. Debs, the Indiana labor leader, became the SPA's most popular spokesman and its candidate for president five times between 1900 and 1920.

In Greenwich Village, socialist supporters founded the magazine *The Masses* in 1911, and the Intercollegiate Socialist Society carried the message to college campuses. The party published over three hundred daily and weekly newspapers, many in foreign languages for immigrant members. The pinnacle of socialist strength came in 1912 when the SPA counted 118,000 members, Debs received over 900,000 (about 6 percent) of the votes for president, and the Socialists elected a congressman along with hundreds of municipal officials.

NATIONAL PROGRESSIVISM PHASE I: ROOSEVELT AND TAFT, 1901–1913

By 1905 localized reform movements had coalesced into a national effort. Symbolically, in 1906 Robert La Follette became a U.S. senator. Five years earlier progressivism had found its first national leader, Theodore Roosevelt.

Bombastic, self-righteous, and jingoistic—but also brilliant, politically masterful, and endlessly interesting—Roosevelt, "TR," became president in 1901. He made the White House a cauldron of political activism. Skillfully orchestrating public opinion, the popular young president pursued his goals: labor mediation, consumer protection, conservation, business virtue, and activism abroad. TR's hand-picked successor, William Howard Taft, lacked his master's political genius, however, and his administration floundered amid sniping among former allies.

In the exciting election of 1912, voters faced a choice among four major presidential candidates who offered differing visions of progressive reform: the conservative Taft; the socialist Eugene V. Debs; Theodore Roosevelt; and political newcomer Woodrow Wilson.

Roosevelt's Path to the White House

On September 6, 1901, in Buffalo, an anarchist shot then-president William McKinley. At first McKinley's survival seemed certain, but when his condition worsened, Vice President Theodore Roosevelt was hastily summoned back from a hiking trip in the Adirondack Mountains. On September 14 McKinley died, and the forty-two-year-old Roosevelt became president.

Reflecting the view of many politicians, Republican kingmaker Mark Hanna exclaimed, "My God, that damned cowboy is in the White House!" Roosevelt displayed many traits associated with the West. The son of an aristocratic New York family and sickly as a child, he used a body-building program and active summers in Wyoming to become a model of physical fitness. Later, two years on a Dakota ranch helped him to struggle past grief over his young wife's death in 1884 and nurtured the physical and mental toughness that he would later extol as "the strenuous life."

Plunging into politics when most of his social class considered it unbefitting gentlemen, Roosevelt held various posts in New York State before leading the Rough Riders in Cuba. He was elected

New York's governor in 1898. Two years later Republican bosses, eager to be rid of him, arranged for his nomination as vice president.

Unexpectedly thrust into the White House, TR energized the presidency. "While President I have been President emphatically," he boasted; "I believe in a strong executive." Roosevelt enjoyed public life and loved the limelight. As a relative wryly observed, he wanted to be the bride at every wedding and the corpse at every funeral. Americans were fascinated by their rambunctious young president, with his toothy grin, machine-gun speech, and passion for the outdoors.

Labor Disputes, Trustbusting, Railroad Regulation

The new president's political skills were quickly tested. In May 1902 the United Mine Workers Union (UMW) called a strike to gain higher wages, shorter hours, and recognition as a union. The mine owners refused to talk to UMW leaders. After five months, with coal reserves dwindling, TR summoned the deadlocked parties to the White House. Threatening to take over the mines, he won reluctant acceptance of an arbitration commission to settle the dispute. In 1903 the commission granted miners a 10-percent wage hike and reduced their workday from ten to nine hours.

TR approached such labor disputes very differently from his predecessors, who had called out federal troops to break strikes. Though not consistently prolabor, he defended labor's right to organize. When a well-known mine owner sanctimoniously claimed that miners' welfare could safely be left to "the Christian men to whom God in his infinite wisdom has given control of the property interests of the country," Roosevelt derided such "arrogant stupidity."

With his elite background, TR neither feared nor much liked business tycoons. Conservative at heart, he had no desire to abolish big corporations, but he embraced the progressive philosophy that corporate behavior must be carefully regulated. A strict moralist, he believed that corporations, like individuals, must meet a high standard of virtue. As a political realist, Roosevelt recognized that many politicians did not share his views. His progressive impulses and his grasp of power realities in capitalist America remained in continuing tension.

J. P. Morgan's formation in 1901 of the United States Steel Company, the nation's first billion-dollar corporation, deepened public uneasiness over business consolidation. Dashing to the head of the parade, TR used his first State of the Union message to advocate "trustbusting," the breakup of business monopolies. Roosevelt's attorney general soon filed suit against the Northern Securities Company, a mammoth holding company formed to control railroading in the Northwest, for violating the Sherman Anti-Trust Act. TR called for a "square deal" for all Americans and denounced special treatment for capitalists. "We don't wish to destroy corporations," he insisted, "but we do wish to make them serve the public good." In 1904, by a 5 to 4 vote, the Supreme Court ordered the Northern Securities Company dissolved.

The Roosevelt administration filed forty-three other antitrust lawsuits. In two key cases in 1911, the Court ordered the breakup of the Standard Oil Company and the reorganization of the American Tobacco Company to make it less monopolistic.

As the 1904 presidential election approached, Roosevelt made peace with the Republicans' big-business wing. When the convention that unanimously nominated Roosevelt adopted a conservative, probusiness platform, $2 million in corporate campaign contributions poured in. The conservative-dominated Democrats meanwhile nominated New York judge Alton B. Parker and wrote a platform firmly embracing the gold standard.

Winning easily, Roosevelt turned to one of his major goals: railroad regulation. He saw regulation, rather than antitrust lawsuits, as the most promising long-term strategy. His work for passage of the Hepburn Act (1906) reflected this shift in outlook. This measure empowered the Interstate Commerce Commission to set maximum railroad rates and to examine railroads' financial records. It also curtailed the railroads' practice of distributing free passes to ministers and other shapers of public opinion. Although the Hepburn Act did not fully satisfy reformers, it did increase the government's regulatory powers, and displayed TR's knack for political bargaining. In one key compromise, he agreed to delay tariff reform in return for railroad regulations.

Consumer Protection and Racial Issues

No progressive reform proved more popular than the fight against unsafe and falsely labeled food, drugs, and medicine. Upton Sinclair's stomach-turning *The Jungle* (1906) described the foul conditions under which sausages and cold cuts were produced. In a vivid passage, Sinclair wrote, "[A] man could run his hand over these piles of meat and sweep off handfuls of dried dung of rats. These rats were nuisances, and the packers would put poisoned bread out for them, they would die, and then rats, bread, and meat would go into the hoppers together." Women's organizations and consumer groups rallied public opinion on this issue, and an Agriculture Department chemist, Harvey W. Wiley, helped shape the proposed legislation. Other muckrakers exposed useless or dangerous patent medicines, many laced with cocaine, opium, or alcohol. One tonic "for treatment of the alcohol habit" contained 26.5 percent alcohol. Peddlers of these nostrums freely claimed that they could cure cancer, grow hair, and restore sexual vigor.

Sensing the public mood, Roosevelt supported the Pure Food and Drug Act and the Meat Inspection Act, both passed in 1906. The former outlawed the sale of adulterated food and drugs and required accurate ingredient labels; the latter imposed strict sanitary rules on meatpackers, set up a quality-rating system, and created a program of federal meat inspection.

h c Primary Source: Attack on the Meat Packers

On racial matters, Roosevelt's record was marginally better than that of other politicians in this racist age. He appointed an African-American as the head of the Charleston customhouse and closed a Mississippi post office rather than yield to demands that he dismiss the black postmistress. In a gesture of symbolic import, he dined with Booker T. Washington at the White House. The worst blot on his record came in 1906 when he approved the dishonorable discharge of an entire regiment of black soldiers in Brownsville, Texas, because some members of the unit, goaded by racist taunts, had killed a local civilian. (In 1972, when most of the men were long dead, Congress removed the dishonorable discharges from their records.)

Environmentalism Progressive-Style

In his first State of the Union message, Roosevelt singled out conservation as "the most vital internal question." By 1900 decades of urban-industrial growth and western expansion had taken a heavy toll on the land. In the West, land use disputes raged as mining and timber interests, farmers, ranchers, sheep growers, and preservationists advanced competing claims.

Western business interests and boosters preached exploitation of the region's resources and farmers pushed for irrigation projects, but organizations such as the Sierra Club battled to preserve large wild areas for their pristine beauty. After Congress in 1891 authorized the president to designate public lands as forest reserves, Presidents Harrison and Cleveland set aside 35 million acres.

A wilderness vogue swept the United States in the early twentieth century. From congested cities and clanging factories, Americans looked to the wilderness for tranquility and spiritual solace. Popular writers evoked the lure of the primitive, and the Boy Scouts (1910) and Girl Scouts (1912) gave city children a taste of the outdoors.

Between the wilderness enthusiasts and the developers stood government professionals like Gifford Pinchot who saw the public domain as a resource to be managed wisely. Named by Roosevelt to head the new U.S. Forest Service in 1905, Pinchot campaigned not for preservation but for conservation—the planned, regulated use of forests for public and commercial purposes.

Wilderness advocates saw Pinchot's Forest Service as a safeguard against mindless exploitation but worried that the multiple-use approach would despoil wilderness areas. A Sierra Club member

TR and Gifford Pinchot
The two allies in the conservation cause aboard the steamboat *Mississippi* on a 1907 tour with the Inland Waterways Commission.

wrote, "It is true that trees are for human use. But there are . . . uses for the spiritual wealth of us all, as well as for the material wealth of some." Professional conservationists dismissed such wilderness advocates as sentimental amateurs.

By temperament, President Roosevelt was a preservationist, a champion of wilderness and wildlife preservation. "When I hear of the destruction of a species," he wrote, "I feel just as if all the works of some greater writer had perished." However, Roosevelt the politician backed the conservationists' call for planned development. He supported the National Reclamation Act of 1902, which earmarked the proceeds of public-land sales for water management in the arid western regions

and established the Reclamation Service to plan dams and irrigation projects.

The Reclamation Act, according to some historians, ranks with the Northwest Ordinance for promoting the development of a vast region of North America. For example, the Roosevelt Dam spurred the growth of Phoenix, Arizona, and the Snake River project converted thousands of barren Idaho acres into fertile farmland. The law required those who benefited from reclamation projects to repay the government for construction costs, thus establishing a revolving fund for other projects. It made possible the transition of the West from a series of isolated "island settlements" into a thriving, interconnected region.

However, competition for scarce water resources sometimes led to bitter political battles. For example, in 1900 the Los Angeles basin had 40 percent of California's population but only 2 percent of its available surface water. In 1907 the city managed to divert, for its own use, water from a Reclamation Act project intended for farmers in the Owens Valley, 230 miles to the north.

President Roosevelt also backed Pinchot's program of multi-use land management and set aside more than 200 million acres of public land as national forests, mineral reserves, and potential water-power sites. But because of opposition in the West, Congress in 1907 rescinded the president's power to create national forests in six timber-rich states. Roosevelt signed the bill—only, however, after designating twenty-one new national forests totaling 16 million acres in those six states.

With Roosevelt's blessing, Pinchot organized a White House conservation conference for the nation's governors in 1908, but John Muir and other wilderness preservationists were not invited. However preservationists won key victories in this era. Initiatives by private citizens saved a large grove of California's giant redwoods and a lovely stretch of the Maine coastline.

While expanding the national forests, TR also created fifty-three wildlife reserves, sixteen national monuments, and five new national parks. As the parks drew more visitors, Congress created the National Park Service in 1916 to manage them. Earlier, the Antiquities Act (1906) had protected archaeological sites, especially in the Southwest, some of which eventually became national parks.

Taft in the White House, 1909–1913

Roosevelt had pledged not to run for a third term in 1908, and to the disappointment of millions, he kept his promise. The Republicans' most conservative wing regained control. Although they nominated Roosevelt's choice, William Howard Taft, for president, they selected a conservative vice-presidential candidate and drafted an extremely conservative platform. The Democrats, meanwhile, nominated William Jennings Bryan for a third and final time. The Democratic platform called for a lower tariff, denounced the trusts, and embraced the cause of labor.

With Roosevelt's endorsement, Taft coasted to victory. But the Democrats made gains and progressive Republican state candidates outran the national ticket. Overall, the outcome suggested a lull in the reform movement, not its end.

Taft differed markedly from Roosevelt. Whereas TR kept in fighting trim and loved boxing, Taft was grossly overweight and played golf. TR loved dramatic public donnybrooks against the forces of evil and greed, but Taft disliked controversy. His happiest days would come later, as chief justice of the Supreme Court.

Pledged to carry on TR's program, Taft supported the Mann-Elkins Act (1910), which strengthened the Interstate Commerce Commission's rate-setting powers and extended its authority to telephone and telegraph companies. The Taft White House filed more antitrust suits than the Roosevelt administration had, but its lack of fanfare left most people considering TR the quintessential "trustbuster."

The reform spotlight, meanwhile, shifted to Congress. During the Roosevelt administration, a small group of reform-minded Republican legislators, nicknamed the Insurgents, had challenged their party's conservative congressional leadership. The Insurgents, who included senators La Follette of Wisconsin and Albert Beveridge of Indiana and congressman George Norris of Nebraska turned against President Taft in 1909 after a tariff struggle.

Taft had originally believed that the tariff should be lowered, but in 1909 he signed the high Payne-Aldrich Tariff, praising it as "the best tariff bill that the Republican party ever passed." The battle between conservative and progressive Republicans was on.

A major Insurgent target was Speaker of the House Joseph G. Cannon of Illinois. With near-absolute power, Cannon prevented most reform bills from reaching a vote. In March 1910 Republican Insurgents joined with Democrats to curtail Cannon's power sharply. This Insurgent victory represented a slap at Taft, who supported Cannon.

The so-called Ballinger-Pinchot affair brought matters to a head. Richard A. Ballinger, Taft's secretary of the interior, was a conservative western lawyer who believed in the private development of natural resources. Ballinger approved the sale of several million acres of public land in Alaska in 1909 to some Seattle businessmen, who promptly sold it to a banking consortium that included J. P. Morgan. When a Department of Interior official protested, he was fired. In true muckraking style, he immediately published an article in *Collier's* blasting Ballinger's actions. When Gifford Pinchot of the Forestry Service publicly criticized Ballinger, he too got the ax. TR's supporters seethed.

When Roosevelt returned to the United States from an African safari in June 1910 Pinchot, met the boat. In the 1910 midterm elections, Roosevelt campaigned for Insurgent candidates. In a speech that alarmed conservatives, he attacked judges who struck down progressive laws and endorsed the radical idea of reversing judicial rulings by popular vote. Borrowing a term from Herbert Croly's *The Promise of American Life*, TR proposed a "New Nationalism" that would powerfully engage the federal government in reform.

Democrats captured the House of Representatives in 1910, and a coalition of Democrats and Insurgents controlled the Senate. As fervor for reform rose, Roosevelt sounded more and more like a presidential candidate.

The Four-Way Election of 1912

In February 1912 Roosevelt announced that he would seek the Republican nomination. With Taft showing no intention of withdrawing, a Republican battle royal loomed. Senator Robert La Follette's candidacy collapsed when TR entered the race.

Roosevelt won virtually all the state primaries and conventions in which he challenged Taft, but Taft controlled the party machinery. When the Republican convention that June disqualified many of Roosevelt's hard-won delegates, TR's outraged supporters stalked out. They reassembled in August to form a third party, the Progressive party.

Roosevelt proclaimed that he felt "as fit as a bull moose," thus giving his party the nickname the Bull Moose party. The euphoric delegates nominated TR by acclamation, with Hiram Johnson as his running mate, and endorsed virtually every reform cause of the day. The charismatic Roosevelt attracted a diverse following to the new party.

Meanwhile, the reform spirit had infused the Democratic party at state and local levels. In New Jersey, voters elected a political novice, Woodrow Wilson, as governor in 1910. A "Wilson for President" boom soon arose, and when the Democrats assembled in Baltimore in June 1912, Wilson won the nomination, defeating several established party leaders.

The Republican Taft essentially gave up. Eugene V. Debs ran on the Socialist platform, demanding an end to capitalism, and Roosevelt and Wilson vied for the moderate reform vote. TR preached his New Nationalism: governmental regulation of big business in the public interest. Wilson called for a "New Freedom," evoking an earlier era of small government, small businesses, and free competition. "The history of liberty is the history of the limitation of government power, not the increase of it," he insisted. The divided Republicans proved no match for the united Democrats. Wilson prevailed and the Democrats took both houses of Congress.

The 1912 election identified the triumphant Democrats with reform, launching a tradition on which Franklin D. Roosevelt would build in the 1930s. The breakaway Progressive party demonstrated the support for reform among grass-roots Republicans while leaving the Republican party in the grip of its most conservative elements.

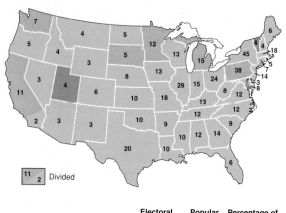

		Electoral Vote	Popular Vote	Percentage of Popular Vote
Democratic Woodrow Wilson		435	6,296,547	41.9
Progressive (Bull Moose) Theodore Roosevelt		88	4,118,571	27.4
Republican William H. Taft		8	3,486,720	23.2
Socialist Eugene V. Debs	–	–	900,672	6.1

MAP 21.2
The Election of 1912

NATIONAL PROGRESSIVISM PHASE II: WOODROW WILSON, 1913–1917

The son and grandson of Presbyterian ministers, Wilson grew up in southern towns in a churchly atmosphere that shaped his oratory and moral outlook. He graduated from Princeton, earned a Ph.D. in political science from Johns Hopkins University, taught at Princeton, and became president there in 1902. He lost support at Princeton because of his unwillingness to compromise and left the academic world for the political arena in

1910. Three years later, he was president of the United States.

Wilson was an eloquent orator. But the idealism that inspired people could also alienate them. At his best, he excelled at political dealmaking. But he could also retreat into a fortress of absolute certitude that tolerated no opposition. During his years as president, all these facets of his personality would come into play. Despite his campaign speeches, Wilson proved ready to use government to address the problems of the new corporate order, and the national progressive movement gained powerful new momentum.

Tariff and Banking Reform

Tariff reform—long a goal of southern and agrarian Democrats—headed Wilson's agenda. A low-tariff bill passed the House but bogged down in the Senate. Showing his flair for drama, Wilson denounced tariff lobbyists, and his censure led to a Senate investigation of lobbyists and of senators who profited from high tariffs. Stung by the publicity, the Senate slashed tariff rates even more than the House had done. The Underwood-Simmons Tariff reduced rates an average of 15 percent.

In June 1913 Wilson called for banking and currency reform. The nation's totally decentralized banking system clearly needed overhauling. But no consensus existed on specifics. Many reformers wanted a publicly controlled central banking system, but the nation's bankers favored private control. Some opposed any central banking authority, public or private.

No banking expert, Wilson listened to all sides. He insisted that the monetary system ultimately be publicly controlled. As the bargaining went on, Wilson played a crucial behind-the-scenes role. The result was the Federal Reserve Act of December 1913. A compromise measure, this law created twelve regional Federal Reserve banks under mixed public and private control. Each regional bank could issue U.S. dollars, called Federal Reserve notes, to the banks in its district to make loans. Overall control of the system was assigned to the heads of the twelve regional banks and a Washington-based Federal Re-

serve Board (FRB), whose members were appointed by the president for fourteen-year terms. (The secretary of the Treasury and the comptroller of the currency were made ex officio members.)

The Federal Reserve Act stands as Wilson's greatest legislative achievement. In time the FRB, nicknamed "the Fed," grew into the strong central monetary institution it remains today, adopting fiscal policies to prevent financial panics, promote economic growth, and dampen inflationary pressures.

Regulating Business; Aiding Workers and Farmers

In 1914 Wilson and his congressional allies turned to that perennial progressive cause, business regulation. Two key regulatory laws resulted, embodying different approaches.

The Federal Trade Commission Act (1914) reflected an administrative approach by creating a "watchdog" agency, the FTC, with power to investigate suspected violations, to require regular reports from corporations, and to issue cease-and-desist orders against unfair methods of competition. The Clayton Antitrust Act (1914) took a legal approach. It remedied the Sherman Anti-Trust Act's vagueness by spelling out a series of illegal practices, such as selling at a loss to undercut competitors. With the added clout of the Clayton Act, the Wilson administration filed antitrust suits against close to a hundred corporations.

The Democrats historically identified with workers, and Wilson supported the American Federation of Labor, defended workers' right to organize, and endorsed a Clayton Act clause that exempted strikes, boycotts, and peaceful picketing from "restraint of trade" injunctions. In 1916 (a campaign year) Wilson and congressional Democrats enacted three important worker-protection laws. The Keating-Owen Act barred from interstate commerce products manufactured by child labor (later declared unconstitutional). The Adamson Act established an eight-hour workday for interstate railway workers. The Workmen's Compensation Act provided accident and injury protection to federal workers.

Wilson also championed the Federal Farm Loan Act and the Federal Warehouse Act (1916), which allowed farmers to secure long-term, low-interest federal loans using land or crops as security. The Federal Highway Act (1916) matched federal funds with state appropriations for highway construction, benefiting the new automobile industry as well as farmers plagued by bad roads.

As with many progressives, Wilson's sympathies for the underdog stopped at the color line. Reared in Georgia, he displayed a patronizing attitude toward blacks and allowed southerners in his cabinet and in Congress to impose rigid segregation on all levels of the government.

Progressivism and the Constitution

The late-nineteenth-century probusiness bias of the courts moderated in the Progressive Era. In 1908 the Supreme Court in *Muller* v. *Oregon* upheld an Oregon law setting maximum hours for women laundry workers at ten hours. To defend the constitutionality of the Oregon law, Boston attorney Louis Brandeis had offered economic, medical, and sociological evidence of how long hours harmed women workers. The Court's acceptance of the "Brandeis brief" marked a breakthrough in the legal system's responsiveness to new social realities.

In 1916 Wilson nominated Brandeis to the Supreme Court. Many conservatives, including Republican leaders in Congress, disapproved of Brandeis's innovative approach to the law and protested. Anti-Semites opposed him because he was a Jew. But Wilson stood by his nominee, and after a fierce battle, the Senate confirmed him.

These years also produced four constitutional amendments. The Sixteenth (ratified in 1913) granted Congress the authority to tax income. An earlier income tax measure had been declared unconstitutional, spurring advocates to campaign for an amendment. Quickly exercising its new authority, Congress in 1913 imposed a graduated federal income tax with a maximum rate of 7 percent on incomes in excess of $500,000. Income tax revenues helped pay for the government's regulatory activi-

ties under progressive-era legislation. The Seventeenth Amendment (1913) completed a Populist crusade by mandating the direct popular election of U.S. senators, until then selected by state legislatures. Popular election, reformers hoped, would reduce corporate influence over senators. The Eighteenth Amendment (1919) established prohibition of "intoxicating liquors." The Nineteenth (1920) granted women the vote. This array of amendments demonstrated how profoundly progressivism had resculpted the political landscape.

1916: Wilson Edges out Hughes

In 1916 Wilson easily won renomination. The Republicans nominated Charles Evans Hughes, Supreme Court justice and former New York governor. Urged by Roosevelt, who was preoccupied with the new war enveloping Europe, the Progressive party endorsed Hughes. With the Republicans more or less reunited, the election was extremely close. Wilson won the popular vote, but the electoral-college outcome remained in doubt for weeks as the California tally seesawed back and forth. Ultimately, Wilson carried the state by less than 4,000 votes, and with it, the election.

After 1916, the progressive movement lost momentum as the nation's attention turned from reform to war. A few ripples of reform in the 1920s, including a 1924 presidential run by La Follette, offered reminders of the progressive agenda. But the movement's zest and drive clearly waned with the coming of World War I.

CONCLUSION   *hc* ACE Practice Test

Progressivism left a remarkable legacy in specific laws and in a changed view of government. By 1916 most Americans agreed that it was proper and necessary for the government to play a central social and economic role. Progressivism had expanded the meaning of democracy and challenged the cynical view that government was nothing more than a tool of the rich. Progressives enlarged the government because they realized that government had to

Chronology

1895	Anti-Saloon League founded.
1898	Charlotte Perkins Gilman, *Women and Economics.*
1899	Thorstein Veblen, *The Theory of the Leisure Class.*
1900	International Ladies' Garment Workers' Union (ILGWU) founded. Socialist Party of America organized. Carrie Chapman Catt becomes president of the National American Woman Suffrage Association (NAWSA).
1901	Assassination of McKinley; Theodore Roosevelt becomes president. J. P. Morgan forms United States Steel Company. Frank Norris, *The Octopus.*
1902	Roosevelt mediates coal strike. Jane Addams, *Democracy and Social Ethics.*
1903	W. E. B. Du Bois, *The Souls of Black Folk. The Great Train Robbery* (movie). Wright Brothers' flight.
1904	Roosevelt elected president. Lincoln Steffens. *The Shame of the Cities.* Ida Tarbell, *History of the Standard Oil Company.*
1905	Industrial Workers of the World (IWW) organized. Niagara Movement established by W. E. B. Du Bois and others. Gifford Pinchot appointed head of U.S. Forest Service.
1906	Upton Sinclair, *The Jungle.*
1907	William James, "Pragmatism."
1908	William Howard Taft elected president. Model T Ford introduced.
1909	Ballinger-Pinchot controversy. National Association for the Advancement of Colored People (NAACP) founded. Herbert Croly, *The Promise of American Life.* Daniel Burnham, *Plan of Chicago.*
1910	Jane Addams, *Twenty Years at Hull House.* Insurgents curb power of House Speaker Joseph Cannon.
1911	Triangle Shirtwaist Company fire. Frederick W. Taylor, *Principles of Scientific Management.*
1912	Republican party split; Progressive (Bull Moose) party founded. Woodrow Wilson elected president. International Opium Treaty. Theodore Dreiser, *The Financier.*
1914	American Social Hygiene Association founded.
1915	D. W. Griffith, *The Birth of a Nation.* Mary Ware Dennett founds National Birth Control League.
1916	Wilson reelected. John Dewey, *Democracy and Education.* Margaret Sanger opens nation's first birth-control clinic in Brooklyn, New York. National Park Service created. Louis Brandeis appointed to Supreme Court. Madison Grant, *The Passing of the Great Race.*

grow in step with gargantuan industries, sprawling cities, and concentrated corporate power if it was to serve the public interest, give people a decent life, and protect vulnerable members of society.

Progressive ideals often faltered in practice, however. Corporations proved remarkably adroit at manipulating the new regulatory state, and bureaucratic routine frequently gutted visionary programs. Unquestionably, too, progressivism had its illiberal and coercive dimensions; on racial justice, its record was miserable.

Nonetheless, the Progressive Era shines as a time when American politics seriously confronted the social upheavals wrought by industrialization. Americans learned to think of their government as neither remote nor a plaything of the powerful, but as an arena of possibility where they could thrash out public issues and social problems. Twenty years later, another great reform movement, the New Deal, would draw heavily on progressivism's legacy.

FURTHER READING

Alan Dawley, *Struggles for Justice: Social Responsibility and the Liberal State* (1991). A thoughtful study placing the progressive movement in a larger historical and ideological context.

Steven J. Diner, *A Very Different Age: Americans of the Progressive Era* (1998). A readable overview stressing the diversity of Progressives and their reforms.

Nan Enstad, *Ladies of Labor, Girls of Adventure: Working Women, Popular Culture, and Labor Politics at the Turn of the Twentieth Century* (1999). An innovative blending of labor history and popular-culture history.

Mark Fiege, *Irrigated Eden: The Making of an Agricultural Landscape in the American West* (1999). A valuable case study of land reclamation in Idaho, with especially good coverage of the Progressive Era.

Leon Fink, *Progressive Intellectuals and the Dilemmas of Democratic Commitment* (1997). Insightful exploration of the tensions between democratic theory and the Progressive Era focus on expertise and specialized knowledge.

Leon Fink, ed., *Major Problems in the Gilded Age and Progressive Era* (2001). Useful, well-chosen collection of primary sources and interpretive essays.

Noralee Frankel and Nancy S. Dye, eds., *Gender, Class, Race, and Reform in the Progressive Era* (1991). Selected essays exploring progressivism from various social perspectives.

Gayle Gullett, *Becoming Citizens: The Emergence and Development of the California Woman's Movement, 1880–1911* (2000). Illuminating case study of the movement in a key Western state.

Christine Stansell, *American Moderns: Bohemian New York and the Creation of a New Century* (2000). A fresh treatment of pre–World War I Greenwich Village, stressing the linkages between cultural and political radicalism.

David Stradling, *Smokestacks and Progressives: Environmentalists, Engineers, and Air Quality in America, 1881–1951* (1999). Well-researched account of the mixed record of the Progressive Era campaign for cleaner air, with attention to the role of civil engineers.

New York City, 1917. Bidding farewell to U.S. troops about to embark for France

22

Global Involvements and World War I, 1902–1920

hc This icon will direct you to additional study and research resources at http://college.hmco.com/history/us/boyer/enduring_concise/5e/students/index.html

The experience of Jane Addams illustrates how World War I touched all Americans, whether they served in the armed forces or not. In addition to her work at Hull House, Addams had long been a peace advocate; in 1915 she helped found the Women's Peace party. Her appeals to President Woodrow Wilson to support arbitration as a way to end the conflict failed. When the United States entered the war in 1917, Addams faced a dilemma: should she join most of her friends and colleagues in supporting the war, or should she follow her conscience in opposing it? Deciding to remain true to her convictions, she faced a hostile reaction: the Daughters of the American Revolution expelled her, editorial writers denounced her, and the American Legion and other patriotic organizations attacked her for "disloyalty." Nonetheless Addams did participate in the war effort in a limited way as part of the Food Administration, traveling the nation to call for increased food production to aid refugees and other innocent war victims.

**This chapter focuses on
five major questions:**

▶ What general aims underlay U.S. involvement in Asia and Latin America in the early
twentieth century?

▶ Why did the United States enter the European war in April 1917?

▶ How did America's war effort affect the
home front?

▶ In what ways did the role of the federal government in the economy and in American
life in general change in 1917–1918?

▶ What was Wilson's role in the creation of the
League of Nations? Why did he fail to win
Senate approval for American membership
in the League?

After the war, Jane Addams continued to work
for peace—she became president of the Women's
International League for Peace and Freedom,
wrote a moving book about her wartime anguish,
and in 1931 won the Nobel Peace Prize. In the
1960s she would serve as a model for some opponents of the Vietnam War.

Whether critics of the war like Jane Addams or
enthusiastic supporters of the effort to make the
world "safe for democracy," millions of Americans
found their lives wrenched apart by the events of
World War I. And the war's social, economic, and
political consequences endured for years.

DEFINING AMERICA'S WORLD ROLE, 1902–1914

The United States' growing determination to assert
its might, to protect and extend American business
interests, and, in true progressive fashion, to impose its own standards of good government
throughout the world led to continued American
involvement in Asia and Latin America as the
twentieth century unfolded.

The "Open Door": Competing for the China Market

As the Philippines war dragged on, Americans
shifted their focus to China. Their aim was not territorial expansion but rather protection of U.S.
commercial opportunities. Textile producers
dreamed of clothing China's millions of people; investors envisioned Chinese railroad construction.
As China's 250-year-old Manchu Ch'ing empire
grew weaker, U.S. businesspeople watched carefully. In 1896 a consortium of New York capitalists
formed a company to promote trade and railroad
investment in China.

China's weakness had drawn other imperialists—including Russia, Germany, and Great
Britain—who had won major concessions of land
and trading rights. In September 1899, fearful of
American businesses being shut out of China, Secretary of State John Hay sent notes to the imperialist powers in China requesting that they open the
ports within their spheres of influence to all comers and not grant special privileges to traders of
their own nations. Although the six nations gave
noncommittal answers, Hay blithely announced
that they had accepted the principle of an "Open
Door" to American business.

Hay's Open Door note illuminated how commercial considerations influenced American foreign policy. It reflected a quest for what has been
called "informal empire," in contrast to the formal
acquisition of overseas territories.

In 1899, even as the Open Door notes were circulating, an antiforeign secret society known as the
Harmonious Righteous Fists (called "Boxers" by
Western journalists) killed thousands of foreigners
and Chinese Christians. In June 1900 the Boxers
occupied Beijing (Peking), China's capital, and besieged the district housing the foreign legations. In
August 1900 an international army, including 2,500
Americans, marched on Beijing, drove back the
Boxers, and rescued the occupants of the threatened legations.

U.S. Troops in China, 1900
On a dirt road flanked by stone elephants, mounted American troops sent by President McKinley prepare to march on Beijing as part of an international force assembled to suppress the Boxer Rebellion. This intervention signaled a deepening U.S. involvement in Asia.

The defeat of the Boxer uprising further weakened China's government. Fearing that the regime's collapse would allow European powers to carve up China, John Hay issued a second, more important, series of Open Door notes in 1900. He reaffirmed the principle of open trade in China for all nations and announced America's determination to preserve China's territorial and administrative integrity. In general, China remained open to U.S. business interests as well as to Christian missionary efforts. In the 1930s, when Japanese expansionism menaced China's survival, Hay's policy helped shape the American response.

The Panama Canal: Hardball Diplomacy

Dreams of a canal across the ribbon of land joining North and South America dated back to the Spanish Conquest. Yellow fever and mismanagement brought a French company's late-nineteenth-century attempt to build a canal to disaster and left a half-completed waterway. To recoup some of the $400 million loss, the company offered to sell its assets, including a concession from Colombia, which then controlled the isthmus, to the United States for $109 million.

Americans considered alternate routes, including a canal across Nicaragua, but in 1901 the French lowered their price to $40 million. President Theodore Roosevelt pressed the offer, but in 1902 the Colombian government refused to ratify the agreement, which would have turned the French concession over to the United States. Furious, Roosevelt privately denounced the Colombians as "greedy little anthropoids."

Roosevelt found a willing collaborator in Philippe Bunau-Varilla, an official of the French company. To prevent the loss of $40 million to his firm, Bunau-Varilla organized a "revolution" in Panama, which was at that time still a Colombian province. Working from a New York hotel room, while his wife stitched a flag, he wrote a declaration of independence and a constitution. On November 3, 1903, the "revolution" erupted on schedule, with a U.S. warship anchored offshore. In short order, Bunau-Varilla proclaimed himself ambassador to Washington, gained American recognition of the newly hatched nation, and signed a treaty guaranteeing the United States a ten-mile-wide strip of land across Panama "in perpetuity" in return for $10 million and an annual payment of $250,000. Roosevelt later summarized the episode, "I took the Canal Zone, and let Congress debate, and while the debate goes on, the canal does also."

Before completing the canal, the United States first had to conquer yellow fever. After Dr. Walter Reed recognized the mosquito as its carrier, the U.S. Army carried out a prodigious drainage project that eradicated the disease-bearing pest. Construction began in 1906, and in August 1914 the first ship sailed through the canal. The Atlantic and Pacific coasts were linked by a short sea route just in time for World War I.

A technical wonder, the canal also symbolized an arrogant American imperialism. For decades, the rancor generated by Roosevelt's high-handed actions, combined with other cases of U.S. interventionism, shadowed U.S.–Latin American relations.

Roosevelt and Taft Assert U.S. Power in Latin America and Asia

Theodore Roosevelt, president from 1901 to 1909, believed that the United States must strengthen its world role, protect U.S. interests in Latin America, and preserve the balance of power in Asia. In 1904, when several European nations threatened to invade the Dominican Republic, a small Caribbean island nation that had defaulted on its debts, Roosevelt reacted swiftly. He feared that the Europeans would turn debt collecting into a permanent occupation. If any big power were to intervene in the region, he felt, it should be the United States. In December 1904 Roosevelt declared that "chronic wrongdoing" by any Latin American nation would justify intervention by the United States, acting as an international policeman.

This pronouncement became known as the Roosevelt Corollary to the Monroe Doctrine. (The original "doctrine," issued in 1823, had warned European powers against meddling in Latin America.) The Roosevelt Corollary announced that in some circumstances the United States had the *right* to meddle. Suiting actions to words, the United States ran the Dominican Republic's customs service for two years and took over the management of the country's foreign debt.

In 1911 a U.S.-supported revolution in Nicaragua brought to power Adolfo Díaz, an officer of an American-owned Nicaraguan mining property. U.S. bankers loaned the Díaz government $1.5 million in exchange for control of the Nicaraguan national bank, the customs service, and the national railroad. A revolt against Díaz in 1912 triggered action under the Roosevelt Corollary: Taft sent in 2,500 marines to protect the American investment. Except for a brief interval, U.S. Marines remained in Managua, Nicaragua's capital, until 1933.

In Asia, too, both Roosevelt and Taft sought to project U.S. power and advance the interests of American business. In 1900 Russia exploited the chaos unleashed by the Boxer uprising by sending troops to occupy Manchuria, China's northeastern province. In February 1904 the Japanese, who had their own plans for Manchuria, launched a surprise attack on Russian forces at Port Arthur, Manchuria. In the Russo-Japanese War that followed, Japan dominated Russia.

Russian expansionism dismayed Roosevelt, but so did the possibility of a total Japanese victory—and disruption of the balance of power that TR considered essential to Asian peace and to the maintenance of America's role in the Philippines. In June 1905 he therefore invited Japan and Russia to a peace conference in Portsmouth, New Hampshire, and in early September the two exhausted foes signed a peace treaty. Russia recognized Japan's rule in Korea and made other territorial concessions. From then on, curbing Japanese expansionism became the United States' chief goal in Asia.

American relations with Japan deteriorated in 1906 when the San Francisco school board ordered Asian children to attend segregated schools. Roosevelt persuaded the board to reverse its decision, however, and in 1907 his administration tried to head off future problems by negotiating a "gentleman's agreement" by which Japan pledged to stop Japanese emigration to the United States. But racist attitudes along the Pacific coast continued to poison U.S.-Japan relations, particularly after 1913, when the California legislature prohibited Japanese aliens from owning land.

As Californians worried about the "yellow peril," Japanese journalists watching America's growing military strength wrote of a "white peril."

In 1907 Roosevelt ordered a flotilla of sixteen gleaming white battleships to steam on a "training operation" to Japan and then around the world. The 1908 visit of the "Great White Fleet" to Japan underscored the United States' growing naval might—and led to huge increases in Japan's naval building program.

Under President Taft, U.S. foreign policy in Asia continued to focus on dollar diplomacy. After a futile attempt to involve American bankers in Manchurian railroad building demonstrated the shortcomings of the Open Door policy, Woodrow Wilson, after he took presidential office in 1913, shelved dollar diplomacy.

Wilson and Latin America

In 1913 the Democrat Wilson repudiated his Republican predecessors' expansionism and pledged that the United States would "never again seek one additional foot of territory by conquest." But he too intervened in Latin America. In 1915 after bloody upheavals in Haiti and the Dominican Republic, Wilson ordered in the marines. A Haitian constitution favorable to American commercial interests was ratified in 1918 by a vote of 69,377 to 355—in a marine-supervised election—and marines brutally suppressed Haitian resistance to American rule. They remained in the Dominican Republic until 1924 and in Haiti until 1934.

From 1913 to 1914, Wilson's major foreign-policy preoccupation was Mexico, a nation divided between a tiny elite of wealthy landowners and a mass of poor peasants. In a particularly turbulent era for Mexico, Wilson tried to promote good government in Mexico City, to protect the large U.S. capital investments in the country, and ultimately to safeguard U.S. citizens traveling in Mexico or living along its border.

In 1911 rebels led by democratic reformer Francisco Madero had overthrown the autocratic Mexican president, Porfirio Díaz. Forty thousand Americans had settled in Mexico under Díaz, and $2 billion in U.S. investments had flowed into the country. Early in 1913, Mexican troops loyal to General Victoriano Huerta ousted and murdered Madero.

Woodrow Wilson, Schoolteacher
This 1914 cartoon captures the patronizing self-righteousness of Wilson's approach to Latin America that planted the seeds of long-term resentments.

Wilson reversed the long-standing American policy of recognizing governments that held power regardless of how they had come to power. "I will not recognize a government of butchers," he declared, refusing to deal with Huerta. Wilson authorized arms sales to Venustiano Carranza, a Huerta foe, and blockaded Vera Cruz to prevent weapons from reaching Huerta. "I am going to teach the South American republics to elect good men," Wilson asserted. In April 1914 American troops occupied Vera Cruz and began fighting Mexican forces. Sixty-five Americans and five hundred Mexicans were killed or wounded. Bowing to U.S. might, Huerta abdicated, Carranza took power, and American troops withdrew.

But the turmoil continued. In January 1916 a bandit chieftain in northern Mexico, Pancho Villa, murdered sixteen American mining engineers and then crossed the border; burned Columbus, New

Mexico; and killed nineteen of its inhabitants. Sharing the public's outrage, Wilson sent into Mexico a punitive expedition that eventually totaled 12,000 U.S. troops. When Villa brazenly staged another raid across the Rio Grande into Texas, Wilson ordered 150,000 National Guardsmen into duty along the border.

Although comparatively minor, these episodes in Latin America and Asia revealed American foreign-policy goals in this era. The United States searched for a world order on U.S. terms—an international system founded on the uniquely American blend of liberalism, democracy, open trade, and capitalism. Washington planners envisioned a harmonious, stable global order of democratic societies that would welcome both American liberal political values and American corporate expansion.

These episodes also foreshadowed the future. The maneuvering between the United States and Japan reflected a growing clash of interests, compounded by racism, that would culminate in war with Japan in 1941. The revolutionary and nationalistic energies stirring in Latin America would explosively transform its politics half a century later. But of more immediate concern, the vision of a world order based on U.S. ideals would soon find expression in Woodrow Wilson's response to the crisis in Europe.

WAR IN EUROPE, 1914–1917

When war engulfed Europe in August 1914, most Americans wanted to remain aloof. For nearly three years, the United States did stay neutral, but then public opinion began to shift. Emotional ties to Britain and France, economic considerations, the vision of a world remade in America's image, and German violations of neutral rights, as defined by President Wilson, combined by April 1917 to draw the United States into the maelstrom.

The Coming of War

With minor exceptions, until the early twentieth century Europe had remained at peace after the conclusion of the Napoleonic Wars in 1815. Problems lurked beneath this serene surface, however. By 1914 a complex network of alliances bound European nations together, even as forces of nationalism threatened to tear some of them apart.

The slow-motion collapse in the 1870s of the ancient Ottoman Empire, centered in Turkey, had created such newly independent Balkan nations as Romania, Bulgaria, and Serbia (later a part of Yugoslavia) and presented opportunities for great-power meddling. Nationalism reached a fever pitch in Serbia, which dreamed of absorbing other South Slavic peoples. Russia, the largest Slavic nation, supported the Serbian dream. Meanwhile, the Austro-Hungarian Empire, itself menaced, saw opportunities for expansion as the Ottoman Empire receded. In 1908 Austria-Hungary annexed Bosnia-Herzogovina, a Slavic land wedged between Austria-Hungary and Serbia. The Russians were alarmed, and the Serbs furious.

Moreover, Germany, under the leadership of Kaiser Wilhelm II, was in an expansionist mood. Many Germans believed that their nation, united only since 1871, was lagging in the quest for national greatness and empire. Expansion, modernization, and military power became the order of the day in Berlin, the German Empire's capital.

Ordinary Europeans experienced a vague restlessness as the twentieth century opened. Life seemed soft, boring, and stale. Like Theodore Roosevelt on the eve of the Spanish-American War, some Europeans openly longed for a war that would strengthen national character and add excitement to a languid age.

In mid-1914, this volatile mixture exploded. In June a terrorist with close links to Serbia gunned down the heir to the Austrian throne and his wife as they rode through the Bosnian capital, Sarajevo. Austria delivered a harsh ultimatum to Serbia and five days later, after an "unacceptable" Serbian response, declared war on its Balkan neighbor. The intricate machinery of the alliance system rumbled into action. Linked to Serbia by a secret treaty, Russia mobilized for war. Germany declared war on Russia and on Russia's ally, France. Great Britain, linked by treaty to France, declared war on

Germany. Thus a lone assassin plunged Europe into a war that altered history.

The Perils of Neutrality

President Wilson immediately proclaimed U.S. neutrality and exhorted the nation to be neutral "in thought as well as in action." Most Americans, grateful that the Atlantic Ocean lay between them and the battlefields, supported Wilson's position. As a popular song said, "I Didn't Raise My Boy to Be a Soldier."

Remaining neutral in sentiment proved difficult. Not only economic ties but also a common language, ancestry, and culture linked many Americans to Britain by strong emotional bonds. Still, not all Americans shared these ties. Because millions were of German origin, many sided with Germany. Irish-Americans, raised for generations on "twisting the [British] lion's tail," had little sympathy for Britain.

By 1917 the American commitment to neutrality had been transformed into strong popular support for war. What caused this turnabout?

First, Wilson's vision of an enlightened world order conflicted with his commitment to neutrality. The international system that he favored, based on liberalism, democracy, and capitalistic enterprise, could never exist in a world dominated by imperial Germany. Wilson also believed that only U.S. leadership could ensure the achievement of this vision, and unless America helped to fight the war, America could not shape the peace.

This global vision influenced Wilson's approach to the first and perhaps most important problem confronting the United States: the question of neutral rights on the high seas. Within days of the war's outbreak, Britain had intercepted American merchant ships bound for Germany. In November 1914 Britain provoked more Wilsonian protests by declaring the North Sea a war zone and planting it with explosive mines. U.S. denunciations had no effect, for Britain had resolved to exploit its naval advantage no matter how it alienated American public opinion.

Ultimately, however, Germany pushed the United States into the war. Determined to take ad-

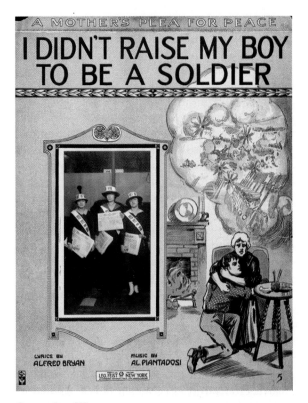

Opposing War

This popular song of 1915 conveys the antiwar sentiment that swept America after the European war began in 1914.

vantage of a new and deadly weapon, the submarine, Germany in February 1915 designated the waters around the British Isles a war zone and warned off all ships, including those of Americans. Wilson warned that Germany would be held to "strict accountability" for the loss of American ships or lives.

Developments in May 1915 underscored the problems of neutrality. Germany placed announcements in U.S. newspapers advising against travel on British or French vessels. Six days later, on May 7, a U-boat sank the British liner *Lusitania*, with a loss of 1,198 lives, including 128 Americans. Wilson demanded specific pledges that Germany would stop its unrestricted submarine warfare. Nonetheless, he also insisted that America could use persuasion, rather than force, to press the belligerents to recognize neutral rights.

The *Lusitania* disaster exposed deep divisions in U.S. public opinion. Many Americans were ready for war. Theodore Roosevelt, strongly pro-British, condemned Wilson for "abject cowardice and weakness." The National Security League, a lobby of bankers and industrialists, led a "preparedness" movement, stirring up patriotism and promoting an arms buildup and military training. By late 1915, Wilson himself called for a military buildup. Many others, however, including pacifists, German-Americans, and those who had taken Wilson's speeches seriously, deplored the drift toward war. Leading feminists and social-justice reformers warned that the war spirit was eroding humanitarian values central to reform. As early as August 1914, fifteen hundred black-clad women marched down New York's Fifth Avenue protesting the war. In 1915 Jane Addams, Carrie Chapman Catt, and other feminists formed the Woman's Peace party, and later that year they and others sailed to Sweden on a ship chartered by industrialist Henry Ford in an attempt to mediate the war and bring peace before Christmas.

Wilson's firm but restrained policy seemed to work. In August 1915 when a U-boat violated orders and sank the *Arabic,* a British liner, with the loss of two American lives, Germany pledged that such an incident would not happen again. But in March 1916 it did, as a German sub sank a French vessel, the *Sussex,* and injured several Americans. Wilson threatened to break diplomatic relations, a first step toward war, and Berlin pledged not to attack merchant vessels without warning. The crisis over neutral rights eased temporarily.

Corporate boardrooms as well as the high seas proved an arena for quarrels over neutral rights. Early in the war, American bankers trying to lend money to the belligerents were told that such loans were "inconsistent with the true spirit of neutrality." The policy did not last. In August 1915 Wilson's cabinet began to warn that only substantial loans to Great Britain could prevent "a serious financial situation" in the United States. Wilson finally permitted the Morgan bank to lend $500 million to the British and French governments. By April 1917 U.S. banks had lent $2.3 billion to the Allies (Great Britain, France, Russia, and Italy) and only $27 million to the Central Powers (Germany and Austria-Hungary). Although the United States remained neutral, Wilson had taken full advantage of the Allies' credit needs to strengthen the nation's commercial and financial position in the world economy.

While Americans focused on neutral rights, the land war in Europe degenerated into a costly stalemate. After Germany's initial offensive drive stalled, the two sides dug in, forming a line of trenches that snaked across France from the English Channel to the Swiss border. For more than three years, this line scarcely changed. A German offensive in 1916 near the French town of Verdun alone cost hundreds of thousands of casualties but did little to break the stalemate. The war in the trenches was nightmarish, a ghastly inferno of mud, lice, rats, artillery bursts, poison gas, and sudden, random death.

Determined to win the propaganda war, Britain bombarded the United States with posters and articles portraying alleged German atrocities, such as the impaling of babies on bayonets. German propaganda proved relatively ineffective.

The war dominated the 1916 presidential election. Democrats praised Woodrow Wilson for keeping the nation out of war, while the Republican candidate, Charles Evans Hughes, vacillated between criticizing Wilson for lack of aggressiveness and criticizing him for policies that brought the country closer to war. Wilson won a close victory, but that victory revealed the strength of the popular desire for peace as late as November 1916.

The United States Enters the War

As the war dragged on, German military leaders pushed for greater and greater use of the submarine. Although such stepped-up German aggression would almost certainly pull the United States into the war, American entry would have no significance, they said. The generals prevailed. On January 9, 1917, the German government decided to return to the policy of unlimited U-boat attacks.

Events now rushed forward. Three days after Germany's formal announcement of the resumption of unrestricted submarine warfare, Wilson broke diplomatic relations. Five American ships fell victim to German torpedoes in February and March. And on February 24, the United States' discovery of the so-called Zimmermann telegram enormously widened the rift between the two nations. Attempting to create problems on the American side of the Atlantic, German foreign secretary Alfred Zimmermann had cabled the German ambassador in Mexico to propose a military alliance of Germany, Mexico, and Japan, with Mexico promised the return of its "lost" territories of Texas, Arizona, and New Mexico. Publication of the telegram raised a furor in the United States.

On April 2 Wilson went before Congress to call for a declaration of war. By wide margins, both the Senate and the House voted for war. Three factors—German attacks on American shipping, U.S. investment in the Allied cause, and American cultural links to the Allies, especially England—had converged to draw the United States into war.

h c Primary Source: Zimmerman Telegram

Mobilizing at Home, Fighting in France, 1917-1918

World War I would leave the United States with relatively few scars. At war for only nineteen months, the nation took comparatively light casualties—112,000 of the 7.5 million dead—and the American homeland remained untouched. Still, the war constituted a major turning point. It changed the lives of almost all Americans, transformed the nation's government and economy, and thrust the United States into the arena of global politics.

Raising, Training, and Testing an Army

A woefully unprepared American military faced war in April 1917. The regular army of 120,000 enlisted men had virtually no combat experience. An aging officer corps was dozing away the years until retirement. There was enough ammunition for only two days of fighting, and the War Department was a snakepit of jealous bureaucrats.

Raising an army and imposing order on the War Department posed a daunting challenge. Wilson's secretary of war, Newton D. Baker, performed brilliantly on the first task, skillfully implementing the Selective Service Act passed in May 1917. Baker cleverly made the first draft registration day a "festival and patriotic occasion." Thanks to a carefully orchestrated public-relations campaign and local civilian draft boards' deft handling of the draft, 24 million men registered by November 1918, of whom nearly 3 million were drafted. In addition, following a precedent-breaking decision by the secretary of the navy, 11,000 women served in the navy during the war. Although not assigned to combat, they performed crucial support functions as nurses, clerical workers, and telephone operators.

World War I training camps not only turned civilians into soldiers but also reinforced prewar moral-control reforms and signaled changes ahead. Beginning in December 1917, all recruits underwent intelligence testing. Eager to demonstrate the usefulness of their new field, psychologists claimed that using tests to measure intelligence (IQ) could help in assigning duties and selecting potential officers; it would "help win the war."

The tests seemed to show that a high percentage of recruits were "morons," and editorial writers bemoaned the wave of imbecility sweeping the nation. In fact, the tests were weighted in favor of educated and culturally sophisticated individuals, not rural Americans. Nonetheless, the testing confirmed racial and ethnic stereotypes: native-born recruits of northern European origin scored well, while African-Americans and recent immigrants scored poorly.

In April 1917 W.E.B. Du Bois urged African-Americans to support the war. Most did. More than 260,000 blacks volunteered or were drafted, and 50,000 went to France. However, racism pervaded the military; the navy assigned blacks only to menial positions and the marines excluded them completely.

One racist senator from Mississippi warned that the sight of "arrogant, strutting" African-American soldiers would trigger race riots in the United States. Tensions reached the breaking point in Houston in August 1917 when some black soldiers, endlessly goaded by local whites, seized weapons from the armory and killed seventeen whites. After a hasty trial with no opportunity for an appeal, thirteen African-American soldiers were hanged, and forty-one went to jail for life.

Organizing the Economy for War

As historian Ellis Hawley has shown, the administrative innovations of the war years accelerated longer-term processes of social reorganization. The war led to greater efficiency in mass production; a wider regulatory role for the government; more extensive collaboration among government, business, and labor; and the rise of new professional and managerial elites. In tracing the roots of the modern American state, the years 1917–1918 are crucial.

The coming of the war in 1917 brought not only military mobilization but also unprecedented government oversight of the economy. The populist and progressive goal of more public control over corporations began to be achieved.

The War Industries Board (WIB) was established in 1917 to coordinate military purchasing, to

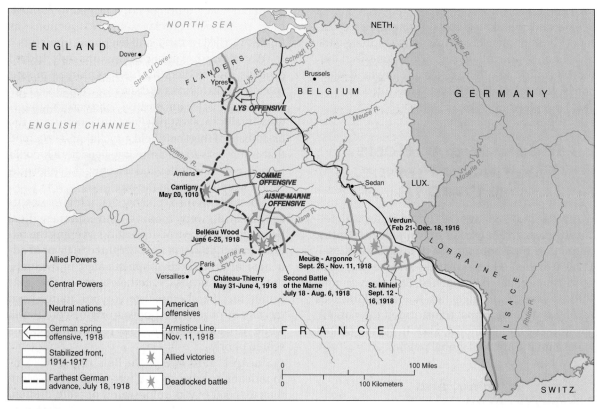

MAP 22.1

The United States on the Western Front, 1918

American troops first saw action in the campaign to throw back Germany's spring 1918 offensive in the Somme and Aisne-Marne sectors. The next heavy American engagement came that autumn as part of the Allies' Meuse-Argonne offensive that ended the war.

hc Interactive Map: American Troops at the Western Front, 1918 fight waste, and to ensure that the military received the weapons, equipment, and supplies it needed. Especially under the wealthy Wall Street speculator Bernard Baruch, whom Wilson appointed to run the WIB in March 1918, the agency exercised enormous control over the industrial sector. In addition to allocating raw materials, the board established production priorities and introduced all kinds of efficiencies. To save steel, rubber, and other scarce commodities, competing companies coordinated their production processes. The standardization of bicycle manufacturing, for example, saved 2,000 tons of steel. The Fuel Administration controlled coal output, regulated fuel prices and consumption, and in March 1918 introduced daylight savings time as a wartime conservation measure.

Baruch's counterpart on the agricultural front was Herbert Hoover, the head of the Food Administration. A mining engineer who had amassed a fortune in Asia, Hoover oversaw the production and distribution of foodstuffs—especially wheat, meat, and sugar—to assure adequate supplies for the army and the food-short Allies. A master of persuasion, Hoover organized a public-relations campaign to convince Americans that they should conserve food. Bombarded with such slogans as "Serve Beans by All Means" and "Don't Let Your Horse Be More Patriotic Than You Are—Eat a Dish of Oatmeal," Americans observed "meatless days" and "wheatless days."

The War Industries Board and the Food Administration represented only the tip of the regulatory iceberg. Nearly 5,000 government agencies supervised home-front activities during the war. When a massive railroad tie-up during the snowy winter of 1917–1918 impeded the flow of supplies to Europe, the government took over and transformed the 3,000 competing companies into an efficient national transportation system.

The war accelerated the corporate consolidation and economic integration as businesses worked together to make production and distribution more rational and more efficient. It was also highly profitable. Despite congressional imposition of an excess-profits tax, wartime corporate profits mushroomed. In place of trustbusting,

moreover, the government actively encouraged industrial cooperation. In 1917 major corporate mergers soared to nearly two hundred, more than twice the annual average for the immediate prewar years.

This colossal regulatory apparatus fell apart when the war ended, but its influence lingered. The old laissez-faire suspicion of government, already eroded, suffered further blows in 1917–1918. In the 1930s when the nation faced a different kind of crisis, the government activism of World War I would be remembered. Indeed, many New Deal agencies (see Chapter 24) resembled the wartime agencies of 1917–1918.

With the American Expeditionary Force in France

About 2 million American soldiers went to France in 1917–1918 as members of the American Expeditionary Force (AEF) under General John J. Pershing. A West Point graduate and commander of the 1916 expedition against Pancho Villa, Pershing was an iron-willed officer with a ramrod bearing, steely eyes, and trim mustache. For most men of the AEF, the war at first seemed a great adventure. After traveling to France on crowded freighters or even captured German liners, they piled aboard freight cars marked "hommes 40, chevaux 8" (40 men, 8 horses) on their way to the front. Once there, they marched, trained, became acquainted with the French—and waited.

Aerial dogfights between German and Allied reconnaissance planes offered spectacular sideshows. Germany's Manfred von Richthofen, the "Red Baron," shot down eighty Allied aircraft before his luck ran out in April 1918. Although Secretary of War Baker was "thoroughly fascinated" by the recently invented airplane's possibilities and pressed Congress to appropriate large sums for aircraft construction, only thirty-seven planes were built.

The war would be won or lost on land and sea, however, and when the United States entered, Allied prospects looked bleak. German submarines took a horrendous toll on Allied shipping: 600,000 tons in March 1917, 900,000 tons in April. A failed French offensive in the spring led to an army mutiny, and an almost equally disastrous British-French offensive in November cost 400,000 casualties to gain four miles.

To make matters worse, Russia left the war in 1917. The all-out effort dictated by the massive war had undermined Russia's already toppling tsarist government, and in March 1917 the imperial government had collapsed. A provisional liberal government attempted to continue the war. Marxist revolutionaries under Vladimir Ilyich Lenin, however, capitalized on the provisional government's instability. On November 6, 1917, Lenin and Leon Trotsky led an armed coup that overthrew the provisional government and began a civil war for the entire Russian empire. In March 1918 Lenin's Bolshevik government signed a separate armistice with Germany, which freed thousands of German troops for transfer to the Western Front in France.

In these desperate circumstances, French and British commanders wanted to incorporate AEF troops into Allied units already at the front. But Pershing insisted that the AEF be "distinct and separate," in part because he scorned the defensive mentality of the Allied commanders and in part because separate combat would strengthen the United States' voice at the peace table.

American forces saw their first real combat in March 1918 when a German offensive threatened France's English Channel ports. The Allies created a unified command under French general Ferdinand Foch, and American troops were thrown into the fighting around Amiens and Armentières that stemmed the German advance. In May 1918 Germany launched the second phase of its spring offensive. By the end of the month, the Germans had broken through the Allied lines and had secured a nearly open road to Paris, only fifty miles away. At this critical moment, Americans spearheaded the forces that finally stopped the German advance at the town of Château-Thierry and nearby Belleau Wood. Eighty-five thousand American troops helped to staunch the final German offensive of the war, a thrust at the ancient cathedral city of Rheims. This Allied victory marked the crucial

turning point of the war. Germany's desperate attempt to take the offensive had failed. Now it was the Allies' turn.

Turning the Tide

In July 18, 1918, the Allies launched their counteroffensive. Of the 1 million American soldiers on French soil, 270,000 participated in a successful drive to push the Germans back.

In September Pershing took his first independent command and assembled nearly 500,000 American and 100,000 French troops to implement his strategy of hard-hitting offense. An American wrote in his diary, "In one instant the entire front as far as the eye could reach in either direction was a sheet of flame, while the heavy artillery made the earth quake."

The war's last great battle began on September 26 as 1.2 million Americans joined the struggle to drive the Germans from the Meuse River and the dense Argonne Forest north of Verdun. Poison gas hung in the air, and bloated rats scurried through the mud, feasting on human remains as the offensive pressed forward over land devastated by four years of trench warfare.

Four black infantry regiments served with distinction under French command. One entire regiment, the 369th, was honored with the French Croix de Guerre, and several hundred individual black soldiers received French decorations for bravery. Most French people, military and civilian alike, treated whites and blacks at least superficially the same. For African-American members of the AEF, this eye-opening experience would remain with them when they returned home.

Theodore Roosevelt's "great adventure" seemed remote indeed in the Meuse-Argonne campaign. Death came in many forms and without ceremony. Bodies, packs, rifles, photos, and letters from home sank into the all-consuming mud as more than 26,000 Americans died in the battle and thousands more perished in an influenza epidemic that would take 50 million lives worldwide. The war's brutality would shape the literature of the 1920s as writers such as Ernest Hemingway forced readers

African-Americans at the Front
Black troops of the 369th Infantry Regiment in the trenches near Maffrecourt, France, in 1918. Most African-American soldiers were assigned to non-combat duty, such as unloading supplies and equipment.

to confront the reality of mass slaughter. By early November the Allied counteroffensive had succeeded, but at terrible cost.

PROMOTING THE WAR AND SUPPRESSING DISSENT

Patriotic fervor pervaded American society in 1917–1918, in part the result of an elaborate government campaign to whip up enthusiasm for the war. In its wake came stifling intellectual conformity and intolerance for dissent. Government authorities and private vigilante groups hounded and arrested socialists, pacifists, and other dissidents and in the process trampled the basic constitutional rights of thousands.

Advertising the War

To President Wilson, selling the war at home was no less important than the war abroad. "It is not an army we must shape and train for war, it is a nation," he declared. The Wilson administration drew on the new professions of advertising and public relations to pursue this goal. Treasury Secretary William Gibbs McAdoo set the patriotic tone, raising enormous sums to defray the expense of the war. Including loans to the Allies, World War I cost the United States $35.5 billion. Almost two-thirds of this amount ($21 billion) came from government bond sales, called Liberty Loan drives, organized by McAdoo.

McAdoo surrounded the Liberty Loan campaigns with great ballyhoo. Posters exhorted citizens to "Fight or Buy Bonds." Parades, rallies, and appearances by movie stars all aided the cause. An undercurrent of coercion also contributed to heavy sales; McAdoo declared that "only a friend of Germany" would refuse to buy bonds.

Stiff taxes supplied the other one-third of the war's funding. Taking advantage of the new power to tax incomes granted by the Sixteenth Amendment (ratified in 1913), Congress imposed wartime income taxes that rose to 63 percent at the top level.

George Creel, a progressive reformer and journalist, headed Washington's most effective wartime propaganda agency, the Committee on Public Information (CPI). Established in April 1917, ostensibly to combat rumors by providing authoritative information, the Creel committee communicated the government's official version of reality and discredited those who questioned it. Posters, news releases, advertisements, and movies all trumpeted the government's sanitized version of events. The CPI poured foreign-language publications into the cities to ensure the loyalty of recent immigrants. Creel also organized the "four-minute men": a network of 75,000 speakers throughout the nation who gave patriotic talks to audiences of all kinds. Creel calculated that this small army of propagandists delivered 7.5 million speeches to listeners totaling 314 million.

Teachers, writers, religious leaders, and magazine editors overwhelmingly supported the war. These custodians of culture viewed the conflict as a struggle to defend threatened values and standards. Historians contrasted Germany's malignant power and glorification of brute force with the Allies' loftier, more civilized ideals. Alan Seeger, a young Harvard graduate who volunteered to fight for France in 1916, wrote highly popular poems romanticizing the war. An artillery barrage became "the magnificent orchestra of war." The "sense of being the instrument of Destiny," wrote Seeger, represented the "supreme experience" of combat. He was killed in action in 1916.

Progressives hoped that the wartime climate of heightened government activism and sacrifice for the common good would encourage further reforms. Herbert Croly, Walter Lippmann, and other progressive intellectuals associated with the *New Republic* zealously supported the war.

John Dewey also joined the prowar chorus. In *New Republic* articles in 1917–1918, Dewey condemned the war's opponents. Socially engaged intellectuals, he wrote, must accept reality as they found it and shape it toward positive social goals, not stand aside in self-righteous indignation. The war presented exciting "social possibilities." Domestically, the wartime growth of government power could be channeled to reform purposes once peace returned. Internationally, America's entry would transform a crude imperialistic clash into a worldwide democratic crusade, Dewey argued.

Wartime Intolerance and Dissent

Responding to this drumfire of propaganda, some Americans became almost hysterical in their hatred of all things German, their hostility to aliens and dissenters, and their strident patriotism. Isolated actions by German saboteurs, including the blowing-up of a New Jersey munitions dump, fanned the antiforeign flames. In Collinsville, Illinois, a mob of 500 lynched a young German-born man in April 1918. When a jury exonerated the mob leaders, a jury member shouted, "Nobody can say we aren't loyal now."

German books vanished from libraries, towns with German names changed them, and "liberty sandwich" and "liberty cabbage" replaced "hamburgers" and "sauerkraut" on restaurant menus. Popular evangelist Billy Sunday proclaimed, "If you turn hell upside down you will find 'Made in Germany' stamped on the bottom." Leopold Stokowski, the conductor of the Philadelphia Orchestra, dropped German opera and songs from the repertoire but asked President Wilson's permission to retain Bach, Beethoven, Mozart, and Brahms.

The zealots of ideological conformity fell with special ferocity on war critics and radicals. A mob hauled a Cincinnati pacifist minister to a wood and whipped him. Theodore Roosevelt, never the voice of moderation, branded antiwar senator Robert La Follette "an unhung traitor." In Bisbee, Arizona, a vigilante mob forced 1,200 miners who belonged to the IWW onto a freight train and shipped them into the New Mexico desert without food, water, or shelter.

Despite the overheated conformist climate, a few Americans refused to support the war. Some were German-Americans with ties to the land of their forebears, and some others belonged to historically pacifist churches. Sixty-five thousand men registered as conscientious objectors, and 21,000 of them were drafted. The army assigned most of these to "noncombatant" duty on military bases.

Socialist party leaders such as Eugene V. Debs opposed the war on political grounds. They viewed it as a capitalist contest for world markets, with the soldiers on both sides mere cannon fodder. The U.S. declaration of war, they insisted, mainly reflected Wall Street's desire to protect its loans to England and France.

Draft resistance extended far beyond the ranks of conscientious objectors. An estimated three million young men failed to register for the draft, and 12 percent either did not respond to being called up or deserted from training camp. The rural South accounted for high levels of draft resistance, especially because the urban elites who ran draft boards were more likely to defer young men of their own class than poor farmers, white or black.

Of southern blacks who registered, one-third were drafted, compared to one-fourth of whites.

White draft boards argued that low-income black families could more easily replace a breadwinner than higher-income white families. At the same time, however, some southern whites feared arming blacks even for military service and favored drafting only whites.

The war's most incisive critic was Randolph Bourne, a young journalist. Although Bourne much admired John Dewey, he rejected his hero's prowar position. Like moths near a flame, Bourne said, intellectuals were mesmerized by the lure of being near the center of action and power. He dismissed as a self-serving delusion the belief that liberal reformers could direct the war to their own purposes. War took on its own terrible momentum, he wrote, and could no more be controlled by intellectuals than a rogue elephant crashing through the bush. Ultimately, Dewey, Lippmann, and other prowar intellectuals agreed with Bourne. By 1919 Dewey had conceded that the war, far from promoting liberalism, had unleashed the most reactionary and intolerant forces in the nation.

Suppressing Dissent by Law

Wartime intolerance also surfaced in federal laws and in the actions of top government officials. The Espionage Act of June 1917 prescribed heavy fines and long prison sentences for a variety of loosely defined antiwar activities. The Sedition Amendment to the Espionage Act (May 1918) imposed heavy penalties on anyone convicted of using "disloyal, profane, scurrilous, or abusive language" about the government, the Constitution, the flag, or the military.

Wilson's reactionary attorney general, Thomas W. Gregory, freely employed these measures to stamp out dissent. Opponents of the war should expect no mercy "from an outraged people and an avenging government," he said. Under this sweeping legislation and equally sweeping state laws, hundreds of pacifists, socialists, and war opponents found themselves imprisoned. Kate Richards O'Hare, a midwestern socialist organizer, spent more than a year in jail for allegedly telling an audience that "the women of the United States are nothing more than brood sows, to raise children to get into the army and be made into fertilizer." Eugene V. Debs was sentenced to ten years in a federal penitentiary for a speech discussing the economic causes of the war.

The Espionage Act also authorized the postmaster general to bar suspect materials from the mail—a provision enthusiastically enforced by Wilson's postmaster general, Albert S. Burleson, a reactionary superpatriot. In January 1919 Congressman-elect Victor Berger received a twenty-year prison sentence (later set aside by the Supreme Court) and was denied his seat in the House for publishing antiwar articles in his socialist newspaper, the *Milwaukee Leader.* Alarm over the Bolshevik revolution in Russia reinforced attacks on domestic radicals.

A few citizens protested. Muckraking novelist Upton Sinclair wrote to President Wilson to deplore that a man of Burleson's "pitiful and childish ignorance" should wield such power. Wilson did little to restrain either his postmaster general or his attorney general. Nor did the Supreme Court. In three 1919 decisions, the Court upheld Espionage Act convictions of people who had spoken out against the war. It also upheld Debs's conviction. Although the war was over, a vindictive Wilson refused to commute Debs's sentence. (President Warren Harding would at last release the ill and aging Debs in December 1921, but the government would not restore his rights as a U.S. citizen.)

Thus wartime idealism and high resolve deteriorated into fearful suspicion, narrow ideological conformity, and the persecution of those who failed to meet the zealots' notion of "100 percent Americanism." The effects of this ugly wartime climate would linger long after the armistice.

Economic and Social Trends in Wartime America

All wars usher in unanticipated economic and social changes, and World War I was no exception. The war affected the lives of millions of industrial workers (including large numbers of African-Americans and women) and farmers. The wartime mood also gave a significant boost to the moral-reform movement. Amid these social changes, a deadly influenza epidemic in 1918 took a grievous toll.

Boom Times in Industry and Agriculture

For all its horrendous human toll, World War I brought glowing prosperity to the American economy. Factory production climbed about 35 percent from 1914 to 1918, and the civilian work force grew by 1.3 million from 1916 to 1918. Wages rose, but prices soared. The real wages of unskilled workers climbed by nearly 20 percent from 1914 to 1918.

Samuel Gompers of the American Federation of Labor urged workers to refrain from striking for the duration of the war. Union membership increased from 2.7 million in 1916 to more than 5 million by 1920. The National War Labor Board guaranteed workers' rights to organize and bargain collectively. It also pressured war plants to introduce the eight-hour workday, which by the war's end had become the standard in U.S. industry.

American agriculture prospered during the war years. With European farm production disrupted, U.S. agricultural prices more than doubled from 1913 to 1918. Cotton jumped from $.12 to $.29 per pound by 1918 and corn from $.70 to $1.52 a bushel. At the same time, farmers' real income rose significantly. But in the long run, this agricultural boom proved a mixed blessing. Farmers borrowed heavily to expand their production, and when the artificially high wartime prices collapsed, they found themselves in a credit squeeze. During an ensuing long agricultural depression in the 1920s and 1930s, farmers would look back to the war years as their last time of real prosperity.

Social disruption as well as prosperity came of the boom. The job seekers streaming into urban industrial centers strained housing, schools, and municipal services. Changes in social behavior occurred, taking many forms. The consumption of cigarettes shot up by 350 percent, to 48 billion a year. Automobile production quadrupled, reaching 1.8 million in 1917. With more cars on the road, American life began to change.

Blacks Migrate Northward

The war sharply accelerated blacks' migration to northern cities. An estimated half-million African-Americans left the South during the war. Chicago's black population swelled from 44,000 in 1910 to 110,000 in 1920 and Cleveland's from 8,000 to 34,000.

Economic opportunity drew them north. When the war sharply reduced immigration from Europe, American industry recruited black workers to take up the slack. The economic inducements found a ready response. To the black sharecropper mired in poverty and confronting blatant racism, the prospect of a salary of three dollars a day, in a region where racism seemed less intense, appeared a heaven-sent opportunity. One black, newly settled near Chicago, wrote his southern relatives, "Nothing here but money, and it is not hard to get." By 1920, 1.5 million African-Americans were working in northern factories or other urban-based jobs.

Once the initial elation faded, African-American migrants often found they had traded one set of problems for another. White workers resented the competition, and white homeowners reacted in fear and hostility as crowded black neighborhoods spilled over into surrounding areas. Bloody violence broke out on July 2, 1917, in East St. Louis, Illinois, home to 10,000 blacks recently arrived from the South. In a well-coordinated action, a white mob torched black homes and then shot the residents as they fled. At least thirty-nine African-Americans were killed. A few weeks later, the newly founded National Association for the Advancement of Colored People (NAACP) organized a silent march down New York's Fifth Avenue to protest racial violence. But racial tensions did not end with the signing of the armistice.

Women in Wartime

From one perspective, World War I seems a supremely male experience. Male politicians and statesmen made the decisions that led to war. Male generals issued the orders that sent untold thousands of other men to their death in battle. Yet any event as vast as war touches all of society. The war affected women differently than men, but it affected them profoundly.

Women activists hoped that the war would lead to equality and greater opportunity for women. One author offered a feminist variation of Woodrow Wilson's theme: women should energetically support the war, she said, in order to win a role in shaping the peace.

For a bright, brief moment, the war promised dramatic gains for women. Thousands of women served in the military and in volunteer agencies and about 1 million women worked in industry in 1917–1918. The woman-suffrage movement sped toward victory on a tide of wartime idealism. By overwhelming margins, Congress passed a woman-suffrage amendment to the Constitution in 1919. This Nineteenth Amendment was ratified in 1920.

But hopes that the war would permanently improve women's status proved unfounded. Relatively few women actually *entered* the work force for the first time in 1917–1918; most simply moved from poorly paying jobs to better-paying positions. And even those in better-paying jobs generally earned less than the men whom they replaced. As soon as the war ended, moreover, women lost their jobs to make room for the returning troops. The New York labor federation stated, "The same patriotism which induced women to enter industry during the war should induce them to vacate their positions after the war."

Despite the short-lived spurt in employment during the war, the percentage of working women fell slightly from 1910 to 1920. As industrial researcher Mary Van Kleeck wrote, when "the immediate dangers" ended, traditional male attitudes "came to life once more." The dark underside of the war spirit—prejudice, intolerance, conformism—demonstrated remarkable tenacity in peace; positive effects such as the beginning of gender equality in the workplace were more fleeting.

Public Health Crisis: The 1918 Influenza Epidemic

Amid battlefield casualties and home-front social changes, the nation coped with influenza, a highly contagious viral infection often complicated by pneumonia. The 1918 epidemic killed as many as 50 million people worldwide.

Moving northward from its origins in southern Africa, the epidemic spread from the war zone in France to U.S. military camps and quickly advanced to the urban population. The flu hit the cities hard. In Philadelphia on September 19, the day after 200,000 people had turned out for a Liberty Loan rally, 635 new influenza cases were reported. Many cities forbade all public gatherings. The worst came in October, when the flu killed 195,000 Americans. The total U.S. death toll was about 550,000, more than six times the total of AEF battle deaths in France.

The War and Progressivism

Exploring the war's impact on progressive reform, historians find a mixed picture. Without question, in the long run the war stifled reform energies and ushered in a decade of repression. During the war, socialists and dissenters endured hostility and persecution. And while the war brought increased corporate regulation, a long-sought progressive goal, wartime regulatory agencies were often dominated by the same business interests they supposedly supervised.

Yet the war also clearly benefited some reform causes. The woman-suffrage campaign prospered, as did the movement to better the lot of the industrial worker. The War Labor Board pushed for greater unionization and for an eight-hour workday, which became standard by the war's end. Social-justice progressives pressed for reforms that would promote social stability and industrial efficiency, both war-related goals. Under pressure from the War Labor Board and the War Department, several states banned child labor, set wage and hour rules, and enacted various protections and benefits for factory laborers. This flurry of social-justice reform activity quieted with the return of peace, but the laws remained on the books as precedents for future reform efforts.

The war strengthened the coercive, moral-reform component of the progressive movement, including the drive for prohibition. Prohibitionists pointed out that most of the nation's biggest breweries bore such German names as Pabst, Schlitz, and Anheuser-Busch. Beer, they hinted, was part of a German plot to undermine the United States' moral fiber and fighting qualities. Furthermore, the use of grain to manufacture whiskey and gin seemed unpatriotic. The Eighteenth Amendment, which banned the manufacture, transportation, and sale of alcoholic beverages, passed in December 1917. It drew wide support as a war measure.

The war also strengthened the antiprostitution movement and encouraged strict sexual morality. The War Department closed all brothels near military bases, and Congress appropriated $4 million to combat prostitution and sexually transmitted disease on the home front. Among the red-light districts closed on military orders was New Orleans's famed Storyville. Many jazz musicians who had been performing in Storyville's brothels and clubs moved up the Mississippi, carrying their music to Memphis, St. Louis, and Chicago. Thus, ironically, the moral reformism of World War I contributed to the diffusion of jazz northward.

Despite some wartime gains, in the long run the war severely retarded the social-justice, prolabor side of progressivism. A reform coalition of progressives, trade unionists, and a handful of socialists had rallied behind Wilson to support a cluster of prolabor laws in 1916. However, wartime repression of radicals and antiwar dissenters fractured this coalition. In 1918 conservative Republicans gained control of both houses of Congress. Not until the 1930s would the reform coalition foreshadowed in 1916 again emerge as a potent political force.

Joyous Armistice, Bitter Aftermath, 1918–1920

In November 1918 the war that had battered Europe for more than four years ground to a halt. Woodrow Wilson took the lead at the peace conference, but he failed in his cherished objective of securing American membership in the League of Nations. At home, racism and intolerance worsened. In the election of 1920, Americans repudiated Wilsonianism and sent conservative Republican Warren G. Harding to the White House.

Wilson's Fourteen Points; The Armistice

President Wilson planned to put a "Made in America" stamp on the peace. American involvement, he believed, could transform a sordid power conflict into something higher and finer—a crusade for a new, more democratic world order.

As the nation had mobilized in 1917, Wilson had striven to translate his vision into specific war aims. The need had grown urgent after Lenin's Bolsheviks seized power in Russia late in 1917 and published many of the self-serving secret treaties signed by the European powers before 1914.

In his Fourteen Points speech to Congress in January 1918, Wilson summed up U.S. war aims. Eight points dealt with territorial settlement in postwar Europe, underscoring Wilson's belief in self-determination and autonomy for peoples formerly ruled by the Austro-Hungarian or the Ottoman empires. A ninth point insisted that colonial disputes be resolved in the interests of the colonial peoples as well as of the European powers. The remaining five points revealed Wilson's larger vision: a world of free navigation, lowered trade barriers, reduced armaments, openly negotiated treaties, and "a general association of nations" to ensure peace and resolve conflicts by negotiation. The Fourteen Points helped to solidify U.S. support for the war, especially among liberals. Such generous and high-minded goals proved that the nation had gone to war for noble objectives. Whether Wilson could achieve his goals remained to be seen.

With the failure of Germany's spring 1918 offensive, and with Allied advances on several fronts, German military leaders acknowledged the inevitable. In early October they proposed to Wilson an armistice based on the Fourteen Points. The British and French hesitated, but in early November they agreed to peace. Meanwhile, political turmoil in Berlin led to the abdication of Kaiser Wilhelm II and the proclamation of a German republic.

As dawn broke over the Forest of Compiègne on November 11, 1918, Marshal Foch and his German counterparts, seated in Foch's private railroad car, signed the armistice. Word spread swiftly: hostilities would cease at 11:00 a.m. As the booming guns fell silent, French, British, American, and German men cautiously approached each other. Rockets burst over the front that night in celebration. Back home, cheering throngs filled the streets. "Everything for which America has fought has been accomplished," Wilson's armistice message stated hopefully.

The Versailles Peace Conference, 1919

The challenge of forging a peace treaty remained. Wilson opted personally to lead the U.S. delegation to the peace conference. This decision was probably a mistake, for Wilson's oratorical skills outstripped his talent for negotiation and compromise. The president compounded his mistake by selecting only one Republican peace commissioner, an elderly diplomat. In the November 1918 congressional elections, Republicans gained control of both houses of Congress, an ominous sign for Wilson.

Wilson received a hero's welcome in Europe. Shouts of "Voodrow Veelson" rang out in Paris as Wilson and the French president headed a parade up the Champs-Elysées, the city's elegant ceremonial boulevard. When Wilson reached Britain, children spread flowers in his path, and in Italy an exuberant official compared his visit to the Second Coming of Jesus Christ.

The euphoria evaporated when the peace conference began on January 18, 1919, at the palace of Versailles near Paris. A Council of Four, comprising the Allied heads of state, dominated the proceedings: Wilson; Italy's Vittorio Orlando; the aged and cynical Georges Clemenceau of France, determined to avenge Germany's humiliating defeat of France in 1871; and David Lloyd George of Great Britain, of whom Wilson said, "He is slippery as an eel, and I never know when to count on him."

These European leaders represented bitter, vindictive nations that had suffered horrendously in the war. Their objectives bore little relationship to Wilson's vision of a liberal peace. As Clemenceau remarked, "God gave us the Ten Commandments and we broke them. Mr. Wilson has given us the Fourteen Points. We shall see." The squabbling among the Allies became intense. Wilson's negotiating position deteriorated in the spring of 1919 after an attack of influenza left him weak and debilitated.

Mirroring this poisonous political climate, the peace treaty signed by a sullen German delegation on June 28, 1919, was harshly punitive. Germany was disarmed, stripped of its colonies, forced to admit sole blame for the war, and saddled with unspecified but potentially enormous reparation payments. In all, Germany lost one-tenth of its population and one-eighth of its territory.

Planting the seeds of future conflict, the treaty makers rejected the efforts of many colonized peoples to free themselves from European rule. For example, Ho Chi Minh, a young Vietnamese nationalist who would later lead his country, visited Versailles in an unsuccessful effort to secure Vietnamese independence from the French.

Wilson's idealism influenced some of the treaty's provisions. Germany's former colonies, as well as those of Turkey in the Middle East, went to various Allies under a trusteeship system by which they eventually, in theory, would become independent. The treaty recognized the independence of Poland; the Baltic states of Estonia, Latvia, and Lithuania, which Germany had seized from Bolshevik Russia; and two new nations, Czechoslovakia and Yugoslavia, carved from the former Austro-Hungarian and Ottoman empires.

On balance, the Versailles treaty was a disaster. Its provisions fed festering resentment in Germany. Its framers, moreover, failed to come to terms with revolutionary Russia. Even as the treaty makers devised territorial settlements in eastern Europe that were designed to keep Russia as weak as possible, the Allies found themselves embroiled in the Russian civil war.

Indeed, in August 1918 a fourteen-nation Allied force had landed in Russian ports in Europe and Asia. The troops soon began assisting the counter-revolutionaries (including both democrats and tsarists) fighting to overthrow Lenin. Wilson approved of American participation. He had welcomed the liberal revolution of March 1917 but viewed Lenin's seizure of power in November 1917 as a betrayal of the Allied cause and of his hopes for a liberal Russian future.

Before leaving Versailles, the Allied leaders agreed to support a Russian military leader, Admiral Aleksandr Kolchak, who was waging an ultimately unsuccessful campaign against the Bolsheviks. Historian David Fogelsong's work makes clear that the Wilson administration played a leading role in the effort to destroy the Bolshevik regime. Not until 1933 would the United States open formal diplomatic relations with the Soviet Union.

The Fight over the League of Nations

Dismayed by the treaty's vindictive features, Wilson increasingly focused on his one shining achievement at Versailles: the League of Nations. The League, whose charter, or "covenant," was written into the treaty itself, represented the highest embodiment of Wilson's vision of a liberal, harmonious, and rational world order.

But Wilson's dream soon lay shattered. Warning signs appeared as early as February 1919, when several leading Republicans, including Senate Majority Leader Henry Cabot Lodge, expressed serious doubts about the League. Wilson told them defiantly, "You cannot dissect the Covenant from the treaty without destroying the whole vital structure."

When Wilson submitted the Versailles treaty to the Senate for ratification, Lodge bottled it up for weeks in the Foreign Relations Committee. Convinced that he could rally popular opinion, Wilson began a speaking tour in early September. He covered more than 9,000 miles and gave thirty-seven speeches in twenty-two days. Large, friendly crowds cheered Wilson's ideal of a world free of war.

But the grueling trip took a terrible toll. On September 25, outside Pueblo, Colorado, Wilson collapsed. Rushed back to Washington, he suffered a major stroke on October 2. Despite a partial recovery, he spent most of the rest of his term in bed or in a wheelchair, a reclusive invalid, his mind clouded, his fragile emotions betraying him into vengeful actions and petulant outbursts. Wilson's strong-willed second wife, Edith Galt, played a highly manipulative role during these difficult months. Fiercely guarding her husband, she and his doctor concealed his condition, controlled his access to information, and decided who could see him and who could not.

The final act of the League drama played itself out. Senators split into three camps: Democrats who supported the Covenant without changes, Republican "Irreconcilables" who opposed the League completely, and Republican "Reservationists," led by Lodge, who demanded significant modifications before they would accept the Covenant. Article 10 of the Covenant, pledging each member nation to preserve the political independence and territorial integrity of all members, concerned the Reservationists. They felt that it infringed on America's freedom of action in foreign affairs and on Congress's right to declare war.

Had Wilson compromised, the Senate would have ratified the treaty and the United States would have joined the League. But the president dug in his heels as his physical and emotional condition aggravated his tendency toward rigidity. He lashed out against the reservations demanded by the Republicans as "a knife thrust at the heart of the treaty." The American people, moreover, did not rise up in support of the League. The wartime reactionary mood persisted and political idealism waned. In November 1919 and again in March 1920, Irreconcilables and Democrats obeying Wilson's orders voted against the treaty that included Lodge's reservations. A president elected amid high popular enthusiasm in 1912, applauded when he called for war in 1917, and adulated when he arrived in Europe in 1918, lay isolated and sick, his political leadership repudiated. What should have been Wilson's supreme triumph turned to ashes in his grasp.

Racism and Red Scare, 1919–1920

The wartime spirit of "100 percent Americanism" left an acrid aftertaste as 1919–1920 saw racial violence and fresh antiradical hysteria. Lynch mobs murdered seventy-six African-Americans in 1919, including ten military veterans, several still in uniform. The bloodiest disorder occurred in 1919 in Chicago, where an influx of southern African-Americans had intensified tensions. On a hot July afternoon, whites at a Lake Michigan beach threw stones at a black youth swimming offshore. He sank and drowned. A thirteen-day reign of terror followed as white and black marauders roamed the streets, randomly attacked innocent victims, and torched buildings. The violence left 15 whites and 23 blacks dead and more than 500 injured.

Wartime antiradical panic, reinforced by the fear and hatred of bolshevism, crested in the Red Scare of 1919–1920. Such emotions deepened as a rash of strikes broke out, representing an accumulation of grievances. When Seattle's labor unions organized an orderly general work stoppage early in 1919, the mayor accused the strikers of trying to "duplicate the anarchy of Russia" and called for federal troops. In April mail bombs were sent to various public officials. One blew off the hands of a senator's maid, and another damaged the U.S. attorney general's home.

The mounting frenzy over supposed radicals took political form. In November 1919 the House of Representatives refused to seat Milwaukee socialist Victor Berger. The New York legislature expelled several socialist members. The Justice Department established a countersubversive division under young J. Edgar Hoover, the future head of the Federal Bureau of Investigation, who arrested hundreds of suspected communists and aliens. In December 1919, 249 Russian-born aliens were deported.

On January 20, 1920, the Justice Department coordinated federal marshals and local police in raids on the homes of suspected radicals and the headquarters of radical organizations. Without search or arrest warrants, authorities arrested more than 4,000 people and ransacked homes and offices. These lightning raids grossly violated civil rights and simple decency. Marshals barged into one woman's bedroom to arrest her. In Lynn, Massachusetts, police arrested thirty-nine men and women meeting to discuss forming a cooperative bakery. The rabidly antiradical and politically ambitious attorney general, A. Mitchell Palmer, coordinated these "Red raids." Palmer had succumbed to the anticommunist hysteria of the early postwar period. He ominously predicted a "blaze of revolution . . . sweeping over every American institution of law and order . . . crawling into the sacred corners of American homes . . . burning up the foundations of society." The Red Scare subsided as Palmer's irrational predictions failed to materialize. When a bomb exploded in New York City's financial district in September 1920, killing thirty-eight people, most Americans concluded that it was the work of an isolated fanatic rather than evidence of an approaching revolution.

The Election of 1920

In this disturbing climate, the nation prepared for the election of 1920. The Democrats, meeting in San Francisco, half-heartedly endorsed Wilson's League

The Election of 1920

Candidates	Parties	Electoral Vote	Popular Vote	Percentage of Popular Vote
Warren G. Harding	Republican	404	16,143,407	60.4
James M. Cox	Democratic	127	9,130,328	34.2
Eugene V. Debs	Socialist		919,799	3.4
P. P. Christensen	Farmer-Labor		265,411	1.0

Chronology

1905	President Theodore Roosevelt mediates the end of the Russo-Japanese War.
1906	San Francisco ends segregation of Asian schoolchildren.
1907	Roosevelt sends the "Great White Fleet" around the world.
1912	U.S. Marines occupy Nicaragua.
1914	U.S. troops occupy Vera Cruz, Mexico. Archduke Franz Ferdinand of Austria assassinated. World War I begins. Wilson protests British interception of U.S. merchant ships.
1915	U.S. Marines occupy Haiti and the Dominican Republic. Woman's Peace party organized. British liner *Lusitania* sunk by German U-boat. U.S. "preparedness" movement begins. Germany restricts U-boat campaign. Wilson permits U.S. bank loans to Allies.
1916	U.S. punitive expedition invades Mexico, seeking Pancho Villa. After *Sussex* sinking, Germany pledges not to attack merchant ships without warning. Wilson reelected as president.
1917	Germany resumes unrestricted U-boat warfare; United States breaks diplomatic relations. United States enters the war. Selective Service Act sets up national draft. War Industries Board, Committee on Public Information, and Food Administration created. Espionage Act passed. NAACP march in New York City. Bolsheviks grab power in Russia; Russia leaves the war. U.S. government seizes the nation's railroads.
1918	Wilson outlines Fourteen Points for peace. Sedition Amendment to Espionage Act. American Expeditionary Force (AEF) helps stop Germans at Château-Thierry and Belleau Wood, closes St. Mihiel salient, and plays key role in the Meuse-Argonne campaign. Armistice signed (November 11).
1919	Eighteenth Amendment added to the Constitution. Peace treaty, including League of Nations covenant, signed at Versailles. Racial violence in Chicago. Wilson suffers paralyzing stroke. Versailles treaty, with League covenant, rejected by Senate.
1920	"Red raids" organized by Justice Department. Nineteenth Amendment added to the Constitution. Warren G. Harding elected president.

position and nominated James M. Cox, the progressive governor of Ohio. They chose as Cox's running mate the young assistant secretary of the navy, Franklin D. Roosevelt, who possessed a potent political name. The confident Republicans turned to Senator Warren G. Harding of Ohio, an amiable politician with few discernable qualifications beyond a lack of enemies. One Republican politician observed, "There ain't any first raters this year. . . . We got a lot of second raters, and Harding is the best of the second raters." For vice president they chose Governor Calvin Coolidge of Massachusetts.

Wilson declared the election a "solemn referendum" on the League, but the nation was spiritually spent, both by the war and by the emotional roller-coaster ride from lofty idealism to cynical disillusionment on which Wilson had taken it. Sensing the popular longing for calm, Harding promised a return to "normalcy." There would be no more idealistic crusades, no more cavalcades of reforms.

Harding and Coolidge piled up a landslide, winning 16 million votes to the Democrats' 9 million. Nearly a million voters defiantly cast their ballots for Socialist Eugene V. Debs, serving time in an Atlanta penitentiary.

The election dashed all hope for American entry into the League of Nations. Harding announced that the question of U.S. membership in the League was "dead." Two decades of reform at home and idealism abroad thus came to an abrupt, embittered end. The sense of national destiny and high purpose that Woodrow Wilson had evoked so eloquently in 1917 survived only as an ironic memory. Americans impatiently turned to a new president, a new decade, and a new era.

CONCLUSION 🎧 ACE Practice Test

The early twentieth century saw intensifying U.S. involvement abroad, reflecting the economic and cultural forces that were reshaping American society. This new globalism initially focused on Latin America and Asia, but after 1914 it centered on the European war, which became an American war as well in 1917.

By conservative estimate, the First World War cost 10 million dead and 20 million wounded worldwide. Included in this staggering toll were 112,000 Americans—49,000 killed in combat, the rest dead of influenza and other diseases.

The war's social, political, economic, and technological impact extended far beyond the battlefield. Many of the technologies of slaughter that would dominate in the rest of the century emerged: torpedoes, bombs, toxic gases, and deadly efficient machine guns. The war furthered the goals of some reformers, particularly the advocates of woman suffrage and prohibition. As a result of war mobilization, government expanded its regulatory power over corporations and took steps to ensure war workers' well-being and efficiency. Ultimately, however, the war undermined the progressive movement's commitment to social justice and its humanitarian concern for the underdog. When Americans repudiated Wilsonian idealism after the war, they also rejected reform. Internationally, the conflict propelled the United States to the center of world politics and left the nation's businesses and financial institutions poised for global expansion.

Some of these changes endured; others were fleeting. Their cumulative effect was profound. The United States that celebrated the armistice in November 1918 was a very different society from the one that Wilson had summoned to war only nineteen months earlier.

FURTHER READING

John M. Barry, *The Great Influenza* (2004). An exhaustive study of the worldwide epidemic, focusing primarily on the United States.

Nancy K. Bristow, *Making Men Moral: Social Engineering During the Great War* (1996). Perceptive study of the Commission on Training Camp Activities.

Robert H. Ferrell, *Woodrow Wilson and World War I, 1917–1921* (1985). A vigorously written critical synthesis; especially good on the peace negotiations.

Martin Gilbert, *The First World War: A Complete History* (1994). Weak on strategy, but vividly conveys the grim experience of ordinary soldiers.

Meiron and Susan Harries, *The Last Days of Innocence: America at War, 1917–1918* (1998). Readable and well-researched overview history of both the military and the home-front aspects of the war.

David M. Kennedy, *Over Here: The First World War and American Society* (1980). Deeply researched interpretive study of the home front during the war.

Thomas J. Knock, *To End All Wars: World War I and the Quest for a New World Order* (1992). A compelling study of the origins of Wilson's internationalism and of the links between domestic reform and foreign policy.

Margaret Macmillan, *Paris 1919: Six Months That Changed the World* (2003). A balanced study of the Versailles negotiations and their complexity.

Ronald Schaffer, *America in the Great War: The Rise of the War Welfare State* (1991). Explores the war's effect on corporate organization and business-government links as well as wartime initiatives to benefit industrial workers.

23

The 1920s: Coping with Change, 1920–1929

hc This icon will direct you to additional study and research resources at http://college.hmco.com/history/us/boyer/enduring_concise/5e/students/index.html

A Pleasure-Mad Decade, 1925

When Sam Groipen of Medford, Massachusetts, saw the meat truck pull up to the A&P supermarket next door, he knew that his days as an independent grocer were numbered. For five years his small grocery, which he and his wife operated, had prospered; they knew their customers and even extended credit to them. But then the chain stores arrived; at first the A&P carried only brand-name groceries, not meat or fish. But Sam understood all too clearly that when the A&P began to carry meat, his business was doomed. "I felt like I was being strangled," he recalled; "those bastard chains were destroying me."

Sam Groipen's experience reflected the economic changes that were overtaking the United States in the 1920s. The American engine of mass production and mass consumption was gaining speed with every passing day.

A NEW ECONOMIC ORDER

With consumer products aplenty, sophisticated advertising, and innovative forms of corporate organization, the economy raced forward in the 1920s. Some key industries declined, and farmers relapsed into chronic economic problems. Still, the overall picture seemed rosy, and most Americans celebrated the nation's thriving business culture.

Booming Business, Ailing Agriculture

The war-induced boom continued until late 1920, when demobilization disrupted the economy. As the government canceled contracts and as veterans swamped labor markets, a recession struck. Business slowed, bankruptcies increased, and unemployment jumped. Recovery came in 1922, and, for the next few years, the economy grew spectacularly. Unemployment dropped as low as 3 percent, prices held steady, and gross national product climbed from $70 billion in 1922 to nearly $100 billion in 1929. By mid-decade the 1920–1922 recession seemed only a minor setback.

Electricity powered the general prosperity. Factories had started to electrify late in the nineteenth century, and by now the construction of hydroelectric generating plants had brought the age of electricity to urban households as well. By the mid-1920s, with more than 60 percent of the nation's homes wired for electricity, a wondrous array of electrical appliances—refrigerators, ranges, washing machines, vacuum cleaners, fans, razors, and mixers—stood gleaming in the stores. Their manufacture provided a potent economic stimulus.

The era's business boom also rested on the automobile. Registrations jumped from 8 million in 1920 to more than 23 million in 1930, when 60 percent of U.S. families owned cars. Ford's Model T led

This chapter focuses on five major questions:

▶ What economic developments underlay the prosperity of the 1920s? How did these affect different social groups?

▶ What were the political values of this period of Republican ascendancy?

▶ How did the Republican administrations of the 1920s promote U.S. economic interests abroad?

▶ What is "mass culture"? How did mass culture arise in the 1920s?

▶ Cultural creativity and social tensions characterized the 1920s. What developments contributed to both creativity and tension?

the market until mid-decade, when General Motors Corporation (GM) spurted ahead by touting a range of colors (the Model T came only in black) and improved passenger comfort. Particularly popular was GM's lowest-price car, named for automotive designer Louis Chevrolet. In response, in 1927 Ford introduced the stylish Model A in a spectrum of colors. By the end of the decade, the automobile industry accounted for 9 percent of all wages in manufacturing and had stimulated such related industries as rubber, gasoline and petroleum, advertising, and highway construction.

American capitalism remained vigorously expansionist. Ford, GM, General Electric, and other large corporations invested heavily in production facilities abroad. Other U.S. firms acquired foreign processing facilities or sources of raw materials. Swift and Armour built meatpacking plants in Argentina; Anaconda Copper acquired Chile's biggest copper mine; and the mammoth United Fruit Company established processing factories throughout Latin America. By 1930 U.S. private investment abroad totaled more than $15 billion.

The era of multinational corporations and thriving international trade still lay in the future. In the 1920s high tariff barriers, the result of economic nationalism, stifled such trade, and U.S. exports as a percentage of the gross national product actually fell. Domestically, however, U.S. industry flexed its muscles and organized for mass consumer production. Manufactured goods, less than half the value of U.S. exports in 1913, rose to 61 percent by the end of the twenties.

The 1920s brought hard times for farmers. Dwindling military purchases and the revival of European agriculture sent prices plummeting. In the period 1919–1921 total farm income fell from $10 billion to $4 billion. Increased production lowered prices even more. The real annual earnings of full-time agricultural workers fell in 1921 and barely inched up for the rest of the decade. Farmers who had borrowed heavily to boost their harvests during the war found themselves unable to pay off loans and mortgages.

New Modes of Producing, Managing, and Selling

In the 1920s assembly-line mass production boosted the per capita output of industrial workers by 40 percent. At the sprawling Ford plants near Detroit, workers stood in one place and performed simple, repetitive tasks as an endless chain conveyed the partly assembled vehicles past them. The technique quickly spread, and *Fordism* became a worldwide synonym for American industrial prowess.

Corporate consolidation continued. By 1930 more than 1,000 companies a year were disappearing through merger. Corporate giants dominated major industries: Ford, GM, and Chrysler in automobiles; General Electric and Westinghouse in electricity; U.S. Steel in the steel industry. Consolidation reached epidemic proportions in public utilities. Samuel Insull of the Chicago Edison Company built an empire of local power companies that by 1929 had assets of $3.5 billion. At the decade's end, 100 corporations controlled nearly half the nation's business activity. Where there were no merg-

ers, companies that made the same product often cooperated on such matters as pricing, product specifications, and division of markets.

Streamlined operations resulted in a more bureaucratic management structure within individual businesses. Like the federal government, corporations nationalized their management in the twenties, establishing specialized divisions for product development, market research, economic forecasting, and employee relations. Professionals trained in management oversaw the day-to-day operations within this new corporate structure.

Wage policies also began to change. Some business leaders argued that employers should not necessarily pay the lowest wages possible; higher wages, they suggested, would generate higher productivity. Henry Ford led the way in 1914 by paying his workers an unprecedented five dollars a day, and other companies followed his lead in the 1920s.

In addition, new systems for distributing goods emerged. Automobiles now reached consumers through vast dealer networks; nearly 10,000 Ford dealerships had sprung up by 1926. A rapidly expanding network of chain stores accounted for about a quarter of all retail sales by 1930. The A&P grocery chain expanded from 5,000 stores in 1922 to 17,500 in 1928. Air conditioning, a new invention, made department stores (as well as movie theaters and restaurants) welcome havens on hot summer days. By 1929, 75 percent of automobiles were bought on credit, and other big-ticket items were increasingly bought on credit as well.

Above all, the 1920s business boom bobbed along on a sea of advertising. In 1919 corporations spent an estimated $1.8 billion promoting their wares. The advertising industry employed 600,000 people. Radio, the newest of the mass media, relied entirely on advertising for its income.

Advertisers used celebrity endorsements ("Nine out of ten screen stars care for their skin with Lux toilet soap"), promises of social success, and threats of social embarrassment. Beneath a picture of a pretty but obviously unhappy young woman, a 1923 Listerine mouthwash ad proclaimed,

> She was a beautiful girl and talented too. She had the advantages of education and better clothes

than most girls of her set. She possessed that culture and poise that travel brings. Yet in the one pursuit that stands foremost in the mind of every girl and woman—marriage—she was a failure.

The young woman's problem was *halitosis,* a hitherto little-known term for bad breath. The remedy, of course, was Listerine, and lots of it.

Beyond touting specific products, advertisers redefined popular aspirations by offering a seductive vision of a new era of consumption. Ads for automobiles, cigarettes, electrical conveniences, clothing, and home furnishings created a fantasy world of elegance, grace, and boundless pleasure.

Business influenced life in the 1920s. A 1921 article summed up the mood: "Among the nations of the earth today America stands for one idea: Business. . . . Thru business, properly conceived, managed, and conducted, the human race is finally to be redeemed." Americans venerated the magnates of business and the new world of material progress they had created. In *The Man Nobody Knows* (1925), ad man Bruce Barton, the son of a Protestant minister, described Jesus Christ as a managerial genius who "picked up twelve men from the bottom ranks of business and forged them into an organization that conquered the world." Observed sociologists Robert and Helen Lynd: "More and more of the activities of life are coming to be strained through the bars of the dollar sign."

🎧 Primary Source: Henry Ford Discusses Manufacturing and Marketing

Women in the New Economic Era

In the decade's ubiquitous advertising, glamorous women smiled behind the steering wheel and happily operated electric appliances. The cosmetics industry flourished, offering women, in the words of one historian, "hope in a jar." Housework became an exciting technological challenge. As one ad said, "Men are judged successful according to their power to delegate work. Similarly the wise woman delegates to electricity all that electricity can do."

In the workplace the assembly line, offering less physically demanding work, should in theory have increased job opportunities for women. In fact, however, the assembly-line work force remained largely male. Although the number of women holding jobs increased by more than 2 million in the twenties, the *proportion* of women working outside the home remained unchanged, at 24 percent. The weakening of the union movement in the 1920s proved especially hard on women workers. By the end of the decade, a minuscule 3 percent of women workers belonged to unions. Wage discrimination continued. In 1929 a male trimmer in the meatpacking industry earned fifty-two cents an hour; a female trimmer, thirty-seven cents an hour.

Corporate bureaucratization increased female employment opportunities. By 1930, 2 million women were working as secretaries, typists, and filing clerks. Few became managers, however. In the professions, women worked in the limited spheres of nursing, librarianship, social work, and public-school teaching. As medical schools imposed a ceiling of 5 percent on female admissions, the number of women physicians declined.

The proportion of female high-school graduates attending college grew from 8 percent to 12 percent during the decade, and nearly 50,000 women received college degrees in 1930. More married women entered the work force, primarily in clerical jobs, in the lower ranks of business, or in traditional "women's professions" such as nursing, social work, and teaching. A handful followed Progressive Era trailblazers to become researchers and scholars in colleges and universities. As today, most found juggling marriage and a career difficult.

Struggling Labor Unions in a Business Age

The labor movement faced tough sledding in the twenties. Several factors led to dwindling union membership, from 5 million in 1920 to 3.4 million in 1929. Overall wage rates crept upward in the 1920s. Despite continuing workplace inequities, employees' fatter pay envelopes helped to undermine the union movement. So did changes in the industrial process. The trade unions' traditional strength lay in established industries such as printing, railroading, and construction. This craft-based pattern of union organization was ill suited to the new mass-production industries.

Management hostility further weakened organized labor. Sometimes this antagonism took physical form, as when Henry Ford hired thugs and spies to intimidate would-be organizers. Typically, however, the anti-union campaign was subtler. Manufacturers' associations renamed the nonunion shop the "open shop" and praised it as the "American Plan" of labor relations. Some companies sponsored their own "unions" and provided cafeterias, better rest rooms, and recreational facilities. Certain big corporations sold company stock to their workers at special prices.

Some corporate leaders heralded this new approach to labor relations as evidence of heightened ethical awareness in American business. General Electric's head insisted that workers' well-being stood second only to productivity in GE's hierarchy of values. Welfare capitalism, as this corporate paternalism was called, was intended to prevent the formation of independent unions.

Black membership in unions remained low. Although the American Federation of Labor (AFL) officially prohibited racial discrimination, the independent unions composing the AFL barred African-Americans from membership. Corporations' hiring of African-Americans as strikebreakers further increased organized labor's hostility toward them.

African-Americans, women, Mexican-Americans, and recent immigrants clustered at the bottom of the wage scale. African-American workers entering the industrial labor force, last hired and first fired, typically performed the most menial jobs. Amid the general prosperity, wages for unskilled workers barely budged.

THE HARDING AND COOLIDGE ADMINISTRATIONS

Politics in the 1920s reflected the decade's business orientation. Republicans controlled Congress and supplied presidents who mirrored the prevailing corporate outlook. In this atmosphere, former progressives and feminists faced difficult times.

Stand Pat Politics in a Decade of Change

In the 1920s the Republicans relied on a base of northern farmers, corporate leaders, small businesspeople, and skilled workers. The Democrats' base remained the white South and the urban political machines.

The conservatives who controlled the 1920 Republican convention selected Senator Warren G. Harding of Ohio as their nominee. A former newspaper editor and a genial backslapper, Harding enjoyed good liquor, good stories, poker with his cronies, and furtive encounters with his mistress. Yet this amiable second-rater won the presidency in a landslide (see Chapter 22). Harding's ordinariness appealed to war-weary voters longing for stability. Compared to Wilson's lofty sermons, Harding's vacuous oratory had a soothing appeal.

Realizing his lack of qualifications, Harding compensated by making some notable appointments: Henry A. Wallace, the respected editor of a farm periodical, became secretary of agriculture; Charles Evans Hughes, a former New York governor and presidential candidate, was named secretary of state; and Andrew Mellon, a Pittsburgh banker and financier, served as treasury secretary. Wartime food administrator Herbert Hoover dominated the cabinet as secretary of commerce. Unfortunately, Harding made some disastrous appointments as well, including Harry Daugherty, his political manager, as attorney general; Albert B. Fall, New Mexico senator, as secretary of the interior; and Charles Forbes, a wartime draft dodger, as director of the Veterans' Bureau. These men draped the Harding years in an aura of back-room sleaze reminiscent of the Grant administration.

By 1922 Washington rumor hinted at criminal activity in high places. Dismayed, Harding confessed, "I have no trouble with my enemies. . . . But . . . my goddamn friends . . . , they're the ones that keep me walking the floor nights." In 1923, returning from an Alaskan cruise, Harding suffered a heart attack and died in San Francisco.

In 1924 a Senate investigation exposed the full scope of the scandals. Charles Forbes, convicted of stealing Veterans' Bureau funds, evaded prison by fleeing abroad. The bureau's general counsel committed suicide, as did an associate of Attorney General Daugherty who had been accused of influence peddling. Daugherty himself, forced from office in 1924, escaped conviction in two criminal trials. The seamiest scandal involved Interior Secretary Fall, who went to jail for secretly leasing government oil reserves in Elk Hills, California, and Teapot Dome, Wyoming, to two oilmen while accepting "loans" from them totaling $400,000. "Teapot Dome" became shorthand, like "Watergate" in the 1970s, for an entire presidential legacy of scandal.

Vice President Calvin Coolidge learned of Harding's death while visiting his family in Vermont. His father, a local magistrate, administered the presidential oath by lantern light. Coolidge brought a distinctly different style to the White House. His determined silence contrasted with Harding's chattiness. Once as he left California, a radio reporter asked for a parting message to the people of the state. "Good-bye," Coolidge responded.

Republican Policymaking in a Probusiness Era

Other than in style, Coolidge's advent meant little change. Tariff rates reached all-time highs, income taxes for the rich fell, and the Supreme Court overturned several progressive measures. Coolidge rejected a request for aid from Mississippi flood victims with the reminder that government had no duty to protect citizens "against the hazards of the elements." (Coolidge did, however, reluctantly sign the Flood Control Act of 1928 and appropriate $325 million for a ten-year program to construct levees along the Mississippi.)

In his 1927 veto of the McNary-Haugen farm bill, introduced in 1924, Coolidge warned against the "tyranny of bureaucratic regulation and control" and denounced the bill for benefiting farmers

at the expense of "the general public welfare." Although his party had long championed high tariffs and other measures of benefit to business, Coolidge balked when farmers pursued the same kind of special-interest politics.

Independent Internationalism

Although the United States participated informally in some League of Nations activities in the 1920s, the country refused to join the League or the World Court. Nonetheless, the United States remained a world power, and Republican presidents pursued what they saw as the national interest—an approach historians have called independent internationalism.

President Harding's most notable achievement was the Washington Naval Arms Conference. To head off an expensive international naval-arms race, Harding called for a conference. When the delegates of various nations met in October 1921, Secretary of State Hughes startled them by proposing the destruction of ships to achieve an agreed-upon ratio of craft among the world's naval powers. Consequently, in February 1924 five nations—Great Britain, the United States, Japan, France, and Italy—signed a treaty pledging to reduce battleship tonnage and to observe a ten-year moratorium on battleship construction. The United States and Japan also agreed to respect each other's territorial holdings in the Pacific. Although the treaty did not prevent war, it represented a pioneering arms-control effort.

America otherwise followed an isolationist foreign policy in the 1920s. Symbolic gestures replaced genuine engagement. For example, in 1928 the United States and France cosponsored the Kellogg-Briand Pact renouncing aggression and calling for the outlawing of war. Lacking enforcement mechanisms, the high-sounding document did nothing to prevent World War II.

U.S. insistence on the full repayment of wartime debts generated ill will among former allies. In 1924 a joint commission scaled back U.S. claims on Allied war debts and German reparations, but tariff barriers, European economic problems, and runaway German inflation made payment of even the reduced amount unrealistic.

The government also worked to advance American business interests overseas. A particular concern was Mexico's effort to reclaim oilfields earlier granted to U.S. companies. With Mexico still in the grip of revolution, many worried that it might go communist, a worry underlined by the Mexican decision to recognize the Soviet Union in 1924, nine years before the United States would do so.

Progressive Stirrings, Democratic Party Divisions

In Congress the progressive spirit had survived. Senator George Norris of Nebraska blocked the Coolidge administration from selling a federal hydroelectric facility at Muscle Shoals, Alabama, to Henry Ford. Congress's creation of the Federal Radio Commission (1927) extended to the fledgling broadcasting industry the progressive principle of government regulation of business.

In 1922 labor and farm groups formed the Conference for Progressive Political Action (CPPA), and in 1924 the CPPA revived the Progressive party. It adopted a prolabor, profarmer platform calling for government ownership of railroads and water-power resources and nominated Senator Robert La Follette for president.

Split between urban and rural wings, the Democratic party held its 1924 convention in New York. The extent of the division became evident when a resolution condemning the Ku Klux Klan failed by one vote. Rural Democrats supported William Gibbs McAdoo, Wilson's treasury secretary; urban Democrats backed Governor Alfred E. Smith of New York, an Irish Roman Catholic. Ballot after ballot left both candidates short of the two-thirds majority necessary for nomination. Humorist Will Rogers observed, "This thing has got to end. New York invited you folks here as guests, not to live." After 102 ballots, exhausted delegates turned to a compromise candidate, John W. Davis.

On the Republican side, Coolidge easily won renomination. The GOP platform praised high tariffs and urged tax and spending cuts. With the economy humming and the opposition divided, Coolidge cruised to victory with about 16 million votes. Davis trailed with 8 million votes, and La Follette collected a little under 5 million.

Women and Politics in the 1920s: A Dream Deferred

Suffragists' belief that votes for women would transform politics died quickly after the war. Women did achieve notable gains: states passed laws permitting them to serve on juries and to hold public office, the League of Women Voters emerged, and the Sheppard-Towner Act of 1921 appropriated $1.2 million for rural prenatal and baby-care centers. Beyond these advances, however, the Nineteenth Amendment had little political impact. With the vote attained, women scattered to all points on the political spectrum, and many withdrew from politics completely.

As the women's movement splintered, it lost focus. Drawing mainly middle-class and professional women, the League of Women Voters abandoned reform activism for the study of civic issues. Carrie Chapman Catt and Jane Addams turned their energies to the peace movement. Meanwhile, Alice Paul and her National Woman's party campaigned for an equal-rights amendment to the Constitution, but many feminists condemned her position. Such an amendment could harm female factory workers by jeopardizing gender-based protective legislation. The proposed amendment got nowhere.

Underlying the disarray in women's ranks was the conservative materialistic mass culture of the 1920s. Right-wing groups accused Jane Addams and other women's rights leaders of communist sympathies. Young women, bombarded by advertising that defined liberation in terms of life-style and the purchase of goods, found civic idealism embarrassingly passé.

In this milieu, reforms achieved by organized women's groups often proved short-lived. The Supreme Court struck down child-labor laws (1922) and women's protective laws (1923). A child-labor constitutional amendment squeezed through Congress in 1924 but won ratification in only a few

states. The Sheppard-Towner program of rural pre-
natal and baby care ended in 1929.

MASS SOCIETY, MASS CULTURE

The new consumer products that roared off the assembly lines in the 1920s heralded profound social
and cultural change. These goods and the corporate order and technological processes that produced them would alter America forever. While
some Americans found these steps toward modernity exhilarating, others found them frightening.

Cities, Cars, Consumer Goods

The 1920 census showed that, for the first time,
America's urban population outnumbered its rural
dwellers. The tally recorded a dozen cities of more
than 600,000. African-Americans constituted a major part of the movement to the cities. By 1930
more than 40 percent of the nation's 12 million
African-Americans lived in cities, notably Chicago,
Detroit, New York, and other northern and western
metropolitan centers.

Increasing urbanization reshaped American
culture. The forces that molded culture—radio, the
movies, corporations, advertising agencies, mass
magazines—operated from cities. Even when they
nostalgically evoked rural values, they did so from
big-city editorial offices and radio studios.

New electrical appliances reduced the hours
and sheer physical effort of housework. In 1925,
nearly 75 percent of working women surveyed said
that they spent less time on housework than their
mothers had. Vacuum cleaners supplanted brooms
and carpet beaters, firing up wood stoves became a
memory, and store-bought clothes replaced hand-
made apparel. Urban wives who had relied on commercial laundries began doing their own wash with
the advent of the electric washing machine and
iron. Cooking and eating patterns shifted. The rise
of the supermarket made sharp inroads on the
practice of canning. Commercially baked bread replaced home-baked bread. Refrigeration, supermarkets, and motor transport made fresh fruits and
vegetables available year-round and led to significant improvement in the national diet.

The automobile, however, had the greatest social and cultural impact. Urban planners worriedly
discussed traffic jams, parking problems, and the
mounting accident rate (more than 26,000 Americans died in traffic accidents in 1924). Like electrical appliances, automobiles reached into the lives
of ordinary Americans. Family vacations and long
drives in the country became popular. The automobile diminished the isolation of rural life and
gave farm dwellers easier access to the city for
shopping and entertainment.

Women of the middle and upper classes welcomed the automobile enthusiastically. Stereotypes of feminine delicacy and timidity faded as
women demonstrated confident mastery of this
new technology. As the editor of an automotive
magazine wrote in 1927, "[E]very time a woman
learns to drive—and thousands do every year—it is
a threat at yesterday's order of things."

For farm families, the automobile reduced isolation and eased work; by 1930 nearly a million
tractors were in use, increasing productivity and
lessening heavy physical labor. However, at the
same time farmers went deeper and deeper into
debt to buy such machinery.

Family cohesion suffered from the new mobility. Young people welcomed the freedom from
parental oversight that the car offered. On a whim,
they could drive to a dance in a distant city. Complained one father, "It's getting so a fellow has to
make a date with his family to see them."

The automobile's impact on individuality was
similarly mixed. Car owners could travel where
they wished, when they wished, freed from fixed
routes and schedules. But the automobile also accelerated the standardization of American life. Millions chugged around in identical black vehicles.
The one-room schoolhouse was abandoned as
buses carried children to consolidated schools.
Neighborhood markets declined as people drove
to chain stores. The automobile age brought the
first suburban department stores, the first shopping center (in Kansas City), and the first fast-food
chain (A &W Root Beer).

Yet even at $300 or $400, the automobile remained too expensive for the poor. The "automobile suburbs" that sprang up beyond the streetcar lines attracted the prosperous, but the urban poor remained behind.

Soaring Energy Consumption and a Threatened Environment

The spread of electrical products and motorized vehicles carried a high environmental price tag. Electrical use tripled in the 1920s, consuming vast quantities of coal, oil, and gas. And the 20 million automobiles clogging the nation's highways by 1929 guzzled fuel. As late as 1916, U.S. refineries

Christmas in Consumerland
Giving a modern twist to an ancient symbol, this advertising catalog of the 1920s offered an enticing array of new electric products for the home.

had produced less than 50 million barrels of gasoline; by 1929 gasoline production had catapulted to 435 million barrels.

Domestic oil production rose by 250 percent, triggering feverish activity in the oilfields of Texas, Oklahoma, and elsewhere. Major oil companies such as Standard, Texaco, Gulf, and Atlantic solidified their dominance of the industry.

The wilderness that had inspired nineteenth-century Americans became more accessible as the automobile, improved roads, and tourist facilities opened the national parks and once-pristine regions to easy access. Thousands of motorized tourists rediscovered the land, putting heavy pressure on wilderness areas.

Intense competition for oil bred massive waste. Natural gas, considered almost worthless, was burned off. The heedless consumption of nonrenewable fossil fuels, which would reach massive proportions after World War II, had begun.

The environment suffered in less obvious ways, too. Power plants, steel mills, and automobile engines spewed tons of pollutants into the atmosphere. As ribbons of asphalt and cement snaked across the land, gas stations, billboards, restaurants, and tourist cabins followed. The wilderness that nineteenth-century Americans had so cherished came under heavy siege.

Isolated voices protested. The Sierra Club and the Audubon Society worked to preserve wilderness and wildlife. Aldo Leopold of the U.S. Forest Service warned that for too long "a stump was our symbol of progress." But few listened. To most Americans of the day, energy resources appeared limitless. Pollution and a vanishing wilderness seemed small prices to pay for the radio, the movies, electric appliances, and cars. The confident generation of the 1920s had little time for the environmental issues that would raise alarms two generations later.

Mass-Produced Entertainment

The routinization of work and the increase in disposable income contributed to rising interest in leisure activities in the 1920s. During their free hours workers sought the fulfillment many found missing in the workplace.

Light reading provided diversion. Mass-circulation magazines flourished. By 1922 ten American magazines boasted circulations of more than 2.5 million each. The *Saturday Evening Post,* with its bucolic Norman Rockwell covers and fiction featuring small-town life, specialized in prepackaged nostalgia. In 1921 DeWitt and Lila Wallace founded *Reader's Digest,* which condensed articles originally published elsewhere. The *Digest* served up traditionalist, probusiness views in simple prose. Pitched to the mass market, it represented the journalistic counterpart of the A&P. Bookselling also saw major changes as publishers began marketing their products through department stores and mail-order organizations such as the Book-of-the-Month Club (1924) and the Literary Guild (1926). Often criticized for debasing literary tastes, these ventures helped sustain a common national culture in an increasingly market-driven society.

Radios and movies standardized culture even more dramatically than literature. The radio era began on November 2, 1920, when station KDKA in Pittsburgh broadcast the news of Warren Harding's election. In 1922, 500 new stations went on the air, and by 1927 radio sales approached 7 million sets.

In 1926 three corporations—General Electric, Westinghouse, and the Radio Corporation of America—formed the first radio network, the National Broadcasting Company (NBC). The Columbia Broadcasting System (CBS) followed in 1927, and the networks soon ruled radio broadcasting. From Maine to California, Americans laughed at the same jokes, hummed the same tunes, and absorbed the same commercials. New York's WEAF broadcast the first commercially sponsored program in 1922, and the commercialization of radio proceeded rapidly. The first network comedy show, the popular (and racist) "Amos 'n' Andy" (1928), brought prosperity to its sponsor, Pepsodent toothpaste.

The motion-picture business evolved similarly. Movies, having expanded from the immigrant slums into elegant uptown theaters with names such as "Majestic," "Ritz," and "Palace," attracted audiences from all social levels. After Al Jolson's *The Jazz Singer* (1927) introduced sound, movies became even more popular and spawned a new generation of screen idols, including the western hero Gary Cooper and the aloof Scandinavian beauty Greta Garbo. Mickey Mouse debuted in 1928. By 1930 weekly movie attendance neared 80 million.

Movies transported their viewers to worlds far removed from reality. One movie ad succinctly promised "all the adventure, all the romance, all the excitement you lack in your daily life." The mass-produced fantasies shaped popular behavior and values, especially among the impressionable young. In the words of novelist John Dos Passos, Hollywood offered "a great bargain sale of five-and-ten-cent lusts and dreams."

Influential as it was, the new standardized mass culture penetrated society unevenly. It made scant inroads in much of rural America and met strong resistance among evangelical Christians deeply suspicious of modernity. Mexican-American farm workers preserved their traditional culture despite "Americanization" efforts by non-Hispanic priests and bosses. Local radio stations carried national networks along with local news, ethnic music, and community announcements. Neighborhood movie theaters provided opportunities for conversation, live music, announcements, and occasionally jeering and catcalls directed at the film being shown. In short, despite the mass culture's growing power, American culture remained vividly diverse in the 1920s.

Celebrity Culture

Fads and media-promoted events preoccupied Americans. In 1921 Atlantic City promoted itself with a new bathing-beauty competition, the Miss America Pageant. In 1924 a crossword-puzzle craze consumed the country.

Larger-than-life celebrities emerged in professional sports: Babe Ruth of the New York Yankees; Ty Cobb of the Detroit Tigers; Jack Dempsey and Gene Tunney, whose two heavyweight title fights drew more than 200,000 spectators and millions of radio listeners. When Tunney won the 1927 bout thanks to a famous "long count" by a referee, five radio listeners dropped dead of heart attacks.

The idolization of celebrities illuminates the anxieties and hopes of ordinary Americans in these years. The young woman trying to define her role in a period of confusing social change could find an ideal in beauty pageants. For the man whose sense of mastery had been shaken by developments from feminism to Fordism, cheering himself hoarse for a towering hero like Dempsey or Ruth could momentarily restore a feeling of personal worth.

Charles Lindbergh, "Lucky Lindy," the young pilot who made the first nonstop flight across the Atlantic, illustrates the hero worship of the times. Lindbergh had been a stunt flyer and airmail pilot before he competed for a $25,000 prize offered for the first nonstop New York–Paris flight. Lindbergh's daring flight on May 20–21, 1927, in his silver-winged *Spirit of St. Louis* attracted a blaze of media attention. Radio, newspapers, magazines, and movie newsreels provided saturation coverage. Many Americans saw his flight as evidence that the individual still counted in an era of standardization and mechanization. To conservatives, Lindbergh's solid virtues proved that the old verities survived.

Clearly, the new mass media had mixed social effects. The technologies of mass communication promoted cultural standardization that eroded local and regional diversity. But radio, the movies, and the mass magazines also helped to forge a national culture and introduced fresh viewpoints and new behaviors. Mass media hammered home a powerful message: personal horizons need no longer be limited by one's immediate environment. The spread of mass culture in the 1920s opened up a large world for ordinary Americans. If that world was often vacuous and tawdry, it was also sometimes exciting and inspiring.

CULTURAL FERMENT AND CREATIVITY

Ferment and creativity also characterized the culture of the 1920s. Writers, artists, musicians, and scientists compiled a record of remarkable achievement. African-Americans asserted their pride through the cultural flowering known as the Harlem Renaissance.

The Jazz Age and the Postwar Crisis of Values

The war and its sour aftermath sharpened the cultural restlessness of the prewar years. The postwar crisis of values took many forms. The younger generation, especially college students, boisterously assailed older conventions of behavior. Taking advantage of prosperity and the mobility afforded by the automobile, they partied, drank bootleg liquor, flocked to jazz clubs, and danced the Charleston.

Charles A. Lindbergh and the *Spirit of St. Louis*
In a celebrity-obsessed decade, Lindbergh rocketed to instant fame after his 1927 solo transatlantic flight.

They also discussed sex freely and sometimes indulged in premarital sexual experimentation. Wrote novelist F. Scott Fitzgerald, "None of the Victorian mothers had any idea how casually their daughters were accustomed to be kissed." The ideas of Sigmund Freud, the Viennese physician whose studies of human sexuality first appeared in the 1890s, enjoyed a popular vogue in the 1920s, often in grossly oversimplified form.

But hard evidence for the "sexual revolution" of the 1920s remains skimpy. Premarital sexual activity may have increased, but it was still widely disapproved of. Courtship patterns did change, however. In earlier periods "courting" implied a serious intention of marriage. In the 1920s the informal ritual of "dating" emerged, allowing young people to test compatibility and to gain social confidence without necessarily contemplating marriage.

The double standard, holding women to a stricter code of sexual conduct than men, remained in force. Young men could boast of their sexual activity, but "fast" women might be ostracized. Nonetheless, the 1920s did see some liberation for women. Female sexuality was acknowledged more openly. Skirts grew shorter, makeup (once the badge of the prostitute) appeared, and petticoats and constricting corsets disappeared. A trim, almost boyish figure replaced the Gibson girl as the ideal beauty. Thousands of young women began smoking cigarettes in defiance of convention.

Moral guardians protested these changes. A Methodist bishop denounced the new dances that brought "the bodies of men and women in unusual relation to each other." In 1925 when the president of the women's college Bryn Mawr permitted students to smoke, others were outraged.

The flapper—a sophisticated, fashionable, pleasure-mad young woman—summed up the "flaming youth" of the twenties. The creation of magazine illustrator John Held, Jr., the flapper symbolized an elaborate complex of cultural values. Her bobbed hair, defiant cigarette, dangling beads, heavy make-up, and shockingly short skirt epitomized the rebelliousness that composed at least a part of the youth culture of the twenties.

Like the flapper, the Jazz Age itself—the "Roaring Twenties"—was partially a mass-media and novelistic creation. F. Scott Fitzgerald's romanticized interpretation of the affluent postwar young, *This Side of Paradise* (1920), spawned many imitators. Fitzgerald himself was only twenty-four when his novel of the "lost generation" appeared. With his sculpted good looks, blond hair, and striking green eyes, he both wrote about and personified the Jazz Age. Flush with royalties, he and his wife, Zelda, partied away the early twenties in New York, Paris, and the French Mediterranean. A moralist at heart, Fitzgerald both admired and deplored his Jazz Age contemporaries. In *The Great Gatsby* (1925) he captured not only the gilded existence of the superrich and social climbers of the 1920s but also the cold-hearted selfishness and romantic illusions that ruled their lives.

The upheaval in manners and morals summed up as the "Jazz Age" was limited to a narrow social stratum. Old values did not vanish overnight. Millions of Americans adhered to traditional ways and traditional standards. Millions more—farmers, blacks, industrial workers, recent immigrants—found economic survival more important than the latest dance craze or the newest flapper fads and fashions.

Nonetheless, stereotypes such as the "flapper" and "Jazz Age" do capture the brassy, urban-based mass culture and hedonism that swamped the idealism and social commitment of earlier years. And during the Great Depression of the 1930s, Americans would look back nostalgically to the supposedly carefree Roaring Twenties.

Alienated Writers

Like Fitzgerald, many other young writers found the cultural turbulence of the 1920s stimulating. They forged a remarkable body of work equally hostile to the moralistic pieties of the old order and the business pieties of the new.

Sinclair Lewis's novels skewered postwar America. In *Main Street* (1920) Lewis caustically depicted the cultural barrenness and smug self-satisfaction of a fictional midwestern farm town.

In *Babbitt* (1922) he wielded his satirical scalpel to dissect George F. Babbitt, a middle-aged real-estate agent trapped in stifling middle-class conformity.

Lewis's pen found a journalistic counterpart in the work of H. L. Mencken, a Baltimore newspaperman who founded and became coeditor of *The American Mercury* (1924), the Bible of the decade's alienated intellectuals. A penetrating stylist, Mencken ridiculed small-town Americans, Protestant fundamentalists, the middle class (the "Booboisie"), and mainstream America generally. His withering essays on Wilson, Harding, Coolidge, and Bryan are classics of American political satire.

Some young American writers spent the 1920s abroad, often in France. Even before the war, T. S. Eliot, Ezra Pound, and Gertrude Stein had become expatriates, and after the armistice others joined them. The most famous expatriate, Ernest Hemingway, had been a reporter before serving as a Red Cross volunteer in Italy during the war. Seriously wounded, he settled in Paris in 1921 and began to write. In *The Sun Also Rises* (1926), he evoked the experiences of a group of young Americans and British, shattered by the war, as they drifted around Spain.

World War I represented a seminal experience for this generation of writers. The best war novel, Hemingway's *A Farewell to Arms* (1929), powerfully depicted the war's futility and leaders' inflated rhetoric and captured the disillusionment of the author's generation. Hemingway and his counterparts gagged at Wilsonian rhetoric, village narrowness, and chamber-of-commerce cant, yet they remained committed to American ideals. A desire to create an authentic national culture inspired their literary efforts, just as it had earlier inspired Hawthorne, Melville, and Whitman.

The social changes of these years energized African-American cultural life as well. The 1920s would spawn the cultural flowering known as the Harlem Renaissance, a surge of creativity that spanned musical reviews, poems, and novels exploring the African-American experience. Cultural nationalists, both black and white, would see it as a step toward an authentic American culture that owed nothing to London or Paris.

Architects, Painters, and Musicians Celebrate Modern America

The creative energies of the 1920s found many outlets. A burst of architectural activity, for example, transformed the skylines of larger cities. By the end of the decade, the United States boasted 377 buildings more than seventy stories tall.

Artists turned to America itself for inspiration—whether the real nation around them or the country that they held in memory. Painter Thomas Hart Benton evoked a half-mythic land of cowboys, pioneers, and riverboat gamblers, while Edward Hopper starkly sketched a nation of faded small towns and lonely cities. Georgia O'Keeffe's early paintings evoked the congestion and excitement of Manhattan; and Charles Sheeler recorded a dramatic series of photographs of Ford's River Rouge plant near Detroit.

The ferment reached the musical world as well. Composer Aaron Copland tapped into folk-music traditions, and other composers evoked the new urban-industrial America. Frederick Converse's 1927 tone poem about the automobile, "Flivver Ten Million," featured "Dawn in Detroit," "May Night by the Roadside," and "The Collision."

Above all, American music in the 1920s meant jazz. The Original Dixieland Jazz Band—five white musicians imitating the black jazz bands of New Orleans—debuted in New York in January 1917, and a jazz vogue was soon under way. But the white bands that introduced jazz drained it of much of its energy. Paul Whiteman, the most popular white band leader of the decade, offered watered-down "jazz" versions of standard tunes and light classical works. Of the white composers who wrote in jazz idiom, George Gershwin, with *Rhapsody in Blue* (1924) and *An American in Paris* (1928), was the most original.

Meanwhile, African-American musicians preserved the spirit of authentic jazz. Guitar picker Huddie Ledbetter (nicknamed Leadbelly) performed his field shouts and raw songs before appreciative African-American audiences in the South. Singers including Bessie Smith and

The Great White Way,
by Howard Thain, 1925
This painting radiates the vibrancy, bright lights, and raucous commercialism of New York City, the nation's premier metropolis in the 1920s.
(© Collection of The New-York Historical Society, ID 1963.150)
hc Interactive Map:
Urbanization, 1890 & 1929

Gertrude ("Ma") Rainey drew packed audiences on Chicago's South Side and sold thousands of records. Trumpeter Louis ("Satchmo") Armstrong and band leader Fletcher Henderson did some of their most creative work in the 1920s, and the enormously talented black pianist, composer, and band leader Duke Ellington performed to packed audiences at Harlem's Cotton Club. Phonographs and radios popularized and standardized jazz, which so captured the spirit of the 1920s.

The Harlem Renaissance

Much of the floodtide of southern black migration washed onto the shores of Manhattan Island. By 1929 New York City had become home to 327,000 African-Americans, the majority crowded into Harlem, formerly an elite suburb. Racism and lack of education condemned most of the new residents to low-paying, unskilled jobs or to unem-

ployment, although black Harlem did boast a small middle class of entrepreneurs, ministers, and funeral directors.

Ironically, amid the social problems spawned by poverty and overcrowding, a vibrant African-American culture emerged in Harlem in the 1920s. The Cotton Club and other Harlem cabarets featured jazz geniuses such as Duke Ellington, Fletcher Henderson, and Jelly Roll Morton. Musical comedy flourished, and muralist Aaron Douglas, concert tenor Roland Hayes, and singer-actor Paul Robeson contributed to the cultural ferment.

Above all, the Harlem Renaissance was a literary movement. Poet Langston Hughes transformed the oral traditions of transplanted southern blacks into *The Weary Blues* (1926), while in *Cane* (1923) Jean Toomer combined poems, drama, and short stories to portray the efforts of a young northern mulatto to penetrate the mysterious, sensual world of the black South. Alain Locke, a Rhodes scholar who taught at historically black Howard University, assembled essays, poems, and short stories in *The New Negro* (1925), a landmark work that hailed the Harlem Renaissance as black America's "spiritual coming of age."

White America quickly took notice. Book publishers courted African-American authors, white patrons funded them, and white writers discovered and sometimes distorted African-American life. Eugene O'Neill's play *The Emperor Jones* (1921) starred Charles Gilpin as a fear-crazed West Indian tyrant. The 1925 novel *Porgy,* by Dubose and Dorothy Heyward, offered a sentimentalized portrait of Charleston's African-American community; as a play, *Porgy* won the Pulitzer Prize in 1927; and as a George Gershwin musical, *Porgy and Bess,* first produced in 1935, it entered the cultural mainstream.

Whites turned to Harlem for the sensuality, eroticism, and escape from taboos of its speakeasies, prostitutes, and readily available drugs. Packing the late-night jazz clubs and the pulsating dance reviews, they praised black culture for its "spontaneous," "primitive," or "spiritual" qualities. Few were aware of, or cared much about, the more prosaic realities of Harlem life. Nor did it bother them that the popular Cotton Club, controlled by gangsters, featured black performers but barred most blacks from the audience. Rebels against Victorian propriety, they romanticized the freedom of black life and ignored its burdens and constraints.

The Harlem Renaissance lacked either a political framework or ties to the larger African-American experience. The writers and artists of the 1920s ignored the racism, discrimination, and economic troubles most blacks faced and reacted with hostility to Marcus Garvey's attempt to mobilize the urban black masses. The stock-market crash in 1929 and the ensuing Great Depression ended the Harlem Renaissance.

Nonetheless, the Harlem Renaissance left an important legacy. The post–World War II literary flowering that began with Ralph Ellison's *Invisible Man* and continued with the works of James Baldwin, Toni Morrison, and Alice Walker, among others, owed a substantial debt to the Harlem Renaissance. A fragile flower withered by the cold winds of the Depression, it nevertheless remains a monument to African-American cultural creativity even under difficult circumstances.

Advances in Science and Medicine

The scientific developments of the 1920s would reverberate for decades. The first long-range television transmission, from New York to Washington, occurred in 1927. Arthur H. Compton won a Nobel Prize for his studies on X rays, and Ernest C. Lawrence laid the theoretical groundwork for the construction of the first cyclotron, a high-energy particle accelerator vital in nuclear-physics research. Physicist Robert Goddard studied rocketry and in 1926 launched the first successful liquid-fuel rocket. His predictions of lunar landings and deep-space exploration, ridiculed at the time, proved prophetic.

In medical research, Harvey Cushing made dramatic advances in neurosurgery, and chemist Harry Steenbock discovered how to create Vitamin D in milk by bombarding it with ultraviolet rays. New discoveries in the treatment of diphtheria, whooping cough, measles, and influenza helped to significantly lengthen life expectancy.

A few observers sensed that a new era of scientific advance was dawning. In 1925 Harvard philosopher Alfred North Whitehead underscored science's growing power. "Individually powerless," White had concluded, scientists were "ultimately the rulers of the world." To many, the prospect of such power was simply part of the array of disorienting social changes that made the 1920s unusually stressful and conflict-ridden.

A SOCIETY IN CONFLICT

Indeed, American society endured deep strains in the 1920s. Immigration, dizzying technological advances, urban growth, and Darwinian theory had shattered the cultural homogeneity of an earlier day. Rural Americans uneasily surveyed the mushrooming cities, native-born Protestants apprehensively eyed the swelling ranks of Catholics and Jews;

and upholders of traditional standards viewed the revolution in manners and morals with dismay.

Immigration Restriction

Fed by wartime superpatriotism, the long-standing impulse to turn America into a nation of like-minded, culturally identical people culminated in the National Origins Act of 1924. This restrictive measure limited the annual number of immigrants allowed from any nation to 2 percent of the total number of that "national origin" living in the United States in 1890. Because the great influx of southern and eastern Europeans had occurred after 1890, the act virtually ended immigration from those areas. Calvin Coolidge observed when he signed the law: "America must be kept American." The law also excluded Asians entirely, deeply insulting the Chinese and Japanese.

In 1929 Congress made 1920 the base year for determining "national origins," but even this slightly liberalized formula kept the quota for Poland at 6,500; for Italy, 5,800; and for Russia, 2,700. This quota system, which survived into the 1960s, represented the most enduring counterattack of rural, native-born America against the immigrant cities. Total immigration plummeted.

Court rulings underscored the nativist message. In *Ozawa* v. *U.S.* (1922) the U.S. Supreme Court rejected a citizenship request by a Japanese-born college student and in 1923 the Court upheld a California law limiting the right of Japanese immigrants to own or lease farmland

Needed Workers/Unwelcome Aliens: Hispanic Newcomers

Most proponents of restriction regarded Asia and southern and eastern Europe as sources of "undesirables," and the laws reflected this bias. No restrictions, however, were placed on immigration from the Western Hemisphere, and consequently immigration from French Canada and Latin America soared during the 1920s. By 1930 at least 2 million Mexican-born people lived in the United States. California's Mexican-American population quadrupled, from 90,000 to nearly 360,000, in the decade.

Many of these newcomers became migratory workers in large-scale agribusiness. Mexican migrant labor sustained California's citrus industry. Cooperatives such as the Southern California Fruit Growers Exchange (Sunkist) hired workers on a seasonal basis and provided substandard housing in isolated settlements the workers called *colonias*. The growers bitterly opposed attempts to form labor unions.

Not all Mexican immigrants were migratory workers; many settled into U.S. communities. While still emotionally linked to "*México Lindo*" (Beautiful Mexico), they formed local support networks and cultural institutions. Mexican-Americans were split, however, between recent arrivals and earlier immigrants who had become U.S. citizens.

Deeply religious, Mexican-Americans found little support from the U.S. Catholic church. Earlier Catholic immigrants had attended ethnic parishes and worshiped in their own languages, but by the 1920s church policy had changed. In "Anglo" parishes with non-Hispanic priests, the Spanish-speaking newcomers faced discrimination and pressure to abandon their language and culture.

Attitudes toward Mexican immigrants were deeply ambivalent. Their labor was needed, but their presence disturbed nativists eager to preserve a "white" and Protestant nation. Would-be Mexican immigrants faced strict literacy and means tests. The Border Patrol was created in 1925; deportations increased; and in 1929 Congress made illegal entry a criminal offense. Nevertheless, an estimated 100,000 illegal Mexican newcomers arrived annually to fill pressing demands in the U.S. labor market.

Nativism, Antiradicalism, and the Sacco-Vanzetti Case

The nativist, antiradical sentiments that produced the 1919 Red Scare and the 1924 National Origins Act emerged starkly in a controversy over a Massachusetts murder case that quickly became a cause célèbre. On April 15, 1920, robbers shot and killed the paymaster and guard of a shoe factory in South Braintree, Massachusetts, and stole nearly $18,000. Three weeks later, two Italian immigrants, Nicola Sacco and Bartolomeo Vanzetti, were arrested and charged with the murders. They were found guilty in 1921.

Bare facts cannot convey the texture of the case or the emotions it aroused. Sacco and Vanzetti were avowed anarchists, and from the beginning the prosecution harped on their radicalism. The judge, a conservative Republican, was openly hostile to the defendants, whom he privately called "those anarchist bastards." The Sacco-Vanzetti case in fact mirrored the larger divisions in society. Nativists dwelled on the defendants' immigrant origins, conservatives insisted that the alien anarchists had to die, and prominent liberals rallied behind them.

In 1927 a commission appointed by the Massachusetts governor to review the case upheld the guilty verdict. Sacco and Vanzetti were executed in the electric chair. But whether they committed the murders remains uncertain. The original case against them was circumstantial and far from airtight. Recent findings, including ballistics tests on Sacco's gun, suggest that at least Sacco may have been guilty. But the poisonous political climate that tainted the trial remains indisputable, as does the case's importance in exposing divisions in American society.

Fundamentalism and the Scopes Trial

In the half-century before 1920, American Protestantism had been severely tried. The prestige of science had increased steadily, challenging religion's cultural standing. Scholars had dissected the Bible's historical origins; psychologists had explained the religious impulse in terms of human emotional needs. Meanwhile, Catholic and Jewish immigrants poured in.

Liberal Protestants responded by accepting the findings of science and emphasizing social service to the immigrants. But a powerful reaction, fundamentalism, was building. Named after *The Fundamentals,* a series of pamphlets published from 1909 to 1914, Protestant fundamentalism insisted on the divine inspiration of every word in the Bible, on the Genesis version of Creation, and on the virgin birth and resurrection of Jesus.

In the early 1920s fundamentalists took aim at the theory of evolution. Charles Darwin's ideas seemed to them a blatant rejection of biblical truth. In 1921–1922 legislators introduced bills to prohibit the teaching of evolution in twenty states' public schools, and several southern states enacted such legislation. Fundamentalism's best-known champion, aging politician William Jennings Bryan, vigorously endorsed the anti-evolution cause.

In 1925, when the Tennessee legislature outlawed the teaching of evolution in public schools, the American Civil Liberties Union (ACLU) volunteered to defend any teacher willing to challenge the law. A young high-school biology teacher in Dayton, Tennessee, John T. Scopes, accepted the offer. Scopes read a description of Darwin's theory to his class and was duly arrested.

Famed criminal lawyer Clarence Darrow headed the ACLU team of lawyers, and William Jennings Bryan enthusiastically assisted the prosecution. Journalists poured into Dayton, and radio stations broadcast the proceedings live. The Scopes "monkey trial" became an overnight sensation.

The trial's symbolic climax came when Darrow cross-examined Bryan on his religious beliefs and scientific knowledge. As Bryan insisted on the literal accuracy of the Bible, his ignorance of vast realms of human knowledge became painfully clear. Darrow succeeded in humiliating Bryan and ridiculing his ideas. The local jury found Scopes guilty, but the larger verdict, the one that really counted, differed. The Dayton trial marked a decisive setback for fundamentalism.

After the trial, fundamentalism diminished in mainstream Protestantism, but many local congregations and scores of radio preachers continued to embrace the traditional faith. Publicity, skilled musicians, and a flamboyant pulpit style enabled evangelist Billy Sunday to preach his fundamentalist message to 10,000 people at a time. Zealous new denominations and "full gospel" churches carried on the cause. Evangelist Aimee Semple McPherson regularly filled the 5,200 seats of her Angelus Temple in Los Angeles and reached thousands more by radio. Her followers embraced the beautiful, white-gowned McPherson's fundamentalist theology while reveling in her mastery of mass entertainment. In many ways she anticipated the television evangelists of a later day. When she died in 1944, her International Church of the Foursquare Gospel had more than 600 branches. Clearly, although fundamentalism had suffered a severe blow at Dayton, Tennessee, it was far from dead.

The Ku Klux Klan and the Garvey Movement

The tensions and hostility tearing at the American social fabric also emerged in the revived Ku Klux Klan. The original Klan had faded in the 1870s, but in November 1915 a group of hooded men met at Stone Mountain, Georgia, to revive it.

In 1920 two Atlanta public-relations specialists propelled the Klan into a national organization by stressing nativism and white supremacy. A recruitment campaign promised money to everyone within an elaborate sales web. The enterprising Atlantans held the exclusive rights to sell everything from Klan robes and masks to the genuine Chattahoochee River water used in initiation rites. This elaborate scam succeeded beyond anyone's wildest dreams. By the mid-1920s, estimates of membership in the Klan and its auxiliary, Women of the Klan, ranged from 2 million to 5 million. The revived Klan, its targets not only blacks but Catholics, Jews, and immigrants, thrived in the Midwest and Far West as well as the South. Most of its members came from blue-collar ranks.

During its brief heyday, the Klan exercised real political power in many areas. In Oklahoma the Klan-controlled legislature impeached and removed an anti-Klan governor. The Klan elected a governor in Oregon and pushed through legislation (later overturned by the Supreme Court) requiring all the state's children to attend public schools.

The Ku Klux Klan in Washington, D.C.

In a brazen display of power, the Ku Klux Klan organized a march in the nation's capital in 1926. By this time, the Klan was already in decline.

Klan bigotry varied from region to region. In the South the antiblack theme loomed large, but Klaverns in the North and West more often targeted Catholics and Jews. In the Southwest the Klan focused on violators of prohibition and traditional morality, including adulterers and men who did not support their families.

The Klan filled important needs for its members. Although corrupt at the top, the organization consisted primarily of ordinary people, not criminals or fanatics. The Klan's promise to restore the nation to an imagined purity—ethnic, moral, and religious—appealed powerfully to ill-educated, deeply religious, and economically marginal Americans disoriented by rapid social and moral change. Klan membership, moreover, bestowed a sense of importance and group cohesion on people who doubted their own worth. The Klan's rituals, ceremonials, and burning crosses lit up drab lives. But while the individual Klansman may seem more pitiful than sinister, the movement as a whole was violent. Klan members used intimidation, threats, beatings, and even murder in their quest for a "purified" America.

In March 1925 Indiana's politically influential Grand Dragon, David Stephenson, pressed bootleg liquor on a young secretary, forced her on a Pullman train, and raped her. When she later swallowed poison, Stephenson and his henchmen refused to call a physician. The woman died, and the Grand Dragon went to jail for first-degree manslaughter. From prison he revealed details of pervasive political corruption in Indiana. Its high moral pretensions shredded, the Klan faded rapidly.

Among African-Americans, the decade's social strains ignited a different kind of mass movement. Blacks' widespread escape from southern rural poverty and racism led only to northern ghetto poverty and racism. Many poor urban African-Americans turned for relief to the spellbinding orator Marcus Garvey and his Universal Negro Improvement Association (UNIA). Garvey glorified all things black, urged black economic solidarity, and founded a chain of UNIA grocery stores and other businesses. He called on the world's blacks to return to "Motherland Africa" and establish a nation "strong enough to lend protection to the members of our race scattered all over the world." An estimated 80,000 blacks joined the UNIA, and thousands more felt the lure of Garvey's hypnotic oratory, the uplift of rousing UNIA parades, and the seduction of Garvey's dream of a mass return to Africa. White Americans were not the only people to find Garvey's mobilization of the black masses unsettling. Middle-class leaders of the African-American church and the NAACP, including W. E. B. Du Bois, were among Garvey's sharpest critics.

In 1923, however, a federal court convicted Garvey of fraud in connection with his Black Star Steamship Company. After two years' imprisonment, he was deported to Jamaica. Without this charismatic leader, the UNIA collapsed. As the first mass movement in black America, however, it revealed the discontent seething in the ghettos and the potential for activism. "In a world where black is despised," wrote an African-American newspaper reporter upon Garvey's deportation, "he taught them that black is beautiful."

Prohibition: Cultures in Conflict

The fissure so evident in the Klan movement and in the Scopes trial also shaped the decade-long struggle to rid America of alcoholic beverages. Prohibition was simultaneously a way to deal with the serious social problems associated with alcohol abuse and a sign of native-born Americans' struggle to maintain cultural and political dominance over the immigrant cities.

When the Eighteenth Amendment took effect in January 1920, prohibitionists rejoiced. Their cause had triumphed. Saloons closed; liquor advertising stopped; arrests for drunkenness dwindled. But by the end of the decade, prohibition was discredited, and in 1933 it ended. What went wrong? Essentially, the prohibition debacle illustrates the virtual impossibility in a democracy of enforcing rules of behavior with which a significant portion of the population disagrees.

From the beginning, enforcement of the Volstead Act, the 1919 law that established the Prohibition Bureau within the Treasury Department, was underbudgeted and largely ineffective, especially in strongly antiprohibition states. New York, for example, repealed its prohibition-enforcement law in 1923. Would-be drinkers grew bold as enforcement faltered. For young people already rebelling against traditional standards, alcohol's illegality added to its appeal. Every city boasted speakeasies where customers could buy drinks, and rumrunners routinely smuggled in liquor. Many people even concocted their own home brew. By 1929 alcohol consumption had risen to 70 percent of the prewar level.

Organized crime entered the liquor business, facilitating efforts to circumvent the law. In Chicago rival gangs engaged in bloody wars to control the liquor business; the 1920s saw 550 gangland killings. By 1929 Chicago mob king Al Capone controlled a network of speakeasies with annual profits of $60 million. Chicago's heavily publicized crime wave appeared dramatic proof of prohibition's failure. A reform designed to produce a more orderly, law-abiding America seemed to be having the opposite effect.

Prohibition became still another battleground in the decade's cultural wars. The "drys"—usually native-born Protestants—praised prohibition as a necessary and legitimate reform. The "wets"—liberals, alienated intellectuals, Jazz Age rebels, urban immigrants—condemned it as moralistic meddling. Prohibition figured prominently in the 1928 presidential campaign. Democratic candidate Al Smith openly endorsed repeal of the Eighteenth Amendment. Republican Herbert Hoover praised prohibition as "a great social and economic experiment, noble in motive and far-reaching in purpose." In 1931 a presidential commission acknowledged the breakdown of prohibition but urged its retention. Nevertheless, in 1933 prohibition ended with the Eighteenth Amendment's repeal.

HOOVER AT THE HELM

Herbert Hoover, overwhelmingly elected president in 1928, seemed ideal to sustain the nation's booming prosperity. He brought a distinctive social and political philosophy that reflected his background in engineering.

The Election of 1928

The presidential candidates of 1928, Al Smith and Herbert Hoover, personified opposite ends of the political and social spectrum. Four-term governor of New York, Smith easily sewed up the Democratic nomination. A Catholic and a "wet," his brown derby perpetually askew, Smith exuded the flavor of immigrant New York. Originally a machine politician, he represented progressivism's urban-immigrant component, championing social welfare and civil rights. Herbert Hoover won the Republican nomination with equal ease. Conservative party leaders, however, remained suspicious of this intelligent but aloof progressive who had never run for public office and had spent most of his pre-1920 adult life overseas. An Iowan orphaned early in life, Hoover had put himself through Stanford University and made a fortune as a mining engineer in China and Australia. His service as wartime food administrator saved millions of lives in Europe and earned him a place in the Harding and Coolidge cabinets.

Eschewing the handshaking and baby kissing of the campaign trail, Hoover delivered radio speeches in a boring monotone. Smith campaigned spiritedly throughout the country—a strategy that may have harmed him, for his big-city wisecracking and accent repelled many Americans.

Smith's Catholicism figured importantly in the campaign as he faced a backlash of prejudice. Although Hoover urged tolerance and Smith denied any conflict between his Catholic faith and the duties of the presidency, many Protestants, especially rural southerners and urban fundamentalists, found the issue of Smith's religion vital. But prosperity, not religion, was the decisive campaign issue. Republicans took credit for the booming economy and warned that Smith would create "soup kitchens instead of busy factories." Hoover predicted "the final triumph over poverty."

Hoover won in a landslide victory, making deep inroads in the Democratic "solid South." Smith carried a meager 87 electoral votes to Hoover's 444. But beneath Hoover's victory lay evidence of an

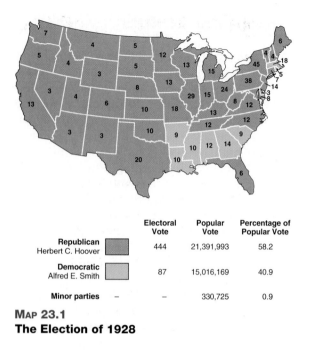

	Electoral Vote	Popular Vote	Percentage of Popular Vote
Republican Herbert C. Hoover	444	21,391,993	58.2
Democratic Alfred E. Smith	87	15,016,169	40.9
Minor parties	–	–	330,725	0.9

MAP 23.1
The Election of 1928

velopment demanded corporate cooperation in marketing, wage policy, raw-material allocation, and product standardization. The economy should operate like a smoothly functioning machine. Capitalism, Hoover argued further, had social obligations. He welcomed the growth of welfare capitalism. But above all, Hoover believed in voluntarism. The cooperative, socially responsive economic order that he envisioned would arise through the voluntary action of capitalist leaders, not through government coercion or power struggles pitting labor against management.

As secretary of commerce, Hoover had reorganized the Commerce Department along rational lines, making it a model for private industry, and tried to accelerate the trend toward corporate consolidation and cooperation. He had convened more than 250 conferences at which business leaders discussed unemployment, pricing, labor-management relations, and the virtues of trade associations. He urged higher wages to increase consumer purchasing power and in 1923 persuaded the steel industry to adopt an eight-hour workday in the name of efficiency. During the disastrous 1927 Mississippi River floods, as President Coolidge remained in Washington, Hoover had rushed to the stricken area and helped mobilize relief efforts.

But Hoover's ideas had limits. He displayed more interest in cooperation among capitalists than among consumers or workers, and he greatly overestimated the role of altruism in business decision making. His unqualified opposition to direct government economic intervention would bring him to grief later in his administration when such intervention became urgently necessary.

Applying his ideology to specific issues, Hoover compiled an impressive record early in his administration. He created commissions to study public-policy issues, gathered data for policy makers' guidance, and established the Federal Farm Board to cope with farmers' problems. Indeed, as the summer of 1929 turned to autumn, the Hoover administration seemed off to a promising start. But a crisis was looming that would overwhelm and destroy the methodical Hoover's presidency.

emerging political realignment. Smith did well in the midwestern farm belt among financially strapped Republicans and in northern cities, where first- and second-generation Catholic and Jewish immigrants voted Democratic in record numbers. In 1924 the nation's twelve largest cities had all gone Republican; in 1928 Smith carried all twelve. If prosperity should end, these signs suggested, the Republican party would face trouble.

Herbert Hoover's Social Thought

Americans looked hopefully to their new president, the Great Engineer. Hoover had a notable record of achievement and a well-developed social philosophy, expounded in his book *American Individualism* (1922). Although his own life followed the classic rags-to-riches formula, Hoover based his social outlook on his Quakerism, humanitarian activities, and engineering experience.

Like Theodore Roosevelt, Hoover disapproved of cutthroat competition. Rational economic de-

Chronology

1915	Modern Ku Klux Klan founded.	**1924**	Teapot Dome scandals investigated.
1919	Volstead Act.		National Origins Act.
1920–1921	Sharp postwar recession; agricultural prices plummet.		Calvin Coolidge elected president.
			McNary-Haugen farm bill introduced.
1920	Warren G. Harding elected president.	**1925**	Scopes trial.
	Eighteenth Amendment takes effect.		Ku Klux Klan scandal in Indiana.
	F. Scott Fitzgerald, *This Side of Paradise*.		Alain Locke, *The New Negro*.
	Sinclair Lewis, *Main Street*.		F. Scott Fitzgerald, *The Great Gatsby*.
1921	Sheppard-Towner Act.	**1926**	Ernest Hemingway, *The Sun Also Rises*.
1921–1922	Washington Naval Arms Conference.		Langston Hughes, *The Weary Blues*.
1922	Recovery from recession; economic boom begins; agriculture remains depressed.	**1927**	*The Jazz Singer,* first sound movie.
			Coolidge vetoes the McNary-Haugen bill.
	Supreme Court declares child-labor laws unconstitutional.		Execution of Sacco and Vanzetti.
			Charles A. Lindbergh's transatlantic flight.
	Herbert Hoover, *American Individualism*.	**1928**	Kellogg-Briand Pact.
	Sinclair Lewis, *Babbitt*.		Herbert Hoover elected president.
1923	Harding dies; Calvin Coolidge becomes president.	**1929**	Sheppard-Towner program terminated.
	Supreme Court strikes down minimum-wage laws for women.		Ernest Hemingway, *A Farewell to Arms*.
	Jean Toomer, *Cane*.		

CONCLUSION ⓗⓒ ACE Practice Test

Reacting against exalted Wilsonian idealism, America in the 1920s shied away from global leadership and pursued a cautious, often unilateral foreign policy. However, aggressive corporate expansion, involvement in Latin America, and the vigorous pursuit of such U.S. interests as reparations and debt repayments continued.

Domestically, the 1920s saw an entire people grappling with massive technological and social change. Almost overnight, it seemed, Americans had to adapt to the rise of an urban world marked by mass culture and mass production. Radio, the automobile, the movies, and electrical appliances were still exciting novelties.

Republican-dominated Washington celebrated, and deferred to, the new corporate, consumerist culture. "The business of America is business," President Calvin Coolidge solemnly stated.

The most interesting responses to these broad changes unfolded outside politics. The stresses and disorientation that produced bitter social conflict also made the 1920s one of the most creative decades in American cultural and intellectual history. Champions of prohibition and fundamentalism, the Ku Klux Klan, rebellious youth, urban blacks who cheered Marcus Garvey, and the novelists and poets who revitalized American literature were all trying to make sense of an unfamiliar, often threatening social order. The twenties saw political failure and reactionary social movements, but the decade also generated positive and lasting achievements.

FURTHER READING

Charles C. Alexander, *Here the Country Lies: Nationalism and the Arts in Twentieth Century America* (1980). A useful revisionist study whose chapters on the 1920s stress the decade's positive achievements.

Loren Baritz, ed., *The Culture of the Twenties* (1970). A rich collection of primary documents with a helpful introductory essay.

John M. Barry, *Rising Tide: The Great Mississippi Flood of 1927 and How It Changed America* (1997). Fascinating study of how a major crisis began to change national government policies about aiding individuals.

Paul Carter, *The Twenties in America* (1968) and *Another Part of the Twenties* (1977). Two short books offering refreshingly personal interpretive judgments.

Lynn Dumenil, *The Modern Temper: America in the 1920s* (1995). A study offering a wealth of fresh insights, especially on often neglected groups and movements.

Ellis W. Hawley, *The Great War and the Search for a Modern Order* (1979). An economic study that traces the emergence (and collapse in 1929) of the first mass-consumption society.

George Hutchinson, *The Harlem Renaissance in Black and White* (1995). Original new study linking the Harlem Renaissance to larger cultural and intellectual movements.

Nancy MacLean, *Behind the Mask of Chivalry: The Making of the Second Ku Klux Klan* (1994). An exploration of Klan members' anxieties about corporate growth, feminism, sexuality, and other issues of the 1920s.

Joan Shelley Rubin, *The Making of Middle-Brow Culture* (1992). An interpretive study of the Book-of-the-Month Club and other 1920s institutions by which high culture reached a larger public.

Young Farm Worker in Western Pennsylvania, 1930s, by Walker Evans

24

The Great Depression and the New Deal, 1929–1939

CHAPTER OUTLINE

Crash and Depression, 1929–1932

The New Deal Takes Shape, 1933–1935

The New Deal Changes Course, 1935–1936

The New Deal's End Stage, 1937–1938

Social Change and Social Action in the 1930s

The American Cultural Scene in the 1930s

hc This icon will direct you to additional study and research resources at http://college.hmco.com/history/us/boyer/enduring_concise/5e/students/index.html

Franklin Delano Roosevelt seemed to have everything. Charming, handsome, and the scion of a well-to-do family, he had found life easy. Not yet forty, he had served as assistant secretary of the Navy during World War I and had been the Democratic vice-presidential candidate in 1920. But in August 1921 an attack of polio left him paralyzed from the waist down and unable to walk. The illness seemed the end of his career, but after enduring years of therapy, he was ready to reenter politics in 1928.

This chapter focuses on five major questions:

▶ What were the main causes of the Great Depression?

▶ What depression-fighting strategy underlay the so-called First New Deal, and why did the Roosevelt administration change course in 1935, giving rise to the so-called Second New Deal?

▶ Which New Deal programs have had the greatest long-term effect, and how did ideas about the role of government change as a result of the New Deal?

▶ How did the depression and the New Deal affect specific groups in the United States?

▶ How did American culture respond to the events of the 1930s?

This chapter focuses on the Great Depression and the New Deal, Roosevelt's economic and social programs to promote national recovery. A dizzying array of approaches, laws, and agencies characterized the New Deal, but certain patterns do emerge. From 1933 to 1935, the first phase of the New Deal emphasized relief and recovery through united national effort. In 1935, facing political challenges on the left and right, Roosevelt charted a more radical course. The so-called Second New Deal (1935–1938) stressed business regulation as well as social programs and tax policies benefiting working people, small farmers, and others at the low end of the economic scale.

The New Deal involved myriad programs, political infighting, and countless individuals. But in the public mind, the New Deal meant Roosevelt. Loved by some almost as a member of the family, and reviled by others as a demagogue, Roosevelt was a consummate politician whose administration set the national political agenda for a generation.

CRASH AND DEPRESSION, 1929–1932

The prosperity of the 1920s collapsed in October 1929 with the stock-market crash. The crash, and the deeper economic problems that underlay it, launched a depression that reached into every household. President Hoover's commitment to private initiative and his horror of governmental coercion handcuffed him. In November 1932 a disillusioned nation gave an overwhelming electoral mandate to the Democratic party and Franklin D. Roosevelt. This election set the stage for a vast expansion in the federal government's role in social and economic issues.

Black Thursday and the Onset of the Depression

Stock prices had climbed throughout the 1920s. Beginning in 1928, optimism turned into frenzy as speculators plunged into the market. In 1925 the market value of all stocks stood at $27 billion; by

By the time he nominated Al Smith at the 1928 Democratic convention, Franklin Roosevelt's long struggle had changed him from a superficial, even arrogant man who relied on charm into a person of greater compassion and far more understanding of the disadvantaged. "If you had spent two years in bed trying to wiggle your big toe," he once said, "after that everything else would seem easy!" The charm remained, but it was now backed up by determination and fortitude. He was elected governor of New York in the fall of 1928.

Eleanor Roosevelt had devoted herself to her husband's care, ultimately encouraging him to return to politics. At the same time, already involved with social issues, she herself joined the executive board of the New York Democratic party and edited the women's division newsletter. Painfully shy, she forced herself to make public speeches. Like her husband, she would soon need the strength of character acquired through adversity.

October 1929 it had hit $87 billion. Nine million Americans "played the market," often with borrowed funds. Optimistic pronouncements drew people in. Former president Calvin Coolidge declared stocks "cheap at current prices." Stockbrokers loaned speculators up to 75 percent of a stock's purchase price, and credit buying became the rule. Treasury Secretary Andrew Mellon's pressure for tax cuts increased the money available for speculation. In 1928–1929 construction declined by 25 percent, but few heeded the warning.

In July 1928 the Federal Reserve Board tried to dampen speculation by increasing interest rates, and early in 1929 it warned member banks to tighten their lending policies. But speculators paid up to 20 percent interest for money to buy more stocks, and lending institutions continued to loan money freely—somewhat like dumping gasoline onto a fire.

On October 24, 1929—"Black Thursday"—the collapse began. As prices plummeted, traders panicked. Some stocks found no buyers at all; they had become worthless. On Tuesday, October 29, a record 16 million stocks changed hands in frantic trading. In the ensuing weeks, feeble upswings alternated with further plunges.

President Hoover, in the first of many optimistic statements, pronounced the economy "sound and prosperous." Few listened. By mid-November the loss in stock value stood at $30 billion. Instead of recovering, as many analysts predicted, the economy went into a long tailspin, producing a full-scale depression.

What caused the depression? Structural weaknesses in the American economy made the 1920s' prosperity unstable. The agricultural sector remained depressed through the decade. Rises in productivity led not to higher wages but to high corporate profits. In 1929 the 40 percent of Americans at the lowest end of the economic scale received only 12 percent of the national income. This reduced consumer purchasing power. At the same time, assembly-line methods encouraged overproduction. By summer 1929 the automobile, housing, textile, tire, and other durable-goods industries were seriously overextended. Further, important sectors of industry—including railroads, steel, textiles, and mining—lagged technologically in the 1930s and could not attract the investment needed to stimulate recovery. Some economists also focus on the banking system's collapse in the early 1930s, which they blame on the Federal Reserve System's tight-money policy.

All analysts link the U.S. depression to a global economic crisis. Enfeebled by massive war-debt payments and a huge trade imbalance with the United States, European economies crashed in 1931. This larger crisis depressed U.S. exports and fed panic.

Statistics tell the bleak story of depression America. The gross national product slumped from $104 billion in 1929 to $59 billion in 1932. Farm prices, already low, fell nearly 60 percent. More than 5,500 banks closed their doors by early 1933. Unemployment reached 25 percent in 1933; 13 million Americans had no jobs, and many who worked faced cuts in wages and hours. Some cities were far worse off. In Toledo in 1932, for example, unemployment hit 80 percent.

Hoover's Response

Historically, Americans had viewed depressions as acts of nature—one simply had to ride them out. Hoover disagreed. Drawing on the legacy of progressive reform and his own experiences as food administrator during World War I, he responded to the crisis boldly. But his course reflected his belief in localism and private initiative.

Business leaders whom Hoover summoned to the White House pledged to maintain wages and employment. Seeing unemployment as a local issue, Hoover called on municipal and state governments to create public-works projects. In October 1930 he established the Emergency Committee for Employment to coordinate voluntary relief efforts, and in 1931 he persuaded the nation's largest bankers to establish the National Credit Corporation to lend smaller banks money for business loans.

The crisis only intensified, and public opinion turned against Hoover. In the 1930 midterm election, the Republicans lost eight Senate seats and control of the House of Representatives. Unemployment mounted, and in 1931 U.S. Steel, General Motors, and other large corporations broke their pledges and announced large wage cuts. Public charities and local welfare agencies faltered. In Philadelphia, joblessness rose to 300,000 by 1932. The city cut relief payments to $4.23 per family per week and then suspended them entirely.

By 1932, with an election looming, Hoover endorsed an unprecedented federal response. In January Congress set up a new agency, the Reconstruction Finance Corporation (RFC), to make loans to economic institutions such as banks, railroads, and insurance companies. By July the RFC had pumped $1.2 billion into the economy. But Hoover gained little political benefit.

Hoover supported these measures reluctantly, warning of "socialism and collectivism." He blamed global forces for the depression and argued that only international measures would help. He advocated a one-year moratorium on war-debt and reparations repayments, a sensible plan but one that seemed irrelevant to hard-pressed Americans.

As Hoover issued press releases urging self-help and local initiative and endlessly saw prosperity "just around the corner," his relations with the news media soured. When he appointed a new press secretary, one reporter called it the first instance of a rat boarding a sinking ship. An administration launched so hopefully in 1929 by a widely admired president was ending in bitterness and failure.

hc Primary Source: Countering the Depression

Mounting Discontent and Protest

A dark mood spread over the nation as hordes of the jobless waited in breadlines, slept on park benches, trudged the streets, and rode freight trains from city to city seeking work. For Americans reared on the ethic of hard work and self-support, unemployment came as a shattering psychic blow. The suicide rate climbed nearly 30 percent between 1928 and 1932. Family savings vanished as banks failed.

Newspapers humanized the crisis. The *New York Times* described a section of Central Park where jobless men lived in boxes and packing crates. In winter they wrapped themselves in layers of newspapers they called Hoover blankets. Violence threatened in some cities when people unable to pay their rent were evicted from homes and apartments.

Hard times battered the nation's farms. Driving through the midwestern farm belt early in 1931, writer Malcolm Cowley found much of it untended and empty. "I wondered," Cowley wrote in the *New Republic,* "how much more of it will be abandoned next spring, after the milch cows have been sold for beef, the tractors and combine harvesters seized by finance corporations, the notes and mortgages allowed to go unpaid." Many farms underwent mortgage foreclosures or forced sales because of tax delinquency. At some forced farm auctions, neighbors bought the foreclosed farm for a trivial sum, and returned it to the evicted family. In 1931, midwestern farmers organized the Farmers' Holiday Association to force prices up by withholding grain and livestock from the market, and dairy farmers dumped thousands of gallons of milk.

World War I veterans mounted the most alarming protest. In 1924 Congress had voted a veterans' bonus to be paid over a twenty-year period. In June 1931, 10,000 veterans, many jobless, descended on Washington to lobby for immediate payment. When Congress refused, several thousand of the "bonus marchers" and their families stayed and built a makeshift settlement of tents and packing crates on the outskirts of Washington, D.C. Hoover called in the army.

On July 28, 1,000 armed soldiers under General Douglas MacArthur, equipped with tear gas, tanks, and machine guns, drove the veterans from their encampment and burned it to the ground. As a journalist described the aftermath, veterans and their families "wandered from street to street or sat in ragged groups, the men exhausted, the women with wet handkerchiefs laid over their smarting eyes, the children waking from sleep to cough and whimper from the tear gas in their lungs." For many, the incident symbolized the Hoover administration's utter bankruptcy.

Matching the mood of the time, American fiction of the early depression exuded disillusionment and despair. In *The 42ⁿᵈ Parallel* (1930), John Dos Passos drew a dark panorama of twentieth-century America as money-mad, exploitive, and lacking spiritual meaning. As one character says, "Everything you've wanted crumbles in your fingers as you grasp it." In *Young Lonigan* (1932), James T. Farrell portrayed the empty existence of Studs Lonigan, a working-class Irish-immigrant youth in Chicago. Unable to find work and feeling betrayed by the American dream, Studs wanders the streets, trying to piece together a coherent worldview from the bits of mass culture that drift his way.

Some radical novelists of the early thirties attacked the capitalist system even more explicitly. The Communist party encouraged such fiction through writers' clubs and contests for working-class writers.

The Election of 1932

Republicans renominated the unopposed Hoover at an intensely gloomy 1932 convention. The Democrats, in contrast, scented victory and drafted a platform to appeal to urban immigrants, farmers, and fiscal conservatives. Rejecting Al Smith, the delegates gave New York's governor, Franklin D. Roosevelt, the nomination.

Breaking precedent, FDR accepted the nomination in person, with a rousing speech promising "a new deal for the American people." But his campaign provided no clear program. He called for "bold, persistent experimentation" and promised more attention to "the forgotten man" while attacking Hoover's "reckless" spending.

Still, Roosevelt exuded confidence. Above all, he was not Hoover. On November 8 FDR and his running mate, John Nance Garner of Texas, received nearly 23 million votes; the Republicans mustered fewer than 16 million. Both houses of Congress went heavily Democratic. What policies would this landslide bring? The nation waited.

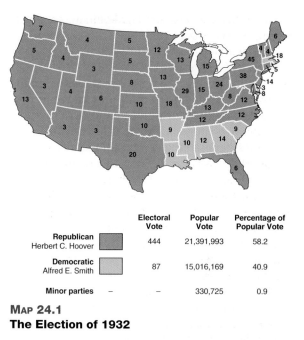

	Electoral Vote	Popular Vote	Percentage of Popular Vote
Republican Herbert C. Hoover	444	21,391,993	58.2
Democratic Alfred E. Smith	87	15,016,169	40.9
Minor parties	–	–	330,725	0.9

MAP 24.1
The Election of 1932

THE NEW DEAL TAKES SHAPE, 1933–1935

The Roosevelt years began with feverish activity as FDR proposed an array of emergency measures and the heavily Democratic Congress passed most by wide margins. The welter of bills carried three basic goals: *industrial recovery* through business-government cooperation and federal spending; *agricultural recovery* through crop reduction; and *short-term emergency relief,* funneled through state and local agencies when possible but provided by the federal government if necessary. Presiding over this bustle, a confident FDR symbolized hope.

Roosevelt and His Circle

FDR's optimistic inaugural address dedicated his administration to helping a people in crisis. "The only thing we have to fear is fear itself," he assured Americans, who responded with half a million approving letters to the White House.

FDR seemed an unlikely popular hero. Like his distant cousin Theodore, he was of the social elite, from a long line of merchants and landed aristocrats. His Harvard-Columbia background highlighted his social status. But as a state senator and governor of New York, he had allied with the Democratic party's urban-immigrant wing, and when the depression struck he had introduced innovative measures such as unemployment insurance and a public-works program. Intent on reviving the economy while preserving capitalism and democracy, Roosevelt had no detailed agenda. He encouraged competing proposals, compromised (or papered over) differences, and then backed the measures he sensed could be sold to Congress and the public.

Roosevelt brought to Washington a circle of advisers, "the brain trust," many of them from universities. FDR sought a wide range of opinions, and his brain trust included both very conservative and very liberal viewpoints. No single ideology controlled the New Deal.

Eleanor Roosevelt played a key role. A niece of Theodore Roosevelt, she had expressed her keen social conscience in settlement-house work and Florence Kelley's National Consumers' League. Through her, FDR met reformers, social workers, and advocates of minority rights. Mrs. Roosevelt traveled ceaselessly, observing depression America firsthand for her wheelchair-bound husband. In 1935 she began writing a syndicated newspaper column, "My Day."

Roosevelt's cabinet reflected the New Deal's diversity. Postmaster General James Farley, FDR's top political adviser, distributed patronage jobs and managed campaigns and relations with state and local Democrats. Secretary of Labor Frances Perkins, the first woman cabinet member, had served as Roosevelt's industrial commissioner in New York. Interior Secretary Harold Ickes had organized liberal Republicans for Roosevelt in 1932. Agriculture Secretary Henry A. Wallace's father had held the same post in the 1920s. Secretary of the Treasury Henry Morgenthau, Jr., FDR's Hudson valley neighbor, though a fiscal conservative, tolerated the unbalanced budgets necessary to finance New Deal programs.

A host of newcomers poured into Washington in 1933—former progressives, liberal-minded pro-

Eleanor Roosevelt Visits a West Virginia Coal Mine, 1933
A *New Yorker* cartoon of 1933 portrayed one coal miner exclaiming to another, "Oh migosh, here comes Mrs. Roosevelt." But reality soon caught up with humor as the First Lady immersed herself in the plight of the poor and the exploited.

fessors, bright young lawyers—who drafted bills, competed for influence, and debated recovery strategies. From this pressure-cooker environment emerged the laws, programs, and agencies that became the New Deal.

The Hundred Days

Between March 9 and June 16, 1933, the "Hundred Days," Congress enacted more than a dozen major bills. Rooted in the Progressive Era, World War I, and the Hoover presidency, these measures sharply expanded federal involvement in the national economy.

The closure of thousands of banks by early 1933 had broken people's faith in the entire system, and the banking crisis was FDR's most urgent challenge. On March 5 he ordered all banks to close for four days. At the end of this "bank holiday," the Emergency Banking Act, which had sailed through Congress, permitted healthy banks to reopen, set up procedures to manage failed banks, increased government oversight, and required that banks separate savings deposits from their investment funds. In the first of a series of "fireside chats" broadcast by radio, FDR assured Americans that they could again trust their banks. In June Congress created the Federal Deposit Insurance Corporation (FDIC) to insure all bank deposits up to $5,000.

Other Hundred Days measures dealt with relief—addressing the urgent plight of Americans struggling to survive. Two new agencies assisted those who were losing their homes. The Home Owners Loan Corporation helped city-dwellers refinance their mortgages. The Farm Credit Administration provided loans to rural Americans to meet their farm payments. In another relief measure, on March 31 Congress created the Civilian Conservation Corps (CCC) to employ jobless youths for reforestation, park maintenance, and erosion control. By 1935 half a million young men, some from families with no income at all, were earning $35 a month in CCC camps.

The principal relief measure of the Hundred Days, the Federal Emergency Relief Act, provided $500 million to fill the empty relief coffers of states and cities. To run this program, Roosevelt appointed New York State relief administrator Harry Hopkins, a gaunt chain smoker who enjoyed parties and who soon emerged as one of the New Deal's most powerful figures.

While dealing with immediate relief, the early New Deal also faced the longer-term challenge of promoting recovery in the agricultural and industrial sectors. Some New Dealers advocated reduced production as a means of raising farm prices. As a first step to cutting production, the government paid southern cotton planters to plow under much of their crop and midwestern farmers to slaughter some 6 million piglets and pregnant sows. Killing pigs at a time of widespread hunger proved a public-relations nightmare. Pursuing the same goal more systematically, Congress passed the Agricultural Adjustment Act in May 1933. This law set up a program by which producers of the major agricultural commodities, such as hogs and wheat, received payments, called subsidies, in return for cutting production. A tax on food processors (a tax ultimately passed along to consumers) financed these subsidies. A new agency, the Agricultural Adjustment Administration (AAA), supervised the program.

The other key recovery measure of the Hundred Days, the National Industrial Recovery Act (NIRA), appropriated $3.3 billion for heavy-duty government public-works programs to provide jobs and

Major Measures Enacted During the "Hundred Days" (March 9–June 16, 1933)

March 9	Emergency Banking Relief Act
20	Economy Act
31	Unemployment Relief Act (Civilian Conservation Corps)
May 12	Agricultural Adjustment Act
12	Federal Emergency Relief Act
18	Tennessee Valley Authority
27	Federal Securities Act
June 13	Home Owners' Refinancing Act
16	Farm Credit Act
16	Banking Act of 1933 (Federal Deposit Insurance Corporation)
16	National Industrial Recovery Act (National Recovery Administration; Public Works Administration)

stimulate the economy. Interior Secretary Harold Ickes headed the agency that ran this program, the Public Works Administration (PWA).

This law also set up the National Recovery Administration (NRA), which brought together business leaders to draft codes of "fair competition" for their industries. These codes set production limits, wages, and working conditions and forbade price cutting and unfair competitive practices. The aim was to promote recovery by breaking the cycle of wage cuts, falling prices, and layoffs. But some New Dealers had further goals. Under pressure from Labor Secretary Frances Perkins, the NRA's textile-industry code banned child labor. And thanks to Senator Robert Wagner of New York, Section 7a of the NIRA affirmed workers' right to organize unions and to bargain collectively.

The NRA's success depended on voluntary support by both business and the public. The NRA's flamboyant head, Hugh Johnson, used parades, billboards, magazine ads, and celebrity events to persuade people to buy only from companies that subscribed to an NRA code and displayed the NRA symbol, a blue eagle, and its slogan, "We Do Our Part."

The Reconstruction Finance Corporation (RFC), dating from the Hoover years, remained active in the New Deal era. The RFC lent billions of dollars to banks, insurance companies, and even new business ventures, making it a potent financial resource for corporate America. The early New Deal thus had a strong probusiness flavor. In his speeches of 1933–1935, FDR always included business as a key player in the "all-American team" fighting the depression.

A few early New Deal measures, however, took a more regulatory approach to business. The 1929 crash had produced a strong antibusiness reaction. A Senate investigation of Wall Street in 1932–1934 discovered that not one of the twenty partners of the giant Morgan Bank had paid any income tax in 1931 or 1932. People jeered when the president of the New York Stock Exchange told a Senate committee considering regulatory legislation, "You gentlemen are making a big mistake. The Exchange is a perfect institution."

Reflecting the public mood, Congress in May 1933 passed the Federal Securities Act. It required corporations to give the Federal Trade Commission full information on all stock offerings and made executives personally liable for any misrepresentation of securities issued. In 1934 Congress curbed the purchase of stock on credit, which had contributed to the 1929 debacle, and created the powerful Securities and Exchange Commission (SEC) to enforce the new regulations.

The most innovative long-range recovery program of the Hundred Days was the Tennessee Valley Authority (TVA). This program advanced the economic and social development of the entire Tennessee River valley, one of the nation's poorest regions. A European visitor in the 1930s described the region's farm houses: "They were lighted by dim, smoking, smelly oil lamps . . . . Ordinarily there is no icebox, so many products that might be grown to vary the horribly monotonous diet are out of the question; they could not be stored." A school administrator wrote of children who could not attend school "Due to insufficient clothing and food."

To remedy such conditions, a series of TVA dams supplied cheap hydroelectric power, bringing electricity to the region. TVA also promoted flood control and erosion prevention and proved one of the New Deal's most popular and enduring achievements.

For many Americans, the burst of laws and the "alphabet-soup" of new agencies during the Hundred Days symbolized both the dynamism and the confusion of the New Deal. How these new programs and agencies would work in practice remained to be seen.

Failures and Controversies Plague the Early New Deal

As the depression persisted, several early New Deal programs faced difficulties. Hugh Johnson's hard-driving, hard-drinking ways created problems for the NRA, but its difficulties went deeper. As the unity of the Hundred Days faded, corporate America chafed at NRA regulation. Small business objected that the codes favored big corporations. The agency itself bogged down in drafting trivial codes. Corporate trade associations used the codes to restrict competition and maintain prices, not to stimulate economic expansion.

In May 1935 the Supreme Court unanimously declared the NRA unconstitutional. The Court ruled that the act gave the president regulatory powers that belonged to Congress and that it regulated commerce within states, violating the Constitution's limitation of federal regulation to commerce between or among states. As an economic-recovery measure, the NRA had failed.

The AAA fared better but also generated controversy. Farm prices did rise as production declined; in 1933–1937, overall farm income increased by 50 percent. But the AAA's crop-reduction payments actually hurt southern tenants and sharecroppers because cotton growers removed acreage from production, evicted the sharecroppers, and banked the subsidy checks. One Georgia sharecropper wrote Harry Hopkins, "I have Bin farming all my life But the man I live with Has Turned me loose . . . I can't get a Job."

Some victims of this process resisted. In 1934 the interracial Southern Tenant Farmers' Union, led by the Socialist party, emerged in the spirit expressed by a black sharecropper at the organizing meeting: "The same chain that holds my people holds your people too. . . . There ain't but one way. . . . That's for us to get together and stay together." Landowners struck back by harassing union organizers.

Debate raged between New Dealers intent on raising total agricultural income and others who urged a focus on helping the poorest farmers. The latter gained influence as a parching drought that began in 1930 turned the Great Plains, from the Dakotas to Texas, into a dust bowl by 1934. Each summer from 1934 through 1939, clouds of dust spread across the nation, darkening cities from Chicago to Boston and Savannah before blowing out to sea.

Survivors never forgot the experience. Even night brought no relief. Recalled a Kansas woman, "A trip for water to rinse the grit from our lips, and then back to bed with washcloths over our noses." Folk singer Woody Guthrie recalled his dust bowl boyhood in his song "The Great Dust Storm." It began: "It fell across our city like a curtain of black rolled down. We thought it was our judgment, we thought it was our doom."

Battered farmers abandoned the land in droves. Some migrated to the cities; others packed their few belongings into old cars and headed west. Though from different states, they all bore the derisive nickname Okies.

Rivalries and policy differences also plagued the New Deal relief program. As unemployment continued, Harry Hopkins convinced Roosevelt to support direct federal relief programs, rather than channeling funds through state and local agencies. Late in 1933 FDR named Hopkins to head a temporary public works agency, the Civil Works Administration (CWA), which through the winter expended nearly a billion dollars on short-term work projects for the jobless. When warm weather returned, FDR abolished the CWA. Like his conservative critics, he feared creating a permanent underclass living on relief. But persistent unemployment that swamped local relief agencies made further federal programs inevitable.

Hopkins and Harold Ickes, head of the PWA, competed to control federal relief policy. The cautious Ickes scrutinized every PWA proposal, leaving billions in relief dollars stalled in the pipeline. The impatient Hopkins sought above all to put people to work and get money circulating. To him, even make-work projects like raking leaves had merit if they provided jobs. Given the urgency of the crisis, Hopkins, not Ickes, became the chief architect of federal relief policy.

1934–1935: Challenges from Right and Left

Despite the New Deal's brave beginnings, the depression persisted. By 1934 national income stood 25 percent above 1933 levels but still far below 1929 figures. Millions had been jobless for three or four years. The rising frustration found expression in

1934 in nearly 2,000 strikes, some of them communist led. With the NRA sinking, conflict flaring over farm policy, and relief spending growing rather than declining, criticism mounted. Conservatives attacked the New Deal as socialistic. In 1934 several business leaders, joined by an embittered Al Smith, formed the anti–New Deal American Liberty League. Anti-Roosevelt jokes circulated among the rich, many of whom denounced him as a traitor to his class.

But the New Deal remained highly popular, and FDR commanded the public stage. Pursuing the national-unity theme, he urged everyone to join the battle for economic recovery as they had united in 1917 against a foreign foe. Although Republican newspaper publishers remained hostile, FDR enjoyed excellent relations with the working press, and reporters painted an overwhelmingly favorable portrait of his administration.

FDR savored public appearances and took naturally to radio. Frances Perkins described his radio talks: "His head would nod and his hands would move in simple, natural, comfortable gestures. His face would smile and light up as though he were actually sitting on the front porch or in the parlor with [his listeners]." Roosevelt's easy mastery of radio provided a model for his successors in the television era.

Major Later New Deal Legislation (November 1933–1938)

1933	Civil Works Administration
1934	Civil Works Emergency Relief Act
	Home Owners' Loan Act
	Securities Exchange Act (Securities and Exchange Commission)
	Communications Act (Federal Communications Commission)
	Federal Farm Bankruptcy Act
	National Housing Act (Federal Housing Administration)
	Taylor Grazing Act
1935	Emergency Relief Appropriations Act (Works Progress Administration)
	National Youth Administration
	National Labor Relations Act (Wagner Act)
	Revenue Act of 1935
	Social Security Act
	Public Utilities Holding Company Act
	Banking Act of 1935
	Resettlement Administration
	Rural Electrification Act
1937	National Housing Act of 1937
	Bankhead-Jones Farm Tenancy Act (Farm Security Administration)
1938	Fair Labor Standards Act
	Agricultural Adjustment Act of 1938

The 1934 midterm election ratified the New Deal's popularity as the Democrats increased their majorities in the House and Senate. Kansas journalist William Allen White observed of FDR that "he's been all but crowned by the people." As the returns rolled in, Harry Hopkins exulted to a group of New Deal friends, "Boys, this is our hour!"

Still, the political scene was highly unstable. Conservatives criticized the New Deal for going too far, and critics on the left attacked it for not going far enough. Socialists and communists ridiculed Roosevelt's efforts to include big business in his "all-American team."

Demagogues peddled more radical social and economic programs. The Detroit Catholic priest and radio spellbinder Charles Coughlin attacked FDR as a "great betrayer and liar," made anti-Semitic allusions, and called for nationalization of the banks. For a time, Coughlin's followers, the mainly lower-middle-class National Union of Social Justice, seemed a potent force.

Meanwhile, California physician Francis E. Townsend proposed that the government pay $200 monthly to retired citizens, stipulating that they spend the money within thirty days. This plan would help elderly Americans and stimulate the economy, Townsend argued, and would open up jobs by encouraging early retirement. Although the scheme would have quickly bankrupted the nation, many older citizens embraced it.

Huey Long, a flamboyant political hell-raiser from Louisiana, became FDR's wiliest rival. A country lawyer who was elected governor in 1928, Long built highways, schools, and public housing. He roared into Washington as a senator in 1933 and preached his "Share Our Wealth" program: a 100 percent tax on annual incomes exceeding $1 million and expropriation of fortunes over $5 million. Every American family, Long promised, could enjoy a comfortable income, a house, a car, old-age benefits, and a free college education. "Every man a king," proclaimed Long. By 1935 he boasted 7.5 million supporters and clearly had his eye on the White House. An assassin's bullet cut him down that September, but Share Our Wealth survived.

THE NEW DEAL CHANGES COURSE, 1935–1936

Roosevelt responded vigorously to his challengers. With the spirit of national unity fading, he shelved the unity theme and veered leftward. In 1935–1936, he recaptured the political high ground with a series of legislative initiatives so impressive that some call this phase the Second New Deal. But while Roosevelt had initially tried to win the support of all Americans including big business, from 1935 on he increasingly criticized the wealthy and the business class and focused on aiding the most disadvantaged Americans.

In his January 1935 State of the Union address, Roosevelt offered six fresh initiatives: an expanded public-works program, assistance to the rural poor, support for organized labor, benefits for retired workers and other needy groups, tougher business regulation, and heavier taxes on the well-to-do. These goals shaped his program thereafter.

Expanding Federal Relief

With unemployment still high, Congress in April 1935 passed the Emergency Relief Appropriation Act. FDR swiftly established the Works Progress Administration (WPA) under Harry Hopkins. Like the CWA of the prior winter, the WPA funneled relief directly to individuals, and FDR insisted that the program provide work, not handouts. In its eight-year life, the WPA put more than 8 million Americans to work, injected $11 billion into the economy, and built or improved 650,000 miles of roads, 124,000 bridges, and 125,000 schools, hospitals, and other public buildings.

The WPA also assisted writers, performers, and artists. The Federal Writers' Project employed out-of-work authors to produce state guides and histories of ethnic and immigrant groups. In the South they collected the reminiscences of ex-slaves. Under the Federal Music Project, unemployed musicians gave free concerts, often featuring American composers. By 1938 more than 30 million Americans had attended an FMP concert.

The Federal Theatre Project employed actors. One FTP project, the Living Newspaper, dramatized contemporary social issues and was criticized as New Deal propaganda. FTP drama companies touring small-town America gave many their first taste of theater. Artists working for the Federal Arts Project designed posters, offered school courses, and decorated post offices and courthouses with murals.

Harold Ickes' Public Works Administration now picked up steam, expending more than $4 billion over its life span. PWA workers completed some 34,000 construction projects, including New York City's Triborough Bridge and Lincoln Tunnel, and the awesome Grand Coulee Dam on the Columbia River.

Monumental relief spending brought monumental budget deficits, cresting at $4.4 billion in 1936. The government borrowed to cover the deficits. British economist John Maynard Keynes had advocated deficit spending on public works during a depression to increase purchasing power and stimulate recovery. However, the New Deal was not Keynesian. Because all the money spent on public-works programs was withdrawn from the economy by taxing or borrowing, the stimulus effect was zero. FDR saw deficits as an unwelcome necessity, not a positive good.

Aiding Migrants, Supporting Unions, Regulating Business, Taxing the Wealthy

The second phase of the New Deal more frankly focused on the interests of workers, the poor, and the disadvantaged. Social-justice advocates like Frances Perkins and Eleanor Roosevelt helped shape this program, but so did hard-headed politics. Looking to 1936, FDR's political advisers feared that Coughlin, Townsend, and Long could siphon off enough votes to cost him the election.

The Second New Deal's agricultural policy addressed the plight of sharecroppers (worsened by the AAA) and other poor farmers. The Resettlement Administration (1935) made loans to help tenant farmers buy their own farms and to enable share-croppers, tenants, and dust-bowl migrants to move to more productive areas. The Rural Electrification Administration, also started in 1935, made low-interest loans to utility companies and farmers' cooperatives to extend electricity to the 90 percent of rural America that lacked it. By 1941, 40 percent of American farms enjoyed electricity.

In January 1936 the Supreme Court declared the processing tax that funded the AAA's subsidies to be an illegal use of the government's tax power. To replace the AAA, Congress passed a soil-conservation act that paid farmers to plant grasses and legumes instead of soil-depleting crops like wheat and cotton (which happened to be the major surplus commodities).

Organized labor won a key victory in 1935, again thanks to Senator Robert Wagner. Despite FDR's opposition during the New Deal's national-unity phase, Wagner built support for a prolabor law. In 1935, the Supreme Court ruled the NIRA unconstitutional, including Section 7a protecting union members' rights, and FDR called for a labor law that would stand up. The National Labor Relations Act of July 1935 guaranteed collective-bargaining rights, permitted closed shops (in which all employees must join a union), and outlawed such management tactics as blacklisting union organizers. The law created the National Labor Relations Board (NLRB) to supervise shop elections and deal with labor-law violations. The Wagner Act, as it was called, stimulated a wave of unionization.

The Second New Deal's more class-conscious thrust shaped other 1935 measures. The Banking Act strengthened the Federal Reserve Board's control over the nation's financial system. The Public Utilities Holding Company Act, targeting the public-utility empires of the 1920s, restricted gas and electric companies to one geographic region. Too, in 1935, Roosevelt called for steeper taxes on the rich. With the Wealth Tax Act, Congress raised taxes on corporations and on the well-to-do to a maximum of 75 percent on incomes above $5 million. Though this law had many loopholes and was not quite the "soak the rich" measure some believed, it did express the Second New Deal's more radical spirit.

The Social Security Act of 1935; End of the Second New Deal

Of all the Second New Deal measures, the Social Security Act of 1935 had the most long-term significance. Drafted by a committee chaired by Frances Perkins, this measure established a mixed federal-state system of workers' pensions, survivors' benefits for victims of industrial accidents, unemployment insurance, and aid for disabled persons and dependent mothers and children. Taxes, paid in part by employers and in part by wages withheld from workers' paychecks, funded pensions and survivors' benefits. Payroll withholding made sense politically because workers would fight the repeal of a pension plan to which they had contributed.

The initial Social Security Act paid low benefits and bypassed farmers, domestic workers, and the self-employed. However, it established the principle of federal responsibility for social welfare and created the framework for a vastly expanded welfare system.

By September 1935, when Congress adjourned, the Second New Deal was complete. Without embracing the panaceas preached by Coughlin, Townsend, or Long, FDR had addressed the grievances they had exploited. Although conservatives called this phase of the New Deal "antibusiness," FDR always insisted that he had saved capitalism by addressing the social problems it spawned. Business remained influential in the 1930s, but as the New Deal evolved, the federal government increasingly acted as a broker for all organized interest groups, including organized labor, not just corporate America. And in 1935, with an election looming, New Deal strategists addressed the troubles of poor and needy Americans who had rarely concerned politicians of the past.

In the process, the New Deal vastly expanded the role of the federal government, as well as the power of the presidency. Americans began to expect presidents to offer national "programs" and shape the terms of public debate. This decisively altered the balance of power between the White House and Congress as the New Deal redefined the scope of the executive branch and, more broadly still, the social role of the state.

The 1936 Roosevelt Landslide and the New Democratic Coalition

With the Second New Deal in place and unemployment declining, FDR faced the 1936 election confidently. "There's one issue . . . ," he told an aide; "it's myself, and people must be either for me or against me."

The Republican party nominated progressive governor Alfred Landon of Kansas, who proved an inept campaigner. When Republicans lambasted Roosevelt's alleged dictatorial ambitions and charged that workers would soon have to wear metal dog tags engraved with their social security numbers, FDR struck back with typical zest. Only the forces of "selfishness and greed" opposed him, he told an election-eve rally in New York; "They are united in their hatred for me—and I welcome their hatred."

In the most crushing electoral victory since 1820, FDR carried every state but Maine and Vermont. The Democrats increased their already-large majorities in Congress. Roosevelt also buried

The Election of 1936

Candidates	Parties	Electoral Vote	Popular Vote	Percentage of Popular Vote
Franklin D. Roosevelt	Democratic	523	27,752,869	60.8
Alfred M. Landon	Republican	8	16,674,665	36.5
William Lemke	Union		882,479	1.9

candidates of the Socialist and Communist parties and of the Union party (a coalition of Coughlin, Townsend, and Share Our Wealth enthusiasts).

FDR's 1936 landslide announced the emergence of a potent new Democratic coalition. Since Reconstruction, the Democrats had counted on three bases of support: the white South, parts of the West, and urban white ethnic voters mobilized by big-city Democratic machines. FDR retained these centers of strength. He rarely challenged state or local party leaders who produced the votes, whether they supported the New Deal or not. In Virginia he even withdrew support from a pro–New Deal governor who clashed with the state's conservative but powerful Democratic senators.

FDR carried the nation's twelve largest cities. Not only did New Deal relief programs aid city-dwellers, but Roosevelt wooed them persuasively. When the presidential entourage swept through cities like New York and Boston, cheering crowds lined the route. FDR also appointed many from urban-immigrant groups, including Catholics and Jews, to New Deal positions.

Expanding the Democratic base, FDR reached out to four partially overlapping groups: farmers, union members, northern blacks, and women. Midwestern farmers, long rock-ribbed Republicans, liked the New Deal's agricultural program and switched to Roosevelt. The unions pumped money into Roosevelt's campaigns (although far less than business gave the Republicans), and union members voted overwhelmingly for FDR, whose reputation as a "friend of labor" proved unassailable.

Although most southern blacks remained disfranchised, northern blacks voted in growing numbers. As late as 1932 two-thirds of them went for Hoover, leading one exasperated African-American editor to advise his readers to "turn Lincoln's picture to the wall. That debt has been paid in full." The New Deal saw a historic shift. In 1936, 76 percent of black voters supported FDR. In economic terms, this shift made sense. Owing mainly to racial discrimination, blacks' unemployment rates in the 1930s surpassed those of the work force as a whole. Thus, jobless blacks benefited heavily from New Deal relief programs.

On issues of racial justice, however, the New Deal's record was mixed at best. Racially discriminatory clauses in some NRA codes led African-American activists to dismiss the agency as "Negroes Ruined Again," and other New Deal agencies tolerated racism. Roosevelt kept aloof from an NAACP campaign to make lynching a federal crime. In 1935 and 1938 he remained passive as antilynching bills were narrowly defeated in Congress.

In limited ways, though, FDR did address racial issues. Assuring an African-American university audience in Washington, D.C., that there would be "no . . . forgotten races" in his administration, FDR worked cautiously to rid New Deal agencies of blatant racism. He appointed more than one hundred African-Americans to policy-level and judicial positions, including educator Mary McLeod Bethune as director of minority affairs in the National Youth Administration. Bethune led the "black cabinet" that served as a link between the New Deal and African-American organizations. In addition, the "Roosevelt Supreme Court" that took shape after 1936 issued antidiscrimination rulings on housing, voting rights, wage discrimination, jury selection, and real-estate transactions.

The New Deal also supported racial justice in symbolic ways. In 1938, when a meeting of an interracial welfare group in Birmingham, Alabama, was segregated in compliance with local statutes, Mrs. Roosevelt pointedly placed her chair halfway between the white and black delegates. In 1939, when the Daughters of the American Revolution barred a performance by black contralto Marian Anderson in Washington's Constitution Hall, Mrs. Roosevelt resigned from the organization, and Harold Ickes arranged for an Easter Sunday concert by Anderson at the Lincoln Memorial. Such symbolic gestures outraged many southern whites.

The Roosevelt administration also courted women voters. Molly Dewson led the effort as head of the Democratic party's women's division. In 1936 she mobilized fifteen thousand women who went door-to-door distributing flyers describing New Deal programs. Dewson did not push a specifically feminist agenda. New Deal programs of economic recovery and social welfare, in her view, served the best interests of both sexes. "We appealed to women's intelligence," she later recalled. Dewson did, however, push for more women in federal policy-level positions. FDR appointed the first woman cabinet member, the first woman ambassador, and more female federal judges than any predecessor. Through Dewson's efforts, the 1936 Democratic platform committee had a fifty-fifty gender balance.

Symbolic gestures and a few appointments should not be overemphasized. Racism and sexism pervaded American society in the 1930s, and Roosevelt, preoccupied with the economic crisis, did relatively little to change things.

The Environment, the West, and Indian Policy

FDR's commitment to conservation ran deep. As early as 1910, he had tried to regulate logging that threatened wildlife in New York. Under his prodding, the Civilian Conservation Corps thinned forests, built hiking trails, and planted trees.

Environmental issues loomed large in the 1930s, and soil conservation became a major priority. The Great Plains dust storms resulted not only from drought but also from overgrazing and unwise farming practices. For decades settlers had used ever more powerful machines to cultivate more land on the Great Plains. They had plowed up the native grasses that anchored the soil, exposing the topsoil to parching winds when drought struck. By the 1930s erosion had destroyed 9 million acres of farmland, with more in jeopardy.

The Department of Agriculture's Soil Conservation Service set up projects across the nation to demonstrate the value of contour plowing, terracing, crop rotation, and soil-strengthening grasses. The Taylor Grazing Act of 1934 restricted the grazing that had compounded the problem on public lands. The TVA helped control floods that worsened soil erosion.

New Deal planners promoted the national-park movement. Washington state's Olympic, Virginia's Shenandoah, and California's Kings Canyon all became National Parks in the 1930s. The administration also established some 160 new national wildlife refuges. Roosevelt even closed a Utah artillery range that threatened a nesting site of the endangered trumpeter swan.

The wilderness movement kept pace. In 1935 Robert Marshall of the U.S. Forest Service and environmentalist Aldo Leopold helped found the Wilderness Society. Pressed by wilderness advocates, Congress set aside a large wilderness area in Kings Canyon National Park.

To be sure, today's environmental issues—pollution, pesticides, dwindling fossil fuels, and so forth—received little attention from most New Dealers. The decade's hydroelectric projects, while necessary when most farmers still lacked electricity, nevertheless celebrated boundless consumption that today seems wasteful and heedless of ecological effects. Research has shown that many New Deal dams disrupted fragile ecosystems—on which many local residents, particularly Native American communities, depended for their livelihood.

Still, viewed in context, the New Deal's environmental record remains impressive. While coping with a grave economic crisis, the Roosevelt administration focused on environmental issues in a way not seen since the Progressive Era, and not to be seen again for a generation.

In the American West, the depression profoundly affected hordes of hard-hit citizens, including dust-bowl refugees who sought a fresh start, especially in California. Continuing a long trend, the West Coast's share of the population spiked upward in the 1930s, and Los Angeles jumped from tenth to fifth among U.S. cities.

With the federal government owning a third or more of the land in eleven western states, the New Deal had an especially big impact. New Deal agencies and laws such as the AAA, the Soil Conservation Service, and the Taylor Grazing Act set new rules for western agriculture, from grain and cattle to citrus groves and truck farms dependent on migrant labor. Some of the largest PWA and WPA projects were built in the West, including thousands of public buildings—not just courthouses and post offices, but even tourist facilities like Timberline Lodge on Oregon's Mount Hood.

Power to the People
The New Deal's massive hydroelectric power projects were celebrated in this 1937 "Living Newspaper" production by the WPA's Federal Theatre Project.

Above all, the PWA in the West built dams—Grand Coulee and Bonneville on the Columbia, Shasta on the Sacramento, Glen Canyon on the Colorado, and others. Boulder (later Hoover) Dam on the Colorado, authorized by Congress in 1928, was completed by the PWA. These great undertakings—among the largest engineering projects in human history—supplied hydroelectric power to vast regions. If their ecological effects were undeniable, so too were their contributions to flood control, irrigation, and soil conservation.

A New Deal initiative particularly important to the West was Harold Ickes's National Resources Planning Board, established in 1934. This agency facilitated state and regional planning for natural resources such as water, soil, timber, and minerals. Despite the West's celebrated "rugged individualism," New Deal planning, in tandem with the PWA's dams and infrastructure development, reshaped the public life of the region.

The 1930s also revived attention to the nation's 330,000 Native Americans, most of whom endured poverty, scant education, poor health care, and bleak prospects. The Dawes Act of 1887 had dissolved the tribes as legal entities, allocated some tribal lands to individuals, and sold the rest. By the early 1930s, whites owned about two-thirds of the land that Native Americans had possessed in 1887, including much of the most valuable acreage. That Indians had been granted full citizenship and voting rights in 1924 did little to improve their lot.

In the 1920s a reform movement arose. One reformer, John Collier, who had lived among the Pueblo Indians of New Mexico, founded the American Indian Defense Association in 1923 to preserve the spiritual beauty and harmony that he saw in traditional Indian life. Gertrude Bonnin, a Yankton Dakota Sioux and president of the National Council of American Indians, while not sharing all of Collier's goals, also pressed for reform.

Appointed commissioner of Indian affairs in 1933, Collier cadged funds from New Deal agencies to build schools, hospitals, and irrigation systems on Indian reservations and to preserve sites of cultural importance. The Civilian Conservation Corps employed twelve thousand Indian youths to work on projects on Indian lands.

Pursuing his vision of renewed tribal life, Collier drafted a bill to halt the sale of tribal land, restore the remaining unallocated lands to tribal control, create new reservations, and expand existing ones. It also envisioned tribal councils with broad governing powers and required Indian schools to teach Native American history and handicrafts. The bill sparked opposition. Some Indian leaders criticized it as a plan to transform the reservations into living museums and to treat Native Americans as exotic and backward. Successful Indian property owners and entrepreneurs rejected the bill's tribalist assumptions. The bill did, indeed, reflect the idealism of well-meaning outsiders rather than the views of the nation's diverse Native American groups.

The Indian Reorganization Act of 1934, a compromise measure, halted the sale of tribal lands and enabled tribes to regain title to unallocated lands. But Congress scaled back Collier's proposals for tribal self-government and dropped measures to renew tribal culture. A majority of tribes approved the law, as required for it to take effect, but opinion was divided. Indian policy clearly remained contentious. But the restoration of tribes as legal entities laid the groundwork for later tribal business ventures as well as tribal lawsuits seeking to enforce long-violated treaty rights.

THE NEW DEAL'S END STAGE, 1937–1938

Buoyed by his enormous victory in the 1936 election, Roosevelt launched an abortive attack on the Supreme Court that weakened him politically. In the wake of this fight, FDR confronted both a stubborn recession and a newly energized conservative opposition; a few final measures in 1937–1938 brought the New Deal to a close.

FDR and the Supreme Court

In 1937 the Supreme Court comprised nine elderly men, four of them archconservatives who despised the New Deal. Joined by moderates, they had invalidated the NRA, the AAA, and progressive state laws. Roosevelt feared a similar fate for key measures of the Second New Deal. Indeed, some lawyers were so sure that the Social Security Act would be found unconstitutional that they advised their clients to ignore it.

In February 1937 FDR proposed a court-reform bill that would have allowed the president to appoint an additional Supreme Court member for each justice over seventy, up to a total of six. Roosevelt blandly insisted that he was concerned

about the heavy workload of aging justices, but his political motivation escaped no one.

Congress and the public greeted the plan with sharp disapproval. The Supreme Court's size (although unspecified in the Constitution) had become almost sacrosanct. Conservatives blasted the "court-packing" scheme. Even some New Dealers disapproved. When the Senate voted down the scheme in July, FDR quietly gave up the fight.

But was it a defeat? One conservative justice retired in May 1937, and others announced plans to step down. In April and May the Court upheld several key New Deal measures, including the Wagner Act and a state minimum-wage law. This outcome may have been FDR's goal all along. He had sent a signal, and the justices heeded it. From 1937 to 1939, FDR appointed four new members to the Court, laying the groundwork for a liberal majority that would endure long after the 1930s.

The Roosevelt Recession

After improving in 1936 and early 1937, the economy plunged ominously in August 1937. Industrial production slumped. Steel output sank to 19 percent of capacity. Jobless rates again reached more than 20 percent.

What caused this relapse? Federal policies that reduced consumer income played a role. Social-security payroll taxes withdrew some $2 billion from circulation. A drastic contraction of the money supply by the Federal Reserve Board to forestall inflation also contributed. Concerned about mounting deficits, FDR had seized upon signs of recovery to end or cut back various New Deal relief programs.

Echoing Hoover, FDR assured his cabinet, "Everything will work out all right if we just sit tight and keep quiet." Some New Dealers, though, took the Keynesian view that deficit spending was the key to recovery. Their warnings of a political backlash if breadlines and soup kitchens returned convinced FDR to authorize new relief spending in April 1938. WPA work-relief checks soon rained down on the parched economy, and the PWA received a new lease on life. By late 1938 unemployment declined and industrial output increased.

A Camera's-Eye View of Depression-Era America

This 1937 image by Dorothea Lange, a photographer with the Farm Security Administration, pictures migrants from the Texas dust bowl gathered at a roadside camp near Calipatria in southern California.

hc Interactive Map: The Dust Bowl

Final Measures; Growing Opposition

Distracted by the Supreme Court fight, the 1937–1938 recession, and a menacing world situation (discussed in Chapter 25), FDR offered few domestic initiatives in his second term. Congress, however, enacted several significant measures. The Farm Tenancy Act of 1937 created the Farm Security Administration (FSA) to replace the Resettlement Administration. Although the FSA did little to help the poorest tenants and sharecroppers, whom it considered bad credit risks, its more than $1 billion in short-term loans by 1941 had enabled thousands of tenant farmers and sharecroppers to buy their own family farms.

The FSA operated camps offering clean, sanitary shelter and medical services to migrant farm workers living in wretched conditions. The FSA also commissioned gifted photographers to record the lives of tenants, migrants, and uprooted dust-bowl families. These FSA photographs helped shape a starkly realistic documentary style that pervaded 1930s popular culture. Today they provide a haunting album of depression-era images.

Other late New Deal measures set precedents. The Housing Act of 1937 appropriated $500 million for urban slum clearance and public housing. The Fair Labor Standards Act of 1938 banned child labor and established a national minimum wage (initially 40 cents an hour) and a maximum workweek of forty hours. Despite many loopholes, the law improved conditions for some and underscored the government's role in regulating employers' abuses.

The Agricultural Adjustment Act of 1938 set up new procedures for limiting the production of basic commodities. It also created a mechanism by which the government, in years of big harvests and low prices, would make loans to farmers and store their surplus crops in government warehouses. When prices rose, farmers could repay their loans and market their commodities. This system set the framework of federal agricultural policy for decades to come.

Overall, however, the New Deal clearly slowed after 1935, in part because of the rise of an anti–New Deal congressional coalition of Republicans and conservative southern Democrats.

The conservative coalition also slashed relief appropriations, cut corporate taxes, and killed the

Federal Theatre Project, a conservative target because of its radicalism. Suspecting that FDR used WPA staff members for political purposes, conservatives in 1939 passed the Hatch Act, forbidding federal workers from participating in electoral campaigns. The Fair Labor Standards Act of 1938 became law only after intense White House lobbying and watering down by conservatives. Congress and the public, Harry Hopkins lamented, seemed "bored with the poor, the unemployed, the insecure."

Although FDR campaigned actively in 1938's midterm election, the Republicans gained heavily in the House and Senate and added thirteen governorships. Roosevelt also tried to purge several prominent anti–New Deal Democratic senators in 1938, but his major targets all won reelection. Focusing mainly on foreign affairs in his January 1939 State of the Union message, FDR proposed no new domestic measures and merely noted the need to "preserve our reforms." The New Deal was over.

Social Change and Social Action in the 1930s

For a fuller picture of American life in the 1930s, we must look beyond the New Deal, to focus on people—the jobless and their families, women in the work force, industrial workers, African-Americans, migrant laborers. For all Americans, the depression's effects were psychological and social as well as economic and political.

The Depression's Psychological and Social Impact

The depression brought untold human suffering. Unemployment never fell below about 14 percent, and for much of the decade it ran considerably higher. Those who were employed often had to take jobs below their qualifications. College alumni pumped gas; business-school graduates sold furniture. Bankruptcies, foreclosures, and abandoned farms multiplied. A quarter of all farm families had to accept public or private assistance during the 1930s.

Psychologists described "unemployment shock": jobless persons who walked the streets seeking work and then lay awake at night worrying. When shoes wore out, heel tacks pushed through, cutting the skin. "You pass . . . shoe-shops where a tack might be bent down," one young man recalled, "but you can't pull off a shoe and ask to have that done—for nothing."

In the face of adversity, some people went to great lengths to maintain appearances. Advertisements for mouthwashes, deodorants, and correspondence courses exploited feelings of shame and failure. Women's magazines described low-cost meals and other strategies for scrimping and saving. As Caroline Bird wrote in *The Invisible Scar*, a social history of the 1930s, the depression for many boiled down to "a dull misery in the bones."

Senator Robert Wagner called the working woman in the depression years "the first orphan in the storm." Indeed, for the 25 percent of women employed in 1930, the depression brought hard times. The female jobless rate hovered above 20 percent through much of the decade. Women desperate to continue working often had to take lower-paying, lower-status jobs. Competition from displaced male workers reduced the proportion of women even in such traditional "women's professions" as library work, social work, and school teaching.

Married women workers faced harsh criticism. Although most worked out of economic necessity, they were accused of stealing jobs from unemployed men. Many cities refused to hire married women as teachers and fired women teachers who married.

Women workers also faced wage discrimination. In 1939 the average woman teacher earned nearly 20 percent less than the average male with comparable experience. Most female office workers earned far less than male factory workers. A number of the NRA codes authorized lower pay for women. The minimum-wage clause of the Fair Labor Standards Act helped some, but did not cover many, including the more than 2 million employed in private households.

A unionization drive of the later 1930s (discussed shortly) had mixed effects on women workers.

Some in the mass-production industries benefited, but the most heavily female sectors—textile, clerical, service, and sales—proved resistant to unionization.

Despite the roadblocks, the proportion of women working for wages crept up in the 1930s. In the face of criticism, the percentage of wage-earning married women increased from under 12 percent to nearly 16 percent as married women took jobs to augment depressed family incomes. One working wife explained, "One day in '32 [my husband] just went fishing . . . and he fished for the rest of the bad times. . . . So at twenty-eight, with two little girls, . . . I took a job as a salesclerk in the J.C. Penney."

As this woman's account suggests, the depression profoundly affected families, old and young alike. Bank failures wiped out the savings of many older Americans. By 1935 a million Americans over sixty-five were on relief. The birthrate fell in the early thirties as married couples postponed a family or limited its size. Family planning became easier with the spread of birth-control devices such as condoms and diaphragms. A declining birthrate plus reduced immigration held population growth in the 1930s to a scant 7 percent, in contrast to an average of 20 percent per decade between 1900 and 1930.

Parents in the 1930s often struggled to make ends meet and hold the family together. They patched clothes, stretched food, and turned to public assistance when necessary. In homes with a tradition of strong male authority, the husband's loss of a job often eroded self-esteem with devastating psychological effect. "I would rather turn on the gas and put an end to the whole family than let my wife support me," one man told a social investigator. Desertions increased, and the divorce rate, after a dip in the early and mid-1930s, edged upward, hitting a then all-time high by 1940.

As for young people, one observer compared them to a team of runners waiting for a starting gun that never sounded. High-school enrollment increased sharply, since many youths, seeing no jobs in view, simply stayed in school. The marriage rate declined as young people facing bleak prospects postponed this step. Many children of the depression wrote sad letters to Eleanor Roosevelt. A Michigan high-school senior described her shame at not having a graduation dress. "I give all I earn for food for the family," she explained. A thirteen-year-old Arkansas girl wrote, "I have to stay out of school because I have no books or clothes to ware."

Out of necessity, many families rediscovered traditional skills. They painted their own houses and repaired their own cars. Home baking and canning revived. Many would look back on the 1930s as a time when adversity encouraged cooperation, savoring simple pleasures, and sharing scant resources.

For the neediest families, among them blacks, Hispanics, and southern sharecroppers, the depression added more misery. In his novel *Native Son* (1940), Richard Wright vividly portrayed the desperate conditions of family life in Chicago's black slums. Yet not all was bleak. Emotional resilience and patterns of mutual aid and survival skills developed through years of oppression helped many black families cope. In New York's Harlem a charismatic black religious leader calling himself Father Divine institutionalized this cooperative spirit by organizing kitchens that distributed thousands of free meals daily.

Industrial Workers Unionize

Between 1900 and 1930, the ranks of factory workers had soared from 3.7 million to 7.7 million. Yet most of these workers remained unorganized. Major industries such as steel, automobiles, and textiles had resisted attempts to unionize their workers. The prosperity and probusiness mood of the 1920s had further weakened the labor movement.

Then in the 1930s, hard times and a favorable government climate led to labor militancy. When the Wagner Act of 1935 guaranteed labor's right to bargain collectively, activism shook the American Federation of Labor (AFL). In November 1935 John L. Lewis of the United Mine Workers (UMW) and Sidney Hillman of the Amalgamated Clothing Workers, chafing at the AFL's slowness in organizing factory workers, started the Committee for Industrial Organization (CIO) within the AFL. CIO activists preached unionization in Pittsburgh's steel mills, Detroit's auto plants, and southern textile factories. Unlike the craft-based, racially exclusive AFL, the CIO unions welcomed all workers in a particular industry.

In 1936 a CIO-sponsored organizing committee geared up for a major strike to win union recognition by the steel industry. (In fact, Lewis had already secretly negotiated a settlement with the head of U.S. Steel, and in March 1937 U.S. Steel recognized the union, granted a wage increase, and accepted a forty-hour workweek.) Other steel companies followed, and soon four hundred thousand steelworkers had signed union cards.

Meanwhile, organizers led by the fiery, socialist-oriented Walter Reuther, mapped a campaign to organize deeply antiunion General Motors. In December 1936 employees at GM's two body plants in Flint, Michigan, stopped work and peacefully occupied the factories, paralyzing GM's production by their "sitdown strike."

GM's management responded by calling in local police to harass the sit-down strikers, sending spies to union meetings, and threatening to fire strikers. A January 1937 showdown with the police at one of the body plants led to the formation of the Women's Emergency Brigade whose members, on 24-hour alert for picket duty, played a key role during the rest of the strike.

GM asked the Roosevelt administration and the governor of Michigan to send troops to expel the strikers by force. Both officials declined. Although FDR disapproved of the sit-down tactic, he refused to intervene with troops. On February 11 GM signed a contract recognizing the United Automobile Workers (UAW). As Chrysler fell into line also, the UAW soon boasted more than 400,000 members. Unionization of the electrical and rubber industries moved forward as well.

In 1938 the Committee for Industrial Organization left the AFL to become the Congress of Industrial Organizations, a 2-million-member association of industrial unions. In response to the CIO challenge, the AFL began to adapt to the changed nature of the labor force. Union membership shot up from under 3 million in 1933 to more than 8 million in 1941.

Some big corporations fought on. Henry Ford hated unions, and his tough lieutenant, Harry Bennett, organized a squad of union-busting thugs to fight the UAW. In 1937 Bennett's men beat Walter Reuther and other UAW officials outside Ford's plant near Detroit. Not until 1941 did Ford yield to union pressure.

The Republic Steel Company, headed by union enemy Tom Girdler, also dug in. Even after U.S. Steel signed with the CIO in March 1937, Republic and other smaller companies known collectively as "Little Steel" resisted. In May 1937 workers in twenty-seven Little Steel plants, including Republic's factory in South Chicago, walked off the job. On May 30, Memorial Day, strikers approached over 250 police officers guarding the plant. Someone threw a large stick at the police, who opened fire, killing four strikers and wounding scores. A blue-ribbon investigation found that the killings had been "clearly avoidable by the police." In 1941 the Little Steel companies finally signed union agreements with the CIO.

Another holdout was the textile industry, whose more than 600,000 workers, mostly in the South and 40 percent female, generally earned very low wages and had no recourse against autocratic bosses. In 1934 the CIO launched an organizing drive. Some 400,000 workers went on strike, but the mill owners viciously fought back. Several strikers were killed, many wounded, and thousands arrested. The strike failed, and the 1930s ended with most textile workers still unorganized.

The union movement bypassed low-paid workers—domestics, farm workers, department-store clerks, restaurant and laundry workers—who tended to be women, blacks, or recent immigrants. More than three-quarters of all nonfarm workers remained unorganized in 1940. Nonetheless, the unionization of key sectors of the industrial work force represents one of the decade's most memorable achievements.

Why did powerful corporations cave in to unions after years of resistance? Workers' militancy and the tactical skills of labor leaders like Reuther were crucial. But labor's successes also reflected the changed government climate. Corporations had once routinely called on the government to help break strikes. Although this still occasionally happened at the state level in the 1930s, the Wagner Act, the Fair Labor Standards Act, and the oversight of the NLRB made clear that Washington would no longer automatically back management in labor disputes. Once corporate managers realized this, unionization soon followed.

Despite its apparent unity at the end of the 1930s, the organized labor movement was increasingly split between hard-core activists, many of whom believed in radical social change, and non-ideological rank-and-file with no desire to overthrow the capitalist system. Indeed, many initially held back from striking, fearful for their jobs. But once the CIO's militant minority showed that picket lines and sit-down strikes could win union contracts and tangible gains, workers signed up by the thou-sands. As they did, the radical organizers lost influence, and the unions became more conservative.

Reuther himself, despite his socialist roots, tried to rein in the radicals in the CIO unions. After World War II, in a different political climate, Reuther purged from the CIO some of the same leftists and communists who had led the battles of the 1930s.

Blacks and Hispanic-Americans Resist Racism and Exploitation

The depression also brought social changes and activism within the African-American and Hispanic communities. Black migration to northern cities continued in the 1930s, though at a slower rate than in the 1920s. Some 400,000 southern blacks moved to northern cities in the 1930s, and by 1940 23 percent of the nation's 12 million blacks lived in the urban North.

Rural or urban, life was hard. Black tenant farmers and sharecroppers often faced eviction.

Labor Organizing, 1930s-Style

Walter Reuther (left) and Richard Frankensteen of the United Auto Workers, after their beating by Ford Motor Company security guards, Detroit, May 1937.

Among black industrial workers, the depression-era jobless rate far outran the rate for whites, largely because of racism and discriminatory hiring policies. Although black workers in some industries benefited from the CIO's nondiscriminatory policy, workplace racism remained a fact of life.

Lynching and miscarriage of justice continued, especially in the South. Twenty-four blacks died by lynching in 1933. In 1931 an all-white jury in Scottsboro, Alabama, sentenced eight black youths to death on highly suspect charges of rape. In 1935 the Supreme Court ordered a new trial for the "Scottsboro Boys" because they had been denied legal counsel and because blacks had been excluded from the jury. Five of the group were again convicted, however, and served long prison terms.

But rising activism signaled changes ahead. The NAACP battled in courts and legislatures against lynching, segregation, and the denial of voting rights. The Urban League campaigned with boycotts and picket lines against businesses in black neighborhoods that employed only whites. In March 1935 hostility toward white-owned businesses in Harlem, fueled by general anger over racism and joblessness, ignited a riot that caused an estimated $200 million in damage and left three blacks dead.

The Communist party publicized lynchings and racial discrimination as part of a depression-era recruitment effort in the black community. A Communist party committee supplied lawyers for the "Scottsboro Boys." But despite a few notable recruits (including the young novelist Richard Wright), few blacks joined the party. Other minority groups also faced discrimination. California continued its efforts to prevent Japanese-Americans from owning land. In 1934 Congress set an annual quota of fifty—lower than that for any other nation—for immigrants from the newly created Commonwealth of the Philippines, still a U.S. colony. Congress also offered free travel "home" for Filipinos long settled in the United States.

The more than 2 million Hispanic-Americans faced trying times as well. Some were citizens with ancestral roots in the Southwest, but most were recent arrivals from Mexico or Caribbean islands such as Cuba and Puerto Rico (a U.S. holding whose residents were and are American citizens). While the Caribbean immigrants (including those from Jamaica, a British colony) settled in East Coast cities, most Mexican newcomers worked as migratory agricultural laborers in the Southwest and elsewhere, or in midwestern steel or meatpacking plants.

As the depression deepened, Mexican-born residents faced mounting hostility. The influx of "Okies" fleeing the dust bowl worsened the job crisis, and by 1937 more than half of the cotton workers in Arizona were out-of-staters who supplanted Mexican born laborers.

With their access to migratory work disrupted, Mexican-Americans poured into the barrios (Hispanic neighborhoods) of southwestern cities. Some signs warned, "no niggers, mexicans, or dogs allowed." Lacking work, half a million Mexicans returned to their native land in the 1930s. Some did so voluntarily, but immigration officials and local authorities expelled thousands.

Mexican-American farm workers faced appalling conditions and near-starvation wages. A wave of protests and strikes swept California. A labor organization called the Confederación de Uniones de Campesinos y Obreros Mexicanos (Confederation of Unions of Mexican Workers and Farm Laborers) emerged from a 1933 strike by grape workers. More strikes erupted in 1935–1936, from the celery fields and citrus groves of the Los Angeles area to the lettuce fields of the Salinas Valley.

Well-financed agribusiness organizations such as the California Fruit Growers Exchange (which marketed citrus under the Sunkist brand name) fought the unions, sometimes with violence. In one incident in 1933, two workers died when bullets ripped into their striking cotton pickers' union hall. Undeterred, the strikers won a 20 percent pay increase, and others achieved a few successes too. Their strikes also awakened some Americans to the plight of one of the nation's most exploited groups.

THE AMERICAN CULTURAL SCENE IN THE 1930s

Hard times and the New Deal shaped American cultural life in the 1930s. While radio and the movies offered escapist fare, novelists, artists, playwrights, and photographers responded to the crisis as well. As the decade wore on, a more positive and affirmative tone in cultural expressions reflected both the renewed hope of the New Deal and apprehension at the deepening threat of war.

Avenues of Escape: Radio and the Movies

The standardization of mass culture continued in the 1930s. Each evening millions of Americans gathered around their radios to listen to news, musical programs, and comedy shows. Radio humor flourished when the real world was grim. Comedian Jack Benny and married team George Burns and Gracie Allen attracted millions.

So, too, did the fifteen-minute afternoon dramas known as soap operas (because soap companies sponsored them). Despite their assembly-line quality, these daily dollops of romance and melodrama won a devoted audience, mostly of housewives. Identifying with the troubled radio heroines, female listeners gained at least temporary escape from their own difficulties. As one put it, "I can get through the day better when I hear they have sorrows, too."

The movies were also extremely popular, and most people could still afford the twenty-five-cent admission. In 1939, 65 percent of Americans went to the movies at least once a week. The motion picture, declared one Hollywood executive, had become "as necessary as any other daily commodity."

A few movies dealt realistically with such social issues as labor unrest and the sharecroppers' plight. Two New Deal documentaries, *The Plow That Broke the Plains*, on the origins of the dust bowl, and *The River*, on erosion and floods in the Mississippi Valley, evoked the human and environmental toll of westward expansion. Warner Brothers studio made a series of movies in 1934–1936

celebrating the New Deal. And in *Mr. Deeds Goes to Town* (1936) and *Mr. Smith Goes to Washington* (1939), director Frank Capra, the son of Italian immigrants, offered the idealistic message that "the people" would always triumph over entrenched interests.

Gangster movies, inspired by actual criminals like Al Capone and John Dillinger, served up a different style of film realism. Films like *Little Caesar* (1930) and *The Public Enemy* (1931) grittily portrayed an urban America of looming skyscrapers and dark, rain-swept streets shredded by the rat-tat-tat of machine guns as rival gangs battled. When civic groups protested the glorification of crime, Hollywood made police and "G-men" (FBI agents) the heroes while retaining the violence. The movie gangsters played by Edward G. Robinson and James Cagney were variants of the Horatio Alger hero struggling upward against adversity. Their portrayals appealed to depression-era moviegoers facing equally heavy odds.

Above all, movies offered escape—the chance to briefly forget the depression. Musicals such as *Gold Diggers of 1933* (with its theme song, "We're in the Money") offered dancing, music, and cheerful plots involving the triumph of pluck over all obstacles. When color movies arrived in the late 1930s, they seemed an omen of better times ahead.

The Marx Brothers provided the decade's zaniest movie moments. In comedies like *Animal Crackers* (1930) and *Duck Soup* (1933), these unrestrained vaudeville troupers created an anarchic world that satirized authority, fractured the English language, and demolished all logic. Amid cynicism about the collapse of 1929, the Marx Brothers' mockery matched the American mood.

African-Americans appeared in movies, if at all, largely as stereotypes. Hollywood confined black performers to such roles as the scatterbrained maid played by Butterfly McQueen in *Gone with the Wind* and the indulgent house servant played by tap dancer Bill Robinson and patronized by child star Shirley Temple in *The Little Colonel* (1935). Under the denigrating screen name Stepin Fetchit, black actor Lincoln Perry played the slow-witted butt of humor in many movies.

In representing women, Hollywood offered mixed messages. Traditional fulfillment through marriage and subordination to a man shaped many roles, but a few films chipped away at the stereotype. Joan Bennett played a strong-willed professional in *The Wedding Present* (1936) and Carol Lombard emerged as a brilliant comedienne in *My Man Godfrey* (1936). Mae West, brassy, openly sexual, and clearly her own woman, mocked conventional stereotypes in *I'm No Angel* and other 1930s hits.

The Later 1930s: Opposing Fascism; Reaffirming Traditional Values

As the 1930s drew to a close, many Americans viewed the nation with a new appreciation. American society had survived the economic crisis. As other societies collapsed into dictatorships, American democracy endured. Among writers, composers, and other cultural creators, despair and pessimism gave way to a more upbeat and patriotic outlook.

A movement known as the Popular Front influenced this shift. In 1935 Russian dictator Joseph Stalin, fearing attack by Nazi Germany, called for a worldwide alliance, or Popular Front, against Adolf Hitler and his Italian ally in fascism, Benito Mussolini. (Fascism is a form of government involving one-party rule, extreme nationalism, hostility to minority groups, and the forcible suppression of dissent.) Parroting the new Soviet line, U.S. communists who in the early 1930s had attacked FDR and the New Deal now praised Roosevelt and summoned writers and intellectuals to the antifascist cause. Many noncommunists, alarmed by developments in Europe, responded to the call.

The high-water mark of the Popular Front came during the Spanish Civil War of 1936–1939. In July 1936 Spanish fascist general Francisco Franco revolted against Spain's legally elected left-wing government. With military aid from Hitler and Mussolini, Franco won backing from Spanish monarchists, landowners, and industrialists and from the Roman Catholic hierarchy.

In America, writers, artists, and intellectuals who backed the Popular Front rallied to support the anti-Franco Spanish Loyalists (those loyal to the elected government). The novelist Ernest Hemingway, who visited Spain in 1936–1937, expressed a newfound sense of worthwhile purpose in *For Whom the Bell Tolls* (1940), the story of a young American volunteer who dies while fighting with a Loyalist guerrilla band. Looking back on these years, Hemingway recalled, "The Spanish Civil War offered something which you could believe in wholly and completely, and in which you felt an absolute brotherhood with the others who were engaged in it."

The Popular Front collapsed on August 24, 1939, when the Soviet Union and Nazi Germany signed a nonaggression pact and divided Poland between them. Enthusiasm for cooperating with the communists under the banner of "antifascism" quickly faded. But while it lasted, the Popular Front helped shape U.S. culture and alerted Americans to dangers abroad.

The New Deal's achievements also contributed to the cultural shift of the later 1930s. The satire and cynicism of the 1920s and early 1930s yielded to a more hopeful view of grass-roots America. In John Steinbeck's best-selling novel *The Grapes of Wrath* (1939), an uprooted dust-bowl family, the Joads, make their difficult way from Oklahoma to California, revealing the strength, endurance, and mutual support shown by ordinary people in depression America. As Ma Joad tells her son Tom, "They ain't gonna wipe us out. Why, we're the people—we go on."

In 1936 writer James Agee and photographer Walker Evans spent weeks living with Alabama sharecroppers to research a magazine article. The result was *Let Us Now Praise Famous Men* (1941). Enhanced by Evans's unforgettable photographs, Agee's masterpiece evoked the strength and decency of those living on society's margins.

This positive mood reached the stage as well. Thornton Wilder's drama *Our Town* (1938) portrayed a New England town where everyday events become, in memory, infinitely precious. William Saroyan's *The Time of Your Life* (1939) celebrated the foibles and virtues of a colorful collection of

American "types" in a San Francisco waterfront bar.

Composers also reflected this spirit of cultural nationalism. In *Billy the Kid* (1938) and other compositions, Aaron Copland drew upon American legends and folk melodies. George Gershwin adapted a popular 1920s play about black street life in Charleston, South Carolina, for his opera *Porgy and Bess* (1935).

And jazz flourished in the later thirties, thanks to the big bands of Benny Goodman, Count Basie, Glenn Miller, and others who developed a flowing, danceable style known as swing. Clarinetist Benny Goodman challenged the color line in jazz, including black musicians like pianist Teddy Wilson and vibraphonist Lionel Hampton along with white performers in his orchestra. A turning point in the acceptance of jazz came in 1938, when Goodman's band performed at New York's Carnegie Hall. In its optimism, innovativeness, and "democratic ethos," historian Lewis Erenberg has argued, swing "expressed in cultural form many of the themes of . . . the New Deal."

The later 1930s also saw a heightened interest in regional literature and art. Zora Neale Hurston's novel *Their Eyes Were Watching God* (1937), exploring a black woman's search for fulfillment, was set in rural Florida. In *Absalom, Absalom!* (1936) William Faulkner continued the saga of his mythic Yoknapatawpha County in Mississippi. Painters Thomas Hart Benton of Missouri, John Steuart Curry of Kansas, and Grant Wood of Iowa struck strongly regional notes in their work.

Galleries displayed Amish quilts, New England weather vanes, and paintings by colonial folk artists. A 1938 show at New York's Museum of Modern Art introduced Horace Pippin, a black Philadelphia laborer whose paintings, such as *John Brown Going to His Hanging*, revealed a genuine, if untutored, talent. In 1939 the same museum featured seventy-nine-year-old Anna "Grandma" Moses of Hoosick Falls, New York, whose memory paintings of her farm girlhood enjoyed great popularity.

This cultural nationalism generated a fascination with the nation's past. Americans flocked to historical re-creations such as Henry Ford's Green-field Village in Michigan and Colonial Williamsburg in Virginia. In 1936–1939 Texans restored the Alamo in San Antonio, the "Cradle of Texas Liberty." Historical novels like Margaret Mitchell's epic of the Old South, *Gone with the Wind* (1936), became best-sellers. These re-creations and fictions often presented a distorted view of history. Slavery was blurred or sentimentalized at Colonial Williamsburg and in Mitchell's novel. "Texas Liberty" had a different meaning for the state's African-American, Indian, and Hispanic populations than it did for those who turned the Alamo into a tourist shrine.

Streamlining and a World's Fair: Corporate America's Utopian Vision

The visual culture of late 1930s' America was also shaped by a design style called streamlining. Industrial designers, inspired by the romance of flight, introduced rounded edges and smoothly flowing curves into the design of commercial products. Streamlining appealed to American business in the 1930s. It made products more attractive to consumers—vital during the depression. When Sears Roebuck streamlined its Coldspot refrigerators, sales surged. Streamlined products also helped corporate America rebuild its tarnished image and present itself as shaping a better future. Products ranging from house trailers to cigarette lighters emerged in sleek new forms poised for takeoff.

Under the theme "The World of Tomorrow," the 1939 New York World's Fair represented the high point of the streamlining vogue and corporate America's public-relations blitz. Inside the fair's hallmark Perisphere, a giant globe, visitors found "Democracity," a diorama showing a harmonious city of the future.

The hit of the fair was General Motors' Futurama, which gave visitors a vision of the United States in the distant year 1960—a nation of complex multilane highways with stacked interchanges. Futurama built public support for the interstate highway system that would soon become a reality. Also featuring such wonders as television and automatic dishwashers, the World's Fair epito-

Chronology

1929	Stock-market crash: onset of depression.
1932	Reconstruction Finance Corporation. Veterans' bonus march. Franklin D. Roosevelt elected president.
1933	Repeal of Eighteenth Amendment. Civilian Conservation Corps (CCC). Federal Emergency Relief Act (FERA). Tennessee Valley Authority (TVA). Agricultural Adjustment Administration (AAA). National Recovery Administration (NRA). Public Works Administration (PWA).
1934	Securities and Exchange Commission (SEC). Taylor Grazing Act. Indian Reorganization Act.
1935	Supreme Court declares NRA unconstitutional. Works Progress Administration (WPA). National Youth Administration. Resettlement Administration. National Labor Relations Act (Wagner Act). Social Security Act. Banking Act. NAACP campaign for federal antilynching law. Huey Long assassinated. Revenue Act raises taxes on corporations and the wealthy. Supreme Court orders a new trial for the "Scottsboro Boys." Harlem riot.
1935–1939	Era of the Popular Front.
1936	Supreme Court declares tax support for the AAA unconstitutional. Roosevelt wins landslide reelection victory. Autoworkers' sit-down strike against General Motors begins (December).
1937	Roosevelt's "court-packing" plan defeated. Farm Security Administration (FSA). GM, U.S. Steel, and Chrysler sign union contracts.
1937–1938	The "Roosevelt recession."
1938	Fair Labor Standards Act. Republicans gain heavily in midterm elections. Congress of Industrial Organizations (CIO) formed. Carnegie Hall concert by Benny Goodman orchestra.
1939	Hatch Act. Marian Anderson concert at Lincoln Memorial. John Steinbeck, *The Grapes of Wrath*.
1940	Ernest Hemingway, *For Whom the Bell Tolls*.

mized corporate capitalism's version of the patriotism and hopefulness that pervaded American culture as the 1930s ended.

The hopefulness was mixed with muted fear. The nation had survived the worst of the depression, but danger loomed overseas. The anxiety triggered by the menacing world situation surfaced on October 31, 1938, when CBS radio aired an adaptation of H. G. Wells's science-fiction story *War of the Worlds,* directed by Orson Welles. In realistic detail, the broadcast reported the landing of a spaceship in New Jersey and the advance of aliens with deadly ray guns toward New York. The show sparked a panic as horrified listeners believed the end was at

hand. Beneath the terror lay a more rational fear: of approaching war. For while Americans had coped with the depression, the international situation had deteriorated. By October 1938 radio news bulletins warned of an impending war between Germany and England. By the time the New York World's Fair offered its vision of "Tomorrow," the actual world of 1939 was very scary indeed.

CONCLUSION 🎧 *c* ACE Practice Test

The Great Depression affected all facets of American life, from individual families to movies and radio programs that entertained millions. It also shaped the outlook of writers and other culture creators. From an initial mood of despair, the cultural climate by the end of the 1930s had become far more hopeful and affirmative.

The New Deal that so dominated the 1930s was hardly an unqualified success. Some New Deal programs failed, and full recovery proved elusive. But as the New Deal evolved, it set a new standard of what citizens could expect of their government, radically redefining the nation's political agenda, the role of the federal government, and the nature of the presidency. For decades after, national political campaigns and public-policy debates would be shaped by differing opinions about the New Deal's legacy.

Any evaluation of the New Deal must confront Franklin D. Roosevelt. Neither saint nor superman, he could be calculating and devious, superficially genial, and breezily casual about details. But for most Americans of the 1930s—and most historians since—his strengths outweighed his liabilities. His open, experimental approach served the nation well in a time of crisis.

Above all, Roosevelt's optimism inspired a demoralized people. "We Americans of today . . . ," he observed to an audience of young people in 1939, "are characters in the living book of democracy. But we are also its author. It falls upon us now to say whether the chapters that are to come will tell a story of retreat or a story of continued advance."

FURTHER READING

Caroline Bird, *The Invisible Scar* (1966). Moving look at the depression's human and psychological toll.

Lizabeth Cohen, *Making a New Deal: Industrial Workers in Chicago, 1919–1939* (1990). Influential, well-researched study of working-class and union culture.

Blanche D. Coll, *Safety Net: Welfare and Social Security, 1929–1979* (1995). Balanced, well-written history of the sources of the Social Security Act and its aftermath.

Lewis Erenberg, *Swingin' the Dream: Big Band Jazz and the Rebirth of American Culture* (1998). Stimulating interpretive study linking New Deal politics and popular music in the later 1930s.

Steve Fraser and Gary Gerstle, eds., *The Rise and Fall of the New Deal Order, 1930–1980* (1989). Incisive critical essays on the New Deal's long-term legacy.

David M. Kennedy, *Freedom from Fear: The American People in Depression and War* (1998). A sweeping synthesis, especially good on Washington politics and the Social Security Act.

William E. Leuchtenberg, *Franklin D. Roosevelt and the New Deal* (1983). A comprehensive, readable overview, rich in illuminating detail.

Albert U. Romasco, *The Politics of Recovery: Roosevelt's New Deal* (1983). A study particularly useful on the New Deal's business policies.

Harvard Sitkoff, *A New Deal for Blacks* (1978). An exploration of the Roosevelt administration's policies toward black Americans.

Robert H. Zieger, *The CIO, 1935–1955* (1995). Valuable on organized labor in the later New Deal, and on tensions between the leadership and the rank-and-file.

Okinawa, 1945

Americans and a World in Crisis, 1933–1945

To most Americans, World War II was "the good war." U.S. losses—some 300,000 dead—paled beside the tens of millions dead in Europe and Asia, and American soil was unscathed. In fact, the war made America once again a land of opportunity and hope as it ended the Depression, redistributed income, and transformed the United States into a largely middle-class society. Many who had been left out of prewar society, women and African-Americans in particular, found liberation in the war. Simultaneously, "the war" fostered an increasingly active and powerful federal government, disrupted families, and laid bare social problems. And war's end found the United States a global leader in a world transformed.

CHAPTER OUTLINE

The United States in a Menacing World, 1933–1939

Into the Storm, 1939–1941

America Mobilizes for War

The Battlefront, 1942–1944

War and American Society

Triumph and Tragedy, 1945

hc This icon will direct you to additional study and research resources at http://college.hmco.com/history/us/boyer/enduring_concise/5e/students/index.html

This chapter focuses on five major questions:

▶ How did the Roosevelt administration and the American people respond to the international crises of the 1930s?

▶ How did war mobilization transform the American economy and government?

▶ What were the major aspects of Allied military strategy in Europe and Asia?

▶ What were the major effects of World War II on American society?

▶ What were the arguments for and against the use of the atomic bomb to end the war with Japan?

THE UNITED STATES IN A MENACING WORLD, 1933–1939

Apart from efforts to improve Latin American relations, the early administration of Franklin D. Roosevelt (FDR) remained largely aloof from the rest of the world. As Italy, Germany, and Japan grew more aggressive and militaristic, American observers reacted with ambivalence. Determined not to stumble into war again, millions of Americans supported neutrality and peace. Others insisted that the United States help embattled democracies abroad. All the while, the world edged steadily closer to the precipice.

Nationalism and the Good Neighbor

President Roosevelt at first put American economic interests above all else. Despite Secretary of State Cordell Hull's urging, FDR showed little interest in free trade or international economic cooperation.

Roosevelt did, however, commit himself to an internationalist approach in Latin America, where bitterness over decades of "Yankee imperialism" ran high. In his 1933 inaugural, he had announced a "Good Neighbor" policy toward Latin America, and at a conference in Uruguay in 1933 the United States endorsed a statement of principles that declared, "No state has the right to intervene in the internal or external affairs of another." Under this policy Roosevelt withdrew the last U.S. troops from Haiti and the Dominican Republic, persuaded American bankers to loosen their grip on Haiti's central banking system, and reduced the U.S. role in Panamanian affairs. However, the United States remained closely identified with the repressive regimes of Raphael Trujillo in the Dominican Republic and Anastasio Somoza in Nicaragua.

Cuba and Mexico provided major tests of the Good Neighbor policy. In Cuba economic problems triggered by high tariffs brought to power a radical leftist, Grau San Martín, in 1933. American opposition to the San Martín administration found expression in indirect action. Early in 1934, a conservative coalition enjoying U.S. support overthrew the San Martín regime. Strongman Fulgencio Batista gained power, aided by American manipulation of sugar quotas. He would retain power off and on until being overthrown by Fidel Castro in 1959.

In 1936 a reform government came to power in Mexico and nationalized several oil companies owned by U.S. and British corporations. The United States did not oppose nationalization but insisted on fair compensation. Economic pressure from Washington led to a compensation agreement that both the Mexican government and the oil companies accepted.

The Good Neighbor policy, in sum, did not terminate American interference in Latin America, but it did end heavy-handed intervention and military occupation. Improved relations became vital when the United States sought hemispheric solidarity in World War II and the Cold War.

The Rise of Aggressive States in Europe and Asia

Meanwhile, powerful forces raged across much of the world. As early as 1922, Italy's economic prob-

MAP 25.1
European Aggression Before World War II

Less than twenty years after the end of World War I, war again loomed in Europe as Hitler launched Germany on a course of military and territorial expansion.

lems and social unrest had opened the way for Benito Mussolini and his Fascist party to seize power in Rome. The regime had swiftly suppressed dissent and imposed one-party rule.

The rise of Adolf Hitler in German proved more menacing. Hitler's National Socialist (Nazi) party had gained broad support as the economy deteriorated, and Hitler had become Germany's chancellor in January 1933. He promptly crushed rivals within the Nazi party and fastened a brutal dictatorship on Germany. A racist who believed that he had to purify Germany of "inferior" taint, Hitler began driving out German Jews, whom he blamed for Germany's defeat in World War I.

In the mid-1930s Hitler pursued a militaristic, expansionist foreign policy that violated the Ver-

sailles treaty by rearming Germany and reoccupying the Rhineland, the strip between the Rhine River and the French border specifically demilitarized at Versailles. Early in 1938 he proclaimed an *Anschluss* (union) between Austria and Germany. Meanwhile, Mussolini, intent on building an empire in Africa, had invaded Ethiopia in 1935. In London, Paris, Washington, and Geneva, the headquarters of the League of Nations, hand wringing but little firm action greeted these aggressive moves.

After Austria, Hitler turned to the Sudetenland, an area of Czechoslovakia containing 3 million ethnic Germans and 700,000 Czechs. Insisting that the Sudetenland was "racially" part of Germany, Hitler made clear his determination to take the area. At a conference in Munich in September 1938—which excluded the Czechs—British prime minister Neville Chamberlain and his French counterpart agreed to turn the Sudetenland over to Germany. Stripped of a third of its population and territory, Czechoslovakia now faced Germany's massed tanks and troops. Viewing this appeasement of Germany as a diplomatic victory, Chamberlain proclaimed "peace in our time." World War II was less than a year away.

In Tokyo, meanwhile, nationalistic militarists had gained control of Japan's government and launched a fateful course of expansion. In 1931–1933 Japanese troops had invaded the Chinese province of Manchuria, installed a puppet government, and forced China, with no outside support, to sign a treaty recognizing Japanese control of the province. In July 1937 Japan launched a full-scale war against China itself.

The American Mood: No More War

The American response reflected a revulsion against war. By the mid-1930s millions of Americans believed that the United States' decision to enter World War I in April 1917 had been a ghastly mistake. In mid-decade a series of books reinforced this conclusion, arguing that banking and corporate interests had dragged the United States into World War I to protect their loans and weapons sales to England and France.

Public concern over the "merchants of death" issue led to a special Senate investigation headed by Republican Gerald Nye, of North Dakota, which concluded that banking and munitions interests had tricked the United States into war to protect loans and weapon sales to the Allies. A January 1937 poll showed that an astonishing 70 percent of

MAP 25.2

Japanese Expansion Before World War II

Dominated by militarists, Japan pursued an expansionist policy in Asia in the 1930s, extending its sphere of economic and political influence. In July 1937, having already occupied the Chinese province of Manchuria, Japan attacked China proper.

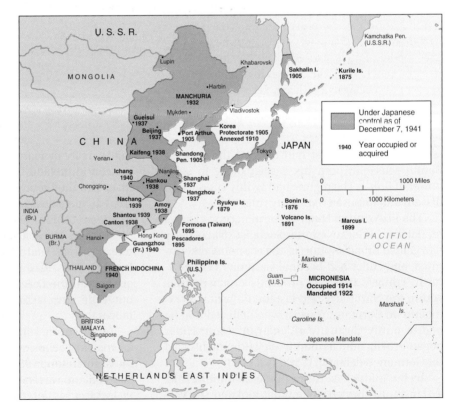

the people believed that the United States should have stayed out of World War I.

Many Americans concluded that the United States, protected by two oceans, could safely remain aloof from the upheavals convulsing other parts of the world. In 1935–1937 a series of Neutrality Acts echoed the longing for peace. To prevent a repetition of 1917, these measures outlawed arms sales and loans to nations at war and forbade Americans from traveling on the ships of belligerent powers. But the high point of peace legislation came early in 1938 when Indiana congressman Louis Ludlow proposed a constitutional amendment requiring a national referendum on any U.S. declaration of war except in cases of direct attack. Only after a direct appeal from FDR, and then by a narrow margin, did Congress reject the Ludlow Amendment.

With the public firmly isolationist and American companies like IBM heavily invested in Nazi Germany, confrontation with fascism came solely in sports. At the 1936 Olympics in Berlin, Jesse Owens, an African-American, made a mockery of Nazi theories of racial superiority by winning four gold medals and breaking or tying three world records. When the black Joe Louis knocked out German Max Schmeling in the first round of their world heavy-weight championship bout, Americans cheered—but still opposed any policy that might involve them in war.

The Gathering Storm: 1938–1939

The interlude of reduced tension that followed the Munich Pact proved tragically brief. "Peace in our time" lasted a mere 5 1/2 months. At 6:00 a.m. on March 15, 1939, Nazi troops thundered across the border into Czechoslovakia. By evening the Nazi flag flew over Prague. Five months later, the signing of the Nazi-Soviet Pact gave Hitler a green light to invade Poland.

In the United States the debate over the American role intensified. Some almost desperately urged the nation to keep free of the approaching conflict. Opponents of intervention warned that American involvement in a war could shatter New

Isolationism vs. Interventionism
In front of the White House in 1941, an American soldier grabs a sign from an isolationist picketing against the United States entering the war in Europe. Isolationists ran the gamut from pacifists who opposed all wars, to progressives who feared the growth of business and centralized power, to ultra-rightists who sympathized with fascism or shared Hitler's anti-Semitism.

Deal reforms and spawn reaction, as it had a generation earlier. But opinion was shifting rapidly. Pacifism and neutralism weakened, and the voices urging activism strengthened. In 1938, warning of the "cancerous spread" of fascism, cultural critic Lewis Mumford issued "A Call to Arms" in the *New Republic*. Archibald MacLeish, having earlier championed the cause of Spain, exhorted his fellow citizens to mobilize against Hitler.

After the fall of Czechoslovakia early in 1939, Roosevelt publicly called on Hitler and Mussolini not to invade thirty-one specific nations. A jeering Hitler ridiculed FDR's message, while in Rome Mussolini mocked Roosevelt's physical disability, joking that the president's paralysis must have reached his brain.

Roosevelt, however, did more than send messages. In October 1938 he asked Congress for a $300 million military appropriation; in November he instructed the Army Air Corps to plan for an annual production of 20,000 planes; in January 1939, he submitted a $1.3 billion defense budget. Hitler and Mussolini, he said, were "two madmen" who "respect force and force alone."

America and the Jewish Refugees

Hitler and the Nazis had translated their hatred of Jews into official policy. The Nuremberg Laws of 1935 had denied German Jews citizenship and many legal rights. Then in 1938 the anti-Jewish campaign became more stringent as the Nazis expelled Jewish students from schools and universities, and required Jews to register their property. When a distraught Jewish youth assassinated a German official in Paris, Hitler levied a "fine" of $400 million on the entire Jewish population of Germany.

This remorseless campaign reached a crescendo of violence on November 9–10, 1938: *Kristallnacht,* the "Night of Broken Glass." Throughout Germany and Austria, Nazis vandalized Jewish homes, burned synagogues, and wrecked and looted thousands of Jewish-owned businesses. Not even Jewish hospitals, old people's homes, or children's boarding schools escaped the terror.

No longer could anyone mistake Hitler's malignant intent. Jews, who had been leaving Germany since 1933, streamed out by the tens of thousands, seeking haven. Between 1933 and 1938, 60,000 had fled to the United States.

Among the victims of fascism who found refuge in America were several hundred distinguished scholars, writers, musicians, artists, and scientists. This remarkable company included pianist Rudolph Serkin, composer Béla Bartók, architect Walter Gropius, political theorist Hannah Arendt, and future secretary of state Henry Kissinger. Also among the refugees were three gifted physicists, Leo Szilard, James Franck, and Enrico Fermi, who would play key roles in building the atomic bomb. American cultural and intellectual life in the second half of the twentieth century would have been much diminished without these refugees.

In general the United States proved reluctant to grant sanctuary to the mass of Hitler's Jewish victims. Congress consistently rejected all efforts to liberalize the immigration law, with its discriminatory quotas. FDR bears some responsibility. While deploring Hitler's persecution of the Jews and helping to establish the Inter-Governmental Committee on Refugees in 1938, he did little else to translate his generalized sympathy for the Jews into political efforts to relax restrictions on immigration.

Most Americans, according to public-opinion polls, condemned the Jews' persecution, but only a minority favored admitting more refugees. In early 1938 when pollsters asked whether the immigration act should be amended to admit "a larger number of Jewish refugees from Germany," 75 percent said no.

The consequences of such attitudes became clear in June 1939 when the *St. Louis,* a German liner jammed with 900 Jewish refugees, asked permission to put its passengers ashore at Fort Lauderdale, Florida. Not only did immigration officials refuse this request, but also, according to the *New York Times,* a Coast Guard cutter stood by "to prevent possible attempts by refugees to jump off and swim ashore." The *St. Louis* turned slowly away from the lights of America and sailed back to Germany, where more than 700 of its passengers would die under Nazi brutality.

INTO THE STORM, 1939–1941

After a decade of crises—worldwide depression and regional conflicts—war erupted in Europe in 1939. Following the lightning German victories in western Europe in spring 1940, President Roosevelt's policy of relying on neutrality to keep America out of the war gave way to a policy of economic intervention. He knew that extending increasing amounts of aid to those resisting aggression by the so-called Rome-Berlin-Tokyo Axis, as well as his toughening conduct toward Germany and Japan, could, as he said, "push" the United States into the crisis of worldwide war. Japan's attack on the U.S. fleet at Pearl Harbor would provide the push.

The European War

Adolf Hitler precipitated war by demanding that Poland return to Germany the city of Danzig (Gdansk), lost after World War I. When Poland refused, Nazi armies poured into Poland at dawn on September 1, 1939, and the Luftwaffe (German air force) devastated Polish cities. Two days later, Britain and France, honoring commitments to Poland, declared war on Germany. Although FDR invoked the Neutrality Acts, he refused to ask Americans to be impartial. Even a neutral, Roosevelt declared, "cannot be asked to close his mind or his conscience."

Determined to avoid an Allied defeat that would leave the United States alone to confront Germany, the president in September 1939 prodded Congress to amend the Neutrality Acts to allow the Allies to purchase weapons on a "cash-and-carry" basis. The cash-and-carry policy reflected a public mood that favored both aiding the Allies and staying out of war.

In spring 1940 Hitler unleashed blitzkrieg (lightning war) against western Europe; the Nazi Wehrmacht (war machine) swept all the way to the English Channel in a scant two months. In early June the British evacuated most of their army, but none of its equipment, from France. And on June 22 France surrendered.

Hitler then turned his fury against Great Britain, pounding the island from the air in preparation for a cross-channel invasion. When the Royal Air Force won the "Battle of Britain," the frustrated Nazi dictator turned to terror-bombing British cities in hopes of forcing a surrender. With Coventry destroyed and much of London in smoking ruins, Prime Minister Winston Churchill pleaded for American aid. Most Americans favored additional support for Britain, but a large minority opposed it as wasteful or as a ruse to involve Americans in a war not vital to U.S. interests.

From Isolation to Intervention

In the United States in 1940, news of the "Battle of Britain" competed with speculation about whether FDR would break with tradition and run for an un-precedented third term. Not until the eve of the Democrats' July convention did he reveal that, given the world crisis, he would consent to a "draft" from his party. The Axis threat forced conservative anti–New Deal Democrats to accept both the third term and the nomination of ultra liberal Henry Wallace as vice president. It had an even greater impact on the Republicans, who nominated Wendell Willkie, an internationalist who championed aid to Britain.

Roosevelt adroitly played the role of a national leader too busy with defense and diplomacy to engage in partisan politics. To undercut GOP criticisms, he appointed Republicans to key cabinet positions: Henry L. Stimson as secretary of war and Frank Knox as secretary of the navy. With bipartisan support in Congress, Roosevelt approved a peacetime draft and a dramatic increase in defense funding. In September he engineered a "destroyers-for-bases" swap with England, sending fifty vintage American ships to Britain in exchange for leases on British air and naval bases in the Western Hemisphere. FDR claimed that the exchange was a way of averting American entry into the war.

Anti-interventionist critics accused Roosevelt of scheming to entangle the United States in the European conflict. Isolationists organized the Committee to Defend America First, which featured Charles Lindbergh as its most popular speaker and proclaimed that "Fortress America" could stand alone. Most Americans supported Roosevelt's attempt to aid Britain while avoiding war. Heartened by FDR's pledge—"I will never send an American boy to fight in a foreign war"—55 percent of Americans voted him into a third term.

Roosevelt now called on the United States to become "the arsenal of democracy." He proposed a "lend-lease" program to supply war materiel to the cash-strapped British. Despite bitter opposition by the isolationists, Congress approved lend-lease in March 1941, and supplies began to flow across the Atlantic. When Hitler's armies invaded the U.S.S.R. in June 1941, FDR dispatched supplies to the Soviets despite American hostility toward communism. To defeat Hitler, FDR said, "I would hold hands with the Devil."

To counter the menace of German submarines that threatened to choke the transatlantic supply line, Roosevelt authorized the U.S. Navy to help the British track U-boats. By summer 1941 the U.S. Navy had begun convoying British ships, with orders to destroy enemy ships if necessary. U.S. forces also occupied Greenland and Iceland to keep them out of Nazi hands.

In mid-August Roosevelt met with Churchill aboard a warship off Newfoundland. They issued a document called the Atlantic Charter that condemned aggression, affirmed national self-determination, and endorsed the principles of collective security and disarmament. After a German submarine fired at an American destroyer in September, Roosevelt authorized naval patrols to shoot on sight all Axis vessels operating in the western Atlantic. On October 31, 1941, a U-boat torpedoed and sank the destroyer *Reuben James,* killing 115 American sailors.

Now on a collision course with Germany, Roosevelt persuaded Congress in November to permit the arming of merchant ships and to allow the transport of lend-lease supplies to belligerent ports in war zones. Virtually nothing remained of the Neutrality Acts. Unprepared for a major war, America was nevertheless fighting a limited one, and full-scale war seemed imminent.

Pearl Harbor and the Coming of War

Hitler's triumphs in western Europe encouraged Japan to expand further into Asia. The United States opposed Japanese expansion virtually alone. Seeing Germany as America's primary threat, the Roosevelt administration tried to apply enough pressure to deter the Japanese without provoking Tokyo to war before the United States had built the "two-ocean navy" authorized by Congress in 1940. "It is terribly important for the control of the Atlantic for us to keep peace in the Pacific," Roosevelt told Harold Ickes, secretary of the interior, in mid-1941. "I simply have not got enough navy to go around—and every episode in the Pacific means fewer ships in the Atlantic."

The Japanese, too, hoped to avoid war, but they would not compromise. Japan's desire to create the Greater East Asia Co-Prosperity Sphere (an empire embracing much of China, Southeast Asia, and the western Pacific) matched America's insistence on the Open Door in China and the status quo in the rest of Asia. Japan saw America's stand as a ploy to block its rise to power, and Americans viewed Japan's talk of legitimate national aspirations as a smoke screen to cloak aggression. Decades of "yellow-peril" propaganda had hardened U.S. attitudes toward Japan, and even those who were isolationist toward Europe tended to be interventionist toward Asia.

Initially Roosevelt employed economic pressure to halt Japanese expansion, ending a long-standing trade treaty and banning the sale of aviation fuel and scrap metal. When Japan responded in September 1940 by signing the Tripartite Pact with Germany and Italy, a pledge by each of the Axis nations to help the others in case of attack by a new enemy, Roosevelt also stopped the sale of steel and other metals. And when Japan occupied northern Indochina, a French colony, the list of embargoed goods lengthened.

In July 1941 the Japanese overran the rest of Indochina. Roosevelt then froze all Japanese assets in the United States and clamped a total embargo on trade with Japan. Tokyo had two choices: submit to the United States to gain a resumption of trade, or conquer new lands to obtain vital resources. In October expansionist war minister General Hideki Tojo became Japan's prime minister. Tojo set the first week in December as the deadline for a preemptive strike if the United States did not yield.

By late November U.S. intelligence's deciphering of Japan's top diplomatic code alerted the Roosevelt administration that war was imminent. Negotiators made no concessions during eleventh-hour negotiations under way in Washington, and Secretary of State Hull told Secretary of War Stimson, "I have washed my hands of it, and it is now in the hands of you and Knox—the Army and the Navy." War warnings went out to all commanders in the Pacific, advising that negotiations were deadlocked and that a Japanese attack was imminent.

U.S. officials believed that the Japanese would strike British or Dutch possessions or even the Philippines—but the Japanese decided to gamble on a knockout punch. They hoped that a surprise Japanese raid on the American naval base at Pearl Harbor would destroy the U.S. Pacific Fleet and compel Roosevelt, preoccupied with Germany, to seek accommodation with Japan.

Waves of Japanese dive-bombers and torpedo planes thundered across the Hawaiian island of Oahu on the morning of December 7, 1941, bombing ships at anchor in Pearl Harbor and strafing planes parked wingtip to wingtip at nearby air bases. American forces suffered their most devastating loss in history. In less than three hours, eight battleships, three light cruisers, and two destroyers had been sunk or crippled, and 360 aircraft destroyed or damaged. The attack killed more than 2,400 Americans and opened the way for Japan's advance to the threshold of Australia in April 1942. Shocked Americans huddled by their radios to hear news of what President Roosevelt called a "date which will live in infamy."

Critics have accused Roosevelt of luring the Japanese into attacking Pearl Harbor in order to bring the United States into the war against Germany. There is no documentary evidence to support this accusation. The real problem was not duplicity—it was prejudice. Americans underestimated the resourcefulness, skill, and daring of the Japanese. Although they knew that war in the Pacific was imminent, civilian and military leaders simply did not believe that Japan would dare to attack a U.S. base five thousand miles from their home islands. However, Japanese leaders also erred. They believed that they could deal the United States a paralyzing blow at Pearl Harbor and compel the Americans to compromise rather than fight. That miscalculation assured an aroused and united nation determined to avenge the attack.

On December 8, when Roosevelt asked Congress to declare war on Japan, only one dissenting vote was cast (by Montana's Jeannette Rankin, who had also voted against entry into World War I). But FDR still hesitated to request a declaration of war against Germany. Hitler resolved the president's dilemma.

Although Hitler's advisers begged him not to add the United States to the long list of anti-Nazi belligerents, he went before a cheering Reichstag on December 11 to declare war on the "half Judaized and the other half Negrified" Americans. Mussolini chimed in with his declaration of war, and Congress reciprocated that same afternoon. America faced a global war that it was not yet ready to fight.

After Pearl Harbor, U-boats wreaked havoc in the North Atlantic and prowled the Caribbean and the East Coast of the United States. Every twenty-four hours, five more Allied vessels went to the bottom. By the end of 1942, U-boat "wolf packs" had destroyed more than a thousand Allied ships, offsetting the pace of American ship production. The United States was losing the Battle of the Atlantic.

The war news from Europe and Africa was, as Roosevelt admitted, "all bad." Hitler's rule covered an enormous swath of territory, from the outskirts of Moscow, deep in Russia, to the Pyrenees on the French-Spanish border, and from northern Norway to the Libyan desert. In spring 1942 Nazi armies inflicted more than 250,000 casualties on the Soviet army in Crimea, and Hitler launched a powerful offensive to seize the Caucasian oil fields. German forces moved relentlessly eastward in North Africa, threatening the Suez Canal, Britain's oil lifeline.

The Japanese inflicted defeat after defeat on Allied Pacific forces. Tojo followed Pearl Harbor with a rampage across the Pacific that put Guam, Wake Island, Hong Kong, Singapore, Burma, and the Netherlands East Indies under Japan's control by the end of April 1942. American forces in the Philippines, besieged for months on the island of Corregidor, surrendered in May. Japan's Rising Sun flag blazed over hundreds of islands in the central and western Pacific and over the entire eastern perimeter of the Asian mainland from the border of Siberia to the border of India.

AMERICA MOBILIZES FOR WAR

In December 1941 American armed forces numbered only 1.6 million, and war production accounted for just 15 percent of U.S. industrial output. Pearl Harbor changed everything. Within a week of the attack, Congress passed the War Powers Act, granting the president unprecedented authority. Volunteers and draftees swelled the army and navy. By war's end 15 million men and nearly 350,000 women had served. To direct this military engine, Roosevelt formed the Joint Chiefs of Staff, made up of representatives of the army, navy, and army air force. The air force grew from a minor "corps" within the army to an autonomous, and vital, part of the military. The changing nature of modern warfare led to the creation of the Office of Strategic Services (OSS) to conduct espionage and to gather the information required for strategic planning. The far-reaching domestic changes under way would outlast the war and significantly alter the nation's attitudes, behavior, and institutions.

Organizing for Victory

Roosevelt established the War Production Board (WPB) to allocate materials, to limit the production of civilian goods, and to distribute contracts. The newly created War Manpower Commission (WMC) supervised the mobilization of men and women for the military, war industry, and agriculture; the National War Labor Board (NWLB) mediated disputes between management and labor; and the Office of Price Administration (OPA) imposed strict price controls to check inflation.

"The Americans can't build planes," a Nazi commander had jeered, "only electric iceboxes and razor blades." But in 1942 the United States achieved a miracle of war production. Car makers retooled to produce planes and tanks; a pinball-machine maker converted to armor-piercing shells. By late 1942, 33 percent of the economy was committed to war production. Whole new industries appeared virtually overnight. Ninety-seven percent of the nation's crude-rubber supply now lay in Japanese-controlled territory, but by 1944, 80 percent of the rubber consumed in the United States came from synthetic-rubber factories that had not existed two years earlier.

America also became the world's greatest weapons manufacturer, producing more war materiel by 1945 than its Axis enemies combined— 300,000 military aircraft, 86,000 tanks, 2.6 million machine guns, and 6 million tons of bombs. The United States built more than 5,000 cargo ships and 86,000 warships. Henry J. Kaiser, who had supervised the construction of Boulder Dam, introduced prefabrication to cut the time needed to build ships. In 1941 the construction of a Liberty-class merchant ship took six months; in 1943, less than two weeks; by 1945, Kaiser and other shipbuilders were completing a cargo ship every day.

Such breakneck production had costs. The size and powers of the government expanded as defense spending zoomed from 9 percent of gross national product (GNP) in 1940 to 46 percent in 1945; the federal budget soared from $9 billion to $98 billion. Federal civilian employees mushroomed from 1.1 million to 3.8 million. An alliance formed between the defense industry and the military. Because the government sought the maximum production in the shortest time, it encouraged corporate profits. "If you are going to try to go to war in a capitalist country," Secretary of War Stimson said, "you have to let business make money out of the process or business won't work."

To encourage business to convert to war production and expand its capacity, the government guaranteed profits, provided generous tax write-offs, and suspended antitrust prosecutions. Two-thirds of all war-production dollars went to the hundred largest firms, and trends toward economic concentration accelerated.

The War Economy

The United States spent $250 million a day to defeat the Axis, ten times the cost of World War I. Wartime spending and the draft not only vanquished unemployment but also stimulated an industrial boom that made most Americans prosper. War expenditures doubled U.S. industrial output and nearly doubled the per capita GNP (to $1,074). By 1945 farm income had doubled from the 1940 level, net corporate profits had leaped 70 percent, and real wages, or purchasing power, had risen 50 percent.

The federal government poured $40 billion into the West, making it an economic powerhouse, the center of massive aircraft and shipbuilding industries. California alone secured more than 10 percent of all federal funds; by 1945 nearly half the personal income in the state came from the federal government.

A dynamic Sun Belt, stretching from the coastal Southeast to the coastal Southwest, was the recipient of billions spent on military bases and the needs of the armed forces—textile, oil and natural gas, chemical, and aluminum industries and their workers prospered. Boom times allowed hundreds of thousands of sharecroppers and tenant farmers to take better-paying industrial jobs.

Full employment, longer workweeks, larger paychecks, and the increased hiring of minorities, women, and the elderly brought a middle-class standard of living to millions of families. In California, the demand for workers opened opportunities in shipyards and aircraft factories for thousands of Chinese-Americans previously confined to menial jobs within their own communities. In San Diego, 40 percent of retirees returned to work. The war years produced the only significant shift toward greater equality in the distribution of income in the twentieth century.

Large-scale commercial farmers prospered, benefiting from a peak parity rate, higher consumer prices, and increased productivity thanks to improved fertilizers and more mechanization. As sharecroppers, tenants, and small farmers left the land, the overall agricultural population fell by 17 percent. Mechanization and consolidation proceeded, farming became "agribusiness," and organized agriculture wielded power equal to organized labor, big government, and big business.

Organized labor grew mightier as union membership rose from 9 million to 14.8 million workers, in part because of the expansion of the labor force. Although the National War Labor Board attempted to limit wage increases to restrain inflation, unions negotiated unprecedented fringe benefits for workers, including paid vacation time and health and pension plans. As most workers honored the "no-strike" pledge that they had given immediately after Pearl Harbor, less than one-tenth of 1 percent of wartime working time was lost to wildcat strikes. However, in 1943 United Mine Workers head John L. Lewis led more than half a million coal-field workers out of the pits and tunnels three times in two months. These strikes cost the union movement dearly as Congress passed the Smith-Connally War Labor Disputes Act in 1943, which limited workers' power to strike at a facility essential to the war effort.

Far more than strikes, inflation threatened the wartime economy. The OPA constantly battled inflation, which was fueled by greater spending power combined with a scarcity of goods. Throughout 1942 prices climbed at a 2 percent a month clip, but at the year's end Congress gave the president authority to freeze wages, prices, and rents. As the OPA clamped down, inflation slowed dramatically: consumer prices went up only 8 percent in the war's last two years.

The OPA also instituted rationing to combat inflation and to conserve scarce materials. Under the slogan "Use it up, wear it out, make it do or do without," the OPA rationed such products as gasoline, coffee, sugar, butter, cheese, and meat. Most Americans cheerfully endured "meatless Tuesdays" and cuffless trousers, formed car pools, planted victory gardens, and recycled paper, fats, rubber, and scrap metal.

The sale of war bonds, like rationing, helped to limit inflation by draining consumer purchasing power. Bond buying gave civilians a sense of involvement in the war. Small investors bought $40 billion in "E" bonds, and wealthy individuals and corporations invested nearly twice that amount. Bond sales raised almost half the money needed to finance the war. FDR wanted to increase taxes to pay for the war, but Congress only grudgingly raised taxes. However, by the war's end the top income-tax rate had risen from 60 percent to 90 percent, and middle- and lower-income Americans were paying income taxes for the first time. The introduction of payroll deductions to withhold income taxes from wages facilitated tax collection.

"A Wizard War"

Recognizing wartime scientific and technological developments, Winston Churchill dubbed World War II "a wizard war." In 1941 FDR created the Office of Scientific Research and Development (OSRD) for the development of new ordnance and medicines. The OSRD spent more than $1 billion to produce improved radar and sonar, rocket weapons, and proximity fuses for mines and artillery shells. It also funded the development of jet aircraft, pressurized cabins, and high-altitude bombsights. Other OSRD research hastened the widespread use of insecticides, contributed to improved blood transfusions, and produced "miracle drugs" such as penicillin. The agency's medical advances saved thousands of lives during the war and would increase life expectancy in peacetime.

The demand for greater accuracy in artillery required the kind of rapid, detailed calculations that only computing machines could supply. By 1944 navy personnel in the basement of Harvard's physics laboratory were operating IBM's Mark I, a cumbersome device 51 feet long and 8 feet high that weighed five tons. A second-generation computer, ENIAC, soon reduced the time to multiply two tenth-place numbers from Mark I's three seconds to less than three-thousandths of a second.

At the same time, however, the environment often became a war casualty. For example, DDT helped control malaria and other insect-borne diseases, but its toxicity was ignored. The production of synthetic rubber fouled the air with sulfur dioxide and carbon monoxide.

The atomic bomb project began in August 1939 when Albert Einstein, a Jewish refugee and Nobel Prize-winning physicist, warned Roosevelt that Nazi scientists were seeking to use atomic physics to construct an extraordinarily destructive weapon. In 1941 FDR launched a massive Anglo-American secret program—the Soviets were excluded—to construct an atomic bomb. The next year the participating physicists, both Americans and Europeans, achieved a controlled chain reaction and acquired the basic knowledge necessary to develop the bomb. In 1943–1944 the Manhattan Engineer-ing District—the code name for the atomic project—stockpiled fissionable materials. By July 1945 the Manhattan Project had employed more than 120,000 people and spent nearly $2 billion.

Just before dawn on July 16, 1945, a blinding fireball with "the brightness of several suns at midday" rose over the desert at Alamogordo, New Mexico, followed by a billowing mushroom cloud. Equivalent to 20,000 tons of TNT, the blast from this first atomic explosion was felt 100 miles away. The awesome spectacle reminded J. Robert Oppenheimer, the scientific director of the Manhattan Project, of a line from Hindu scripture: "Now I am become Death, the destroyer of worlds." The atomic age had begun.

Propaganda and Politics

People as well as science and machinery had to be mobilized. To sustain a spirit of unity, the Roosevelt administration carefully managed public opinion. The Office of Censorship, established in December 1941, examined all letters going overseas and worked with publishers and broadcasters to suppress information that might damage the war effort, such as details of troop movements. Much was concealed. A year passed, for example, before the casualty and damage figures from Pearl Harbor were disclosed.

To shape public opinion, FDR created the Office of War Information (OWI) in June 1942. The OWI employed more than 4,000 writers, artists, and advertising specialists to explain the war and to counter enemy propaganda. The OWI depicted the war as a moral struggle between good and evil—the enemy had to be destroyed, not merely defeated.

While the Roosevelt administration concentrated on the war, Republican critics seized the initiative in domestic politics. Full employment and high wages undermined the Democrats' class appeal, and many of the urban and working-class voters essential to the Roosevelt coalition were serving in the armed forces and did not vote in the 1942 elections. As Republicans gained nine seats in the Senate and forty-six in the House, congressional politics shifted to the right. Conservative Republicans and southern Democrats held the power to make or break legislation. Resentful of the wartime expansion of executive authority and determined to curb labor unions and welfare spending, the conservatives abolished the CCC and the WPA and rebuffed attempts to extend the New Deal.

Despite the strength of the conservative coalition, the war enormously expanded governmental and executive power. As never before, Washington managed the economy, molded public opinion, funded scientific research, and influenced people's daily lives.

THE BATTLEFRONT, 1942–1944

America's industrial might and Soviet manpower turned the tides of war. Diplomacy followed the fortunes of war, with Allied unity gradually diminishing as Germany and Japan weakened, and as the United States, Britain, and the Soviet Union each sought wartime strategies and postwar arrangements best suited to its own interests.

Liberating Europe

After Pearl Harbor, British and American officials agreed to concentrate first on defeating Germany and then on smashing Japan. But they differed on where to mount an attack. Stalin demanded a second front, an invasion of western Europe to force Hitler to transfer troops west and thus to relieve pressure on the Russians, who faced the full fury of the Nazi armies. Prime Minister Churchill insisted on clearing the Mediterranean before invading France. He feared that a premature landing in France could mean slaughter, and he wanted American aid in North Africa to protect the Suez Canal, vital to the British. Over Soviet protests, Churchill persuaded Roosevelt to postpone the "second front" in western Europe and to invade North Africa instead. In November 1942 in Operation Torch, American and British troops under General Dwight D. Eisenhower landed in Morocco

and Algeria. Pushing eastward, they trapped the German and Italian armies being driven westward by the British, and in May 1943 some 260,000 German-Italian troops surrendered.

Left alone to face two-thirds of the Nazi force, the Soviet Union hung on and, in the turning point of the European war, defeated Germany in the protracted Battle of Stalingrad (August 1942–January 1943). After destroying an entire German army—more than 600,000 men—at Stalingrad, the Red Army went on the offensive along a thousand-mile front. Stalingrad cost the Soviet Union more battle deaths in four months than the United States suffered in the entire war.

Although Stalin renewed his plea for a second front, Churchill again objected, and Roosevelt again agreed to a British plan: the invasion of Sicily. In summer 1943 Anglo-American forces gained control of Sicily in less than a month. Italian military leaders deposed Mussolini and surrendered to the Allies on September 8. As Allied forces moved up the Italian peninsula, German troops poured into Italy. Facing elite Nazi divisions in strong defensive positions, the Allies spent eight months inching their way 150 miles to Rome and were still battling through the mud and snow of northern Italy when the war in Europe ended.

In 1943 and 1944 the United States and Britain turned the tide in the Atlantic and sent thousands of bombers over Germany. To the east, Soviet troops kept the Nazis in retreat. American science and industry, as much as the American navy, won the Battle of the Atlantic. Advanced radar systems, high-frequency detection finders, and improved depth charges and torpedoes moved from laboratories to the ocean. Planes and ships poured from American factories. Moreover, at the start of 1943 British and American air forces began round-the-clock bombardment, raining thousands of tons of bombs on German cities. In raids on Hamburg in July 1943, Allied planes dropping incendiary bombs created terrible firestorms, killing nearly 100,000 people and leveling the city, much as they had done earlier at Cologne.

Meanwhile, in 1943 as the Soviet offensive reclaimed Russian cities and towns from the Nazis,

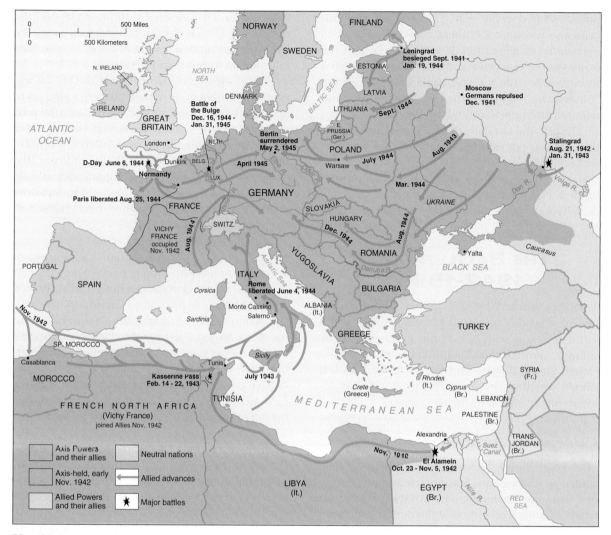

MAP 25.3
World War II in Europe and Africa
The momentous German defeats at Stalingrad and in Tunisia early in 1943 marked the turning point in the war against the Axis. By 1945 the Allied conquest of Hitler's "thousand year" Reich was imminent.

the German armies fell into perpetual retreat across the vast north European plain. Advancing swiftly, the Red Army drove the Germans out of Soviet territory by mid-1944 and plunged into Poland, where the Soviets set up a puppet government. Late summer and early fall saw Soviet troops seize Romania and Bulgaria and aid communist guerillas under Josip Broz Tito in liberating Yugoslavia.

As the Soviets swept across eastern Europe, Allied forces finally opened the long-delayed second front. On June 6, 1944—D-Day—nearly 200,000 Allied troops landed in Normandy in northwestern France, gaining a toehold on French soil. Within six weeks another million Allied troops had waded ashore. Under General Eisenhower, the Allies liberated Paris in August and reached the German border by the end of summer. However, in the face of supply problems and stiffened German resistance, the Allied offensive ground to a halt.

In mid-December as the Allies prepared for a full-scale assault on the German heartland, Hitler in a desperate gamble threw his last reserves against American positions. The Battle of the Bulge—named for the "bulge" eighty miles long and fifty miles wide that Hitler's troops drove into the Allies' line—raged for nearly a month, and when it ended American troops stood on the banks of the Rhine. It had cost the United States fifty-five thousand soldiers dead or wounded and 18,000 taken prisoner. But the way to Germany lay open, and the end of the European war was in sight.

War in the Pacific

The day after the Philippines fell to Japan in mid-May 1942, U.S. and Japanese fleets confronted each other in the Coral Sea off northeastern Australia, the first naval battle in history fought entirely from aircraft carriers. Both sides took heavy losses, but the Battle of the Coral Sea stopped the Japanese advance on Australia. Less than a month later, a Japanese armada turned toward Midway Island, the crucial American outpost between Hawaii and Japan. Because the U.S. Signal Corps had broken the Japanese naval code, Japan's plans and the locations of her ships were known. American carriers and their planes consequently won a decisive victory, sinking four Japanese carriers and destroying several hundred enemy planes. Suddenly on the defensive, the stunned Japanese could now only try to hold what they had already won.

On the offensive, U.S. Marines waded ashore at Guadalcanal in the Solomon Islands in August 1942. Tropical diseases—malaria, fungus, dysentery—afflicted both sides, but in six months of bloody fighting the United States drove the Japanese out of the Solomons. Japan left behind 25,000 dead, a gruesome preview of island battles to come.

In fall 1943 American forces began a two-pronged advance toward Japan. Under General Douglas MacArthur, the army advanced north from Australia, "leapfrogging" from one strategic island to another. A second force under Admiral Chester Nimitz "island-hopped" across the central Pacific, isolating Japanese troops behind American lines and seizing key islands to serve as bases for American bombers sent against Japan itself. Capture of the Marianas in summer 1944 put Tokyo within range of the new B-29 bombers, which by late 1944 were incinerating Japanese cities. In fall 1944 the American navy annihilated what remained of the imperial fleet at the battles of the Philippine Sea and Leyte Gulf. Japan's sea and air power were now totally shattered. Still, Japanese military leaders stymied attempts by civilians in the government to negotiate peace.

The Grand Alliance

Two primary goals underlay Roosevelt's wartime strategies: the total defeat of the Axis at the least possible cost in American lives, and the establishment of a world order strong enough to preserve peace, open trade, and ensure national self-determination in the postwar era. Aware that only a common enemy fused the Grand Alliance together, FDR tried to promote harmony by concentrating on military victory and postponing divisive postwar matters.

But Churchill and Stalin had other goals. Britain sought to retain its imperial possessions and a balance of power against the U.S.S.R. in Europe. The Soviet Union wanted a permanently weakened Germany and a sphere of influence in eastern Europe in order to protect itself against future attacks from the West. To hold together this uneasy alliance, FDR used personal diplomacy to mediate conflicts.

In January 1943 Roosevelt and Churchill had met at Casablanca, Morocco's main port, where they had resolved to attack Italy before invading France, and proclaimed that the war would continue until the Axis accepted "unconditional surrender." In this proclamation they sought to reduce Soviet mistrust of the West, which had deepened because of the postponement of the second front. Then in November 1943, at Cairo, Roosevelt had met with Churchill and Jiang Jieshi (Chiang

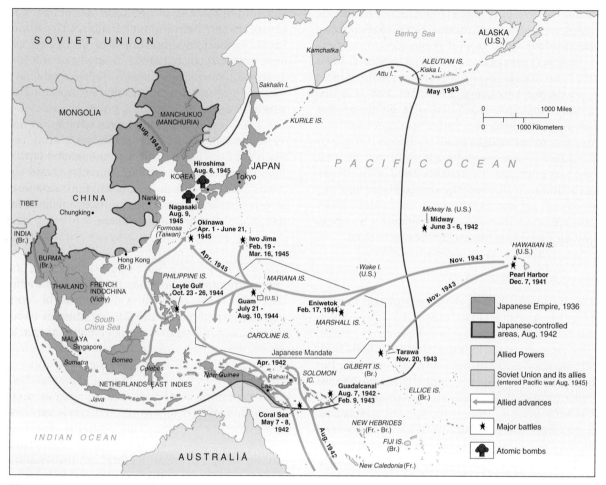

MAP 25.4

World War II in the Pacific

American ships and planes stemmed the Japanese offensive at the Battles of the Coral Sea and Midway Island. Thereafter, the Japanese were on the defensive against American amphibious assaults and air strikes. **hc** Interactive Map: The Pacific War

Kai-shek), head of the Chinese government. To keep China in the war, FDR promised the return of Manchuria and Taiwan to China and guaranteed a free and independent Korea.

FDR and Churchill had continued on from Cairo to Tehran, Iran's capital, to confer with Stalin. Here they had set the invasion of France for June 1944 and agreed to divide Germany into zones of occupation and to impose reparations on the Reich. Most important to Roosevelt, at Tehran

Stalin had also pledged to enter the Pacific war after Hitler's defeat.

Roosevelt then turned his attention to domestic politics. Conservative gains in both the Republican and the Democratic parties drove FDR to dump the liberal Henry A. Wallace from the ticket and accept Harry S Truman as his vice-presidential candidate. A moderate senator from Missouri, Truman was not strongly opposed by any major Democratic faction, and was called "the new Missouri

Compromise." He restored a semblance of unity to the party for the 1944 campaign. The Republicans, hoping that unity would carry *them* to victory, nominated moderate New York governor Thomas E. Dewey. The campaign focused more on personalities than issues, with the Republicans harping on FDR's failing health and FDR touting American military victories.

In November the American electorate handed FDR an unprecedented fourth term, but with his narrowest margin ever—only 53 percent of the popular vote. Roosevelt owed his triumph largely to the urban vote and the support of organized labor. Weary and frail, the president now directed his waning energies toward defeating the Axis and constructing a new international order.

WAR AND AMERICAN SOCIETY

The crisis of war altered the most basic patterns of American life, powerfully affecting those on the home front as well as those who served in the armed forces. Few families were untouched: more than 15 million Americans went to the war, an equal number were on the move, and unprecedented numbers of women went to work outside the home. As well, the war opened some doors of opportunity for African-Americans and other minorities, although most remained closed. It heightened minority aspirations and widened cracks in the wall of white racist attitudes and policy, while maintaining much of America's racial caste system, thereby tilling the ground for future crises.

The GIs' War

Fifteen million American men and 350,000 U.S. women went to war, grousing that they were as "GI"—government-issue—as their uniforms and equipment. More interested in dry socks than in ideology, they knew little of the big strategies, and cared less. They wanted to defeat Hitler, avenge Pearl Harbor, and return to a secure, familiar United States.

But the GIs' war dragged on for almost four years, transforming its participants. Millions who had never been far from home traveled to unfamiliar cities and remote lands. Sharing tents and foxholes with fellow Americans of different religions, nationalities, and social backgrounds helped to erase deep-seated prejudices.

Physical misery, chronic exhaustion, and intense combat left psychological as well as physical wounds. In the Pacific, both American and Japanese troops saw the others in racist terms, as animals to be exterminated. Both sides sometimes behaved brutally, machine-gunning pilots parachuting from damaged planes, torturing and killing prisoners, and mutilating enemy dead. Atrocities also occurred in the war against Germany, although on a lesser scale; for example, one armored battalion boasted that it shot all the SS soldiers it captured. Some became cynical about human life; others, haunted by nightmares about the war, would long languish in veterans' hospitals.

The Home Front

Nothing transformed the social topography more than the vast internal migration of an already mobile people. Americans swarmed to the centers of war production, especially the Pacific coast states, which manufactured one-half of the nation's wartime ships and airplanes. Six million people left farms to work in cities, and several million southern whites and blacks migrated northward and westward. This mass uprooting made Americans both more cosmopolitan and tolerant of differences and more lonely, alienated, and frustrated.

Life-styles became freewheeling as Americans moved far from their hometowns, leaving behind their traditional values. Housing shortages left millions living in converted garages, tent cities, trailer camps, or even their own cars. Overcrowding as well as wartime separations strained family and community life. High rates of divorce, family violence, and juvenile delinquency reflected the disruptions. Urban blight and conflicts between newcomers and old-timers accelerated.

Millions of American women donned pants, put their hair in bandannas, and went to work in defense plants. Reversing a decade of efforts to exclude women from the labor force, the federal government in 1942 urged women into war production. Songs such as "We're the Janes Who Make the Planes" appealed to women to take up war work, and propaganda called on them to fill jobs to release able-bodied men for fighting. More than 6 million women entered the labor force during the war, bringing the number of employed women to 19 million. Less than a quarter of the labor force in 1940, women constituted well over a third of all workers in 1945.

The characteristics of female wage earners changed. Before the war women workers were predominantly young and single, but 75 percent of the new female workers were married, 60 percent were over thirty-five, and more than 33 percent had children under age fourteen. Women tended blast furnaces, operated cranes, drove taxis, welded hulls, and worked in shipyards. "Rosie the Riveter," her muscular arms cradling a pneumatic gun, symbolized the woman war worker; she was, as a popular song put it, "making history working for victory."

Women war workers implicitly challenged ideas of sexual inequality, but wartime strengthened traditional convictions. Men, not women, fought and died. This mindset allowed gender discrimination to flourish throughout the war, with women earning only 65 percent of what men did for the same work. Government propaganda portrayed women's war work as a temporary response to an emergency, and few women challenged traditional views of gender roles. "A woman is a substitute," asserted a War Department brochure, "like plastic instead of metal." Work was pictured as an extension of women's traditional roles as wives and mothers. A newspaperwoman wrote of the "deep satisfaction which a woman of today knows who has made a rubber boat which may save the life of her aviator husband, or helped fashion a bullet which may avenge her son!" Given the concern about jobs for veterans after the war, attitudes toward women's employment changed little; in 1945 only 18 percent of respondents in a poll approved of married women working.

Traditional notions about a woman's place also shaped government resistance to establishing child-care centers for women employed in defense. "A mother's primary duty is to her home and children," the Labor Department's Children's Bureau stated. Funds for federal child-care centers covered few defense workers' children, and the young suffered. New terms such as *eight-hour orphans* and *latchkey children* described children forced to fend for themselves. Feeding the fears of

Rosie the Riveter
Memorialized in song and story, "Rosie the Riveter" symbolized the women war workers who assumed jobs in heavy industry to take up the slack for the absent 15 million men in the armed services. Here a very real Rosie the Riveter is doing her job in April 1943 at the Baltimore manufacturing plant for Martin PMB Mariners.

those who believed that having women work outside the home would cause the family to disintegrate, juvenile delinquency increased fivefold and the divorce rate nearly doubled.

The impact of war on women and children was multifaceted and even contradictory. Divorce rates soared, but so did marriage rates and birthrates. Although some women remained content to roll bandages for the Red Cross, 350,000 women joined the armed forces and for the first time served in positions there other than nurse. Female workers gained unprecedented employment opportunities and public recognition. Although many eagerly gave up their jobs at the end of the war, just as many did not relish losing their income and newfound independence. Overall, the war gave women a new sense of their potential. Most women still hoped to be wives and mothers, but the war had widened women's worlds and challenged traditional notions as nothing before ever had.

The war production boom that created both overcrowded communities and ghost towns played havoc with the nation's school systems. More than 350,000 teachers joined the armed services or took on better-paying war work, leaving schools badly understaffed. Students abandoned school in record numbers. High-school enrollments sank as full-time teenage employment rose from 900,000 in 1940 to 3 million in 1944.

The loss of students to the armed services and war production forced colleges to admit large numbers of women and to contract themselves out to the military. Military training programs sent nearly a million servicemen and women to college campuses to acquire skills in engineering, foreign languages, economics, and the sciences. Higher education became more dependent on the federal government, and universities competed for federal contracts and subsidies.

The war profoundly affected American culture. Spending on books and theater entertainment more than doubled. More than sixty million people (in a population of 135 million) attended movies weekly. Hollywood turned out a spate of war films that reinforced the image of Nazis and Japanese as fiends, portrayed GIs as freedom-loving heroes, and intensified Americans' appetites for unconditional victory. But as the war dragged on, people tired of propaganda, and Hollywood reemphasized romance and adventure.

Early in the war popular music featured patriotic themes. "Goodbye, Mama, I'm Off to Yokohama" was the first hit of 1942. As the war continued, themes of lost love and loneliness dominated songs. By 1945 bitterness pervaded the lyrics of best-selling records, and such hits as "Saturday Night Is the Loneliest Night of the Week" revealed an impatience for the war's end.

In bookstores, nonfiction crowded the shelves, and every newsmagazine increased its circulation. Wendell Willkie's *One World* (1943) became the fastest-selling title in publishing history to that time, with 2 million copies snapped up in two years. A vision of a world without military alliances and spheres of influence, this brief volume expressed hope that an international organization would extend peace and democracy through the postwar world. The Government Printing Office published Armed Services Editions, paperback reprints of classics and new releases, and nearly 350 million copies were distributed free to soldiers.

Americans also stayed glued to their radios during the war. The quest for up-to-date information kept radio audiences at record levels. Networks increased their news programs from 4 percent to nearly 40 percent of their daily schedule. Daytime serials, such as those featuring Dick Tracy tracking down Axis spies, reached the height of their popularity; a platoon of new comic book superheroes, including Captain America and Captain Marvel, saw action on the battlefield. Even Bugs Bunny put on a uniform to combat America's foes.

Racism and New Opportunities

Realizing that the government needed the loyalty and work of a united people in order to win the war, African-American leaders saw new pathways to securing equal rights. In 1942 civil-rights spokesmen insisted that African-American support of the war hinged on the United States' commitment to racial justice. They demanded a double campaign: to gain victory over racial discrimination at home as well as over the Axis abroad.

Membership in the National Association for the Advancement of Colored People multiplied nearly ten times, reaching 500,000 in 1945. The association pressed for anti–poll tax and antilynching legislation, decried discrimination in defense industries and the armed services, and sought to end African-American disfranchisement. The campaign for black voting rights gained momentum when the Supreme Court, in *Smith* v. *Allwright* (1944), ruled Texas's all-white primary unconstitutional. This decision eliminated a barrier that had existed in eight states, although these states promptly resorted to other devices to minimize African-American voting.

A new civil-rights organization, the Congress of Racial Equality (CORE), was founded in 1942. Employing the strategy of nonviolent resistance to challenge Jim Crow, CORE sought to desegregate public facilities in northern cities. Also proposing nonviolent direct action was A. Philip Randolph, president of the Brotherhood of Sleeping Car Porters. In 1941 Randolph called for a "thundering march" of 100,000 blacks on Washington "to wake up and shock white America." He had warned Roosevelt that if the president did not abolish discrimination in the armed services and the defense industry, African-Americans would besiege the nation's capital. FDR had agreed to compromise, in June 1941 issuing Executive Order 8802, the first presidential directive on race since Reconstruction. It prohibited discriminatory employment practices by federal agencies and all unions and companies engaged in war-related work and established the Fair Employment Practices Commission (FEPC) to enforce this policy. Although the FEPC did not apply to the armed forces and lacked effective enforcement powers, roaring war production and a shrinking labor pool resulted in the employment of 2 million African-Americans in industry and 200,000 in the federal civil service. Between 1942 and 1945 the proportion of blacks in war production shot up from 3 percent to 9 percent. African-American membership in labor unions doubled, and the number of skilled and semi-skilled African-American workers tripled. Average earnings for blacks increased from $457 to $1,976 a year, compared to $2,600 for whites.

About 1 million African-Americans served in the armed forces. Wartime needs forced the military to end policies of excluding blacks from combat units. The all-black 761st Tank Battalion gained distinction fighting in Germany, and the 99th Pursuit Squadron won eighty Distinguished Flying Crosses in combat against the Luftwaffe. Although the army and navy began experiments with integration in 1944, most blacks served in segregated units under white officers. Ironically, the Red Cross maintained separate black and white blood banks, even though a black physician, Dr. Charles Drew, had invented the process of storing blood plasma. The failure of military authorities to protect African-American servicemen off the post and the use of white military police to keep African-Americans "in their place" sparked conflict on many army bases. At least fifty African-American soldiers died in wartime racial encounters in the United States.

Violence within the military mirrored growing racial tensions at home. As African-Americans militantly protested against discrimination, many whites resisted all efforts by blacks to improve their economic and social status. Numerous clashes occurred. In mid-1943 scores of cities reported pitched battles between whites and African-Americans. The bloodiest race riot exploded in Detroit that June. By its end, twenty-five blacks and nine whites lay dead, more than seven hundred had been injured, and more than $2 million in property had been destroyed. Fear of more violence led white liberals to emphasize racial tolerance and African-American leaders to reduce their militancy.

These wartime developments would lead to eventual success in the drive for black civil rights. As more than 700,000 blacks migrated from the South, blacks' status in society became a national concern. African-Americans were experiencing a new attitude of independence, and their greater educational and employment opportunities engendered hopefulness. With growing numbers of blacks voting in northern industrial cities, African-Americans could hold the balance of power in close elections. Consequently, politicians extended greater recognition to African-Americans and paid more attention to civil rights.

Blacks' optimism also flowed from the new prominence of the United States as a major power in a nonwhite world. As Japanese propaganda directed at Asians and Latin Americans emphasized lynchings of blacks and race riots in the United States, Americans confronted the peril that white racism posed to their national security. In addition, the horrors of Nazi racism made Americans sensitive to the harm caused by their own white-supremacist attitudes and practices. A former Alabama governor lamented that Nazism had "wrecked the theories of the master race with which we were so contented so long."

In a massive study of race problems entitled *An American Dilemma* (1944), Swedish economist Gunnar Myrdal concluded that "not since Reconstruction had there been more reason to anticipate fundamental changes in American race relations." Returning black veterans, and African-Americans who had served the nation on the home front, resolved as never before to gain all the rights enjoyed by whites.

War and Diversity

Wartime winds of change brought new opportunities, and problems, to other American minorities. Twenty-five thousand Native Americans served in the armed forces, including Navajo "code-talkers" who confounded the Japanese by relaying secret messages in an unbreakable code based on their native tongue. Another 50,000 Indians left reservations to work in defense. For most, it was the first experience of living in a non-Indian world, and after the war some would remain in the cities. Continued discrimination, however, would force a majority back to their reservations, which suffered severely from budget cuts during the war and the immediate postwar years. Prodded by those who coveted Indian lands, lawmakers demanded that Indians be taken off the backs of taxpayers and "freed from the reservations" to make their own way like other Americans. To mobilize against the

campaign to end all reservations and trust protections, Native Americans in 1944 organized the National Congress of American Indians.

To relieve agricultural labor shortages, the federal government negotiated an agreement with Mexico to import temporary workers, *braceros.* Classified as foreign workers, not immigrants, an estimated 200,000 *braceros* received short-term contracts. Farm owners frequently violated these contracts and also encouraged an influx of illegal immigrants.

Unable to complain about prejudice and the way they were treated without risking deportation, hundreds of thousands of Mexicans were exploited by Anglo planters and ranchers. At the same time, large numbers of Mexicans and Mexican-Americans moved to Los Angeles, Chicago, Detroit, and other large cities, where they found jobs in defense plants, garment factories, shipyards, and steel mills. Even as their occupational status and material conditions improved, most Mexican-Americans remained in communities segregated from the larger society.

In the military itself, Spanish-speaking Americans, like blacks, suffered discrimination. Nevertheless, nearly 350,000 Chicanos served in the armed forces, earning a disproportionate number of citations for distinguished service and Congressional Medals of Honor. And much like black and Indian veterans, Mexican-American veterans organized new groups to press for equal rights.

Thousands of gay men and lesbians who served in the armed forces also found new wartime opportunities. Although the military officially barred those they defined as "sexual perverts," the urgency of building a massive armed forces led to just four to five thousand men out of eighteen million examined for induction to be excluded because of homosexuality. For the vast majority of gays not excluded, being emancipated from traditional expectations and the close scrutiny of family and neighbors, and living in overwhelmingly all-male or all-female environments, brought freedom to meet like-minded gay men and women and to express their sexual orientation. Like other minorities, many gays saw the war as a chance to prove their worth under fire. On one American warship, the most highly regarded officer was "a notorious Queen" who wore a hair net. Yet others suspected of being gay were dishonorably discharged, sent to psychiatric hospitals, or imprisoned in so-called queer stockades, to be abused by military police. In 1945 gay veterans established the Veteran's Benevolent Association, the first major gay organization in the United States to combat discrimination.

The Internment of Japanese-Americans

Far more than any other minority in the United States, Japanese suffered grievously during the war. The internment of 112,000 Japanese-Americans, two-thirds of them native-born U.S. citizens, in relocation centers guarded by military police, was a tragic reminder of the fragility of civil liberties in wartime.

The policy reflected forty years of anti-Japanese sentiment on the West Coast, rooted in racial prejudice and economic rivalry. Self-serving politicians and farmers who wanted Japanese-American land had long decried the "yellow peril," and after the attack on Pearl Harbor they whipped up the rage and fears of many white Californians. In February 1942 Roosevelt gave in to the pressure and authorized the evacuation of all Japanese-Americans from the West Coast, despite the fact that not a single Japanese-American had been apprehended for espionage or sedition and neither the Federal Bureau of Investigation nor military intelligence had uncovered any disloyal behavior by Japanese-Americans.

Interestingly, only Japanese-Americans on the mainland fell victim to the internment policy. The Hawaiian islands were home to approximately 160,000 people of Japanese ancestry, one-third of the entire population. Nonetheless, despite the potential damage that saboteurs could have inflicted, Hawaiian officials maintained their tradition of interracial harmony. "This is America and we must do things the American way," announced Hawaii's military governor. Hawaii's Japanese committed no acts of sabotage; indeed, many became "super-patriots" in order to honor their obligations to the United States.

But on the mainland Japanese-Americans, forced to sell their lands and homes at whatever prices they could obtain, were herded into barbed-wire-encircled detention camps in desolate areas of the West. The Supreme Court, in *Korematsu* v. *U.S.* (1944), upheld the constitutionality of the evacuation, stating that it would not question government claims of military necessity during the war. By then, however, the hysteria had subsided, and the government had begun a program of gradual release. In 1982 a special government commission would formally blame the Roosevelt administration's action on "race prejudice, war hysteria, and a failure of political leadership" and would apologize to Japanese-Americans for "a grave injustice." In 1988 Congress voted to pay $20,000 as compensation to each of the nearly 60,000 Japanese-American internees still alive.

TRIUMPH AND TRAGEDY, 1945

Spring and summer 1945 brought stunning changes. In Europe the collapse of the Nazi Third Reich saw a new balance of power emerge. In Asia continued Japanese resistance and reluctance to surrender led to the use of the atomic bomb. And in the United States, a new president, Harry Truman, presided over the end of World War II and the beginning of a new, "cold" war.

The Yalta Conference

By the time Roosevelt, Churchill, and Stalin met at the Soviet city of Yalta in February 1945, the military situation favored the Soviet Union. The Red Army had overrun Poland, Romania, and Bulgaria; driven the Nazis out of Yugoslavia; penetrated Austria, Hungary, and Czechoslovakia; and was massed only fifty miles from Berlin. American forces, in contrast, were still recovering from the Battle of the Bulge and faced stiff resistance on the route to Japan. The Joint Chiefs of Staff, predicting

Yalta Conference, 1945
The palaces where Churchill, Roosevelt, Stalin, and their
advisers gathered were still standing, but the rest of Yalta had
been reduced to ruin during the German occupation.

ence to establish a permanent international organization for collective security.

Stalin, however, proved adamant about Soviet domination in eastern Europe, particularly Poland. Twice in the twentieth century, German troops had used Poland as a pathway for invading Russia. Stalin would not expose his land again, and after the Red Army had captured Warsaw in January 1945, he brutally subdued the noncommunist majority. Roosevelt and Churchill refused to recognize the communist Lublin regime, but they accepted Stalin's pledge to include noncommunist Poles in the new government and to allow free elections. They could do little else. Short of going to war against the Soviet Union while battling Germany and Japan, FDR could only hope that Stalin would keep his word.

that an invasion of Japan would cost 1 million American casualties, insisted that obtaining Stalin's help in Asia was worth almost any price. Stalin was in a position to make demands. Roosevelt and Churchill could do little about Stalin's domination of eastern Europe but considered Soviet aid essential in Asia. The United States anticipated a long, bloody battle against Japan. Stalin, however, had the luxury of deciding whether or not to enter the Pacific war.

The Yalta agreements mirrored these realities. Stalin again promised to declare war on Japan "two or three months" after Germany's surrender, and in return Roosevelt and Churchill reneged on their arrangement with Jiang Jieshi (made earlier at Cairo) and promised the Soviet Union concessions in Manchuria and the territories that it had lost in the Russo-Japanese War forty years before. Stalin accepted the temporary partitioning of Germany and the postponement of discussions about reparations. On the matter dearest to FDR's heart, Stalin approved plans for a United Nations confer-

Victory in Europe

Meanwhile, Allied armies closed the vise on Germany. In early March 1945 American troops captured Cologne and encircled Germany's industrial heartland. To counter the threat of Soviet power in postwar Europe, Churchill proposed a rapid thrust to Berlin, but Eisenhower, with Roosevelt's backing, overruled the British. Instead, to minimize their casualties and to reassure Stalin, the Americans advanced methodically on a broad front until they met the Russians at the Elbe River at the end of April. By then the Red Army had overrun Vienna and reached the suburbs of Berlin. On April 30 Hitler committed suicide in a bunker under the ruins of Berlin; the city fell to the Soviets on May 2. A hastily assembled German government surrendered unconditionally on May 8.

Jubilant Americans celebrated Victory in Europe (V-E) Day less than a month after they had mourned the death of FDR. On April 12 the exhausted president died of a cerebral hemorrhage. His unprepared successor inherited leadership of the most powerful nation in history—as well as troubles with the Soviet Union that seemed more intractable every day.

Harry S Truman had little familiarity with world affairs. Perhaps sensing his own inadequacies, he adopted a tough pose and counted on American military power to maintain the peace. In office less than two weeks, he lashed out at Soviet ambassador V. M. Molotov that the United States was tired of waiting for Moscow to allow free elections in Poland, and he threatened to cut off lend-lease aid if the Soviet Union did not cooperate. The Truman administration then reduced U.S. economic assistance to the Soviets and stalled on their request for a $1 billion reconstruction loan. Stalin consequently broke his Yalta promises and strengthened his control of eastern Europe.

The Truman administration neither conceded the Soviet sphere of influence in eastern Europe nor tried to end it. Truman still sought Stalin's cooperation in establishing the United Nations and in defeating Japan, but Soviet-American relations rapidly deteriorated. By June 1945, when the Allied countries framed the United Nations Charter in San Francisco, hopes for a peaceful new international order had dimmed, and the United Nations emerged as a diplomatic battleground. Truman, Churchill, and Stalin met at Potsdam, Germany, from July 16 to August 2, to complete the postwar arrangements begun at Yalta. Each trying to preserve and enlarge his nation's sphere of influence, the allies could barely agree even to demilitarize Germany and to punish Nazi war criminals. All the major divisive issues were postponed. Given the diplomatic impasse, military power would determine the contours of the postwar world.

The Holocaust

When news of the Holocaust—the term later given to the Nazis' extermination of European Jewry—first leaked out in early 1942, many Americans discounted the reports. Not until November did the State Department admit knowledge of the massacres. A month later the American broadcaster Edward R. Murrow, listened to nationwide, reported on the systematic killing of millions of Jews, "It is a picture of mass murder and moral depravity unequalled in the history of the world. It is a horror beyond what imagination can grasp. . . . There are no longer 'concentration camps'—we must speak now only of 'extermination camps'."

Nevertheless, most Americans considered the annihilation of Europe's six million Jews beyond belief. There were no photographs to prove it, and, some argued, the atrocities attributed to the Germans in World War I had turned out to be false. So few took issue with the military's view that the way to liberate those enslaved by Hitler was by speedily winning the war. Pleas by American Jews for the Allies to bomb the death camps and the railroad tracks leading to them fell on deaf ears. In fall 1944 U.S. planes flying over Auschwitz in southern Poland bombed nearby factories but left the gas chambers and crematoria intact, in order, American officials explained, not to divert air power from more vital raids elsewhere.

How much could have been done remains uncertain. Still, the U.S. government never seriously considered rescue schemes or searched for a way to curtail the Nazis' "final solution" to the "Jewish question." Its feeble response was due to its overwhelming focus on winning the war as quickly as possible, congressional and public fears of an influx of destitute Jews into the United States, Britain's wish to placate the Arabs by keeping Jewish settlers out of Palestine, and the fear of some Jewish-American leaders that pressing the issue would increase anti-Semitism at home. The War Refugee Board managed to save the lives of just two hundred thousand Jews and twenty thousand non-Jews. Six million other Jews, about 75 percent of the European Jewish population, were gassed, shot, or incinerated, as were several million gypsies, communists, homosexuals, Polish Catholics, and others deemed unfit to live in the Third Reich.

"The things I saw beggar description,' wrote General Eisenhower after visiting the first death camp liberated by the U.S. army. He sent immediately for a delegation of congressional leaders and newspaper editors to make sure Americans would never forget the gas chambers and human ovens. Only after viewing the photographs and newsreels of corpses stacked like cordwood, boxcars heaped with the bones of dead prisoners, bulldozers shoving emaciated bodies into hastily dug ditches, and liberated, barely alive living skeletons lying in their own filth, their vacant, sunken eyes staring through

Bergen-Belsen Concentration Camp
Entering Germany in 1945, American troops discovered the horrors that the Nazis had perpetrated on European Jews and others. Here, General Eisenhower and U.S. soldiers view the bodies of victims at Bergen-Belsen.

barbed wire, did most Americans see that the Holocaust was no myth.

The Atomic Bombs

In the Pacific, the war with Japan ground on. Early in 1945 marines landed on the tiny island of Iwo Jima, 700 miles from Japan. Because Japanese soldiers had hidden in tunnels and behind concrete bunkers and pillboxes, securing the island cost 25,000 marine casualties. A month later Americans landed on Okinawa, a key staging area for the planned invasion of the Japanese home islands, only 350 miles distant. In nearly three months of ferocious combat, U.S. forces sustained 40,000 casualties, while more than 110,000 Japanese military died and Japanese civilians took 80,000 casualties.

If the capture of these small islands had entailed such bloodshed, military planners asked, what would the invasion of Japan itself be like? Although a naval blockade had strangled Japan's commerce and its lands lay defenseless to U.S.

bombers, the imperial government showed little disposition to surrender. Truman scheduled an invasion of Kyushu, the first of the home islands, for late 1945.

But the successful test of an atomic weapon at Alamogordo in mid-July presented an alternative. While at Potsdam, Truman, on July 25, ordered that an atomic bomb be used if Japan did not surrender before August 3. He publicly warned Japan to surrender unconditionally or face "prompt and utter destruction." When Japan rejected this Potsdam Declaration, Truman gave the military the go-ahead. On August 6 a B-29 named *Enola Gay* dropped a uranium bomb on Hiroshima, creating "a hell of unspeakable torments." A searing flash of heat, a fireball estimated at 300,000 degrees centigrade, incinerated buildings and vaporized people. Nearly seventy thousand died from the blast and another 70,000 later died of burns and radiation poisoning. On August 8, as promised, Stalin declared war on Japan. The next day much of Nagasaki disappeared under the mushroom cloud of a plutonium bomb. Finally, on August 14 Japan surrendered, leaving the emperor on the throne but powerless. On September 2 General MacArthur, aboard the battleship *Missouri* in Tokyo Bay, formally accepted the Japanese surrender.

Many have questioned whether the war had to end with the atomic bombings. Some believe that racist American attitudes toward Japan motivated the decision to use the bombs. Yet from the beginning of the Manhattan Project, Germany had been the target; and considering the indiscriminate ferocity of the Allied bombings of Hamburg and Dresden, which killed tens of thousands of civilians, there is little reason to assume that the Allies would not have used atomic bombs against Germany had they been available. Others contend that demonstrating the bomb's destructiveness on an uninhabited island would have moved Japan to surrender. But American policy makers considered a demonstration too risky. Still others argue that Japan was ready to surrender and that an invasion of the home islands was unnecessary. We cannot know for sure. But we do know that as late as July 28, 1945, Japan rejected a demand for surrender and that not until after the Hiroshima bombing did the Japanese government discuss acceptance of the Potsdam Declaration.

Rapidly worsening relations between the United States and the U.S.S.R. convinced some that Truman dropped the atomic bomb primarily to intimidate Stalin. The failure of the Americans and Soviets to resolve their differences had led Truman to seek an end to the Pacific war before Stalin could enter. Truman recognized that such an awesome weapon might give the United States leverage to oust the communists from eastern Europe. Just before the Alamogordo test, Truman had said, "If it explodes, as I think it will, I'll certainly have a hammer on [Stalin]." Truman's new secretary of state, James Byrnes, thought that the bomb would "put us in a position to dictate our own terms at the end of the war."

Although the president and his advisers believed that the atomic bomb would strengthen their hand against the Soviets, that was not the main reason that the bombs were dropped. Throughout the war Americans had relied on production and technology to win the war with a minimum loss of American life. Every new weapon was used. "Total war" included the terror bombing of masses of civilians, and within this context the atomic bomb seemed simply one more weapon in an arsenal that had already wreaked enormous destruction on the enemy. No responsible official suggested that the United States accept the deaths of thousands of Americans while not using a weapon developed with 2 billion taxpayer dollars. Indeed, to the vast majority of Americans, the atomic bomb was, in Churchill's words, "a miracle of deliverance" that shortened the war and saved lives.

hc Primary Source: Announcing the Use of the A-Bomb at Hiroshima

CONCLUSION   **hc** ACE Practice Test

The atomic bombs ended the deadliest war in history. More than 20 million combatants, including 300,000 Americans, had died. Another 25 million civilians had perished. Much of Europe and Asia was rubble. Although physically unscathed, the United States had changed profoundly. Mobilization had altered the structure of the economy; accelerated trends toward bigness in business, agriculture, and labor; and enlarged the role of the military. World War II had also transformed the scope and authority of the federal government, especially the presidency, and catalyzed vital changes in racial and social relations. Winning the greatest war in history infused an entire generation with a "can-do" spirit.

Each of the allies pursued wartime strategies best suited to preserve or enlarge its sphere of influence. To keep the Allies united and force the unconditional surrender of the Axis, Roosevelt yielded to Churchill's pleas to delay a second front in Europe and reluctantly accepted Soviet dominance in eastern Europe. The use of atomic bombs on Japan not only ended the war but also destroyed whatever was left of American isolationism. The United States had become a superpower engaged in a new conflict, the Cold War, which would lead it to play a global role inconceivable to most Americans only a few years earlier.

Chronology

1933	Adolf Hitler becomes chancellor of Germany.
1935–1937	Neutrality Acts.
1937	Japan invades China.
1938	Germany annexes Austria; Munich Pact gives Sudetenland to Germany. *Kristallnacht*, night of Nazi terror against German and Austrian Jews.
1939	Germany invades Poland; World War II begins.
1940	Germany conquers the Netherlands, Belgium, France, Denmark, Norway, and Luxembourg. Germany, Italy, and Japan sign the Tripartite Pact. Selective Service Act. Franklin Roosevelt elected to a third term.
1941	Lend-Lease Act. Roosevelt establishes the Fair Employment Practices Commission (FEPC). Germany invades the Soviet Union. Japan attacks Pearl Harbor; the United States enters World War II. War Powers Act.
1942	Battle of Midway halts Japanese offensive. Internment of Japanese-Americans. Revenue Act expands graduated income-tax system. Allies invade North Africa (Operation Torch). First successful atomic chain reaction. Congress of Racial Equality (CORE) founded.
1943	Soviet victory in Battle of Stalingrad. Coal miners strike; Smith-Connally War Labor Disputes Act. Detroit race riot. Allied invasion of Italy. Big Three meet in Tehran.
1944	D-Day: the Allied invasion of France (Operation Overlord). Roosevelt wins fourth term. Battle of the Bulge.
1945	Big Three meet in Yalta. Battles of Iwo Jima and Okinawa. Roosevelt dies; Harry S Truman becomes president. Germany surrenders. Truman, Churchill, and Stalin meet in Potsdam. United States drops atomic bombs on Hiroshima and Nagasaki; Japan surrenders.

FURTHER READING

Michael C.C. Adams, *The Best War Ever* (1994). A wide-ranging interpretation of the experience of war on the home front and abroad.

Beth Bailey and David Farber, *The First Strange Place: The Alchemy of Race and Sex in World War II Hawaii* (1992). A wide-ranging survey of the war's impact on Hawaiian society.

John Dower, *War Without Mercy* (1986). An insightful look at racism among the Americans and the Japanese.

John Keegan, *The Second World War* (1990). The standard account of the military aspects of the war.

Warren Kimball, *The Juggler: Franklin Roosevelt as Wartime Statesman* (1991). A study of the president's war aims and postwar vision.

Neil McMillen, ed., *Remaking Dixie: The Impact of World War II on the American South* (1997). Ten essays assess the war as a watershed in southern history.

Gerald D. Nash, *The American West Transformed: The Impact of World War II* (1985) and *World War II and the West: Reshaping the Economy* (1990). In-depth examinations of the changes in the West wrought by the war.

Holly Cowan Shulman, *The Voice of America* (1991). An in-depth account of America's wartime propaganda policies and programs.

E. B. Sledge, *With the Old Breed at Peleliu and Okinawa* (1990). A candid memoir of a marine's war in the Pacific.

David Wyman, *The Abandonment of the Jews* (1985). A critical assessment of the United States' role in the Holocaust.

26

The Cold War Abroad and at Home, 1945–1952

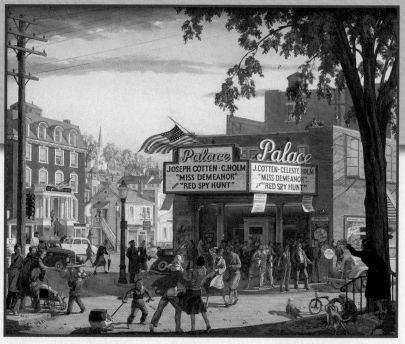

McCarthyism and the Hollywood Witch Hunts, by Thomas Maitland Cleland

hc This icon will direct you to additional study and research resources at http://college.hmco.com/history/us/boyer/enduring_concise/5e/students/index.html

Optimistic that there would not soon be another war and confident that the nation could solve any problems, ordinary Americans of the postwar years rushed to grab a share of the good life. They married, had babies, made Dr. Benjamin Spock's child care manual the hottest book since best-seller lists had begun, bought cars with automatic transmissions, and moved to new split-level houses in suburbs. However, the peace of mind that they yearned for eluded them, for World War II had wrought decisive and disturbing changes in society and in the global balance of power.

Disagreement over Eastern Europe's postwar fate sparked a confrontation in which the Soviet Union and the United States each sought to reshape the world to serve its own interests. An uncompromising Harry S Truman squared off against an obsessive Joseph Stalin, each intensifying the insecurities of the other. A new form of international conflict—the Cold War—emerged, in which the two superpowers avoided direct military clashes while using all their resources to thwart the other's objectives.

The Cold War changed America. Abandoning its historical aloofness from events outside the Western Hemisphere, the United States now plunged into a global struggle to contain the Soviet Union and to stop communism. The nation that only a few years before had no military alliances, a small defense budget, and no troops on foreign soil created a giant military establishment, signed mutual-defense pacts with forty countries, directly intervened in the affairs of allies and enemies alike, built military bases on every continent, and embarked on a seemingly limitless nuclear-arms race.

The Cold War's political and social effects at home proved equally decisive. Preoccupation with the Soviet threat discredited the political Left and sapped liberalism's vitality. Conservatives remained convinced that the federal government's power should be strictly limited, but at the same time they applauded the growth of federal power when military expansion, sniffing out domestic disloyalty, and leading the world fight against communism were at issue. Socially, the free expression of ideas suffered during the Cold War, as popular fears of communist aggression and domestic subversion led to witch hunts against suspected communists that undermined civil liberties. In 1952 Americans turned hopefully to Dwight D. Eisenhower to deliver the stability for which they longed.

THE POSTWAR POLITICAL SETTING, 1945–1946

The emerging Cold War profoundly changed the United States for better and for worse. It spurred a quarter of a century of economic growth and prosperity, the longest such period in American history. It propelled research in medicine and science that, for the most part, made lives longer and better. And it contributed to a vast expansion of higher education that enabled many Americans to become middle class.

Demobilization and Reconversion

When the war ended, GIs and civilians alike wanted all those who had served overseas "home

This chapter focuses on five major questions:

▶ How did both the United States and the Soviet Union contribute to the start of the Cold War?

▶ What was the doctrine of containment, and how was it implemented from 1947 to 1952?

▶ Why did the New Deal spirit diminish after World War II, and what effect did this have on Truman's domestic programs?

▶ How did the Cold War affect the rights of African-Americans?

▶ What led to the postwar Red Scare, and why did Americans react to it as they did? "

alive in '45." Troops demanding transport ships barraged Congress with threats of "no boats, no votes." On a single day in December 1945, 60,000 postcards arrived at the White House with the message "Bring the Boys Home by Christmas." Truman bowed to popular demand, and by 1948 American military strength had dropped from 12 million at war's end to just 1.5 million.

Returning veterans faced readjustment problems intensified by a soaring divorce rate and a drastic housing shortage. As war plants closed, moreover, veterans and civilians feared the return of mass unemployment and economic depression. Defense spending plummeted from $76 billion in 1945 to under $20 billion in 1946, and more than a million defense jobs vanished.

By the end of the decade more women were working outside the home than during World War II. They took jobs in traditional women's fields, especially office work and sales, to pay for family needs. Although the postwar economy created new openings for women in the labor market, many public figures urged women to seek fulfillment at home. Popular culture romanticized married bliss and demonized career women as a threat to social stability.

The GI Bill of Rights

The Servicemen's Readjustment Act of 1944, the "GI Bill of Rights," was designed to forestall the expected recession by easing veterans back into the work force, as well as to reward the "soldier boys" and reduce their fears of female competition. The GI Bill gave veterans priority for many jobs, occupational guidance, and, if need be, fifty-two weeks of unemployment benefits. It also established veterans' hospitals and provided low-interest loans to returning GIs who were starting businesses or buying homes or farms. Almost four million veterans bought homes with government loans, fueling a baby boom, suburbanization, and a record demand for new goods and services.

Most vitally in the long run, the government promised to pay millions of veterans for up to four years of further education or job training. Not all Americans approved. Some opposed it as opening the door to socialism or to demands by minorities to special entitlements. Many university administrators, fearing that riffraff would sully their bastions of privilege, echoed the complaint of the University of Chicago president that their hallowed halls of learning would become "educational hobo jungles."

By 1950 some six million veterans had used the GI Bill to enroll in colleges, universities, and vocational training programs; by 1956 the number had risen to nearly ten million. Often married and the fathers of young children, they were less interested in knowledge than in a degree and a higher-paying job. To accommodate them, colleges converted old military barracks and Quonset huts into so-called Veterans' Village housing units and featured accelerated programs and more vocational or career-oriented courses.

To make room for the millions of GIs pursuing higher education after the war, many colleges limited the percentage of women admitted or barred students from out of state. The percentage of female college graduates dropped from 40 percent in 1949 to 25 percent in 1950. By then most women students were the working wives of the eight million veterans who took advantage of the GI Bill to go college.

The GI Bill democratized higher education. It allowed many more Americans (most the first in their families to attend) to go to college. Later those GIs expected their children to follow suit, and higher education became an accepted part of the American Dream. No longer a citadel of privilege, universities awarded almost half a million degrees in 1950, more than twice as many as in 1940.

The cost to the government was huge, but the money was well spent. The more than $15 billion that veterans received sent them to school, helped them buy homes, and financed their new businesses. It propelled millions of veterans into middle-class status in employment, education, and residence, accelerating the postwar demand for goods and services.

The Economic Boom Begins

In addition to the assistance given to returning servicemen, a 1945 tax cut of $6 billion spurred corporate investment in new factories and equipment and helped produce an economic boom that began in late 1946. Wartime savings and a pent-up demand for consumer goods further kindled postwar growth and prosperity. The men and women who had endured the Great Depression and the Second World War craved the "good life," and by the end of 1945, they possessed $140 billion in bank accounts and government bonds to purchase it. Advertisements promising "a Ford in your future" and an "all-electric kitchen-of-the-future" became reality as sales of homes, furniture, cars, appliances, and clothing skyrocketed. Scores of new products—televisions, filter cigarettes, electric clothes dryers, freezers, automatic transmissions, air conditioners, hi-fis—emerged as hallmarks of the middle-class life-style.

The Bretton Woods agreement (1944) among the Allies had set the stage for the United States to become economic leader of the noncommunist world. In addition to valuing ("pegging") other cur-

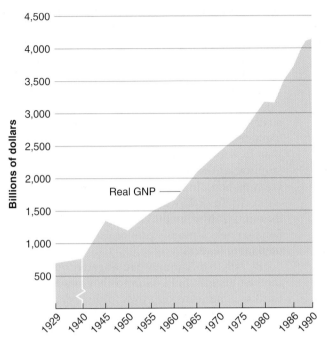

Gross National Product, 1929–1990
Following World War II, the United States achieved the highest living standard in world history. Between 1950 and 1970, the real GNP, which factors out inflation and reveals the actual amount of goods and services produced, steadily increased. However, in 1972, 1974–1975, 1980, and 1982 the real GNP declined.

rencies in relation to the dollar, Bretton Woods created several institutions to oversee international trade and finance: the International Monetary Fund (IMF), the General Agreement on Tariffs and Trade (GATT), and the World Bank.

The United States' favorable position in international trade and finance bolstered the idea that "the American century" of world peace and prosperity was at hand. Fears of depression were replaced by visions of limitless growth. With many nations in ruins, American firms could import cheap raw materials; with little competition from other industrial nations, they could increase their export sales to record levels. Wartime advances in science and technology, especially electronics and synthetic materials, led to the development of new industries and drove up productivity in others.

Truman's Domestic Program

Americans' hunger for the fruits of affluence left them little appetite for extension of the New Deal. Truman's only major legislative accomplishment in

the Seventy-ninth Congress, the Employment Act of 1946, committed the federal government to assuring economic growth and established the president's Council of Economic Advisers. Congress, however, had gutted from the proposed bill the goal of providing *full* employment, as well as the broad executive authority necessary to achieve that goal. Congress also blocked Truman's requests for public housing, a higher minimum wage, social-security expansion, a permanent Fair Employment Practices Commission, an anti–poll tax bill, federal aid to education, and government medical insurance.

Congressional eagerness to dismantle wartime controls, and inconsistent presidential leadership, hobbled the administration's ability to handle the major postwar economic problem: inflation. Consumer demand outran the supply of goods, putting intense pressure on prices. The Office of Price Administration (OPA) continued to set price controls after the war, but food producers, manufacturers, and retailers opposed controls strenuously. Many consumers favored preserving the OPA, but others saw the agency as a symbol of irksome wartime

President Truman with Union Supporters
Following his veto of the Taft-Hartley bill and 1948 election victory, won, in large part, by the strong backing of organized labor, a smiling Truman dons a hard hat with copper miners in Butte, Montana.

regulation. In June 1946, when Congress passed a bill that extended the OPA's life but removed its powers, Truman vetoed the bill. Within a week food costs rose 16 percent and the price of beef doubled.

Congress passed, and Truman signed, a second bill extending price controls in weakened form. Protesting any price controls, however, farmers and meat producers threatened to withhold food from the market. Observing that "meatless voters are opposition voters," Truman lifted controls on food prices just before the November 1946 midterm elections. Democratic candidates fared badly at the polls anyhow. By the time Truman lifted all price controls, shortly after the election, the consumer price index had already jumped nearly 25 percent.

Sharp price rises and shrinking paychecks goaded organized labor to demand higher wages. In 1946 alone, more than 4.5 million men and women went on strike. After a United Mine Work-

ers walkout paralyzed the economy for forty days, President Truman ordered government seizure of the mines. A week later the miners returned to work, after Truman had pressured owners to grant most of the demands. Six months later the drama repeated itself.

In spring 1946 railway engineers and trainmen struck, shutting down the railway system. Truman exploded. "If you think I'm going to sit here and let you tie up this whole country," the president shouted at the heads of the two unions, "you're crazy as hell." In May Truman asked Congress for authority to draft workers who struck in vital industries. Only when the rail workers gave in did the Senate reject Truman's proposals. His threat alienated labor leaders.

By fall 1946 Truman had angered most major interest groups; polls showed that less than one-third of Americans approved of his performance. Summing up public discontent, Republicans asked, "Had enough?" In the 1946 elections they captured twenty-five governorships and, for the first time since 1928, won control of Congress.

The public mood reflected more than just economic discontent. Under the surface laughter at bartenders mixing atomic cocktails ran a new, deep current of fear, symbolized by the rash of "flying saucer" sightings that had begun after the war. An NBC radio program depicted a nuclear attack on Chicago in which most people died instantly. There was much talk of urban dispersal—resettling people in small communities in the country's vast open spaces—and of how to protect oneself in a nuclear attack. Schoolchildren practiced crawling under their desks and putting their hands over their heads—"Duck and Cover"—to protect themselves from the bomb. The end of World War II had brought an uneasy peace.

ANTICOMMUNISM AND CONTAINMENT, 1946–1952

By the end of 1946, smoldering antagonisms between Moscow and Washington had flared up. With the Nazis defeated, the "shotgun wedding" between the United States and the Soviet Union dissolved into a struggle to fill the power vacuum left by the defeat of Germany and Japan, the exhaustion and bankruptcy of Western Europe, and the crumbling of colonial empires in Asia and Africa. Misperception and misunderstanding proliferated as the two nations sought security, each feeding the other's fears. The Cold War was the result.

Polarization and Cold War

The destiny of Eastern Europe, especially Poland, remained at the heart of U.S.-Soviet contention. Wanting to end the Soviet Union's vulnerability to invasions from the west, Stalin insisted on a demilitarized Germany and a buffer of nations friendly to the Soviet Union along its western flank. He considered a Soviet sphere of influence in Eastern Europe essential to national security, a just reward for the U.S.S.R.'s bearing the brunt of the war against Germany, and no different from the American spheres of influence in Western Europe, Japan, and Latin America. Stalin also believed that at Yalta, Roosevelt and Churchill had implicitly accepted a Soviet zone in Eastern Europe.

With the Red Army occupying half of Europe at the war's end, Stalin installed pro-Soviet governments in Bulgaria, Hungary, and Romania, while communist governments independent of Moscow came to power in Albania and Yugoslavia. Ignoring the Yalta Declaration of Liberated Europe, the Soviet Union barred free elections in Poland and brutally suppressed Polish democratic parties.

Stalin's refusal to abandon dominance in Eastern Europe collided with Truman's unwillingness to concede Soviet supremacy beyond Russia's borders. What Stalin saw as critical to Russian security, Truman viewed as a violation of the right of national self-determination, a betrayal of democratic principles, and a cover for communist aggression. Furthermore, Truman and his advisers believed that history taught that the appeasement of dictators only fed their appetites for expansion. Many in Truman's inner circle believed that traditional European balance-of-power politics and spheres of influence had precipitated both world wars. Only a new world order based on the self-determination of all nations working in good faith within the United Nations could guarantee peace.

Truman also thought that accepting the "enforced sovietization" of Eastern Europe would betray American war aims and condemn nations rescued from Hitler's tyranny to another totalitarian dictatorship. Too, Truman worried, a Soviet stranglehold in Eastern Europe would imperil the health of an American economy that depended on exports and on access to raw materials in the countries that Stalin appeared resolute to control solely for Soviet economic betterment.

Domestic political considerations also shaped Truman's response to Stalin. The Democratic party contained 6 million Polish-Americans as well as millions of other Americans of Eastern European origin, all of whom remained keenly interested in the fates of their homelands. The president realized that the Democratic party courted disaster by reneging on the Yalta agreements. He also recognized the strength of anticommunism in American politics and was determined not to appear "soft on communism."

Combativeness fit the temperament of the feisty Truman. Eager to demonstrate that he was in command, the president matched Stalin's intransigence on Polish elections with his own demands for Polish democracy. Emboldened by America's monopoly of atomic bombs and its undisputed position as the world's economic superpower, the president hoped that the United States could control the terms of postwar settlement.

The Iron Curtain Descends

But Truman's assertiveness inflamed Stalin's mistrust of the West and deepened Soviet obsession with their own security. Stalin stepped up his confiscation of materials and factories from occupied territories and forced his satellite nations to close their doors to American trade and influence. In February 1946 he warned that there could be no lasting peace with capitalism and vowed to overcome the American edge in weapons.

Two weeks later a sixteen-page telegram from George F. Kennan, the American chargé d'affaires in Moscow, reached Washington. A leading student of Soviet politics, Kennan warned that the only way to deal with Soviet intransigence was "a long-term, patient but firm and vigilant containment of Russian expansive tendencies." Truman, who had already insisted that it was time "to get tough with Russia," accepted the idea of containment, as did many others in Washington who wanted "no compromise" with the communists. Containment soon became gospel.

In early March 1946 Truman accompanied Winston Churchill to Westminster College in Missouri, where the former British prime minister warned of a new threat to democracy, this time from Moscow. Stalin, he said, had drawn an iron curtain across the eastern half of Europe. Churchill called for an alliance of the English-speaking peoples against the Soviet Union and the maintenance of an Anglo-American monopoly on atomic weapons.

Convinced that American firmness could check Soviet expansionism, Truman in the spring of 1946 dispatched part of the Sixth Fleet to the Black Sea and threatened to send in American combat troops unless the Soviets withdrew from oil-rich Iran. In June Truman submitted to the United Nations an atomic-energy control plan requiring the Soviet Union to stop all work on nuclear weapons and to submit to a system of U.N. control and inspection before the United States would destroy its own atomic arsenal. As expected, the Soviets rejected the American proposal and offered an alternative plan equally unacceptable to the United States. As mutual hostility escalated, the Soviets and Americans rushed to develop doomsday weapons. In 1946 Congress established the Atomic Energy Commission (AEC) to regulate nuclear development. Although Congress specified that fissionable materials should be used for civilian purposes "so far as practicable," at least 90 percent of the AEC's effort focused on weapons.

Thus, less than a year after American and Soviet soldiers had jubilantly met at the Elbe River to celebrate Hitler's defeat, the Cold War had begun. Economic pressure, nuclear intimidation, propaganda, and subversion, rather than military confrontation, characterized this conflict. Nonetheless, it would affect American life as decisively as any military engagement that the nation had fought.

Containing Communism

In early 1947 America formally stated its commitment to combat Soviet power. On February 21 the British informed the United States that they could no longer afford to assist the governments of Greece and Turkey in their struggles against communist-supplied guerrilla insurgencies and against Soviet pressure for access to the Mediterranean. Britain asked the United States to assume the costs of thwarting communism in the eastern Mediterranean. The harsh European winter, the most severe in memory, heightened the sense of urgency in Washington. The economies of Western Europe had ground to a halt, famine and tuberculosis plagued the Continent, and colonies in Africa and Asia had risen in rebellion. Communist parties in France and Italy appeared ready to topple democratic coalition governments. Truman resolved to meet the Soviet challenge.

He first had to mobilize support for a radical departure from the American tradition of avoiding entangling alliances. In a tense White House meeting on February 27, the new secretary of state, former army chief of staff George C. Marshall, presented the case for massive aid to Greece and Turkey. Congressional leaders balked, more concerned about U.S. inflation than civil war in Greece. But Dean Acheson, the newly appointed undersecretary of state, seized the moment. The issue, he said, was not one of assisting the repressive Greek oligarchy and Turkey's military dictatorship—it was, rather, a universal struggle of freedom versus tyranny. "Like apples in a barrel infected by the corruption of one rotten one," he warned, the fall of Greece or Turkey would open Asia, Western Europe, and the oil fields of the Middle East to the Red menace. Shaken, the congressional leaders agreed to support the administration's request—if Truman could "scare hell out of the country."

Truman could and did. On March 12, 1947, addressing a joint session of Congress he painted global politics as a stark confrontation between liberty and oppression and asked for military aid for Greece and Turkey. Outlining what became known as the Truman Doctrine, the president declared that the United States must support any free people "resisting attempted subjugation by armed minorities or by outside pressures." This unilateral declaration proclaimed the national intention to become a global policeman everywhere on guard against advances by the Soviet Union and its allies. Endorsed by the Republican Congress, the Truman Doctrine laid the foundation for American Cold War policy that would endure for much of the next four decades.

In June the administration proposed massive U.S. assistance for European recovery. First proposed by the secretary of state and thus called the Marshall Plan, such aid would become another weapon in the arsenal against the spread of communism. Truman wanted to end the economic devastation in Europe that he believed could readily be exploited by communist revolutionaries. Although the Marshall Plan ostensibly would help the hungry and homeless of *all* European countries, Truman calculated, correctly, that the U.S.S.R. and its communist allies would reject it because of the conditions and controls that were linked to the aid. The administration also accurately foresaw that Western European economic recovery would lead to an expansion in the sales of American goods abroad and thus promote domestic prosperity.

The Marshall Plan fulfilled its sponsors' hopes. Over a five-year period Congress appropriated $17 billion for economic recovery in sixteen nations, and by 1952 the economic and social chaos that could have proved a fertile seedbed for communism had died down. Western Europe revived, prospered, and achieved an unprecedented unity. U.S. business, not coincidentally, boomed.

Confrontation in Germany

The Soviet Union reacted to the Truman Doctrine and the Marshall Plan by tightening its grip on Eastern Europe. Then in 1947–1948 communist coups added Hungary and Czechoslovakia to the Soviet bloc, and Stalin turned his sights on Germany.

The Potsdam Agreement had divided Germany into four separate zones (administered by France, Great Britain, the Soviet Union, and the United States) and created a joint four-power administration for Germany's capital, Berlin, which lay 110 miles inside the Soviet-occupied eastern zone. As the Cold War intensified, the Western nations began to see a revived Germany as a buffer against Soviet expansion and they gradually united their zones. In June 1948 Stalin responded by blocking all rail and highway routes through the Soviet zone into Berlin. Stalin calculated that the Western powers, unable to feed the 2 million pro-Western Berliners under their control, would either have to abandon plans to create an independent West Germany or accept a communist Berlin.

Truman resolved neither to abandon Berlin nor to shoot his way into the city—and possibly trigger World War III. Instead, he ordered a massive airlift to provide Berliners with the food and fuel necessary for survival. American cargo planes landed at West Berlin's Templehof Airport virtually every three minutes, around the clock, carrying a mountain of supplies. Then in July 1948 Truman hinted that he would use "the bomb" if necessary and sent a fleet of B-29s, the only planes capable of delivering atomic bombs, to English bases. As tensions rose, Truman confided to his diary that "we are very close to war." The Berlin airlift continued for nearly a year.

In May 1949 the Soviets ended the blockade. Stalin's gambit had failed. The airlift highlighted American determination and technological prowess, revealed Stalin's willingness to use innocent citizens as pawns, and dramatically heightened anti-Soviet feeling in the West. In late 1948 U.S. public-opinion polls revealed an overwhelming demand for "firmness and increased 'toughness' in relations with Russia."

Continuing fears of a Soviet attack on Western Europe fostered support for a revitalized West German state and for an Atlantic collective-security alliance. Thus in May 1949 the United States, Britain, and France ended their occupation of Germany and approved the creation of the Federal Republic of Germany (West Germany). A month earlier ten nations of Western Europe had signed the North

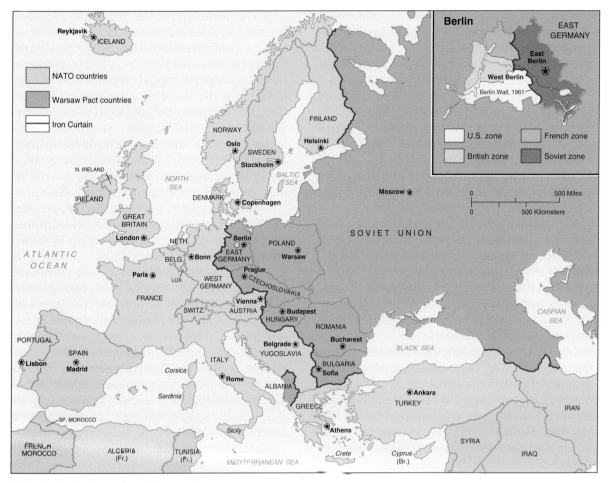

MAP 26.1
The Postwar Division of Europe
The wartime dispute between the Soviet Union and the Western Allies over Poland's future hardened after World War II into a cold war that split Europe into competing American and Soviet spheres of influence. Across an "iron curtain," NATO countries faced the Warsaw Pact nations. ⚫️ Interactive Map: Divided Europe

Atlantic Treaty, establishing a military alliance with the United States and Canada and declaring that an attack on any member would be considered an attack against all. For the first time in its history, the United States entered into a peacetime military alliance. After overwhelming Senate approval, the United States officially joined the North Atlantic Treaty Organization (NATO).

Two days after Senate ratification, Truman asked Congress to authorize $1.3 billion for mili-

tary assistance to NATO countries. To underscore his determination to contain communism, Truman persuaded General Dwight D. Eisenhower to become supreme commander of the new mutual-defense force and authorized the stationing of four U.S. army divisions in Europe as the nucleus of the NATO armed force. The Soviet Union responded by creating the German Democratic Republic (East Germany) in 1949, by exploding its own atomic bomb that same year, and by forming an Eastern bloc military alliance, the Warsaw Pact, in 1955. The United States and Soviet Union had divided Europe into two armed camps.

The Cold War in Asia

Moscow-Washington hostility also carved Asia into contending military and economic camps. The Russians created a sphere of influence in Manchuria, the United States denied Moscow a role in postwar Japan, and the two superpowers partitioned a helpless Korea.

As the head of the U.S. occupation forces in Japan, General Douglas MacArthur oversaw the country's transformation from an empire in ruins into a prosperous democracy. In 1952 the occupation ended, but a military security treaty allowed the United States to retain its Japanese bases on the Soviet-Asian perimeter and brought Japan under the American "nuclear umbrella." Both benefited: Japan could devote most of its resources to economic development, and the United States gained a staunch anticommunist ally. The containment policy in Asia also led the United States to help crush a procommunist guerrilla movement in the Philippines and to aid French efforts to reestablish colonial rule in Indochina (Vietnam, Laos, and Cambodia), despite American declarations in favor of national self-determination and against imperialism.

In China, however, U.S. efforts to block communism failed. The Truman administration initially tried to mediate the civil war raging between Jiang Jieshi's Nationalist government and Mao Zedong's communist forces. Between 1945 and 1949 the United States sent nearly $3 billion to the Nationalists. But American dollars could not force Jiang's corrupt government to reform itself and to win the support of the Chinese people, whom it had widely alienated. As Mao's well-disciplined and motivated forces marched south, Jiang's soldiers mutinied and surrendered without a fight. Unable to stem revolutionary sentiment or to build loyalty among the peasants, Jiang's regime collapsed, and he fled to exile on the island of Taiwan (Formosa).

Mao's establishment of the communist People's Republic of China shocked Americans. The most populous nation in the world, seen as a counterforce to Asian communism and a market for American trade, had become "Red China." Although the Truman administration insisted that it could have done little to alter the outcome and placed responsibility for Jiang's defeat on his failure to reform China, most Americans were unconvinced. China's fall to communism particularly embittered those conservatives who believed that America's future lay in Asia, not Europe. They launched an angry campaign to discover "Who lost China?" and assumed that the answer lay in the United States.

As the China debate raged, the president announced in September 1949 that the Soviet Union had exploded an atomic bomb. The loss of the nuclear monopoly shattered illusions of American invincibility. Combined with Mao's victory, this development would spawn an anticommunist hysteria and lead to irrational searches for scapegoats and subversives to explain American setbacks in world affairs.

In January 1950, stung by charges that he was soft on communism, Truman ordered the development of a fusion-based hydrogen bomb (H-bomb), hundreds of times more powerful than an atomic bomb. In November 1952 the United States exploded its first H-bomb in the Marshall Islands, projecting a radioactive cloud twenty-five miles into the atmosphere and blasting a canyon a mile long and 175 feet deep in the ocean floor. Nine months later the Soviets detonated their own hydrogen bomb. The balance of terror escalated.

In April 1950 a presidentially appointed committee issued a top-secret review of defense policy. The report, NSC-68, emphasized the Soviet Union's aggressive intentions and military strength. To counter the U.S.S.R.'s "design for world domination"—the mortal challenge posed by the Soviet Union "not only to this Republic but to civilization itself"—NSC-68 called for a vast American military buildup, a large standing army, and a quadrupling of the defense budget to wage a global struggle against communism.

Truman hesitated to swallow his advisers' expensive medicine. An aide to Secretary of State Acheson recalled, "We were sweating over it, and

U.S. Marines Battling for Seoul, September 1950
From the start Truman believed that the Soviet Union had orchestrated the North Korean invasion of South Korea. He steadfastly maintained that "if the Russian totalitarian state was intending to follow in the path of the dictatorship of Hitler and Mussolini, they [had to] be met head on in Korea."

then, with regard to NSC-68, thank God Korea came along." By the end of 1950, Truman would order the implementation of NSC-68 and triple the defense budget.

The Korean War, 1950–1953

After Japan's defeat in World War II, the Soviet Union and United States temporarily divided Korea at the thirty-eighth parallel for purposes of military occupation. The dividing line had solidified into a political frontier between the Soviet-backed People's Democratic Republic in North Korea and the American-supported Republic of Korea, each claiming the sole right to rule Korea.

On June 24, 1950, North Korean troops swept across the thirty-eighth parallel to attack South Korea. Truman saw the invasion as Soviet-directed aggression. He never doubted that Stalin was testing American will. The president maintained, "If we are tough enough now, if we stand up to [the Soviets] . . . they won't take any next steps." Mindful of the failure of appeasement at Munich in 1938, Truman said that failure to act would lead to a bloody "third world war, just as similar incidents had

brought on the second world war." Truman also had to prove to Republican critics that the Democrats would not allow another country to "fall" to the communists.

The president decided to intervene in Korea. Without consulting Congress or asking for a formal declaration of war, Truman secured the United Nations' sanction for a "police action" against the aggressor. Boycotting the Security Council in a dispute over recognition of the People's Republic of China, the Soviet Union could not veto this policy. On June 27 Truman ordered American air and sea forces to South Korea's aid and appointed General MacArthur to command the U.N. effort in Korea. Within three days American soldiers were fighting in Korea. U.S. forces provided most of the air and navy support and almost 50 percent of the troops fighting under the U.N. flag; South Korea supplied 43 percent of the forces, and fourteen other nations contributed less than 10 percent.

North Korea rapidly pushed the U.N. forces to the southeastern tip of the Korean peninsula. Then in mid-September a brilliant amphibious movement designed by MacArthur landed U.N. troops at Inchon, north of Seoul, and forced a North

Korean retreat. Heartened, Truman permitted MacArthur to order U.N. armies across the thirty-eighth parallel toward the Yalu River, the boundary between Korea and China. The police action to restore the original border between the two Koreas was being transformed into a war of liberation to create "a unified, independent, and democratic" nation of Korea.

As U.N. troops approached the Yalu River, the Chinese warned that they would not "stand idly by" if their border was threatened. Ignoring this assertion, an overconfident MacArthur deployed his forces in a thin line below the river. On November 25 thirty-three Chinese divisions (about 300,000 men) counterattacked, driving stunned U.N. forces back below the thirty-eighth parallel. By March 1951 the fighting was stabilized at roughly the original dividing line between the two Koreas.

In spring 1951 Truman again reversed course and sought a negotiated peace based on the objective of restoring the integrity of South Korea. MacArthur rocked the boat, however, urging that he be allowed to bomb and blockade China, "unleash" Jiang Jieshi's troops against Mao's regime, and seek a total victory even at the risk of an all-out war with China. Truman refused: "We are trying to prevent a world war—not to start one." Worried that American involvement in Asia might tempt Soviet aggression in Europe, he sought a limited war for a limited objective: to hold the line in Korea. But MacArthur would not accept a stalemate. "In war," he said, "there is no substitute for victory."

When MacArthur refused to stop criticizing administration policy, Truman relieved him of command, on April 10, 1951. To the president, the issue was civilian control of the military, a control that seemed threatened by MacArthur's public insubordination. Public opinion, however, backed the general. The very idea of limited war baffled many Americans, and a mounting casualty list added anger to the mix. It seemed so senseless. Despite warnings from the chairman of the Joint Chiefs of Staff that MacArthur's proposals would result in "the wrong war at the wrong place in the wrong time and with the wrong enemy," a growing number of Americans listened sympathetically to

Republican charges that Soviet-directed agents controlled American policy.

In July 1951 truce talks began, but they dragged on for two years as both sides continued their restricted but deadly war. By the time that wrangling over prisoner repatriation and the cease-fire line ended on July 26, 1953, the "limited war" had cost

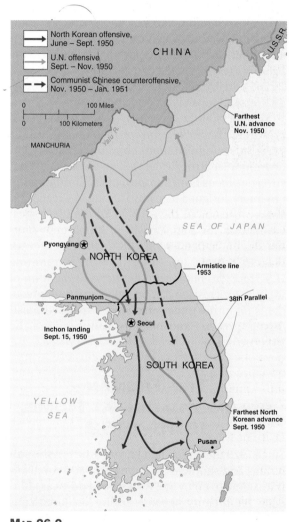

MAP 26.2
The Korean War, 1950–1953
The experience of fighting an undeclared and limited war for the limited objective of containing communism confused the generation of Americans who had just fought an all-out war for the total defeat of the Axis.

the United States almost 55,000 American lives, another 103,284 wounded or missing, and $54 billion. The conflict also accelerated implementation of NSC-68 and the expansion of containment into a global policy. From 1950 to 1953 defense spending zoomed from one-third to two-thirds of the entire federal budget. The United States acquired new bases around the world, committed itself to rearm West Germany, and joined a mutual-defense pact with Australia and New Zealand. Increased military aid flowed to Jiang Jieshi's troops on Taiwan, and American dollars supported the French army fighting the communist Ho Chi Minh in Indochina. By 1954 the United States was paying about three-quarters of French war costs in Vietnam.

Truman's intervention in Korea preserved a precarious balance of power in Asia and underscored the administration's commitment to the anticommunist struggle, as well as the shift of that struggle's focus from Europe to Asia. Containment, originally designed to justify U.S. aid to Greece and Turkey, became in the early 1950s the ideological foundation for a major war in Korea and, ominously, for a deepening U.S. involvement with France's colonial war in Vietnam. By committing U.S. troops to battle with neither a declaration of war nor congressional approval, Truman set precedents for future undeclared wars, expanded presidential powers, and helped institutionalize the "warfare" state.

THE TRUMAN ADMINISTRATION AT HOME, 1945–1952

Since 1929 the nation had known little but the sufferings and shortages of depression and war. Now it was time to enjoy life! Widespread postwar affluence let dreams become reality as Americans flocked to the suburbs, launched a "baby boom" of howling proportions, and rushed to buy stoves, refrigerators, televisions, and cars.

Not all Americans shared the good times. Poverty remained a stark fact of life for millions. African-Americans experienced the grim reality of racism, but from the early postwar period there emerged a civil-rights movement that in a few years would sweep the nation.

Family and career, not public issues, preoccupied most Americans, however, and New Deal reform energies subsided into a mood of complacency. Although Truman sought to extend reform, the times were against him. Congressional conservatives wanted to reduce, not expand, federal power. Anticommunism intensified the American tendency to identify social radicalism with disloyalty, and undercut efforts to alter the status quo.

The Eightieth Congress, 1947–1948

Many Republicans in the Eightieth Congress, which convened in January 1947, interpreted the 1946 elections as a mandate to reverse the New Deal. Republican-controlled, Congress defeated proposals to raise the minimum wage and provide federal funds for education and housing.

Truman and the conservatives waged their major battle over the pro-union Wagner Act of 1935 (see Chapter 24). Postwar strikes had whipped up a national consensus for curbing union power. In 1947 Congress passed the Taft-Hartley Act (the Labor-Management Relations Act), which barred the closed shop and permitted the president to call a sixty-day cooling-off period to delay any strike that might endanger national safety or health. Unions termed the law a "slave labor bill" and demanded a presidential veto.

Truman did veto the measure, and Congress easily overrode the veto. But Truman had taken a major step toward regaining organized labor's support. This move reflected his recognition that his only hope for election in 1948 lay in reforging the New Deal coalition. To this end, he played the role of staunch New Dealer to the hilt, proposing a series of liberal reform bills—federal aid to education, housing, and health insurance; repeal of Taft-Hartley; and high farm-price supports.

Truman courted voters of Eastern European ancestry by emphasizing his opposition to the Iron Curtain. He overrode the objections of the State

Department, which feared alienating the oil-rich Arab world, to extend diplomatic recognition to the new state of Israel immediately after it proclaimed independence. This move reflected both his deep sympathy toward Holocaust survivors who had immigrated to Israel and the strategic importance of Jewish-American voters.

The Politics of Civil Rights and the Election of 1948

In 1947 Jackie Robinson, grandson of a slave, joined the Brooklyn Dodgers and broke major-league baseball's color barrier. Fans showered insults on him, opposing players spiked him, and pitchers tried to bean him, but Robinson endured and triumphed, becoming Rookie of the Year, Most Valuable Player, and a member of the Hall of Fame. In the wake of Robinson's success, professional football and other baseball teams also integrated. "World War II has immeasurably magnified the Negro's awareness of the disparity between the American profession and practice of democracy," noted the president of the NAACP.

Many African-Americans, especially veterans, demanded the right to vote after the war. Aggressive voter-registration drives raised the number of blacks registered to vote in the South from 2 percent in 1940 to 12 percent in 1947. Southern blacks risked intimidation, repression, and even murder in pursuing their right to vote, for white-supremacist politicians urged their followers to use any means to keep African-Americans from exercising that right.

Fearful of black assertiveness in seeking the vote and of other signs of a bold new spirit among African-Americans, some southern whites reacted brutally. In 1946 in rural Georgia, whites killed several black veterans who had voted that year, and in South Carolina whites blinded a black soldier for failing to sit in the rear of a bus. In Columbia, Tennessee, in 1946, whites rioted against blacks who insisted on their rights. Police arrested seventy blacks and looked the other way as a white mob broke into the jail to murder two African-American prisoners.

In September 1946 Truman met with a delegation of civil-rights leaders. Horrified by their ac-

Jackie Robinson, 1947
Robinson's brilliant play for the Brooklyn Dodgers did not save him from racial taunts of fans and players or exclusion from restaurants and hotels that catered to his white teammates.

counts, he vowed to act. Truman believed that every American should enjoy the full rights of citizenship. He also understood the importance of the growing African-American vote, particularly in northern cities. The president realized, too, that white racism damaged U.S. relations with much of the world. The Soviet Union highlighted the mistreatment of American blacks, both to undercut U.S. appeals to racially diverse peoples in Africa, Asia, and Latin America and to counter U.S. condemnation of repression behind the Iron Curtain.

After the 1946 elections, Truman established the President's Committee on Civil Rights to investigate race relations. The committee's report, *To Secure These Rights,* published in 1947, called for the eradication of racial discrimination and segregation and proposed antilynching and anti–poll tax legislation. Boldly, Truman in February 1948 sent a special message to Congress urging lawmakers to enact most of the committee's proposals.

Southern segregationists denounced Truman's "stab in the back" and warned of a boycott of the national Democratic ticket. Truman backtracked, flinching at the prospect of major southern defections. He dropped his plans to submit specific civil-rights bills to Congress and endorsed a weak civil-rights plank for the Democratic platform.

At the Democratic convention in July 1948, liberals and urban politicians who needed African-American votes rejected the president's feeble civil-rights plank and committed the party to action on Truman's original proposals. Thirty-five delegates from Mississippi and Alabama responded by stalking out of the convention. They joined other southern segregationists to form the States' Rights Democratic party and nominated Governor Strom Thurmond of South Carolina for the presidency. The "Dixiecrats" hoped to restore their dominance in the Democratic party and to preserve the segregationist "southern way of life." They placed their electors on the ballot as the regular Democratic ticket in several states, posing a major roadblock to Truman's chances of victory.

Truman's electoral hopes further faded when left-wing Democrats joined with communists to launch a new Progressive party and nominated Henry A. Wallace for president. The Wallace candidacy threatened Truman's chances in northern states, where many urban Democrats saw Wallace as the heir of New Deal liberalism.

To capitalize on Democratic divisions, Republicans tried to play it safe. They nominated the moderate governor of New York, Thomas E. Dewey, and ran a complacent campaign designed to offend the fewest people. Truman, in contrast, campaigned tirelessly, blasting the "no-good, do-nothing" Republican-controlled Eightieth Congress. To shouts of "Give 'em hell, Harry," the president hammered away at the GOP as the party of "privilege, pride, and plunder." Pollsters applauded Truman's spunk but predicted a sure Dewey victory.

A surprised nation awoke the day after the election to learn that the president had won in the biggest electoral upset in U.S. history. Ironically, the Progressives and Dixiecrats had helped Truman. Their radicalism had kept both moderate liberals and moderate conservatives safely in the Democratic fold. The attorney general of Virginia explained, "The only sane and constructive course to follow is to remain in the house of our fathers—even though the roof leaks, and there be bats in the belfry, rats in the pantry, cockroaches in the kitchen, and skunks in the parlor." Moreover, Dixiecrat defections had freed Truman to campaign as a proponent of civil rights.

In July 1948 Truman had issued executive orders barring discrimination in federal employment and creating a committee to ensure "equality of treatment and opportunity for all persons in the armed services without regard to race, color, religion or national origin." Truman had also benefited from two Supreme Court decisions. In 1946 the Court had declared segregation in interstate bus transportation unconstitutional, and in 1948 it had outlawed restrictive housing covenants that forbade the sale or rental of property to minorities.

Truman succeeded in 1948 by re-creating the New Deal coalition. He had seized every opportunity to remind farmers and laborers that the Republican "gluttons of privilege" planned to "turn the clock back" and strip away New Deal benefits.

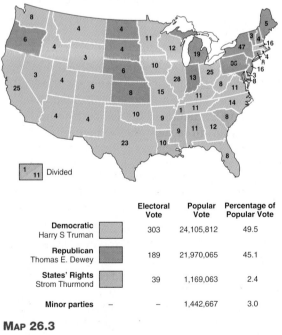

	Electoral Vote	Popular Vote	Percentage of Popular Vote
Democratic Harry S Truman	303	24,105,812	49.5
Republican Thomas E. Dewey	189	21,970,065	45.1
States' Rights Strom Thurmond	39	1,169,063	2.4
Minor parties	–	1,442,667	3.0

MAP 26.3
The Election of 1948

The Fair Deal

Despite his narrow victory margin, Truman tried to translate his election into a mandate for liberalism. In his 1949 State of the Union message, he proposed an ambitious social and economic program, the Fair Deal. He asked Congress to enlarge New Deal programs in economic security, conservation, and housing and to go beyond the New Deal in other areas.

The Eighty-first Congress complied with the extension of existing programs but rejected new measures. Lawmakers raised the minimum wage; increased social-security coverage and benefits; expanded appropriations for public power, conservation, and slum clearance; and authorized the construction of nearly a million low-income housing units. But they rejected federal aid to education, national health insurance, civil-rights legislation, larger farm subsidies, and the repeal of Taft-Hartley.

Congress's rejection of most Fair Deal proposals stemmed from Truman's own lessening commitment to domestic reform in favor of foreign policy, as well as from the strengthening of the congressional conservative coalition. And widespread prosperity sapped public enthusiasm for more reform. The postwar congresses mirrored the sense of well-being that most Americans enjoyed and reflected the popular apprehensions over communism that doomed hope for liberal reform.

THE POLITICS OF ANTICOMMUNISM

As the Cold War worsened, some Americans concluded that the roots of the nation's foreign difficulties lay in domestic treason and subversion. How else could the communists have taken China and built an atomic bomb? Millions of fearful Americans would eventually enlist in a crusade that would find scapegoats for the nation's problems and would equate dissent with disloyalty.

Since 1938 the House Committee on Un-American Activities (later called the House Un-American Activities Committee, or HUAC) had served as a platform for conservatives' denunciation of the New Deal as a communist plot. At first only the extreme Right had embraced this viewpoint seriously, but after World War II mounting numbers of Democrats and Republicans climbed aboard the anti-Red bandwagon.

The Great Fear influenced both governmental and personal actions. Millions of Americans were subjected to loyalty oaths and security investigations after the war. The anticommunist hysteria would destroy the Left, discredit liberalism, and undermine labor militancy. The purge of controversial government officials, furthermore, would ensure foreign-policy rigidity and the postponement of domestic social change.

Loyalty and Security

The Cold War raised legitimate concerns about American security. The Communist party had claimed 80,000 members during World War II, and no one knew how many occupied sensitive government positions. In mid-1945 a raid of the offices of a procommunist magazine revealed that classified documents had been given to the periodical by two State Department employees and a naval intelligence officer. Ten months later the Canadian government exposed a major spy network that had passed American military information and atomic secrets to the Soviets during the war. Republicans accused the administration of being "soft on communism."

In March 1947 Truman issued Executive Order 9835 establishing the Federal Employee Loyalty Program to provide a loyalty check on all government workers. The drive for absolute security soon overran concerns about rights, however, as civil servants suspected of disloyalty were allowed neither to face their accusers nor to require investigators to reveal sources. Instead of focusing on potential subversives in high-risk areas, the probe extended to the associations and beliefs of *every* government worker.

Mere criticism of American foreign policy could result in an accusation of disloyalty. People could lose their jobs if they liked foreign films, associated with radical friends or family members, or were past members of organizations now declared disloyal. Between 1947 and 1951 loyalty boards forced nearly 3,000 government employees to resign and fired 300 on charges of disloyalty. The probe uncovered no evidence of subversion or espionage, but it did spread fear among government employees. "If communists like apple pie and I do," said one federal worker, "I see no reason why I should stop eating it. But I would."

hc Primary Source: Duck Test

The Anticommunist Crusade

The very existence of a federal loyalty inquest fed mounting anticommunist hysteria. Federal investigators promoted fears of communist infiltration and legitimized other efforts to expose subversives. Universities banned controversial speakers, and popular magazines ran articles like "Reds Are After Your Child." Even comic books joined the fray: "Beware, commies, spies, traitors, and foreign agents! Captain America, with all loyal, free men behind him, is looking for you." By the end of Truman's term, thirty-nine states had created loyalty programs, most with virtually no procedural safe-

guards. Schoolteachers, college professors, and state and city employees throughout the nation signed loyalty oaths or lost their jobs.

In 1947 the House Un-American Activities Committee began hearings to expose communist influence in American life. HUAC's probes blurred distinctions between dissent and disloyalty, between radicalism and subversion. People who refused to answer HUAC questions often lost their livelihoods. Labor unions expelled communist members and avoided progressive causes, concentrating on securing better pay and benefits and becoming bureaucratic special-interest pressure groups. HUAC also left its mark on the entertainment industry. When several prominent film directors and screenwriters refused to cooperate in 1947, HUAC had them cited for contempt and sent to federal prison. Blacklists in Hollywood and in radio broadcasting barred the employment of anyone with a slightly questionable past, thereby silencing many talented people.

The 1948 presidential campaign fed national anxieties. Truman lambasted Henry Wallace as a Stalinist dupe and accused the Republicans of being "unwittingly the ally of the communists in this country." In turn, the GOP dubbed the Democrats "the

The Red Menace, 1949

Although Hollywood generally avoided overtly political films, it released a few dozen explicitly anticommunist films in the postwar era. Depicting American communists as vicious hypocrites, if not hardened criminals, Cold War movies were an effort to protect Hollywood's imperiled public image after HUAC's widely publicized investigation of the movie industry.

party of treason." A rising Republican star, Richard M. Nixon of California, charged that Democrats bore responsibility for "the unimpeded growth of the communist conspiracy in the United States."

To blunt the force of such accusations, the Justice Department prosecuted eleven top leaders of the American Communist party under the Smith Act of 1940, which outlawed any conspiracy advocating the overthrow of the government. In 1951 the Supreme Court upheld the Smith Act's constitutionality, declaring that Congress could curtail freedom of speech if national security demanded such restrictions.

Ironically, the Communist party was fading into obscurity at the very time that politicians were magnifying the threat it posed. By 1950 its membership had shrunk to less than 30,000. Yet Truman's attorney general warned that American Reds "are everywhere—in factories, offices, on street corners, in private businesses—and each carries in himself the germ of death for society."

Alger Hiss and the Rosenbergs

Nothing set off more alarms about the diabolic Red conspiracy in the federal government than the case of Alger Hiss. During the 1948 presidential campaign, HUAC conducted a sensational hearing in which Whittaker Chambers, a senior editor at *Time* and a former Soviet agent who had broken with the communists in 1938, identified Hiss as an underground party member in the 1930s.

In the hearing, Chambers appeared a tortured soul crusading to save the West from the Red peril. The elegant and cultured Hiss, in contrast, seemed the very symbol of the liberal establishment; a Harvard Law School graduate, he had clerked for Justice Oliver Wendell Holmes, served as a presidential adviser on foreign affairs (including the Yalta conference), and headed the Carnegie Endowment for International Peace. Hiss denied any communist affiliation and claimed not to know Chambers. Most liberals believed Hiss. They saw him as the victim of conservatives bent on tarnishing New Deal liberalism. Rushing to Hiss's defense, Truman denounced Chambers's allegations as a "red her-

ring" to deflect attention from the failures of the Eightieth Congress.

To those suspicious of the Rooseveltian liberal tradition, Chambers's persistence and Hiss's fumbling retreat intensified fears that the Democratic administration was teeming with communists. Under rigorous questioning by Richard Nixon, Hiss admitted that he had known Chambers but denied having been a communist. Chambers broadened his accusation, claiming that Hiss had committed espionage in the 1930s by giving him secret State Department documents to be sent to the Soviet Union. Hiss protested his innocence, but a grand jury indicted him for perjury, or lying under oath. In January 1950 Hiss was convicted and received a five-year prison sentence. Emboldened congressional conservatives stalked other Hisses.

Just as the Hiss affair ended, another case shocked Americans. In early February 1950 the British arrested Klaus Fuchs, a German-born scientist involved in the Manhattan Project, for passing atomic secrets to the Soviets. Fuchs's confession led to the arrest of two Americans, Ethel and Julius Rosenberg, as coconspirators. The Rosenbergs insisted that they were victims of anti-Semitism and were being prosecuted for their leftist beliefs. But in March 1951 a jury found them guilty of conspiring to commit espionage, and on June 19, 1953, the husband and wife were executed, although they maintained their innocence to the end. Soviet documents released in the 1990s implicated both Hiss and Julius Rosenberg.

McCarthyism

At this point, some Americans could not separate fact from fantasy. For them, only conspiracy could explain U.S. weakness and Soviet might. Frustrated by unexpected failure in 1948, Republicans eagerly exploited public apprehension. Doomed to four more years of exile from the White House, the GOP in 1949 hurled a series of reckless accusations at the administration.

No individual would inflict so many wounds on the Democrats as Republican senator Joseph R. McCarthy of Wisconsin. Desperate for an issue to run for reelection on in 1952, McCarthy had noted the success of fellow Republicans who had labeled the Democrats "soft on communism." In February 1950 McCarthy boldly told a West Virginia audience that communists in the State Department had betrayed America. "I have here in my hand a list of 205," McCarthy reported as he waved a laundry list, "a list of names known to the Secretary of State as being members of the Communist party and who nevertheless are still working and shaping policy." Although he could produce no evidence to support his accusations, his senatorial stature and brazen style gave him a national forum. McCarthy soon repeated his charges, though lowering his numbers and reducing his indictment from "card-carrying communists" to "subversives" to "bad risks." A Senate committee found McCarthy's accusations "a fraud and a hoax," but he persisted.

As the Korean War dragged on, McCarthy's efforts to "root out the skunks" escalated. He ridiculed Secretary of State Dean Acheson as the "Red Dean" and called Truman's dismissal of MacArthur "the greatest victory the communists have ever won." Buoyed by the partisan usefulness of McCarthy's onslaught, many Republicans encouraged him. McCarthyism especially appealed to midwestern party members opposed to the welfare state, restrictions on business, and the Europe-first emphasis of Truman's foreign policy. For them, anticommunism was a weapon of revenge against liberals and internationalists and a means to regain the controlling position that conservatism had once held. McCarthy also won a devoted following among blue-collar workers. His flag-waving patriotism appealed to traditionally Catholic ethnics, who wanted to gain acceptance as "100 percent Americans" through a show of anticommunist zeal. Countless Americans also shared McCarthy's scorn for privilege and gentility, for the "bright young men who are born with silver spoons in their mouths." And his conspiracy theory offered a simple answer to the perplexing questions of the Cold War.

McCarthy's political power rested on the Republican establishment and Democrats fearful of antagonizing him. The GOP support that Mc-Carthy enjoyed made Democrats' condemnation look like mere partisan criticism. In the 1950 elections when he helped Republicans to defeat Democrats who had denounced him, McCarthy appeared invincible. "Joe will go that extra mile to destroy you," warned the new Senate majority leader, Lyndon B. Johnson of Texas.

Over Truman's veto, Congress in 1950 adopted the McCarran Internal Security Act, which required organizations deemed communist by the attorney general to register with the Department of Justice. The McCarran Act authorized the arrest and detention during a national emergency of "any person as to whom there is reason to believe might engage in acts of espionage or sabotage." The McCarran-Walter Immigration and Nationality Act of 1952, also adopted over a presidential veto, maintained the quota system that gave immigrants from northern and Western Europe 85 percent of available slots, although it did end Asian exclusion. The new law also strengthened the attorney general's authority to exclude or deport aliens suspected of supporting communism.

The Election of 1952

By 1952 public apprehension about the loyalty of government employees combined with frustration over the Korean stalemate to sink Democratic presidential hopes to their lowest level since the 1920s. Both business and labor also resented Truman's freeze on wages and prices during the Korean conflict. In addition, revelations of bribery and influence peddling by some of Truman's old political associates gave Republicans ammunition for charging the Democrats with "plunder at home, and blunder abroad."

When Truman decided not to seek reelection, dispirited Democrats drafted Governor Adlai E. Stevenson of Illinois. But Stevenson could not separate himself from Truman, and his lofty speeches did not stir the average voter. Above all, Stevenson could not overcome the sentiment that twenty years of Democratic rule was enough.

The GOP nominated the hugely popular war hero Dwight D. Eisenhower. Essentially apolitical,

Chronology

1945	Truman proposes economic reforms.	**1949**	North Atlantic Treaty Organization (NATO) established.
1946	Winston Churchill delivers his "iron curtain" speech.		East and West Germany founded as separate nations.
	Coal miners' strike.		Communist victory in China.
	More than a million GIs enroll in college.		Soviet Union detonates an atomic bomb.
	Republicans win control of Congress.	**1950**	Truman authorizes building a hydrogen bomb.
1947	Truman Doctrine.		Alger Hiss convicted of perjury.
	Federal Employee Loyalty Program.		Joseph McCarthy launches anticommunist crusade.
	Marshall Plan proposed to aid Europe.		Korean War begins.
	President's Committee on Civil Rights publishes *To Secure These Rights*.		McCarran Internal Security Act.
			Truman accepts NSC-68.
1948	Communist coup in Czechoslovakia.		China enters the Korean War.
	State of Israel founded.	**1951**	Douglas MacArthur dismissed from his Korean command.
	Soviet Union blockades Berlin; United States begins airlift.		Supreme Court upholds Smith Act.
	Truman orders an end to segregation in the armed forces.		Julius and Ethel Rosenberg convicted of espionage.
	Communist leaders put on trial under the Smith Act.	**1952**	First hydrogen bomb exploded.
			Dwight D. Eisenhower elected president.

Eisenhower had once insisted that "lifelong professional soldiers should abstain from seeking higher political office," but he answered the call of the moderate wing of the Republican party and accepted the nomination. "Ike" chose as his running mate Richard M. Nixon, the former HUAC Red hunter.

Eisenhower and Nixon proved unbeatable. With a captivating grin and an unimpeachable record of public service, Eisenhower projected both personal warmth and the vigorous authority associated with military command. His smile, wrote one commentator, "was a smile of infinite reassurance." Indeed, Eisenhower symbolized the stability for which Americans yearned. At the same time, Nixon kept public apprehensions at the boiling point. Accusing the Democrats of treason, he charged that a Democratic victory would bring "more Alger Hisses, more atomic spies."

The GOP ticket stumbled when newspapers revealed the existence of a "slush fund" that California business leaders had created to keep Nixon in "financial comfort." But Nixon saved himself with a heart-tugging television defense. He explained the gifts, which included a cocker spaniel named Checkers given to his daughters, as intended to benefit his family. His appeal worked. The Republican ticket won 55 percent of the popular vote, cracked the solid South to carry thirty-nine states, and amassed 442 electoral votes. Enough Republicans rode Ike's coattails to give the GOP control of both houses of Congress by small margins.

CONCLUSION *hc* ACE Practice Test

The 1952 election ended two decades of Democratic control of the White House and closed the first phase of the Cold War, in which an assertive United States, eager to protect and expand its influence and power, faced off against a Soviet Union obsessed with its own security and self-interest. In the name of containment, the United States aided Greece and Turkey, established the Marshall Plan, airlifted supplies into Berlin, approved the creation of the Federal Republic of Germany (West Germany), established NATO, and went to war in Korea.

American fear of global communism spawned anxiety about domestic communism. Truman's own Cold War rhetoric encouraged others to seek scapegoats for the failure of the United States to get its way everywhere in the world and legitimated conservative accusations that equated dissent with disloyalty. This Red Scare, combined with economic prosperity and pent-up demand for consumer goods, weakened attempts at liberal reform. The New Deal stood, but Truman's attempts to gain education, health insurance, and civil-rights reforms failed. Although bold proposals to end racial discrimination and segregation had little chance in the midst of the Great Fear, the U.S. need to appeal to nonwhites brought racial issues to the fore in American politics. They would remain there as a Republican assumed the presidency.

FURTHER READING

Gary Donaldson, *Truman Defeats Dewey* (1999). An interpretation of Truman's political fortunes.

Mary L. Dudziak, *Cold War Civil Rights: Race and the Image of American Democracy* (2000). A key study of the effect of the Cold War on civil rights.

Elizabeth Fones-Wolf, *Selling Free Enterprise: The Business Assault on Labor and Liberalism, 1945–1960* (1994). An important examination of the postwar relationship between government and business.

Richard M. Fried, *The Russians Are Coming! The Russians Are Coming! Pageantry and Patriotism in Cold-War America* (1999). A balanced introduction to some of the social consequences of the Cold War.

John Earl Haynes and Harvey Klehr, *Venona: Recoding Soviet Espionage in America* (1999). Soviet spying in the United States, as disclosed by recently declassified yet sometimes ambiguous evidence.

Michael Hogan, *A Cross of Iron: Harry S Truman and the Origins of the National Security State* (1998). A vital analysis of postwar national defense policies.

Robbie Lieberman, *The Strangest Dream: Communism, Anticommunism, and the U.S. Peace Movement, 1945–1963* (2000). A wide-ranging assessment of the Great Fear's effect on antiwar activism.

Stanley Sandler, *The Korean War: No Victors, No Vanquished* (1999). An indispensable account of the war.

Sean Savage, *Truman and the Democratic Party* (1998). Another interpretation of Truman's political fortunes.

William Stueck, *The Korean War* (1995). Another indispensable account of the war.

Allen Weinstein and Alexander Vassiliev, *The Haunted Wood: Soviet Espionage in America—The Stalin Era* (1999). More on Soviet spying in the United States.

America at Midcentury, 1952–1960

The 1950s College Graduate, by Norman Rockwell

CHAPTER OUTLINE

hc This icon will direct you to additional study and research resources at http://college.hmco.com/history/us/boyer/enduring_concise/5e/students/index.html

Nostalgia has painted the 1950s as a decade of tranquility, abundance, easy living, new homes in the suburbs, family togetherness, big cars, and cheap gasoline. In movies and television, the fifties are a sunny time when everybody liked Ike, loved Lucy, and idolized Elvis.

Behind these stereotypes lies a reality far more complex, and often far darker. Yet, Americans did enjoy the fruits of the decade's consumer culture. Having survived a depression and global war, they reveled in prosperity. They

This chapter focuses on five major questions:

▶ What domestic policies support the notion of Eisenhower as a centrist or moderate politician?

▶ In what ways did Eisenhower continue Truman's foreign policy, and in what ways did he change it? How successfully did Eisenhower accomplish his foreign policy goals?

▶ What were the main sources, and consequences, of economic prosperity in the 1950s?

▶ How accurate is the image of the 1950s as a period of conservatism and conformity?

▶ What strategies did minorities adopt in order to gain greater equality in the 1950s, and how successful were they?

trusted Dwight D. Eisenhower and welcomed the thaw in the Cold War that came after the Korean War.

At the same time, the fifties saw the birth of the space age and of hydrogen bombs. Senator Joseph McCarthy, the Warren Court, and Martin Luther King, Jr. kindled intense political passions. The arrival of an automated society and television's growing power transformed life, as did the "baby boom" and mass suburbanization. Midcentury America encompassed peace and a widening Cold War, prosperity and persistent poverty, civil-rights triumphs and rampant racism.

THE EISENHOWER PRESIDENCY

Rarely in U.S. history has a president better fit the national mood than Dwight David Eisenhower. Ex-

hausted by a quarter century of upheaval—the stock-market crash, the Great Depression, World War II, the Cold War—Americans craved stability and peace. And Eisenhower delivered. Elected in 1952, Eisenhower gave people weary of partisanship a sense of unity, and he inspired confidence. Most Americans approved his neither expanding nor dismantling New Deal programs. He also neither publicly challenged Joseph McCarthy nor supported desegregation of public education, until events forced his hand.

"Dynamic Conservatism"

The most distinguished general of World War II, Eisenhower projected the image of a plain but good man. He expressed complicated issues in simple terms while governing a complex, urban, technological society and comforting an anxious people.

Born on October 14, 1890, in Denison, Texas, Eisenhower grew up in Abilene, Kansas, in a poor, strongly religious family. More athletic than studious, he graduated from the U.S. Military Academy at West Point in 1915. In directing the Allied invasion of North Africa in 1942 and of Western Europe in 1944, he revealed himself to be a brilliant war planner, respected for his managerial ability and talent for conciliation.

Eisenhower's approach to the presidency reflected his wartime leadership style. He concentrated on major matters, delegated authority, and worked to reconcile contending factions. His restrained view of presidential authority stemmed from his respect for the constitutional balance of power and for the dignity of the Oval Office. Eisenhower rarely intervened publicly in the legislative process, shunned using his office as a "bully pulpit," and assured his cabinet members that he would "stay out of [their] hair." This low-key style, combined with frequent fishing and golfing vacations, led Democrats to scoff at Eisenhower as a leader who "reigned but did not rule."

The image of passivity masked an active and occasionally ruthless politician. Determined to govern the nation on business principles, Eisenhower staffed his administration with corporate executives. "Eight millionaires and a plumber," wrote one journalist. Eisenhower initially worked with the Republican-controlled Congress to reduce the size of government and to slash the federal budget. He also promoted the private development of hydroelectric and nuclear power and persuaded Congress to turn over to coastal states the oil-rich "tidelands" that the Supreme Court had awarded to the federal government.

For the most part, however, the Eisenhower administration followed a centrist course. More pragmatic than ideological, the president wished to reduce taxes, contain inflation, and govern efficiently. Milton Eisenhower, the president's brother and adviser, summed up Ike's views: "We should keep what we have, catch our breath for a while, and improve administration; it does not mean moving backward."

Eager to avoid a depression, Eisenhower relied heavily on the Council of Economic Advisers (CEA) despite conservative calls for its abolition. He followed the advice of CEA head Arthur Burns to "fine-tune" the economy. When recessions struck in 1953 and 1957, Eisenhower abandoned a balanced budget and increased spending to restore prosperity.

Eisenhower labeled his ideas "dynamic conservatism" and "modern Republicanism." Whatever the slogan, he supported extending social-security benefits, raising the minimum wage, adding 4 million workers to those eligible for unemployment benefits, and providing federally financed public housing for low-income families. He also approved construction of the St. Lawrence Seaway, linking the Great Lakes and the Atlantic Ocean, and creation of the Department of Health, Education, and Welfare. In 1956 Eisenhower backed the largest and most expensive public-works program in American history: the Interstate Highway Act, authorizing construction of a 41,000-mile system of expressways. Freeways would soon snake across America, accelerating suburban growth, heightening dependence on cars and trucks, contributing to urban decay and air pollution, and drastically increasing gasoline consumption.

Republicans renominated Ike by acclamation in 1956, and voters gave him a landslide victory over Democrat Adlai Stevenson. With the GOP crowing, "Everything's booming but the guns," the president won by the greatest popular majority since FDR's victory in 1936.

The Downfall of Joseph McCarthy

Although he despised Joseph McCarthy, Eisenhower feared battling the senator. Instead, he allowed McCarthy to grab plenty of rope in hopes that the demagogue would hang himself. He did. In 1954 McCarthy accused the army of harboring communist spies, and the army charged McCarthy with using his influence to gain preferential treatment for a staff member who had been drafted.

In the resulting televised Senate investigation—the Army-McCarthy hearings—in 1954, a national audience witnessed McCarthy's boorish behavior. His dark scowl, endless interruptions, and disregard for the rights of others repelled many viewers. In June, when McCarthy smeared the reputation of a young lawyer assisting Joseph Welch, the army counsel, the mild-mannered Welch suddenly struck back: "Until this moment, Senator, I think I really never gauged your cruelty or your recklessness. . . . Have you no sense of decency?" The gallery burst into applause.

The spell of the inquisitor broken, the Senate in December 1954 censured the Wisconsin senator for contemptuous behavior. This powerful rebuke demolished McCarthy as a political force. In 1957 he died a broken man. But the fears he exploited lingered. Congress annually funded the House Un-American Activities Committee. State and local governments continued to require loyalty oaths from teachers.

McCarthyism also remained a rallying call of conservatives disenchanted with the postwar consensus. Young conservatives like William F. Buckley, Jr. and the Christian Anti-Communist Crusade continued to claim that domestic communism was a major subversive threat. The John Birch Society denounced Eisenhower as a conscious agent of the communist conspiracy and equated liberalism with treason. Its grass-roots network of as many as a hundred thousand activists promoted right-wing political candidates while waging local struggles against taxes, gun control, and sex education in the schools. Although few saw all the lurking dangers that the John Birch Society did, Barry Goldwater, George Wallace, and Ronald Reagan, among others, used its anticommunist, antigovernment rhetoric to advantage. Stressing victory over communism, rather than its containment, the self-proclaimed "new conservatives" (or radical right, as their opponents called them) criticized the "creeping socialism" of Eisenhower, advocated a return to traditional moral standards, and condemned the liberal rulings of the Supreme Court.

Jim Crow in Court

Led by a new chief justice, Earl Warren (1953), the Supreme Court drew conservatives' wrath for defending the rights of those accused of subversive beliefs. In a 1957 decision, the Court held that the accused had the right to inspect government files used by the prosecution, and that same year the justices overturned convictions of Communist party officials under the Smith Act. Right-wing opponents plastered "Impeach Earl Warren" posters on highway billboards.

These condemnations paled beside those of segregationists after the *Brown* v. *Board of Education of Topeka* (May 1954) ruling. Unanimously reversing *Plessy* v. *Ferguson* and its separate but equal doctrine, the Court held that separating schoolchildren "solely because of their race generates a feeling of inferiority . . . that may affect their hearts and minds in a way unlikely ever to be undone," thereby violating the equal-protection clause of the Fourteenth Amendment. The justices concluded that "separate educational facilities are inherently unequal." A year later the Court ordered the states to desegregate their schools "with all deliberate speed."

The border states complied, but white politicians in the South vowed resistance. Eisenhower refused to force them. "I don't believe you can change the hearts of men with laws or decisions," he observed. Although not a racist, he never publicly endorsed the *Brown* decision, and privately he called his appointment of Earl Warren "the biggest damn fool mistake I ever made."

Polls indicated that 80 percent of white southerners were against the Brown decision and, encouraged by Ike's silence, opposition stiffened. White Citizens Councils sprang up, and the Ku Klux Klan revived. Declaring the *Brown* decision "null, void, and of no effect," southern legislatures denied state aid to school systems that desegregated or closed them down. They also permitted school boards to assign black and white children to different schools.

In 1956, more than one hundred members of Congress signed the Southern Manifesto, denouncing *Brown* as "a clear abuse of judicial power." An Alabama gubernatorial candidate promised to go to jail to defend segregation, and his opponent promptly vowed to die for it. Segregationists also used violence and economic reprisals against blacks. At the end of 1956, not a single African-American attended school with whites in the Deep South, and few did so in the Upper South.

The Laws of the Land

Southern resistance reached a climax in September 1957 when Arkansas governor Orval Faubus mobilized the state's National Guard to bar nine African-American students from entering Little Rock's Central High School under a federal court order. After another court order forced Faubus to withdraw the guardsmen, jeering whites blocked the black students' entry.

Eisenhower sought to avoid the civil-rights issue, but he believed he had to uphold federal law. He also understood that racism at home hampered American efforts to gain the support of nonwhite Third World nations. The Soviets, he feared, were "gloating over this incident and using it everywhere to misrepresent our whole nation." The president dispatched federal troops to protect blacks' rights, and soldiers patrolled Central High for the rest of the year. Rather than accept integration, Faubus shut down Little Rock's public high schools for two years. At the end of the decade, fewer than 1 percent of African-American students in the Deep South attended desegregated schools.

Little Rock only strengthened African-Americans' determination to end Jim Crow. The crisis foreshadowed television's vital role in the civil-rights movement by airing images of howling whites abusing resolute black students. A 1957 public-opinion poll showed that 90 percent of whites outside the South approved the use of federal troops in Little Rock.

Most northern whites also favored legislation to enfranchise southern blacks, and during the 1956 campaign Eisenhower proposed a voting-rights bill. The Civil Rights Act of 1957, the first civil-rights law since Reconstruction, established a permanent commission on civil rights with broad investigatory powers but did little to guarantee the ballot to blacks. The Civil Rights Act of 1960 only slightly strengthened the first measure. Like the

Little Rock, 1957
Elizabeth Eckford, age 15, one of the nine black students to desegregate Central High School, endures abuse on her way to school, September 4, 1957. Forty years later, the young white woman shouting insults asked for forgiveness.

Brown decision, however, these laws implied a changing federal attitude about race and encouraged blacks to fight for their rights.

THE COLD WAR CONTINUES

Eisenhower maintained Truman's containment policy. Stalin's death in 1953 and Eisenhower's resolve to reduce the risk of nuclear war brought a thaw in the Cold War, but the United States and the U.S.S.R. remained deadlocked. The Cold War did not end, nor did American determination to check communism waver. Global fear of a nuclear holocaust mounted in step with both countries' increasingly destructive weapons.

Honoring his campaign pledge, Eisenhower visited Korea in December 1952, but the fate of thousands of prisoners of war who did not want to return to communist rule remained the sticking point preventing a settlement. After Stalin's death, the uncertainty in the communist world, and Eisenhower's veiled threat to use nuclear weapons broke the stalemate. The armistice signed in July 1953 set the boundary between North and South Korea once again at the thirty-eighth parallel and established a panel from neutral nations to oversee the return of prisoners of war. Some Americans claimed that communist aggression had been thwarted and containment vindicated; others condemned the truce as peace without honor.

hc Primary Source: The War that Could Have Set Off WWIII

Ike and Dulles

Eager to ease Cold War hostilities, Eisenhower first had to quiet the GOP right-wing's clamor to roll back the Red tide. To do so he chose as his secretary of state John Foster Dulles, a rigid, humorless Presbyterian who advocated a holy war against "atheistic communism," backed by the threat of "instant, massive retaliation" with nuclear weapons. Dulles called for "liberation" of the captive peoples of Eastern Europe and for unleashing Jiang Jieshi against Communist China. Believing that the Soviet Union understood only force, Dulles insisted on the necessity of "brinksmanship," the art of never backing down in a crisis, even at the risk of war.

Such saber rattling pleased the Right, but Eisenhower preferred conciliation. Partly because he feared a nuclear war—the Soviet Union had tested its own hydrogen bomb in 1953—Eisenhower refused to translate Dulles's rhetoric into action. Too, the president understood the limits of American power. When the U.S.S.R. crushed insurrections in East Germany (1953) and Hungary (1956), the United States did not intervene.

As multimegaton thermonuclear weapons replaced atomic bombs in U.S. and Soviet arsenals, Eisenhower worked to reduce the probability of mutual annihilation. He proposed "atoms for peace," whereby both superpowers would contribute fissionable materials to a new U.N. agency for use in industrial projects. In the absence of a positive Soviet response, the government began construction of an electronic air defense system to provide early warning of a missile attack.

Work also began on commercial nuclear plants in the mid-1950s, promising electricity "too cheap to meter." However, most money continued to go for nuclear research that was military-related. Radioactive fallout from atomic tests, especially the 1954 U.S. tests that spread strontium 90 over a wide area, heightened world concern about the nuclear-arms race.

In 1955 Eisenhower and Soviet leaders met in Geneva for the first East-West conference since World War II. Discussions produced no concrete plan for arms control, but mutual talk of "peaceful coexistence" led reporters to hail the "spirit of Geneva." In March 1958 Moscow suspended atmospheric tests of nuclear weapons, and the United States followed suit.

But the Cold War continued. Dulles negotiated mutual-defense pacts with any nation that opposed communism. His "pactomania" committed the United States to the defense of forty-three nations. The United States' "New Look" defense program guaranteed "more bang for the buck" by emphasizing nuclear weapons and reducing conventional forces. It spurred the Soviets to seek "more rubble for the ruble" by enlarging their nuclear stockpile.

Meanwhile, the focus of the Cold War shifted from Europe to the Third World, the largely nonwhite developing nations. There the two superpowers waged war by proxy, using local guerrillas and military juntas. There, too, the Central Intelligence Agency (CIA) fought covert wars against those thought to imperil American interests.

CIA Covert Actions

To command the CIA, Eisenhower appointed Allen Dulles, a veteran of wartime OSS operations and the brother of the secretary of state. Established in 1947 to conduct foreign intelligence gathering, the CIA soon began to carry out undercover operations to topple regimes friendly to communism. By 1957 half its personnel and 80 percent of its budget were devoted to "covert action." To woo influential foreign thinkers away from communism, the CIA also sponsored intellectual conferences and jazz concerts. It bankrolled anticommunist cultural events, subsidized magazines to publish articles supporting Washington, and recruited college students and businessmen traveling abroad as "fronts" in clandestine CIA activities.

In 1953 the CIA orchestrated a coup to overthrow the government of Iran. Fearing that the prime minister, who had nationalized oil fields, might open oil-rich Iran to the Soviets, the CIA replaced him with pro-American Shah Reza Pahlavi. The United States thus gained a loyal ally on the Soviet border, and American oil companies prospered when the Shah made low-priced oil available to them. But Iranian hatred of America took root—an enmity that would haunt the United States a quarter-century later.

Also in 1953 the CIA intervened in Philippine elections to ensure a pro-American government. In 1954 in Guatemala a CIA-supported band of mercenaries overthrew the elected communist-influenced regime, which had seized land from the American-owned United Fruit Company. The new pro-American government restored United Fruit's properties and trampled political opposition.

The Vietnam Domino

The most extensive CIA covert operations during the 1950s took place in Indochina. As a result of the Korean War and Mao Zedong's victory in China, the United States viewed Indochina as a Cold War battleground. The Truman administration had provided France with large-scale military assistance to fight the Vietminh, a broad-based Vietnamese nationalist coalition led by the communist Ho Chi Minh. By 1954 American aid accounted for 75 percent of French expenditures, but the French were losing. In early 1954 the Vietminh besieged twelve thousand French troops in the valley of Dienbienphu.

France appealed for U.S. intervention, and some American officials toyed with the idea of a nuclear strike, which Eisenhower flatly rejected. When the Democratic majority leader, Senator Lyndon Johnson of Texas, opposed "sending American GIs . . . to perpetuate colonialism and white man's exploitation in Asia," Ike refused to commit U.S. troops. In May the French surrendered at Dienbienphu. An international conference in Geneva arranged a cease-fire and divided Vietnam at the seventeenth parallel, pending elections in 1956 to choose the government of a unified nation.

Although Eisenhower would not take the United States into an Asian land war, he also would not permit a communist takeover of all of Vietnam. In what became known as the "domino theory," Eisenhower warned that if Vietnam fell to the communists, then Thailand, Burma, Indonesia, and ultimately all of Asia would follow. The United States refused to sign the Geneva Peace Accords, and in late 1954 created the Southeast Asia Treaty Organization (SEATO), a military alliance patterned on NATO.

In June 1954 the CIA installed Ngo Dinh Diem, a fiercely anticommunist Catholic, as premier and then president of an independent South Vietnam. CIA agents helped him train his armed forces and secret police, eliminate political opposition, and block the election to reunify Vietnam specified by the Geneva agreements. As Eisenhower later admitted, "possibly 80 percent of the population would have voted for the communist Ho Chi Minh as their leader." Washington pinned its hopes on Diem to maintain a noncommunist South Vietnam with American dollars rather than American lives.

But the autocratic Diem's Catholicism alienated the predominantly Buddhist population, and his refusal to institute land reform and to end corruption spurred opposition. In December 1960 opposition to Diem coalesced in the National Liberation Front (NLF). Backed by North Vietnam, the insurgency attracted broad support and soon controlled half of South Vietnam. The administration's commitment to "sink or swim with Ngo Dinh Diem" had cost over $1 billion, and Diem was sinking.

Troubles in the Third World

Eisenhower faced his greatest crisis in the Middle East. In 1954 Gamal Abdel Nasser came to power in Egypt determined to modernize his nation. To woo him, the United States offered financing for a dam at Aswan to harness the Nile River. But when Nasser purchased arms from Czechoslovakia, John Foster Dulles canceled the loan and Nasser nationalized the British-owned Suez Canal.

Viewing the canal as the lifeline of its empire, Britain planned to take it back by force. Supporting the British were France, which feared Arab nationalism in their Algerian colony, and Israel, which feared the Egyptian arms buildup. The three countries, America's closest allies, coordinated an attack on Egypt in October 1956 without consulting Eisenhower. Ike fumed that the military action would drive the Arab world and its precious oil to the Russians. When Moscow threatened to intervene, Eisenhower forced his allies to withdraw their troops.

The Suez crisis had major consequences. It swelled Third World antiwestern sentiment, and the United States replaced Britain and France as the protector of western interests in the Middle East. Determined to guarantee the flow of oil to the West, in 1957 the president announced the Eisenhower Doctrine, a proclamation that the United States would send military aid and, if necessary, troops to any Middle Eastern nation threatened by "Communist aggression." To prove he meant it, in July 1958 Eisenhower ordered fourteen thousand marines into Lebanon to quell a threatened revolt against its prowestern regime.

Such interventions intensified anti-American feelings in Third World nations. Shouting "yanqui imperialism," angry crowds in Peru and Venezuela spat at Vice President Nixon and stoned his car in 1958. In 1959 Fidel Castro overturned a dictatorial regime in Cuba and confiscated American properties without compensation. Anti-American riots in Japan in 1960 forced Eisenhower to cancel a trip there.

A tougher blow struck on May 1, 1960, two weeks before a scheduled summit conference with Soviet premier Nikita Khrushchev, when the Soviets shot down a U.S. spy plane far inside their border. Khrushchev displayed the captured CIA U-2 pilot and photos taken of Soviet missile sites. Eisenhower refused to apologize and the summit collapsed.

The Eisenhower Legacy

Just before leaving office, Eisenhower offered Americans a farewell and a warning. The demands of national security, he stated, had produced the "conjunction of an immense military establishment and a large arms industry." Swollen defense budgets had yoked American economic health to military expenditures, and military contracts had become the staff of life for research scholars, politicians, and America's largest corporations. This combination of interests, Eisenhower believed, exerted enormous leverage and threatened the traditional subordination of the military in American life. "We must guard against the acquisition of unwarranted influence . . . by the military-industrial complex. The potential for the disastrous rise of misplaced power exists and will persist."

The president concluded by saying that although he had avoided war, lasting peace was not in sight. Most scholars agreed. Eisenhower had ended the Korean War, avoided direct intervention in Vietnam, begun relaxing tensions with the Soviet Union, and suspended atmospheric nuclear testing. He had also presided over an accelerating nuclear-arms race and a widening Cold War, and he had loosed the CIA to intervene in local conflicts around the globe.

The moderate Eisenhower pleased neither Left nor Right. His acceptance of New Deal social-welfare measures angered the Republican Right, while liberal Democrats faulted his passivity toward McCarthyism and racism. But Ike had given the majority of Americans what they most wanted—prosperity, reassurance, and a breathing spell in which to relish the comforts of life.

THE AFFLUENT SOCIETY

In 1958 economist John Kenneth Galbraith published *The Affluent Society,* a study of postwar America. The title reflected the broad-based prosperity that made the 1950s seem the fulfillment of the American dream. By the end of the decade, 60 percent of American families owned homes; 75 percent, cars; and 87 percent, at least one TV. Government spending, a huge upsurge in productivity, and steadily increasing consumer demand pushed the gross national product (GNP) up 50 percent.

Three brief recessions and a rising national debt, almost $290 billion by 1961, evoked concern but did little to stifle economic growth or optimism. The United States had achieved the world's highest living standard ever. By 1960 the average worker's income, adjusted for inflation, was 35 percent higher than in 1945. With just 6 percent of the world's population, the United States produced and consumed nearly 50 percent of everything made and sold on earth.

The New Industrial Society

Federal spending constituted a major source of economic growth, nearly doubling in the 1950s to $180 billion. The outlays of state and local governments kept pace. Federal expenditures, just 1 percent of the GNP in 1929, reached 17 percent by the mid-1950s. These funds built roads and airports, financed home mortgages, supported farm prices, and provided stipends for education. More than half the federal budget—10 percent of the GNP—went to defense spending. With continued superpower rivalry in atomic weapons, missile-delivery systems, and the space race, the federal government remained the nation's chief sponsor of scientific and technological research and development (R&D).

Particularly for the West, it was as if World War II had never ended. Politicians from both parties labored to keep defense spending flowing westward. By the late 1950s California alone received half the space budget and a quarter of all major military contracts. Denver had the largest number of federal employees outside Washington, D.C. Over a third of workers in Los Angeles depended on defense industries. Utah, once the Mormon dream of an agricultural utopia, received the nation's highest per capita expenditures on space and defense research. Government spending transformed the West of rugged individualists into a new West of bureaucrats, defense contractors, and scientists dependent on federal funds.

Science increasingly became a ward of the state, with government funding and control transforming both the U.S. military and industry sectors. Financed by the Atomic Energy Commission and using navy scientists, the nation's first nuclear power plant came on line in 1957. The chemical industry surged from fiftieth place in the industrial economy before the war to fourth. Americans enjoyed their Dacron suits and Teflon-coated pans and marveled at the Saran Wrap–covered produce that crowded store shelves, unaware that chemical fertilizers and pesticides were contaminating groundwater and nearly indestructible plastics were reducing landfill space.

Electronics became the fifth-largest American industry. Electricity consumption tripled in the 1950s as industry automated and consumers learned to "live better electrically," as commercials urged, by buying all manner of appliances. Cheap oil fueled expansion in both the chemical and the electronics industries. Domestic oil production and foreign imports rose steeply, and by 1960 oil had replaced coal as the nation's main energy source. Hardly anyone paid attention when a physicist warned in 1953 that "adding 6 billion tons of carbon dioxide to the atmosphere each year is warming up the Earth."

Plentiful cheap gasoline fed the growth of the automobile and aircraft industries. Aerospace, the nation's third-largest industry in the 1950s, depended on defense spending and federally funded research. Seattle, Dallas–Fort Worth, San Diego, and Los Angeles accounted for nearly all the nation's aircraft production. The automobile industry, still the nation's industrial titan, also applied technological R&D. Where machines had earlier replaced some human workers, automation now controlled the machines. Between 1945 and 1960 the industry halved the number of hours and workers needed to produce a car. Other industries followed, investing $10 billion a year throughout the fifties on labor-saving machinery.

The Age of Computers

The computer was a key to technological revolution. In 1944 International Business Machines (IBM), cooperating with Harvard scientists, had produced the Mark I calculator, a slow, cumbersome machine with five hundred miles of wiring. In late 1945 to improve artillery accuracy, the military devised ENIAC, the first electronic computer. Still unwieldy, with eighteen thousand vacuum tubes, ENIAC could perform five thousand calculations per second. Next came the development of operating instructions, or programs, that could be stored in the computer's memory and the replacement of wires by printed circuits. Then, in 1948, Bell Labs invented tiny, solid-state transistors that ended reliance on radio tubes and initiated the age of computers.

Sales of electronic computers to industry rose from twenty in 1954 to more than two thousand in 1960. Major manufacturers used them to monitor production lines, track inventory, and ensure quality control. In government, computers were as indispensable to Pentagon strategists playing war games as to the Census Bureau and the Internal Revenue Service. By the mid-1960s more than thirty thousand mainframe computers would be used by banks, hospitals, and universities. In time, the development of integrated circuits would lead to the Internet and transform the nature of work and its landscape.

The high-tech complex known as Silicon Valley began with the 1951 opening of the Stanford

Industrial Park in the Santa Clara Valley. Hoping to attract financial aid from business and the military, Stanford University used its science and engineering faculties to design and produce products for Fairchild Semiconductor and Hewlett-Packard. This relationship became a model for other high-tech firms, and apricot and cherry orchards gave way to industrial parks for computer firms and pharmaceutical laboratories. Initially far from the dirt and noise of eastern factories, these campus-like facilities would eventually choke the valley with traffic congestion, housing developments, and smog.

The Costs of Bigness

Rapid technological advances accelerated the growth and power of big business. In 1950 twenty-two firms had assets of more than $1 billion; by 1960, fifty did. By then, one-half of 1 percent of corporations earned more than half the total corporate income in the United States. Wealthy firms, able to afford huge R&D outlays, swallowed weak competitors and became oligopolies. Three television networks monopolized the nation's airwaves; three automobile and three aluminum companies produced 90 percent of America's cars and aluminum; and large corporations controlled the lion's share of assets and sales in steel, petroleum, chemicals, and electrical machinery. Corporations formed conglomerates by merging companies in unrelated industries, and they acquired overseas facilities to become "multinational" enterprises.

Growth and consolidation meant greater bureaucratization. "Executives" replaced "capitalists." Success required conformity not creativity, teamwork not individuality. According to sociologist David Riesman, the new "company people" were "other-directed," eager to follow the cues from their peers and not think innovatively or act independently.

Changes in agriculture paralleled those in industry. Farming grew increasingly scientific and mechanized. Between 1945 and 1960, technology cut the work hours necessary to grow crops by half.

Many farm families migrated to cities. In 1956 alone, one-eleventh of the farm population left the land. Meanwhile, heavily capitalized farm businesses prospered by using more and more machines and chemicals.

Few Americans understood the extent to which fertilizers, herbicides, and pesticides poisoned the environment until the publication of Rachel Carson's *Silent Spring* in 1962. A former researcher for the Fish and Wildlife Service, Carson demonstrated how the indiscriminately used insecticide DDT spread through the food chain. (Her book's title referred to the death of songbirds from DDT toxicity.) Many states banned DDT's use, and the federal government followed suit. But the incentives for cultivating more land led to further ravages. The Army Corps of Engineers and the Bureau of Reclamation dammed the waters of the West, turning the Columbia and Missouri Rivers into rows of slack-water reservoirs, killing fish and wildlife, and inundating hundreds of square miles of Indian tribal lands.

Blue-Collar Blues

Consolidation also transformed the labor movement. In 1955 the AFL and CIO merged, bringing 85 percent of union members into a single unit. Although leaders promised aggressive unionism, organized labor fell victim to its success at the bargaining table. Higher wages, a shorter workweek, paid vacations, health-care coverage, and automatic wage hikes tied to the cost of living led most workers to view themselves as middle class, not an aggrieved proletariat. Strikes occurred far less than they did in the 1930s.

A decrease in the number of blue-collar workers also sapped labor's momentum. Automation cut membership in the coal, auto, and steelworkers' unions by more than half. Most of the new jobs in the 1950s were in the service sector and in public employment, which banned collective bargaining by labor unions.

In 1956, for the first time in U.S. history, white-collar workers outnumbered blue-collar workers.

Although most service jobs were as routinized as any factory job, few unions wooed white-collar workers. The percentage of the labor force in unions dropped from a high of 36 percent in 1953 to 31 percent in 1960, and kept falling.

Prosperity and the Suburbs

As real income (adjusted for inflation) rose, Americans spent less of their income on necessities and more on powered lawn mowers and air conditioners. They heaped their shopping carts with frozen, dehydrated, and fortified foods. When they lacked cash, they borrowed. In 1950 Diners' Club issued the first credit card, and American Express followed in 1958. Installment buying, home mortgages, and auto loans tripled Americans' private indebtedness in the 1950s. Advertising expenditures also tripled. Appealing to the desire for status and glamor in its effort to convince people to buy what they did not need, business spent more on advertising than the nation did on public schools.

Americans purchased 58 million new cars during the 1950s. Manufacturers enticed people to trade in and up by offering flashier models, two-tone color, tail fins, and more powerful engines, such as Pontiac's 1955 "Sensational Strato-Streak V-8," which could go more than twice as fast as any speed limit. The results were increases in highway deaths, air pollution, oil consumption, and "auto-sclerosis"—clogged urban arteries.

Government policy as well as "auto-mania" spurred white Americans' exodus to the suburbs. Federal spending on highways skyrocketed from $79 million in 1946 to $2.6 billion in 1960. Once-remote areas came within "commuting distance" for urban workers. The income tax code stimulated home sales by allowing deductions for home-mortgage interest payments and for property taxes. The Federal Housing Administration (FHA) and the

Made for Each Other
The two-tone '55 Chevy Bel Air convertible and a California suburban drive-in. As Americans flocked to the new suburban communities, the number of cars in the country increased by 133 percent between 1945 and 1960; and as Americans raced to buy the latest, flashiest model, almost as many cars were junked each year in the mid-1950s as were manufactured.

Veterans Administration (VA) offered low-interest loans; neither promoted housing desegregation.

Eighty-five percent of the 13 million new homes built in the 1950s were in the suburbs. While social critics lampooned the "ticky-tacky" houses in "disturbia," suburban life embodied the American dream for many families who longed for their own home, good schools, a safe environment for children, and neighbors like themselves.

Park Forest, Illinois, a thirty-mile commute from Chicago, was planned to be a "complete community for middle-income families with children." In 1947 Long Island, some thirty miles from Manhattan, Alfred and William Levitt used mass production techniques to construct thousands of look-alike 720-square-foot houses as quickly as possible. Property deeds mandated regular lawn mowing and a tree was planted every twenty-eight feet along streets that all curved at the same angle.

In the greatest internal migration in its history, some 20 million Americans moved to the suburbs in the 1950s—doubling the numbers and making the suburban population equal to that of the central cities. By 1960 over 60 percent of American families owned their homes—the symbol of the affluent society.

Americans also moved South and West, into the Sunbelt, lured by job opportunities, the climate, and the pace of life. California, where the population went from 9 to 19 million between 1945 and 1964, supplanted New York as the most populous state. Los Angeles boasted the highest per capita ownership of private homes and cars of any city. Bulldozers ripped out three thousand acres of orange groves a day in Los Angeles County to make way for housing developments.

Industry also headed South and West, drawn by low taxes, low energy costs, and anti-union right-to-work laws. Senior citizens headed to the easier climate. Both groups brought a conservative outlook. By 1980 the population of the Sunbelt, which stretched from the Old Confederacy across Texas to southern California, exceeded that of the North and East. The political power of the Republican party rose accordingly.

hc Interactive Map: Population Increase in the Sun Belt States

CONSENSUS AND CONSERVATISM

Not everyone embraced the conformity of 1950s consumer culture. Intellectuals found a wide audience for their attack on "organization men" bent on getting ahead by going along and on "status seekers" pursuing external rewards to compensate for inner insecurities. Others took aim at the consumerist middle-class: "all items in a national supermarket—categorized, processed, labeled, priced, and readied for merchandising."

This criticism oversimplified reality. It ignored ethnic and class diversity, the acquisitiveness and conformity of earlier generations, and the currents of dissent swirling beneath the surface. But it rightly spotlighted the elevation of comfort over challenge, and of private pleasures over public affairs. Americans, indeed, sought refuge in "the good life," and a large majority shared agreed-on values, rejecting radicalism at home and opposing the spread of communism abroad.

Togetherness and the Baby Boom

In 1954 *McCall's* magazine coined the term *togetherness* to celebrate the ideal couple: the man and woman who centered their lives on home and children. Americans in the 1950s tended to marry young, to have babies quickly, and to have lots of them. The fertility rate (the number of births per one thousand women) peaked at 123 in 1957, when an American baby was born every seven seconds.

New antibiotics subdued diphtheria and whooping cough, while the Salk and Sabin vaccines eliminated polio. The plunge in childhood mortality helped to raise American life expectancy from 65.9 years in 1945 to 70.9 years in 1970. Coupled with the baby boom, this led to a 19 percent population spurt during the 1950s. By 1960 children under fourteen constituted one-third of the population.

The sheer size of the baby-boom generation ensured its impact. In the 1950s school construction boomed, as did college enrollments in the

1960s. The 1970s through the 1990s would see peaks in home construction, as the boomers had families, and in retirement investments. In the 1950s the baby boom made child rearing a foremost concern and reinforced the idea that women's place was in the home. With Americans convinced of the psychological potency of early childhood experiences, motherhood became an increasingly vital, demanding calling.

No one did more to emphasize the link between full-time mothers and healthy children than Dr. Benjamin Spock; only the Bible outsold his *Baby and Child Care* (1946) in the fifties. Spock urged mothers not to work outside the home, in order to create an atmosphere of warmth and intimacy for their children. Crying babies were to be comforted; breast-feeding came back into vogue. At best, Spock's advice meant less spanking and more "democratic" family discussions; at worst, it produced a "filiarchy" allowing kids to rule the roost and unduly burdening mothers.

Domesticity

Popular culture throughout the fifties glorified marriage and parenthood, painting a woman's devotion to life in the home with her children as the most cherished goal. Television almost always pictured mother at home. Hollywood perpetuated the stereotype of career women as neurotic. As Debbie Reynolds declared in *The Tender Trap* (1955), "A woman isn't a woman until she's been married and had children."

Education reinforced these ideas. Alongside academic subjects, girls studied typing, etiquette, and cooking. Guidance counselors cautioned young women not to miss out on marriage by pursuing higher education. "Men are not interested in college degrees, but in the warmth and humanness of the girls they marry," stressed a textbook on family living. More men than women went to college, and only one-third of college women completed their degrees.

However, profound changes were under way. Despite the wave of layoffs of women workers when World War II ended, women had quickly returned to the work force. By 1960 nearly 40 percent of American women held full- or part-time jobs; 40 percent of working women had school-age children.

Most women worked to augment family income, not to challenge stereotypes, and took low-paying, low-prestige jobs. Organized feminism ebbed to its lowest point of the century during the fifties. Yet many working women developed a heightened sense of expectations and empowerment that, transmitted to their daughters, would fuel a feminist resurgence in the late 1960s.

Religion and Education

"Today in the U.S.," *Time* claimed in 1954, "the Christian faith is back in the center of things." Religious popularizers—fiery evangelist Billy Graham, riveting Roman Catholic bishop Fulton J. Sheen, and "positive-thinking" Protestant minister Norman Vincent Peale—had syndicated newspaper columns, best-selling books, and radio and television programs. Hollywood religious extravaganzas such as *The Robe* (1953) and *The Ten Commandments* (1956) became box-office hits, and TV commercials pronounced that "the family that prays together stays together."

Millions embraced evangelical fundamentalism and became "born-again" Christians—a trend that would escalate. Billy Graham and Oral Roberts among others developed huge followings by preaching against the hedonism and secularism of modern life; they appealed mainly to Americans alienated by rapid cultural and social change. President Eisenhower declared, "Everybody should have a religious faith, and I don't care what it is." Despite the aura of religiosity in the fifties, the *intensity* of faith diminished for many people as mainstream churches downplayed sin and evil and preached Americanism and fellowship.

Similarly, while education flourished in the 1950s, it seemed shallower. The baby boom inflated primary-school enrollment by 10 million. California opened a new school every week throughout the decade and still faced a classroom shortage. The proportion of college-age Americans in higher education climbed from 15 percent in

1940 to more than 40 percent by the 1960s. "Progressive" educators promoted sociability and self-expression over science, math, and history. The "well-rounded" student became more prized than the highly skilled or knowledgeable pupil. Surveys of college students found them conservative, conformist, and careerist, a "silent generation" primarily seeking security and comfort.

Among faculty, few challenged the economic structure or ideology of the United States, or addressed the problems of minorities and the poor or class issues. Historians highlighted the pragmatic ideas and values shared by most Americans. Many asserted that America owed its unique national character primarily to economic abundance.

The Culture of the Fifties

American culture reflected the spirit of a prosperous era as well as Cold War anxiety. Enjoying more leisure time and bigger paychecks, Americans spent one-seventh of the GNP in 1950 on entertainment. People visited national parks in droves. Spectator sports boomed, new symphony halls opened, and book sales doubled.

New York replaced Paris as the capital of the art world. Like the abstract canvases of Jackson Pollock and the cool jazz trumpet of Miles Davis, the major novels of the fifties displayed introspection and improvisation. John Cheever's *The Wapshot Chronicles* and John Updike's *Rabbit Run* (1960) presented characters vaguely dissatisfied with jobs and home, longing for a more vital and authentic existence but incapable of decisive action.

Southern, African-American, and Jewish-American writers turned out the decade's most vital fiction. William Faulkner continued his dense saga of a family in Yoknapatawpha County, Mississippi, in *The Town* (1957) and *The Mansion* (1960), while Eudora Welty evoked small-town Mississippi life in *The Ponder Heart* (1954). The black experience found memorable expression in James Baldwin's *Go Tell It on the Mountain* (1953) and Ralph Ellison's *Invisible Man* (1951). Bernard Malamud's *The Assistant* (1957) depicted the Jewish immigrant world of New York's Lower East Side; Philip Roth's

Goodbye, Columbus (1959) dissected the world of upwardly mobile Jews.

Hollywood reflected the diminished concern with political issues, churning out westerns, musicals, and costume spectacles. Movies about the 1950s portrayed Americans as one happy, white, middle-class family. Minorities and the poor remained invisible, and women appeared largely as "dumb blondes" or cute helpmates. But as TV viewing soared, movie attendance dropped by 50 percent, and 20 percent of the nation's theaters became bowling alleys or supermarkets.

The Message of the Medium

No cultural medium ever grew so huge so quickly as television. In 1946 one in every eighteen thousand households had a TV set; by 1960, 90 percent of all households owned at least one TV, and more Americans had televisions than had bathrooms.

Business capitalized on the phenomenon. The three main radio networks—ABC, CBS, and NBC—gobbled up virtually every TV station in the country. *TV Guide* soon outsold all other periodicals; in 1960 fifty-three separate editions were published. First marketed in 1954, the TV dinner changed the nation's eating habits. It seemed that TV could sell anything. By the mid-fifties the three major networks *each* had larger advertising revenues than any other communications medium in the world.

The TV Culture

Initially, TV showcased talent and creativity. Opera performances appeared in prime time, as did sophisticated comedies and dramas and documentaries like Edward R. Murrow's *See It Now*. Early situation comedies such as *The Life of Riley* featured ethnic working-class families. As the price of TV sets fell and the chill of McCarthyism spread, the networks' appetite for a mass audience transformed TV into a cautious celebration of conformity and consumerism. Nearly all situation comedies featured suburban upper-middle-class families; most, like *Leave It to Beaver*, portrayed perfectly coiffed moms who loved to vacuum in high heels, frisky yet ultimately obedient kids, and all-knowing dads. Even Lucille Ball and Desi Arnaz in *I Love Lucy*—which no network initially wanted because an all-American redhead was married to a Cuban—had a baby and left New York for suburbia.

Decrying television's mediocrity, in 1961 the head of the Federal Communications Commission called it "a vast wasteland." A steady parade of soaps, unsophisticated comedies, and violent westerns led others to call TV "the idiot box."

Measuring television's impact is difficult. Different people read the "texts" of TV (or of movies or books) in their own way and so receive their own messages from the medium. In the main, television reflected American society and stimulated the desire to be included in that society. It spawned mass fads for Barbie dolls and hula hoops and spread the message of consumerism. It reinforced gender and racial stereotypes, rarely showing African-Americans and Latinos—except in servile roles or prison scenes—and extolling male violence in fighting evil; it portrayed women as zany madcaps or self-effacing moms. While promoting professional baseball and football into truly national phenomena, TV virtually ended network radio and decreased the audience of movies and of magazines such as *Look* and *Life*.

Television also changed political life. Politicians could effectively appeal to the voters over the heads of party leaders, and appearance mattered more than content. At least 20 million watched Senator Joseph McCarthy bully and slander witnesses. Richard Nixon reached 58 million and saved his political career with his appeal in the "Checkers" speech. And Eisenhower's pioneering use of brief "spot advertisements" combined with Stevenson's avoidance of televised appearances to clinch Ike's smashing presidential victories. In 1960 John F. Kennedy's "telegenic" image would play a significant role in his successful campaign.

All in all, television helped produce a more-national culture, diminishing provincialism and regional differences. Its overwhelming portrayal of a contented citizenry reinforced complacency and hid the reality of "the other America."

THE OTHER AMERICA

"I am an invisible man," declared the African-American narrator of Ralph Ellison's *Invisible Man;* "I am invisible . . . because people refuse to see me." Indeed, few white middle-class Americans of the fifties perceived the extent of social injustice in the United States. "White flight" from cities to suburbs physically separated races and classes. Popular culture focused on affluent white Americans enjoying the "good life." But poverty and racial discrimination were rife and dire, and the struggles for social justice intensified.

Poverty and Urban Blight

Although the percentage of poor families declined from 1947 to 1960, in 1960 some 35 million Americans, one-fifth of the nation, lived below the poverty line. Some 8 million elderly had yearly incomes of less than a thousand dollars.

One-third of the poor lived in depressed rural areas, and two million migrant farm workers lived in the most abject poverty. Observing a Texas migratory-labor camp in 1955, a journalist reported that 96 percent of the children had had no milk in the previous six months, eight out of ten adults had eaten no meat, and most slept "on the ground, in a cave, under a tree, or in a chicken house." In California's Imperial Valley, the infant death rate among migrant workers was more than seven times the statewide average.

The bulk of the poor huddled in decaying inner-city slums. Displaced southern blacks and Appalachian whites, Native Americans forced off reservations, and newly arrived Hispanics strained cities' inadequate facilities. Nearly two hundred thousand Mexican-Americans herded into San Antonio's Westside barrio; a local newspaper described them as living like cattle in a stockyard, "with roofed-over corrals for homes and chutes for streets." As described by Michael Harrington in *The Other America: Poverty in the United States* (1962), the poor lived trapped in a cycle of want and poverty. Unable to afford a nutritious diet or doctors, the poor got sick more often and for longer

North Chicago Slum
Life was not the "nifty fifties" for all Americans. Nearly one in four lived below the poverty line, which was calculated by the federal government to be $2,973 for a family of four in 1959.

than affluent Americans. Children of the poor started school at a disadvantage and rapidly fell behind; many dropped out. Living with neither hope nor skills, the poor bequeathed a similar legacy to their children.

The pressing need for low-cost housing went unanswered. Slum-clearance and urban-renewal projects shunted the poor from one ghetto to another to make room for parking garages and cultural centers. Bulldozers razed the Los Angeles barrio of Chavez Ravine to make way for Dodger Stadium. Landlords, realtors, and bankers deliberately excluded nonwhites from decent housing. Half of the housing in New York's Harlem predated 1900. There, a dozen people might share a tiny apartment with broken windows, faulty plumbing, and gaping holes in the walls. Harlem's rates of illegitimacy, infant deaths, narcotics use, and crime towered above city and national averages. "Where flies and maggots breed . . . where rats bite helpless children," an African-American social psychologist observed, "the conditions of life are brutal and inhumane."

Blacks' Struggle for Justice

The collision between the hopes raised by the 1954 *Brown* decision and the indignities of persistent segregation sparked a new phase in the civil-rights movement. African-Americans developed new tactics, founded new organizations, and followed new leaders. They used nonviolent direct-action protest to engage large numbers of blacks in their own freedom fight and to arouse white America's conscience.

Racism touched even the smallest details of daily life. In Montgomery, Alabama, although the city's black bus riders represented more than three-fourths of all passengers, they had to sit in the rear and give up their seats to any standing white riders. In December 1955, when Rosa Parks, an officer of the Montgomery NAACP who would not drink from "colored only" fountains and who climbed stairs rather than use a segregated elevator, refused to get up so that a white man could sit, she was arrested. Montgomery's black leaders organized a massive boycott. "There comes a time when people get tired, tired of being segregated and humiliated," declared Martin Luther King, Jr., a twenty-seven-year-old minister who articulated the anger of Montgomery blacks. The time had come, he continued, to stop being patient "with anything less than freedom and justice." Accordingly, fifty-thousand black Montgomerians boycotted the buses for a year, organizing car pools and often walking miles to work. "My soul has been tired for a long time," an old woman said; "now my feet are tired, and my soul is resting." When city leaders would not budge, blacks filed suit, challenging bus segregation. In November 1956 the Supreme Court affirmed a lower-court decision outlawing such segregation.

The bus boycott demonstrated black strength and determination. It shattered the myth that African-Americans approved of segregation and that only outside agitators fought Jim Crow. It affirmed the possibility of social change. It vaulted Dr. King, whose oratory simultaneously inspired black activism and touched white consciences, into the national spotlight.

King's philosophy of civil disobedience fused the spirit of Christianity with the strategy of nonviolent resistance. His emphasis on direct action gave every African-American an opportunity to become involved, and his insistence on nonviolence diminished the threat of bloodshed. Preaching that they must lay their bodies on the line to provoke crises that would force whites to confront their racism, he urged his followers to love their enemies. In this way, he believed, blacks would convert their oppressors and bring "redemption and reconciliation." In 1957 King and a network of black ministers formed the Southern Christian Leadership Conference (SCLC) to help lead the fight against Jim Crow. But the movement's triumphs rested not on its leaders but on the domestic servants who walked instead of riding the buses, the children on the front lines of the battle for school desegregation, and the tens of thousands of ordinary people who marched, rallied, and demonstrated.

Latinos and Latinas

Hispanic-Americans initially made less headway in ending discrimination. High unemployment on the Caribbean island brought a steady stream of Puerto Ricans, who as U.S. citizens could enter the mainland without restriction. By 1960 nearly a million lived in El Barrio in New York City's East Harlem.

In New York they suffered from inadequate housing and schools and from police harassment; they were denied decent jobs and political recognition. Family frictions flared in the transition to unaccustomed ways. Parents felt upstaged by children who learned English and obtained jobs that were closed to them. The relationship between husbands and wives changed as women found readier access to jobs than did men. One migrant explained, "Whether I have a husband or not I work . . . and if my husband dare to complain, I throw him out. That is the difference; in Puerto Rico I should have to stand for anything a man asks me to do because he pays the rent. Here I belong to myself." Yet however much they tried to embrace American ways, many Puerto Ricans could not enjoy the promise of the American Dream because of their skin color and Spanish language.

Mexican-Americans suffered the same indignities. Most were underpaid and segregated from mainstream American life. After World War II, new irrigation systems added 7.5 million acres to the agricultural lands of the Southwest, stimulating demand for cheap Mexican labor. In 1951, to stem the resulting tide of illegal Mexican immigrants, Congress reintroduced the wartime "temporary worker" program that brought in seasonal farm laborers called *braceros*. Many stayed without authorization, joining a growing number of Latinos who entered the country illegally.

During the 1953–1955 recession, the Eisenhower administration's "Operation Wetback" (a term of derision for illegal Mexican immigrants) deported some 3 million allegedly undocumented entrants. Periodic roundups, however, did not stop the millions of Mexicans who continued to cross the poorly guarded border. The *bracero* program itself peaked in 1959, admitting 450,000 workers.

The swelling Mexican-American population became more urban. In Los Angeles County it doubled to more than six hundred thousand, and the *colonias* of Denver, El Paso, Phoenix, and San Antonio grew proportionately as large. By 1970, 85 percent of Mexican-Americans lived in urban areas. As service in World War II gave Hispanics an increased sense of their own American identity and a claim on their rights as American citizens, urbanization gave them better educational and employment opportunities. The *Asociación Nacional México-Americana* was founded in 1950. Unions like the United Cannery, Agricultural, Packing and Allied Workers of America sought higher wages and better working conditions for their Mexican-American members, and such middle-class organizations as the League of United Latin American Citizens (LULAC), the GI Forum, and the Unity League campaigned to desegregate schools and public facilities.

In 1954 the Supreme Court banned the exclusion of Mexican-Americans from Texas jury lists, and in 1958 El Paso elected the first Mexican-American mayor. Latinos also took pride in baseball star Roberto Clemente and their growing numbers in the major leagues, in Nobel Prize winners like biologist Severo Ochoa, and in such Hollywood stars as Anthony Quinn. But the existence of millions of undocumented aliens and the continuation of the *bracero* program stigmatized all people of Spanish descent and depressed their wages. The median income of Hispanics was less than two-thirds that of Anglos. At least a third lived in poverty.

Native Americans

Native Americans remained the poorest, most ignored minority. Their death rate was three times the national average, and unemployment on reservations ran a staggering 70 to 86 percent for some tribes. Congress again changed course, moving away from efforts to reassert Indian sovereignty and cultural autonomy and back toward the goal of assimilation. Between 1954 and 1962 Congress terminated treaties and withdrew financial support from sixty-one reservations. First applied to the

Menominees of Wisconsin and the Klamaths of Oregon, who owned valuable timberlands, the policy was disastrous. Further impoverishing the tribes, it transferred more than 500,000 acres of Native American lands to non-Indians. The federal Voluntary Relocation Program, designed to lure Indians off the reservations, provided Native Americans with moving costs, assistance in finding housing and jobs, and living expenses until they obtained work.

By 1960 about sixty thousand Indians had been relocated to cities. Some became middle class, some ended up in run-down urban shantytowns, and nearly a third eventually returned to their reservations. The National Congress of American Indians vigorously opposed termination, and most tribal politicians advocated Indian sovereignty, treaty rights, and federal trusteeship.

SEEDS OF DISQUIET

Late in the 1950s apprehension ruffled the placid surface of American life. Questions about the nation's goals and values, periodic recessions, rising unemployment, and the ballooning national debt made Khrushchev's boast that "your grandchildren will live under communist rule" ring in American ears. Third World anticolonialism, especially in Cuba, diminished Americans' national pride. So did the growing alienation of American youth and a technological breakthrough by the Soviet Union.

Sputnik

On October 4, 1957, the Soviet Union launched the first artificial satellite, *Sputnik* ("Fellow Traveler"). Weighing 184 pounds and only twenty-two inches in diameter, it circled the earth at eighteen thousand miles per hour. When *Sputnik II*, carrying a dog, went into a more distant orbit on November 3, critics indignantly said that Eisenhower had allowed a "technological Pearl Harbor."

The Eisenhower administration disparaged the Soviet achievement but behind the scenes pushed to have the American Vanguard missile readied to launch a satellite. On December 6, with millions watching on TV, Vanguard rose six feet into the air and exploded. Newspapers wrote of America's "Flopnik."

Eisenhower didn't laugh. Instead he doubled the funds for missile development to $4.3 billion in 1958 and then raised the level to $5.3 billion in 1959. He also established the Science Advisory Committee, whose recommendations led to creation of the National Aeronautics and Space Administration (NASA) in July 1958. By decade's end, the United States had launched several space probes and successfully tested the Atlas intercontinental ballistic missile (ICBM).

Critics had long complained that Americans honored football stars more than outstanding students and warned that the Soviet Union produced twice as many scientists and engineers as the United States. Spurred by *Sputnik*, Americans embarked on a crash program to raise educational standards. Federal funding built new classrooms and laboratories, raised teachers' salaries, and installed instructional television systems in schools. In 1958 Congress passed the National Defense Education Act, providing loans to college students and funds for teacher training and for the development of new instructional materials in science, mathematics, and foreign languages.

America now banked on higher education to ensure national security. The number of college students skyrocketed from 1.5 million in 1940 to 3.6 million by 1960. That year, the government funneled $1.5 billion to universities, a hundred-fold increase over 1940. Linked directly to the Cold War, this hike in educational spending raised unsettling questions. By 1960 nearly a third of scientists and engineers on university faculties worked full-time on government research, primarily defense projects. Some observers feared that a military-industrial-*educational* complex was emerging.

A Different Beat

Few adults considered the implications of affluence for the young or the consequences of having a generation of teenagers who could stay in school instead of working. Few thought about the effects of growing up in an age when traditional values such as thrift and self-denial had declining relevance among youth with the leisure and money to shape their own subculture. And despite talk of togetherness, fathers were often too busy to give their children much attention, and mothers sometimes spent more time chauffeuring adolescents than listening to them. Much of what adults knew about teenagers they learned from the mass media, which focused on the sensational and the superficial.

Accounts of juvenile delinquency abounded. News stories painted high schools as war zones and streets as jungles ruled by gangs. In truth, teenage crime barely increased. But male teenagers sporting black-leather motorcycle jackets, their hair slicked into "ducktails," aroused adult alarm.

Too, young Americans embraced rock-and-roll. In 1952 Cleveland radio host Alan Freed, having observed white teenagers dancing to rhythm-and-blues records by black performers, started a new radio program, "Moondog's Rock and Roll Party," to play "race music." It was popular, and in 1954 Freed took the program to New York, creating a national craze for rock-and-roll.

White performers transformed black rhythm-and-blues, with its heavy beat and suggestive lyrics, into "Top Ten" rock-and-roll. In 1954 Bill Haley and the Comets dropped some of the sexual allusions from Joe Turner's "Shake, Rattle, and Roll," added country-and-western guitar riffs, and produced the first major white rock-and-roll hit. When Haley performed "Rock Around the Clock" in *The Blackboard Jungle,* a 1955 film about juvenile delinquency, many parents linked rock-and-roll with disobedience and crime. Red-hunters saw it as a communist plot to corrupt youth. Segregationists claimed it was a ploy "to mix the races." Psychiatrists feared it was "a communicable disease." Some churches condemned it as the "devil's music."

Elvis Presley confirmed the worst fears. Born in Tupelo, Mississippi, Elvis was a nineteen-year-old truck driver in 1954 when he paid four dollars to record two songs at a Memphis studio. He melded the Pentecostal music of his boyhood with the powerful beat and sexual energy of rhythm-and-blues, and in songs like "Hound Dog" and "All Shook Up" he seemed to proclaim teenage "separateness." Presley's smirking lips and bucking hips shocked white middle-class adults. The more adults condemned rock-and-roll, the more teenagers loved it. Record sales tripled between 1954 and 1960, and Dick Clark's *American Bandstand* became the decade's biggest TV hit. As teens listened to it in their own rooms and cars, their music, by such "outsiders" as Buddy Holly from West Texas and Richie Valens from East Los Angeles, nourished the roots of the coming youth revolt.

Portents of Change

In other genres, teens elevated rebellious characters like James Dean in *Rebel Without a Cause* (1955) to cult status for overturning respectable mores. They delighted in *Mad* magazine's ridicule of the phony and pretentious in middle-class America. They customized their cars to reject Detroit's standards. All were signs of their distinctiveness from the adult world.

Nonconformist writers known as the Beats expressed a more fundamental revolt against middle-class society. In works such as Allen Ginsberg's *Howl* (1956) and Jack Kerouac's *On the Road* (1957), the Beats scorned the conformity and materialism of "square" America, described by Kerouac as "rows of well-to-do houses with lawns and television sets in each living room with everybody looking at the same thing and thinking the same thing at the same time." The Beats romanticized society's outcasts and glorified uninhibited sexuality and spontaneity in the search for "It," the ultimate authentic experience.

The mass media scorned the Beats, as they did all dissenters. But some admiring college youth

Chronology

1946	ENIAC, the first electronic computer, begins operation.
1947	Levittown, New York, development started.
1948	Bell Labs develops the transistor.
1950	Asociación Nacional México-Americana established.
1952	Dwight D. Eisenhower elected president.
1953	Korean War truce signed. CIA supported coup in Iran. Earl Warren appointed U.S. chief justice. Operation Wetback begins.
1954	Army-McCarthy hearings. *Brown* v. *Board of Education of Topeka*. Fall of Dienbienphu; Geneva Conference.
1955	Salk polio vaccine developed. AFL-CIO merger. First postwar U.S.-Soviet summit meeting. James Dean stars in *Rebel Without a Cause*. Montgomery bus boycott begins.
1956	Interstate Highway Act. Suez crisis. Soviet intervention in Hungary.
1957	Eisenhower Doctrine announced. Civil Rights Act (first since Reconstruction). Little Rock school-desegregation crisis. Soviet Union launches *Sputnik*. Peak of baby boom (4.3 million births). Southern Christian Leadership Conference founded.
1958	National Defense Education Act. United States and Soviet Union halt atmospheric atomic tests. National Aeronautics and Space Administration (NASA) founded.
1959	Fidel Castro comes to power in Cuba. Khrushchev and Eisenhower meet at Camp David.
1960	U-2 incident. Second Civil Rights Act.
1962	Rachel Carson, *Silent Spring*. Suburban population almost equals that of central city.

took up the Beat message. Students protested capital punishment and demonstrated against the continuing investigations of the House Un-American Activities Committee. Others decried the nuclear-arms race. In 1958 and 1959 thousands participated in Youth Marches for Integrated Schools in Washington. Together with the Beats and rock music, this vocal minority of the "silent generation" heralded a youth movement that would explode in the 1960s.

CONCLUSION 🅗🅒 ACE Practice Test

In the 1950s the United States, mightier than any nation in history, basked in prosperity. Most Americans applauded Eisenhower's minimal expansion of the welfare state and the start of new projects like the interstate highway system. They were relieved by the relaxation of tensions with the Soviet Union after the end of the Korean War. The nation focused on the search for the good life, and idealized traditional gender roles, domesticity, and togetherness. Young families went on a buying spree, snapping up new cars and television sets; television programs reaffirmed existing values and prejudices and reinforced conformity, consumerism, and complacency.

Enjoying their larger paychecks and increased leisure time, most white middle-class Americans ignored social inequities and troubling trends such as the arms race. They left for another decade the problems of poverty, urban decay, and racial injustice and the explosive consequences of a younger generation unwilling to accept their parents' embrace of the status quo.

FURTHER READING

David Anderson, *Trapped by Success: The Eisenhower Administration and Vietnam, 1953–1961* (1993). An analysis of America's policy of supporting South Vietnam.

Robert Bowie and Richard Immerman, *Waging Peace: How Eisenhower Shaped an Enduring Cold War Strategy* (2000). A thoughtful and provocative account.

Mary Dudziak, *Cold War Civil Rights: Race and the Image of American Democracy* (2000). An important analysis of how the Cold War furthered and constrained the civil-rights movement.

William Graebner, *Coming of Age in Buffalo* (1990). An excellent autobiographical study of teenage life.

Julia Grant, *Raising Baby by the Book: The Education of American Mothers* (1998). The influence of pediatrician Benjamin Spock is assessed.

Margot Henriksen, *Dr. Strangelove's America: Society and Culture in the Atomic Age* (1997). An imaginative look at the impact of the Cold War on popular culture.

Joanne Meyerowitz, ed., *Not June Cleaver: Women and Gender in Postwar America, 1945–1960* (1994). A wide-ranging collection of essays examining American women from diverse perspectives.

Thomas Sugrue, *The Origins of the Urban Crisis: Race and Inequality in Postwar Detroit* (1996). An award-winning account of racial and economic inequality.

Jessica Weiss, *To Have and To Hold: Marriage, the Baby Boom, and Social Change* (2000). An incisive study that places the family patterns of the 1950s in historical perspective.

Stephen J. Whitfield, *The Culture of the Cold War* (1991). A keen-sighted meditation on postwar cultural phenomena.

28

The Liberal Era, 1960–1968

hc This icon will direct you to additional study and research resources at http://college.hmco.com/history/us/boyer/enduring_concise/5e/students/index.html

Selma to Montgomery March, 1965

On February 1, 1960, four African-American students at North Carolina Agricultural and Technical College in Greensboro sat down at the lunch counter at the local Woolworth's and asked for coffee and doughnuts. When the waitress announced "We don't serve colored here," the students remained seated, staying until the store closed. By the end of the week, hundreds of students had joined the sit-in. By April 1960 sit-ins had spread to seventy-eight southern communities, and by September 1961 some seventy thousand African-American students had targeted segregated restaurants, churches, libraries, and movie theaters.

The sit-ins helped redefine liberalism. In managing the economy, liberals now placed greater emphasis on equalizing opportunity and targeting benefits to those who had been ignored. Liberalism was also redefined by others, including Ralph Nader, who sounded the alarm that many automobiles were "unsafe at any speed"; Betty Friedan, who wrote *The Feminine Mystique* to denounce "the housewife trap"; and students who protested what they saw as an immoral war in Vietnam.

These endeavors symbolized a spirit of new beginnings. The impatience and idealism of the young would lead many to embrace John F. Kennedy's New Frontier and to rally behind Lyndon Johnson's Great Society. Both liberal administrations' rhetorical emphasis on social change and activism would generate fervent hopes and lofty expectations. But assassinations of cherished leaders, ongoing racial strife, and a deepening quagmire in Vietnam would dampen optimism, while a reaction by the majority who opposed radical change would curtail reform. A decade that began with bright promise would end in discord and disillusionment.

THE KENNEDY PRESIDENCY, 1960–1963

Projecting an image of youth and vigor, John F. Kennedy personified the self-confident liberal who believed that an activist state could improve life at home and confront the communist challenge abroad. His wealthy father, Joseph P. Kennedy, seethed with ambition and instilled in his sons a passion to excel and to attain political power. Despite a severe back injury, John Kennedy served in the navy in World War II, and the elder Kennedy persuaded a popular novelist to write articles lauding John's heroism in rescuing his crew after their PT boat had been sunk in the South Pacific.

Esteemed as a war hero, John Kennedy used his charm and his father's connections to win election in 1946 to the House of Representatives from a

This chapter focuses on five major questions:

▶ How liberal was the New Frontier in civil rights and economic matters?

▶ What was the new liberalism of the 1960s, and how did Lyndon Johnson's Great Society exemplify it?

▶ What were the major successes and failures of the black movements for civil rights and socioeconomic progress from 1964 to 1968?

▶ In what ways did 1960's liberalism affect other minorities and women, and how did minorities and women affect liberalism?

▶ How did the United States get involved in Vietnam, and to what extent was President Johnson responsible for the tragedy of Vietnam?

Boston district where he had never lived. Although Kennedy earned little distinction in Congress, Massachusetts voters sent him to the Senate in 1952 and overwhelmingly reelected him in 1958. By then he had a beautiful wife, Jacqueline, and a Pulitzer Prize for *Profiles in Courage* (1956), written largely by a staff member.

Despite the obstacle of his Roman Catholic faith, the popular Kennedy won a first-ballot victory at the 1960 Democratic convention. Just forty-two years old, he sounded the theme of a "New Frontier" to "get America moving again" by liberal activism at home and abroad.

A New Beginning

Recalled a University of Nebraska student, "All at once you had something exciting. . . . Kennedy was talking about pumping new life into the nation and steering it in new directions." But most voters, middle-aged and middle class, wanted the stability, security, and continuation of Eisenhower's "middle way" that the Republican candidate, Vice President Richard M. Nixon, promised. Although scorned by liberals for his McCarthyism, Nixon was better known and more experienced than Kennedy, a Protestant, and identified with the still-popular Ike.

Nixon fumbled his opportunity, agreeing to meet Kennedy in televised debates. More than 70 million tuned in to the first televised debate between presidential candidates—a broadcast that secured the dominance of television in American politics. Nixon, sweating visibly, appeared haggard and insecure; in a striking contrast, the tanned, telegenic Democrat radiated confidence. Radio listeners called the debate a draw, but television viewers declared Kennedy the victor. He shot up in the polls, and Nixon never regained the lead.

Kennedy also benefited from an economic recession and from his choice of a southern Protestant, Senate majority leader Lyndon B. Johnson, as his running mate. Still, the election was the closest since 1884. Only 120,000 votes separated the two candidates. Kennedy's religion cost him millions of popular votes, but the Catholic vote in the closely contested midwestern and northeastern states delivered crucial electoral college votes, enabling him to squeak to victory.

Kennedy's inauguration set the tone of a new era: "the torch has been passed to a new generation of Americans." In sharp contrast to the Eisenhower administration's reliance on business leaders, Kennedy surrounded himself with liberal intellectuals—the "best and the brightest," author David Halberstam called them. For attorney general he selected his brother Robert Kennedy; "I see nothing wrong with giving Robert some legal expertise before he goes out to practice law," JFK joked.

Kennedy seemed more a celebrity than a politician, and his dash played well on TV. Aided by his wife, he adorned his presidency with the trappings of culture and excellence, inviting distinguished artists to perform at the White House and studding his speeches with quotations from Emerson. Awed by his grace and wit, the media extolled him as a vibrant leader and adoring husband. The public knew nothing of his fragile health, frequent use of mood-altering drugs to relieve pain, and extramarital affairs.

Kennedy's Domestic Record

Media images obscured Kennedy's lackluster domestic record. The conservative coalition of Republicans and southern Democrats that had stifled Truman's Fair Deal doomed the New Frontier. Lacking the votes, Kennedy rarely pressed Congress for social legislation, maintaining that "there is no sense in raising hell and then not being successful."

JFK made economic growth his domestic priority. To stimulate the economy, he combined higher defense and space expenditures with investment incentives for private enterprise. In 1961 he persuaded Congress to boost the defense budget by 20 percent. He vastly increased America's nuclear stockpile and strengthened the military's conventional forces. Kennedy also convinced Congress to finance a "race to the moon," which Americans

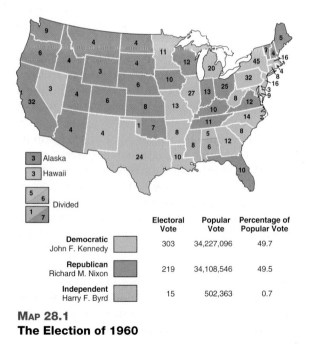

	Electoral Vote	Popular Vote	Percentage of Popular Vote
Democratic John F. Kennedy	303	34,227,096	49.7
Republican Richard M. Nixon	219	34,108,546	49.5
Independent Harry F. Byrd	15	502,363	0.7

MAP 28.1
The Election of 1960

would win, at a cost of more than $25 billion, with the first lunar landing in 1969. Most importantly, Kennedy took his liberal advisers' Keynesian advice to call for a huge cut in corporate taxes that would greatly increase the deficit but would presumably provide capital for business to invest, stimulating the economy and thus increasing tax revenues. In this way, government would be able to pay for Kennedy's proposed federal aid to education, medical care for the elderly, and urban renewal. Thus, economic growth was the way for the government to create a better life for all Americans.

When the Kennedy presidency ended tragically in November 1963, the proposed tax cut was bottled up in Congress, but JFK's economic program had doubled the rate of economic growth, decreased unemployment, and held inflation at 1.3 percent a year. The United States was in the midst of its longest uninterrupted boom.

The boom would both cause further ecological damage and provide the affluence that enabled Americans to care about the environment. The fallout scare of the 1950s raised questions about the well-being of the planet. The publication in 1962 of Rachel Carson's *Silent Spring* documenting the hazards of pesticides, intensified concern. Additionally, with postwar prosperity many Americans were concerned less with increased production and more with the quality of life. In response, Kennedy appointed an advisory committee that warned against widespread pesticide use. In 1963 Congress passed a Clean Air Act, regulating automotive and industrial emissions. After decades of heedless pollution, Washington hesitantly began to address environmental problems.

Cold War Activism

In his inaugural address Kennedy proclaimed, "we shall pay any price, bear any burden, . . . oppose any foe to assure the survival and success of liberty." He launched a major military buildup and surrounded himself with Cold Warriors who shared his belief that American security depended on superior force and the willingness to use it. At the same time, he gained congressional backing for

economic assistance to Third World countries to counter the appeal of communism. The Peace Corps, created in 1961, exemplified the New Frontier's liberal anticommunism. By 1963 five thousand Peace Corps volunteers were serving two-year stints as teachers, sanitation engineers, crop specialists, and health workers in more than forty Third World nations. They were, according to historian and Kennedy aide Arthur Schlesinger, Jr., "reform-minded missionaries of democracy."

In early 1961 a crisis flared in Laos, a tiny nation in Southeast Asia, where a civil war between American-supported forces and Pathet Lao rebels seemed headed toward a communist triumph. In July 1962 Kennedy agreed to a face-saving compromise that restored a neutralist government but left communist forces dominant in the countryside.

Spring 1961 brought Kennedy's first major foreign-policy crisis. To eliminate a communist outpost on the United States' doorstep, he approved a CIA plan, drawn up under Eisenhower, to invade Cuba. In mid-April 1961, fifteen hundred anti-Castro exiles landed at Cuba's Bay of Pigs, assuming that their arrival would trigger a general uprising to overthrow Fidel Castro. The invasion was a fiasco. Deprived of air cover because Kennedy wanted to conceal U.S. involvement, the invaders had no chance against Castro's superior forces. Although Kennedy accepted blame for the failure, he neither apologized for nor ended attempts to overthrow Castro.

In July 1961, on the heels of the Bay of Pigs failure, Kennedy met in Vienna with Soviet premier Nikita Khrushchev to try to resolve a peace treaty with Germany. Comparing American troops in the divided city of Berlin to "a bone stuck in the throat," Khrushchev threatened war unless the West retreated. A shaken Kennedy returned to the United States and declared the defense of West Berlin essential to the Free World. He mobilized 150,000 reservists and called for higher defense spending. The threat of nuclear war escalated until mid-August, when Moscow constructed a wall to seal off Soviet-held East Berlin and end the exodus of brains and talent to the West. The Berlin Wall became an enduring symbol of communism's denial of personal freedom until it fell in 1989.

To the Brink of Nuclear War

In mid-October 1962 aerial photographs revealed that the Soviet Union had built bases for intermediate-range nuclear missiles, capable of striking most U.S. soil, in Cuba. Smarting from the Bay of Pigs disaster, fearing unchecked Soviet interference in the Western Hemisphere, and believing his credibility at stake, Kennedy responded forcefully. In a somber televised address he denounced the "provocative threat to world peace" and announced that the United States would "quarantine" Cuba—impose a naval blockade—to prevent delivery of more missiles and would dismantle by force the missiles already in Cuba if the Soviet Union did not do so.

The world held its breath. The two superpowers appeared to be on a collision course toward nuclear war. Soviet technicians worked feverishly to complete the missile launch pads, and Soviet missile-carrying ships steamed toward the blockade; B-52s armed with nuclear weapons took to the air; and nearly 250,000 troops assembled in Florida to invade Cuba. Secretary of State Dean Rusk reported, "We're eyeball to eyeball."

"I think the other fellow just blinked," a relieved Rusk announced on October 25. Kennedy received a message from Khrushchev promising to remove the missiles if the United States pledged never to invade Cuba. As Kennedy prepared to respond positively, a second, more belligerent message arrived from the Soviet leader insisting that American missiles be withdrawn from Turkey as part of the deal. Hours later an American U-2 reconnaissance plane was shot down over Cuba. It was "the blackest hour of the crisis," recalled one participant. Robert Kennedy persuaded his brother to accept the first message and simply ignore the second one. In the early morning hours of October 28, Khrushchev pledged to remove the missiles in return for Kennedy's noninvasion promise. Less publicly, Kennedy later removed U.S. missiles from Turkey.

Only in January 1992 were the full dimensions of the crisis revealed: Soviet forces in Cuba had possessed thirty-six nuclear warheads and nine tactical nuclear weapons for battlefield use. Soviet field commanders had independent authority to use them. Worst of all, Kennedy did not know that the Soviets already had the ability to launch a nuclear strike from Cuba. Former secretary of defense Robert S. McNamara, speaking in 1992, recalled the pressure for an invasion in late October 1962. "We can predict the results with certainty. . . . U.S. troops could [not] have been attacked by tactical nuclear warheads without the U.S.'s responding with nuclear warheads. . . . Where would it have ended? In utter disaster."

Chastened by coming so close to the brink of nuclear war, Kennedy and Khrushchev installed a telephone "hot line" so that the two sides could communicate instantly in future crises. In June 1963 JFK advocated a relaxation of superpower tensions, and two months later the two nations agreed to a treaty prohibiting atmospheric and undersea nuclear testing.

These efforts signaled the beginning of a new phase of the Cold War, later called détente, as the superpowers moved from confrontation to negotiation. At the same time, the Cuban missile crisis escalated the arms race by convincing both sides of the need for nuclear superiority.

The Thousand-Day Presidency

On November 22, 1963, during a trip to Texas to shore up his reelection chances, a smiling JFK rode in an open car along Dallas streets lined with cheering crowds. Shots rang out. The president slumped, dying, his skull and throat shattered. Soon after, aboard Air Force One, Lyndon B. Johnson was sworn in as president.

Grief and disbelief numbed the nation as most Americans spent the next four days in front of their television sets staring at replays of the murder of accused assassin Lee Harvey Oswald; at the somber state funeral, with the small boy saluting his father's casket; at the grieving family lighting an eternal flame at Arlington National Cemetery. Few who watched would forget. Kennedy had helped make TV central to politics; now, in death, it made him the fallen hero-king of Camelot.

Kennedy loyalists have stressed his intelligence and his ability to change and grow. His detractors, however, point to his unfulfilled liberal rhetoric and the discrepancy between his public image and his private philandering. Kennedy's rhetoric expressed the new liberalism, but he rarely made liberal ideas a reality. Against the background of his frequent compromises with conservatives and segregationists in Congress, economic expansion came from spending on missiles and the space race, not on social welfare and human needs. Partly because his own personal behavior made him beholden to FBI Director J. Edgar Hoover, JFK allowed the agency to infringe on civil liberties, even as the CIA plotted with the Mafia to assassinate Fidel Castro. (Scholars are still untangling the plots and policies that enmeshed the Kennedy brothers, Hoover, organized crime, and the national security agencies.) He increased the powers of the presidency and, as never before, a small group of loyal aides secretly dominated policy making. Finally, the New Frontier barely existed for environmental protection or for women. (Compared to his predecessors, JFK appointed few women to policy positions and none to the cabinet.)

Internationally, Kennedy left a mixed record. He signed the world's first nuclear-test-ban treaty yet undertook a massive arms buildup. He compromised on Laos but deepened U.S. involvement in Vietnam. He came to question the need for U.S.-Soviet confrontation yet insisted on U.S. global superiority and aggressively prosecuted the Cold War.

Still, JFK gave liberals new hope, aroused the disadvantaged, and stimulated the young to activism. And he died with his glory untarnished. He left his successor a liberal agenda, soaring expectations at home, and a deteriorating entanglement in Vietnam. His legacy would combine with later events to shatter illusions, leading millions of Americans to lose confidence in their government and their future.

LIBERALISM ASCENDANT, 1963–1968

Distrusted by liberals as "a Machiavelli in a Stetson," regarded as a usurper by Kennedy loyalists, Lyndon Baines Johnson had achieved his highest ambition through the assassination of a popular president in Johnson's home state of Texas. Though just nine years older than Kennedy, he seemed a relic of the past, a back-room wheeler-dealer as crude as his predecessor was smooth.

Yet Johnson had substantial political assets. He had served in Washington almost continuously since 1932, accruing enormous experience and a close association with the Capitol Hill power brokers who helped pass bills. He excelled at wooing allies, neutralizing opponents, forging coalitions, and achieving results.

Johnson's first three years in office demonstrated his determination to prove himself to liberals. He deftly handled the transition of power, won a landslide victory in 1964, and guided through Congress the greatest array of liberal legislation in U.S. history, surpassing the New Deal agenda. Nevertheless, LBJ's swollen yet fragile ego stung at the sniping of the Kennedy loyalists, and he frequently complained that the media did not give him "a fair shake." Wondering aloud, "Why don't people like me?" Johnson pressed both to ensure that everyone shared in the promise of the American Dream and to vanquish all foes at home and abroad. Ironically, in seeking consensus and affection, Johnson would divide the nation and leave office repudiated.

Johnson Takes Over

Calling for early passage of the tax-cut and civil-rights bills as a memorial to Kennedy, Johnson used his legislative skills to good effect, winning passage of the Civil Rights Act of 1964 (discussed later) and a $10 billion tax-reduction bill, which produced a surge in capital investment and personal consumption that spurred economic growth and shrank the budget deficit. More boldly, Johnson declared "unconditional war on poverty in America."

Largely invisible in an affluent America, according to Michael Harrington's *The Other America* (1962), some 40 million people dwelled in substandard housing and subsisted on inadequate diets. Living in a "culture of poverty," they lacked the education, medical care, and employment opportunities that most Americans took for granted. To be poor, Harrington asserted, is "to grow up in a culture that is radically different from the one that dominates the society."

LBJ championed a campaign to bring these "internal exiles" into the mainstream. Designed to offer a "hand up, not a handout," the Economic Opportunity Act established the Office of Economic Opportunity to fund and coordinate a job corps to train young people in marketable skills; VISTA (Volunteers in Service to America), a domestic peace corps; Project Head Start, to provide compensatory education for preschoolers from disadvantaged families; and an assortment of public-works and training programs.

Summing up his goals in 1964, Johnson offered his vision of the Great Society. First must come "an end to poverty and racial injustice." But that would be just the beginning. The Great Society would also be a place where all children could enrich their minds and enlarge their talents, where people could renew their contact with nature, and where citizens would be deeply concerned with the quality of their goals.

The 1964 Election

Johnson's Great Society horrified the "new conservatives," such as William F. Buckley, Jr., and the college students of Young Americans for Freedom. The most persuasive critic was Arizona senator Barry Goldwater, an outsider fighting the Washington establishment, a fervent anticommunist, and an advocate of individual freedom. His opposition to big government, deficit spending, racial liberalism, and social-welfare programs found receptive audiences on Sun Belt golf courses and in working-class neighborhoods.

Racial liberalism frightened southern segregationists and blue-collar workers in northern cities who dreaded the integration of their neighborhoods, schools, and workplaces. Their support of Alabama's segregationist governor George Wallace in early 1964 presidential primaries heralded a "white backlash" against the civil-rights movement.

Buoyed by this backlash, conservatives in 1964 gained control of the GOP. They nominated Barry Goldwater for the presidency and adopted a platform totally opposed to the new liberalism. Determined to offer the nation "a choice, not an echo,"

Goldwater extolled his opposition to the civil-rights act and the censure of McCarthy. He denounced the War on Poverty and suggested scrapping social security, and he hinted that he might use nuclear weapons against Cuba and North Vietnam. "We have gotten where we are," he declared, "not because of government, but in spite of government." Goldwater's stance appealed to Americans disturbed by the Cold War stalemate and the federal government's growing decision-making power. His campaign slogan, "In your heart you know he's right," allowed his liberal opponents to quip "In your guts, you know he's nuts."

Goldwater's conservative crusade let LBJ run as a liberal reformer but still be the more moderate candidate. LBJ and his running mate, Senator Hubert Humphrey of Minnesota, painted Goldwater as an extremist not to be trusted with the nuclear trigger. When Goldwater charged that the Democrats had not pursued total victory in Vietnam, Johnson appeared the apostle of restraint: "We are not going to send American boys . . . to do what Asian boys ought to be doing for themselves."

LBJ won a landslide victory, 43 million votes to Goldwater's 27 million. The GOP lost five hundred seats in state legislatures in addition to thirty-eight congressional and two senate seats. Many proclaimed the death of conservatism. But Goldwater's coalition of antigovernment westerners, economic and religious conservatives, and anti-integrationist whites presaged conservatism's future triumph. His candidacy transformed the Republicans from a moderate, Eastern-dominated party to one decidedly conservative, southern, and western. It built a national base of financial support for conservative candidates and mobilized future leaders of the party, like Ronald Reagan. But in the short run, the liberals had a working majority.

Triumphant Liberalism

"Hurry, boys, hurry," LBJ urged his aides. "Get that legislation up to the hill and out. Eighteen months from now ol' Landslide Lyndon will be Lame Duck Lyndon." Johnson flooded Congress with liberal proposals, sixty-three in 1965 alone. And he got most of what he requested.

The Eighty-ninth Congress enlarged the War on Poverty and passed another milestone civil-rights act. It enacted Medicare to provide health insurance for the aged under social security, and a Medicaid health plan for the poor. By 1975 the two would serve 47 million people and account for a quarter of the nation's health-care expenditures. The legislators appropriated funds for public education and housing and for urban revitalization, and they created new departments of transportation and of housing and urban development and the National Endowments for the Arts and the Humanities.

Of enormous future significance, Congress enacted a new immigration law, abolishing the national-origins quotas of the 1920s. Annual legal immigration would increase from about 250,000 before the act to well over a million, and the vast majority of new immigrants would come from Asia and Latin America. Less than 1 percent of the U.S. population in 1960, Asian-Americans would be nearly 4 percent in 2000, and the Hispanic population would increase from 4.5 percent in 1970 to about 11 percent in 2000. The so-called browning of America enormously expanded the nation's culinary, linguistic, musical, and religious spectrum.

The Great Society also sought to protect the environment. In 1964 Congress set aside 9.1 million acres of wild lands. It established Redwood National Park and defeated efforts to dam the Colorado River and flood the lower Grand Canyon; strengthened the Clean Water and Clean Air Acts; and protected endangered species. Responding to the uproar caused by Ralph Nader's revelations about unsafe cars, Congress set the first federal safety standards for automobiles and required states to establish highway safety programs.

The Great Society improved the lives of millions. The poor, 22 percent of the population in 1960, shrank to 13 percent in 1969. African-American family income rose from 54 percent to 61 percent of white family income, and the segment of blacks living below the poverty line plummeted from 40 percent to 20 percent. But in part because

Johnson oversold the Great Society and Congress underfunded it, liberal aspirations outdistanced results.

For many in need, the Great Society remained more a dream than a reality. The war against poverty was, in the words of Martin Luther King, Jr., "shot down on the battlefields of Vietnam." In 1966 Johnson spent twenty times more to wage war in Vietnam than to fight poverty in the United States. Yet the perceived liberality of federal programs and the "ungratefulness" of rioting blacks would alienate many middle- and working-class whites. Increasing numbers of Americans feared the growing intrusiveness of the liberal state in managing their daily lives. The Democrats' loss of forty-seven House seats in 1966 sealed liberalism's fate.

The Warren Court in the Sixties

The Supreme Court did much to support and promote the liberal agenda. A liberal majority on the Court, led by Chief Justice Earl Warren, acted to expand individual rights to a greater extent than ever before in American history. Kennedy appointed two liberals to the Court, and Johnson two more, including the Court's first black justice, Thurgood Marshall. In the resulting series of landmark cases, the Court prohibited Bible reading and prayer in public schools, limited local power to censor books and films, and overturned state bans on contraceptives. In *Baker* v. *Carr* (1962) and related decisions, the Court ruled that "one person, one vote" must prevail in both state and national elections, reducing the political power of rural and small-town America.

The Court's upholding of the rights of the accused in criminal cases, at a time of soaring crime rates, particularly incensed many Americans. In 1966 criticism reached a crescendo when the Court ruled in *Miranda* v. *Arizona* that police must warn all suspects that anything they say can be used against them in court and that they may remain silent. In 1968 both Richard Nixon and George Wallace would promise to appoint judges who would emphasize "law and order" over individual liberties.

THE STRUGGLE FOR BLACK EQUALITY, 1961–1968

JFK neither anticipated nor welcomed the crusade for civil rights that engulfed the South. Fearful that a struggle over civil rights would divide the nation, split the Democratic party, and entangle Congress in lengthy filibusters, he straddled the issue for two years.

To JFK, racial problems were a thorny thicket to tiptoe around, not a moral issue requiring decisive leadership. He appointed an unprecedented number of African-Americans to high offices but also named white racists to federal judgeships. Kennedy remained aloof from attempts by congressional liberals to enact civil-rights legislation and stalled for two years before issuing a weak executive order banning discrimination in federally financed housing.

Nonviolence and Violence

In the spring of 1961, the Congress of Racial Equality (CORE) organized a "freedom ride" through the Deep South to dramatize widespread violation of a 1960 Supreme Court decision banning segregation in interstate transportation. In Anniston, Alabama, Ku Klux Klansmen savagely beat the freedom riders and burned their bus, while in Birmingham a white mob mauled a CORE group. When whites in Montgomery viciously assaulted the freedom riders, Kennedy finally dispatched federal marshals to end the violence. Scores more freedom rides and the arrest of hundreds of young protesters forced the president to press the Interstate Commerce Commission to enforce the Supreme Court's ruling.

In fall 1962 Kennedy again applied federal force to quell white racist violence. When a federal court ordered the University of Mississippi to enroll James Meredith, a black air force veteran, angry whites rioted. Rallying behind Confederate flags, students and troublemakers attacked federal marshals escorting Meredith to "Ole Miss." The clash left two dead, hundreds injured, and the campus shrouded in tear gas. Federal troops finally restored order and upheld the right of a black American to attend the university of his home state.

The African-American Revolution

As television coverage brought mounting numbers of African-Americans into the struggle for racial equality, civil-rights leaders pressured Kennedy to act decisively. Dismantling segregation piecemeal would take generations, they realized; only comprehensive national legislation, backed by the power of the federal government, could guarantee full citizenship for African-Americans. To get this they needed a crisis that would outrage the conscience of the white majority and force the president's hand.

In Birmingham on Good Friday 1963, Martin Luther King, Jr., determined to expose the violent extremism of southern white racism and to force the president's hand, organized a series of marches, sit-ins, and pray-ins. With each protest bringing more arrests, police commissioner Eugene "Bull" Connor scoffed that King would soon "run out of niggers." Resorting to force, Connor unleashed his men, armed with electric cattle prods, high-pressure water hoses, and snarling attack dogs, on the nonviolent demonstrators. The ferocity of the attack, chronicled on television news programs, filled the world with revulsion.

"The civil-rights movement should thank God for Bull Connor," JFK remarked. "He's helped it as much as Abraham Lincoln." Indeed, the combination of African-American activism and growing white support for equal rights pushed Kennedy to arrange a behind-the-scenes compromise ending the Birmingham demonstrations in return for desegregating stores and upgrading the status of African-American workers. By mid-1963 the rallying cry "Freedom Now!" reverberated across the nation as the number and magnitude of protests grew. Increasingly concerned about America's image abroad and the "fires of frustration and discord" at home, Kennedy feared that if the federal government did not lead the way toward "peaceful and constructive" changes in race relations, blacks would turn to militancy. Accordingly, when Alabama governor George Wallace in June 1963

Birmingham, 1963
President Kennedy said this photograph of an African-American being attacked by a police dog during the protest demonstrations in Birmingham made him "sick." It helped galvanize the nation's conscience, leading Kennedy to submit a comprehensive civil-rights bill to Congress.

refused to allow two African-American students to enter the University of Alabama, Kennedy forced Wallace—who had pledged "Segregation now! Segregation tomorrow! Segregation forever!"—to capitulate to a court desegregation order.

On June 11 JFK went on television to define civil rights as "a moral issue" and to assert that "race has no place in American life or law." Describing the plight of blacks in Jim Crow America, he asked, "Who among us would be content to have the color of his skin changed and stand in his place? Who among us would then be content with the counsels of patience and delay?" A week later, Kennedy proposed a comprehensive civil-rights measure—which most members of Congress ignored.

The March on Washington, 1963

To compel Congress to act, nearly 250,000 Americans converged on the Capitol on August 28, 1963. There they heard the ringing words of Martin Luther King, Jr., proclaiming that he had a dream, a dream of brotherhood, of freedom and justice, a dream that "all of God's children, black men and white men, Jews and Gentiles, Protestants and Catholics, will be able to join hands and sing in the words of the old Negro spiritual, 'Free at last! Free at last! Thank God Almighty, we are free at last!'" King had turned a political rally into a historic event with one of the great speeches of history.

Neither Kennedy's nor King's eloquence could quell the anger of white racists. On the night of the president's address, Medgar Evers, the head of the Mississippi branch of the National Association for the Advancement of Colored People, was murdered by a sniper in Jackson. In September the bombing of a black church in Birmingham killed four girls. And still, southern obstructionism kept the civil-rights bill stymied in Congress, with little hope of passage.

The Civil Rights and Voting Rights Acts

As a southerner who had earlier opposed civil rights for blacks, LBJ thought he had to prove himself on this issue or the liberals "would get me . . . I had to produce a civil rights bill that was even stronger than the one they'd have gotten if Kennedy had lived."

The resulting Civil Rights Act of 1964, the most significant civil-rights law in U.S. history, banned racial discrimination and segregation in public accommodations. It outlawed bias in federally funded programs, granted the federal government new powers to fight school segregation, and created the Equal Employment Opportunity Commission (EEOC) to enforce a ban on job discrimination on the basis of race, religion, national origin, or gender.

In 1964 CORE and SNCC (Student Nonviolent Coordinating Committee) activists, believing that the ballot box held the key to power for southern blacks, mounted a major campaign to register African-American voters. Focusing on the state most hostile to equal rights, field workers organized the Mississippi Freedom Summer Project of 1964. One thousand college-student volunteers assisted blacks in registering to vote and in organizing "Freedom Schools" that taught black history and emphasized African-American self-worth. Harassed by Mississippi law-enforcement officials and Ku Klux Klansmen, the volunteers endured the firebombing of black churches and civil-rights headquarters as well as arrests and even murders.

Although they registered only twelve hundred African-Americans to vote, the workers enrolled nearly sixty thousand disfranchised blacks in the Mississippi Freedom Democratic party (MFDP) and took their case to the national Democratic convention in August 1964. They insisted that the convention seat MFDP delegates instead of the all-white delegation chosen by the Mississippi Democratic party. LBJ, trying to head off white southern walkouts, forged a compromise that granted two at-large seats to the MFDP and barred from all future conventions any delegations from states that discriminated against African-Americans. The compromise alienated militants in the civil-rights movement.

Martin Luther King, Jr., and the Southern Christian Leadership Conference (SCLC), resolved to gain a voting-rights act, organized mass protests in Selma, Alabama, in March 1965. African-Americans made up half the voting-age population in Dallas County, where Selma was located, but only 1 percent were registered to vote. Selma's county sheriff Jim Clark was every bit as violence prone as Birmingham's Bull Connor, and Clark's men attacked black protesters and bystanders indiscriminately and brutally. Showcased on TV, the attacks provoked national outrage and increased support for a voting-rights bill.

Signed by the president in August 1965, the Voting Rights Act expanded black suffrage and transformed southern politics. It authorized federal examiners to register voters and to suspend literacy tests in areas where fewer than one-half the minority residents of voting age were registered. Together with the Twenty-third Amendment, ratified in 1964, which outlawed the poll tax in federal elections, and a 1966 Supreme Court decision striking down the poll tax in *all* elections, the Voting Rights Act by 1968 had boosted the number of registered African-American voters in the South from 1 million to 3.1 million. For the first time since Reconstruction, blacks were a force to be reckoned with in southern politics.

The number of blacks holding office in the South mushroomed from fewer than two dozen to nearly twelve hundred by 1972. That meant jobs for African-Americans, contracts for black businesses, and improvements in facilities and services in black neighborhoods. Most importantly, as Fannie Lou Hamer recalled, when African-Americans could not vote, "white folks would drive past your house in a pickup truck with guns hanging up in the back and give you hate stares. . . . Those same people now call me Mrs. Hamer."

Fire in the Streets

The civil-rights movement altered, rather than revolutionized, race relations. Black voting power defeated some white supremacists while stirring other once-ardent segregationists prudently to seek black support. Equal access to public accommodations gave African-Americans a new sense of dignity. But with discrimination lingering in many spheres and African-American unemployment still disproportionately high, the anger bubbling below the surface of the urban ghetto boiled over.

On August 11, 1965, five days after the Voting Rights Act had been signed, a confrontation between white police and young blacks in Watts, Los Angeles's largest black district, ignited the most destructive race riot in decades. For six days nearly fifty thousand African-Americans looted shops, fire-bombed white-owned businesses, and sniped at police officers, fire fighters, and National Guard troops. When the riot ended, thirty-four people had been killed, nine hundred injured, and four thousand arrested, and $30 million worth of property had been devastated. In rapid succession African-Americans in Chicago and in Springfield,

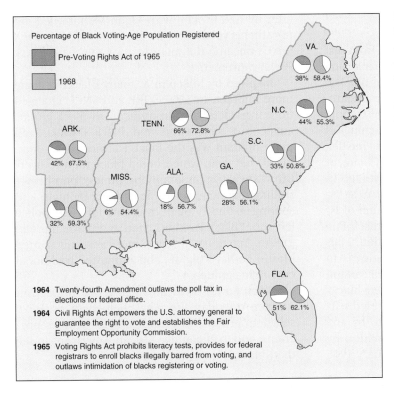

Percentage of Black Voting-Age Population Registered

Pre-Voting Rights Act of 1965

1968

VA. 38% 58.4%

ARK. 42% 67.5%

TENN. 66% 72.8%

N.C. 44% 55.3%

S.C. 33% 50.8%

MISS. 6% 54.4%

ALA. 18% 56.7%

GA. 28% 56.1%

LA. 32% 59.3%

FLA. 51% 62.1%

1964 Twenty-fourth Amendment outlaws the poll tax in elections for federal office.

1964 Civil Rights Act empowers the U.S. attorney general to guarantee the right to vote and establishes the Fair Employment Opportunity Commission.

1965 Voting Rights Act prohibits literacy tests, provides for federal registrars to enroll blacks illegally barred from voting, and outlaws intimidation of blacks registering or voting.

MAP 28.2
Voter Registration of African-Americans in the South, 1964–1968
As blacks overwhelmingly registered to vote as Democrats, some former segregationist politicians, among them George Wallace, started to court the African-American vote, and many southern whites began to cast their ballots for Republicans, inaugurating an era of real two-party competition in the South.

Massachusetts, took to the streets, looting, burning, and battling police.

In summer 1966 rioting erupted in more than a score of northern ghettos, forcing whites to heed the squalor of the slums, the savage behavior of police in the ghetto, and urban poverty—issues that the civil-rights movement had ignored. The following summer brought nearly 150 racial outbreaks and 40 riots, the most intense and destructive period of racial violence that the United States had ever witnessed. In 1968 riots again would flare in the ghettos of more than one hundred cities after the assassination of Martin Luther King, Jr. (see Chapter 31). The 1964–1968 riot toll would include two hundred dead, seven thousand injured, forty thousand arrested, and $500 million worth of property wrecked.

A frightened, bewildered nation asked why such widespread rioting was occurring just as African-Americans were beginning to achieve their goals. Explanations abounded. Militant blacks saw

the uprisings as revolutionary violence directed at a racist, reactionary society. Conservatives described them as senseless outbursts by troublemakers. The National Advisory Commission on Civil Disorders (the Kerner Commission) indicted white racism for fostering "an explosive mixture" of poverty, slum housing, poor education, and police brutality. Warning that "our nation is moving toward two societies, one black, one white—separate and unequal," the commission recommended the creation of 2 million new jobs, the construction of 6 million units of public housing, an end to de facto school segregation in the North, and funding for a "national system of income supplementation." Aware of a swelling white backlash, LBJ ignored the commission's advice, and most whites approved of his inaction. Alarmed by demands for "Black Power" that had risen in recent riots, they preferred that their taxes be spent on strengthening local police forces instead of on improving ghetto conditions.

"Black Power"

Demands for Black Power in 1966 flowed from disappointment at the slow pace of racial change and from outrage toward a white society that blocked even minimal advances by African-Americans. Less an ideology than a cry of fury and frustration, Black Power rhetoric evolved from the teachings of Malcolm X. A former drug addict and street hustler, Malcolm X had converted to the Nation of Islam, or Black Muslim faith, while in prison. Founded in Detroit in 1931 by Elijah Poole (who took the Islamic name Elijah Muhammed), the Nation of Islam insisted that blacks practice self-discipline and self-respect, and it rejected integration. Malcolm X accordingly urged African-Americans to separate themselves from the "white devil" and to take pride in their African roots and their blackness. Blacks, he claimed, had to rely on armed self-defense and had to seize their freedom "by any means necessary." Malcolm X's assassination by members of the Nation of Islam in February 1965 after he had broken with Elijah Muhammed did not still his voice. *The Autobiography of Malcolm X* (1965) became the main text for the rising Black Power movement.

Inspired by Malcolm X, many blacks became more militant. In 1966 CORE and SNCC changed from interracial organizations to all-black groups advocating separatism and Black Power. Even more militant was the Black Panther party, organized that year, which urged black men to overthrow their oppressors by becoming "panthers—smiling, cunning, scientific, striking by night and sparing no one." Violent confrontations with police left some Black Panthers dead and many more in prison. Yet most African-Americans still lauded Martin Luther King, Jr., and supported traditional civil-rights groups.

Black Power advocates had a real impact on African-American life. They helped to organize self-help groups, to establish black studies programs, and to encourage African-Americans to see that "black is beautiful."

Black Power
Rejecting the faith long held by African-Americans in the United States and In the professed intentions of white America to remedy injustices, black power advocates insisted on controlling their own movement and institutions, shaping their own agenda and programs, and defining their own demands and destiny.

Young SCLC leader Jesse Jackson asked students to repeat after him, "I may have lost hope, but I am . . . somebody. . . . I am . . . black . . . beautiful . . . proud. . . . I must be respected." Similar themes would reverberate through other social movements in the sixties.

VOICES OF PROTEST

The aura of liberalism in the 1960s markedly affected Native Americans, Hispanic-Americans, and women. With younger members pushing radical approaches, each followed the black example in demanding full and equal citizenship rights and emphasizing group identity and pride.

Native American Activism

In 1961 representatives of sixty-seven tribes drew up a Declaration of Purposes, and in 1964 hundreds of Indians assembled in Washington to lobby for recognition in the War on Poverty. Indians suffered the worst poverty, the highest disease and death rates, and the poorest education and housing of any American group. President Johnson established the National Council on Indian Opportunity in 1965. It funneled more federal funds onto reservations than any previous program. Johnson rejected the termination policy and advocated "the right of the First Americans to remain Indians while exercising their rights as Americans."

By 1968 younger Indian activists, calling themselves "Native Americans," demanded "Red Power." They protested the lack of protection for Indian land and water rights and the desecration of Indian sacred sites. They established reservation cultural programs to reawaken spiritual beliefs and teach Native languages. The Puyallup asserted old treaty rights to fish in the Columbia River and Puget Sound. The Navajo and Hopi protested strip-mining in the Southwest. The Chippewas, Sioux, and Ojibwa founded the militant American Indian Movement (AIM) in 1968. Among its goals was preventing police harassment of Indians in urban "red ghettos." To dramatize the Indian cause, in late 1969 an armed AIM contingent occupied Alcatraz Island, citing a treaty right, and held the island for nineteen months.

AIM's militancy aroused Native American pride. AIM members "had a new look about them, not that hangdog reservation look I was used to," Mary Crow Dog remembered, and they "loosened a sort of earthquake inside me."

Hispanic-Americans Organize

The fastest-growing minority, Latinos, or Hispanic-Americans, also grew impatient with their establishment organizations, which had been unable to better the dismal conditions facing most Hispanic-Americans. Turning to the more militant tactics of the civil-rights movement, Latinos found a charismatic leader in César Chávez. In 1965 Chávez led a strike by grape pickers of the San Joaquin Valley. Similar efforts had been smashed in the past. But Chávez and United Farm Worker (UFW) cofounder Dolores Huerta organized consumer boycotts of table grapes. They made *La Causa* both a community struggle and part of the larger national movement for civil rights and social justice. Chávez combined religion, labor militancy, and Mexican heritage to stimulate ethnic pride and politicization. For the first time, farm workers gained the right to unionize.

Also in the mid-1960s young Hispanic activists began using the formerly pejorative terms *Chicano* and *Chicana* to express a militant collective identity. Rejecting assimilation, Chicano student organizations came together in 1967 in *El Movimiento Estudiantil Chicano de Aztlan (MEChA)* to demand bilingual education and more Latino teachers in high schools as well as Chicano Studies programs and organizations at colleges.

Activism also led to the founding of the Crusade for Justice in Colorado to fight police brutality and improve job opportunities, and to the creation in 1967 of an alternative political party in Texas, *La Raza Unida,* to elect Latinos and instill cultural pride. As "brown is beautiful" came into vogue, David Sanchez organized the paramilitary Brown Berets in East Los Angeles.

"History and Evolution of the Chicano in the United States"
This mural, painted in 1974 by the MEChA club at Santa Ana College in Los Angeles, depicts the history of Mexico on the left side and the Chicano experience in the United States on the right. Joining the two sides is an animated skeleton wearing a pachuco hat and military garb of the 1910 Mexican Revolution.

Puerto Ricans in New York City founded the Young Lords, which they modeled on the Brown Berets. They published *Palante* ("forward in the struggle"), which popularized strategies and aims. The Young Lords started drug treatment programs and demonstrated to demand better medical services and improved sanitation services in Latino neighborhoods.

Like their counterparts, young activists with roots in the Far East rejected the term *Oriental* and adopted *Asian-American* to signify a new ethnic consciousness. They too campaigned for special educational programs and for the election of Asian-Americans. Formed at the University of California in 1968, the Asian American Political Alliance encouraged Asian-American students to claim their own cultural identity.

Though the fervor of the late sixties would moderate, each of these movements elevated the consciousness and nurtured the confidence of the younger generation. And each contributed to the politics of identity that would continue to grow in importance.

A Second Feminist Wave

The rising tempo of activism in the 1960s also stirred new self-awareness and dissatisfaction among educated women. Several events fanned the embers of discontent into a flame. The 1963 report of the Presidential Commission on the Status of Women, established by Kennedy, documented occupational inequities that were comparable to those endured by minorities. Women received less pay than men for comparable work. And they made up only 7 percent of the nation's doctors and less than 4 percent of its lawyers. The women who served on the presidential commission successfully urged that the Civil Rights Act of 1964 prohibit gender-based as well as racial discrimination in employment.

Dismayed by the Equal Employment Opportunity Commission's reluctance to enforce the ban on sex discrimination, these women formed the National Organization for Women (NOW) in 1966. A civil-rights group for women, NOW lobbied for equal opportunity, filed lawsuits against gender discrimination, and mobilized public opinion.

NOW's popularity owed much to the publication in 1963 of Betty Friedan's *The Feminine Mystique.* Calling it "the problem that has no name," Friedan deplored the narrow view that women should seek fulfillment solely as wives and mothers. Suburban domesticity—the "velvet ghetto"—left many women with feelings of emptiness, with no sense of accomplishment, and afraid to ask "the silent question—'Is this all?'" Friedan wanted women to pursue careers and establish "goals that will permit them to find their own identity." Friedan's message informed unfulfilled women that they were not alone. It rang true to many educated middle-class women who found the rewards of homemaking and motherhood exaggerated.

Still another catalyst for feminism came from the involvement of young women in the civil-rights and anti-Vietnam War movements. Women activists gained confidence in their own potential, an ideology to describe oppression, and experience in the strategy and tactics of protest. They also became conscious of their second-class status, as they were sexually exploited and relegated to menial jobs by male activists. By 1967 female activists had created a women's liberation movement more critical of sexual inequality than was NOW.

Women's Liberation

In 1968 militant feminists adopted "consciousness-raising" as a recruitment device and a means of transforming women's perceptions of themselves and society. Tens of thousands of women across the United States assembled in small groups to share their experiences and air grievances. Women learned from such meetings that their individual, personal problems were in fact shared problems with social causes and political solutions—"the personal is political." This new consciousness begot a sense that "sisterhood is powerful." Radical feminists set up "freedom trash cans" into which women could discard high-heeled shoes, bras, girdles, and other symbols of subjugation. They established health collectives and day-care centers and fought negative portrayals of women in the media, in advertising, and in language. Terms like *male chauvinist pig* entered the American vocabulary and those like *chicks* exited. Some radical feminists claimed the power of men to be the main cause of all oppression and exploitation.

The right to control their own sexuality and decisions whether to have children also became a feminist rallying cry. In 1960 "the Pill" came on the market, giving women greater freedom to be sexually active without the risk of pregnancy. Many women, aware of the dangers of illegal abortions, pushed for their legalization.

Despite a gulf between radicals and liberals, in August 1970 feminist factions put aside their differences to join the largest women's rights demonstration ever. Commemorating the fiftieth anniversary of woman suffrage, the Women's Strike for Equality brought out tens of thousands of women across the nation to parade for the right to equal employment and to safe, legal abortions. By then the women's movement had already pressured many financial institutions to issue credit to single women and to married women in their own name. Such pressure had also ended newspapers' practice of listing employment opportunities under "Male" and "Female" headings and had secured guidelines that required corporations receiving federal funds to adopt nondiscriminatory hiring practices and equal pay scales. By 1970, more than 40 percent of all women held full-time jobs outside the home.

THE LIBERAL CRUSADE IN VIETNAM, 1961–1968

The activist liberals who boldly tried to uplift the downtrodden went to war on the other side of the globe to contain communism. Kennedy escalated Eisenhower's efforts in Vietnam to hold "the cornerstone of the Free World in Southeast Asia." Johnson resolved, "I am not going to lose Vietnam, I am not going to be the president who saw Southeast Asia go the way China went." The war in Vietnam pursued by liberals ended the era of liberalism. By the time the nation's longest war was over, the United States would be more divided than at any time since the Civil War.

Kennedy and Vietnam

After the compromise in Laos, Kennedy, who was resolved not to give further ground in Southeast Asia, ordered large shipments of weapons to South Vietnam and increased the number of American forces there from less than seven hundred in early

MAP 28.3

The Vietnam War, to 1968

Wishing to guarantee an independent, noncommunist government in South Vietnam, Lyndon Johnson remarked in 1965, "We fight because we must fight if we are to live in a world where every country can shape its own destiny. To withdraw from one battlefield means only to prepare for the next."

Interactive Map: The Vietnam War, 1954–1975

1961 to more than sixteen thousand by late 1963. He accepted Eisenhower's "domino theory" and viewed international communism as a monolithic force, a single global entity controlled by Moscow and Beijing. He wanted to prove that the United States was not the "paper tiger" mocked by Mao Zedong.

To counter communist Vietcong gains in South Vietnam, the United States uprooted Vietnamese peasants and moved them into fortified villages. But South Vietnamese president Diem rejected American pressure to gain popular support through re-form measures, instead crushing demonstrations by students and Buddhists. By mid-1963 Buddhist monks were setting themselves on fire to protest Diem's repression, and Diem's own generals were plotting a coup.

Frustrated American policy makers concluded that only a new government could stave off a Vietcong victory and secretly backed the coup efforts. On November 1 military leaders staged their coup, captured Diem and his brother, and shot them. Although the United States promptly recognized the new government, it made little headway against the Vietcong. JFK now faced two unpalatable alternatives: to use American combat forces or to withdraw and seek a negotiated settlement.

What Kennedy would have done remains unknown. Less than a month after Diem's death, John F. Kennedy himself fell to an assassin's bullet. His admirers contend that by late 1963 he was favoring the withdrawal of American forces after the 1964 election. JFK publicly proclaimed in fall 1963 that "it is their war. . . . it is their people and their government who have to win or lose the struggle." Skeptics note that the president followed this comment with a ringing restatement of the domino theory and a promise that the United States would not withdraw from the conflict. Virtually all his closest advisers held that an American victory was essential to check communism in Asia. They would counsel Kennedy's successor accordingly.

Escalation of the War

Now it was Johnson who had to choose between intervening decisively or withdrawing. While privately describing Vietnam as "a raggedy-ass fourth-rate country," LBJ feared that an all-out American military effort might lead to World War III. He foresaw that a full-scale U.S. engagement in "that bitch of a war" would destroy "the woman I really loved—the Great Society." Yet Johnson thought that only American resolve would prevent a wider war. The president also worried that a pullout would leave him vulnerable to conservative attack and threaten his liberal programs.

Trapped between unacceptable alternatives, Johnson expanded the war, hoping that U.S. firepower would force Ho Chi Minh to the bargaining table. But the North Vietnamese calculated that they could gain more by outlasting the United States than by negotiating.

In 1964 LBJ took bold steps to impress the North Vietnamese with American resolve and to block his opponent, Barry Goldwater, from capitalizing on Vietnam in the presidential campaign. In February he ordered the Pentagon to prepare for air strikes against North Vietnam. In May his advisers drafted a congressional resolution authorizing an escalation of American military action, and in July LBJ appointed General Maxwell Taylor, an

LBJ and Vietnam
The Vietnam War spelled Johnson's undoing. Here, peace demonstrators express their feelings about the president's role in the war during a massive antiwar protest at the Pentagon in October 1967.

advocate of greater American involvement, as ambassador to Saigon.

In early August, North Vietnamese patrol boats reportedly clashed with two U.S. destroyers patrolling the Gulf of Tonkin. Evidence of the attack was unclear, yet Johnson announced that Americans had been victims of "open aggression on the high seas." Never admitting that the U.S. destroyers had been aiding the South Vietnamese in clandestine raids against North Vietnam, the president condemned the attacks as unprovoked and called on Congress to pass the previously prepared resolution giving him the authority to "take all necessary measures to repel any armed attack against the forces of the United States and to prevent further aggression." Assured that this power would lead to no "extension of the present conflict," the Senate passed the Gulf of Tonkin Resolution by a vote of 98 to 2 and the House, by 416 to 0. Privately, Johnson called the resolution "grandma's nightshirt—it covered everything." He considered it a mandate to commit U.S. forces as he saw fit. The blank check to determine the level of force made massive intervention more likely. But the resolution would eventually allow opponents of the war to charge that Johnson had misled Congress and lied to the American people.

The Endless War

Early in 1965 Johnson ordered the sustained bombing of North Vietnam. It neither convinced Hanoi to negotiate nor stopped the flow of soldiers and supplies southward from North Vietnam. So LBJ escalated the air war. The United States dropped eight hundred tons of bombs daily on North Vietnam from 1965 to 1968, three times the tonnage used by all combatants in World War II.

Unable to turn the tide by bombing, Johnson committed U.S. combat troops. Adopting a "meatgrinder" strategy, Johnson intended to inflict unacceptable casualties on the communists to force them to the peace table. Johnson sent 485,000 troops to Vietnam by the end of 1967. But North Vietnam had matched each American troop increase with its own, and there was no end in sight.

Doves Versus Hawks

First on college campuses and then in the wider society, a growing number of Americans began to oppose the Vietnam War. In March 1965, students and faculty at the University of Michigan staged the first teach-in to raise questions about U.S. involvement. Later that spring, twenty-five thousand people, mainly students, rallied in Washington to protest the escalation. In 1966 large-scale campus antiwar protests erupted. Students demonstrated against the draft and university research for the Pentagon.

hc Primary Source: Letters Home from Vietnam

Intellectuals and clergy joined the chorus of opposition to the war. Some decried the massive bombing of an undeveloped nation; some doubted that the United States could win at any reasonable cost; some feared the demise of liberalism. In 1967 critics, who included Robert Kennedy and Martin Luther King, Jr., spurred hundreds of thousands to participate in antiwar protests.

Critics noted that the war fell especially hard on the poor. Because of college deferments, the use of influence, and a military assignment system that shunted the better educated to desk jobs, lower-class youths were twice as likely to be drafted and, if drafted, twice as likely to see combat duty as middle-class youths. About 80 percent of the enlisted men who fought in Vietnam were from poor or working-class families.

TV coverage of the war further eroded support. Scenes of children maimed by U.S. bombs and of dying Americans, replayed in living rooms night after night, undercut the optimistic reports of government officials. Americans shuddered in horror as they watched napalm (a burning glue that clings to skin and clothing) and defoliants lay waste Vietnam's countryside and leave thousands of civilians dead or mutilated. They saw American troops, supposedly winning the hearts and minds of the Vietnamese, uproot peasants and burn their villages.

Yet most Americans still either supported the war or remained undecided. The desire to get out but not give up became a common sentiment. People were not prepared to accept a communist victory over the United States. In mid-1967 Secretary

Chronology

1960	Sit-ins to protest segregation begin. John F. Kennedy elected president.
1961	Peace Corps created. Bay of Pigs invasion. Freedom rides. Berlin Wall erected.
1962	Michael Harrington, *The Other America.* Cuban missile crisis.
1963	Civil-rights demonstrations in Birmingham. March on Washington. Test-Ban Treaty between the Soviet Union and the United States. Kennedy assassinated; Lyndon B. Johnson becomes president. Betty Friedan, *The Feminine Mystique.*
1964	Freedom Summer in Mississippi. Civil Rights Act. Gulf of Tonkin incident and resolution. Economic Opportunity Act initiates War on Poverty. Johnson elected president.
1965	Bombing of North Vietnam and Americanization of the war begin. Assassination of Malcolm X. Civil-rights march from Selma to Montgomery. César Chávez's United Farm Workers strike in California. Teach-ins to question U.S. involvement in the war in Vietnam. Voting Rights Act. Watts riot in Los Angeles.
1966	Black Panthers formed. National Organization for Women (NOW) founded.
1967	Massive antiwar demonstrations. Race riots in Newark, Detroit, and other cities.

of Defense McNamara admitted that "the picture of the world's greatest superpower killing or seriously injuring a thousand noncombatants a week, while trying to pound a tiny backward country into submission on an issue whose merits are hotly disputed, is not a pretty one."

Equally disturbing was how polarized the nation had grown. "Hawks" would accept little short of total victory, whereas "doves" insisted on negotiating, not fighting. Civility vanished. Demonstrators paraded past the White House chanting, "Hey, hey, LBJ, how many kids did you kill today?" By 1968 the president had become a prisoner in the White House, unable to speak in public without being shouted down, and an era of hope and liberalism lay in ruins.

CONCLUSION *hc* ACE Practice Test

The Kennedy "style"—charm, vigor, intellectual curiosity, and glamor—obscured the administration's so-so domestic record. It was left to Johnson to persuade Congress to pass Kennedy's most significant proposals, a civil-rights bill and a tax cut. LBJ also pushed Congress to create the Great Society, promoting health, education, voting rights, urban renewal, immigration reform, environmental protection, and the war against poverty. The United States became a more caring and just nation. His landmark Civil Rights Act ended Jim Crow, provided education and jobs, and inspired a continued fight for equality and dignity—but left untouched the maladies of the black urban ghetto. There, unfulfilled expectations and frustrated hopes exploded into urban rioting, in turn triggering a white backlash that undermined support for the liberal agenda.

At the same time, the struggle for racial justice inspired other minorities to fight for equality and dignity. Native Americans, Hispanic-Americans, and women all took to the streets.

Most of all, the Vietnam War destroyed both the liberal consensus and the Johnson presidency. At

Kennedy's death, LBJ inherited a deteriorating war. Hoping to force a North Vietnamese compromise, Johnson steadily escalated the war and the level of violence but only sank deeper into the quagmire, polarizing the country and fragmenting the Democratic party. Although administration officials claimed to see the light at the end of the tunnel, critics saw the light as a speeding train about to crash American society.

FURTHER READING

John A. Andrew, *Lyndon Johnson and the Great Society* (1998). A sound, brief overview.

George Pierre Castile, *To Show Heart: Native American Self-Determination and Federal Indian Policy, 1960–1975* (1998). An analysis of Indian activism and liberal government policies.

Elizabeth Cobbs Hoffman, *All You Need Is Love: The Peace Corps and the Spirit of the 1960s* (1998). A thoughtful view of liberal idealism.

Michael Friedland, *Lift Up Your Voice Like a Trumpet: White Clergy and the Civil Rights and Antiwar Movements, 1954–1973* (1998). An interesting perspective on the era's protests.

Ignacio M. Garcia, *Viva Kennedy: Mexican Americans in Search of Camelot* (2000). An assessment of ethnicity and the new liberalism.

Fredrik Logevall, *Choosing War: The Lost Chance for Peace and the Escalation of War in Vietnam* (1999), and David Kaiser, *American Tragedy: Kennedy, Johnson, and the Vietnam War* (2000). Two important analyses of the Americanizing of the war in Vietnam.

Lisa McGirr, *Suburban Warriors, The Origins of the New American Right* (2001). An excellent interpretation focused on California.

Timothy Thurber, *The Politics of Equality: Hubert H. Humphrey and the African-American Freedom Struggle* (1999). A balanced view of the relationship between liberalism and the civil-rights movement.

Bong Son, Vietnam, by Henri Huet, 1966.

A Time of Upheaval, 1968–1974

hc This icon will direct you to additional study and research resources at http://college.hmco.com/history/us/boyer/enduring_concise/5e/students/index.html

The Free Speech Movement . . . Students for a Democratic Society . . . "Make Love, Not War." . . . The baby boomers who deluged college campuses in the 1960s espousing these and other outlooks and causes spawned a tumultuous student movement and counterculture that gave the decade its distinctive aura of upheaval. They exploded the well-kept world of the 1950s, when "nice" girls did not have sex or pursue careers and when African-Americans feared to vote or to assert themselves. They revived both the left and the right. Then, disillusioned with the slow pace of change, many became, and remained, preoccupied with themselves, which again transformed the nation.

This chapter focuses on five major questions:

▶ In what ways did the furor over the war in Vietnam affect the student movement?

▶ What were the main causes and consequences of the politics of upheaval in 1968?

▶ What fundamental changes in American foreign policy were made by President Nixon?

▶ How did Richard Nixon's political strategy reflect the racial upheavals and radicalism of this era?

▶ What were the main causes of the Watergate scandal?

Both agent in and beneficiary of the era's realignment, Republican Richard M. Nixon won the presidency in 1968 and gained a stunning reelection victory in 1972. Winning high marks for his management of world affairs, Nixon ended U.S. involvement in Vietnam and inaugurated a period of reduced tensions with China and the Soviet Union. In 1974, however, having flouted the very law and order that he had pledged to uphold on the domestic front, Nixon resigned in disgrace to avoid impeachment. He left as his legacy a public disrespect for the political system unparalleled in U.S. history.

THE YOUTH MOVEMENT

In the 1950s the number of American students pursuing higher education rose from 1 million to 4 million, and in the 1960s the number doubled again, to 8 million. By then more than half the U.S. population was under age thirty. Their sheer numbers gave the baby boomers a collective identity and guaranteed that their actions would have impact.

Most baby boomers followed conventional paths in the 1960s. If they went to college—and

fewer than half did—they typically took business and other career-oriented degrees. Whether they attended college or entered the work force directly after high school, the vast majority had their eyes fixed on a good job, a new car, a family, and a pleasant home. They had little incentive to turn radical. In fact, many young Americans disdained the long-haired protesters and displayed the same bumper stickers as their elders: "My Country—Right or Wrong" or "America—Love It or Leave It."

Tens of thousands of baby boomers mobilized on the right, idolizing Barry Goldwater, supporting the war in Vietnam, and embracing traditional values. Some moved beyond traditional conservatism to become libertarians. On the right or on the left, student activists shared a common conviction: they were part of an upheaval that would fundamentally change America.

Toward a New Left

An insurgent minority of liberal arts majors and graduate students at prestigious universities attracted considerable notice. This liberal-minded student minority welcomed the idealism of the civil-rights movement, the rousing call of John F. Kennedy for service to the nation, and the campaign against nuclear testing that had led to the 1963 test ban treaty. Determined not to be a "silent generation," they admired the mavericks and outsiders of the 1950s: iconoclastic comedian Mort Sahl, Beat poet Allen Ginsberg, and pop-culture rebels like James Dean.

In June 1962 sixty students adopted the Port Huron (Michigan) Manifesto, a broad critique of American society and a call for more genuine human relationships. It announced the formation of a "new left"—Students for a Democratic Society (SDS). Citing the success of civil-rights activists' sit-ins and freedom rides, SDS envisioned a nonviolent youth movement transforming the United States into a "participatory democracy" in which individuals would directly control the decisions that affected their lives and could end materialism, militarism, and racism.

Many idealistic students never joined SDS and instead associated themselves with what they vaguely called "the Movement." No matter what the label, a generation of activists found its agenda in the Port Huron Manifesto. Thousands of students became radicalized in the sixties by what they saw as the impersonality and rigidity of campus administrators, the insensitivity of the nation's bureaucratic processes, and mainstream liberalism's inability to achieve deep, swift change. Only a radical rejection of compromise and consensus, they concluded, could restructure society along humane and democratic lines.

From Protest to Resistance

The first wave of student protest washed across the campus of the University of California, Berkeley. In fall 1964 civil-rights activists who were veterans of the Mississippi Freedom Summer Project tried to solicit funds and to recruit volunteers near the campus gate, a spot traditionally open to political activities. Prodded by local conservatives, however, the university suddenly banned such enterprises from the area. Organizing as the Berkeley Free Speech Movement, a coalition of student groups insisted on the right to campus political activity. The arrest of one student led to the occupation of the university administration building, more arrests, and a strike by nearly 70 percent of the student body. Mario Savio, a philosophy major, tried to place the Free Speech Movement in a broader context by claiming that the university not only greedily served the interests of corporate America but also treated students as interchangeable robots. Likening the university to a giant machine, Savio insisted, "There is a time when the operation of the machine becomes so odious, makes you so sick to heart, that . . . you've got to make it stop."

As unrest spread to other campuses, protest took many forms. Students sat in to halt compulsory ROTC (Reserve Officers' Training Corps) programs, rallied to protest dress codes, marched to demand fewer required courses, and threatened to close down universities unless they admitted more minority students and stopped research for the military-in-

dustrial complex. The escalation of the Vietnam War in 1965 gave the New Left an opportunity to kindle a mass social movement. When the Johnson administration abolished automatic student deferments for the draft in January 1966, more than two hundred new campus chapters of SDS appeared.

In 1966 SDS disrupted ROTC classes, organized draft-card burnings, and harassed campus recruiters for the military and for Dow Chemical Company, the chief producer of napalm and Agent Orange, chemicals used in Vietnam to burn villages and to defoliate forests. By 1967 SDS leaders were encouraging more provocative acts of defiance, orchestrating civil disobedience at selective-service centers, and counseling students to flee to Canada or Sweden rather than be drafted. At the Spring Mobilization to End the War in Vietnam, which attracted nearly a half-million protesters to New York's Central Park, SDS members led chants of "Burn cards, not people" and "Hell, no, we won't go!"

Spring 1968 saw at least forty thousand students on one hundred campuses demonstrate against war and racism. Although the student movement was overwhelmingly peaceful, occasionally confrontations turned violent. In April, denouncing the university's proposed expansion into Harlem to construct a gymnasium, militant Columbia University students shouting "Gym Crow must go" took over the administration building and held a dean captive. The protest expanded into a demonstration against the war and university military research. A thousand students occupied other campus buildings and made them "revolutionary communes." Galvanized by the brutality of the police who retook the buildings, the moderate majority of Columbia students joined a general boycott of classes that shut down the university.

August 1969 saw the high point of the movement with the New Mobilization, a series of huge antiwar demonstrations culminating in mid-November with the March Against Death in Washington, D.C. The three hundred thousand protesters who descended on the nation's capital marched single file through a cold drizzle, carrying candles and signs with the names of soldiers killed or villages destroyed in Vietnam.

Kent State–Jackson State

A crescendo of violence in spring 1970 marked the effective end of the student movement as a political force. On April 30, 1970, President Richard M. Nixon, Lyndon Johnson's successor, jolted a war-weary nation by announcing that he had ordered U.S. troops to invade Cambodia, a neutral Indochinese nation that had become a staging area for North Vietnamese forces. Nixon had decided to extricate the United States from Vietnam by "Vietnamizing" the ground conflict and intensifying bombing. Students lulled by periodic announcements of troop withdrawals from Vietnam now felt betrayed. They exploded in hatred for Nixon and the war.

At Kent State University in Ohio, as elsewhere, these frustrations unleashed new turmoil. Radicals broke windows and tried to firebomb the ROTC building. Nixon lashed out at them as "bums." Ohio governor James Rhodes slapped martial law on the university and ordered three thousand National Guardsmen to Kent. In full battle gear, the troops rolled onto the Kent State campus in armored personnel carriers.

On May 4, the day after the Guard's arrival, six hundred Kent State students peacefully demonstrated against the Cambodian invasion. Suddenly a campus policeman boomed through a bullhorn, "This assembly is unlawful! This is an order—disperse immediately!" Students shouted back, "Pigs off campus!" Some threw stones. With bayonets fixed, the guardsmen moved toward the rally and laid down a blanket of tear gas. Hundreds of demonstrators and onlookers, choking and weeping, ran from the advancing troops. Guardsmen in Troop G, poorly trained in crowd control, raised their rifles and fired a volley into the retreating crowd. When the shooting stopped, eleven students lay wounded; four were dead. None was a campus radical; two had simply been passing by on their way to lunch.

Then on May 15 highway patrolmen looking into a campus demonstration fired into a women's dormitory at Jackson State College in Mississippi, killing two students and wounding eleven. Protests against such senseless violence, the war, and President Nixon thundered across campuses, and more than four hundred colleges and universities shut down as students boycotted classes.

The nation was polarized. Although most students blamed Nixon for widening the war and applauded the demonstrators' goals, more Americans blamed the *victims* for the deaths at Kent State and criticized campus protesters for undermining U.S. foreign policy. Underlying these attitudes were a deep resentment of privileged college students and an impatience for an end to the social chaos. Symptomatically, Kent State students expressed profound alienation after the shootings, while a local merchant said that the National Guard "made only one mistake—they should have fired sooner and longer."

Legacy of Student Frenzy

The campus protests after Kent State and Jackson State represented the final spasm of a fragmenting movement. When a bomb planted by three antiwar radicals destroyed a science building at the University of Wisconsin in summer 1970, killing a graduate student, most students deplored the tactic. With the resumption of classes in the fall, the campus mood had changed dramatically. Frustrated by the failure to end the war, much less to revolutionize American society, antiwar activists at Wisconsin and elsewhere turned to other causes or to communes, careers, or parenthood. A handful of frustrated radicals went underground, engaging in terrorist acts that justified the government's repression of the remnants of the antiwar movement. The New Left fell victim to government harassment, to its own internal contradictions, and to Nixon's success in winding down the Vietnam War.

The aftereffects of campus activism outlived the New Left. Student radicalism had catalyzed the resentments of millions of people into a rejection of liberalism. Evangelical Protestants, white southerners, and blue-collar workers united in a new conservatism.

Early stirrings of this backlash propelled Ronald Reagan to prominence. In 1966 he won California's governorship, in part because of his opposition to Berkeley demonstrators. The actor-turned-politician won a resounding reelection victory by railing against radicals: "If it takes a bloodbath," he said, "let's get it over with. No more appeasement." Nationwide, other conservatives gained office with similar promises. And memories of student radicalism would strengthen conservatism's appeal for the rest of the century.

At the same time, the New Left catalyzed public opposition to the Vietnam War. It mobilized the campuses into a force that the government could not ignore, and it made continued U.S. involvement in Indochina difficult. The movement had also aided in liberalizing many facets of campus life and making university governance less authoritarian. Dress codes and curfews virtually disappeared; ROTC became an elective, not a requirement; schools recruited minorities; and students now assisted in shaping their own education.

Some New Left veterans would remain active in post-1970 causes, including environmentalism, consumer advocacy, and the antinuclear movement. Female students who took part in the antiwar movement would form the backbone of a resurgent women's movement in the seventies. These involvements, however, fell short of the original New Left vision of remaking the social and political order. Masses of students could be mobilized in the short run against the Vietnam War, but only a few had made long-term commitments to radical politics.

THE COUNTERCULTURE

The alienation and hunger for change that drew some youth to politics led others to cultural rebellion. In communes and tribes, these "hippies" denounced individualism and private property, and in urban areas such as Chicago's Old Town or Atlanta's Fourteenth Street, "places where you could take a trip without a ticket," they experimented with drugs. Historian Theodore Roszack called them "a 'counter culture' . . . a culture so radically

"My God, They're Killing Us"
Following rioting downtown and the firebombing of the ROTC building, Ohio Governor James Rhodes called in the National Guard to stop the antiwar protests at Kent State University. On May 4, after retreating from rock-throwing students, nervous guardsmen turned and began to shoot. When the firing stopped, four students lay dead and eleven were left wounded.
hc Interactive Map: Disturbances on College and University Campuses, 1967–1969

disaffiliated from the mainstream assumptions of our society that it scarcely looks to many as a culture at all, but takes on the alarming appearance of a barbarian intrusion."

Hippies and Drugs

Illustrative of the gap between the two cultures, one saw marijuana as a "killer weed," a menace to health and life, and the other thought it a harmless social relaxant. In the absence of scientific evidence that the drug was dangerous, at least half the college students in the late sixties tried marijuana. A minority used mind-altering drugs, especially LSD and mescaline. Many youths, distancing themselves from middle-class respectability, flaunted outrageous personal styles. They showed disdain for consumerism by wearing surplus military clothing, torn jeans, and tie-dyed T-shirts. Especially galling to adults, young men sported shaggy beards and long hair, the badge of the counterculture.

Musical Revolution

Popular music both echoed and influenced the youth culture. In the early sixties, college students listened to folk music. Songs protesting racism and injustice mirrored the idealistic, nonviolent commitment of the civil-rights movement. Bob Dylan sang hopefully of changes "blowin' in the wind" that would transform society. Then in 1964 Beatlemania swept the United States. Moving beyond their early romantic songs, the Beatles gloried in the youth culture's drugs ("I'd love to turn you on"), sex ("Why don't we do it in the road?"), and radicalism ("You say you want a revolution"). The Grateful Dead, Jefferson Airplane, and other bands launched "acid rock," which blended a heavy beat with lyrics extolling "sex, drugs, and rock-and-roll."

In August 1969, four hundred thousand young people gathered for the Woodstock festival in New York's Catskill Mountains to celebrate their vision of freedom and harmony. For three days and nights they reveled in the music of dozens of rock stars and openly shared drugs, sexual partners, and con-

tempt for the Establishment. The counterculture heralded Woodstock as the dawning of an era of love and peace, the Age of Aquarius.

In fact, the counterculture was disintegrating. Pilgrimages of "flower children" to San Francisco's Haight-Ashbury district and to New York's East Village in the mid-sixties had brought in their wake a train of muggers, rapists, and dope peddlers pushing hard drugs. In December 1969 the deranged Charles Manson and his "family" of runaways ritually murdered a pregnant movie actress and four of her friends. Then a Rolling Stones concert at the Altamont Raceway near San Francisco deteriorated into a violent melee in which four concertgoers died. In July 1970 the Beatles disbanded. John Lennon sang, "The dream is over. What can I say?"

Although cynics concluded that counterculture values were not deeply held, the optimistic view of human nature and skeptical view of authority continued to influence American education and society long after the 1960s. Self-fulfillment remained a goal, and the repressive sexual standards of the 1950s did not return.

The Sexual Revolution

The counterculture's "if it feels good, do it" approach to sex fit into an overall atmosphere of greater permissiveness. These shifts in attitude and behavior unleashed a sexual revolution that would flourish until the mid-1980s, when the AIDS epidemic and the "graying" of the youth movement chilled the ardor of open sexuality.

Most commentators linked the sexual revolution to waning fears of unwanted pregnancy. In 1960 oral contraceptives reached the market, and by 1970, 12 million women were taking "the Pill." Even more women used the intrauterine device (later banned as unsafe) or the diaphragm for birth control. And states gradually legalized abortion. In 1970 in New York State, one fetus was legally aborted for every two babies born. The Supreme Court's *Roe* v. *Wade* decision (1973) struck down all remaining state laws infringing on a woman's right to abortion during the first three months of pregnancy.

The Court also threw out most laws restricting "sexually explicit" materials, and mass culture quickly exploited the new permissiveness. *Playboy* magazine featured ever-more-explicit erotica, and women's periodicals encouraged their readers to enjoy recreational sex. Hollywood filled movie screens with scenes of explicit sex; Broadway presented plays featuring frontal nudity, mimed sex acts, and mock orgies; and even television presented frank discussions of once forbidden subjects.

The casual acceptance of sexuality influenced Americans' behavior. Many couples lived together without being married. Surveys showed that by the mid-1970s three-quarters of all college students had engaged in sexual intercourse before their senior year. The use of contraceptives (and to some extent, abortion) spread to women of all religious backgrounds—including Roman Catholics, despite the Catholic church's impassioned stand against "artificial" birth control.

Gay Liberation

In 1969 gay liberation emerged publicly from the semiunderground gay communities that had sprouted in major cities. During a routine raid by New York City police, the homosexual patrons of the Stonewall Inn, a gay bar in Greenwich Village, unexpectedly fought back. The furor triggered a surge of "gay pride," a new sense of identity and self-acceptance, and widespread activism. The Gay Liberation movement that emerged asserted, "We are going to be who we are."

By 1973 eight hundred openly gay groups campaigned for equal rights for homosexuals, the incorporation of lesbianism into the women's movement, and the removal of the stigmas of immorality and depravity attached to being gay. That year the American Psychiatric Association officially ended its classification of homosexuality as a mental disorder.

Simultaneously, several cities and states began to broaden their civil-rights statutes to include "sexual orientation" as a protected status, and in 1975 the U.S. Civil Service Commission officially ended its ban on the employment of homosexuals.

Millions of gays had "come out," demanding public acceptance of their sexual identity.

In a few years, the baby boomers had transformed sexual relations as well as gender and racial relations. The institutions of marriage and family were fundamentally altered. Women could have access to birth control, abortion, and an active sex life with or without a male partner.

What some hailed as sexual liberation, others bemoaned as moral decay. Offended by "topless" bars, X-rated theaters, and "adult" bookstores, many Americans applauded politicians who promised a war on smut. The public association of the counterculture and the sexual revolution with student demonstrations and ghetto riots swelled the tide of conservatism as the sixties ended.

1968: THE POLITICS OF UPHEAVAL

The social and cultural turmoil of the 1960s unfolded against a backdrop of frustration with the Vietnam War and an intensifying domestic political crisis. The stormy year 1968 brought these elements together explosively. Converging in the presidential campaign of 1968, the swirling currents of strife precipitated the first major realignment of American politics since the New Deal.

The Tet Offensive in Vietnam

In January 1968 liberal Democratic senator Eugene McCarthy of Minnesota, a Vietnam War critic, announced that he would challenge Lyndon B. Johnson for the presidential nomination. Pundits scoffed that McCarthy had no chance of unseating Johnson, who had won the presidency in 1964 by the largest margin in U.S. history. But McCarthy persisted, determined that at least one Democrat enter the primaries on an antiwar platform.

Suddenly, America's hopes for victory in Vietnam sank, and with them LBJ's political fortunes. On January 31, the first day of Tet, the Vietnamese New Year, National Liberation Front (NLF) and North Vietnamese forces mounted a huge offensive, attacking more than one hundred towns in South Vietnam and even the U.S. Embassy in Saigon. U.S. troops repulsed the offensive after a month of ferocious fighting, inflicting a major military defeat on the communists.

The media, however, emphasized the staggering number of American casualties and the scope of the offensive. Americans at home reacted sharply to the realization that no area of South Vietnam was secure from the enemy and that a foe that the president had claimed was beaten could initiate such daring attacks. Many stopped believing reports of battlefield successes streaming from the White House and doubted that the United States could win the war at an acceptable cost.

After Tet, McCarthy's criticism of the war won new sympathizers. *Time, Newsweek,* and the *Wall Street Journal* published editorials urging a negotiated settlement. The nation's most respected newscaster, Walter Cronkite of CBS, observed that "it seems now more certain than ever that the bloody experience of Vietnam is to end in a stalemate." "If I've lost Walter," LBJ sighed, "then it's over. I've lost Mr. Average Citizen." Johnson's approval rating dropped to 35 percent. The number of Americans who described themselves as prowar "hawks" slipped from 62 percent in January to 41 percent in March, while the antiwar "doves" jumped from 22 percent to 42 percent.

A Shaken President

Beleaguered, Johnson pondered a change in American policy. When the Joint Chiefs of Staff sought an additional 206,000 men for Vietnam, he consulted with advisers. Dean Acheson, the former secretary of state and a venerable Cold Warrior, told LBJ that "the Joint Chiefs of Staff don't know what they're talking about." Clark Clifford, the new secretary of defense, became convinced that the American course was hopeless.

Meanwhile, nearly five thousand college students had swarmed to New Hampshire to stuff envelopes and ring doorbells for Eugene McCarthy. To be "Clean for Gene," they cut their long hair and dressed conservatively. McCarthy astonished the experts by winning nearly half the popular vote and twenty of twenty-four nominating-convention delegates in the primary contest of a state usually regarded as conservative.

After this upset, twice as many students converged on Wisconsin to canvass its more liberal Democratic voters, anticipating a resounding McCarthy triumph in the nation's second primary. Hurriedly, on March 16 Senator Robert Kennedy entered the Democratic contest, also promising to end the war. Projecting the familiar Kennedy glamor and magnetism, Kennedy was the one candidate whom Johnson feared could deny him renomination. Indeed, millions viewed Kennedy as the rightful heir to the White House. Appealing to minorities, the poor, and working-class ethnic whites, Kennedy became, according to one columnist, "our first politician for the pariahs, our great national outsider."

On March 31 LBJ informed a television audience that he was halting the bombing of North Vietnam. Saying that he wanted to devote all his efforts to the search for peace, Johnson then startlingly announced, "I shall not seek, and I will not accept, the nomination of my party for another term as your president." Embittered by the personal abuse that he had endured, and reluctant to polarize the nation further, the president called it quits. "The only difference between the Kennedy assassination and mine," he lamented, "is that I am alive and it has been more tortuous." Two days later, McCarthy trounced the president in the Wisconsin primary.

All but forgotten in retirement, Johnson died of a heart attack in January 1973—ironically, on the very day that the Paris Peace Accords ended America's direct combat role in Vietnam. In many ways a tragic figure, he had carried out Vietnam policies shaped by his predecessors and received little acclaim for his domestic achievements, especially in civil rights. Although he often displayed high idealism and generosity of spirit, the enduring image of LBJ is that of a crude, overbearing politician with an outsized ego that masked deep insecurities.

Assassinations and Turmoil

On April 4, three days after the Wisconsin primary, Martin Luther King, Jr., was killed in Memphis, Tennessee, where he had gone to support striking sanitation workers. The assassin was James Earl Ray, a white escaped convict. As the news spread, black ghettos burst into violence in 125 cities. Twenty blocks of Chicago's West Side went up in flames, and Mayor Richard Daley ordered police to shoot to kill arsonists. In Washington, D.C., under night skies illuminated by seven hundred fires, army units in combat gear set up machine-gun emplacements outside the Capitol and White House. The rioting left 46 dead and 3,000 injured.

The Democratic contest for the presidential nomination became a three-cornered scramble as LBJ's vice president, Hubert Humphrey, entered the race as the standard-bearer of the New Deal coalition. McCarthy remained the candidate of the "new politics"—a moral crusade against war and injustice directed to affluent and educated liberals. And Kennedy campaigned as the tribune of the less privileged, the only candidate who appealed to white ethnics and the minority poor. But on June 5, 1968, as he celebrated victory in the California primary at a Los Angeles hotel, the brother of the murdered president was himself assassinated by a Palestinian refugee, Sirhan Sirhan, who loathed Kennedy's pro-Israel views.

The dream of peace and racial justice turned to despair. "I won't vote," one youth said. "Every good man we get they kill." Kennedy's death cleared the way for Humphrey's nomination, but Democrats were far from united.

Some Democrats looked to third-party candidate George Wallace or to Republican nominee Richard M. Nixon. Nixon promised to end the war in Vietnam with honor, to restore "law and order," and to heed "the voice of the great majority of Americans, the forgotten Americans, the non-shouters, the non-demonstrators, those who do not break the law, people who pay their taxes and go to work, who send their children to school, who go to their churches, . . . who love this country."

George Wallace tapped into the same wellspring of angry reaction as Nixon. Wallace pitched his message to blue-collar workers and southern whites fed up with antiwar protesters, black militants, hippies, and liberal intellectuals.

In August 1968 violence outside the Democratic National Convention in Chicago reinforced the appeal of both Wallace and Nixon. Thousands descended on the city to protest the Vietnam War. Radicals among the protesters wanted to provoke a confrontation to discredit the Democrats, and a handful ridiculed the system by creating their own "Youth International Party." These "Yippies'" guerrilla-theater stunts fascinated the media, which repeated with a straight face Yippie threats to dump LSD into Chicago's water system or to release greased pigs in the city's crowded Loop area.

Determined to avoid the rioting that had wracked Chicago after the assassination of Martin Luther King, Jr., Mayor Richard Daley gave police a green light to attack "the hippies, the Yippies, and the flippies." The result was a police riot, televised live to a huge national audience. As protesters chanted, "The whole world is watching," Chicago police clubbed demonstrators and bystanders alike. The brutality on the streets overshadowed Humphrey's nomination and tore the Democrats further apart, fixing Americans' image of them as the party of dissent and disorder.

Conservative Resurgence

Nixon capitalized on the tumult. His TV campaign commercials flashed images of campus and ghetto uprisings. He portrayed himself as the representative of the Silent Majority, castigated the Supreme Court for safeguarding criminals at the expense of law-abiding citizens, and told white southerners that "our schools are for education—not integration."

George Wallace, also appealing to the broad revulsion against radicalism, raged across the political landscape. He stoked the fury of the working class against school integrationists, welfare mothers, and radical professors alike. Promising to keep peace even if it took "thirty thousand troops armed with three-foot bayonets," he vowed that "if any demonstrator ever lays down in front of my car, it'll be the last car he'll ever lie down in front of."

By September Wallace had climbed to 21 percent in voter-preference polls. Although many liked Wallace's views, few believed that he had any chance of winning and either did not vote or grudgingly supported one of his opponents. Still, nearly 14 percent of the electorate voted for Wallace in November.

Nixon squeaked to victory with 43.4 percent of the popular vote. He garnered only 301 electoral votes, the narrowest victory since Woodrow Wilson's slender triumph in 1916. A conservative majority had supplanted the New Deal coalition—Humphrey received just 38 percent of the white vote.

The 57 percent of the electorate who chose Nixon or Wallace would dominate American politics for the rest of the century. While the national Democratic party fractured into a welter of single-issue groups, the Republicans attracted a new ma-

jority who lived in the suburbs and the Sun Belt, regarded the federal government as wasteful, opposed the forced busing of schoolchildren, and objected to special efforts to assist minorities and those on welfare. Yearning for restraint abroad and stability at home, a new majority looked hopefully to the new president to end the Vietnam War and to reestablish social harmony.

NIXON AND WORLD POLITICS

A Californian of Quaker roots, Richard Milhous Nixon was elected to Congress as a Navy veteran in 1946. He won prominence for his role in the HUAC investigation of Alger Hiss and advanced to the Senate in 1950 by accusing his Democratic opponent of disloyalty. He served two terms as Eisenhower's vice president but lost the presidency to Kennedy in 1960 and the California governorship in 1962. Ignoring what seemed a political death sentence, Nixon campaigned vigorously for GOP candidates in 1966 and won his party's nomination and the presidency in 1968 by promising to restore domestic tranquility.

In office, Nixon focused mainly on foreign affairs. Considering himself a master of realpolitik—a pragmatic approach stressing the advancement of the national interest rather than theoretical or ethical goals—he sought to check Soviet expansionism and to reduce superpower conflict, to limit the nuclear-arms race, and to enhance the United States' economic well-being. He planned to move the United States out of Vietnam and into an era of détente—an easing of tensions—with the communist world. To manage diplomacy, Nixon chose Henry Kissinger, a refugee from Hitler's Germany and a Harvard professor of international relations who shared Nixon's desire to concentrate decision-making power in the White House.

Vietnamization

Nixon's grand design hinged on ending the Vietnam War. The war was sapping American military strength, worsening inflation, and thwarting détente. In August 1969 the president unveiled what

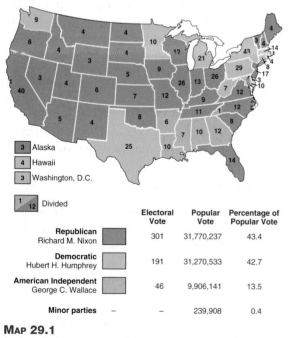

	Electoral Vote	Popular Vote	Percentage of Popular Vote
Republican Richard M. Nixon	301	31,770,237	43.4
Democratic Hubert H. Humphrey	191	31,270,533	42.7
American Independent George C. Wallace	46	9,906,141	13.5
Minor parties	–	–	239,908	0.4

MAP 29.1
The Election of 1968

became known as the Nixon Doctrine, in which he redefined the United States' role in the Third World as that of a helpful partner rather than a military protector. Nations facing communist subversion could count on American financial and moral support, but they would have to defend themselves.

The Nixon Doctrine reflected the president's understanding of the war weariness of both the electorate and the U.S. troops in Vietnam. Johnson's decision to negotiate, rather than to escalate, had left American troops with the sense that nothing mattered except survival. Morale plummeted and discipline collapsed. Army desertions rocketed from twenty-seven thousand in 1967 to seventy-six thousand in 1970. Racial conflict became commonplace and drug use soared. The army reported hundreds of cases of "fragging"—enlisted men killing officers.

The toll of atrocities against the Vietnamese mounted. In March 1968 an army unit led by an inexperienced lieutenant, William Calley, massacred several hundred defenseless civilians. Soldiers gang-raped girls, lined up women and old men in ditches and shot them, and then burned the village, My Lai. Revelations of such incidents, and the rising number of returned soldiers who joined Vietnam Veterans Against the War, undercut the already diminished support for the war.

Despite pressure to end the war, Nixon would not sacrifice America's prestige. Seeking "peace with honor," Nixon pursued three simultaneous courses. First, he implemented "Vietnamization," replacing American troops with South Vietnamese. By 1972 U.S. forces in Vietnam had dropped from half a million to thirty thousand. Second, Nixon bypassed South Vietnamese leaders by sending Kissinger to negotiate secretly with North Vietnam's foreign minister, Le Duc Tho. Third, to force the communists to compromise despite U.S. withdrawal, the president radically escalated American bombing. To maximize the harm done to the enemy, Nixon in March 1969 secretly ordered the bombing of North Vietnamese supply routes in Cambodia and Laos and the intensification of bombing raids on North Vietnam. He told an aide, "We'll just slip the word to them that 'you know

Nixon is obsessed about communism. We can't restrain him when he's angry—and he has his hand on the nuclear button'—and Ho Chi Minh . . . will be . . . begging for peace.'"

LBJ's War Becomes Nixon's War

The secret B-52 raids against Cambodia neither made Hanoi beg for peace nor disrupted communist supply bases. They did, however, undermine the stability of that tiny republic. In early 1970 North Vietnam increased its infiltration of troops into Cambodia, both to aid the Cambodian communists (the Khmer Rouge) and to escalate its war in South Vietnam. Nixon ordered a joint U.S.–South Vietnamese incursion into Cambodia at the end of April 1970. The invaders seized large caches of arms and bought time for Vietnamization. But the costs were high. The invasion ended Cambodia's neutrality, widened the war throughout Indochina, and provoked massive American protests against the war, culminating in the student deaths at Kent State and Jackson State universities.

In 1971 Nixon combined Vietnamization with renewed blows against the enemy. In February, at the administration's initiative, the South Vietnamese army invaded Laos to destroy communist bases there and to restrict the flow of supplies southward from North Vietnam. The South Vietnamese, however, were routed. Emboldened, the North Vietnamese in 1972 mounted the so-called Easter Offensive, their largest campaign since 1968. Nixon retaliated by mining North Vietnam's harbors and unleashing B-52s against its major cities.

America's Longest War Ends

On October 26, just days before the 1972 presidential election, Kissinger announced that "peace is at hand." The cease-fire agreement that he had secretly negotiated required the withdrawal of all American troops, provided for the return of U.S. prisoners of war, and allowed North Vietnamese troops to remain in South Vietnam.

Kissinger's negotiations had sealed Nixon's reelection, but South Vietnam's President Thieu refused to sign a cease-fire agreement permitting North Vietnamese troops to remain in the South. Angered by Thieu's rebuff, Le Duc Tho pressed for additional concessions. President Nixon again resorted to B-52 raids. The 1972 Christmas bombings of Hanoi and Haiphong, the most destructive of the war, roused fierce opposition domestically and globally but broke the deadlock. Nixon's secret reassurance to Thieu that the United States would "respond with full force should the settlement be violated by North Vietnam" ended Saigon's recalcitrance.

The Paris Accords, signed in late January 1973, essentially restated the terms of the October truce. The agreement ended hostilities between the United States and North Vietnam but left unresolved the differences between North and South Vietnam, guaranteeing that Vietnam's future would yet be settled on the battlefield.

The war in Vietnam would continue despite fifty-eight thousand American deaths, three hundred thousand wounded, and the expenditure of at least $150 billion. Twenty percent of those who served, nearly five hundred thousand, received less-than-honorable discharges, a measure of the desertion rate, drug usage, strength of antiwar sentiment in the military, and immaturity of the troops (the average U.S. soldier in Vietnam was just nineteen years old, seven years younger than the average GI in World War II).

Virtually all who survived, wrote one marine, returned "as immigrants to a new world. For the culture we had known dissolved while we were in Vietnam, and the culture of combat we lived in . . . made us aliens when we returned." Beyond occasional media attention to the psychological difficulties that they faced in adjusting to civilian life, the nation paid little heed to its Vietnam veterans.

Relieved that the long nightmare had ended, most Americans wanted to forget the war. The bitterness of many veterans moderated with time. Few Americans gave much thought to how the war had devastated Vietnam, inflicting 2 million casualties. Laos, too, had suffered, but Cambodia had paid the highest price. After the war engulfed this previously peaceful land, the fanatical Khmer Rouge emerged victorious in 1975. Three million Cambodians—40 percent of the nation's population—died on the "killing fields."

Détente

Disengagement from Vietnam helped Nixon to achieve a turnabout in Chinese-American relations and détente with the communist superpowers. These developments, the most significant shift in U.S. foreign policy since the start of the Cold War, created a new relationship among the United States, China, and the Soviet Union.

The United States had refused to recognize the People's Republic of China in 1949. The United States had vetoed the admission of "Red China" to the United Nations and pressured American allies to restrict trade with the communist giant. But by 1969 a widening Chinese-Soviet split made the prospect of improved relations attractive to both Nixon and Mao Zedong. China wanted to end its isolation, the United States wanted to play one communist power against the other, and both wanted to thwart Soviet expansionism in Asia.

In fall 1970, Nixon played "the China card" by calling China the People's Republic rather than Red China. In June 1971 Kissinger made a secret trip to China, and a month later Nixon announced that he would travel to the People's Republic "to seek the normalization of relations." In February 1972 the president's plane landed in China, beginning the first trip ever by a sitting American president to the largest nation in the world. Although differences between the two powers delayed official diplomatic relations until 1979, Nixon's visit signaled the end of more than twenty years of Chinese-American hostility.

Equally significantly, Nixon went to Moscow in May 1972 to sign agreements with the Soviets on trade and technological cooperation. The Strategic Arms Limitation Talks (SALT I) limited each nation to two antiballistic missile systems, froze each side's offensive nuclear missiles for five years, and committed both superpowers to strategic equality rather than nuclear superiority. Although it did not end the arms race, SALT I moved both countries to-

Nixon in China
One of the great triumphs of his administration was the rapprochement with the People's Republic of China. Planned in total secrecy, Nixon's trip to China in February 1972 stunned the world and gave the president the aura of a bold, imaginative statesman.

ward "peaceful coexistence" and, in an election year, enhanced Nixon's stature.

Shuttle Diplomacy

Not even rapprochement with China and détente with the Soviet Union could ensure global stability. In 1967 Israel, fearing that a massive Arab attack was imminent, launched a preemptive strike on its Arab neighbors, routing them in six days. Israel occupied the Egyptian-controlled Sinai and Gaza Strip, the Jordanian-ruled West Bank and East Jerusalem, and Syria's Golan Heights. Israel prom-

ised to give up most of the occupied lands in exchange for direct negotiations and peace, but the Arab states refused to negotiate with Israel or to recognize its right to exist. Palestinians, many of them refugees, turned to the Palestine Liberation Organization (PLO), which called for Israel's destruction.

War exploded again in 1973 when Egypt and Syria launched surprise attacks against Israel on the Jewish high holy day of Yom Kippur. Israel reeled under the attacks but, with military equipment airlifted by the United States, counterattacked. In retaliation, the oil-producing Arab states, through the Organization of Petroleum Exporting Countries (OPEC), embargoed shipments of crude oil to the United States and its allies from October 1973 to March 1974. Acute oil shortages and soaring costs—the price of a barrel of crude oil soared from $3 to more than $12—fed inflation and spurred the use of nuclear power.

The dual shocks of the energy crisis at home and renewed Soviet influence among Arab hardliners spurred Nixon and Kissinger to pursue "shuttle diplomacy." Flying from one Middle East capital to another for two years, Kissinger negotiated a cease-fire, pressed Israel to cede additional captured Arab territory, and persuaded the Arabs to end the oil embargo. Although shuttle diplomacy left the Palestinian issue still festering, it successfully excluded the Soviets from a major role in Middle Eastern affairs.

To counter Soviet influence and to protect American interests, the Nixon administration liberally supplied arms to the shah of Iran, to President Ferdinand Marcos in the Philippines, and to the white-supremacist regime of South Africa. Nixon-Kissinger realpolitik based American aid on a nation's willingness to oppose the Soviet Union, not on the nature of its government. Thus, the administration provided aid to antidemocratic regimes in Brazil and South Korea as well as to Portuguese colonial authorities in Angola.

When Chileans elected a Marxist, Salvador Allende, president in 1970, Nixon secretly funneled $10 million to the CIA to fund opponents of Allende's leftist regime. The United States also cut off economic aid to Chile, blocked banks from granting loans, and pressed the World Bank to drop Chile's credit rating. In September 1973 a military junta overthrew the Chilean government and killed Allende. Nixon quickly recognized the dictatorship, and economic aid and investment again flowed to Chile.

The administration's active opposition to Allende reflected the extent to which American policy remained committed to containing communist influence. At the same time, Nixon understood the limits of U.S. power and the changed realities of world affairs. Discarding the vision of a bipolar world that had shaped American foreign policy since 1945, Nixon took advantage of the Chinese-Soviet split to improve American relations with both nations. The administration also ended American involvement in Vietnam and improved the U.S. position in the Middle East. The politician who had built his reputation as a staunch Cold Warrior initiated a new era of détente with the communist powers.

DOMESTIC PROBLEMS AND DIVISIONS

Although Richard M. Nixon yearned to be remembered as an international statesman, domestic affairs kept intruding. He displayed creativity, reforming welfare and grappling with other complex economic problems. But another side of the Nixon personality appealed to the darker recesses of national character and intensified the fears and divisions among Americans.

Richard Nixon: Man and Politician

Close observers of Nixon noted the multiple levels of his personality. Beneath the calculated public persona of the politician hid a shadowy man who rarely revealed himself. Nixon the politician was highly intelligent, but also displayed the rigid self-control of a man monitoring his own every move. When the private Nixon did emerge, he was suspicious, insecure, and filled with anger. Nixon's conviction that enemies lurked everywhere, waiting to

destroy him, verged on paranoia. He sought to annihilate his partisan enemies, especially the "eastern liberal establishment" that had long opposed him.

Probing the source of his insecurities, some observers viewed Nixon as the classic outsider: reared in pinched surroundings, physically awkward, unable to relate easily to others. Although at the height of national power, Nixon remained fearful that he would never be accepted. In the early Nixon years, the president's strengths were most apparent. Nixon spoke of national reconciliation, took bold initiatives internationally, and dealt with domestic problems responsibly. But the darker side ultimately prevailed and drove him from office in disgrace.

The Nixon Presidency

Nixon began his presidency with a moderation reminiscent of Eisenhower. Symbolic of this positive start, the nation joined the new president in celebrating the first successful manned mission to the moon on July 20, 1969, as astronaut Neil Armstrong descended from the lunar lander *Eagle* to the surface of the Sea of Tranquillity, announcing to enthralled television audiences back on Earth, "That's one small step for man, one giant leap for mankind." Americans thrilled as Armstrong and Buzz Aldrin planted an American flag, collected rock and soil samples, and erected a plaque reading "We came in peace for all mankind." Five more lunar expeditions followed, but in 1975 the space race essentially ended with the United States and Soviet Union engaging in cooperative efforts to explore the rest of the universe.

The first newly elected president since 1849 whose party controlled neither house of Congress, Nixon initially signed bills to increase social-security benefits, to build subsidized housing, to expand the Job Corps, and to grant the vote to eighteen-year-olds. More grudgingly, he accepted legislation targeting the adverse effects of material growth. New laws limited pesticide use, protected endangered species, regulated consumer-product safety, and established maximum levels for the emission of pollutants into the air. The National

A Walk on the Moon, 1969

Ten years after John F. Kennedy challenged America to put a person on the moon, astronaut Neil Armstrong stepped down from his lunar module onto the surface of the moon. From the White House, President Nixon told the astronauts and the nation, "this has to be the proudest day of our lives."

Environmental Policy Act (1969) required environmental-impact analysis statements for proposed federal projects and established the Environmental Protection Agency in 1970. Congress also created the Occupational Safety and Health Administration to ensure workers' safety and well-being.

Growing environmental awareness culminated in the celebration of the first Earth Day in April 1970. Earth Day spotlighted such problems as thermal pollution, dying lakes, oil spills, and dwindling resources. It introduced Americans to the idea of "living lightly on the earth." Organic gardening, vegetarianism, solar power, recycling, and preventive health care came into vogue, as did zero population growth, the idea that the birthrate should not exceed the death rate.

Conservatives grumbled as government grew larger and more intrusive and as race-conscious employment policies, including quotas, were mandated for all federal contractors. And conservatives grew still angrier when Nixon unveiled the Family Assistance Plan (FAP) in 1969. A bold effort to overhaul the welfare system, FAP proposed a guaranteed annual income for all Americans. Caught between liberals who considered it inadequate and conservatives who opposed it on principle, FAP made it through the House but died in the Senate.

A Troubled Economy

Nixon inherited the fiscal consequences of Lyndon B. Johnson's effort to wage the Vietnam War and finance the Great Society by deficit financing, to have both "guns and butter." Facing a large budget deficit, $25 billion, and an inflation rate of 5 percent. Nixon initially encouraged the Federal Reserve Board to raise interest rates and contract the money supply. The result was a combination of inflation and stagnation soon christened "stagflation."

Accelerating inflation lowered the standard of living for many families and sparked a wave of strikes as workers sought wage hikes to keep up with the cost of living. It also encouraged the

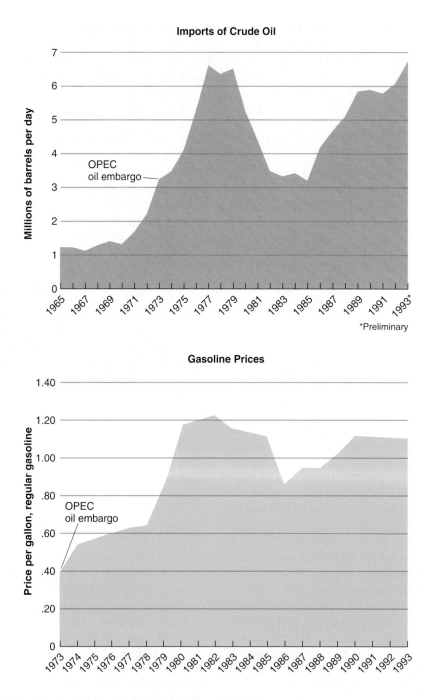

The Energy Crisis: Crude-Oil Imports and Gasoline Prices

Not until the 1980s, through the combination of a deep recession and fuel conservation, did U.S. petroleum imports finally begin dropping off (top). OPEC's ability to act as a supercartel in setting oil prices sent the cost of filling a car's gas tank skyrocketing in the 1970s (bottom).

Source: Energy Information Administration, Annual Energy Review, 1993.

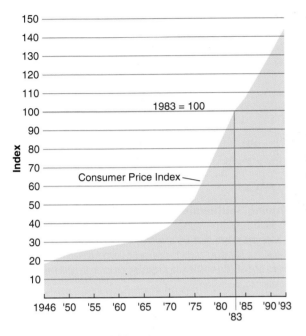

Inflation, 1946–1993
Inflation, which had been moderate during the two decades following the Second World War, began to soar with the escalation of the war in Vietnam in the mid-1960s. In 1979 and 1980 the nation experienced double-digit inflation in two consecutive years for the first time since World War I.

wealthy to invest in art and real estate instead of technology and factories. More plants shut down, industrial jobs dwindled, and millions of displaced workers lost their savings, their health and pension benefits, and their homes.

Throughout 1971 Nixon lurched from policy to policy. Declaring "I am now a Keynesian," he increased deficit spending to stimulate the private sector; gross national product spurted, as did the budget deficit, but economic decline continued. Nixon devalued the dollar, allowing it to "float" in international monetary exchanges in a desperate attempt to correct the balance-of-payment deficit. Finally, he froze wages, prices, and rents for ninety days, a Band-Aid that worked until after the 1972 election. Then Nixon again reversed course, replacing controls with voluntary—and ineffective—guidelines. Inflation and sluggish growth would dog the U.S. economy throughout the decade.

Law and Order

Despite his public appeals for unity, Nixon actually intensified social tensions when he tried to outflank George Wallace and appeal to southern whites, northern ethnics, blue-collar workers, and suburbanites—voters that political strategist Kevin Phillips vividly described as "in motion between a Democratic past and a Republican future." This strategy included a tough stand against crime, drug use, and radicalism.

To combat the militants he despised, Nixon used full federal government resources. The Internal Revenue Service (IRS) audited their tax returns; the Small Business Administration denied them loans; and the FBI illegally wiretapped them. The Justice Department and the FBI worked with local officials to disrupt and immobilize Black Panthers. The CIA illegally investigated and compiled dossiers on thousands of American citizens. The Department of Justice prosecuted antiwar activists and militant blacks in highly publicized trials.

In 1970 Nixon widened his offensive against the antiwar movement by approving the Huston Plan, which would use the CIA and FBI in various illegal missions. The plan called for extensive wiretapping and electronic surveillance, break-ins to find or plant evidence of illegal activity, and a new agency to centralize domestic covert operations under White House supervision. But FBI chief J. Edgar Hoover opposed the Huston Plan as a threat to the FBI's independence. Blocked, Nixon secretly created his own White House unit to discredit his opposition and to ensure executive security. Nicknamed the plumbers because of their assignment to plug government leaks, the team was headed by ex-FBI agent G. Gordon Liddy and former CIA operative E. Howard Hunt.

The plumbers first targeted Daniel Ellsberg, a former Defense Department analyst who had turned over to the press the Pentagon Papers, a secret documentary history of U.S. involvement in Vietnam. On June 13, 1971, the *New York Times* began publishing the Pentagon Papers, which revealed a long history of government lies to foreign leaders, Congress, and the American people.

Although the papers contained nothing damaging about his administration, Nixon feared that they would undermine public trust in government and establish a precedent for publishing classified material. The Supreme Court ultimately ruled that the documents' publication was protected under the First Amendment. Livid, Nixon directed the Justice Department to indict Ellsberg for theft and ordered the plumbers to break into the office of Ellsberg's psychiatrist in search of information against the man who had become an instant hero to the antiwar movement.

The Southern Strategy

While attacking radicalism, Nixon courted whites upset by the drive for racial equality. The administration opposed extension of the Voting Rights Act of 1965, sought to cripple enforcement of the Fair Housing Act of 1968, pleaded for the postponement of desegregation in Mississippi schools, and filed suits to prohibit the busing of children to desegregate schools. In 1971 when the Supreme Court upheld busing as a constitutional and necessary tactic, Nixon condemned the ruling and asked Congress to enact a moratorium on busing.

The strategy of wooing white southerners dictated Nixon's Supreme Court nominations. To reverse the Warren court's liberalism, he sought strict constructionists, judges who would not "meddle" in social issues or be "soft" on criminals. In 1969 he appointed Warren Burger as chief justice. Nixon then tried to appoint a Deep South conservative, but the Senate rejected both of his nominees. However, by 1972 Nixon had succeeded in appointing to the Supreme Court three justices with reputations as strict constructionists: Harry Blackmun of Minnesota, Lewis Powell of Virginia, and William Rehnquist of Arizona. The Nixon appointees would steer the court in a moderate direction. Although ruling liberally in cases involving abortion, desegregation, and the death penalty, the Burger court would shift to the right in rulings on civil liberties, community censorship, and police power.

As the 1970 elections neared, Nixon encouraged his vice president, Spiro T. Agnew, to step up

Driving Southward and Backward
To outflank George Wallace and win the votes of both southern whites and urban blue-collar workers in the North, Nixon's "southern strategy" included delaying school desegregation plans and strong opposition to busing children to achieve racial balance in the schools.

attacks on the liberal opposition. Agnew assailed students as "parasites of passions," Democrats as "sniveling hand-wringers," intellectuals as "an effete corps of intellectual snobs," and the news media as "nattering nabobs of negativism." Liberals deplored Agnew's alarming alliterative allegations, but much of the country found them on target. The 1970 elections were a draw, with the Democrats gaining nine House seats and the Republicans two Senate seats.

THE CRISIS OF THE PRESIDENCY

In his second inaugural, Nixon pledged to make the next four years "the best four years in American history." Ironically, they would rank among its sorriest. His vice president would resign in disgrace, his closest confidants would go to jail, and he would serve barely a year and a half of his second term before resigning to avoid impeachment.

The Election of 1972

Nixon's reelection in 1972 appeared certain. He counted on his diplomatic successes and his winding down of the Vietnam War to win over moderate voters. He expected his southern strategy and law-and-order posture to attract Wallace voters. Continuing Democratic divisions boosted Nixon's optimism. Nixon's only major worry, another third-party candidacy by George Wallace, vanished on May 15, 1972. During a campaign stop, Wallace was shot and paralyzed from the waist down. He withdrew from the race, leaving Nixon a monopoly on the white backlash.

The Senate's most outspoken dove, George McGovern of South Dakota, capitalized on the support of antiwar activists to blitz the Democratic primaries. New party rules requiring state delegations to include minority, female, and youthful delegates in approximate proportion to their numbers aided the liberal McGovern. A disapproving labor leader complained about "too much hair and not enough cigars at this convention," but McGovern won the nomination on the first ballot.

Perceptions of McGovern as inept and radical drove away all but the most committed supporters. After pledging to stand behind his vice-presidential running mate, Thomas Eagleton, "1,000 percent" when it became known that Eagleton had received electric-shock therapy for depression, McGovern dumped him and was embarrassed when several prominent Democrats declined to run with him. McGovern's endorsement of income redistribution, decriminalization of marijuana, immediate withdrawal from Vietnam, a $30 billion defense-budget cut, and pardons for those who had fled the United States to avoid the draft exposed him to GOP ridicule as the candidate of the radical fringe.

Meanwhile, Nixon, remembering his narrow loss to Kennedy in 1960 as well as his narrow victory in 1968, left no stone unturned. He created the Committee to Re-Elect the President (CREEP) to do everything necessary to ensure his reelection, and he appointed Attorney General John Mitchell as its head. Millions in contributions financed a series of "dirty tricks" that spread dissension among Democrats and paid for a special espionage unit to spy on the opposition. Led by Liddy and Hunt of the White House plumbers, the Republican undercover team received Mitchell's approval to wiretap

telephones at the Democratic National Committee headquarters in the Watergate apartment and office complex in Washington. Early one morning in June 1972, a security guard foiled the break-in to install the bugs. Arrested were James McCord, the security coordinator of CREEP, and several other Liddy and Hunt associates.

A White House cover-up began immediately. Publicly, Nixon stated "categorically" that "no one in the White House staff, no one in this administration, presently employed, was involved in this bizarre incident." Privately, Nixon ordered staff members to expunge Hunt's name from the White House telephone directory, to buy the silence of those arrested with $400,000 in hush money and hints of a presidential pardon, and to direct the CIA to halt the FBI's investigation of the Watergate break-in on the pretext that the inquiry would damage national security.

With the McGovern campaign a shambles and Watergate seemingly contained, Nixon won the election overwhelmingly, amassing nearly 61 percent of the popular vote and 520 electoral votes. Strongly supported only by minorities and low-income voters, McGovern carried just Massachusetts and the District of Columbia. The election solidified the 1968 realignment.

However, the GOP gained only twelve seats in the House and lost two in the Senate. The outcome demonstrated the growing difficulty of unseating incumbents, the prevalence of ticket splitting among voters, and the decline of party loyalty. Only 55.7 percent of eligible voters went to the polls, down from 63.8 percent in 1960. Whether indifferent to politics or disenchanted with the choices offered, a growing number of citizens no longer bothered to participate in the electoral process.

The Watergate Upheaval

The scheme to conceal links between the White House and the accused Watergate burglars had succeeded during the 1972 campaign. But after the election, federal judge John Sirica refused to accept the defendants' claim that they had acted on their own. Threatening severe prison sentences, Sirica coerced James McCord of CREEP into confessing that highly placed White House aides knew in advance of the break-in and that the defendants had committed perjury during the trial. Two *Washington Post* reporters, Carl Bernstein and Bob Woodward, following clues furnished by "Deep Throat," an unnamed informant, wrote a succession of front-page stories tying the break-in to illegal contributions and "dirty tricks" by CREEP.

In February 1973 the Senate established the Special Committee on Presidential Campaign Activities to investigate. As the trail of revelations led closer to the Oval Office, Nixon fired his special counsel, John Dean, who refused to be a scapegoat, and announced the resignations of his principal aides, H. R. Haldeman and John Ehrlichman. Pledging to get to the bottom of the scandal, he appointed Secretary of Defense Elliott Richardson, a Boston patrician of unassailable integrity, as his new attorney general and bowing to Senate demands, instructed Richardson to appoint a special Watergate prosecutor with broad powers of investigation and subpoena. Richardson selected Archibald Cox, a Harvard law professor and Democrat.

In May the special Senate committee began a televised investigation. Chaired by Sam Ervin of North Carolina, an expert on constitutional law, the hearings revealed the existence of the "enemies list," the president's use of governmental agencies to harass his opponents, and administration favors in return for illegal campaign donations. Most damaging to Nixon, the hearings exposed the White House's active involvement in the Watergate cover-up. But the Senate still lacked concrete evidence of the president's criminality, the "smoking gun" that would prove Nixon's guilt. Because it was simply his word against that of John Dean, who testified that Nixon personally directed the cover-up, the president expected to survive the crisis.

Then another presidential aide revealed that Nixon had installed a secret taping system that recorded all conversations in the Oval Office. The Ervin committee and Cox insisted on access to the tapes, but Nixon refused, claiming executive privilege. In October, when Cox sought a court order to obtain the tapes, Nixon ordered Attorney General Richardson to fire him. Richardson resigned in protest, as did the deputy attorney general, leaving the third-ranking official in the Department of Justice to dump Cox. The furor raised by the "Saturday Night Massacre" sent Nixon's public-approval rating plunging downward. As Nixon named a new special prosecutor, Leon Jaworski, the House Judiciary Committee began impeachment proceedings.

h c Primary Source: Nixon Incriminates Himself

A President Disgraced

Adding to Nixon's woes that October, Vice President Agnew, charged with income-tax evasion and acceptance of bribes, pleaded no contest—"the full equivalent of a plea of guilty," according to the trial judge. Agnew left office with a three-year suspended sentence and a $10,000 fine. House minority leader Gerald R. Ford replaced Agnew.

In March 1974 Jaworski and the House Judiciary Committee subpoenaed the president for the tape recordings of Oval Office conversations after the Watergate break-in. Nixon released edited transcripts of the tapes, filled with gaps and the phrase "expletive deleted." Despite the excisions, the president emerged as petty and vindictive.

Nixon's sanitized version of the tapes satisfied neither Jaworski nor the House Judiciary Committee. Both pressed for unedited tapes. In late July the Supreme Court rebuffed the president's claim of executive privilege. Chief Justice Burger cited the president's obligation to provide evidence necessary for the due process of law and ordered Nixon to release the unexpurgated tapes.

In late July the House Judiciary Committee adopted three articles of impeachment, accusing the president of obstruction of justice for impeding the Watergate investigation; abuse of power, especially his partisan use of the FBI and IRS; and of contempt of Congress for refusing to obey a congressional subpoena for the tapes.

Checkmated, Nixon conceded in a televised address on August 5 that he had withheld relevant evidence. He then surrendered the tapes, which contained the smoking gun proving that the president had ordered the cover-up, obstructed justice, sub-

Chronology

1960	Birth-control pill marketed.
1964	Berkeley Free Speech Movement.
	The Beatles arrive in the United States. "I Want to Hold Your Hand" tops the charts.
1966	Abolition of automatic student deferments from the draft.
1967	Israeli-Arab Six-Day War.
1968	Tet offensive.
	President Lyndon Johnson announces that he will not seek reelection.
	Martin Luther King, Jr., assassinated; race riots sweep nation.
	Student strike at Columbia University.
	Robert F. Kennedy assassinated.
	Violence mars Democratic convention in Chicago.
	My Lai massacre.
	Vietnam peace talks open in Paris.
	Richard Nixon elected president.
1969	*Apollo 11* lands first Americans on the moon.
	Nixon begins withdrawal of U.S. troops from Vietnam.
	Woodstock festival.
	March Against Death in Washington, D.C.
1970	United States invades Cambodia.
	Students killed at Kent State University and Jackson State College.
	Nixon proposes Huston Plan.
	Environmental Protection Agency established.
	Earth Day first celebrated.
1971	United States invades Laos.
	New York Times publishes Pentagon Papers.
	Nixon institutes wage-and-price freeze.
	South Vietnam invades Laos.
1972	Nixon visits China and the Soviet Union.
	Strategic Arms Limitation Talks (SALT I) agreement approved.
	Watergate break-in.
	Nixon reelected in landslide victory.
	Christmas bombing of North Vietnam.
1973	Vietnam cease-fire agreement signed.
	Trial of Watergate burglars.
	Senate establishes Special Committee on Presidential Campaign Activities to investigate Watergate.
	President Salvador Allende murdered in Chile.
	Vice President Spiro Agnew resigns; Gerald Ford appointed vice president.
	Roe v. *Wade*.
	Yom Kippur War; Organization of Petroleum Exporting Countries (OPEC) begins embargo of oil to the West.
	Saturday Night Massacre.
1974	Supreme Court orders Nixon to release Watergate tapes.
	House Judiciary Committee votes to impeach Nixon.
	Nixon resigns; Ford becomes president.

verted one government agency to prevent another from investigating a crime, and lied about his role for more than two years.

Impeachment and conviction were now certain. On August 9, 1974, Richard M. Nixon became the first American president to resign. Gerald Ford took office as the nation's first chief executive who had not been elected either president or vice president.

CONCLUSION ACE Practice Test

Baby boomers took material comfort and their own importance for granted. Longing for meaning in their lives and personal liberty, they sought a more humane democracy, a less racist and materialistic society, and an end to the war in Vietnam, and they reveled in "sex, drugs, and rock-and-roll." The United States did become a more tolerant and open society and the war in Vietnam did finally end, but not before it claimed a second presidential casualty, Richard Nixon.

The youth rebellion and the war in Vietnam brought politics to a boil in 1968, costing Lyndon Johnson the White House, making Richard Nixon president by a narrow margin, and triggering a major political realignment. Pursuing realpolitik,

Nixon withdrew U.S. troops from Vietnam, lessened Cold War hostilities, and pursued a domestic program that courted the white backlash.

But soon his secret schemes against his political "enemies" began to unravel. The arrest of the Watergate burglars and the attempted cover-up of White House involvement led to the indictment of nearly fifty administration officials, the jailing of scores of Nixon's associates, and a House Judiciary Committee vote to impeach the president himself. To avoid certain conviction, Nixon resigned. Despite the Ford administration's soothing continuity and solidity, a deepening public distrust of politicians and disillusionment with government grew.

FURTHER READING

David Allyn, *Make Love, Not War: The Sexual Revolution, An Unfettered History* (2000). A well-written and illuminating narrative.

Howard Brick, *Age of Contradiction: American Thought and Culture in the 1960s* (2000). An excellent, insightful survey.

Alice Echols, *Scars of Sweet Paradise: The Life and Times of Janis Joplin* (1999). A fascinating biography that sheds much light on the history of the counterculture.

Ignacio Garcia, *Chicanismo: The Forging of a Militant Ethos Among Mexican Americans* (2000). A balanced assessment of this vital development.

Paul Lyons, *New Left, New Right, and the Legacy of the Sixties* (1996). A fair overview filled with acute observations and interpretations.

Melvin Small, *The Presidency of Richard Nixon* (1999). The best overview to date.

David Szamarty, *Rockin' in Time: A Social History of Rock-and-Roll* (1999). A fresh, and refreshing, account.

James E. Westheider, *Fighting on Two Fronts: African Americans and the Vietnam War* (1997). A comprehensive and engaging analysis.

Progreso, by Jesse Treviño, 1977

Society, Politics, and World Events from Ford to Reagan, 1974–1989

CHAPTER OUTLINE

hc This icon will direct you to additional study and research resources at http://college.hmco.com/history/us/boyer/enduring_concise/5e/students/index.html

Discount chains such as Wal-Mart changed mass marketing in the United States after 1960. During the 1970s high unemployment and high inflation eroded consumer buying power in conventional stores, and Wal-Mart's rock-bottom prices were a boon to low-income families. One hundred shares of stock bought for $1,650 in 1970 soared to a value of $3 million by 1990. Sam Walton, the chain's founder, became both rich and famous; in 1992 he received the Medal of Freedom, the nation's highest civilian award.

Wal-Mart, like the other discount chains, had its critics. For example, Wal-Mart fought off unionization of its low-paid employees by establishing a profit-sharing plan. Its most vociferous critics were small-town merchants driven

**This chapter focuses on
five major questions:**

▶ How were the cultural climate and social
activism of 1974–1989 influenced by the
1960s?

▶ What social developments most affected
farmers, middle-class women, African-
Americans, and Native Americans in these
years, and how did patterns of immigration
change?

▶ What core beliefs shaped Ronald Reagan's
political ideology, and what steps did his
administration take to translate this ideology into practice?

▶ How did U.S.-Soviet relations evolve from
the late 1970s through 1988?

▶ In what respects did the international situation improve during these years, from the
U.S. perspective, and in what ways did it
grow more threatening?

out of business by Wal-Mart's aggressive high
volume, price-slashing approach to marketing.
Nonetheless, by 1997 Wal-Mart had more than five
thousand stores with annual sales of nearly $100
billion.

The Wal-Mart phenomenon was part of a transformation of the American economy in the 1970s
and 1980s. The service sector grew rapidly as discount stores and fast-food outlets spread, and
high-tech industries prospered. But the "old economy"—steel mills, auto plants, and factories in the
industrial heartland—grew weaker, battered by
imports. For many dependent on the industrial
economy, the American dream seemed to fade.

This chapter, which traces American history
from the Nixon resignation to the end of the second Reagan administration, 1974–1989, focuses on
two key themes: the continuing impact of the

1960s on U.S. culture and politics, and the continuing importance of events abroad despite the end
of the Vietnam war.

THE LONG SHADOW OF THE 1960S: CULTURAL CHANGES AND CONTINUITIES

Both the afterglow of the 1960s activism and reaction against that turbulent decade shaped American social and cultural trends in the 1970s and beyond. Environmentalism and feminism gained
ground, but the violence that scarred the years
from 1968 to 1970 turned many young adults toward personal goals and materialism. Radicals in
the 1960s had celebrated sexual freedom and feminists had demanded reproductive choice, but the
post-1970 years brought sexual caution as acquired immune deficiency syndrome (AIDS) took a
fearsome toll and abortion rights became the center of fierce debate. Individuals unsettled by rapid
change sought moral certitude and spiritual solace, and organized religion prospered.

The Post-1960s Mood: Personal Preoccupations; New Activist Energies

On the Left, the wreckage of the Kennedy-Johnson
liberal consensus and the fragmentation of the New
Left produced a vacuum of political leadership; on
the Right, the Watergate debacle temporarily had
the same effect. With politics in disarray, personal
concerns beckoned. The "campus radical" of the
sixties became the "yuppie" (young urban professional), preoccupied with physical fitness and
material consumption. But self-absorption too frequently became selfishness; writer Tom Wolfe
christened yuppies the "Me Generation."

Average daily TV viewing crept upward from six
hours in 1970 to seven hours by 1990. Prime-time
soap operas such as *Dallas*, chronicling the steamy
affairs of a mythical Texas oil family, engrossed millions. Cable television featured specialized programming for everything from the stock market to

rock music, and the major networks watched their market share shrink. Disneyworld, opened in Florida in 1982, thrived, while blockbuster movies such as *Jaws, Close Encounters of the Third Kind, E.T.*, and *Star Wars* offered escapist fare for millions. Professional sports drew huge television audiences, and superstar sports celebrities won multimillion-dollar salaries and product endorsements. The politically engaged songs of the 1960s gave way to bland disco music. A fitting symbol for this aspect of the 1970s, historian Bruce Schulman suggested, was the pet rock, "which just sat there doing nothing."

Videocassette recorders (VCRs) allowed Americans to tape TV shows for later viewing and to rent movies. By the early 1990s, 70 percent of U.S. households had VCRs. Entertainment became privatized as families could "go to the movies" at home. Using laser beams to digitize sound waves, compact discs (CDs) offered remarkably high-quality sound.

And the personal computer arrived. In the late 1970s two young Californians, Steven Jobs and Stephen Wozniak, reduced computers from room size to desk-top size and marketed the phenomenally successful Apple computer. As Apple sales shot up, computer manufacturers multiplied, especially in California's "Silicon Valley." In 1981 IBM launched its PC (personal computer) and quickly grabbed 40 percent of the market, but computer entrepreneurs continued to proliferate. By 1997, 44 percent of American households owned personal computers.

American life in these years was not all escapism and technological novelties. The protest mood of the 1960s survived. The songs of Bruce Springsteen evoked the stresses of blue-collar life and offered a bleak view of widening class divisions in post-Vietnam, post-Watergate America. Bob Dylan, best known for his 1960s protest songs, produced some of his best work in the 1970s. His 1974 album *Blood on the Tracks* expressed distrust of authority and the difficulty of personal relationships while celebrating outlaws and outsiders who defied the established order.

Along with escapist fare, directors also produced some brilliant films exploring the darker side of American life in the 1970s. Robert Altman's *Nashville* (1975) offered a disturbing vision of cynical mass-culture producers, manipulative politicians, and lonely, alienated drifters. Roman Polanski's *Chinatown* (1974) probed the personal and political corruption beneath the sunny surface of Southern California life.

The Environmental Movement Gains Support

The movement to protect the environment against the effects of heedless exploitation, a legacy of the 1960s, built upon a decade of activism triggered by Rachel Carson's *Silent Spring* of 1962, the environmental laws of the 1960s, and the inauguration of Earth Day in 1970.

Greenpeace was founded in 1971 when Canadian activists protested a planned U.S. nuclear test at Amchitka Island in the Bering Sea. Addressing a range of environmental issues, including the preservation of old-growth forests and protection of the world's oceans, by 2000 Greenpeace had 2.5 million members worldwide. The Save the Whales campaign, launched by the Animal Welfare Institute in 1971, mobilized opposition to the killing of the world's largest mammals to provide pet food for dogs and cats.

In the later 1970s environmentalists targeted the nuclear-power industry. Reviving protest techniques first used in the civil-rights and antiwar campaigns, activists across America staged rallies at planned nuclear-power plants. The movement crested in 1979 when a partial meltdown crippled the Three Mile Island nuclear-power plant in Pennsylvania.

The Women's Movement: Gains and Uncertainties

Of all the legacies of the 1960s, perhaps the most far-reaching was a revitalized women's movement. Millions of young, middle-class women had begun to reexamine their subordinate status in society. The fifty thousand members of NOW (National Organization for Women), feminist support groups, and *Ms.* and other magazines spread the message.

Activism meant political clout—exemplified by the National Women's Political Caucus (1971), which promoted a feminist agenda. By 1972 many states had liberalized their abortion laws and outlawed gender discrimination in hiring. That same year, Congress passed the Equal Rights Amendment (ERA) to the Constitution: "equality of rights under the law shall not be denied or abridged by the United States or any State on the basis of sex." Twenty-eight states quickly ratified it, and adoption seemed sure. In 1973 the Supreme Court, in *Roe* v. *Wade,* proclaimed women's constitutional right to abortion; the decision relied heavily on the right to privacy, grounded in the due-process clause of the Fourteenth Amendment.

By the early 1980s, however, the women's movement had splintered as moderates deplored the radicals' sometimes strident rhetoric. Betty Friedan's *The Second Stage* (1981) urged feminists who had downgraded family values to incorporate family issues into their campaign rather than leave this potent agenda to their opponents.

By 1992, 58 percent of women worked outside the home, up from 35 percent in 1960, as the through-the-roof cost of living sent women into the work force to supplement family income. Many women workers remained at the low end of the wage scale. Increasing numbers, however, entered corporate management and professions such as law and medicine. Top management remained primarily a masculine preserve as women encountered "the glass ceiling." Conservatives increasingly voiced fears about the breakdown of the family.

The baby boom yielded to the baby bust as birthrates reached a low in 1976. By 1980 the statistically average American family had 1.6 children. The number of unmarried couples living together rose steadily, reaching 2.8 million by 1990, and the divorce rate catapulted to 480 per 1,000 marriages, up from 258 per 1,000 in 1960.

Feminists recognized that a long road lay ahead in overcoming ingrained gender discrimination. Working women's wages still lagged behind those of men. Gender segregation of the workplace largely persisted. Nursing and secretarial work remained overwhelmingly female, and, despite inroads by women, men still dominated high-prestige professions, especially at the upper ranks.

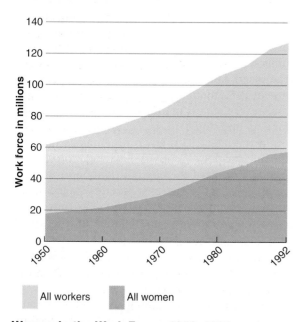

All workers   All women

Women in the Work Force, 1950–1992:
After 1960 the proportion of American women who were gainfully employed surged upward. As a result, young women coming of age in the 1990s had far different expectations about their lives than had their grandmothers or even their mothers.

Sources: *Statistical Abstract of the United States*, 1988 (Washington, D.C.: U.S. Government Printing Office, 1987), 373; *World Almanac and Book of Facts*, 1989 (New York: Pharos Books, 1988), 152; *Statistical Abstract of the United States, 1993* (Washington, D.C., U.S. Government Printing Office, 1993), 400, 401

Changing Patterns of Sexual Behavior; the Looming Specter of AIDS

The long shadow of the 1960s was evident in the realm of sexual behavior. The 1960s counterculture had challenged the prevailing sexual code, and the loosening of old taboos that resulted had long-lasting effects. In 1960 about 30 percent of unwed nineteen-year-old U.S. women had sexual experience. By 1980 more than half did, and the figure soared still higher by 2000. The number of unmarried couples living together jumped from 523,000 in 1970 to 3.5 million by 1993. This trend, too, accelerated as the twentieth century wore on. Beginning in the early 1970s, many gay men and women "came out of the closet" to acknowledge their sexual orientation openly. In 1977 "Gay Pride" marches drew seventy-five thousand marchers in New York City and three hundred thousand in San Francisco, a center of gay activism; two years later one hundred thousand participated in the first national gay rights parade in Washington, D.C.

Increasingly lesbians and gays demanded the repeal of anti-gay laws and passage of legislation to protect the rights of homosexuals. Many states and cities repealed laws against same-sex relationships between consenting adults.

The loosening of traditional sexual mores received a jolting setback in the 1980s with the proliferation of sexually transmitted diseases, including AIDS, which was first diagnosed in the United States in 1981. By 1998 more than three hundred eighty thousand Americans had died of AIDS, and a million more carried HIV (human immunodeficiency virus), the causative virus. Public-health officials warned that a vaccine lay far in the future. Although confined largely to sexually active gays and bisexuals, intravenous drug users, and those having intercourse with these high-risk groups, AIDS appeared in the general population, too, and medical authorities warned of the need for caution and the use of condoms. This somber message was driven home in 1991 when basketball superstar Earvin ("Magic") Johnson announced that he had tested positive for HIV.

AIDS provided some Americans with an excuse to express their hatred of homosexuality. Others responded more sympathetically. Research on the mysterious disease received massive funding. Hospices opened to provide care and support for patients, and a quilt bearing the names of AIDS victims toured the nation and grew steadily larger; candlelight marches memorialized the dead.

Fearful of exposure to AIDS, herpes, and other sexually transmitted diseases, Americans grew more cautious in their sexual behavior. The exuberant 1960s slogan "Make Love, Not War" gave way to "Safer Sex."

Conservative Backlash and Evangelical Renaissance

Another legacy of the 1960s was a conservative reaction. An early target was *Roe* v. *Wade*. In the wake of the Supreme Court's legalization of abortion, conservative Protestants and Roman Catholics organized a "Right to Life" movement and pressed for a constitutional amendment outlawing abortion. They charged that abortion was "the murder of the unborn." Congress in 1976 halted Medicaid funding for most abortions, thus putting the procedure out of the reach of the poor. Most feminists took a "pro-choice" stance, arguing that individual women and their doctors, not laws, should dictate the decision. Polls showed that a majority of Americans agreed.

As the women's movement gained visibility, it too faced a backlash. In 1972 President Nixon had vetoed a bill to establish a national network of day-care centers. The ERA died in 1982, three states short of the three-fourths required for ratification.

The gay and lesbian movement particularly inflamed conservatives. Religious conservatives deplored this trend as evidence of society's moral disintegration. Evangelist Jerry Falwell proclaimed, "Homosexuality is . . . so abominable in the sight of God that he destroyed the cities of Sodom and Gomorrah because of this terrible sin." In 1977 singer Anita Bryant led a crusade against a Miami ordinance protecting the civil rights of homosexuals: "God created Adam and Eve, not Adam and Bruce," she said. Miami soon repealed the law, and other cities would follow suit.

A revival of religion and spiritual questing accompanied this conservative reaction. Cults such as the Reverend Sun Myung Moon's Unification Church and the International Society for Krishna Consciousness prospered. Evangelical Protestant denominations, including the 2-million-member Assemblies of God and the 14-million-strong Southern Baptist Convention, grew rapidly. All these groups believed in the Bible's literal truth, in "born-again" religious experience, and in an earthly life governed by personal piety and strict morality.

Evangelical Christians had pursued social reform before the Civil War, and many twentieth-century evangelicals also turned to political activism. In 1980 and 1984 Jerry Falwell's pro-Reagan Moral Majority registered nearly 2 million new voters. While targeting domestic issues—abortion, pornography, and public-school prayer—evangelicals embraced a strongly conservative, anticommunist world view. Falwell disbanded his organization after 1984, but the Reverend Pat Robertson's well-organized Christian Coalition took its place, with the long-range goal of expanding conservative Christian influence at the state and national levels.

Fueling this rejuvenation was a network of Christian bookstores, radio stations featuring religious programming, and, above all, television evangelists. Jerry Falwell, Pat Robertson, Jim and Tammy Bakker, Oral Roberts, and Jimmy Swaggart, among others, accounted for countless hours of broadcasting. Robertson's Christian Broadcasting Network became the nation's fourth-largest cable network. Televangelists repelled many Americans with their endless pleas for money, but millions of others found their spiritual message reassuring.

Sexual and financial scandals tarnished the "electronic church" after 1987, but the influence of evangelical religion continued. In a world of change, evangelicals found certitude in their faith and profoundly influenced American life.

PATTERNS OF SOCIAL CHANGE IN POST-1960s AMERICA

While white, urban, middle-class Americans pursued the good life or embraced reform causes, other groups grappled with economic worries and struggled to move up the ladder. Family farmers became an endangered species amid the proliferation of giant agribusinesses. Although many African-Americans successfully pursued the academic and professional avenues opened by the civil-rights movement, others remained trapped in poverty. While Native Americans continued to face many hurdles, the 1970s brought brighter eco-

nomic prospects and a new assertiveness in pursuing long-ignored treaty rights. New patterns of immigration, meanwhile, changed the nation's ethnic and demographic profile, with profound implications for the future.

Decline of the Family Farm

The family farm, historically revered as the backbone of America, continued its long decline in these years. In 1960 about 6 percent of the U.S. labor force worked on farms; by 1994 the figure was 2.5 percent. The farm population was aging, as young people sought opportunities in the cities. The small-farm operators who still hung on often held second jobs to make ends meet.

Total farm production increased, however, thanks to factory farms and agribusinesses. Big operators bought up failing farms, demolished the homes that had sheltered successive generations, and consolidated them into large-scale operations involving major capital investment and heavy-duty equipment. Mass-production factory farms dominated poultry and hog production. Although politicians paid lip service to the family farm, federal crop subsidy programs accelerated the process of consolidation, as they had since the 1930s.

While the family farm disappeared, movies, novels, and songs kept it vivid in the nation's collective memory. In 1985, country singer Willie Nelson, combining show-business savvy with a genuine desire to help small farmers, began a popular series of annual concerts he called "Farm Aid." By 1999 Farm Aid had contributed nearly $15 million to programs designed to help small farmers survive.

Like much else in the 1970s, the movement to recapture a vanishing rural past owed a debt to the 1960s. As the sixties ended, many members of the counterculture formed rural communes to escape the urban-corporate world and live in harmony with nature. Several thousand rural communes soon arose across America. Periodicals like *The Whole Earth Catalog* and *The Mother Earth News* provided guidance on organic farming and sold simple, hand-operated products for rural living.

The Two Worlds of Black America

The story of African-Americans in these years is really two very different stories. Millions of blacks moved upward as the civil-rights movement opened doors. In 1965 African-American students had accounted for only 5 percent of college enrollment; by 1990, the figure reached 12 percent. And by 1990 some 46 percent of African-American workers held white-collar jobs.

But outside this world lay a second, much grimmer realm of inner-city slums. A third of all African-Americans inhabited this world, in which half the young people never finished high school and the jobless rate hovered around 60 percent.

Economic trends as well as racism played a role. Structural changes in the American economy had eliminated many unskilled jobs once held by the urban poor. Recessions in the 1970s and early 1980s, moreover, battered the already struggling African-American underclass, and job cuts in steel, automaking, and other basic industries hit skilled African-American workers. Demands for a well-educated work force further battered the poor and uneducated, and welfare payments lagged behind the rising cost of living.

Cocaine and other drugs pervaded the inner cities. Some black children recruited as lookouts for drug dealers became dealers themselves when they reached their early teens. With drugs came violence. In the 1980s a young black male was six times as likely to be murdered as a young white male. In 1987 two major youth gangs, the Bloods and the Crips, accounted for more than four hundred killings in Los Angeles. One observer summed up the situation in 1988: "Young black males in America's inner cities are an endangered species. . . . They are [the] rejects of our affluent society."

Single women, most of them young, poor, and uneducated, accounted for 63 percent of all black births in 1988. Millions of them, scarcely more than children, depended on welfare payments for survival. Caught in a cycle of dependence, they raised the specter of a permanent American underclass.

Buffeted by complex social and economic forces, America's predominantly nonwhite inner cities posed a major social challenge. Governments used various strategies to address these problems: "affirmative action" to aid groups previously discriminated against, "set-asides" to guarantee building contracts for minority contractors, and reserved spots for minorities at educational institutions. However, the Supreme Court overturned a California medical school's affirmative-action plan in 1978 and a Richmond, Virginia, set-aside requirement in 1979.

The conservative backlash affected African-Americans. The Reagan administration's general contempt for government fueled a reluctance to use government powers to remedy racial injustice. This governmental foot-dragging came at a time of worsening crisis for the African-American community.

Brightening Prospects for Native Americans

In the 1950s, the federal government had promoted Indians' absorption into the general population. Aroused by this destructive and ill-conceived policy, and influenced by the social-protest climate of the sixties, members of the militant American Indian Movement (AIM) had dramatized their cause by occupying Alcatraz Island in San Francisco Bay in 1969, the Bureau of Indian Affairs in Washington in 1972, and a trading post at Wounded Knee, South Dakota (the site of the 1890 massacre) in 1973.

hc Primary Source: AIM Occupation

Indians' militancy worked. In 1970 President Nixon rejected the "termination" approach and the federal government's traditional paternalism toward Indians and called for greater autonomy for Native Americans. The Indian Self-Determination Act of 1974 granted tribes control of federal-aid programs on reservations and oversight of their schools.

By 1990 more than 1.7 million persons identified themselves as Native Americans, up from 800,000 in 1970. Natural increase could not account for this growth, and census analysts concluded simply that more people than before chose to identify themselves as Indians. This upsurge reflected not only ethnic pride but also advantages associated with tribal membership, such as employment opportunities under affirmative-action guidelines.

Ethnic pride inspired economic development. Tribal ventures ranged from resorts to mining and logging enterprises. Food-processors, electronics firms, and other businesses built factories that created much-needed jobs on tribal lands. Certain tribes took advantage of their exemption from state gambling laws to open casinos, despite opposition from Native Americans who saw the casinos as a threat to Indian culture.

Indian tribes also reasserted long-ignored treaty rights. In 1971 native peoples in Alaska won 40 million acres of land and $1 billion in settlement of long-standing claims. In 1980 the Sioux received $107 million for South Dakota land taken from them illegally a century earlier, and the Penobscots of Maine won claims based on a 1790 law. In 1988 the tiny Puyallup tribe of Washington State was given $162 million to settle claims that the city of Tacoma occupied land granted them by treaty in the 1850s. The Puyallups announced plans to restore the salmon runs of the Puyallup River and to construct a deep-water port on Puget Sound.

High rates of unemployment, alcoholism, and disease persisted for Native Americans. But the renewal of tribal life, new federal policy, and the courts' willingness to honor ancient treaties represented an advance. Movies such as *Little Big Man* (1970) and *Dances with Wolves* (1990) reflected changing attitudes; although they tended to sentimentalize Indian culture, they were a vast improvement over the hostile stereotypes of earlier cowboys-and-Indians films.

New Patterns of Immigration

America's population growth—from 204 million in 1970 to more than 275 million in 2000—reflected a steady influx of both legal and illegal immigrants. Whereas most immigrants once came from Europe, 45 percent of the new immigrants hailed from the Western Hemisphere and 30 percent from Asia.

Immigration and a high birthrate made Hispanics the nation's fastest-growing ethnic group. In 1997 the Hispanic population stood at more than 27 mil-

lion, up from 9 million in 1970. Mexican-Americans concentrated in the Southwest, while Cubans, Puerto Ricans, and other West Indians lived mainly in New York, Florida, Illinois, and New Jersey.

Desperate economic conditions drove these newcomers to America. The collapse of world oil prices intensified unemployment and chronic poverty in Mexico during the 1980s, spurring many to seek opportunity in the north. These recent immigrants often faced hardship and poverty. In 1990 nearly 20 percent of Mexican-Americans and 30 percent of Puerto Ricans lived below the poverty line.

Proud of their language and traditions, Hispanic newcomers influenced U.S. culture. In some areas of Los Angeles, home to nearly a million Mexican-Americans, one could drive for miles in the 1980s and see only Spanish business signs and movie marquees. Large parts of Miami seemed wholly Hispanic.

By 1990 estimates of the number of illegal immigrants in the United States ranged as high as 12 million. Working long hours under harsh conditions with few legal protections, these impoverished immigrants, primarily Mexican and Haitian, sweated in the garment trades, cleaned homes and cared for children, and bent their backs in agricultural fields. The Immigration Reform and Control Act of 1986 outlawed the hiring of illegal immigrants and strengthened immigration controls at the border. The law also offered legal status to those immigrants who could prove that they had lived in the United States since January 1, 1982.

Immigration from Asia rose as newcomers from Korea, Vietnam, and the Philippines arrived in California and migrated eastward. These newest Americans worked hard, sought higher education, and moved up rapidly. All these trends made contemporary America a far more diverse and vibrant place than it had been a generation earlier.

YEARS OF MALAISE: POST-WATERGATE POLITICS AND DIPLOMACY, 1974–1980

With Richard Nixon's graceless exit from the presidency, the nation lost spirit and direction. His successors, Republican Gerald R. Ford and Democrat Jimmy Carter, grappled with a tangle of domestic and foreign problems—inflation, unemployment, and recession—and a foreboding sense of limits gripped many Americans.

Globally the years from 1974 to 1980 brought humiliations, from the withdrawal from Vietnam to the seizures of American hostages in Iran. The stark simplicities of the Cold War blurred as complex problems arose in the Third World (Asia, the Middle East, Africa, and Latin America).

Americans felt adrift in an increasingly hostile world. Long convinced that it was immune to the historical forces that hedged in other societies, the United States now seemed buffeted by forces beyond its control. By 1980 accumulating frustration and anger were generating a powerful political revolt.

The Caretaker Presidency of Gerald Ford, 1974–1976

Gerald Ford became president on August 9, 1974, after Richard M. Nixon's resignation. A former Michigan congressman who had served as Republican minority leader before becoming vice president, Ford displayed human decency, if little evidence of brilliance. Most Americans found him a welcome relief after Nixon. Only a month into his term, however, Ford strained his popularity by pardoning Nixon for "any and all crimes" committed while in office, thus shielding the ex-president from prosecution for his Watergate role. Ford insisted that the pardon would help to heal the body politic, but many Americans were outraged.

More conservative than Nixon on domestic issues, Ford vetoed environmental, social-welfare, and public-interest measures, but the heavily Democratic Congress overrode most of the vetoes. Economic problems especially bedeviled Ford. Oil prices had shot up in 1973 as a result of the Arab oil embargo and OPEC (Organization of Petroleum Exporting Countries) price hikes. These blows fell hard on the United States, which imported one-third of its oil. The soaring cost of gasoline, home heating oil, and other petroleum-based products worsened already serious inflation. Consumer prices rose 12 percent in 1974 and 11 percent in 1975.

In October 1974 Ford initiated a program of voluntary restraint called Whip Inflation Now (WIN), but prices continued to rise. When the Federal Reserve attempted to cool the economy by raising the discount rate, a severe recession resulted in 1974–1975. Unemployment climbed to nearly 11 percent in 1975, tax receipts dropped as business stagnated, and the federal deficit increased. Although Ford proposed a tax cut and measures to coax consumer spending, economic headaches persisted.

The oil crisis battered the U.S. auto industry. Americans stopped buying gas-guzzlers and turned to smaller, more fuel-efficient imports. General Motors, Ford, and Chrysler laid off 225,000 workers in 1974, and imports doubled their share of the U.S. market, reaching 33 percent by 1980.

In April 1975 battered American morale suffered a heavy blow when the South Vietnamese government fell. The triumphant northerners swiftly changed the name of Saigon to Ho Chi Minh City. TV chronicled desperate helicopter evacuations from the roof of the U. S. Embassy. A few weeks later, the new communist government in Cambodia seized an American merchant ship, the *Mayagüez*. Ford ordered a military rescue that freed the thirty-nine *Mayagüez* crewmen but cost the lives of forty-one U.S. servicemen.

Americans found little to cheer as the nation entered 1976, an election year and the bicentennial of the Declaration of Independence.

The Outsider as Insider: President Jimmy Carter, 1977–1980

President Ford won the Republican nomination in 1976. The Democratic nomination went to a little-known Georgia politician and peanut farmer, Jimmy Carter, who carried out a brilliant primary campaign. The folksy Carter made a virtue of his status as an outsider to Washington, pledged never to lie to the American people, and freely avowed his "born-again" Christianity.

The Democrats won by a narrow margin—49.9 percent of the popular vote to Ford's 47.9 and 297 electoral votes to the Republican's 240. The vote broke sharply along class lines: the well-to-do voted heavily for Ford; the disadvantaged, overwhelmingly for Carter. The Georgian swept the South and received 90 percent of the African-American vote.

As president, Carter rejected the trappings of what some in Nixon's day had called the imperial presidency. On inauguration day, he walked from the Capitol to the White House. In an attempt to echo FDR's radio chats, he later delivered some televised speeches from an easy chair by a fireplace.

But such symbolism could not ensure a successful presidency. Because Carter had entered the White House without a clear political philosophy, liberals and conservatives alike claimed him. Moreover, the intensely private Carter relied on a tight circle of young staff members from Georgia and avoided socializing with politicians. "Carter couldn't get the Pledge of Allegiance through Congress," groused one legislator. Disciplined and intelligent, Carter focused well on specific problems but lacked a larger political vision.

In his first year Carter used a tax cut and public-works programs to fight the recession. The unemployment rate dropped to 5 percent by late 1978. However, Carter showed little sympathy for social-welfare measures involving federal spending. Carter also introduced administrative reforms in civil service and the executive branch early in his presidency. But poor relations with Congress frustrated his attempts to promote national health insurance, to overhaul the welfare system, and to reform loophole-ridden income-tax laws. Responding to major social movements, he did appoint a substantial number of women and members of minority groups to federal judgeships.

Environmental issues loomed large for Carter and for many Americans, particularly with the eruption of a major environmental crisis in Niagara Falls, New York. For years the Hooker Chemical and Plastics Corporation had dumped tons of waste products in a district known as the Love Canal. In 1953, as the landfill reached capacity,

Hooker covered the site with earth and sold it to the city; houses, apartment buildings, and schools soon sprang up. Residents complained of strange odors and of substances oozing from the ground, and in the late 1970s tests confirmed that a witches' brew of toxic chemicals, including dioxin, was seeping into basements, polluting the air, and discharging into the Niagara River. Love Canal inhabitants had elevated rates of miscarriage, cancer, and birth defects.

By 1980 Carter had declared Love Canal a national emergency, making available federal funds for relocation of families and for clean-up. The fact that Love Canal lay just a few miles from Niagara Falls, once a symbol of America's unspoiled wilderness, added both irony and poignancy to the situation.

Carter did better on foreign affairs, but even here the negatives outweighed the positives. Carter and his secretary of state, Cyrus Vance, worked vigorously to inject human rights into foreign policy and to combat abuses in Chile, Argentina, Ethiopia, South Africa, and other nations. Human-rights violations by American allies such as South Korea and the Philippines received far more gingerly treatment. Trying to adapt U.S. policy to a multipolar world, Carter also sought better relations with the new black nations of Africa.

Carter also pursued initiatives launched by his predecessors. Earlier administrations had begun negotiating a more equitable treaty relationship with Panama. The Carter administration completed negotiations on two treaties transferring the Panama Canal and the Canal Zone to the Panamanians by 1999. Although the agreements protected U.S. interests, conservatives attacked them as proof of the United States' post-Vietnam loss of nerve. In 1977 the Senate ratified both treaties.

The strengthening of ties with China accelerated after Mao Zedong's death in 1976. Carter initiated full diplomatic relations with the People's Republic of China on January 1, 1979, opening the door to scientific, cultural, and commercial exchanges. Toward the Soviet Union, Carter showed both toughness and conciliation. In 1979 Carter and Brezhnev signed SALT II. Critics, however, charged that the agreement favored the Soviets, and after the U.S.S.R. invaded neighboring Afghanistan in January 1980, Carter withdrew the treaty from the Senate and took a series of hard-line measures against the Soviet Union, including a boycott of the 1980 Moscow Olympics. This get-tough policy reflected the views of Carter's national security adviser, Zbigniew Brzezinski, a Polish-born political scientist who harbored hostility toward the Soviet Union and viewed détente with suspicion.

The Middle East: Peace Accords and Hostages

Carter's proudest achievement and his most bitter setback both came in the Middle East. In September 1978 he hosted Egyptian leader Anwar el-Sadat and Israeli leader Menachem Begin at Camp David, where they agreed upon a peace framework; six months later they signed a formal peace treaty which also set a timetable for greater autonomy for Palestinians in the West Bank and Gaza Strip. The president's hopes for a comprehensive Middle East settlement collapsed as the Israeli government continued to build Jewish settlements in the occupied territories, despite fierce Palestinian protests, and Islamic fundamentalists assassinated Sadat in 1981. Nonetheless, Camp David was the high point of Carter's presidency.

The low point of his presidency also came in the Middle East. Protests against the repressive regime headed by the shah of Iran, a long-time American client and ally, swelled throughout 1978 and climaxed in January 1979 as the shah left Iran. Ayatollah Ruhollah Khomeini, who had orchestrated the anti-shah movement from exile in Paris, returned triumphantly to Tehran to impose strict Islamic rule and preach hatred of "the great Satan," the United States.

When Carter allowed the shah to enter the United States for cancer treatment, Khomeini supporters stormed the American embassy in Tehran and seized more than fifty American hostages. For the next 444 days the Carter administration was virtually paralyzed as appalled Americans watched TV images of blindfolded hostages, anti-American mobs, and burning U.S. flags. The hostages were freed on January 20, 1981, as Ronald Reagan took the presidential oath of office.

Iran Hostage Crisis, 1979
As the Iranians staged scenes like this at the U.S. embassy in Tehran for the TV cameras, American frustration soared and President Carter's political fortunes plunged.

Troubles and Frustration at the End of Carter's Term

Inflation reached horrendous levels as Carter's term wore on. Prices vaulted by more than 13 percent in both 1979 and 1980. As OPEC boosted oil prices, Americans who were used to paying $.30 for a gallon of gasoline saw prices edge toward $1 a gallon. Lines formed at gas stations and tempers flared. In 1979 alone, Americans paid $16.4 billion in added costs related to oil-price increases. Carter's Council on Wage and Price Stability urged workers and manufacturers to hold the line, but repeated hikes in oil prices thwarted his efforts.

As the Federal Reserve Board pushed the discount rate higher, bank interest rates reached an unheard of 20 percent by 1980. Mortgages and business loans consequently dried up, and economic activity remained in the doldrums.

Carter had drawn a larger lesson from the oil crisis: that the nation's wasteful consumption of dwindling fossil fuels must yield to conservation. He recognized that two key factors underlying a generation of economic growth—cheap, unlimited energy and the lack of foreign competition—were about to disappear. In 1975 Congress had set fuel-efficiency standards for cars and mandated a national speed limit of fifty-five miles per hour. Convinced that more had to be done, Carter in 1977 had created the Department of Energy and proposed taxes on oil and gasoline consumption, tax credits for conservation measures, and research on alternative energy resources. In 1978 Congress had passed a watered-down energy bill.

Americans turned against the remote figure in the White House. Carter's approval rating plummeted to 26 percent in summer 1979. The president delivered a televised address discussing "national malaise" and "loss of confidence," but the speech only deepened the spreading suspicion that Carter himself was a large part of the problem. By mid-1980 his approval rating had sunk to 23 percent. The Democrats glumly renominated Jimmy Carter in 1980, but defeat in November loomed.

Carter remains a fascinating political figure. His sudden emergence vividly illustrates the power of television, which permitted an unknown candidate to bypass power brokers and interest groups. He seemed to offer the integrity that Americans longed to see restored to the presidency. He identified issues that would dominate the national agenda in the future: energy policy; tax, welfare, and health-care reform; and the need to redefine America's world role. But he lacked the political skills to work well with Congress and to inspire the nation. By the end of his term, a victim of his own flaws and of forces largely beyond his control, Carter was discredited. A post-presidential career devoted to humanitarian service and the resolution of international conflicts restored Carter's reputation and brought him the Nobel Peace Prize in 2002, but few were sorry to see him leave in January 1981.

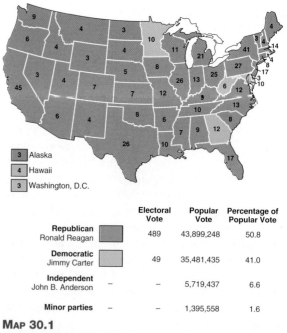

		Electoral Vote	Popular Vote	Percentage of Popular Vote
Republican Ronald Reagan		489	43,899,248	50.8
Democratic Jimmy Carter		49	35,481,435	41.0
Independent John B. Anderson	–	–	5,719,437	6.6
Minor parties	–	–	1,395,558	1.6

MAP 30.1

The Election of 1980

Jimmy Carter's unpopularity and Ronald Reagan's telegenic appeal combined to give Reagan a crushing electoral victory.

THE REAGAN REVOLUTION, 1981–1984

In 1980 voters turned to a presidential candidate who promised to break with the recent past—Ronald Reagan. His unabashed patriotism appealed to a nation still traumatized by Vietnam. His denunciation of "tax-and-spend" policies and his attacks on liberal ideology resonated with millions of Americans.

As president, Reagan revived national pride. His economic policies lowered inflation and triggered a consumer buying spree and a surge of speculative investment. They also laid the groundwork for serious economic difficulties after his departure. President Reagan revived the belligerent rhetoric of the early Cold War, raised the stakes in the arms race with the Soviets, and supplied money and weapons to anticommunist forces in Latin America. But Reagan soon found himself enmeshed in foreign problems that did not easily fit into his Cold War world view.

Background of the Reagan Revolution

Several economic, ideological, and social trends contributed to Reagan's appeal. First, stagflation frightened and angered voters, and Reagan promoted a simple idea: a dramatic tax cut would stimulate the economy, boost federal tax revenues, and achieve a balanced budget. Although George Bush, his chief rival for the Republican nomination, ridiculed these ideas as "voodoo economics," many voters thought them worth trying. Moreover, a belief in self-help and private enterprise had remained entrenched despite the New Deal–Great Society ideology of government activism. Decades of Cold War rhetoric had left Americans determined to remain ahead of the Soviets militarily and to play a forceful world role. Reagan's uncomplicated patriotism and eloquent assertions of the United States' continued greatness soothed a wounded national psyche.

Reagan also embraced the ideology of the New Right: a cultural conservatism stressing social and moral issues. Upset by social turmoil, the sexual revolution, the women's movement, rising rates of divorce and abortion, and "secular humanism," millions of Americans called for a restoration of morality and "traditional values." Jerry Falwell's Moral Majority and other groups eagerly translated public concerns into political action.

Demographics also played a role in Reagan's success. During the 1970s New York, Chicago, and the other cities of the Northeast and upper Midwest had lost population as Texas, Florida, California, and the Sun Belt had grown rapidly. These areas were historically conservative and suspicious of Washington. Westerners had organized the "Sagebrush Revolution" to demand less government control and the return of federal lands to state control.

A skillful actor with a likeable manner and a ready smile, Ronald Reagan combined these themes into a potent message. Belying his sixty-nine years, he exuded youthful zest and jauntiness and offered a jittery nation confident leadership. Time would reveal a considerable gap between substance and image in Reagan's program, but in 1980 a majority of voters found it irresistible.

Reagan grew up in Dixon, Illinois, the son of an alcoholic father and a pious mother. After graduating from Eureka College, he worked as a sports announcer before striking out for Hollywood in 1937. His fifty-four films enjoyed only moderate success, but after 1954 he made a name for himself as a spokesperson for General Electric. A former New Dealer, Reagan moved to the right in the 1950s and won prominence through a TV speech for Barry Goldwater in 1964, praising individualism and free enterprise.

Recognizing Reagan's flair for politics, a group of California millionaires engineered his election as governor in 1966. He popularized conservative ideas while demonstrating an ability to compromise. After nearly winning the Republican presidential nomination in 1976, Reagan in 1980 had little trouble disposing of his principal opponent, George Bush, whom he then made his running mate.

Reagan promised Americans a new deal. Unlike FDR's New Deal, however, Reagan's offered smaller government, reduced taxes and spending, and untrammeled enterprise.

Asking "Are you better off now than you were four years ago?" Reagan captured 51 percent of the popular vote to Carter's 41 percent. Reaping the benefits of Nixon's southern strategy, Reagan carried every southern state except Carter's own Georgia and every state west of the Mississippi. More than half the nation's blue-collar workers voted Republican. Only African-American voters remained firmly Democratic. Republicans also gained eleven Senate seats and, for the first time since 1955, a majority. These Senate victories reflected the power of conservative political action committees using computerized mass mailings to focus on such hot-button issues as abortion and gun control.

Although the Reagan victory clearly stemmed at least as much from Reagan's personal charm as from public acceptance of his ideas, he and his advisors arrived in Washington determined to change the role of government in American life through what became known as "the Reagan Revolution."

Reaganomics

"Reaganomics," the new president's economic program, boiled down to the belief that American capitalism, freed of heavy taxes and government regulation, would achieve wonders of productivity. Reagan's first budget message proposed a five-year, $750 billion tax cut built around a 30 percent reduction in federal income taxes over three years. Trimming the proposal slightly, Congress in May 1981 voted a 25 percent income-tax cut over three years.

To make up for the lost revenues, Reagan proposed massive cuts for school lunches, student loans, job training, and urban mass transit. Congress slashed more than $40 billion from domestic spending in 1981 (less than Reagan had requested). Conservative Democrats supported the reductions. Although mainstream economists warned that the tax cut would produce catastrophic federal deficits, Reagan remained convinced that lower tax rates would stimulate economic growth and raise total tax revenues. He was wrong.

Appointees to key agencies implemented another component of Reaganomics, radical cutbacks in the federal regulation of business. Dereg-ulation, begun under Carter, was extended to banking, the savings-and-loan industry, transportation, and communications. The head of the Federal Communications Commission gutted federal rules governing the broadcast industry, and the secretary of transportation trimmed regulations reducing air pollution and increasing efficiency and safety in cars and trucks. Secretary of the Interior James Watt, a leader in the Sagebrush Rebellion, opened public lands in the West to commercial developers. Despite deregulation, Reagan's attack on "big government" had little effect on checking the steady growth of the federal budget and of the federal bureaucracy.

While implementing Reaganomics, the administration also had to cope with the immediate problem of inflation. The Federal Reserve Board led the charge, pushing the discount rate ever higher. This harsh medicine, coupled with a sharp downturn in world oil prices, worked. Inflation dropped to 4 percent in 1983 and held steady thereafter.

Recession and Boom Times

The high interest rates necessary to curb inflation spawned another severe recession. By late 1982 unemployment stood at 10 percent. Falling exports added to the Reagan recession. As high U.S. interest rates lured foreign investors, the dollar rose in value vis-à-vis foreign currencies, making American goods more expensive abroad. The decline in U.S. exports—accompanied by enormous increases in imported TVs, stereos, and cars—propelled the U.S. trade deficit (the gap between exports and imports) from $31 billion in 1981 to $111 billion in 1984.

The industrial heartland reeled under the triple blow of slumping exports, foreign competition, and technological obsolescence. The aging steel mills, automobile companies, and other smokestack industries of the Midwest and Great Lakes laid off hordes of workers. Some plants closed. From 1979 through 1983, 11.5 million Americans lost jobs as a result of plant shutdowns or slack work. The drop in exports hurt farmers as well. From 1980 to 1985 wheat exports fell 38 percent and corn exports, 49 percent. Some lost farms that their families had run for generations.

Soaring federal deficits compounded the economic muddle. Reagan's tax cuts reduced federal revenues without immediately stimulating business, and increases in military spending more than offset domestic spending cuts. In 1982–1983, with the economy in crisis, the government awash in red ink, and critics denouncing him as callous, Reagan accepted a reduced rate of military spending, slower funding cuts in social programs, emergency job programs, and tax increases euphemistically described as "revenue-enhancement measures."

As recession's grip remained tight through 1982, the Democrats gained twenty-six House seats in the fall elections. The Reagan presidency appeared headed toward failure until early 1983 when the economy rebounded. Encouraged by tax cuts, declining interest rates, and evidence that inflation had been tamed, consumers went on a buying spree. The stock market surged, unemployment dropped, and Reagan's popularity rebounded.

Better times unleashed a wave of stock-market speculation reminiscent of the 1920s. The bull market began on August 12, 1982, and lasted five years. Entrepreneurs such as Manhattan real-estate tycoon Donald Trump and stock analyst Ivan Boesky became celebrities. Corporate mergers burgeoned. Chevron bought Gulf for $13 billion; GE acquired RCA for $6.3 billion. Meanwhile, the stock market steadily roared on. Banks and savings-and-loan companies, newly deregulated, loaned billions to developers for the construction of shopping malls, luxury apartments, retirement villages, and office buildings.

In the mid-1980s the dark side of this feeding frenzy emerged. The E. F. Hutton brokerage firm pleaded guilty to manipulating funds and defrauding hundreds of banks. Ivan Boesky went to prison after his 1986 conviction for insider trading. On October 19, 1987, "Black Monday," the Dow Jones plunged 508 points as one-fifth of the paper value of the nation's stocks evaporated. The downslide was eerily similar to the 1929 crash that precipitated the Great Depression, but prompt government action prevented another collapse.

Even at the height of the bull market, economic problems remained. The trade gap persisted, the deficit surpassed $200 billion in 1986, and farmers, the poor, and former industrial workers did not share in the renewed prosperity. The United States had been transformed from the world's largest creditor to the world's largest debtor. But—just in time to brighten Reagan's reelection prospects—the overall economic picture looked brighter than it had in years.

Reagan Confronts the "Evil Empire" and Crises in the Middle East

Anti-Soviet rhetoric escalated when Ronald Reagan took office. The president blasted the Soviet Union as an "evil empire" and "the focus of evil in the modern world." Anti-Soviet sentiment crested in September 1983 when the Soviets shot down a Korean passenger aircraft that had strayed into their airspace, killing 269. Moscow claimed that the plane had been spying, but most Americans rejected this explanation.

Obsession with the Soviets also influenced Reagan policy in El Salvador and Nicaragua, two poor Central American nations caught up in revolutionary turmoil. In El Salvador the administration supported the ruling military junta in its ruthless suppression of a leftist insurgency backed by Cuba and Nicaragua. Even after a moderate won the 1984 presidential election with U.S. support, death squads continued to operate. In Nicaragua, where Carter had at first aided the Sandinista revolutionaries who overthrew dictator Anastasio Somoza in 1979, Reagan accused the Sandinistas of creating another Cuba and a staging area for Soviet expansion. The Central Intelligence Agency in 1982 organized and financed a ten-thousand-man guerrilla army, the contras, based in Honduras and Costa Rica. The contras, many with links to the Somoza regime, conducted raids, planted mines, and carried out sabotage inside Nicaragua.

Fearing another Vietnam, Americans grew alarmed as details of this "covert" war leaked out. Congress imposed a series of bans on military aid to the contras from 1984 to 1986, but Reagan's enthusiasm for the contras, whom he labeled "the moral equivalent of our Founding Fathers," held steady. Secret contra aid, organized within the White House, continued despite congressional prohibitions. In 1988 Reagan, still hoping for a contra victory, grudgingly supported a truce between the Sandinistas and the contras.

Reagan's militarization of American policy fell heavily on the West Indian island of Grenada, ruled by a radical leftist regime. In October 1983, two thousand U.S. Marines invaded Grenada, overthrew the government, and installed one friendly to the United States. Most Grenadians expressed their approval.

The continuing turmoil and conflict in the Middle East that had so frustrated President Carter also preoccupied the Reagan administration. Hoping to stem Islamic fundamentalism, the United States tilted toward Saddam Hussein's Iraq in its long war with Iran, although U.S. officials also courted "moderates" in Iran. Cold War policies dictated other U.S. actions in the Middle East as well.

Meanwhile, the conflict among Israel, the Palestinians, and Israel's Arab foes dragged on. The United States had vital interests in the region. Many Americans felt a deep emotional bond with Israel, which was the recipient of large amounts of military aid and other assistance. At the same time the United States also gave extensive aid to Egypt

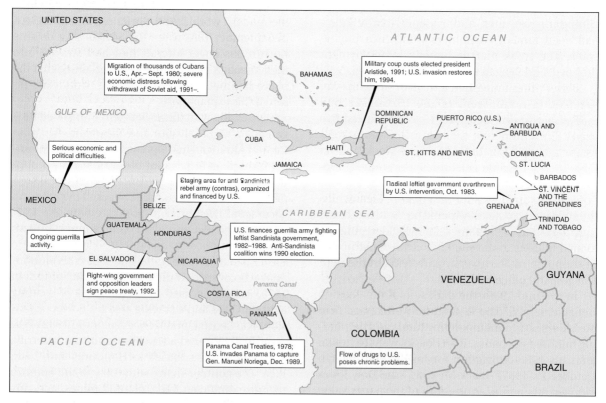

MAP 30.2

The United States in Latin America and the Caribbean

Plagued by poverty, population pressures, repressive regimes, and drug trafficking, Latin America saw turmoil and conflict—but also some hopeful developments—in the 1980s and 1990s.   Interactive Map: The U.S. in the Caribbean & Central America

and relied heavily on oil from Saudi Arabia and other Arab states, some of which were violently anti-Israel.

In August 1981 Israel and the Palestine Liberation Organization (PLO) concluded a cease-fire, but the PLO continued building up its forces and carved out a sanctuary in southern Lebanon. In June 1982 when PLO extremists critically wounded the Israeli ambassador to Great Britain, Israeli troops under General Ariel Sharon invaded Lebanon, defeated the PLO militarily, and forced its leaders to leave Lebanon. It also intensified civil war among Lebanese Christian and Islamic factions. With Sharon's approval a Lebanese Christian militia force entered the Shatila refugee camp near Beirut and massacred 700–800 camp residents, including women and children. An Israeli inquiry found no evidence that Sharon knew of the planned massacre in advance, but he resigned as defense minister.

In the aftermath of the Shatila massacre, the Reagan administration deployed 2,000 U.S. Marines to Beirut as part of a multinational peace-keeping force. Muslim militias saw the Americans as favoring Israel and Lebanon's Christian parties. In October 1983 a Shiite Muslim crashed a truck laden with explosives into poorly guarded barracks, killing 239 marines. Reagan had never defined American interests in Lebanon, and the disaster underscored the failure of his Lebanese policy. By early 1984 the marines had withdrawn.

Disappointment also dogged Reagan's attempt to promote a wider Middle East settlement. In September 1982 the president tried to jump-start Arab-Israeli peace talks along the lines envisioned by the Camp David Accords. Over the next four years, the administration tried to bring PLO leader Yasir Arafat and Jordan's King Hussein together for a "Jordanian solution" to the West Bank question. But Reagan's efforts were scuttled by Syria's opposition, stemming from that nation's exclusion from the process; by PLO reluctance; and by Israeli security fears.

At the same time the United States began covertly to supply massive amounts of weapons and ammunition to the mujahideen, Afghan fighters trying to drive Soviet forces from their country. Ironically, many of those whom the U.S. supported during the 1980s were the same Islamic fundamentalists who later became major figures in anti-American terrorism.

Military Buildup and Antinuclear Protest

Convinced that the United States had grown dangerously weak militarily, Reagan launched a massive military expansion. From 1981 to 1985, the Pentagon's budget swelled from $171 billion to more than $300 billion. Nuclear weapons were a key element of the U.S. buildup. In 1983 the administration deployed 572 cruise and Pershing II missiles in Western Europe, counterbalancing Soviet missiles in Eastern Europe. Reagan's supporters would later claim that the U.S.S.R.'s collapse in the late 1980s came from its efforts to match this American stockpiling. Others, however, would see the collapse as the result of structural weaknesses within the U.S.S.R. itself.

On the domestic front, the Federal Emergency Management Agency designed an elaborate civil-defense plan whereby city residents would flee to remote "host communities" if nuclear war threatened. A Defense Department official averred that backyard shelters would save millions of people in a nuclear holocaust. "With enough shovels," he asserted, "everybody's going to make it." Such talk, coupled with the military buildup and the faltering of arms control, sparked a grass-roots reaction as millions of Americans felt a growing threat of nuclear war. Concerned citizens campaigned for a freeze on the manufacture and deployment of nuclear weapons. In June 1982, eight hundred thousand antinuclear protesters rallied in New York's Central Park. Nine states passed freeze resolutions in the following fall elections.

Responding to the "No nukes!" clamor, the administration in June 1982 proposed the removal of medium-range nuclear missiles from Europe and resumed talks with the Soviets on strategic-arms reductions. In March 1983 Reagan proposed the Strategic Defense Initiative (SDI), a space-based defense system against nuclear missiles. Nicknamed

Star Wars, SDI reflected America's deep faith in technology. But even as the Pentagon launched an SDI research program, critics pointed out not only the project's prohibitive cost and technological implausibility but also the likelihood that it would further escalate the arms race.

Reagan Reelected

As the 1984 election neared, liberal Democrats and independents criticized Reagan for runaway military spending, worsening Cold War tensions, yawning budget deficits, sharp cuts in social programs, and the assault on regulatory functions. To critics, Reaganism meant jingoism abroad and selfishness at home.

But many Americans applauded Reagan's attacks on big government as well as his get-tough policy toward the Soviets. Rhetoric aside, the administration *had* ended inflation and created a booming economy. Reagan's popularity remained high; some dubbed him the Teflon president because nothing bad seemed to stick to him. By 1984 many Americans believed that Reagan had revitalized the free-enterprise system, rebuilt U.S. military might, and made the nation "stand tall" in the world. Buoyed by evidence of broad support, Reagan confidently prepared to campaign for a second term. The 1984 Republican convention, scripted for TV, accentuated patriotism, prosperity, and the personality of Ronald Reagan.

Democratic hopefuls included Jesse Jackson, an African-American Chicago minister and one-time associate of Martin Luther King, Jr. Jackson attempted to build a broad "rainbow coalition" of African-Americans, Hispanic-Americans, displaced workers, and other outsiders in Reagan's America. Former vice president Walter Mondale, however, won the Democratic nomination. He ignited little enthusiasm, despite his choice of a woman, New York representative Geraldine Ferraro, as his running mate.

Reagan and Bush collected 59 percent of the popular vote and carried every state but Minnesota and the District of Columbia. Reagan's popular ideology and mastery of television teamed with a booming economy to secure his solid victory. Democrats remained in control of Congress, but Republican dominance of presidential politics, broken only by Carter's single term, held firm.

In 1985, some centrist Democrats sought to erase their image as "big government . . . tax and spend" liberals and formed the Democratic Leadership Council. In a few years Arkansas governor Bill Clinton would use his chairmanship of the group as a springboard to the Democratic presidential nomination.

A Sea of Problems in Reagan's Second Term, 1985–1989

In his first term, Ronald Reagan set the political agenda: tax cuts, deregulation, and expanded military spending. In his second term, a growing budget deficit and trade gap, and the Iran-contra scandal, overtook him. Foreign affairs temporarily eclipsed domestic issues, however, as a new era of Soviet-American cooperation and friendship replaced the "evil empire" confrontation of Reagan's first term; however, continued conflict in the Middle East and a wave of terrorist bombings made clear that even with the end of the Cold War, the world was still a dangerous place.

Budget Deficits and Trade Gaps

Reagan achieved significant legislative victories in his second term, including a new immigration law and tax reform. To make the system fairer, the tax-reform law eliminated many deductions, established uniform rates for people at comparable income levels, and removed 6 million low-income Americans from the tax rolls.

But sky-high federal deficits, the legacy of Reaganomics, persisted. In 1985 and 1986, the budget deficit reached $221 billion before settling at $150 billion in 1987 and 1988. Enormous federal debts and an escalating trade gap, which hit $154 billion in 1987, were Reagan's economic legacy.

The Iran-Contra Affair and Other Scandals

The Middle East spawned a crisis that would rock the Reagan presidency. Late in 1986 a Beirut newspaper reported that in 1985 the United States had shipped 508 antitank missiles to the anti-American Iranian government. Acknowledging the sale, Reagan said that his goal had been to encourage "moderate elements" in Iran and to secure the release of American hostages held in Lebanon by pro-Iranian radicals. In February 1987 a presidential investigative panel placed heavy blame on Chief of Staff Donald Regan, who soon resigned.

Soon more details surfaced. The most explosive revelation was that Lieutenant Colonel Oliver North, a National Security Council aide, had diverted millions in profits from the arms sales to the Nicaraguan contras at a time when Congress had made such aid illegal. In November 1986 North and his secretary had altered or deleted computer files and had held a "shredding party" to destroy incriminating documents.

In May 1987 a joint House-Senate committee investigated the charges. A fascinated nation watched "Ollie" North, resplendent in his military uniform, portray himself as a true patriot. Former national-security adviser John Poindexter testified that he had deliberately concealed the diversion of funds from Reagan.

The committee found no evidence that President Reagan personally knew of illegalities, but it severely criticized the casual management style and disregard for the law that had fed the scandal. In early 1988 a court-appointed special prosecutor, Lawrence Walsh, won criminal indictments against Poindexter, North, and others. In 1989 a federal jury convicted North of obstructing a congressional inquiry and destroying and falsifying National Security Council documents, but the conviction was later reversed on the technical grounds that certain incriminating testimony had been given under a promise of immunity. The Iran-contra scandal dogged the Reagan administration's final years.

Other revelations, some of them involving the president's closest associates, plagued Reagan's sec-

ond term. His old friend Attorney General Edwin Meese was accused of influence peddling and resigned in July 1988. That same year, former chief of staff Donald Regan's *For the Record* painted Reagan as little more than an automaton: "Every moment of every public appearance, every word was scripted, every place where Reagan was expected to stand was chalked with toe marks." In 1989 came revelation that former interior secretary James Watt and other prominent Republicans accepted hundreds of thousands of dollars for interceding with the Department of Housing and Urban Development on behalf of developers seeking federal subsidies.

But the dirty linen did not sully Reagan's own popularity. The source of his success lay far deeper, in his uncanny ability to articulate the beliefs, fears, and hopes of millions of Americans. Moreover, Reagan benefited from an unanticipated turn of events abroad that would end his presidency on a note of triumph.

Reagan's Mission to Moscow

The Cold War thawed dramatically in Reagan's second term. Meeting in Switzerland in 1985 and Iceland in 1986, Reagan and Soviet leader Mikhail Gorbachev revived the stalled arms-control talks. Beset by economic crisis at home, Gorbachev pursued an easing of superpower tensions to gain breathing space for domestic reform.

In 1987 Gorbachev came to Washington to sign the Intermediate Nuclear Forces (INF) Treaty. Providing for the removal of twenty-five hundred American and Soviet missiles from Europe, this treaty revived the arms-control process and for the first time eliminated an entire class of nuclear weapons. INF also provided on-site inspections to verify compliance. In May 1988 Reagan made a historic visit to Moscow, where he and Gorbachev established a cordial personal relationship.

The Dangerous Middle East: Continued Tension and Terrorism

As relations with Moscow improved in Reagan's second term, the situation in the Middle East

President Reagan Visits Red Square
As the Cold War crumbled, President Reagan flew to Moscow in 1988 to celebrate a nuclear-arms reduction treaty with Soviet premier Mikhail Gorbachev.

worsened. In December 1987 the Intifada, a Palestinian uprising against Israeli occupation, began in Gaza and spread to the West Bank. U.S. Secretary of State George Shultz attempted in 1988 to bring Jordan and the Palestinians into negotiations with Israel over a plan for Palestinian autonomy. But the Israeli government rejected the "land for peace" formula and refused to negotiate until the Intifada ended; and the Palestinians rejected Shultz's proposals for not going far enough toward establishing a Palestinian state. Israel continued to build Jewish settlements on the West Bank.

In the late 1980s the Middle East conflict generated a deadly by-product: kidnappings, airplane hijackings, airport attacks, and other terrorist acts. In April 1986 after terrorists bombed a Berlin nightclub popular with American GIs, President Reagan ordered a retaliatory air attack on Libya, which had been implicated in the bombing. In the worst of the terrorist incidents, a bomb exploded aboard a Pan Am jet over Scotland in December 1988, killing all 259 aboard, many of them Americans. In 1991 the U.S. and British governments formally blamed Libya for the bombing. Colonel Muammar el-Qaddafi, Libya's ruler, denied the charges and refused to extradite the accused officials until 1999.

Assessing the Reagan Years

After Nixon's disgrace, Ford's caretaker presidency, and Carter's rocky tenure, Reagan's two full terms helped restored a sense of stability to American politics. Reagan's domestic record was mixed: inflation was tamed and the economy turned upward, but federal deficits soared and the administration ignored festering social issues, environmental concerns, and long-term economic problems.

Reagan's critics dismissed his two terms as a triumph of nostalgia and drift over achievement during which individualism all too easily translated into selfishness and greed.

Reagan's admirers dismissed these criticisms and focused on his reassertion of traditional values such as self-reliance and free enterprise. His military build-up had helped bring down the Soviet Union, they proclaimed, and his infectious optimism and patriotism had helped restore national pride.

Ronald Reagan had had the good fortune to hold office as the Cold War thawed and the Soviet Union began to disintegrate. By the end of his term, détente was once more barreling along. The shadow world of international terrorism, however, had announced itself with assassinations, bombs, and crashing airplanes, signaling new challenges ahead. In his post-presidential years, as Reagan moved into the dark world of Alzheimer's disease,

Chronology

1972	Equal Rights Amendment passed by Congress.
1973	Major rise in Organization of Petroleum Exporting Countries (OPEC) prices: Arab oil boycott. *Roe* v. *Wade.*
1974	Richard Nixon resigns presidency; Gerald Ford sworn in. Whip Inflation Now (WIN) program. Indian Self-Determination Act.
1975	South Vietnamese government falls. *Mayagüez* incident.
1976	Jimmy Carter elected president.
1977	Panama Canal treaties ratified.
1978–1980	Double-digit inflation and soaring interest rates.
1979	Menachem Begin and Anwar el-Sadat sign peace treaty at White House. Second round of OPEC price increases. Accident at Three Mile Island nuclear plant. Carter and Leonid Brezhnev sign Strategic Arms Limitation Treaty (SALT) II. Carter restores full diplomatic relations with the People's Republic of China.
1980	Carter withdraws SALT II agreement from Senate after Soviet invasion of Afghanistan. Iran hostage crisis preoccupies nation. Ronald Reagan elected president.
1981	Major cuts in taxes and domestic spending, coupled with large increases in military budget. AIDS first diagnosed.
1981–1983	Severe recession (late 1981–early 1983).
1982	Equal Rights Amendment dies. Central Intelligence Agency organizes contra war against Nicaragua's Sandinista government. Nuclear-freeze rally in Central Park. Stock-market boom begins.
1983	239 U.S. Marines die in Beirut terrorist attack. U.S. invasion of Grenada. Reagan proposes Strategic Defense Initiative (SDI).
1984	Reagan defeats Walter Mondale in landslide.
1984–1986	Congress bars military aid to contras.
1985	Rash of airline hijackings and other terrorist acts.
1986	Immigration Reform and Control Act. Federal deficit rises to $221 billion. U.S. air raid on Libya.
1987	Congressional hearings on Iran-contra scandal. Intermediate Nuclear Forces Treaty signed. Stock-market crash.
1988	Oliver North, John Poindexter, and other Iran-contra figures indicted.

the "Reagan Revolution" continued in some ways to shape the terms of American politics. The former president's death in 2004 brought a brief resurgence of a "morning in America" spirit (see Chapter 31) that soon faded.

CONCLUSION 🄷🄲 ACE Practice Test

In the 1970s and 1980s American culture revealed sharp contradictions. Activism faded into conservatism as millions of middle-class Americans and even ex-radicals turned to personal pursuits and careerist goals. At the same time, reformist energies poured into a revived women's movement, a gay-rights campaign, and a variety of environmental and consumer causes.

The economic scene was equally diverse. Stagnation and inflation soured the national mood and shadowed the presidencies of Gerald Ford and Jimmy Carter, while a fleeting midterm boom in the Reagan years was bracketed by recessions. Millions of Americans—mostly in the inner cities and mostly darker-skinned minorities—remained frozen out of a high-tech economy that demanded education and specialized skills. Family farms proved unable to compete with large agribusinesses. Many African-Americans entered the ranks of the middle class and the professions, but a large minority remained trapped in poverty. Native Americans faced continuing deprivation but also new economic opportunities and the prospect of benefiting from long-ignored treaty rights. Throughout the era growing immigration from Latin America and Asia reshaped the nation's ethnic and demographic profile.

Presidents Ford, Carter, and Reagan all grappled with a rapidly changing world. U.S.-Soviet relations worsened in the late 1970s and early 1980s, but improved dramatically in Reagan's second term. Economic and social problems in the Soviet Union—perhaps hastened by Reagan's heavy defense spending—signaled the end of the Cold War, an amazing development that would fully unfold during the presidency of Reagan's successor, George Bush.

Brightening prospects on one front were matched by heightened menace elsewhere. The Middle East, in particular, brought moments of illusory hope interspersed with frustration and tragedy. As the 1980s ended, a rising tempo of terrorist attacks suggested that the nation was entering a period no less dangerous, in its own way, than that which Americans had faced during the darkest days of the Cold War.

FURTHER READING

Robert Bellah et al., *Habits of the Heart* (1985). Reflections on the discontents of the American middle class in the early 1980s, drawn from extensive interviews.

Paul Boyer, ed., *Reagan as President* (1990). Contemporary speeches, articles, and editorials commenting on Reagan and his program, with an introduction by the editor.

Peter Carroll, *It Seemed Like Nothing Happened* (1983). A perceptive, readable overview history of the 1970s.

George Crile, *Charlie Wilson's War* (2003). A fascinating account of a Texas congressman's manipulation of the CIA and Congress in order to support Afghan mujahideen.

Thomas Byrne Edsall with Mary D. Edsall, *Chain Reaction: The Impact of Race, Rights, and Taxes on American Politics* (1992). Insightful analysis of the social and economic sources of the rise of a conservative voting majority.

Haynes Johnson, *Sleepwalking Through History: America in the Reagan Years* (1991). A highly readable account of American politics and culture in the 1980s by a seasoned *Washington Post* reporter.

Joane Nagel, *American Indian Ethnic Renewal: Red Power and the Resurgence of Identity and Culture* (1996). Interpretive study of recent Indian history and culture.

Carl H. Nightingale, *On the Edge: A History of Poor Black Children and Their American Dreams* (1993). Moving presentation of the effect of inner-city poverty on its most vulnerable victims.

Bruce J. Schulman, *The Seventies: The Great Shift in American Culture, Society, and Politics* (2001). An engaging history stressing the rise of a "populist conservatism" featuring religious revival and suspicion of authority.

John W. Sloan, *The Reagan Effect: Economics and Presidential Leadership* (1999). A generally positive revisionist study arguing that Reagan, for all his antigovernment rhetoric, used government effectively.

Robert A. Strong, *Working in the World: Jimmy Carter and the Making of American Foreign Policy* (2000). Presenting nine case studies, the author argues that Carter's foreign-policy record is impressive.

Massachusetts high school students and a teacher admire their computer Web page

Beyond the Cold War: Charting a New Course, 1988–1995

The end of the Cold War and the global events of the immediate post–Cold War era provide the framework of the early parts of this chapter. At first, the Soviet Union's shocking collapse brought an enormous sigh of relief in the United States. An era of great danger was over; surely the future would be safer and more tranquil. As the initial euphoria faded, however, Americans realized that the world remained a threatening and unsettled place. While U.S. leaders struggled to come to terms with the new post–Cold War world order, an immediate crisis arose in the Middle East as Saddam Hussein's Iraq invaded oil-rich Kuwait, forcing Reagan's successor, President George Bush, to respond.

Changes were underway at home as well as abroad. When Bill Clinton replaced George Bush in the White House in 1993, domestic policy moved front and center. This chapter also discusses home-front politics and culture in the 1990s, as well as long-term social and economic trends, the effect of which became particularly visible in this eventful decade. U.S. history has always been a story of change, and the changes came at a dizzying pace as the twentieth century ended.

CHAPTER OUTLINE

ℏ𝒸 This icon will direct you to additional study and research resources at http://college.hmco.com/history/us/boyer/enduring_concise/5e/students/index.html

This chapter focuses on five major questions:

▶ What major events marked the end of the Cold War, and why did the long conflict between the United States and the Soviet Union end so suddenly?

▶ How effectively did George Bush, President Reagan's successor, cope with the "new world order" that emerged with the end of the Cold War?

▶ What key themes dominated Bill Clinton's 1992 presidential campaign and the early years of his presidency?

▶ What long-term social and economic trends had the greatest effect on the United States at the end of the twentieth century?

▶ How did U.S. popular culture reflect the prosperity of the 1990s, and what issues divided Americans in the "culture wars" of these years?

THE BUSH YEARS: GLOBAL RESOLVE, DOMESTIC DRIFT, 1988–1993

Ronald Reagan's vice president, George Bush, elected president in his own right in 1988, was a patrician in politics. The son of a powerful Connecticut senator, he had fought in World War II and attended Yale before entering the Texas oil business. He had served in Congress, lost a Senate race, directed the Central Intelligence Agency (CIA), and fought for the 1980 Republican nomination before being tapped as Ronald Reagan's running mate in 1980.

As president, Bush compiled a curiously uneven record. Despite a series of international triumphs, especially orchestration of the Gulf War, in the domestic theater Bush substituted platitudes for policy. In retrospect, the Bush interlude seems primarily a postscript to the Reagan era.

The Election of 1988

As the 1988 election approached, Vice President George Bush easily won the Republican presidential nomination. A seven-way battle among Democrats narrowed to a contest between Jesse Jackson and Massachusetts governor Michael Dukakis. Preaching concern for the poor and urging a full-scale war on drugs, Jackson ran well in the primaries. However, Dukakis victories in major primary states, including New York and California, proved decisive. He chose Texas senator Lloyd Bentsen as his running mate. On the Republican side, Bush surprised everyone by choosing a little-known conservative senator from Indiana, J. Danforth ("Dan") Quayle III, as his running mate.

Bush called for a "kinder, gentler America" and promised no new taxes. He emphasized peace and prosperity, pointing to better superpower relations, low inflation, and the 14 million new jobs created during the eighties. While Bush personally took the high road, some of his commercials took the low road. One campaign ad, playing on racist stereotypes, featured a black man who had committed rape and murder after his release under a Massachusetts prisoner-furlough program. Bush assailed Dukakis's veto of a bill requiring Massachusetts schoolchildren to recite the Pledge of Allegiance, although the Supreme Court had already declared such a law unconstitutional. For his part, Dukakis stressed that "this election is not about ideology, it's about competence." Boasting his accomplishments as governor, he hammered at the failures of the "Swiss-cheese" Reagan economy. But Dukakis seemed edgy and defensive, and his dismissal of ideology made it difficult for him to define his vision of America.

Both candidates avoided serious issues in favor of TV-oriented "photo opportunities" and "sound bites." Bush visited flag factories and military plants; Dukakis looked spectacularly out of place posing in a tank. Editorial writers grumbled about the "junk-food" campaign, but images, catchy phrases, and twenty-second spots on the evening news became the essence of presidential politics. On November 8 Bush gained 54 percent of the vote, won forty states, and emerged with a lopsided 426 to 112 electoral margin. The Democrats retained control of both houses of Congress.

The Cold War Ends

Soviet power collapsed with breathtaking speed. In May 1989 Soviet President Mikhail Gorbachev announced that Moscow would no longer use its power to prop up Eastern Europe's unpopular communist regimes. One by one, these governments fell. New democratic governments sprang up behind what had been the iron curtain. In November 1989 exuberant Germans tore down the Berlin Wall, and within a year Germany was reunited for the first time since 1945. The Baltic republics—Latvia, Lithuania, and Estonia—forcibly annexed by the Soviet Union on the eve of World War II, declared their independence. Other Soviet republics followed.

The Cold War was over; the arms race, the Cold War's evil twin, seemed to wind down as well. In August 1991 President Bush and Gorbachev signed a treaty reducing their strategic arsenals by 25 percent. Secretary of Defense Dick Cheney proposed a 25 percent reduction in U.S. military forces over five years. With the Warsaw Pact gone, the North Atlantic Treaty Organization (NATO) planned a 50 percent troop reduction.

In August 1991 as the Soviet Union inched toward a market economy, increasing economic chaos led hard-line Communist party leaders to stage a coup against Gorbachev. Rallied by Boris Yeltsin, the president of the Russian Republic, the Russian people protectively surrounded the Russian parliament to defy the plotters and their tanks. Gorbachev returned to power, but Yeltsin assumed a dominant role.

Exultant crowds toppled statues of Lenin and other communist leaders across the nation, and Leningrad reverted to its tsarist name, St. Petersburg. As the Soviet republics rushed to independence, Gorbachev was overwhelmed by the forces that he had released. The August 1991 coup stripped the last shred of legitimacy from the Soviet Communist party. Later that year, the Soviet republics proclaimed the end of the U.S.S.R. Bowing to the inevitable, Gorbachev resigned and was replaced by Boris Yeltsin.

Secretary of State James Baker and President Bush proceeded cautiously as the Soviet empire disintegrated. American influence was limited, in any event, as nationalism and ethnic issues exploded in Eastern Europe and the former Soviet Union.

The future of the Soviet arsenal, twenty-seven thousand nuclear weapons, based not only in Russia but also in newly independent Ukraine, Belarus, and Kazakhstan, remained a particularly vital concern. Baker worked, with limited success, to assure the security and orderly dismantling of these weapons and to prevent the flow of nuclear technology to Third World nations and to nonnuclear European nations. Early in 1992, as strategic talks progressed, Bush announced major reductions in the American nuclear arsenal.

The Cold War's end offered opportunities for the resolution of regional conflicts elsewhere in the world. For decades, the superpowers had aided allies, client states, and rebel forces throughout the Third World. As the Cold War faded, the prospects for resolving local disputes brightened.

In Latin America, the Bush administration abandoned its predecessors' financing of the Nicaraguan contras and worked at reintegrating them into Nicaragua's life and politics. Victory in the 1990 elections went to an anti-Sandinista coalition.

Enormous problems linked to poverty, ignorance, and economic exploitation still plagued Latin America. Open guerrilla warfare continued in Peru. Cocaine and heroin flowed from South and Central America to U.S. cities. In December 1989 concern over the drug traffic led to a U.S. invasion of Panama to capture the nation's strongman ruler, General Manuel Noriega. Formerly on the CIA payroll, Noriega accepted huge bribes to allow Panama to serve as a conduit for the northward movement of drugs. Convicted in a U.S. court, Noriega received a life prison term for drug trafficking.

America's relations with the Philippines, a former colony and longtime ally, shifted as well. In 1991 the Philippines legislature ended long-term American leases on two military bases. In the post–Cold War climate of eased world tensions, the Bush administration accepted this decision and withdrew from the bases.

South Africa had become a focus of debate in Reagan's second term. In 1986 Congress, over Reagan's veto, imposed stiff sanctions, banning South African products and prohibiting U.S. investments there. Worldwide sanctions helped to bring extraordinary changes to South Africa. In 1990 the government released black leader Nelson Mandela after twenty-seven years in prison and opened negotiations with his African National Congress. The South African parliament scrapped most apartheid laws in 1991, and Bush lifted U.S. sanctions.

China proved a major exception to the world trend toward democracy. In 1989 U.S. relations with China suffered a serious setback when the Chinese army brutally crushed a prodemocracy demonstration by thousands of unarmed students in Beijing's Tiananmen Square. As many as one thousand students died, and repression, arrests, and public executions followed. The Bush administration protested but neither broke diplomatic relations nor canceled trade agreements with China.

As Cold War worries waned, international trade issues loomed large. The towering U.S. trade deficit with Japan, which ranged from $40 billion to $55 billion in the late 1980s, aroused particular concern. In early 1992 President Bush led a high-level trade mission to Japan, accompanied by the heads of the "big three" U.S. auto companies. But efforts to open Japanese markets proved futile. When Bush collapsed from the flu during a state dinner in Tokyo, the mishap seemed unhappily symbolic.

Operation Desert Storm

As the Bush administration grappled with a tangle of global issues, one regional provocation elicited a dramatic response. On August 2, 1990, the Middle Eastern nation of Iraq invaded its oil-rich neighbor, Kuwait. Iraq's dictator, Saddam Hussein, had dismissed Kuwait's nation-state status as a creation of western imperialists and asserted Iraq's claim to the area.

Under Saddam, Iraq had for years threatened not only its Arab neighbors but also Israel. Iraq's military buildup, including chemical- and nuclear-weapons programs, had worried many governments in the 1980s. However, during the Iraq-Iran war (1980–1988), the United States had tilted toward Iraq because of Iran's rabid anti-Americanism. But lessened Iranian hostility after Ayatollah Khomeini's death in 1989 had removed the United States' incentive to placate Iraq. When Iraq invaded Kuwait, Washington acted quickly.

Determined to avoid the mistakes of the Vietnam era, Bush carefully built a consensus for anti-Iraqi action in Congress, in the United Nations, and among the American people. He also articulated a clear military objective—Iraqi withdrawal from Kuwait—and provided the necessary military force. More than four hundred thousand troops were shuttled to Saudi Arabia.

The United Nations imposed economic sanctions on Iraq and insisted that Saddam withdraw from Kuwait by January 15, 1991. On January 12, after somber debate, both houses of Congress endorsed military action against Iraq. Most Democrats, however, voted against war, favoring continued economic sanctions.

On January 16 a massive air assault opened the war. For nearly six weeks both American and allied land- and carrier-based planes pounded troops, supply depots, and command targets in Iraq's capital, Baghdad. They flew up to three thousand sorties daily. Saddam ordered Soviet-made Scud missiles fired against Israeli and Saudi Arabian cities. Americans watched transfixed as the Cable News Network carried live coverage of U.S. Patriot missiles streaking off to intercept incoming Scuds. Carefully edited for mass television viewers, the war often seemed a glorified video game. The reality of many thousands of Iraqi deaths, both military and civilian, hardly impinged on Americans' consciousness.

Kuwait, 1991
Burning oilfields, set ablaze by retreating Iraqis, provide an eerie backdrop to motorized U.S. troops participating in Operation Desert Storm, the high point of the Bush presidency.
Interactive Map: Operation Desert Storm: The Ground War

On February 23, two hundred thousand U.S. forces under General H. Norman Schwarzkopf advanced across the desert toward Kuwait. Within three days Iraqi soldiers were in full flight or surrendering en masse. U.S. forces destroyed thirty-seven hundred Iraqi tanks while losing only three. One hundred hours after the ground war had begun, with Iraqi resistance crushed and Kuwait City liberated, President Bush declared a cease-fire. American casualties numbered 148 dead, including 35 killed by "friendly fire," and 467 wounded.

As victory celebrations receded, the war's political aftermath came into focus. Saddam clung to power, and his army brutally suppressed rebellions by Shiite Muslims in the south and by a large Kurdish ethnic minority in the north. U.N. inspectors found convincing evidence of an advanced nuclear-weapons project under way in Iraq, and its discontinuance brought general relief. Within a few years Saddam would restart secret nuclear-weapons development. What had seemed a stunning military victory in 1991 largely evaporated as Iraq continued to preoccupy the United States and its allies.

Home-Front Discontents: Economic, Racial, and Environmental Problems

The tax cuts, Pentagon spending, and deregulatory fever of the "Reagan revolution" had unleashed entrepreneurial energies, powered a stock-market surge and a wave of corporate takeovers, and set off an economic boom that gave the 1980s a patina of prosperity. But in the 1990s the longer-term effects of Reaganism began to be felt. As the economy slowed, the go-go eighties seemed remote. Bush's term brought economic discontent, especially to the middle class.

First came the collapse of the savings-and-loan (S&L) industry, long a source of home loans to borrowers and of a secure return to depositors. In the late seventies, S&Ls had paid high interest rates to attract depositors, even though their assets were tied up in fixed-rate mortgages. In the early eighties, capital freed up by the Reagan tax cuts had flowed to S&Ls just as they were deregulated. Caught up in the high-flying mood of the eighties, S&Ls made risky loans on speculative real-estate ventures. As the economy cooled, many such investments went bad. In the period 1988–1990, nearly six hundred S&Ls failed, wiping out thousands of depositors' savings.

Because the federal government insures S&L deposits, the Bush administration in 1989 set up a program to repay depositors and to sell millions of dollars' worth of foreclosed office towers and apartment buildings in a depressed real-estate market. Estimates of the cost of the bailout topped $400 billion.

Meanwhile, the federal deficit, already worsened by the Reagan tax cuts and military spending, mounted. In fall 1990 Congress and Bush agreed on a five-year deficit-reduction package that clipped government spending and increased taxes. Bush would pay a high price for abandoning his "Read my lips: no new taxes" campaign pledge. But the red ink flowed on; the deficit reached $269 billion in 1991 and $290 billion in 1992. The Gulf War, the S&L bailout, and soaring welfare and Medicare-Medicaid payments shattered the budget-balancing effort.

Making matters worse, a recession struck in summer 1990. Retail sales slumped, housing starts declined, and unemployment rose. Troubled times continued into 1992, with a jobless rate of more than 7 percent. Hard-pressed states gutted social-welfare funding—Michigan cut Aid to Families with Dependent Children payments by 17 percent As the number of Americans below the poverty line rose by 2.1 million, the plight of the poor roused more resentment than sympathy. Ohio's governor declared, "Most Ohioans have had enough welfare, enough poverty, enough drugs, enough crime." The middle class, political strategists discovered, were suffering from "compassion fatigue."

Economic jitters made many Americans look back on Reagan's policies skeptically. If 1984 was "morning in America," wrote a columnist, quoting a Reagan campaign slogan, 1989–1990 was the "morning after."

Hard times worsened already bleak inner-city conditions. In April 1992 violence erupted in a poor black section of Los Angeles and quickly spread. The immediate trigger was the Rodney King case. Videotapes showed white California po-lice officers beating an African-American motorist, Rodney King, who seemed to be trying to escape. When an all-white jury acquitted the four officers, the predominantly black south-central section of Los Angeles exploded into riots that left forty dead and reminded the nation again of the desperate conditions in its inner cities.

The Bush administration did little to address these issues. In 1990 Bush vetoed a bill broadening federal protection against job discrimination, claiming that it would encourage "racial quotas." In 1991 he signed a similar bill. When Bush came to Atlanta in 1992 on the birthday of Martin Luther King, Jr., King's daughter, the Reverend Bernice King, asked bitterly, "How dare we celebrate in the midst of a recession, when nobody is sure whether their jobs are secure?"

The recession also stung school budgets. Bush proclaimed himself the "education president" but addressed the issue only fitfully. Bush called for standardized national testing of schoolchildren, supported a voucher system by which parents could enroll their children in private schools at public expense, and urged corporate America to support a fund for experimental schools. These proposals hardly matched the magnitude of the problem.

One Bush-supported measure, the Americans with Disabilities Act, did have significant implications for education. The law, which barred discrimination against the disabled and improved job and educational opportunities for the handicapped, led to an increase of more than a million physically or cognitively impaired children in public schools.

The environmental issue was spotlighted in March 1989 when a 987-foot oil tanker, the *Exxon Valdez*, ran aground in Alaska's beautiful Prince William Sound and spilled more than 10 million gallons of crude oil. The accident fouled six hundred acres of coastal and marine habitats, killed thousands of sea otters and shore birds, and jeopardized salmon and herring industries. Then in summer 1989 the Environmental Protection Agency (EPA) reported that air pollution exceeded federal standards in more than one hundred cities. In 1991 the EPA reported that pollutants were depleting the ozone shield—the layer that protects humans from cancer-causing solar radiation—over the United States at twice the rate that scientists had predicted.

Caught between public pressure for change and corporate calls for a go-slow policy, the Bush administration compiled a mixed environmental record. Bush deplored the *Exxon Valdez* spill but defended offshore oil exploration and drilling. In a rare bipartisan effort, the White House and the Democratic Congress passed a tough Federal Clean Air Act in 1990. The government also began the multibillion-dollar task of disposing of radioactive waste and cleaning up nuclear-weapons facilities and nuclear-power plants that had been contaminating soil and ground water for years.

Aftermath of the *Exxon Valdez* Disaster
Fisherman John Thomas rescues an oil-soaked bird after the massive oil spill in Alaska's Prince William Sound in March 1989.

But the Bush administration generally dismissed environmental concerns. Vice President Dan Quayle ridiculed environmentalists; the administration scuttled international treaties on global warming and mining in Antarctica, recommended oil exploration in the Alaskan wilderness, and proposed opening vast tracts of protected wetlands to development. In 1992 Bush addressed the Earth Summit, a United Nations–sponsored environmental conference in Brazil, but his defensive, self-serving speech further alienated environmentalists.

The Supreme Court Moves Right

Like all presidents, Reagan and Bush sought to perpetuate their political ideology through Supreme Court appointments. In addition to nominating Sandra Day O'Connor, Reagan in 1986 elevated William Rehnquist to chief justice and chose judicial conservative Antonin Scalia to fill the vacant seat. Then in 1987 Reagan named Robert Bork, a judge and legal scholar whose rigidity and doctrinaire opposition to judicial activism led the Senate to reject him. Reagan's next nominee withdrew after admitting that he had smoked marijuana, but Reagan's third choice, Anthony Kennedy, also very conservative, won speedy confirmation.

President Bush made two nominations, in 1990 and 1991: David Souter and Clarence Thomas. Souter, a New Hampshire judge, gained easy confirmation, but the Thomas nomination proved controversial. Bush nominated him to fill the seat vacated by Thurgood Marshall, a black who had fought segregation as an NAACP lawyer. Thomas, also an African-American, espoused a conservative political ideology and opposed affirmative-action programs. The head of the Equal Employment Opportunity Commission (EEOC) under Reagan, Thomas saw individual effort, not government programs, as the avenue for black progress. Noting Thomas's thin record as a federal judge, critics charged Bush with playing racial politics.

The nomination drew even more challenges when a former Thomas associate at EEOC, law professor Anita Hill, charged him with sexual harassment. For several days, the Senate Judiciary

Committee's hearings on Hill's accusations filled the nation's TV screens. Thomas narrowly won confirmation, 52 to 48.

These Reagan-Bush appointments blunted the liberal social activism that had characterized the Court from the New Deal through the Earl Warren years. In the 1990–1991 term, the Court narrowed the rights of an arrested person and upheld regulations barring physicians in federally funded family-planning clinics from discussing abortion with their patients. Then in a 5-to-4 decision in June 1992, the Supreme Court upheld a Pennsylvania law placing various restrictions on abortion. At the same time, however, the majority affirmed *Roe* v. *Wade* (1973), the decision that had upheld women's constitutional right to abortion.

The Politics of Frustration

In the afterglow of Operation Desert Storm, Bush's approval ratings shot up to 88 percent, only to plummet below 50 percent as the recession eroded national confidence. In late 1991, a *New York Times* editorial damningly described him as "shrewd and energetic in foreign policy . . . , clumsy and irresolute at home. . . . The domestic Bush flops like a fish, leaving the impression that he doesn't know what he thinks or doesn't much care, apart from the political gains to be extracted from an issue." In January 1992 Bush unveiled a recession-fighting package, including tax breaks for home buyers, lower taxes on capital gains, and tax incentives for business investment. Democrats dismissed Bush's belated attention to domestic issues as politically motivated and inadequate.

In the 1992 race for the White House, the Bush-Quayle ticket coasted to renomination. But the Republican right dominated the convention and platform, while moderates deplored this rightward turn. Undaunted by Bush's apparent invulnerability after Desert Storm, Governor William ("Bill") Clinton of Arkansas withstood doubts about his character and accusations of marital infidelities to defeat his opponents in the primaries and win the Democratic presidential nomination. Choosing Senator Albert Gore of Tennessee, an advocate for the environment, as his running mate, Clinton pledged an activist government and oriented the Democratic party toward middle-class concerns.

Folksy Texas billionaire H. Ross Perot presented a political challenge to politics-as-usual. His insistence that the nation's economic problems were simple, and that only party politics stood in the way of their solution, carried Perot to a nearly 40 percent peak in the polls. However, the Texan's autocratic ways and thin-skinned response to criticism turned off many supporters. In July 1992 he left the race for poorly explained reasons, but he returned in October 1992 and participated in televised presidential debates.

Bush attacked Clinton's character and charged that the Arkansas governor had been a draft dodger during the Vietnam War. Clinton called for an industrial policy that would give Washington an active role in promoting economic recovery and innovative technologies, and he put health-care reform high on his agenda.

The voters spoke on November 3 when 43 percent chose Clinton. Bush trailed with 38 percent, and Perot amassed 19 percent—the largest share for a third party since Teddy Roosevelt's 1912 Bull Moose party.

Clinton's electoral success rested largely on his ability to resurrect the Democratic coalition, luring blue-collar and "Reagan Democrat" voters as well as reclaiming parts of the South. The new Congress itself was more representative of U.S. society as a whole as thirty-eight African-Americans and seventeen Hispanic-Americans won election to the 1993–1994 session, up from twenty-five and ten, respectively. And the new Congress included fifty-three women: six in the Senate and forty-seven in the House. This outcome buoyed those who had declared 1992 the "Year of the Woman."

hc Primary Source: Clinton Bus Tour

THE CLINTON ERA I: DEBATING DOMESTIC POLICY, 1993–1997

George Bush was a World War II veteran, shaped by Pearl Harbor, FDR, and Bing Crosby. William Jefferson Clinton—Bill Clinton, as he preferred—was the first baby-boomer president: born after World War II, shaped by JFK, the Beatles, and Vietnam. Born in Arkansas in 1946, he attended Georgetown University and then, after a stint at Oxford as a Rhodes Scholar, Yale Law School. Fascinated by politics, he returned to Arkansas, married his law-school classmate Hillary Rodham, and won the governorship in 1979, at thirty-two.

Clinton began his presidency with energy, but he quickly encountered rough seas. When disgruntled voters gave the Republicans a stunning victory in the 1994 midterm election, Clinton moved right.

Shaping a Domestic Agenda

In contrast to predecessors like Nixon and Bush, Clinton preferred domestic issues to foreign policy. No modern president can avoid global involvement, and Clinton would confront myriad international problems (for a full discussion, see Chapter 32), but for the most part domestic issues dominated the Clinton era.

Both Clinton and Vice President Al Gore belonged to the New Democratic Coalition, a group of fiscal moderates who stood for economic growth, attention to the economic concerns of the middle class, and reduced federal spending on social programs. Clinton's campaign, designed to lure blue-collar and middle-class voters back to the Democratic fold, stressed economic growth, middle-class tax relief, health-care reform, and welfare programs based on work rather than the dole. The campaign also echoed themes of the sixties and seventies such as feminism, abortion rights, and environmental concerns.

Clinton named women to head several cabinet departments and other high-level federal agencies. In 1997 he appointed Madeleine Albright secretary of state, making her the highest-ranking woman in U.S. government history. One of his two Supreme Court appointments, Ruth Bader Ginsburg, was a champion of women's rights. (His second appointment to the Court was moderate liberal Stephen G. Breyer of Boston.) And he appointed his wife Hillary Rodham Clinton to head the task force on national health-care reform.

The transition from campaigning to governing proved rocky for Clinton. His effort to implement a campaign pledge to end the exclusion of homosexuals from military service stirred up controversy. He soon retreated to a compromise position summed up in the phrase "Don't ask, don't tell."

A slogan on the wall of Clinton's campaign headquarters had proclaimed, "It's the Economy, Stupid," and, as president, Clinton offered an economic program to cut the deficit and stimulate long-term growth. After six months of debate, Congress narrowly passed a five-year economic plan that cut military spending, increased taxes on upper-income families, and trimmed the projected budget deficit—but omitted a $169 billion package intended to stimulate job creation and economic expansion.

Clinton also endorsed the North American Free Trade Agreement (NAFTA), negotiated by the Bush administration, which admitted Mexico to the free-trade zone created earlier by the United States and Canada. Although critics warned that jobs would be lost as U.S. companies rushed to take advantage of cheap labor in Mexico, supporters predicted a net gain in jobs as Mexican markets opened to U.S. products. In late 1993 Congress approved NAFTA by a comfortable margin.

By 1993 the economy was rebounding from its earlier slump; by 1995 unemployment fell to 5.4 percent, the lowest level in four years, as 3.5 million new jobs appeared. Inflation remained low, thanks in part to interest-rate increases by the Federal Reserve Board. A weakening of the OPEC oil cartel also helped check inflation; in constant dollars, oil in 1993 cost about the same as it had in 1973, before the cycle of price spurts. And, in 1994, the federal budget deficit dropped to $220 billion, with further declines in prospect.

Clinton touted health-care reform as his central domestic goal. Although Americans in general enjoyed the world's best health care, the system had serious problems, including the fact that some 37 million citizens lacked health insurance and the cost of Medicare and Medicaid was spiraling. If unchecked, analysts calculated, health costs would eat up nearly 20 percent of the gross domestic product by 2000, twice the rate of other industrialized nations.

Led by Hillary Rodham Clinton, the task force on health-care reform devised a sweeping plan that the president presented to Congress in September 1993. As insurance-industry lobbyists and the health-care professions criticized aspects of the plan, polls made clear that the public favored incremental, rather than radical, reform. The key role of Hillary Clinton, who held no elective office or official government position, in shaping the proposal also rankled many voters. Ultimately the health-care bill died.

Clinton scored a major success on another front, however, with enactment of the administration's anticrime bill, which provided $30 billion for drug treatment, more prisons and more police officers, and boot camps for first-time offenders. It also included a controversial ban on assault weapons.

During his presidential campaign, driven by concerns that the largest welfare program, Aid to Families with Dependent Children, was creating a permanent underclass, Clinton had pledged to "end welfare as we know it." Although Congress took no action on a bill the president introduced in 1994, welfare reform remained high on the national agenda.

Despite the successes mixed in with his problems, Clinton's approval rating had dropped to 42 percent by mid-1994. Many found him too willing to compromise and too unfocused.

The Clintons' Arkansas financial dealings, especially their real-estate venture with the Whitewater Development Company, presented critics with ammunition and led to Senate hearings and the appointment of a special counsel. By 1996 Whitewater had resulted in several criminal convictions, including Clinton's successor as Arkansas's governor, but had not directly implicated the Clintons. Other issues dogged the White House as well, including Hillary Clinton's $100,000 profit on a $1,000 commodities investment; the suicide of White House aide Vincent Foster, a close Clinton friend and former law partner of Hillary Clinton; controversy over the firing of the White House Travel Office staff; White House mishandling of confidential Federal Bureau of Investigation files; and a sexual harassment lawsuit filed against the president by Paula Jones, a former Arkansas state employee.

The political climate turned nasty, even vicious. Radio commentator Rush Limbaugh won celebrity with his jeering attacks on liberals. Televangelist Jerry Falwell offered for sale a videotape suggesting that Clinton had arranged the murder of political enemies. The Christian Coalition, founded by TV preacher—and former presidential candidate—Pat Robertson, mobilized voters at the local level. The religious Right, with its passion and organizational energy, became a potent and unpredictable force in American politics during the 1990s.

1994: A Sharp Right Turn

Clinton had won in 1992 as a "New Democrat," but by 1994 many voters saw him as an old Democrat of the "tax-and-spend" variety. The failure of his health-care plan seemed to epitomize the top-down reform approach of the New Deal and the Great Society.

At the same time, a movement to downsize government, reform welfare, slash taxes and spending, and shift power to the states gained momentum among the middle class. A bubbling brew of cultural and social issues—abortion, school prayer, "radical feminism," and "family values"—reinforced disaffection with the president, as did a reaction against affirmative action programs to benefit minority groups. A network of conservative organizations including the Christian Coalition and the National Rifle Association orchestrated the rightward swing, while the radio waves vibrated to denunciations of the "liberal elite" by right-wing commentators and talk-show hosts. Prosperity did little to aid Clinton; the average worker's buying power remained flat because of automation, foreign competition, and organized labor's weakness.

Newt Gingrich, a Republican congressman from Georgia, capitalized on the sour mood by drafting a conservative "Contract with America" and bringing some three hundred GOP candidates to Washington to sign it. This strategy turned the midterm elections, normally dominated by local issues, into a national referendum. In a landslide that galvanized conservatives and stunned liberals, voters gave Republicans control of both houses of Congress for the first time since 1954. The number of Republican governors swelled to thirty-one; among the ousted were Democratic luminaries Mario Cuomo of New York and Ann Richards of Texas.

Evangelical Christians had flocked to the polls, mostly to vote for GOP candidates. Republicans hailed the election as the death knell of activist "big" government and insisted that the states, not Washington, D.C., represented the best source of policy ideas. Bob Dole of Kansas became majority leader of the Senate; the reactionary Jesse Helms chaired the Foreign Relations Committee; and ninety-two-year-old Strom Thurmond, presidential candidate of the racist southern Dixiecrat party in 1948, headed the Armed Services Committee.

In the House, a jubilant horde of Republicans, including seventy-three freshmen, chose Gingrich as Speaker of the House and rapidly enacted most of the provisions of the Contract with America. These measures—including a balanced-budget amendment, repeal of the assault-weapon ban, and major tax cuts—soon bogged down in the Senate, however. On the cultural front, House Republicans also targeted "liberal elite" institutions such as the National Endowment for the Arts. Congress also passed legislation to combat obscenity in the mass media and to curb pornography on the Internet.

GOP leaders promised an array of tax credits and benefits to the middle class and the wealthy. The promise of tax cuts coupled with increased defense spending threatened deeper budget deficits, but Republican leaders insisted that large savings could be carved out of other parts of the budget. Exactly where the surgery would take place was unclear, since the biggest budget items other than defense were interest payments on the national debt and two programs sacred to the middle class, social security and Medicare.

The torrent of bills, hearings, and press releases of early 1995 recalled the heady days of the Great Society or even FDR's first Hundred Days—but now the activist energy came from conservatives, not liberals.

At the center of this whirlwind was Newt Gingrich. The new Speaker seemed to be everywhere, appearing on talk shows, giving interviews, calling press conferences. However, his loquacious "shoot-from-the-lip" style and his glib rhetoric, a blend of computer-age technobabble and harsh, sink-or-swim individualism, alienated many. An ethically dubious $4.5 million book advance (which he eventually repudiated) further tarnished Gingrich's reputation.

In a troubling demonstration of voter apathy, only 38 percent of eligible voters had gone to the polls in 1994; about one-fifth of the electorate actually created the great shift rightward. Still, a significant ideological change did appear to be underway, challenging a social-welfare tradition stretching back to the Progressive Era.

In foreign relations, the 1994 Republican landslide signaled a turn inward. The "Contract with America" had largely ignored foreign policy, and key Republican legislators pushed isolationist views. Jesse Helms, chair of the Senate Committee on Foreign Relations, saw little good in United Nations' peacekeeping programs or U.S. foreign aid. Congressional Republicans refused to pay America's $1 billion in past-due U.N. dues.

Welfare Reform

With the Republicans riding high, welfare reform took on fresh urgency. Critics of the existing system offered two main arguments: the economic argument that welfare programs were too costly and the ideological argument that the system undermined the work ethic and trapped the poor in a cycle of dependence.

The debate raised serious ethical as well as policy issues. Would cutting welfare penalize children for their parents' actions? Would the government provide jobs if no private-sector jobs were available? Historian Joel Handler dismissed the welfare-reform campaign as largely symbolic; without fundamental changes in the labor market and the political and social climate, he wrote, "for the vast majority of mothers and their families, life will go on much as before."

But the warning went unheeded in the rush to "end welfare as we know it." In August 1996, having vetoed two earlier bills, Clinton agreed to sign a Republican welfare-reform bill—thereby depriving the GOP of a potent campaign issue. Ending a sixty-year commitment of unconditional support to those in need, this bill turned responsibility for welfare back to the states, which would receive lump-sum grants to devise their own programs. Along with sharp cuts in overall welfare spending, the bill set a five-year lifetime limit on benefits, required all able-bodied adults to work after two years on the dole, cut the federal food stamp program, and denied all but emergency aid to legal immigrants. Serious questions about job training, work programs, and the fate of those destined to be cut off from public assistance—including millions of children—remained unanswered.

Clinton's approval of a Republican welfare bill disappointed liberals and such mainstays of the Democratic coalition as women's groups, minority organizations, and advocacy groups for children and the poor. However, in the short term the law seemed successful: by December 1998, with the economy booming, welfare rolls had dropped by 38 percent to a thirty-year low of 7.6 million people, down from 14.1 million in January 1993. However, it had yet to be tested in an economic downturn.

SOCIAL AND CULTURAL TRENDS IN 1990S AMERICA

As the economy expanded through most of the 1990s, Americans continued to move to the thriving South and West, and immigrants poured in from Asia and Latin America. Not all Americans prospered. Minorities in the inner cities, including recent immigrants, struggled under harsh conditions to make ends meet. Long-term changes in the economy affected the lives of millions of citizens, benefiting some and creating serious difficulties for others.

U.S. culture of the 1990s reflected the general prosperity, with a heavy emphasis on consumerism, leisure pursuits, and mass-media diversions. But uneasiness stirred beneath the surface, and the good times did not prevent bitter conflicts over issues of morality and belief.

America in the 1990s: A People in Transition

Historically, U.S. society has been marked by rapid growth, geographic mobility, and ethnic diversity, and—as the 2000 census revealed—this remained true as a new century began. The total population in 2000 stood at more than 281 million, some 33 million more than in 1990, the largest ten-year increase ever. The historic shift of population to the South and West continued, reflecting both internal migration and immigration patterns. The West added 10.4 million residents in the 1990s, with California alone increasing by more than 4 million. The South expanded by nearly 15 million people in the decade. Georgia, which outpaced Florida as the most rapidly expanding southern state, grew by more than 26 percent.

The graying of the baby-boom generation (those born between 1946 and 1964) pushed the median age from around 33 in 1990 to 35.3 in 2000, the highest since census records began. The 45 to 54 age group grew by nearly 50 percent in the decade. Government planners braced for pressures on the social-security system and old-age facilities as the baby boomers reached retirement age.

The census also revealed changing living arrangements and family patterns. The proportion of "traditional" nuclear-family households headed by a married couple fell from 74 percent in 1960 to 52 percent in 2000. People living alone made up more than one-quarter of all households, while the proportion of households maintained by unmarried partners continued to increase, reaching 5 percent in 2000. Commenting on the census data, the *New York Times* observed, "[T]he nuclear family is not the only kind of family or even the only healthy kind of family. In modern America no type of family can really be recognized to the exclusion of all others."

The overall crime rate fell nearly 20 percent between 1992 and 2000. Experts attributed the decline to a variety of factors, including the decade's prosperity, stricter gun-control laws, a drop in the young male population, the waning crack-cocaine epidemic, and tougher law enforcement and sentencing rules. The U.S. prison population increased sharply throughout the decade, approaching 2 million by 2000.

Despite the falling crime rate, public fears of crime and violence remained high, fed in part by the appalling annual toll of gun deaths, which exceeded thirty thousand in 1998. A rash of school shootings proved particularly unsettling. In April 1999 two heavily armed students in Littleton, Colorado, shot and killed a teacher and twelve students before killing themselves. These episodes produced anxious discussions of America's obsession with firearms, the breakdown of parental authority, and the influence of mass-media violence on young people. President Clinton intensified his campaign for tougher gun-control laws, to little effect.

Public-health statistics, by contrast, brought encouraging news. Average life expectancy at birth rose from seventy-four to seventy-seven between 1980 and 1999. (Life expectancy differed by gender, race, and other variables, however.) Total health expenditures hit $1.2 trillion in 2000, up 17 percent from 1990. The decline in cigarette smoking by Americans continued, falling to under 25 percent of the population in 2000.

The U.S. AIDS epidemic peaked at last, thanks to safer-sex practices and advances in drug therapies. After cresting in 1995, AIDS deaths and new HIV/AIDS cases both declined. Health officials warned against complacency: AIDS remained deadly, producing some forty-one thousand new cases in 2000, with African-Americans and Hispanics especially at risk. New (and expensive) drugs slowed the progression from HIV to full-blown AIDS, but no cure had been found.

Globally, the AIDS epidemic raged on, with 22 million deaths and an estimated 36 million HIV/AIDS cases worldwide by 2001. Sub-Saharan Africa, with 25 million cases, was devastated by the disease, and many women and children were among the victims.

The 2000 census underscored the nation's growing racial and ethnic diversity. The U.S. population at century's end was about 13 percent Hispanic, 12 percent African-American, 4 percent Asian, and 1 percent American Indian. The Asian category included persons whose origins lay in the Philippines, China and Hong Kong, Vietnam, India, Korea, and elsewhere. The Hispanics (who may be of any race, and are linked by a shared language, Spanish) were nearly 60 percent of Mexican origin, with Puerto Ricans, Cubans, and Salvadorans comprising most of the balance. The number of persons with ancestral roots in Haiti (where the languages are Creole and French) increased as well, reaching 385,000 by 2000.

Growing immigration from Asia and Latin America reversed a long decline in the proportion of foreign-born persons in the population. From a low of about 5 percent in 1970, the figure rose steadily, reaching more than 10 percent in 2000. As in earlier immigration cycles, the new immigrants mostly settled in cities, from Los Angeles and Seattle to New York City and Miami. In New York, Catholic priests regularly said mass in thirty-five different languages!

Challenges and Opportunities in a Multiethnic Society

At century's end the African-American community continued to present diverse social, educational, and economic characteristics. In a decade of prosperity, many African-Americans made significant advances. The black unemployment rate fell from more than 11 percent in 1990 to 6.7 percent in 2000, and the proportion of blacks below the government's poverty line dropped from 32 percent to less than 24 percent.

By 2000, black families' median income stood at nearly $28,000, a record high, close to that of non-Hispanic white families. The earnings of college-educated blacks was significantly higher. But in the inner cities in particular, blacks continued to be mired in poverty and scarred by its consequences. By 1997 more than eight hundred thousand African-Americans languished in prison; tragically, a black male aged twenty was statistically more likely to be in prison than in college. Drug-related carnage took a fearful toll. Young people living in housing projects or slums sometimes had to duck bullets as they walked to school. A black third-grader in New Orleans, James Darby, gained national attention when he wrote President Clinton about his fears of urban violence; a week after the president received his letter, James was shot dead. Out-of-wedlock births to teenage black mothers peaked in the mid-nineties and began to decline, but more than half of all black children continued to live with a single parent, usually the mother, curtailing educational and economic opportunities for both generations.

Native Americans continued to reassert tribal pride and activism. Many tribes went to court to enforce treaties signed long ago. Others sought economic salvation through business enterprises, particularly gambling casinos. By the late 1990s huge casinos such as the Foxwoods Casino run by the Mashantucket Pequots in Connecticut were earning $6 billion annually. Some Indian communities prospered from this inflow of money, but many non-Indians deplored the spread of gambling, and states battled to extract more tax revenues from the casinos. Many within the Native American community lamented the erosion of traditional values.

New patterns of immigration continued to redefine the U.S. population. The mounting numbers of Hispanic immigrants and high birthrates among Hispanic women led demographers to predict that Hispanics would become the nation's largest minority in the early 2000s and comprise 25 percent of the total population by 2050.

The highly diverse Hispanic population resisted easy generalization. Many were well educated and upwardly mobile; for example, Henry Cisneros became a member of the Clinton cabinet. Many others, however, remained trapped in an inner-city world of gangs, drugs, failing schools, and teen pregnancy. Many of the new immigrants were young and poorly educated, with few options other than low-paying, low-status jobs as gardeners, maids, or migrant agricultural workers.

One thing was clear: the burgeoning Hispanic population was changing America. In June 2001 *Time* magazine devoted a special issue to what it called "Amexica," a Southwestern border region of 24 million people, growing at double the national rate. "The border is vanishing before our eyes," declared *Time,* creating a new nation within a nation

"where hearts and minds and money and culture merge."

Asian newcomers also presented a highly variegated picture. Prizing education, supported by close family networks, and often possessing needed skills and entrepreneurial talent, many Asian immigrants moved rapidly up the economic ladder. Chinese and other Asian immigrant groups often followed a similar pattern of assimilation and upward mobility. In Fremont, California, near San Francisco, the Asian population increased from 19 percent in 1990 to 37 percent in 2000. Many of the newcomers worked as engineers and businesspeople in nearby Silicon Valley. On campuses and in city neighborhoods, Asian-Americans organized to promote their interests, sometimes acting collectively and sometimes in specific national groups.

Rethinking Citizenship in an Era of Diversity

Population experts calculate that by 2050 America will have no single racial or ethnic majority. At the start of the millennium increasing numbers of Americans already reflected mixed racial and ethnic origins. Golfer Tiger Woods, for example, could boast of Thai, Native American, and African-American ancestors. Questions were rising about what being an American would mean in a diverse, multiethnic society. Separatist pressures among various ethnic groups were strong; for example, at the UCLA law school, blacks, Latinos, and Asians each had their own student association and law review.

Language itself became a battleground. Some advocates for immigrant groups sought instruction in a child's native tongue or at least bilingual education, while some Anglo politicians campaigned to make English the nation's "official language." Urban populations changed rapidly as "white flight" emptied inner cities of all but minority and immigrant populations. Some observers feared the fragmentation of the nation into enclaves determined by ethnicity or skin color. Racial and ethnic identities remained strong; not surprisingly, Americans confronting modern mass society sought security and reassurance in a group identity.

Americanization, Twenty-first Century Style
Recent immigrants from Afghanistan join a fitness class in Fremont, California, in 2001.

At the start of the twentieth century, America was seen as a "melting pot," in which all ethnic groups would become assimilated; by the end of that century, many were starting to describe the country not as a melting pot but as a "salad bowl," in which people of diverse backgrounds retained their ethnic identity. What would hold such a society together? Would forces such as consumerism and mass culture be strong enough to bind citizens into a nation? The answers remained unclear.

The "New Economy"

As the twentieth century ended, a transformation was reshaping the U.S. economy: the decline of the industrial sector and the rise of a service-based economy. Manufacturing continued, of course, but it faded as a major source of employment. In 1960 about half of the male labor force worked in industry or in related jobs such as truck driving. By the late 1990s this figure had fallen to under 40 percent.

In the same period, the percentage of professional, technical, and service workers continued its century-long upward trend. In 1960 such workers had comprised about 42 percent of the male labor force; by 1998 the figure was 58 percent. The percentage of women workers in the service sector was even higher.

The service economy was highly segmented. At one end were low-paying jobs in fast-food outlets, video rental stores, nursing homes, and chain stores such as Wal-Mart. At the other end were lawyers and physicians; money managers and accountants; and workers in the entertainment and telecommunications fields. The latter category expanded rapidly with the growth of high-speed telecommunications systems and the rise of the personal computer with its Internet-based spinoffs.

The decline of the industrial economy and the rise of the service economy had different meanings for different groups. Young people with the education, skills, and contacts to enter the new high-tech industries often found exciting challenges and substantial economic rewards. For less-privileged youths, supermarkets, fast-food outlets, or discount superstores could provide entry-level work, but doubtful job security and long-term career prospects. For older workers displaced from industrial jobs, the impact could be devastating both economically and emotionally. The rise of the new economy and its implications for social change affected almost all Americans.

Changing Patterns of Work, 1900–2000

This chart illustrates the sweeping changes in the male U.S. labor force in the twentieth century. Farming, fish, forestry, and mining industry participation fell dramatically while the number of workers in the service, technical, managerial, sales, clerical, and professional categories rose steadily.

Source: *Historical Statistics of the United States, Colonial Times to 1970* (1975); Statistical Abstract of the United States, 2002; Caplow, Hicks, and Wattenberg, *The First Measured Century: An Illustrated Guide to Trends in America* (Washington, D.C.: The AEI Press, 2001).

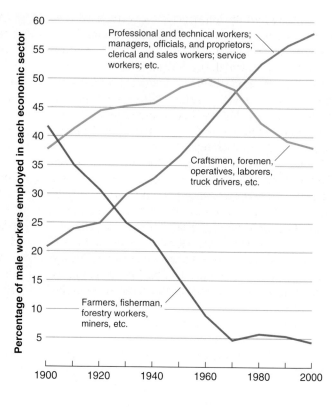

Affluence, Conspicuous Consumption, a Search for Heroes

The economic boom that began in 1992 and roared through the Clinton years produced instant fortunes for some and an orgy of consumption that set the tone of the decade. Wall Street and Silicon Valley spawned thousands of twenty-something millionaires. Tales circulated of elegant restaurants offering obscenely expensive cigars and rare wines, and exclusive shops selling $13,000 handbags.

The economic boom also encouraged what some considered a smug, hard-edged "winner take all" mentality, with those at the top turning their backs on the larger society. In *Bowling Alone: The Collapse and Revival of American Community* (2000), political scientist Robert Putnam sharply criticized American public life. Putnam found diminished civic engagement and weakened interest in public issues, as evidenced by declines in voter participation, political activism, and participation in civic organizations. He even found less informal socializing, from dinner with friends to card parties and bowling leagues, as Americans pursued purely personal goals.

With the stock market surging, the Cold War over, and other threats only beginning to come into focus, many Americans set out to enjoy themselves. Attendance at the Disney theme parks in Florida and California neared 30 million in 2000. The sales of massive sport-utility vehicles (SUVs) soared, despite environmentalists' laments about their fuel inefficiency.

As in the 1980s, the media offered escapist fare. The 1997 blockbuster film *Titanic,* with spectacular special effects, grossed $600 million. The top-rated TV show of 1999–2000, *Who Wants to Be a Millionaire?,* unabashedly celebrated greed. So-called "reality" TV shows like *Survivor,* popular as the decade ended, offered viewers a risk-free taste of the hazards that American life itself (at least for the affluent) conspicuously lacked.

Millions avidly followed TV coverage of the 1995 murder trial of O. J. Simpson, a former football star, while the 2001 disappearance of a young government intern after an alleged affair with her congressman similarly mesmerized the public. The sex scandals that swirled around President Clinton and eventually led to his impeachment often seemed to be no more than another media diversion in a sensation-hungry decade.

Again, as was true of the 1980s, other evidence from the popular culture suggests a more complex picture. Some critics interpreted *Titanic*, which sided with its working-class hero in steerage against the rich snobs in first class, as a subtle comment on a decade when class differences in America were blatantly on display. *American Beauty* (1999) explored dark and murderous currents beneath the facade of a comfortable suburban family.

The Clint Eastwood western *Unforgiven* (1991) seemed to express nostalgia for an earlier era when life presented rugged challenges and hard moral choices. The same longings, some suggested, underlay the outpouring of admiring biographies of larger-than-life heroes from the past, such as Stephen Ambrose's *Eisenhower* (1991) and David McCullough's *Truman* (1993) and *John Adams* (2001).

The decade also reveled in the heroic era of World War II, featuring it in a series of TV specials, books such as Tom Brokaw's *The Greatest Generation* (1998), and movies like *Saving Private Ryan* (1998) and *Pearl Harbor (2001)*.

A Truce in the Culture Wars?

Elsewhere on the cultural landscape, the 1990s also saw a continuation of the moralistic battles that had begun in the 1970s, which some viewed as nothing less than a struggle for the nation's soul. Historically, American culture wars have raged along sectarian lines, with native-born Protestants battling Catholic and Jewish immigrants. During the Cold War, the source of evil seemed clear: communism. Now, many Americans translated the same apocalyptic world view to the home front and searched for the enemy within.

As the abortion controversy continued, some opponents of abortion turned from protest to violence. In 1995 an anti-abortion activist fatally shot a doctor and his bodyguard outside a Florida abortion clinic, and an unstable young man shot seven people, killing two, at a clinic near Boston. In 1997 bombers struck clinics in Tulsa and Atlanta. Anti-abortion sites on the Internet carried lists of physicians who performed abortions with a line through the names of doctors already killed; to many in the pro-choice camp, these seemed chillingly like "hit lists."

The worst domestic terrorism was the April 19, 1995, bombing of the Murrah Federal Building in Oklahoma City; 168 died, including many children who had been in a day-care facility there. The Oklahoma City bombing came exactly two years after a long stand-off in Waco, Texas, between federal authorities and Branch Davidians, an apocalyptic sect charged with firearms violations; the Waco incident had ended in violence, when tanks closed in and flames swept through the Branch Davidian compound, killing 80 people. In 1997 Timothy McVeigh, a Gulf War veteran with vague links to one of many secretive right-wing militia groups that had sprung up in the 1990s, was found guilty of the Oklahoma City bombing and sentenced to die. These right-wing organizations were often racist, anti-Semitic, obsessed with conspiracy theories, and deeply suspicious of the federal government, claiming Waco as an example of the abuse of federal power.

However, words and symbols were the main weapons of the culture wars. Conservatives denounced the National Endowment for the Arts for funding "indecent" art and cut funding for the Public Broadcasting System on the grounds that it was too liberal and "elitist." Conservative culture warriors called for constitutional amendments outlawing abortion and permitting prayer in public schools, and demanded a renewal of religion, morality, and "family values." History texts came under fire for promoting multiculturalism and not being sufficiently patriotic. Conflict raged between scholars who carried out traditional literary analysis and "deconstructionists" who probed the ways in which writers of the past had reinforced an imperialist and patriarchal social order.

Chronology

1988	George Bush elected president.		**1993**	Congress enacts modified version of Clinton economic plan. Congress approves North American Free Trade Agreement (NAFTA). Recession ends. Congress debates health-care reform (1993–1994).
1989	Massive Alaskan oil spill by *Exxon Valdez*. U.S. invasion of Panama; Manuel Noriega overthrown. China's rulers crush prodemocracy movement. Berlin Wall is opened.			
1990	Federal Clean Air Act passed. Iraq invades Kuwait. Recession begins. Germany reunified; Soviet troops start withdrawal from Eastern Europe.		**1994**	Republican victory in 1994 elections.
			1995	Bombing of Murrah Federal Building in Oklahoma City. AIDS epidemic peaks in the United States, continues worldwide. Sweeping changes in welfare enacted. Clinton reelected.
1991	Gulf War (Operation Desert Storm). United States and U.S.S.R. sign treaty reducing strategic nuclear arms by 25 percent. Upheavals in Soviet Union as economy nears collapse and Soviet republics declare independence.			
			1996	Timothy McVeigh found guilty in Oklahoma City bombing.
1992	Supreme Court approves Pennsylvania restriction on abortion but upholds *Roe* v. *Wade*. Bill Clinton elected president.		**2000**	Census finds population surge in West and South, sharp increase in Hispanic and Asian populations, and changing family patterns.

As the year 2000 approached, popularizers of biblical prophecy warned that history's final crisis, "the end times," was near. Pat Robertson's *The New World Order* (1991) portrayed American history as a vast conspiracy that would soon culminate in the rule of the Antichrist. Although the new millennium arrived without the Apocalypse, a series of novels portraying the trials of those "left behind" by the Rapture sold millions of copies. The charges of adultery and perjury that swirled around President Clinton simply underscored to conservatives the moral rot they saw eating away at America.

As the 1990s ended, the culture wars seemed to be diminishing. The Christian Coalition lost momentum with the resignation of its politically savvy director, Ralph Reed. And its members and other religious conservatives became openly frustrated with Republican politicians who courted their vote but ignored their cultural agenda once in office.

One Nation After All, a 1998 study of middle-class Americans by sociologist Alan Wolfe, found in the course of extensive interviews that most were suspicious of extremist views and broadly accepting of diversity. Tolerance and the philosophy of live-and-let-live seemed to be thriving in middle America. Although the study omitted the views of the poor and immigrant newcomers, as well as extremists, it illuminated the generosity of spirit of the American middle class. The optimism and pragmatism of this vast group struck an encouraging note for the new century and for the realization at last of America's elusive but enduring vision of a more fully just and humane society.

CONCLUSION   *hc* ACE Practice Test

Both America and the world changed with dizzying speed in the 1990s. The sudden collapse of the Soviet Union radically altered global politics; Reagan's successor, George Bush, sought a "new world order" and successfully met the first post–Cold War international crisis, the Iraqi invasion of Kuwait, but faltered on the domestic front. In 1992 Bush lost the presidency to Bill Clinton, who emphasized the theme of economic recovery.

Clinton was a highly intelligent man with a mastery of policy issues, but he came with character flaws that continually undermined his strengths. His failure to achieve health-care reform laid the groundwork for a Republican landslide in the 1994 midterm election and brought into the spotlight, at least briefly, Newt Gingrich and "the Contract with America," a laundry list of conservative programs and policies.

The 1990s seemed to glow with prosperity, but the good times were unevenly distributed and the problems of the inner city left unsolved. Long-term social and economic trends reshaped America: the population shift to the south and the west continued, as did high levels of immigration from Latin America and Asia, giving the nation an ever more multiethnic and multicultural flavor. New information technologies—especially the rise of the personal computer—contributed to a fundamental economic restructuring, as the old factory-based economy yielded to the new knowledge-based service economy.

Cultural conservatives grew increasingly vocal, hammering on "hot-button" issues such as abortion, homosexuality, and what they saw as the nation's moral decay. The culture wars seemed to ease as the decade ended, and Americans looked to the new century with confidence.

On the political front, the economic boom worked in Democrats' favor, as did Gingrich's self-destruction, and Clinton easily won a second term in 1996. But the years after 1996 would bring political scandal, recession, and the most horrendous act of terrorism the nation had ever experienced.

FURTHER READING

Discussions of trends in contemporary America may be found in such journals as *The American Prospect, The Atlantic Monthly, Business Week, Christianity Today, Commentary, The Economist* (London), *Fortune, Harper's Magazine, Monthly Labor Review* (U.S. Department of Labor), *The New Repub-*

lic, National Review, The Nation, Nation's Business, New York Times Magazine, The Progressive, Scientific American, and *U.S. News and World Report.*

Mary Jo Bane and David T. Ellwood, *Welfare Realities: From Rhetoric to Reform* (1994). Ellwood, assistant secretary of health and human services in the Clinton administration, and his coauthor explore the complexities of welfare reform.

Michael R. Beschloss and Strobe Talbott, *At the Highest Levels: The Inside Story of the End of the Cold War* (1994). A historian and a journalist-turned-diplomat collaborate on an early but valuable account of the Cold War's demise.

Haynes Johnson, *The Best of Times: America in the Clinton Years* (2001). A Washington journalist offers an informed, critical view of Clinton and his era.

David Maraniss, *First in His Class: A Biography of Bill Clinton* (1995). Explores the sources of Clinton's political drive and his almost desperate need to be liked.

Gwendolyn Mink, ed., *Whose Welfare?* (1999). Essays on welfare policy and the effects of the 1996 welfare-reform act.

Richard J. Payne, *Getting Beyond Race: The Changing American Culture* (1998). An argument for moving beyond the emphasis on division and difference.

Robert D. Putnam, *Bowling Alone: The Collapse and Revival of American Community* (2000). A well-researched and carefully argued assessment of the decline of civic engagement and human connectedness in late-twentieth century America.

Rickie Solinger, ed., *Abortion Wars: A Half Century of Struggle* (1998). Scholars offer historical perspectives on a contentious issue.

Roberto Suro, *Strangers Among Us: How Latino Immigration Is Transforming America* (1998). A rich and perceptive assessment, based on careful research and firsthand interviews, of sweeping demographic trends that are changing the United States in profound ways.

U.S. Bureau of the Census, *Statistical Abstract of the United States, 2002. The National Data Book* (2002). An annual treasure trove of information on economic and social trends, from the federal budget to college enrollments.

Alan Wolfe, *One Nation After All: What Middle Class Americans Really Think . . .* (1998). A sociologist reports on his extensive firsthand interviews, and finds reason for optimism about middle-class attitudes on a variety of issues.

32

New Century, New Challenges, 1996 to the Present

hc This icon will direct you to additional study and research resources at http://college.hmco.com/history/us/boyer/enduring_concise/5e/students/index.html

A candlelight vigil in Grayslake, Illinois, after the terrorist attacks of September 11, 2001

Friday, February 26, 1993, began like most other business days at New York's World Trade Center, two 110-story towers soaring over lower Manhattan. But suddenly, at 12:18 p.m., a bomb containing over one thousand pounds of explosives ripped through Level B2 of the parking garage under the north tower. The blast cut off electricity, plunging the building into darkness. Fifty thousand workers hastily evacuated, and hundreds were trapped in stalled elevators. Six persons died in the blast, and more than one thousand were injured.

The first investigators found an eerie scene: a giant hole extending five stories underground, fires from ruptured automobile gasoline tanks, water and sewage cascading from broken pipes, car alarms wailing in the darkness. The FBI quickly identified the vehicle that had carried the bomb into the garage: a Ford Econoline van rented in Jersey City. Five Islamic militants, including a blind Egyptian sheik, Omar Abdel Rahman, the alleged mastermind, were arrested and convicted of conspiracy and other crimes. Three, including Sheik Omar, were found guilty of murder and received life sentences.

Shocking as it was, the attack could have been far worse: at least the tower had survived, and comparatively few lives had been lost. In reality, this event was one of a nightmarish series of attacks that would take a heavy toll in life and property as the upsurge of terrorist attacks in the 1980s (see Chapter 30) continued. In November 1995 a bomb shattered a U.S. military training center in Riyadh, Saudi Arabia, killing seven, including five Americans. In June 1996 another bomb ripped through a U.S. military barracks in Saudi Arabia, leaving nineteen U.S. airmen dead.

Like distant thunder signaling an approaching storm, the attacks were ominous warnings of worse ahead. On September 11, 2001, terrorists again struck the World Trade Center, as well as the Pentagon, this time with horrendous consequences.

Much of this chapter focuses on the impact of escalating terrorist attacks, particularly the aftermath of September 11, at home and abroad. As Americans faced these dangers, they also coped with domestic political battles and economic turmoil. Amid calls for unity, deep divisions remained. A White House scandal in Bill Clinton's second term, a disputed presidential election in 2000, and the policies of Clinton's successor, George W. Bush, who seemed to favor the privileged and powerful and took the nation into a preemptive war in Iraq, all proved highly divisive. As prosperity gave way to recession, bankruptcies and charges of fraud hit some of the nation's largest companies, undermining investors' confidence and tarnishing the reputation of the corporate world.

This chapter focuses on six major questions:

▶ What domestic initiatives marked Bill Clinton's second term, and how did the scandals that swirled around him in 1998–1999 affect his ability to govern?

▶ On balance, was President Clinton's foreign-policy record a success?

▶ What factors fueled the economic boom of the 1990s, and why did it end?

▶ What key domestic policies did George W. Bush propose early in his presidency?

▶ How did the government respond to the terrorist attacks of September 2001, domestically and internationally? Was the response appropriate? Was it effective?

▶ What factors contributed to President Bush's reelection in 2004?

THE CLINTON ERA II: DOMESTIC POLITICS, SCANDALS, IMPEACHMENT, 1996–2000

Moving to the political center, Bill Clinton won a second term in 1996. Apart from his support for tough regulation of the tobacco industry, Clinton's second term is remembered mainly for a sex scandal that led to an impeachment effort by his Republican foes. This effort further poisoned an already highly partisan political climate.

Campaign 1996 and After

After the rout of 1994, Clinton's reelection prospects looked bleak, but the self-styled "Comeback Kid" again hit the campaign trail. The budget-balancing and welfare-reform bills helped him, as did the choice of a weak Republican opponent, Senator Bob Dole of Kansas. A party stalwart whose useless arm was a constant reminder of his World War II heroism and sacrifice, the seventy-three-year-old Dole ran a lethargic campaign.

Clinton won with just under 50 percent of the vote; Dole received 41 percent, and H. Ross Perot 8 percent. Congress remained Republican, although at times the GOP legislators seemed more concerned with intraparty intrigues than with new proposals.

Launching his second term, Clinton cautiously distanced himself from the New Deal–Great Society past. For example, in 1997 he signed a Republican bill providing some tax cuts while establishing a timetable for a balanced budget by 2002. (Thanks to the economic boom, Clinton beat the deadline by three years.) Many Clinton proposals involved more cheerleading than expenditures: school uniforms, parents' reading to their children, and a citizens' commission to lead a national dialogue on race. Public opinion among non-Hispanic whites increasingly turned against affirmative action. In 1995 the Supreme Court restricted the awarding of federal contracts on the basis of race, and in 1996 California voters barred racial or ethnic preferences in state agencies, including the state's university system.

Campaign-finance reform emerged as another hot issue in Clinton's second term. Television costs had driven campaign expenses to ruinously high levels, which showed no signs of lessening. Abuses abounded. One Democratic fundraiser with links to Indonesian and possibly Chinese corporate interests had raised $3.4 million; more than half of that was returned as illegal. President Clinton, an aggressive fundraiser himself, was accused of auctioning off the White House Lincoln bedroom to wealthy donors.

Neither party leapt to curb such abuses. Early in 1998, the Senate shelved a modest campaign-finance bill sponsored by Republican John McCain of Arizona and Democrat Russ Feingold of Wisconsin. (McCain, continuing to crusade for campaign-finance reform, made it the centerpiece of his run for the Republican presidential nomination in 2000.) In reality, politicians seemed addicted to the contributions that poured in from lobbying groups. As scandal concerning Clinton's sexual behavior began to swirl about the White House, momentum for such reform dwindled.

In his January 1998 State of the Union address, Clinton continued his policy of incremental proposals appealing to progressives and moderates alike. He called for tax credits for college tuition costs, grants to hire more teachers, more medical research, Medicare for poor children, and other modest social programs. The pending budget surplus, Clinton insisted, should be used to pay down the national debt and "Save Social Security First." Although some die-hard liberals jeered at his ideas as "Progressivism Lite," Clinton's politically astute program would normally have been a major step toward his political comeback, offering assurance that history would judge his legacy positively.

Scandal Grips the White House

However, conditions were far from normal. Even as Clinton spoke, scandal gripped the White House. Adultery charges had long clung to Clinton, and Paula Jones's sexual harassment suit was still in the courts. Subpoenaed to testify by Jones's lawyers, the president on January 17 was also quizzed about reports of a sexual relationship with a White House intern, Monica Lewinsky. He denied any such relationship and insisted to his family, advisers, cabinet members, and the American people that the stories were completely false.

But, like Richard Nixon earlier, Clinton was undone by a tape recorder. In hours of telephone conversations secretly and illegally taped by her "friend" Linda Tripp, Lewinsky graphically described an intermittent sexual relationship with Clinton that had begun when she was twenty-one. In early January 1998 Tripp had passed the tapes to Kenneth Starr, the independent counsel investigating Whitewater.

Although a judge dismissed the Jones suit, Starr secured permission to broaden his inquiry and focused on whether Clinton had committed perjury in his Jones testimony and had tried to persuade Lewinsky to lie as well. In August, after threats of a long jail term and promises of immunity, Lewinsky acknowledged the affair in testimony before Starr's grand jury. Clinton continued to insist that his testimony had been technically accurate but admitted misleading the American people.

Impeachment

In a September 1998 report to the House Judiciary Committee, Starr narrated the Clinton-Lewinsky affair in lurid detail and found "substantial and credible" grounds for impeachment on charges of perjury and obstruction of justice. After acrimonious hearings and a straight party-line vote, the partisan Judiciary Committee forwarded four articles of impeachment to the full House. In December the House, in an equally partisan vote, approved and sent to the Senate two articles of impeachment: perjury and obstruction of justice. Clinton thus became only the second president, and the first in more than 130 years, to be impeached.

Opinion polls sent the Republicans an ominous message: most Americans opposed impeachment. The 1998 midterm elections saw Democratic gains in the House and drove Speaker Newt Gingrich to resign as both speaker and representative.

Conviction and removal of the president required a two-thirds vote of the Senate; Republicans held only a fifty-five to forty-five majority, which made this unlikely. Nevertheless in early 1999 the Senate conducted a full-scale trial, with Chief Justice William Rehnquist, resplendent in a black robe with gold stripes on the sleeves, presiding.

Polls showed that the public's opinion of Clinton's performance as president remained high, reaching 70 percent in the middle of the trial. While most people deplored Clinton's personal behavior, few believed that it met the "high crimes and misdemeanors" specified by the Constitution as the only grounds for impeachment and removal. The feeling grew that Clinton had been targeted by conservative Republican zealots grimly determined to drive him from office.

On February 12, 1999, the Senate rejected both articles of impeachment; neither charge won even a simple majority. President Clinton again expressed contrition and urged the nation to move on. Most Americans simply seemed relieved that the long ordeal was over.

On the last full day of his presidency, Bill Clinton reached a deal with Robert Ray, Kenneth Starr's successor as independent counsel. Clinton admitted lying in his grand jury testimony and agreed to the suspension of his law license for five years. In turn, Ray dropped all charges against the president and agreed not to indict him once he left office.

Clinton clearly had suffered grievous damage—mostly self-inflicted. Despite his enormous political skills and other strengths, his character flaws had overtaken him at last, eroding his leadership and tarnishing his historical standing. Ironically, in the short run the Republican party had been damaged even more by its apparent surrender to its most extreme and moralistic elements.

hc Primary Source: Clothespin Vote

CLINTON'S FOREIGN POLICY: BEYOND THE COLD WAR

Bill Clinton preferred domestic issues to foreign policy. Yet the United States, as the world's only remaining superpower, could not escape its global role. Bill Clinton faced two key challenges abroad: using American power wisely in the post–Cold War era and responding to terrorist attacks against the United States and the threat of further attacks.

The Balkans, Russia, and Eastern Europe in the Post-Soviet Era

The collapse of Soviet hegemony in Eastern Europe unleashed ancient ethnic hatreds. While the Czechs and Slovaks peacefully divided Czechoslovakia into two separate nations, attempts at ethnic separation in Yugoslavia proved catastrophic. In pursuit of a "Greater Serbia," Orthodox Christian Serbs seized territory from Roman Catholic Croats and Muslim Bosnians (with the Croats occasionally joining the Serbs in attacking the Bosnians) and carried out a brutal "ethnic cleansing" all too reminiscent of Nazi genocide. The bloody conflict dragged on until 1995 when the Clinton administration brought leaders of the warring groups to Dayton, Ohio, to sign a peace treaty and arrange a partition of Serbian, Croatian, and Bosnian lands. At the end of

1995, Clinton dispatched some twenty thousand U.S. troops to Bosnia-Herzegovina as part of a NATO peacekeeping contingent, despite serious misgivings by many Americans.

By 1998 the Balkans were again aflame, this time as the Serbian leader, Slobodan Milosevic, launched a new ethnic cleansing campaign against ethnic Albanians living in the southern province of Kosovo. Under U.S. leadership, NATO bombed Serbian military and government facilities, including the capital of Belgrade. Hundreds of thousands of ethnic Albanians, primarily Muslim, were driven from their homes, creating the worst refugee crisis in Europe since World War II. Slobodan Milosevic was overthrown in 2001, and a more democratic Yugoslav government, eager for Western aid, delivered him for trial before a war-crimes tribunal at The Hague.

These developments affected U.S. relations with Russia. Although Russia protested the air attacks on its traditional ally, Serbia, Russian forces joined in NATO's occupation of Kosovo. Facing unrest among its own Muslim population, Russia in 1995–1996 waged war against the breakaway Muslim republic of Chechnya. Some called this unpopular, inconclusive conflict Russia's Vietnam.

Amid these troubles, Russia endured inflation, shortages, and economic chaos as centralized control yielded to a market-oriented system. The Clinton administration supported President Boris Yeltsin, Russia's first democratically elected leader, and pledged economic aid. American-Russian relations remained testy as Russia adopted an independent foreign-policy course, but destruction of nuclear weapons continued, as did cooperation on the International Space Station. When Vladimir Putin succeeded Yeltsin in March 2000, the United States applauded the continuation, however shaky, of democracy in Russia.

Symbolic Gestures in Africa; a Modest Success in Haiti

Clinton was stirred by conditions in Africa, a continent wracked by poverty, AIDS, tribal conflict, and authoritarian regimes. His engagement, however, proved mainly symbolic.

In December 1992, President Bush had committed twenty-six thousand U.S. troops to a U.N. mission to the East African nation of Somalia, afflicted by civil war and famine. The mission was intended to provide humanitarian aid and end the fighting. As the warring factions battled, forty-four Americans were killed and many more injured, and President Clinton withdrew the U.S. force in 1994. The U.N. mission ended a year later. Traumatized by this fiasco, Clinton failed to intervene in other African conflicts, including an appalling human tragedy in Rwanda, where as many as half a million people died and thousands more became refugees in intertribal massacres.

During Clinton's presidency South Africa ended apartheid and became a multiracial democracy—a transformation hastened by U.S. and other nations' economic sanctions. In 1994 Nelson Mandela, long imprisoned by South Africa's white government, was elected president. Touring Africa in 1998, President Clinton visited South Africa and greeted Mandela. Calling upon six nations in eleven days, he offered modest aid assistance.

Closer to home, in Haiti, a 1991 military junta overthrew President Jean-Bertrand Aristide and terrorized his supporters. Thousands of Haitians fleeing poverty and repression set out for Florida in small, leaky boats. African-American leaders demanded U.S. action, as did Haitians born in the United States. Clinton assembled an invasion flotilla off Haiti's coast in 1994, and former president Jimmy Carter persuaded the junta's leaders to accept voluntary exile. Backed by a U.S. occupation force, Aristide resumed the presidency, giving Clinton a modest diplomatic success.

The Middle East: Seeking an Elusive Peace, Combating a Wily Foe

In the Middle East, the 1987 Palestinian uprising, or Intifada, against Israel's military occupation of the West Bank and Gaza (see Chapter 30) continued into the 1990s. Peace prospects brightened in 1993, however, after Israeli and Palestinian nego-

MAP 32.1

The Mideast Crises, 1980–2004

With terrorist attacks, the Iran-Iraq War, the Persian Gulf War, Iraq's secretive weapons program, and the ongoing struggle between Israel and the Palestinians, the Middle East was the site of almost unending violence, conflict, and tension in these years.

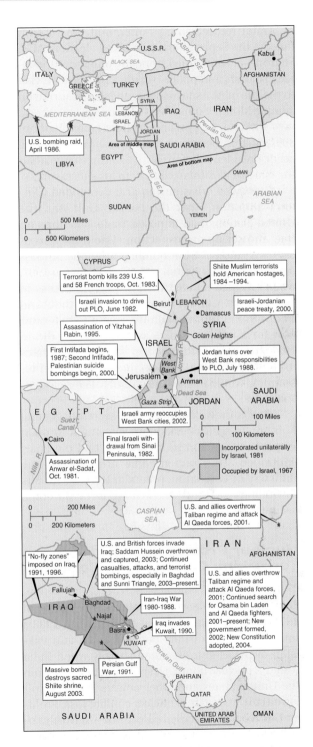

tiators who met in Norway agreed on a six-year timetable for peace.

The so-called Oslo Accords provided for a Palestinian state, the return of most Israeli-held land in the West Bank and Gaza to the Palestinians, and further talks on the claims of Palestinian refugees. In 1994 President Clinton presided as Israeli prime minister Yitzhak Rabin and Yasir Arafat, head of the Palestine Liberation Organization, signed the agreement at the White House.

Rabin was assassinated in 1995 by a young Israeli opposed to the Oslo Accords. Israel's next election brought Benjamin Netanyahu of the hardline Likud party to power. Despite American prodding, and because of a series of terrorist bombings by Palestinian extremists, Netanyahu stalled the withdrawal of Israeli troops from the West Bank and permitted housing construction to continue. Under U.S. pressure Netanyahu in 1998 agreed to withdraw Israeli forces from some West Bank areas in return for security guarantees. But as terrorist attacks continued, Netanyahu halted the withdrawal. More Jewish housing was built in Palestinian territory, and by 2000 an estimated two hundred thousand Israeli settlers were living there.

Ehud Barak of Israel's more moderate Labour party became prime minister in 1999. In July 2000 Clinton invited Barak and Arafat to Camp David. Barak made unprecedented concessions based on the principle of "land for peace." According to press reports, he agreed to Israeli withdrawal from 95 percent of the West Bank and all of Gaza; the creation of a Palestinian state; Palestinian control of East Jerusalem; and the transfer of control over Jerusalem's Temple Mount, sacred to both Muslims and Jews, from Israel to a vaguely defined "religious authority." In return, Arafat would declare an end to hostilities and give up further claims on Israel.

Arafat refused Barak's offer, and the summit failed. In September the Likud leader Ariel Sharon—accompanied by nearly one thousand Israeli soldiers and police—made a provocative visit to the site of Al-Asqa Mosque, an Islamic shrine on Temple Mount. Soon after, Palestinians launched a new Intifada, or uprising, against Israel. Early in 2001, Sharon became Israel's prime minister. Like other presidents before him, Clinton bequeathed the Israeli-Palestinian conflict to his successor.

A renewed crisis in Iraq also demanded Clinton's attention. After the Persian Gulf War, the United Nations had imposed trade sanctions on Iraq and set up an inspection system to prevent Saddam Hussein from building weapons of mass destruction. This system was effective, but in 1997, when Hussein refused U.N. inspectors access to certain sites, Clinton dispatched thirty thousand troops to the Persian Gulf. He sought to rally support for a military strike, as George Bush did in 1991, but France, Russia, and various Arab states resisted. At home, critics questioned whether bombing would further the goal of unrestricted inspections.

Clinton drew back after U.N. secretary general Kofi Annan secured Saddam's agreement to open inspection. Saddam soon reneged, and the crisis continued. The Iraqi muddle underscored the difficulty of combating potential terrorist threats by military actions whose long-term outcome seemed murky.

Nuclear Proliferation and Terrorism: Confronting Global Security Challenges

Despite the Nuclear Nonproliferation Treaty of 1970, the proliferation threat continued. In 1998 a long-simmering dispute between India and Pakistan over Kashmir escalated sharply when India tested a nuclear bomb. Despite urgent pleas from the United States and other powers, Pakistan followed suit, and fears of nuclear conflict rose. Proliferation fears also focused on communist North Korea, which, in violation of the 1970 treaty, began a program of nuclear-weapons development and

missile testing. In 1994, facing U.N. economic sanctions and the loss of $9 billion in international assistance (and following a visit by Jimmy Carter), North Korea pledged to halt this program. In 1999, confronting famine and economic crisis, North Korea agreed to suspend long-range missile testing in return for an easing of U.S. trade and travel restrictions. North Korea's continued violation of these pledges caused ongoing concern, however.

Nuclear dangers also arose in the former Soviet Union. In the 1993 Strategic Arms Reduction Treaty (START II), the United States and Russia agreed to cut their long-range nuclear arsenals by half. This left many nuclear weapons in Russia and in three nations once part of the Soviet Union: Ukraine, Kazakhstan, and Belarus. With unrest and economic crisis in the region, Washington feared that foreign powers or terrorist groups might acquire nuclear weapons or know-how through espionage or bribery. The Bush and Clinton administrations expended much money and diplomatic effort to speed the dismantling and secure disposal of nuclear weapons in Russia and elsewhere in the former Soviet Union.

The cycle of terrorism continued in the Clinton years. On August 7, 1998, powerful bombs destroyed the U.S. embassies in Nairobi, Kenya, and Dar-es-Salaam, Tanzania, killing 220 people, including Americans and many Kenyans and Tanzanians. U.S. antiterrorism specialists pinpointed a wealthy Saudi Arabian, Osama bin Laden, who in 1982 had moved to Afghanistan, where he established and financed terrorist training camps. In the 1990s he had spent time in Sudan.

After the embassy bombings, Clinton ordered cruise missile strikes on a suspected chemical-weapons factory in Sudan allegedly financed by bin Laden and on a training camp in Afghanistan. A U.S. grand jury indicted bin Laden on charges of planning the embassy attacks and also of inciting the killing of GIs in Somalia in 1993. Clinton called for new measures to cope with rogue states and terrorist groups that might acquire nuclear, chemical, or biological weapons. Secretary of State Albright, foreseeing "a long-term struggle," declared: "This is, unfortunately, the war of the future."

Underscoring Albright's grim assessment, on October 12, 2000, a bomb aboard a small boat in the harbor of Aden, Yemen, ripped a gaping hole in the U.S. destroyer *Cole,* killing seventeen sailors. The peaceful post–Cold War era that many had anticipated seemed an ever-receding mirage.

A New World Order?

Like George Bush, Bill Clinton had little success in designing a coherent American foreign policy to cope with the complexity of the post–Cold War world. And foreign policy was low on the list of American concerns; from 1988 to 1995 foreign news coverage on network television fell by more than 50 percent, and by 1998 only 20 percent of Americans said that they followed foreign news.

Four large-scale developments defined America's post–Cold War global role. The first was the growing importance of economic and trade issues. In the new, trade-driven era, commercial considerations, multinational corporations, and global systems of finance, marketing, and communications largely shaped international relations.

Second, in contrast to economic globalization, the world saw a rise of fundamentalism. Islamic, Jewish, Hindu, and Christian fundamentalists all challenged regional or even global order as they decried secularism, modernization, and change. The struggle between fundamentalism on one side and rapid modernization and globalization on the other presented challenges to diplomats and other officials worldwide.

Third, a growing gulf separated prosperous, industrialized societies with high living standards and stable birthrates, and regions scourged by poverty, disease, illiteracy, spiraling population growth, and a dangerous gap between the masses and the elites. The vast disparity created conditions ripe for conflict, including the spreading menace of terrorism.

Finally, the Cold War's end left the future of international organizations uncertain. Some Americans either turned to isolationism or favored unilateralist, go-it-alone approaches. Others, however, continued to hope that the United Nations, long a pawn of the superpowers' conflict, could at last function as its founders had envisioned in 1945. Indeed, in 2003 some forty-three thousand U.N. peacekeeping forces and civilian personnel were serving in trouble spots around the world. U.N. agencies also addressed global environmental and public-health issues.

THE ECONOMIC BOOM OF THE 1990S

The 1990s saw one of the longest periods of sustained economic growth in U.S. history. Productivity increased, unemployment fell, and inflation remained under control. Prosperity helped bring crime rates down and reduce welfare rolls. Federal deficits gave way to surpluses as tax revenues increased.

For some, the surging stock market stimulated the urge to get rich quick and enjoy the good times. But real wages did not keep pace with the stock market, and workers who lacked the skills required by the new economy remained stuck in dead-end jobs. America's participation in the global economy fueled growth, but when foreign economies faltered, Americans felt the effects as well.

Economic Upturn; Surging Stock Market

Although Bill Clinton targeted the sluggish economy in the 1992 campaign, a turnaround had already begun. Economists differ over the reasons, but the new products, efficiencies, and business opportunities associated with the personal computer and the information revolution were certainly crucial. Rising international trade and high consumer confidence helped sustain the boom, as did low inflation, the Federal Reserve Board's low interest rates, and a steady flow of immigrants eager to work.

Whatever its sources, the fact of the boom is clear. Unemployment fell from 7.5 percent in 1992 to 4 percent by 2000. Corporate profits soared. The gross domestic product, a key economic indicator, rose nearly 80 percent in the decade.

The stock market reflected and then outran the economic upturn as the stock of many companies far outpaced their actual value or earnings prospects. From under 3,000 in 1991, the Dow Jones Industrial Average edged toward 12,000 by early 2001. New investors flocked into the market. As early as 1996 Alan Greenspan, chairman of the Federal Reserve Board, warned of "irrational exuberance" in the stock market, but it only surged higher. By 1998 nearly 50 percent of American families owned stock directly or through their pension plans. With so many Americans speculating in stocks rather than investing in more secure forms of savings, some economists warned, the inevitable downturn could have severe consequences.

An Uneven Prosperity

The benefits of the boom were unevenly distributed. From 1979 to 1996 the portion of total income going to the wealthiest 20 percent of the population increased by 13 percent, while the share going to the poorest 20 percent dropped by 22 percent. Commented Harvard economist Richard Freeman in 1998, "The U.S. has the most unequal distribution of income among advanced countries—and the degree of inequality has increased more here than in any comparable country." While stockholding was widely diffused by the later 1990s, the top 5 percent of the owners held 80 percent of all stock.

As corporations maintained profits through mergers, "downsizing," and cost cutting, job worries increased. Adjusted for inflation, the wages of industrial workers rose only slightly in the 1990s. The rapidly growing service sector included not only high-income positions but also low-paying, low-skilled jobs in sales, fast-food outlets, custodial work, telemarketing, and so forth. Overall union membership stood at only 13.5 percent of the labor force by 2000, weakening this means by which workers had historically improved their wages and job conditions. Unions' political clout weakened as well. Congress ratified the 1993 NAFTA treaty, for example, despite protests from organized labor.

Job-market success increasingly required special training and skills, posing problems for young people, displaced industrial workers, and welfare recipients thrown into the labor force. Overall employment statistics also concealed racial and ethnic variables. In 2000 the jobless rate for blacks and Hispanics, despite having dropped, remained significantly higher than the rate for whites. In short, the economic boom brought real benefits to many, but also left millions behind.

America and the Global Economy

Expanding foreign trade ranked high on Clinton's agenda. "Trade as much as troops," Clinton proclaimed, "will . . . define the ties that bind nations in the twenty-first century." When the U.S. trade deficit shot up to $133 billion in 1993, after several years of decline, and included a $59 billion trade gap with Japan, Clinton pressured the Japanese to buy more U.S. goods.

Clinton also opted to preserve trading ties with China despite Beijing's human-rights abuses; restrictive trade practices; threats to Taiwan; and pirating of U.S. movies, CDs, and computer software. Brushing aside protests from human-rights activists, Clinton welcomed Chinese president Jiang Zemin in 1997 and returned the visit in 1998.

Clinton's China policy reflected hard economic realities: with U.S. imports from China surpassing $100 billion annually, China was America's fourth largest trading partner, after Canada, Mexico, and Japan. In 2000 Congress permanently granted China the same trading status as America's other trading partners, rather than making trade agreements with China dependent on year-by-year congressional action, as in the past.

Economic calculations also defined U.S. relations with Europe, which became a powerful trading competitor in 1993 when fifteen nations created the European Union (EU) to integrate their economic policies and work toward a common currency, the Euro, adopted in 2001.

In 1994 the Senate ratified a new global trading agreement that created the World Trade Organization (WTO) to replace the old General Agreement on Tariffs and Trade (GATT) established in 1947. The WTO agreement, which went effect in 1995, provided for a gradual lowering of trade barriers and set up mechanisms for resolving trade disputes.

Several events underscored the interconnectedness of the new global economy. When the Mexican peso collapsed in 1995, jeopardizing U.S.-Mexican trade and threatening to increase the flow of illegal migrants northward, Clinton quickly granted Mexico $40 billion in loan guarantees. Conditions became especially dangerous in Indonesia, the world's fourth-most-populous nation. Working through the International Monetary Fund, the administration sought to bail out Indonesia's faltering economy and to reduce corruption in the regime.

The once-sizzling Japanese economy stumbled as Asia's economic crisis spread. The Tokyo stock market fell and the yen lost value, unsettling the U.S. stock market and further jeopardizing U.S. exports and investments in Asia. Again recognizing the threat to U.S. prosperity, the Clinton administration urged Japan to undertake needed economic reforms. By 1999, as the economies of Brazil, Argentina, and other South American nations sank into recession as well, analysts questioned how long the American boom could continue.

With globalization, foreign investors flocked into the American market. By 2000 foreign investment in the United States totaled a staggering $1.24 trillion. Investment flowed the other way as well. As American fast-food chains, soft drinks, movies, pop music, and TV programs spread globally, other nations fretted about being swamped by U.S. mass culture.

Globalization aroused opposition in other quarters as well. Union leaders and environmentalists warned that multinational corporations could build plants in poor countries, bypassing U.S. environmental and worker-protection laws. Activists pressured companies selling goods made in poor nations to upgrade labor conditions in their factories. At a 1999 WTO conference in Seattle, opposition demonstrators representing a variety of causes nearly shut down the city.

DISPUTED ELECTION; CONSERVATIVE ADMINISTRATION, 2000–2002

The 2000 election highlighted the acrimony pervading U.S. politics. The disputed election ended the Democrats' hold on the White House, but only after the Supreme Court intervened on behalf of the Republican candidate, George W. Bush. Pursuing his father's unfulfilled agenda, Bush advocated policies supported by corporate America and by religious conservatives. On the military front, Bush pursued a missile-defense system first proposed by Ronald Reagan. In its approach to the world, the administration followed a go-it-alone policy, arousing widespread criticism abroad.

Election 2000: Bush Versus Gore

The 2000 campaign shaped up as a contest of personalities. The Democrats, bouncing back from the impeachment crisis, confidently nominated Al Gore for president. As his running mate, Gore chose Connecticut Senator Joseph Lieberman, making him the first Jewish-American candidate on a major party ticket. The fact that Lieberman had denounced Clinton's extramarital affair and his efforts to cover up the scandal helped insulate Gore from the "sleaze factor" in the Clinton legacy.

The Republican contest pitted Senator John McCain of Arizona, a former prisoner of war in Vietnam, against Texas governor George W. Bush, son of the former president. McCain, a champion of campaign-finance reform and a critic of corporate influences in his party, made a strong bid. Bush, however, with powerful backers and a folksy manner, won the nomination. His running mate Dick Cheney had been defense secretary in the first Bush administration and then head of the Halliburton Corporation, a Dallas-based energy company. Conservative columnist Pat Buchanan won the nomination of Ross Perot's Reform party. The Green party nominated consumer advocate Ralph Nader.

Both Gore and Bush courted the center while trying to hold their bases. For Bush, this meant corporate interests, religious conservatives, and the so-called Reagan Democrats in the white middle and working classes. Gore's base, by contrast, consisted of liberals, academics and professionals, union members, African-Americans, and many Hispanics.

Gore's prospects looked good. He pointed to the nation's prosperity and pledged to extend health-care coverage and protect social security. In televised debates Gore displayed greater mastery of detail than his opponent.

Bush, while projecting a likeable manner, had little national or foreign-policy experience. Many saw him as a lightweight who owed his political success to family influence. But he campaigned hard, pledging tax cuts, education reform, and a missile-defense system. Calling himself a "compassionate conservative," Bush subtly reminded voters of Clinton's misdeeds by promising to restore dignity to the White House.

Polls showed that most voters agreed with Gore on the issues, approved the Democrats' economic policies, and conceded Gore's intellectual edge. Ominously for Gore, however, they preferred Bush as a person. The election seemed a toss-up.

Feuding in Florida

The intensely partisan politics so vividly on display in the impeachment crisis was further symbolized by a bitter dispute over the election outcome. Gore won the popular vote by a margin of more than 500,000. The electoral college, however, remained up for grabs. Soon the struggle narrowed to Florida, whose 25 electoral votes would give either candidate the presidency.

Flaws in Florida's electoral process quickly became apparent. In Palm Beach County, a poorly designed ballot led several thousand Gore supporters to vote for Buchanan by mistake. In other counties, particularly those with many poor and African-American voters, antiquated vote-counting machines threw out thousands of ballots in which the paper tabs, called "chads," were not fully punched out. Gore supporters demanded a hand

count of these rejected ballots. Bush's lawyers filed suit to halt the recounts.

When Florida's secretary of state, Katherine Harris, refused to extend the deadline for certifying the Florida vote to allow time for a hand recount, Democrats cried foul, since Harris was also cochair of Bush's Florida campaign and a political ally of Florida Governor Jeb Bush, the candidate's brother.

As various counties conducted hand counts, election officials scrutinized ballots to see whether the chads were detached, dangling, or "pregnant" (partially pushed out). On November 21 the Florida Supreme Court unanimously held that the hand count should constitute the official results. However, Bush's legal team appealed to the U.S. Supreme Court. Overturning the Florida justices' ruling, the U.S. Supreme Court on December 4 sent the case back to Tallahassee for clarification.

Meanwhile, Secretary of State Harris had certified the Florida vote, awarding Bush the state by 527 votes. But on December 8, the Florida Supreme Court ordered an immediate recount of all ballots statewide. The U.S. Supreme Court again heard an appeal, and on December 12, in a 5 to 4 vote, ordered an end to the recounting. Republican appointees to the court generally supported Bush. Five Supreme Court justices had made George W. Bush president.

Ralph Nader, though winning only 3 percent of the vote, also helped put Bush in the White House. Had it not been for the 97,488 Floridians who voted for Nader, Gore would have won the state.

The election produced an evenly divided Senate, giving Vice President Cheney the deciding vote. (The Republicans narrowly held the House of Representatives.) Hillary Rodham Clinton won election as senator from New York, becoming the first presidential wife to pursue a political career. Overall, the new Senate included thirteen women, a record number.

The George W. Bush Administration: A Conservative Turn in Domestic Politics

The election crisis over, Americans focused on the incoming president, fifty-four-year-old George W.

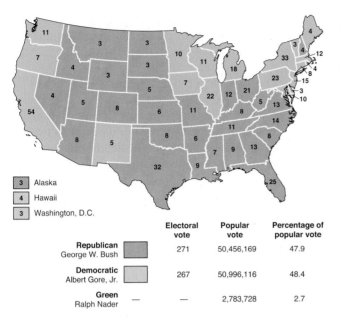

MAP 32.2

The Election of 2000

For the first time since 1888, the winner of the popular vote, Al Gore, failed to win the presidency. The electoral-college system and the Supreme Court's intervention in the disputed Florida vote put George W. Bush in the White House.

	Electoral vote	Popular vote	Percentage of popular vote
Republican George W. Bush	271	50,456,169	47.9
Democratic Albert Gore, Jr.	267	50,996,116	48.4
Green Ralph Nader	—	2,783,728	2.7

Bush. After graduating from Yale, sitting out the Vietnam War in the Texas Air National Guard, and attending Harvard Business School, Bush returned to Texas and entered the oil business. Known for partying and heavy drinking since his college days, he was convicted of drunk driving in 1976; he experienced a religious conversion and eventually quit drinking altogether in 1986, at age 40. Bush's business ventures did not thrive, but in 1989 he joined a consortium that bought the Texas Rangers baseball team. Frequently appearing at games, he used this visibility, plus his family connections, to win the Texas governorship in 1994.

Attention soon focused on the team Bush assembled. Colin Powell, former head of the Joint Chiefs of Staff, became secretary of state and the highest ranking African-American ever to serve in a presidential administration. As national security adviser Bush named Condoleezza Rice of Stanford University, also an African-American.

Other Bush appointees were, like Vice President Cheney, veterans of earlier Republican administrations with strong corporate ties. Secretary of Defense Donald Rumsfeld had held the same post under President Ford and later headed a large

pharmaceutical company. Army Secretary Thomas E. White came from Houston's Enron Corporation. To appease his party's right wing, Bush named ultra-conservative John Ashcroft, who had just lost a bid for reelection to the Senate, as attorney general.

Despite his razor-thin victory, Bush did not move to the center, as many had expected. Rather he tailored his policies to reflect the interests of the wealthy, corporate leaders, and the religious right. His probusiness outlook, combined with the influence of businesspeople in his inner circle and a desire to win favor with religious conservatives (whose alienation had helped defeat his father in 1992), shaped his administration.

Evangelical Protestants had voted overwhelmingly for Bush, and his policy proposals reflected the views of evangelicals and cultural conservatives. Pursuing his so-called faith-based initiative, he set up a White House office to funnel federal funds to religious organizations providing social services. National Park Service officials permitted religious groups to erect mottos containing Bible verses in national parks. When a Massachusetts court in 2003 found no constitutional bar to gay marriage, Bush called for a constitutional amendment banning such unions and urged Congress to appropriate $1.2 billion to promote marriage among heterosexual couples.

Bush's education program, called No Child Left Behind, proposed standardized national basic-skills tests from grades three through eight, with penalties for schools that failed to measure up. He also called for a voucher system by which children could attend private or religious schools at taxpayers' expense. In December 2001 Congress mandated annual testing and provided funds for tutors in poorly performing schools, but rejected the controversial voucher provision.

In February 2001, fulfilling a campaign promise, Bush proposed a bill to cut taxes by $1.6 trillion over a ten-year period. The cuts would stimulate investment, he argued, as the economy faltered (see discussion later in this chapter). Democrats attacked the bill for giving the greatest tax breaks to the wealthiest taxpayers. Recalling the huge deficits that followed the 1981 Reagan tax cut, they also charged that Bush's plan reflected overly optimistic economic projections. In May Congress passed a $1.35 trillion tax cut—lower than Bush's proposal and somewhat less tilted toward the rich. As the economy worsened, second thoughts about Bush's tax cut increased. The *New York Times,* esti-mating the lost federal revenue over a twenty-year period at a staggering $4 trillion, warned that the shortfall could be covered only by dipping into social security and Medicare trust funds.

Bush's energy bill reflected the industry's influence in the administration. Kenneth Lay, for example, head of Houston's Enron Corporation and a major GOP contributor, enjoyed access to top administration officials and the heads of federal regulatory agencies. The bill was drafted in secret meetings between Dick Cheney and energy-company executives.

Warning of America's dependence on imported oil, Bush proposed two thousand new electric power plants, including more nuclear power plants, and vastly expanded coal, oil, and natural-gas production, including mining and drilling in environmentally fragile regions such as Alaska's Arctic National Wildlife Refuge (ANWR). Energy conservation and research on renewable energy barely figured in the bill.

The Republican House passed a bill favored by the White House. It provided $27 billion in incentives for the domestic oil, gas, and coal industries and permitted drilling in the ANWR. In April 2002 the Democratic Senate passed a very different bill featuring tax breaks and other incentives to promote energy conservation and the use of renewable fuels, and forbid-

Musk Oxen in Alaska's Arctic National Wildlife Refuge
Proposals by the George W. Bush administration to permit oil drilling in the refuge stirred bitter controversy.

ding drilling in the ANWR. The two bills went to a joint House-Senate conference committee.

The bill that finally emerged late in 2003 closely paralleled Bush's original proposal, without the controversial authorization of drilling in the ANWR. It provided many tax breaks and other incentives to energy companies, with little emphasis on conservation or environmental protection. Despite heavy administration pressure, however, the Senate took no action. The process illustrated the difficulties of governing in a climate of sharp partisan divisions.

Bush's attempt to placate the religious right without alienating moderate voters was evident in his maneuvering on the emotional issue of research on stem cells, which are produced during an early stage of human embryo development. Bush's compromise, announced in August 2001, permitted federal funding of research on stem-cell lines already held by laboratories but barred funding for research on stem cells taken from embryos in the future.

A Go-It-Alone Foreign Policy; Pursuing Missile Defense

The administration of George W. Bush at first proceeded with scant regard for other nations' views. This contrasted with his father's more internationalist approach. On military matters, the younger Bush pursued programs initiated by his Republican predecessors. For example, the Bush administration was determined to build the antimissile system first proposed by President Reagan in 1983. Reagan's "Star Wars" initiative had been criticized as a fantasy, and its strategic rationale seemingly evaporated with the Cold War's end. Clinton had downgraded the program, but George W. Bush gave it high priority. True believers and military contractors argued that the technical problems could be solved. As for its strategic rationale, they now focused on possible missile attacks from "rogue states" such as North Korea.

Bush's enthusiasm for missile defense had diplomatic implications, because such a system would violate the 1972 Anti-Ballistic Missile (ABM) Treaty. Russian president Vladimir Putin, eager for U.S. investment and for a greater role in NATO,

agreed to discuss dropping the ABM Treaty if both sides further reduced their remaining nuclear arsenals. The Bush administration, which valued Russia as an ally in the war against terrorism and as a potential supplier of oil should imports from the Middle East be disrupted, accepted Putin's terms. In 2002, despite protests from other nations and arms-control specialists, the United States allowed the ABM Treaty to lapse. Soon after, Bush and Putin signed a treaty pledging to cut their nuclear arsenals by two-thirds within ten years. Fulfilling another of Moscow's objectives, NATO granted Russia a close consultative relationship.

In 2002 work began at Fort Greely, Alaska, on a missile defense facility that planners hoped would be operational by 2004. Alaskans who were worried about the state's economy welcomed the infusion of jobs and federal dollars the project promised. Pentagon planners envisioned a much expanded and extremely costly future system, including warship-based interceptors and modified laser-firing Boeing 747s.

Other U.S. actions underscored the administration's go-it-alone approach. In 2001 the United States boycotted a U.N. conference in Bonn, Germany, considering an international treaty aimed at reducing global warming (see "Environmental Issues Persist" later in this chapter). When most other nations, including the EU and Japan, agreed to strengthen a 1972 treaty banning biological weapons, the United States balked. The administration refused to join the International Criminal Court, created by the U.N. in 1998 to prosecute individuals charged with war crimes or crimes against humanity, claiming that U.S. officials might be unjustly prosecuted. The Bush administration also rejected a U.N. agreement to regulate the global trade in handguns, a treaty banning discrimination against women ratified by 169 other nations, and a U.N. effort to reduce smoking worldwide.

The United Nations had long been a target of conservatives skeptical of international commitments. Beginning in 1994, conservatives in Congress led by Republican Jesse Helms of North Carolina had withheld payment of America's U.N. dues. By 2001 the back debt totaled $2.3 billion. Early in

2001 the Senate Foreign Relations Committee agreed to pay part of this sum and to resume payment of future dues at a reduced percentage rate. In 2001, in a symbolic action underscoring the growing resentment of America's strong-arm tactics, the United States was voted off the U.N. Human Rights Commission, on which it had served since 1947.

The Bush administration, like its predecessors, actively promoted U.S. trade interests, a fact underscored by its relations with China. In April 2001 a U.S. spy plane off China's coast collided with a Chinese aircraft monitoring it. The Chinese plane crashed, killing the pilot, and the damaged U.S. plane landed in China. Angry words followed, but $120 billion in annual trade spoke more loudly, and after negotiations China released the U.S. crew. Later that year President Bush attended an Asia-Pacific economic cooperation conference hosted by Beijing, and China formally entered the World Trade Organization.

Despite Bush's commitment to foreign trade, domestic pressures influenced him as well. In 2002, responding to demands from U.S. steel producers and the steelworkers' union, Bush slapped tariffs of up to 30 percent on imported steel products for a three-year period. While the tariffs did not apply to Canada, Mexico, or certain developing nations, they did hit China, Japan, Russia, South Korea, and the EU, which protested this violation of free-trade principles. Whether the U.S. steel industry, with its steadily shrinking labor force and high production costs, could long survive even with tariff protection remained an open question.

Recession Woes; Campaign-Finance Battles; Environmental Debates

A sharp recession abruptly ended the prosperity of the 1990s and raised questions about the wisdom of the tax cut. Disagreements over economic policy, combined with criticism of Bush's environmental actions and a long-running battle over campaign-finance reform, helped perpetuate the climate of intense political partisanship as the Bush administration began.

End of the Economic Boom

The stock-market boom of the later 1990s barely outlasted the decade. As Asian and Latin American economies faltered, the U.S. economy suffered as well. In March 2001, the stock market recorded its worst week since 1989, falling by 6 percent. Millions of stockholders felt the pain. Consumer confidence fell, corporate profits plunged, and businesses announced layoffs. The unemployment rate rose from under 4 percent in 2000 to nearly 6 percent by November 2001. In that month alone, three hundred thousand workers lost their jobs.

The bursting of the Internet bubble worsened the downturn. By one calculation, nearly 250 dot-com businesses collapsed in a few months' time. The market value of the companies that did survive fell sharply. Instant millionaires watched their portfolios melt away.

To stimulate the economy, the Federal Reserve Board cut interest rates eleven times in 2001, to a forty-year low. The Bush administration, having based its tax-cut plan on the assumption of continued budget surpluses, now projected years of deficits. Democrats attacked the administration's overly optimistic economic projections and warned about threats to social security and Medicare funds. As an antirecession stimulus package, the administration proposed generous new tax breaks for corporations and the wealthy, and a speeding up of tax cuts already approved.

Retirees with pension plans invested in the stock market and low-paid workers lacking job security suffered as the recession that began in Silicon Valley and Wall Street spread ominously. Industrial production declined, and every state lost jobs. Service-sector employment fell faster in the last quarter of 2001 than in any three-month period since World War II. Unskilled workers and former welfare recipients seeking entry-level jobs faced problems. Openings for temporary workers dropped precipitously. The long economic boom ended with a thud, and the impact spread through society. An anemic recovery began in 2002, but it was slowed by business scandals that eroded investor confidence (see "Bankruptcies and Scandals in Corporate America" later in this chapter).

The Rocky Path of Campaign-Finance Reform

In Congress, meanwhile, two senators—Arizona Republican John McCain and Wisconsin Democrat Russ Feingold—carried on the battle for campaign-finance reform. They targeted so-called soft-money contributions made to political parties (rather than to specific candidates) by individuals and lobbying organizations seeking to influence legislation. Given the soaring cost of TV advertising, soft money loomed increasingly large in electoral campaigns. In the 1997–1998 electoral cycle the national parties raised more than $190 million in soft money. In the 2000 election, soft-money contributions reached nearly $500 million.

Finally, in 2002, a committee reconciled the House and Senate versions of the campaign-finance bill originally sponsored by McCain and Feingold, and Bush signed the bill. It banned soft-money contributions to national parties by lobbying organizations and phony TV "issue ads" that were really aimed at influencing elections. The law faced legal challenges on free-speech grounds, but in December 2003 the Supreme Court upheld all its major provisions. Whether the new law would achieve its purpose remained unclear as politicians and special-interest groups searched for ways to circumvent it.

Environmental Issues Persist

Modern technology's environmental risks and long-term environmental changes gravely jeopardized human well-being. The late twentieth and early twenty-first centuries brought growing environmental awareness along with a mixed record of environmental action.

With the Cold War over, Americans faced the estimated $150-billion cost of cleaning up nuclear-

weapons facilities, including disposing of 70,000 tons of highly radioactive uranium and plutonium from dismantled nuclear weapons and aging nuclear-power plants. In 1997 scientists reported water seepage into the vast cave intended for nuclear-waste storage at Nevada's Yucca Mountain. In 2002, over objections from environmentalists, Nevada politicians, and Las Vegas civic leaders, the Senate approved the Yucca Mountain site for storage beginning in 2010. Lawsuits and controversy continued, however.

Other environmental and health risks arose from atmospheric changes linked to industrial processes. Acid rain carrying sulfur dioxide and other pollutants from U.S. factories and auto exhaust threatened Appalachian forests and Canadian lakes. Fluorocarbons from spray cans, refrigeration equipment, and other sources depleted the upper-atmosphere ozone layer, allowing higher levels of solar radiation to reach Earth's surface, increasing skin-cancer risks and other health hazards.

The threat of global warming seemed especially urgent. As carbon dioxide and other gases produced by fossil-fuel emissions and deforestation (as well as naturally occurring sources) accumulated in the lower atmosphere, the resulting "greenhouse effect" prevented Earth's heat from escaping. Scientists predicted a 40 percent increase in carbon dioxide emissions by 2020. Long-term global warming could disrupt agricultural production and plant and animal ecosystems. In the most dire scenario, rising sea levels from melting polar ice could flood low-lying coastal regions.

Heightening global-warming fears, the ten hottest years of the twentieth century all occurred after 1985. In Alaska, where the average annual temperature rose seven degrees from 1972 to 2002, rising water levels in the Chukchi Sea threatened coastal villages, and a new species of beetle that arrived with the warmer weather devastated spruce forests. Highways buckled as the permafrost melted, and engineers warned that the Alaska pipeline stretching from Prudhoe Bay to Valdez could be destabilized.

Some environmental gains were recorded. U.S. emissions of the principal air pollutants fell more than 60 percent from 1970 to 1999. In 1996–1997, Congress strengthened pesticide regulation and the Environmental Protection Agency (EPA) announced new air-quality standards to reduce soot and ground-level ozone. (In 2001 the Supreme Court unanimously upheld the EPA's right to establish such standards.) In 1997 the EPA created an environmental "superfund" to clean up hazardous-waste sites. By 2001 more than thirteen hundred such sites had been designated, though the pace of cleanup proved slow.

The policies of the George W. Bush administration dismayed environmentalists. On taking office, Bush announced that he would not implement proposed EPA measures to reduce carbon dioxide emissions from power plants. His energy program, which stressed increased production and less regulation, roused particular opposition. An order permitting higher levels of arsenic in drinking water proved a public-relations nightmare. The proposed oil drilling in the Arctic National Wildlife Reserve and other public lands stirred intense resistance.

The United States under Bush, alone among 178 nations, boycotted a U.N.-sponsored effort launched at a conference in Kyoto, Japan, in 1997, to combat global warming by setting emissions standards for industrialized nations. Bush charged that the treaty threatened America's economic growth and standard of living. The administration also refused to participate in an international conference in Bonn, Germany, called specifically to meet U.S. objections to the Kyoto treaty. These actions came at a time when the United States, with less than 5 percent of the world's population, accounted for 25 percent of global energy consumption.

The administration's environmental insensitivity flew in the face of mounting scientific evidence. A National Science Foundation report in 2001 concluded that global warming was real, and likely to become more serious.

Thanks in part to his approach to energy and environmental issues, Bush's approval rating stood at only about 50 percent midway through his first year. But suddenly, politics as usual went out the window, as the nation faced a crisis that would test it to the limit.

SEPTEMBER 11 AND BEYOND

The course of American history changed profoundly in September 2001, when a terrorist attack left the nation in shock. The nation's priorities shifted at home and abroad as President Bush summoned the country to a war on terrorism. At home, the administration took far-reaching measures to enhance security. While all Americans agreed on the objective of these actions, some saw a threat to civil liberties in the vast strengthening of governmental powers of surveillance and detention.

Having shown little concern for world opinion earlier, Bush now called upon all nations to join the United States in a drive to eradicate terrorism. A broad coalition of nations supported the U.S. effort to uproot Osama bin Laden's Al Qaeda organization, the group responsible for the 9/11 attacks, from its base in Afghanistan. However, America's subsequent invasion of Iraq proved far more controversial. Despite the administration's single-minded focus on the antiterrorism campaign, other world issues demanded attention, particularly the Israeli-Palestinian conflict.

Despite the post–September 11 unity impulse, major differences soon arose over Bush's domestic and international policies. Contentiousness deepened as Americans reacted to revelations of greed, deception, and fraud in some of the nation's largest corporations during the boom years of the 1990s.

America Under Attack

Throughout American history, surprise attacks have marked historic turning points. The Confederates' attack on Fort Sumter in Charleston harbor on April 12, 1861, began the Civil War. The Japanese attack on Pearl Harbor on December 7, 1941, drew the United States into World War II.

Another such pivotal moment came on the morning of September 11, 2001. As Americans watched their televisions in horror, the blazing twin towers of New York's World Trade Center crashed to the earth, carrying more than 2,600 men and women to their deaths, including nearly 350 firefighters. A simultaneous attack on the Pentagon left

125 dead on the ground, and a plane crash in western Pennsylvania directly related to these events killed still more innocent people. Along with the dead on the ground, 246 passengers and crew, plus 19 hijackers, died in the four planes. Only the Civil War battle of Antietam, in which 3,650 soldiers died, brought a higher single-day toll of American dead.

The World Trade Center towers and the Pentagon had been struck by three commercial aircraft piloted by hijackers in a carefully planned assault on these highly visible symbols of U.S. economic and military power. The Pennsylvania crash occurred when heroic passengers prevented terrorists from diverting the plane to another target, possibly the White House. The government soon identified the hijackers, all from the Middle East, and traced their pre-9/11 actions, including enrollment in Florida flight-training schools.

In a few hours, a new and menacing era began. Terrorism—whether assassinations or bombed buildings, buses, ships, and planes—was familiar elsewhere, of course, and U.S. citizens, civilian and military, had died in terrorist attacks in the 1980s and 1990s. The 1995 bombing of the Oklahoma City federal building had made clear that America was not immune to such attacks. But now foreign terrorism had erupted on U.S. soil.

A wave of patriotism swept the nation as political divisions were put aside. Flags flew, "God Bless America" became the anthem of the moment, and the banners proclaimed, "United We Stand." President Bush visited a mosque to urge Americans to distinguish between a handful of terrorists and the world's 1.2 billion Muslims, including as many as 6 million in the United States. Nevertheless, Middle Easterners in America faced hostility and even violence in the post-attack period.

The damaged New York Stock Exchange closed for six days. When it reopened, stock prices plunged. Even after stocks slowly edged upward, retail sales declined and consumer confidence remained fragile. The airline and travel industries reeled as jittery travelers canceled trips or chose ground transportation. A $15 billion bailout of the airlines by Congress helped, but travel and tourism industries suffered.

Post–September 11 anxieties deepened in early October when an editor at the Florida offices of the tabloid newspaper *National Enquirer* died of anthrax, a rare and deadly bacterial disease contracted from spores sent in a letter. Letters containing high-grade anthrax spores next appeared in the office of NBC news anchor Tom Brokaw and Senators Tom Daschle and Patrick Leahy. The Senate

America Under Attack
Rescuers remove a flag-draped body from the ruins of the World Trade Center.
hc Interactive Map: Afghanistan

Office Building was closed for decontamination. Four other persons, two of them postal workers, died from anthrax-tainted mail.

Analysis indicated that the anthrax spores had probably been made in a U.S. research laboratory, and investigators focused on finding a domestic source of the deadly mailings. Fears revived in February 2004 when a letter containing the poison ricin reached the office of Senator Bill Frist, the majority leader.

Battling Terrorist Networks Abroad

President Bush, speaking from the White House on September 12, declared the attacks an "act of war." On September 15, the Senate unanimously authorized Bush to use "all necessary and appropriate force" to respond.

On September 20, addressing a joint session of Congress, a somber Bush blamed the attack on the Al Qaeda terrorist network headed by Osama bin Laden from headquarters in Afghanistan. Bin Laden, already under indictment for the 1998 attack on U.S. embassies in Africa, had long denounced America for supporting Saudi Arabia's corrupt regime, stationing "infidel" troops on Saudi soil, backing Israel, and spreading wickedness through its sinful mass culture. (Ironically, the United States had aided bin Laden in the 1980s, when he was fighting Russian forces in Afghanistan.) In a videotape discovered later in Afghanistan, bin Laden described how he planned the attack and even laughed about the massive damage. Bin Laden invoked the name of Allah and claimed to have acted on behalf of Islam.

Bush announced a military campaign to uproot Al Qaeda and its protectors, the Pakistan-trained Islamist group called the Taliban, which had seized power in Afghanistan in 1996. As part of a program to disrupt the terrorists' money supply, Bush froze the assets of organizations with possible terrorist links. Despite pro-Taliban sympathies in Pakistan, Bush enlisted the cooperation of Pakistan's military government. Complicating U.S. military planning was Afghanistan's forbidding terrain and patch-

work of ethnic and tribal groups. The major anti-Taliban force, the Northern Alliance, was an uneasy coalition of rival warlords.

The military phase of the antiterrorist operation, launched on October 7, achieved impressive success. Battered by U.S. bombing and an offensive by Northern Alliance forces, the Taliban soon surrendered Kabul (the Afghan capital) and other strongholds. British, Canadian, Pakistani, and other forces played an important role in this campaign. By mid-December, despite sporadic resistance, the United States claimed victory. More than six hundred captured Al Qaeda fighters, or persons caught up in the fighting, were transferred to prison facilities at the U.S. base in Guantanamo, Cuba. As more U.S. Special Forces arrived, a remnant of Al Qaeda fighters retreated to Pakistan or to fortified caves in the rugged mountains of eastern Afghanistan between Kabul and the Khyber Pass. The whereabouts of Osama bin Laden remained unknown.

A British-led international force was mobilized to maintain law and order in Kabul, but the diplomatic challenge of welding rival factions into a post-Taliban government proved difficult. In June 2002, with U.S. support, an assembly of Afghan regional and ethnic leaders, called a loya jirga, established a new government and chose an interim prime minister, Hamid Karzai. The nation-building effort had the blessing of Afghanistan's eighty-nine-year-old former king, who returned to Kabul after years in exile.

The loya jirga initially bogged down in rancorous debate between Afghanistan's two major ethnic and linguistic groups, the majority Pashtuns and the Tajiks. But early in 2004, thanks to the negotiating skills of a seasoned U.N. envoy from Algeria, the loya jirga approved a constitution that protected women's rights, finessed the competing claims of Pashtuns and Tajiks, and established Afghanistan as an Islamic republic with an elected president and assembly and an independent judiciary. In November 2004, Karzai was elected president in the first election of the new democracy.

But Afghanistan remained violent and unstable. Al Qaeda and Taliban insurgents carried out periodic bombings and other attacks. President Karzai and other officials faced assassination attempts, and outside Kabul, regional warlords and their heavily armed followers controlled the countryside. U.S. efforts to ferret out Al Qaeda and Taliban fighters sometimes killed innocent noncombatants, stirring bitter resentment. Adding to the tension, Arabic television and radio broadcast video and audio recordings in which Osama bin Laden, still at large, urged more attacks on the United States. Western nations only partially fulfilled pledges of billions in reconstruction and development aid. Once again, the opium poppy became Afghanistan's leading crop. As Washington's attention turned elsewhere, Afghanistan's future remained uncertain.

Shadowing the post–September 11 strategic debate was a troubling question: would breaking up Al Qaeda's centers of power end the terrorist threat? While most Arab leaders repudiated bin Laden, many among the impoverished, ill-educated Arab masses were receptive to his anti-American harangues. Ending terrorism, clearly, involved not only military operations, but also long-term diplomatic, political, and ideological efforts.

Tightening Home-Front Security

Americans supported the Bush administration's campaign in Afghanistan. The administration's domestic antiterrorism campaign proved more controversial, however. Despite Republicans' traditional hostility to big government, the administration and Congress significantly expanded the federal government's role in many aspects of American life.

On September 20, 2001, Bush appointed former Pennsylvania governor Tom Ridge to head a new White House office of homeland security. Ridge and the Congress gave high priority to the newly urgent issue of aviation security. Late in 2001, Congress required all security personnel to be U.S. citizens and to meet rigorous job criteria and performance requirements set by a newly created Transportation Security Administration.

The USA-Patriot Act, the administration's sweeping antiterrorist law, was overwhelmingly passed by Congress in October 2001. This law ex-tended the government's powers to monitor telephone and e-mail communications, including conversations between prisoners and their lawyers. It also authorized authorities to seize suspects' financial, medical, computer, and even library records. Both conservatives and liberals were troubled by these vastly expanded federal powers.

In May 2002 news media reported disturbing evidence of missed clues before the terrorist attack. In August 2001, for example, a flight school in Minnesota warned the FBI of a suspicious person named Zacarias Moussaoui who had tried to enroll. Moussaoui had been arrested on immigration charges, but the Justice Department had denied a request by the Minneapolis FBI office for permission to check his computer. In response, Congress created a bipartisan national commission to investigate intelligence failures and other circumstances relevant to the 9/11 attacks, including a lack of communication among and within various government agencies, notably the FBI and the CIA.

In November 2002, Congress approved a new cabinet-level Department of Homeland Security to coordinate the domestic antiterrorism effort. The new department, with 170,000 employees, absorbed twenty-two government agencies, including the Coast Guard, the Customs Service, the Immigration and Naturalization Service, and the Federal Emergency Management Agency. It did not, however, include the FBI or the CIA.

After September 11, the Justice Department detained more than one thousand Middle Easterners living in the United States, some for visa violations, and held them for questioning without filing charges or, in most cases, revealing their names. Some local police officials refused to cooperate in the wholesale roundup of persons not accused of crimes simply on the basis of their ethnicity or national origin.

In November, without consulting Congress, Bush signed an executive order empowering the government to try noncitizens accused of fomenting terrorism in secret military tribunals rather than in the civilian justice system. While precedent existed for such tribunals in wartime, this proposal roused opposition from civil libertarians and others. Opinion polls found Americans divided on the use of military tribunals, but strongly at odds with Bush's failure to consult Congress.

While few questioned the need for heightened security, the civil-liberties implications of all these measures raised growing concern. Over 150 cities and towns passed resolutions criticizing the Patriot Act for infringing citizens' rights. In July 2003, Congress repealed a Patriot Act provision that allowed the FBI to search suspects' homes without informing them.

In December 2003, a New York federal appeals court heard a case involving José Padilla, a U.S. citizen arrested in May 2002 on suspicion of planning a bombing and imprisoned him as an "enemy combatant" with no access to a lawyer or family members. The court ruled that the government had violated Padilla's Fifth Amendment right to due process of law. The Justice Department appealed, and in June 2004 the Supreme Court ruled against the Bush administration, affirming that the government may not deny a U.S. citizen the right to federal court review of his detention. With key provisions of the Patriot Act scheduled to expire in 2005, President Bush in his 2004 State of the Union address called on Congress to extend the law. Opponents mobilized to insist on modifications.

Meanwhile, despite protests by the International Red Cross, Amnesty International, and civil-liberties organizations, the U.S. military continued to hold at Guantanamo around 650 prisoners, some in their early teens, most captured in Afghanistan or Pakistan, with no legal representation or outside contact. In December 2003, in a case involving 3 Guantanamo prisoners, a California federal appeals court ordered their release or transfer to the civil-court system. The Justice Department appealed this ruling, too, to the Supreme Court. In June 2004 the Supreme Court ruled against the Justice Department, saying that those regarded as enemy combatants must be allowed to challenge their detention before a judge or other neutral "decision maker." The government decided not to bring the three defendants to trial, and they were released.

WAR IN IRAQ AND ITS PAINFUL AFTERMATH

While the military action against Al Qaeda and its Taliban protectors in Afghanistan enjoyed broad support, the next front in Bush's war on terrorism was highly controversial. In his 2002 State of the Union address, Bush had identified three nations as an "Axis of Evil" that menaced U.S. security: Iraq, Iran, and North Korea. Of these, Iraq topped the list. Iraqi president Saddam Hussein had remained a troublemaker since the Persian Gulf War, which had left him weakened but still in power.

In a barrage of speeches in 2002–2003, Bush, Cheney, and other administration officials accused Saddam of complicity in the 9/11 attacks. They suggested that Saddam possessed "weapons of mass destruction" in the form of chemical and biological weapons and was actively pursuing a nuclear-weapons capability. U.N. weapons inspectors, sent to Iraq after the Persian Gulf War to monitor Iraq's weapons programs, had departed in 1998 when the Iraqis denied them access to Saddam's presidential palaces. Clearly, the administration insisted, Saddam posed an imminent threat to American security. Further, they suggested, overthrowing Saddam could lead to other regime changes in the Middle East and promote peace and democracy in the region. They also noted Saddam's well-documented brutality against his opponents, including restive Kurds in the north and Islamic Shiites in the south. In short, the administration claimed, Saddam's ouster would not only advance the war on terrorism but also transform the entire Middle East.

Those opposed to the administration position, charging that a preemptive war would violate U.S. principles, challenged the administration to produce evidence that Saddam posed an immediate threat and warned that such a war could unleash turmoil across the Arab world and bog down U.S. forces for years. Critics also cautioned that the preoccupation with Saddam could undermine the larger antiterrorist campaign. British Prime Minister Tony Blair backed the administration, as did Italy, Spain, Poland, and other smaller nations. France,

Germany, other European nations, as well as Canada, Mexico, and most Arab leaders objected. To counter the rush to war, they called for a U.N. resolution demanding that Iraq grant complete and unrestricted access to U.N. weapons inspectors.

Under pressure to secure U.N. backing, President Bush in September 2002 presented the case against Saddam in a U.N. address. In October the House and Senate passed resolutions authorizing U.S. military action against Iraq. On November 8, the U.N. Security Council unanimously adopted a resolution imposing tough new weapons inspections on Iraq. Baghdad agreed and U.N. inspectors returned.

The U.S. administration continued the buildup for war, unleashing protests at home and abroad. Antiwar marchers rallied in London, Paris, Rome, and other cities, as the level of anti-American sentiment grew. In a February 2003 U.N. address, Secretary of State Colin Powell again insisted that Iraq possessed weapons of mass destruction. However, the U.N. Security Council refused to authorize an attack, calling instead for continued pressure on Iraq to cooperate with the weapons-inspection process.

Nevertheless, on March 20, 2003, after an extended military buildup, a U.S. force in excess of one hundred thousand, supplemented by ten thousand British troops, invaded southern Iraq. While the British seized the southern city of Basra, a center of Iraq's oil industry, the Americans moved north toward Baghdad, the capital, which fell on April 5. (Saddam Hussein eluded capture until December.) Except for officials and supporters of Saddam's Baath party, most Iraqis, particularly the Shiites and Kurds, welcomed Saddam's overthrow.

President Bush named L. Paul Bremer III to administer postwar Iraq. Bremer set up a Governing Council representing Iraq's religious and ethnic groups, but it initially exercised little authority. Bremer also worked to restore Iraq's electric power, communications, transportation, educational system, and medical services, as well as the nation's vital oil industry, its main source of income, all suffering from the effects of war and neglect. Multimillion-dollar reconstruction contracts went to large U.S. businesses, some of which, such as the Halliburton Corporation, formerly headed by Vice President Cheney, had close ties to the administration and were major Republican contributors.

In September 2003, Congress appropriated $87 billion for expenses connected with Iraq's occupation and reconstruction. The monumental task was complicated by continued violence in Iraq. Bombings, sniper attacks, and land mines planted on roadways took a steady toll of GIs and innocent bystanders. Surface-to-air missiles brought down several U.S. helicopters. British, Spanish, and Italian occupation forces suffered casualties as well. Much of the violence erupted in the so-called "Sunni Triangle" north of Baghdad, a center of pro-Saddam sentiment. U.S. authorities claimed steady progress against the insurgents, but as GIs conducted raids and searched houses, Iraqi resentment deepened.

The insurgents' campaign of disruption also targeted international organizations and Iraqis cooperating with the Americans. Ministers of the U.S.-appointed Governing Council were assassinated. In August 2003, a truck bomb destroyed the U.N.'s Baghdad headquarters, killing 17, including the U.N.'s chief envoy in Iraq. Soon after, a massive car bomb in the sacred Shiite city of Najaf killed 125, including a leading Shiite cleric whose brother served on the Governing Council. In October, terrorists bombed the International Red Cross's Baghdad office.

As conditions deteriorated, President Bush in November 2003 instructed Bremer to transfer governing power to Iraqis by June 30, 2004. Complicating this task, Iraq's leading Shiite cleric, Grand Ayatollah Ali al-Sistani, rejected a U.S. plan for choosing the new government by regional caucuses and instead demanded direct national elections—a procedure that would assure the Shiite majority a leading role. In response to a U.S. request, U.N. secretary general Kofi Annan agreed to send a team to Iraq to help prepare election procedures.

As the casualties and costs mounted in Iraq, many Americans criticized Washington's inadequate planning for the postwar phase. The administration's arguments for starting the war met with increasing skepticism. No evidence proved Saddam's involvement in the 9/11 attacks. The

U.S. ground troops, like those seen here, faced threats of insurgent attacks and anti-coalition violence through 2005.

claim that Saddam possessed weapons of mass destruction (WMD) proved similarly unfounded, as the administration reluctantly admitted in January 2005. After the invasion, the Bush administration sent twelve hundred weapons inspectors to Iraq, but no WMD were found. Debate centered on whether prewar intelligence had been faulty or whether administration officials had exaggerated the WMD danger to build support for a war they were predisposed to wage.

More broadly, critics argued that the United States should have supported strengthened U.N. inspections, which had successfully monitored Iraq's weapons programs in 1991–1998, and again briefly in 2003, rather than launching a costly war that squandered world support for America after 9/11. The administration's defenders responded that despite the problems, the Iraq war was worthwhile and a necessary extension of the war on terrorism.

Meanwhile, the situation in Iraq continued to deteriorate. When American authorities shut down the newspaper of a violently anti-American young Shiite cleric, Moqtada Sadr, in March 2004, his militant supporters unleashed a bloody anti-Ameri-

can uprising as Sadr took refuge in the holy city of Najaf. Farther north, in the Sunni Triangle, insurgents in Fallujah ambushed four American civilian contract workers in late March, burned their truck, and brutalized their charred bodies. As fighting raged around Najaf and Fallujah, and attacks, including the kidnapping and videotaped beheading of foreigners, continued in Baghdad and elsewhere, the situation looked grim.

As conditions worsened, the coalition of governments with troops in Iraq weakened. On March 11, 2004, bombs planted on crowded commuter trains in Madrid killed 191 and injured 1,800. Spanish authorities soon arrested suspects belonging to a Morocco-based Islamic extremist group. On March 14, Spanish voters defeated the pro-U.S. government and elected a socialist government that proceeded to withdraw all Spanish troops from Iraq.

Despite these conditions, the Bush administration turned over power to an Iraqi authority on June 30. To facilitate the process, the United States relied on a special U.N. envoy, Lakhdar Brahimi, who proposed a plan for an interim authority to exercise limited powers until elections could be held. Having earlier dismissed the U.N., the administration now needed the world body to help resolve the crisis.

U.S. authorities made clear that American forces would remain in Iraq for the indefinite future, however, and that the U.S. military would continue to control security matters. A fresh crisis for the administration arose in May 2004 with the publication of photographs of the abuse of Iraqi prisoners held in U.S. custody. As the International Red Cross confirmed reports of more widespread abuses of prisoners, Americans reacted in disgust and disbelief, anti-Americanism in the Arab world and in Europe intensified, and Iraqis demanded ever more vehemently that the Americans leave the country.

Although the continuing violence reflected a deteriorating security situation in much of Iraq, the United States and the Iraqi interim authority insisted on general elections to be held on January 30, 2005. Meanwhile, the U.S. military suffered at least 348 deaths over the final four months of 2004, more than in any other similar period since the invasion in March 2003. The number of GIs killed since the war began totaled more than 1,400. The number of wounded surpassed 10,000, with more than a quarter of those injured in the last four months of 2004. President Bush continued to insist that the goal of installing a free and democratic regime in Iraq remained unchanged, but the final outcome of his venture into Iraq, launched with such bravado, remained uncertain.

Despite a sharp escalation in violence, directed primarily against Iraqis, the elections took place as scheduled. Election officials reported a voter turnout of nearly sixty percent, although most Sunnis did not participate, and hope for a democratic Iraq rose.

The Israeli-Palestinian Conflict Worsens

Although the war on terrorism diverted attention from the conflict between Israel and the Palestinians, the issues were linked, since a major grievance of the terrorists was U.S. economic and military support of Israel and Israel's occupation of, and promotion of Jewish settlements in, the Palestinian territories of Gaza and the West Bank.

With Yasir Arafat's rejection of Israel's peace plan at Camp David and the launching of a second Intifada in 2000, violence in the region exploded. Suicide bombings took many Israeli lives as the bombers deliberately chose crowded targets such as buses and restaurants.

Israel retaliated against Palestinian targets in the West Bank and Gaza and assassinated leaders of Hamas, a violently anti-Israel organization responsible for many of the bombings. The Israelis periodically closed border crossings for security reasons, keeping Palestinian laborers from jobs in Israel and deepening Palestinian anger. None of these measures stopped the suicide attacks; indeed, they increased.

Prime Minister Ariel Sharon demanded an end to violence before peace talks could resume and denounced Arafat's failure to stop the terrorists or to end corruption within the Palestinian Authority. Arafat, in turn, insisted that as long as Israel fostered Jewish settlements in the West Bank and Gaza, dominated the region militarily, controlled water rights and highway access, and in other ways behaved as a colonial power, the anger that fueled the violence would continue.

In March 2002, after a devastating round of suicide bombings, Israel launched a major assault in the West Bank. Parts of the city of Jenin, a center of terrorist activity, were reduced to rubble. A standoff between armed Palestinians and Israeli troops unfolded around Bethlehem's Church of the Nativity. The Israelis besieged Arafat's compound in Ramallah, confining him in a single building for days. Eventually the Israelis withdrew, but conditions remained tense.

In a June 2002 speech offering a "road map" for peace, President Bush called for creation of a Palestinian state, Israeli withdrawal from the occupied Palestinian territories, and the resolution of other disputed issues. He also demanded an end to terrorism and recognition of Israel's right to exist secure within its borders, and he embraced the Israeli position that Arafat must go.

In June 2003 Bush met with Israeli and Palestinian leaders in Jordan to promote the "road map," but a brief truce collapsed after a deadly bus bombing in Jerusalem. From September 2000 to late 2003, the conflict had killed eight hundred Israelis and twenty-three hundred Palestinians.

As violence continued, Israel began construction of a massive security fence separating Israel from the West Bank and Gaza. In places this fence extended into Palestinian territory and divided Palestinian communities from their lands. In 2004, Sharon proposed withdrawing Jewish settlements and outposts from Gaza and a few from the West Bank while insisting that the largest Jewish settlements in the West Bank must remain. Sharon also authorized the assassination of two successive heads of Hamas, accusing them of being nothing but terrorists. When President Bush endorsed Sharon's West Bank plan, Arab leaders reacted with fury, accusing him of siding with Israel and abandoning America's role as an honest broker between the two sides.

Arafat died in November 2004. In January 2005, Mahmoud Abbas, his longtime aide and successor as PLO chief, won election as president of the Palestinian National Authority. Israel and the United States viewed Abbas as a moderate willing to compromise and to take a harder line against violence by radical Palestinian groups. His emergence raised hopes for a negotiated settlement of the long conflict.

Settlement of the Israeli-Palestinian conflict seemed essential to any comprehensive plan to combat terrorism by Islamic extremists. Yet since 1948 the United States had tried without success to broker an enduring peace in the region. Would Arafat's death finally break the familiar pattern of fresh initiatives by each new administration, followed by frustration and defeat?

Bankruptcies and Scandals in Corporate America

Economic matters also vied for attention as the recession led to a series of high-profile bankruptcies among energy and telecommunications companies that had thrived in the high-flying 1990s. Accusations of accounting fraud and other criminal behavior soon followed, producing a crisis of confidence in the integrity of corporate America.

First to fall was Houston's Enron Corporation, with close ties to the Bush administration. Selling electric power in advance at guaranteed rates, Enron flourished in the freewheeling climate of the 1990s and expanded into utilities and telecommunications. Hailed as a model of the new economy, the company charmed investors. In 2000, claiming assets of $62 billion, it ranked seventh in *Fortune* magazine's list of America's top corporations.

Suddenly, the house of cards collapsed. Late in 2001, Enron filed for bankruptcy and admitted to vastly overstating profits. Thousands of Enron workers lost not only their jobs but also their retirement funds, which consisted mostly of Enron stock. A number of high-ranking Enron executives faced criminal proceedings and several are already serving prison terms.

Enron was only the beginning. The overbuilt fiber-optics industry, having laid 100 million miles of optical fiber worldwide in 1999–2001, suffered staggering blows. Lucent Technologies, a telecommunications giant, cut nearly one hundred thousand jobs in 2001. Global Crossing, a high-speed voice and data carrier, declared bankruptcy in 2002, the fourth largest in U.S. history. In June 2002 WorldCom, America's second-largest telecommunications company and long-distance carrier, with eighty-five thousand employees in 65 countries, announced that its chief financial officer had overstated profits by $3.8 billion. As WorldCom stock dropped to nine cents a share, the company fired seventeen thousand employees and filed for bankruptcy.

The Justice Department brought criminal charges, including the deliberate destruction of incriminating files and e-mail, against Arthur Andersen, a giant Chicago accounting firm that had certified the accuracy of the financial reports of Enron, WorldCom, and other troubled companies. A grand jury found the firm guilty, and it faced dissolution. The integrity of the accounting industry as a whole, so crucial to investor confidence, fell under suspicion.

In July 2002, in the first of what promised to be a series of criminal prosecutions, John J. Rigas and two of his sons, who had allegedly looted bankrupt Adelphia Communications, the family-owned TV-cable business, of $1 billion, were arrested and held for trial.

Public outrage deepened amid reports of corporate executives who made millions selling their own stock holdings just before their companies collapsed. Attention focused, too, on the stratospheric salaries and stock benefits these CEOs had earned. In his 2002 book *Wealth and Democracy,* Kevin Phillips reported that America's top ten CEOs earned an average of $154 million each in 2000.

The bankruptcies of seemingly healthy companies and the disclosures of deception in the business world slowed the economic recovery. Despite positive economic news, the stock market sank through much of 2002, as distrustful investors stayed away.

At a deeper level, the escalating scandals eroded the standing of corporate America. Executives who had been celebrities in the 1990s now faced deep public skepticism if not criminal charges. Declared the chairman of Goldman Sachs, a major Wall Street investment bank, "I cannot think of a time when business . . . has been held in less repute."

Politicians and government agencies scrambled to respond to mounting public anger. Presi-dent Bush delivered a stern speech about the need for business morality. The head of the Securities and Exchange Commission, the watchdog agency created in the 1930s, pledged to pursue wrongdoers, but he himself resigned in November 2002 amid conflict-of-interest charges.

To reassure investors, Congress passed a new regulatory law imposing stricter accounting rules, tightening procedures for corporate financial reporting, and toughening criminal penalties for business fraud. But the wave of scandals rolled on. Famed home-decorating guru Martha Stewart was convicted in March 2004 of obstructing justice and lying to officials investigating charges that she had profited from insider trading in the stock of a pharmaceutical company whose head was a personal friend.

All these scandals were nurtured by the get-rich-quick mood of the booming 1990s, when investors came to expect stock prices to move ever higher, pressuring corporations to issue glowing reports of endless growth and soaring profits. The scandals also arose in a laissez-faire political climate that left regulatory agencies like the SEC understaffed, underfunded, and vulnerable to politicians and corporate leaders hostile to the entire notion of government regulation.

The widespread disgust with big business evoked memories of the Progressive Era, when reformers had denounced corporate greed and ruthlessness. It also recalled the early 1930s, when once-admired business leaders faced public hostility as hard times sank in. The pendulum would no doubt swing again, but for the moment the status of corporate America could hardly have been lower.

Martha Stewart Outside the Courthouse
"Domestic diva" Martha Stewart leaves the federal courthouse in March 2004 during her trial for obstruction of justice and lying to officials.

Elections of 2002 and 2004

The corporate scandals posed dangers for the Bush administration, with its close ties to big business. Bush's tax, energy, and environmental policies all served the interests of corporate America. His original tax-cut proposal (later scaled back by Congress) would have given lucrative tax breaks to America's biggest corporations, including a $254 million windfall to Enron. Bush's own well-timed and highly profitable 1990 sale of his stock in a failing Texas energy company of which he was a director came up for fresh examination.

Nevertheless, in the November elections of 2002, Republicans regained control of the Senate and increased their House majority. President Bush, enjoying popularity ratings close to 70 percent, had campaigned tirelessly, stressing the antiterrorism campaign. The Democrats proved unable to shift focus to the economy and corporate scandals. In the wake of the defeat, Representative Richard Gephardt of Missouri resigned as House Democratic leader. He was replaced by Nancy Pelosi of California, who became the first woman of either party to hold such a major leadership position in Congress.

By early 2004, with another presidential election looming, Bush's approval ratings had sunk to around 50 percent, presaging another close contest. An improving economy helped the president's cause. The stock market had recovered most of its losses and other economic indicators looked good. Unemployment in March 2004 stood at 5.7 percent, down from 6.5 percent in January 2003, and the jobs picture looked brighter. Bush took credit

for the recovery, pointing to the stimulus effect of his tax cuts. But many jobs had been lost in the recession, including 2.8 million in manufacturing, as corporations shifted production to foreign countries with lower wage scales and fewer employee benefits. The southern textile industry was especially hard hit. The shift of manufacturing overseas emerged as a major campaign issue. "America's greatest export is jobs," went one Democratic campaign slogan. Supporters of NAFTA and the WTO vigorously insisted that despite job losses in some sectors, globalization and lower trade barriers benefited the U.S. economy overall.

Bush continued to hammer on security issues and to defend the Iraq war. His 2004 State of the Union address mentioned "war" twelve times and "terror," "terrorism," or "terrorists" twenty times. The administration's 2005 budget proposed a 7 percent increase in military spending (not including upwards of $50 billion more for the continuing Iraq operations) and a 10 percent increase for homeland security. (On the cost-cutting side, Bush proposed to slash the Environmental Protection Agency's budget by 7 percent.)

Bush gained some support among senior citizens in 2003 when Congress passed his Medicare reform bill providing limited prescription-drug benefits beginning in 2006. Hispanics and many employers welcomed his 2004 proposal to issue temporary work permits to some 8 million illegal immigrants, mostly from Mexico, working for low wages and no job security in the shadow economy.

As Democrats moved into election mode in 2004, they charged the administration with favoritism to big business, a needlessly belligerent and unilateralist foreign policy, and an unwise rush to war in Iraq. Pointing to a record federal deficit of $521 billion, they portrayed Bush as a profligate spender concerned only with short-term political calculations. Challenging the Republicans' reputation for fiscal restraint, the senior Democrat on the Senate Budget Committee, Kent Conrad of North Dakota, attacked Bush as "the most fiscally irresponsible [president] in the nation's history." (Many Republican leaders, while not attacking Bush so openly, shared this view as well.)

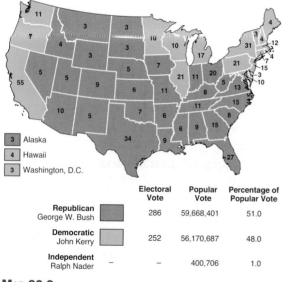

3	Alaska
4	Hawaii
3	Washington, D.C.

		Electoral Vote	Popular Vote	Percentage of Popular Vote
Republican George W. Bush		286	59,668,401	51.0
Democratic John Kerry		252	56,170,687	48.0
Independent Ralph Nader	–	–	400,706	1.0

MAP 32.3
The Election of 2004

As for the president's Medicare reform, Democrats charged that the massive cost of the new drug coverage ($540 billion in the first ten years) would worsen the federal deficit and noted that the law placed no restraints on drug-company prices and prevented seniors from buying less-expensive prescription drugs from Canada. Democrats especially criticized a provision that permitted seniors to opt out of Medicare and join private for-profit health-maintenance organizations, arguing that this could potentially destroy the Medicare system.

In July the Democrats nominated Senator John Kerry of Massachusetts, a Yale graduate (like George W. Bush) and decorated Vietnam War veteran, for president. Kerry chose North Carolina Senator John Edwards as his running mate. Some early straw polls put Kerry slightly ahead of Bush. But the president, focusing on post-9/11 dangers and the war on terrorism, defeated his Democratic

Chronology

1994	Oslo Accords establish framework for peace between Israel and Palestinians.
1995	World Trade Organization (WTO) replaces GATT as regulator of world trade. Dayton Accords establish cease-fire in Bosnia.
1996	Clinton reelected.
1997	Kyoto Accords on emission standards.
1998	Terrorist bombings of U.S. embassies in Kenya and Tanzania. House of Representatives impeaches Clinton.
1999	NATO offensive drives Yugoslav forces out of Kosovo. Senate trial acquits Clinton.
2000	Congress normalizes trade relations with China. End of economic boom. Yasir Arafat rejects Israeli peace plan; second Intifada begins. U.S.S. *Cole* bombed in Aden harbor, Yemen. Presidential election: Al Gore wins popular vote; George W. Bush chosen by electoral college after Supreme Court intervenes to resolve disputed Florida vote. Senate evenly split between Republicans and Democrats; Republicans retain control of House.
2001	Bush administration repudiates Kyoto protocol on emission standards. Congress passes $1.35 trillion tax-cut bill. September 11 terrorist attacks on World Trade Center, Pentagon. U.S. and allied forces oust Taliban regime in Afghanistan and attack Al Qaeda terrorist network. United States announces intention to allow ABM (Anti-Ballistic Missile) Treaty to lapse and authorizes construction of missile defense system. USA-Patriot Act passed. Collapse of Enron Corporation; wave of corporate bankruptcies and accounting scandals.
2002	Bipartisan Campaign Reform Act. Department of Homeland Security created. Palestinian suicide bombings; Israeli invasion of West Bank. Republicans regain Senate in midterm elections.
2003	U.S. and British forces invade and occupy Iraq (March). Insurgent attacks on U.S. troops and Iraqi supporters. U.N. headquarters and major Shiite shrine in Iraq bombed. Saddam Hussein captured (December). Medicare reform provides prescription drug benefits for seniors. Federal courts challenge government treatment of security suspects.
2004	Insurgency in Iraq continues. Loya jirga in Afghanistan approves new constitution. Turnover of authority to new interim Iraqi government (June 30). Federal deficit reaches $521 billion. Bush reelected. Office of Director of National Intelligence created.
2005	Iraqi elections appear successful.

challenger. Polls showed that a majority of Americans agreed with Democratic policies, but President Bush's personal popularity, coupled with a poor campaign by the Kerry camp and a brilliantly orchestrated campaign designed by presidential advisor Karl Rove, gave the Republican candidate a 3 million vote majority. Postelection analysis focused on the chasm between conservative Republicans, who described themselves as concerned primarily with "moral issues," and Democrats; clearly the religious right believed it had played a decisive role in the election and would be entitled to a large role in shaping policy during the second Bush administration.

The GOP widened its majorities in both houses of Congress. In the election's aftermath, Bush moved quickly to consolidate his control over governmental agencies and to pursue his goals abroad and domestically, including bringing democracy to Iraq; making his tax cuts permanent; appointing conservative judges; and partially privatizing social security, a legacy of the New Deal. In December 2004, following the recommendations of a blue-ribbon inquiry into the 9/11 disaster, Congress created a new post, Director of National Intelligence, to manage the U.S. intelligence budget, coordinate terrorism-related intelligence, and oversee a National Counterterrorism Center responsible for strategic antiterrorism planning.

CONCLUSION   *hc* ACE Practice Test

Brief as it was, the interval spanning Bill Clinton's second term and George W. Bush's first term brought many changes. The Republican administration that emerged from the disputed 2000 election pursued a conservative, probusiness domestic agenda, advocating fiscal and environmental policies that many critics denounced as irresponsible, and a go-it-alone approach to foreign policy. The humming economy of the 1990s stalled in 2000–2001, leading to a recession and, indirectly, to a wave of business failures and corporate scandals. And, as we saw in Chapter 30, America's social and demographic profile continued to change as the population grew older, the surging growth of the Sun Belt continued, and the Hispanic and Asian populations increased at a rapid pace.

On September 11, 2001, a shocking act of mass terrorism transformed America. Like Pearl Harbor sixty years before, the shattering events of that day opened a new chapter in U.S. history. The 9/11 attacks initially produced a world outpouring of sympathy and a spirit of unity at home. However, as the Bush administration pursued security measures that many believed jeopardized civil liberties and launched a preemptive war in Iraq without a clear international mandate, controversy arose at home and abroad.

A post–Cold War future that had looked so promising only a few years earlier had suddenly become more menacing, adding a dark strand of apprehension to Americans' traditional optimism and confidence. Coping with the complex new realities of a post-9/11 world would clearly challenge the tolerance and wisdom of all citizens. Yet the enduring vision of what America at its best might become, despite the dangers stalking an uncertain world, remained strong.

FURTHER READING

The journals of political and cultural commentary listed in the "Further Reading" section of Chapter 31 are relevant to this chapter as well, as is the annual government publication *Statistical Abstract of the United States,* with its wealth of economic, social, and demographic information.

David Barney, *Prometheus Wired: The Hope for Democracy in the Age of Network Technology* (2000). Reflections on the civic and political implications of the new information technologies.

David Brooks, *Bobos in Paradise: The New Upper Class and How They Got There* (2000). Witty and shrewd cultural profile of the baby-boom generation in the affluent 1990s.

James W. Caesar and Andrew E. Busch, *The Perfect Tie: The True Story of the 2000 Presidential Election* (2001). A thoughtful and readable account of the Bush-Gore campaign.

Fred Halliday, *Two Hours That Shook the World: September 11, 2001: Causes and Consequences* (2001). A British international-affairs specialist views terrorism in the context of political and ideological struggles within the Arab world.

Chalmers Johnson, *Blowback: The Costs and Consequences of American Empire* (2001). A diplomatic historian examines the domestic and international consequences of America's global economic expansion.

Haynes Johnson, *The Best of Times: America in the Clinton Years* (2001). Thoughtful reflections on American culture in the 1990s.

Anthony Lake, *Six Nightmares: Real Threats in a Dangerous World and How America Can Meet Them* (2001). A foreign-affairs specialist explores a variety of terrorist threats and offers recommendations for responding to them.

Kevin Phillips, *Wealth and Democracy* (2002). Critical analysis of the corporate practices of the 1990s and their implications for American democracy.

Paul Pillar, *Terrorism and U.S. Foreign Policy* (2001). A counterterrorism specialist argues that effective intelligence work and cooperation with other nations offer the best hope.

Cass R. Sunstein and Richard A. Epstein, eds., *The Vote: Bush, Gore, and the Supreme Court* (2001). Scholars representing a broad spectrum of viewpoints analyze the legal struggle to resolve the 2000 election controversy.

Peter Trubowitz, *Defining the National Interest: Conflict and Change in American Foreign Policy* (1998). Explores the domestic economic and political calculations that help shape U.S. diplomacy.

William Julius Wilson, *When Work Disappears: The World of the New Urban Poor* (1996). A sociologist looks at those left behind by the high-tech, high-skilled economy.

Appendix

DECLARATION OF INDEPENDENCE

IN CONGRESS, JULY 4, 1776

The Unanimous Declaration of the Thirteen United States of America

When, in the course of human events, it becomes necessary for one people to dissolve the political bands which have connected them with another, and to assume, among the powers of the earth, the separate and equal station to which the laws of nature and of nature's God entitle them, a decent respect to the opinions of mankind requires that they should declare the causes which impel them to the separation.

We hold these truths to be self-evident: That all men are created equal; that they are endowed by their Creator with certain unalienable rights; that among these are life, liberty, and the pursuit of happiness; that, to secure these rights, governments are instituted among men, deriving their just powers from the consent of the governed; that whenever any form of government becomes destructive of these ends, it is the right of the people to alter or to abolish it, and to institute new government, laying its foundation on such principles, and organizing its powers in such form, as to them shall seem most likely to effect their safety and happiness. Prudence, indeed, will dictate that governments long established should not be changed for light and transient causes; and accordingly all experience hath shown that mankind are more disposed to suffer, while evils are sufferable, than to right themselves by abolishing the forms to which they are accustomed. But when a long train of abuses and usurpations, pursuing invariably the same object, evinces a design to reduce them under absolute despotism, it is their right, it is their duty, to throw off such government, and to provide new guards for their future security. Such has been the patient sufferance of these colonies; and such is now the necessity which constrains them to alter their former systems of government. The history of the present King of Great Britain is a history of repeated injuries and usurpations, all having in direct object the establishment of an absolute tyranny over these states. To prove this, let facts be submitted to a candid world.

He has refused his assent to laws, the most wholesome and necessary for the public good.

He has forbidden his governors to pass laws of immediate and pressing importance, unless suspended in their operation till his assent should be obtained; and, when so suspended, he has utterly neglected to attend to them.

He has refused to pass other laws for the accommodation of large districts of people, unless those people would relinquish the right of representation in the legislature, a right inestimable to them, and formidable to tyrants only.

He has called together legislative bodies at places unusual, uncomfortable, and distant from the depository of their public records, for the sole purpose of fatiguing them into compliance with his measures.

He has dissolved representative houses repeatedly, for opposing, with manly firmness, his invasions on the rights of the people.

He has refused for a long time, after such dissolutions, to cause others to be elected; whereby the legislative powers, incapable of annihilation, have returned to the people at large for their exercise;

the state remaining, in the mean time, exposed to all the dangers of invasions from without and convulsions within.

He has endeavored to prevent the population of these states; for that purpose obstructing the laws of naturalization of foreigners; refusing to pass others to encourage their migration hither, and raising the conditions of new appropriation of lands.

He has obstructed the administration of justice, by refusing his assent to laws for establishing judiciary powers.

He has made judges dependent on his will alone, for the tenure of their offices, and the amount and payment of their salaries.

He has erected a multitude of new offices, and sent hither swarms of officers to harass our people and eat out their substance.

He has kept among us, in times of peace, standing armies, without the consent of our legislatures.

He has affected to render the military independent of, and superior to, the civil power.

He has combined with others to subject us to a jurisdiction foreign to our constitution, and unacknowledged by our laws, giving his assent to their acts of pretended legislation:

For quartering large bodies of armed troops among us;

For protecting them, by a mock trial, from punishment for any murders which they should commit on the inhabitants of these states;

For cutting off our trade with all parts of the world;

For imposing taxes on us without our consent;

For depriving us, in many cases, of the benefits of trial by jury;

For transporting us beyond seas, to be tried for pretended offenses;

For abolishing the free system of English laws in a neighboring province, establishing therein an arbitrary government, and enlarging its boundaries, so as to render it at once an example and fit instrument for introducing the same absolute rule into these colonies;

For taking away our charters, abolishing our most valuable laws, and altering fundamentally the forms of our governments;

For suspending our own legislatures, and declaring themselves invested with power to legislate for us in all cases whatsoever.

He has abdicated government here, by declaring us out of his protection and waging war against us.

He has plundered our seas, ravaged our coasts, burned our towns, and destroyed the lives of our people.

He is at this time transporting large armies of foreign mercenaries to complete the works of death, desolation, and tyranny already begun with circumstances of cruelty and perfidy scarcely paralleled in the most barbarous ages, and totally unworthy of the head of a civilized nation.

He has constrained our fellow-citizens, taken captive on the high seas, to bear arms against their country, to become the executioners of their friends and brethren, or to fall themselves by their hands.

He has excited domestic insurrection among us, and has endeavored to bring on the inhabitants of our frontiers the merciless Indian savages, whose known rule of warfare is an undistinguished destruction of all ages, sexes, and conditions.

In every stage of these oppressions we have petitioned for redress in the most humble terms; our repeated petitions have been answered only by repeated injury. A prince, whose character is thus marked by every act which may define a tyrant, is unfit to be the ruler of a free people.

Nor have we been wanting in our attentions to our British brethren. We have warned them, from time to time, of attempts by their legislature to extend an unwarrantable jurisdiction over us. We have reminded them of the circumstances of our emigration and settlement here. We have appealed to their native justice and magnanimity; and we have conjured them by the ties of our common kindred, to disavow these usurpations, which would inevitably interrupt our connections and correspondence. They, too, have been deaf to the voice of justice and of consanguinity. We must, therefore, acquiesce in the necessity which denounces our separation, and hold them, as we hold the rest of mankind, enemies in war, in peace friends.

We, therefore, the representatives of the United States of America, in General Congress assembled, appealing to the Supreme Judge of the world for the rectitude of our intentions, do, in the name and by the authority of the good people of these colonies, solemnly publish and declare, that these United Colonies are, and of right ought to be, FREE AND INDEPENDENT STATES; that they are absolved from all allegiance to the British crown, and that all political connection between them and the state of Great Britain is, and ought to be, totally dissolved; and that, as free and independent states, they have full power to levy war, conclude peace, contract alliances, establish commerce, and do all other acts and things which independent states may of right do. And for the support of this declaration, with a firm reliance on the protection of Divine Providence, we mutually pledge to each other our lives, our fortunes, and our sacred honor.

JOHN HANCOCK [*President*]
[*and fifty-five others*]

CONSTITUTION OF THE UNITED STATES OF AMERICA

PREAMBLE

We the people of the United States, in order to form a more perfect union, establish justice, insure domestic tranquility, provide for the common defense, promote the general welfare, and secure the blessings of liberty to ourselves and our posterity, do ordain and establish this CONSTITUTION for the United States of America.

ARTICLE I

Section 1. All legislative powers herein granted shall be vested in a Congress of the United States, which shall consist of a Senate and a House of Representatives.

Section 2. The House of Representatives shall be composed of members chosen every second year by the people of the several States, and the electors in each State shall have the qualifications requisite for electors of the most numerous branch of the State Legislature.

No person shall be a Representative who shall not have attained to the age of twenty-five years, and been seven years a citizen of the United States, and who shall not, when elected, be an inhabitant of that State in which he shall be chosen.

Representatives and direct taxes shall be apportioned among the several States which may be included within this Union, according to their respective numbers, *which shall be determined by adding to the whole number of free persons, including those bound to service for a term of years and excluding Indians not taxed, three-fifths of all other persons.* The actual enumeration shall be made within three years after the first meeting of the Congress of the United States, and within every subsequent term of ten years, in such manner as they shall by law direct. The number of Representatives shall not exceed one for every thirty thousand, but each State shall have at least one Representative; *and until such enumeration shall be made, the State of New Hampshire shall be entitled to choose three, Massachusetts eight, Rhode Island and Providence Plantations one, Connecticut five, New York six, New Jersey four, Pennsylvania eight, Delaware one, Maryland six, Virginia ten, North Carolina five, South Carolina five, and Georgia three.*

When vacancies happen in the representation from any State, the Executive authority thereof shall issue writs of election to fill such vacancies.

The House of Representatives shall choose their Speaker and other officers; and shall have the sole power of impeachment.

Section 3. The Senate of the United States shall be composed of two Senators from each State, *chosen by the legislature thereof,* for six years; and each Senator shall have one vote.

Immediately after they shall be assembled in consequence of the first election, they shall be divided as equally as may be into three classes. The seats of the Senators of the first class shall be vacated at the expiration of the second year, of the second class at the expiration of the fourth year, and of the third class at the expiration of the sixth year, so that one-third may be chosen every second year; and if vacancies happen by resignation or otherwise, during the recess of the legislature of any State, the Executive thereof may make temporary appointments until the next meeting of the legislature, which shall then fill such vacancies.

No person shall be a Senator who shall not have attained to the age of thirty years, and been nine years a citizen of the United States, and who shall not, when elected, be an inhabitant of that State for which he shall be chosen.

The Vice President of the United States shall be President of the Senate, but shall have no vote, unless they be equally divided.

Note: Passages no longer in effect are printed in italic type.

The Senate shall choose their other officers, and also a President *pro tempore,* in the absence of the Vice President, or when he shall exercise the office of the President of the United States.

The Senate shall have the sole power to try all impeachments. When sitting for that purpose, they shall be on oath or affirmation. When the President of the United States is tried, the Chief Justice shall preside: and no person shall be convicted without the concurrence of two-thirds of the members present.

Judgment in cases of impeachment shall not extend further than to removal from the office, and disqualification to hold and enjoy any office of honor, trust or profit under the United States; but the party convicted shall nevertheless be liable and subject to indictment, trial, judgment and punishment, according to law.

Section 4. The times, places and manner of holding elections for Senators and Representatives shall be prescribed in each State by the legislature thereof; but the Congress may at any time by law make or alter such regulations, except as to the places of choosing Senators.

The Congress shall assemble at least once in every year, and such meeting *shall be on the first Monday in December, unless they shall by law appoint a different day.*

Section 5. Each house shall be the judge of the elections, returns and qualifications of its own members, and a majority of each shall constitute a quorum to do business; but a smaller number may adjourn from day to day, and may be authorized to compel the attendance of absent members, in such manner, and under such penalties, as each house may provide.

Each house may determine the rules of its proceedings, punish its members for disorderly behavior, and with the concurrence of two-thirds, expel a member.

Each house shall keep a journal of its proceedings, and from time to time publish the same, excepting such parts as may in their judgment require secrecy; and the yeas and nays of the members of either house on any question shall, at the desire of one-fifth of those present, be entered on the journal.

Neither house, during the session of Congress, shall, without the consent of the other, adjourn for more than three days, nor to any other place than that in which the two houses shall be sitting.

Section 6. The Senators and Representatives shall receive a compensation for their services, to be ascertained by law and paid out of the treasury of the United States. They shall in all cases except treason, felony and breach of the peace, be privileged from arrest during their attendance at the session of their respective houses, and in going to and returning from the same; and for any speech or debate in either house, they shall not be questioned in any other place.

No Senator or Representative shall, during the time for which he was elected, be appointed to any civil office under the authority of the United States, which shall have been created, or the emoluments whereof shall have been increased, during such time; and no person holding any office under the United States shall be a member of either house during his continuance in office.

Section 7. All bills for raising revenue shall originate in the House of Representatives; but the Senate may propose or concur with amendments as on other bills.

Every bill which shall have passed the House of Representatives and the Senate, shall, before it become a law, be presented to the President of the United States; if he approve he shall sign it, but if not he shall return it with objections to that house in which it originated, who shall enter the objections at large on their journal, and proceed to reconsider it. If after such reconsideration two-thirds of that house shall agree to pass the bill, it shall be sent, together with the objections, to the other house, by which it shall likewise be reconsidered, and, if approved by two-thirds of that house, it shall become a law. But in all such cases the votes of both houses shall be determined by yeas and nays, and the names of the persons voting for and against the bill shall be entered on the journal of each house respectively. If any bill shall not be returned by the President within ten days (Sundays excepted) after it shall have been presented to him, the same shall be a law, in like manner as if he had signed it, unless the Congress by their adjournment prevent its return, in which case it shall not be a law.

Every order, resolution, or vote to which the concurrence of the Senate and House of Representatives may be necessary (except on a question of adjournment) shall be presented to the President of the United States; and before the same shall take effect, shall be approved by him, or being disapproved by him, shall be repassed by two-thirds of the Senate and House of Representatives, according to the rules and limitations prescribed in the case of a bill.

Section 8.   The Congress shall have power

To lay and collect taxes, duties, imposts, and excises, to pay the debts and provide for the common defense and general welfare of the United States; but all duties, imposts and excises shall be uniform throughout the United States;

To borrow money on the credit of the United States;

To regulate commerce with foreign nations, and among the several States, and with the Indian tribes;

To establish an uniform rule of naturalization, and uniform laws on the subject of bankruptcies throughout the United States;

To coin money, regulate the value thereof, and of foreign coin, and fix the standard of weights and measures;

To provide for the punishment of counterfeiting the securities and current coin of the United States;

To establish post offices and post roads;

To promote the progress of science and useful arts by securing for limited times to authors and inventors the exclusive right to their respective writings and discoveries;

To constitute tribunals inferior to the Supreme Court;

To define and punish piracies and felonies committed on the high seas and offenses against the law of nations;

To declare war, grant letters of marque and reprisal, and make rules concerning captures on land and water;

To raise and support armies, but no appropriation of money to that use shall be for a longer term than two years;

To provide and maintain a navy;

To make rules for the government and regulation of the land and naval forces;

To provide for calling forth the militia to execute the laws of the Union, suppress insurrections, and repel invasions;

To provide for organizing, arming, and disciplining the militia, and for governing such part of them as may be employed in the service of the United States, reserving to the States respectively the appointment of the officers, and the authority of training the militia according to the discipline prescribed by Congress;

To exercise exclusive legislation in all cases whatsoever, over such district (not exceeding ten miles square) as may, by cession of particular States, and the acceptance of Congress, become the seat of government of the United States, and to exercise like authority over all places purchased by the consent of the legislature of the State, in which the same shall be, for erection of forts, magazines, arsenals, dock-yards, and other needful buildings;—and

To make all laws which shall be necessary and proper for carrying into execution the foregoing powers, and all other powers vested by this Constitution in the government of the United States, or in any department or officer thereof.

Section 9.   *The migration or importation of such persons as any of the States now existing shall think proper to admit shall not be prohibited by the Congress prior to the year 1808; but a tax or duty may be imposed on such importation, not exceeding $10 for each person.*

The privilege of the writ of habeas corpus shall not be suspended, unless when in cases of rebellion or invasion the public safety may require it.

No bill of attainder or ex post facto law shall be passed.

No capitation, or other direct, tax shall be laid, unless in proportion to the census or enumeration herein before directed to be taken.

No tax or duty shall be laid on articles exported from any State.

No preference shall be given by any regulation of commerce or revenue to the ports of one State over those of another; nor shall vessels bound to, or from, one State, be obliged to enter, clear, or pay duties in another.

No money shall be drawn from the treasury, but in consequence of appropriations made by law; and a regular statement and account of the receipts and expenditures of all public money shall be published from time to time.

No title of nobility shall be granted by the United States: and no person holding any office of profit or trust under them, shall, without the consent of the Congress, accept of any present, emolument, office, or title, of any kind whatever, from any king, prince, or foreign state.

Section 10.   No State shall enter into any treaty, alliance, or confederation; grant letters of marque and reprisal; coin money; emit bills of credit; make anything but gold and silver coin a tender in payment of debts; pass any bill of attainder, ex post facto law, or law impairing the obligation of contracts, or grant any title of nobility.

No State shall, without the consent of Congress, lay any imposts or duties on imports or exports, except what may be absolutely necessary for executing its inspection laws: and the net produce of all duties and imposts, laid by any State on imports or exports, shall be for the use of the treasury of the United States; and all such laws shall be subject to the revision and control of the Congress.

No State shall, without the consent of Congress, lay any duty of tonnage, keep troops or ships of war in time of peace, enter into any agreement or compact with another State, or with a foreign power, or engage in war, unless actually invaded, or in such imminent danger as will not admit of delay.

ARTICLE II

Section 1.   The executive power shall be vested in a President of the United States of America. He shall hold his office during the term of four years, and, together with the Vice President, chosen for the same term, be elected as follows:

Each state shall appoint, in such manner as the legislature thereof may direct, a number of electors, equal to the whole number of Senators and Representatives to which the State may be entitled in the Congress; but no Senator or Representative, or person holding an office of trust or profit under the United States, shall be appointed an elector.

The electors shall meet in their respective States, and vote by ballot for two persons, of whom one at least shall not be an inhabitant of the same State with themselves. And they shall make a list of all the persons voted for, and of the number of votes for each; which list they shall sign and certify, and transmit sealed to the seat of government of the United States, directed to the President of the Senate. The President of the Senate shall, in the presence of the Senate and the House of Representatives, open all the certificates, and the votes shall then be counted. The person having the greatest number of votes shall be the President, if such number be a majority of the whole number of electors appointed; and if there be more than one who have such majority, and have an equal number of votes, then the House of Representatives shall immediately choose by ballot one of them for President; and if no person have a majority, then from the five highest on the list said house shall in like manner choose the President. But in choosing the President the votes shall be taken by States, the representation from each State having one vote; a quorum for this purpose shall consist of a member or members from two-thirds of the States, and a majority of all the States shall be necessary to a choice. In every case, after the choice of the President, the person having the greatest number of votes of the electors shall be the Vice President. But if there should remain two or more who have equal votes, the Senate shall choose from them by ballot the Vice President.

The Congress may determine the time of choosing the electors and the day on which they shall give their votes; which day shall be the same throughout the United States.

No person except a natural-born citizen, *or a citizen of the United States at the time of the adoption of this Constitution,* shall be eligible to the office of President; neither shall any person be eligible to that office who shall not have attained to the age of thirty-five years, and been fourteen years a resident within the United States.

In case of the removal of the President from office or of his death, resignation, or inability to discharge the powers and duties of the said office, the same shall devolve on the Vice President, and the Congress may by law provide for the case of removal, death, resignation, or inability, both of the President and Vice President, declaring what officer shall then act as President, and such officer shall act accordingly, until the disability be removed, or a President shall be elected.

The President shall, at stated times, receive for his services a compensation, which shall neither be increased nor diminished during the period for which he shall have been elected, and he shall not receive within that period any other emolument from the United States, or any of them.

Before he enter on the execution of his office, he shall take the following oath or affirmation:—"I do solemnly swear (or affirm) that I will faithfully execute the office of the President of the United States, and will to the best of my ability preserve, protect and defend the Constitution of the United States."

Section 2.   The President shall be commander in chief of the army and navy of the United States, and of the militia of the several States, when called into the actual service of the United States; he may require the opinion, in writing, of the principal officer in each of the executive departments, upon any subject relating to the duties of their respective offices, and he shall have power to grant reprieves and pardons for offenses against the United States, except in cases of impeachment.

He shall have power, by and with the advice and consent of the Senate, to make treaties, provided two-thirds of the Senators present concur; and he shall nominate, and by and with the advice and

consent of the Senate, shall appoint ambassadors, other public ministers and consuls, judges of the Supreme Court, and all other officers of the United States, whose appointments are not herein otherwise provided for, and which shall be established by law: but Congress may by law vest the appointment of such inferior officers, as they think proper, in the President alone, in the courts of law, or in the heads of departments.

The President shall have power to fill up all vacancies that may happen during the recess of the Senate, by granting commissions which shall expire at the end of their next session.

Section 3.   He shall from time to time give to the Congress information of the state of the Union, and recommend to their consideration such measures as he shall judge necessary and expedient; he may, on extraordinary occasions, convene both houses, or either of them, and in case of disagreement between them, with respect to the time of adjournment, he may adjourn them to such time as he shall think proper; he shall receive ambassadors and other public ministers; he shall take care that the laws be faithfully executed, and shall commission all the officers of the United States.

Section 4.   The President, Vice President and all civil officers of the United States shall be removed from office on impeachment for, and on conviction of, treason, bribery, or other high crimes and misdemeanors.

ARTICLE III

Section 1.   The judicial power of the United States shall be vested in one Supreme Court, and in such inferior courts as the Congress may from time to time ordain and establish. The judges, both of the Supreme and inferior courts, shall hold their offices during good behavior, and shall, at stated times, receive for their services a compensation which shall not be diminished during their continuance in office.

Section 2.   The judicial power shall extend to all cases, in law and equity, arising under this Constitution, the laws of the United States, and treaties made, or which shall be made, under their authority;—to all cases affecting ambassadors, other public ministers and consuls;—to all cases of admiralty and maritime jurisdiction;—to controversies to which the United States shall be a party;—to controversies between two or more States;—*between a State and citizens of another State;*—between citizens of different States;—between citizens of the same State claiming lands under grants of different States, and between a State, or the citizens thereof, and foreign states, citizens or subjects.

In all cases affecting ambassadors, other public ministers and consuls, and those in which a State shall be party, the Supreme Court shall have original jurisdiction. In all the other cases before mentioned, the Supreme Court shall have appellate jurisdiction, both as to law and fact, with such exceptions, and under such regulations, as the Congress shall make.

The trial of all crimes, except in cases of impeachment, shall be by jury; and such trial shall be held in the State where said crimes shall have been committed; but when not committed within any State, the trial shall be at such place or places as the Congress may by law have directed.

Section 3. Treason against the United States shall consist only in levying war against them, or in adhering to their enemies, giving them aid and comfort. No person shall be convicted of treason unless on the testimony of two witnesses to the same overt act, or on confession in open court.

The Congress shall have power to declare the punishment of treason, but no attainder of treason shall work corruption of blood, or forfeiture except during the life of the person attainted.

ARTICLE IV

Section 1. Full faith and credit shall be given in each State to the public acts, records, and judicial proceedings of every other State. And the Congress may by general laws prescribe the manner in which such acts, records, and proceedings shall be proved, and the effect thereof.

Section 2. The citizens of each State shall be entitled to all privileges and immunities of citizens in the several States.

A person charged in any State with treason, felony, or other crime, who shall flee from justice, and be found in another State, shall on demand of the executive authority of the State from which he fled, be delivered up, to be removed to the State having jurisdiction of the crime.

No person held to service or labor in one State, under the laws thereof, escaping into another, shall, in consequence of any law or regulation therein, be discharged from such service or labor, but shall be delivered up on claim of the party to whom such service or labor may be due.

Section 3. New States may be admitted by the Congress into this Union; but no new State shall be formed or erected within the jurisdiction of any other State; nor any State be formed by the junction of two or more States, or parts of States, without the consent of the legislatures of the States concerned as well as of the Congress.

The Congress shall have power to dispose of and make all needful rules and regulations respecting the territory or other property belonging to the United States; and nothing in this Constitution shall be so construed as to prejudice any claims of the United States, or of any particular State.

Section 4. The United States shall guarantee to every State in this Union a republican form of government, and shall protect each of them against invasion; and on application of the legislature, or of the executive (when the legislature cannot be convened); against domestic violence.

ARTICLE V

The Congress, whenever two-thirds of both houses shall deem it necessary, shall propose amendments to this Constitution, or, on the application of the legislatures of two-thirds of the several States, shall call a convention for proposing amendments, which, in either case, shall be valid to all intents and purposes, as part of this Constitution, when ratified by the legislatures of three-fourths of the several States, or by conventions in three-fourths thereof, as the one or the other mode of ratification may be proposed by the Congress; provided *that no amendments which may be made prior to the year one thousand eight hundred and eight shall in any manner affect the first and fourth clauses in the ninth section of the first article;* and that no State, without its consent, shall be deprived of its equal suffrage in the Senate.

ARTICLE VI

All debts contracted and engagements entered into, before the adoption of this Constitution, shall be as valid against the United States under this Constitution, as under the Confederation.

This Constitution, and the laws of the United States which shall be made in pursuance thereof; and all treaties made, or which shall be made, under the authority of the United States, shall be the supreme law of the land; and the judges in every State shall be bound thereby, anything in the Constitution or laws of any State to the contrary notwithstanding.

The Senators and Representatives before mentioned, and the members of the several State legislatures, and all executive and judicial officers, both of the United States and of the several States, shall be bound by oath or affirmation to support this Constitution; but no religious test shall ever be required as a qualification to any office or public trust under the United States.

ARTICLE VII

The ratification of the conventions of nine States shall be sufficient for the establishment of this Constitution between the States so ratifying the same.

Done in Convention by the unanimous consent of the States present, the seventeenth day of September in the year of our Lord one thousand seven hundred and eighty-seven and of the Independence of the United States of America the twelfth. In witness whereof we have hereunto subscribed our names.

[Signed by]
G° WASHINGTON
Presidt and Deputy from Virginia
[*and thirty-eight others*]

AMENDMENTS TO THE CONSTITUTION

AMENDMENT I*

Congress shall make no law respecting an establishment of religion, or prohibiting the free exercise thereof; or abridging the freedom of speech, or of the press; or the right of the people peaceably to assemble, and to petition the government for a redress of grievances.

AMENDMENT II

A well-regulated militia being necessary to the security of a free State, the right of the people to keep and bear arms shall not be infringed.

AMENDMENT III

No soldier shall, in time of peace, be quartered in any house without the consent of the owner, nor in time of war, but in a manner to be prescribed by law.

AMENDMENT IV

The right of the people to be secure in their persons, houses, papers, and effects, against unreasonable searches and seizures, shall not be violated, and no warrants shall issue but upon probable cause, supported by oath or affirmation, and particularly describing the place to be searched, and the persons or things to be seized.

* The first ten Amendments (Bill of Rights) were adopted in 1791.

AMENDMENT V

No person shall be held to answer for a capital, or otherwise infamous crime, unless on a presentment or indictment of a grand jury, except in cases arising in the land or naval forces, or in the militia, when in actual service in time of war or public danger; nor shall any person be subject for the same offense to be twice put in jeopardy of life or limb; nor shall be compelled in any criminal case to be a witness against himself, nor be deprived of life, liberty, or property, without due process of law; nor shall private property be taken for public use without just compensation.

AMENDMENT VI

In all criminal prosecutions, the accused shall enjoy the right to a speedy and public trial, by an impartial jury of the State and district wherein the crime shall have been committed, which district shall have been previously ascertained by law, and to be informed of the nature and cause of the accusation; to be confronted with the witnesses against him; to have compulsory process for obtaining witnesses in his favor, and to have the assistance of counsel for his defense.

AMENDMENT VII

In suits at common law, where the value in controversy shall exceed twenty dollars, the right of trial by jury shall be preserved, and no fact tried by a jury shall be otherwise reexamined in any court of the United States, than according to the rules of the common law.

AMENDMENT VIII

Excessive bail shall not be required, nor excessive fines imposed, nor cruel and unusual punishments inflicted.

AMENDMENT IX

The enumeration in the Constitution, of certain rights, shall not be construed to deny or disparage others retained by the people.

AMENDMENT X

The powers not delegated to the United States by the Constitution, not prohibited by it to the States, are reserved to the States respectively, or to the people.

AMENDMENT XI   [*Adopted 1798*]

The judicial power of the United States shall not be construed to extend to any suit in law or equity, commenced or prosecuted against one of the United States by citizens of another State, or by citizens or subjects of any foreign state.

AMENDMENT XII   [*Adopted 1804*]

The electors shall meet in their respective States, and vote by ballot for President and Vice President, one of whom, at least, shall not be an inhabitant of the same State with themselves; they shall name in their ballots the person voted for as President, and in distinct ballots the person voted for as Vice President, and they shall make distinct lists of all persons voted for as President, and of all persons voted for as Vice President, and of the number of votes for each, which lists they shall sign and certify, and transmit sealed to the seat of government of the United States, directed to the President of the Senate;—the President of the Senate shall, in the presence of the Senate and House of Representatives, open all the certificates and the votes shall then be counted;—the person having the greatest number of votes for President shall be the President, if such number be a majority of the whole number of electors appointed; and if no person have such majority, then from the persons having the highest numbers not exceeding three on the list of those voted for as President, the House of Representatives shall choose immediately, by ballot, the President. But in choosing the President, the votes shall be taken by States, the representation from each State having one vote; a quorum for this purpose shall consist of a member or members from two-thirds of the States, and a majority of all the States shall be necessary to a choice. And if the House of Representatives shall not choose a President whenever the right of choice shall devolve upon them, before *the fourth day of March* next following, then the Vice President shall act as President, as in the case of the death or other constitutional disability of the President.

The person having the greatest number of votes as Vice President shall be the Vice President, if such a number be a majority of the whole number of electors appointed; and if no person have a majority, then from the two highest numbers on the list the Senate shall choose the Vice President; a quorum for the purpose shall consist of two-thirds of the whole number of Senators, and a majority of the whole number shall be necessary to a choice. But no person constitutionally ineligible to the office of President shall be eligible to that of Vice President of the United States.

AMENDMENT XIII   [*Adopted 1865*]

Section 1.   Neither slavery nor involuntary servitude, except as a punishment for crime whereof the party shall have been duly convicted, shall exist within the United States, or any place subject to their jurisdiction.

Section 2.   Congress shall have power to enforce this article by appropriate legislation.

AMENDMENT XIV   [*Adopted 1868*]

Section 1.   All persons born or naturalized in the United States, and subject to the jurisdiction thereof, are citizens of the United States and of the State wherein they reside. No State shall make or enforce any law which shall abridge the privileges or immunities of citizens of the United States; nor shall any State deprive any person of life, liberty, or property, without due process of law; nor deny to any person within its jurisdiction the equal protection of the laws.

Section 2.   Representatives shall be apportioned among the several States according to their respective numbers, counting the whole number of persons in each State, excluding Indians not taxed. But when the right to vote at any election for the choice of Electors for President and Vice President of the United States, Representatives in Congress, the executive and judicial officers of a State, or the members of the legislature thereof, is denied to any of the male inhabitants of such State, being twenty-one years of age and citizens of the United States, or in any way abridged, except for participation in rebellion, or other crime, the basis of representation therein shall be reduced in the proportion which the number of such male citizens shall bear to the whole number of male citizens twenty-one years of age in such State.

Section 3.   No person shall be a Senator or Representative in Congress or Elector of President and Vice President, or hold any office, civil or military, under the United States, or under any State, who, having previously taken an oath, as a member of Congress, or as an officer of the United States, or as a member of any State legislature, or as an executive or judicial officer of any State, to support the Constitution of the United States, shall have engaged in insurrection or rebellion against the same, or given aid and comfort to the enemies thereof. Congress may, by a vote of two-thirds of each house, remove such disability.

Section 4.   The validity of the public debt of the United States, authorized by law, including debts incurred for payment of pensions and bounties for services in suppressing insurrection or rebellion, shall not be questioned. But neither the United States nor any State shall assume or pay any debt or obligation incurred in aid of insurrection or rebellion against the United States, or any claim for the loss or emancipation of any slave; but all such debts, obligations, and claims shall be held illegal and void.

Section 5.   The Congress shall have the power to enforce, by appropriate legislation, the provisions of this article.

AMENDMENT XV [*Adopted 1870*]

Section 1. The right of citizens of the United States to vote shall not be denied or abridged by the United States or by any State on account of race, color, or previous condition of servitude.

Section 2. The Congress shall have power to enforce this article by appropriate legislation.

AMENDMENT XVI [*Adopted 1913*]

The Congress shall have power to lay and collect taxes on incomes, from whatever source derived, without apportionment among the several States, and without regard to any census or enumeration.

AMENDMENT XVII [*Adopted 1913*]

Section 1. The Senate of the United States shall be composed of two Senators from each State, elected by the people thereof, for six years; and each Senator shall have one vote. The electors in each State shall have the qualifications requisite for electors of [voters for] the most numerous branch of the State legislatures.

Section 2. When vacancies happen in the representation of any State in the Senate, the executive authority of such State shall issue writs of election to fill such vacancies: Provided, that the Legislature of any State may empower the executive thereof to make temporary appointments until the people fill the vacancies by election as the Legislature may direct.

Section 3. This amendment shall not be so construed as to affect the election or term of any Senator chosen before it becomes valid as part of the Constitution.

AMENDMENT XVIII
[*Adopted 1919; repealed 1933*]

Section 1. *After one year from the ratification of this article the manufacture, sale, or transportation of intoxicating liquors within, the importation thereof into, or the exportation thereof from the United States and all territory subject to the jurisdiction thereof, for beverage purposes, is hereby prohibited.*

Section 2. *The Congress and the several States shall have concurrent power to enforce this article by appropriate legislation.*

Section 3. *This article shall be inoperative unless it shall have been ratified as an amendment to the Constitution by the legislatures of the several States, as provided by the Constitution, within seven years from the date of the submission thereof to the States by the Congress.*

AMENDMENT XIX [*Adopted 1920*]

Section 1. The right of citizens of the United States to vote shall not be denied or abridged by the United States or by any State on account of sex.

Section 2. The Congress shall have the power to enforce this article by appropriate legislation.

AMENDMENT XX [*Adopted 1933*]

Section 1. The terms of the President and Vice President shall end at noon on the 20th day of January, and the terms of Senators and Representatives at noon on the 3d day of January, of the years in which such terms would have ended if this article had not been ratified; and the terms of their successors shall then begin.

Section 2. The Congress shall assemble at least once in every year, and such meeting shall begin at noon on the 3d day of January, unless they shall by law appoint a different day.

Section 3. If, at the time fixed for the beginning of the term of the President, the President-elect shall have died, the Vice President-elect shall become President. If a President shall not have been chosen before the time fixed for the beginning of his term, or if the President-elect shall have failed to qualify, then the Vice President-elect shall act as President until a President shall have qualified; and the Congress may by law provide for the case wherein neither a President-elect nor a Vice President-elect shall have qualified, declaring who shall then act as President, or the manner in which one who is to act shall be selected, and such persons shall act accordingly until a President or Vice President shall have qualified.

Section 4.   The Congress may by law provide for the case of the death of any of the persons from whom the House of Representatives may choose a President whenever the right of choice shall have devolved upon them, and for the case of the death of any of the persons from whom the Senate may choose a Vice President whenever the right of choice shall have devolved upon them.

Section 5.   Sections 1 and 2 shall take effect on the 15th day of October following the ratification of this article.

Section 6.   This article shall be inoperative unless it shall have been ratified as an amendment to the Constitution by the Legislatures of three-fourths of the several States within seven years from the date of its submission.

AMENDMENT XXI   [*Adopted 1933*]

Section 1.   The eighteenth article of amendment to the Constitution of the United States is hereby repealed.

Section 2.   The transportation or importation into any State, Territory, or Possession of the United States for delivery or use therein of intoxicating liquors, in violation of the laws thereof, is hereby prohibited.

Section 3.   This article shall be inoperative unless it shall have been ratified as an amendment to the Constitution by conventions in the several States, as provided in the Constitution, within seven years from the date of submission thereof to the States by the Congress.

AMENDMENT XXII   [*Adopted 1951*]

Section 1.   No person shall be elected to the office of President more than twice, and no person who has held the office of President, or acted as President, for more than two years of a term to which some other person was elected President shall be elected to the office of President more than once. But this article shall not apply to any person holding the office of President when this article was proposed by the Congress, and shall not prevent any person who may be holding the office of President, or acting as President, during the term within which this article becomes operative from holding the office of President or acting as President during the remainder of such term.

Section 2.   This article shall be inoperative unless it shall have been ratified as an amendment to the Constitution by the legislatures of three-fourths of the several States within seven years from the date of its submission to the States by the Congress.

AMENDMENT XXIII   [*Adopted 1961*]

Section 1.   The District constituting the seat of Government of the United States shall appoint in such manner as the Congress may direct:

A number of electors of President and Vice President equal to the whole number of Senators and Representatives in Congress to which the District would be entitled if it were a State, but in no event more than the least populous State; they shall be in addition to those appointed by the States, but they shall be considered for the purposes of the election of President and Vice President, to be electors appointed by a State; and they shall meet in the District and perform such duties as provided by the twelfth article of amendment.

Section 2.   The Congress shall have the power to enforce this article by appropriate legislation.

AMENDMENT XXIV   [*Adopted 1964*]

Section 1.   The right of citizens of the United States to vote in any primary or other election for

President or Vice President, for electors for President or Vice President, or for Senator or Representative in Congress, shall not be denied or abridged by the United States or any State by reason of failure to pay any poll tax or other tax.

Section 2. The Congress shall have the power to enforce this article by appropriate legislation.

AMENDMENT XXV [Adopted 1967]

Section 1. In case of the removal of the President from office or of his death or resignation, the Vice President shall become President.

Section 2. Whenever there is a vacancy in the office of the Vice President, the President shall nominate a Vice President who shall take office upon confirmation by a majority vote of both Houses of Congress.

Section 3. Whenever the President transmits to the President pro tempore of the Senate and the Speaker of the House of Representatives his written declaration that he is unable to discharge the powers and duties of his office, and until he transmits to them a written declaration to the contrary, such powers and duties shall be discharged by the Vice President as Acting President.

Section 4. Whenever the Vice President and a majority of either the principal officers of the executive departments or of such other body as Congress may by law provide, transmit to the President pro tempore of the Senate and the Speaker of the House of Representatives their written declaration that the President is unable to discharge the powers and duties of his office, the Vice President shall immediately assume the powers and duties of the office as Acting President.

Thereafter, when the President transmits to the President pro tempore of the Senate and the Speaker of the House of Representatives his written declaration that no inability exists, he shall resume the powers and duties of his office unless the Vice President and a majority of either the principal officers of the executive department[s] or of such other body as Congress may by law provide,

transmit within four days to the President pro tempore of the Senate and the Speaker of the House of Representatives their written declaration that the President is unable to discharge the powers and duties of his office. Thereupon Congress shall decide the issue, assembling within forty-eight hours for that purpose if not in session. If the Congress, within twenty-one days after receipt of the latter written declaration, or, if Congress is not in session, within twenty-one days after Congress is required to assemble, determines by two-thirds vote of both Houses that the President is unable to discharge the powers and duties of his office, the Vice President shall continue to discharge the same as Acting President; otherwise, the President shall resume the powers and duties of his office.

AMENDMENT XXVI [Adopted 1971]

Section 1. The right of citizens of the United States, who are eighteen years of age or older, to vote shall not be denied or abridged by the United States or by any State on account of age.

Section 2. The Congress shall have power to enforce this article by appropriate legislation.

AMENDMENT XXVII* [Adopted 1992]

No law, varying the compensation for services of the Senators and Representatives, shall take effect, until an election of Representatives shall have intervened.

---

* Originally proposed in 1789 by James Madison, this amendment failed to win ratification along with the other parts of what became the Bill of Rights. However, the proposed amendment contained no deadline for ratification, and over the years other state legislatures voted to add it to the Constitution; many such ratifications occurred during the 1980s and early 1990s as public frustration with Congress's performance mounted. In May 1992 the Archivist of the United States certified that, with the Michigan legislature's ratification, the article had been approved by three-fourths of the states and thus automatically became part of the Constitution. But congressional leaders and constitutional specialists questioned whether an amendment that took 202 years to win ratification was valid, and the issue had not been resolved by the time this book went to press.

Presidential Elections, 1789–2004

Year	States in the Union	Candidates	Parties	Electoral Vote	Popular Vote	Percentage of Popular Vote
1789	11	GEORGE WASHINGTON	No party designations	69		
		John Adams		34		
		Minor candidates		35		
1792	15	GEORGE WASHINGTON	No party designations	132		
		John Adams		77		
		George Clinton		50		
		Minor candidates		5		
1796	16	JOHN ADAMS	Federalist	71		
		Thomas Jefferson	Democratic-Republican	68		
		Thomas Pinckney	Federalist	59		
		Aaron Burr	Democratic-Republican	30		
		Minor candidates		48		
1800	16	THOMAS JEFFERSON	Democratic-Republican	73		
		Aaron Burr	Democratic-Republican	73		
		John Adams	Federalist	65		
		Charles C. Pinckney	Federalist	64		
		John Jay	Federalist	1		
1804	17	THOMAS JEFFERSON	Democratic-Republican	162		
		Charles C. Pinckney	Federalist	14		
1808	17	JAMES MADISON	Democratic-Republican	122		
		Charles C. Pinckney	Federalist	47		
		George Clinton	Democratic-Republican	6		
1812	18	JAMES MADISON	Democratic-Republican	128		
		DeWitt Clinton	Federalist	89		
1816	19	JAMES MONROE	Democratic-Republican	183		
		Rufus King	Federalist	34		
1820	24	JAMES MONROE	Democratic-Republican	231		
		John Quincy Adams	Independent Republican	1		
1824	24	JOHN QUINCY ADAMS	Democratic-Republican	84	108,740	30.5
		Andrew Jackson	Democratic-Republican	99	153,544	43.1
		William H. Crawford	Democratic-Republican	41	46,618	13.1
		Henry Clay	Democratic-Republican	37	47,136	13.2
1828	24	ANDREW JACKSON	Democratic	178	642,553	56.0
		John Quincy Adams	National Republican	83	500,897	44.0
1832	24	ANDREW JACKSON	Democratic	219	687,502	55.0
		Henry Clay	National Republican	49	530,189	42.4
		William Wirt	Anti-Masonic	7	33,108	2.6
		John Floyd	National Republican	11		
1836	26	MARTIN VAN BUREN	Democratic	170	765,483	50.9
		William H. Harrison	Whig	73		
		Hugh L. White	Whig	26	739,795	49.1
		Daniel Webster	Whig	14		
		W. P. Mangum	Whig	11		

Because candidates receiving less than 1 percent of the popular vote are omitted, the percentage of popular vote may not total 100 percent.

Before the Twelfth Amendment was passed in 1804, the electoral college voted for two presidential candidates; the runner-up became vice president.

(cont.)

Year	States in the Union	Candidates	Parties	Electoral Vote	Popular Vote	Percentage of Popular Vote
1840	26	WILLIAM H. HARRISON	Whig	234	1,274,624	53.1
		Martin Van Buren	Democratic	60	1,127,781	46.9
1844	26	JAMES K. POLK	Democratic	170	1,338,464	49.6
		Henry Clay	Whig	105	1,300,097	48.1
		James G. Birney	Liberty		62,300	2.3
1848	30	ZACHARY TAYLOR	Whig	163	1,360,967	47.4
		Lewis Cass	Democratic	127	1,222,342	42.5
		Martin Van Buren	Free Soil		291,263	10.1
1852	31	FRANKLIN PIERCE	Democratic	254	1,601,117	50.9
		Winfield Scott	Whig	42	1,385,453	44.1
		John P. Hale	Free Soil		155,825	5.0
1856	31	JAMES BUCHANAN	Democratic	174	1,832,955	45.3
		John C. Frémont	Republican	114	1,339,932	33.1
		Millard Fillmore	American	8	871,731	21.6
1860	33	ABRAHAM LINCOLN	Republican	180	1,865,593	39.8
		Stephen A. Douglas	Democratic	12	1,382,713	29.5
		John C. Breckinridge	Democratic	72	848,356	18.1
		John Bell	Constitutional Union	39	592,906	12.6
1864	36	ABRAHAM LINCOLN	Republican	212	2,206,938	55.0
		George B. McClellan	Democratic	21	1,803,787	45.0
1868	37	ULYSSES S. GRANT	Republican	214	3,013,421	52.7
		Horatio Seymour	Democratic	80	2,706,829	47.3
1872	37	ULYSSES S. GRANT	Republican	286	3,596,745	55.6
		Horace Greeley	Democratic	*	2,843,446	43.9
1876	38	RUTHERFORD B. HAYES	Republican	185	4,034,311	48.0
		Samuel J. Tilden	Democratic	184	4,288,546	51.0
		Peter Cooper	Greenback		75,973	1.0
1880	38	JAMES A. GARFIELD	Republican	214	4,453,295	48.5
		Winfield S. Hancock	Democratic	155	4,414,082	48.1
		James B. Weaver	Greenback-Labor		308,578	3.4
1884	38	GROVER CLEVELAND	Democratic	219	4,879,507	48.5
		James G. Blaine	Republican	182	4,850,293	48.2
		Benjamin F. Butler	Greenback-Labor		175,370	1.8
		John P. St. John	Prohibition		150,369	1.5
1888	38	BENJAMIN HARRISON	Republican	233	5,477,129	47.9
		Grover Cleveland	Democratic	168	5,537,857	48.6
		Clinton B. Fisk	Prohibition		249,506	2.2
		Anson J. Streeter	Union Labor		146,935	1.3
1892	44	GROVER CLEVELAND	Democratic	277	5,555,426	46.1
		Benjamin Harrison	Republican	145	5,182,690	43.0
		James B. Weaver	People's	22	1,029,846	8.5
		John Bidwell	Prohibition		264,133	2.2
1896	45	WILLIAM MCKINLEY	Republican	271	7,102,246	51.1
		William J. Bryan	Democratic	176	6,492,559	47.7

*When Greeley died shortly after the election, his supporters divided their votes among the minor candidates.
Because candidates receiving less than 1 percent of the popular vote are omitted, the percentage of popular vote may not total 100 percent.

(cont.)

Year	States in the Union	Candidates	Parties	Electoral Vote	Popular Vote	Percentage of Popular Vote
1900	45	WILLIAM MCKINLEY	Republican	292	7,218,491	51.7
		William J. Bryan	Democratic; Populist	155	6,356,734	45.5
		John C. Wooley	Prohibition		208,914	1.5
1904	45	THEODORE ROOSEVELT	Republican	336	7,628,461	57.4
		Alton B. Parker	Democratic	140	5,084,223	37.6
		Eugene V. Debs	Socialist		402,283	3.0
		Silas C. Swallow	Prohibition		258,536	1.9
1908	46	WILLIAM H. TAFT	Republican	321	7,675,320	51.6
		William J. Bryan	Democratic	162	6,412,294	43.1
		Eugene V. Debs	Socialist		420,793	2.8
		Eugene W. Chafin	Prohibition		253,840	1.7
1912	48	WOODROW WILSON	Democratic	435	6,296,547	41.9
		Theodore Roosevelt	Progressive	88	4,118,571	27.4
		William H. Taft	Republican	8	3,486,720	23.2
		Eugene V. Debs	Socialist		900,672	6.0
		Eugene W. Chafin	Prohibition		206,275	1.4
1916	48	WOODROW WILSON	Democratic	277	9,127,695	49.4
		Charles E. Hughes	Republican	254	8,533,507	46.2
		A. L. Benson	Socialist		585,113	3.2
		J. Frank Hanly	Prohibition		220,506	1.2
1920	48	WARREN G. HARDING	Republican	404	16,143,407	60.4
		James N. Cox	Democratic	127	9,130,328	34.2
		Eugene V. Debs	Socialist		919,799	3.4
		P. P. Christensen	Farmer-Labor		265,411	1.0
1924	48	CALVIN COOLIDGE	Republican	382	15,718,211	54.0
		John W. Davis	Democratic	136	8,385,283	28.8
		Robert M. La Follette	Progressive	13	4,831,289	16.6
1928	48	HERBERT C. HOOVER	Republican	444	21,391,993	58.2
		Alfred E. Smith	Democratic	87	15,016,169	40.9
1932	48	FRANKLIN D. ROOSEVELT	Democratic	472	22,809,638	57.4
		Herbert C. Hoover	Republican	59	15,758,901	39.7
		Norman Thomas	Socialist		881,951	2.2
1936	48	FRANKLIN D. ROOSEVELT	Democratic	523	27,752,869	60.8
		Alfred M. Landon	Republican	8	16,674,665	36.5
		William Lemke	Union		882,479	1.9
1940	48	FRANKLIN D. ROOSEVELT	Democratic	449	27,307,819	54.8
		Wendell L. Willkie	Republican	82	22,321,018	44.8
1944	48	FRANKLIN D. ROOSEVELT	Democratic	432	25,606,585	53.5
		Thomas E. Dewey	Republican	99	22,014,745	46.0
1948	48	HARRY S TRUMAN	Democratic	303	24,105,812	49.5
		Thomas E. Dewey	Republican	189	21,970,065	45.1
		Strom Thurmond	States' Rights	39	1,169,063	2.4
		Henry A. Wallace	Progressive		1,157,172	2.4

Because candidates receiving less than 1 percent of the popular vote are omitted, the percentage of popular vote may not total 100 percent.

(cont.)

Year	States in the Union	Candidates	Parties	Electoral Vote	Popular Vote	Percentage of Popular Vote
1952	48	DWIGHT D. EISENHOWER	Republican	442	33,936,234	55.1
		Adlai E. Stevenson	Democratic	89	27,314,992	44.4
1956	48	DWIGHT D. EISENHOWER	Republican	457	35,590,472	57.6
		Adlai E. Stevenson	Democratic	73	26,022,752	42.1
1960	50	JOHN F. KENNEDY	Democratic	303	34,227,096	49.7
		Richard M. Nixon	Republican	219	34,108,546	49.5
		Harry F. Byrd	Independent	15	502,363	.7
1964	50	LYNDON B. JOHNSON	Democratic	486	43,126,506	61.1
		Barry M. Goldwater	Republican	52	27,176,799	38.5
1968	50	RICHARD M. NIXON	Republican	301	31,770,237	43.4
		Hubert H. Humphrey	Democratic	191	31,270,533	42.7
		George C. Wallace	American Independent	46	9,906,141	13.5
1972	50	RICHARD M. NIXON	Republican	520	47,169,911	60.7
		George S. McGovern	Democratic	17	29,170,383	37.5
1976	50	JIMMY CARTER	Democratic	297	40,827,394	49.9
		Gerald R. Ford	Republican	240	39,145,977	47.9
1980	50	RONALD W. REAGAN	Republican	489	43,899,248	50.8
		Jimmy Carter	Democratic	49	35,481,435	41.0
		John B. Anderson	Independent		5,719,437	6.6
		Ed Clark	Libertarian		920,859	1.0
1984	50	RONALD W. REAGAN	Republican	525	54,451,521	58.8
		Walter F. Mondale	Democratic	13	37,565,334	40.5
1988	50	GEORGE H. W. BUSH	Republican	426	47,946,422	54.0
		Michael S. Dukakis	Democratic	112	41,016,429	46.0
1992	50	WILLIAM J. CLINTON	Democratic	370	43,728,275	43.2
		George H. W. Bush	Republican	168	38,167,416	37.7
		H. Ross Perot	Independent		19,237,247	19.0
1996	50	WILLIAM J. CLINTON	Democratic	379	47,401,185	49.2
		Robert Dole	Republican	159	39,197,469	40.7
		H. Ross Perot	Reform		8,085,294	8.4
2000	50	GEORGE W. BUSH	Republican	271	50,456,141	47.9
		Albert Gore Jr.	Democratic	266	50,996,039	48.4
		Ralph Nader	Green		2,882,807	2.7
2004	50	GEORGE W. BUSH	Republican	286	60,608,582	51.0
		John Kerry	Democratic	252	57,288,974	48.0
		Ralph Nader	Independent		406,924	1.0

Because candidates receiving less than 1 percent of the popular vote are omitted, the percentage of popular vote may not total 100 percent.

Photograph Credits

Chapter 16   *p. 320*, The William Gladstone Collection; *p. 323, Harper's Weekly,* 1866; *p. 330,* © Bettmann/Corbis; *p. 332,* The William Gladstone Collection.

Chapter 17   *p. 344,* National Anthropological Archives, neg. 3238E, National Museum of Natural History, Smithsonian Institution, Washington D.C.; *p. 346,* Courtesy of the Burton Historical Collection, Detroit Public Library; *p. 352,* Courtesy of the Burton Historical Collection, Detroit Public Library; *p. 357,* painting by Francis X. Grosshenney, Courtesy Museum of New Mexico, Neg. 37916; *p. 363,* Smithsonian American Art Museum, Washington, D.C./Art Resource, New York.

Chapter 18   *p. 366,* Chicago Historical Society, ICHi-06185; *p. 368,* Hagley Museum and Library; *p. 373,* National Park Service: Edison National Historic Site; *p. 375,* Courtesy of the Boston Public Library, Print Department; *p. 379,* Library of Congress; *p. 382,* Library of Congress.

Chapter 19   *p. 388,* George Eastman House; *p. 391,* National Park Service: Statue of Liberty National Monument; *p. 395,* The Granger Collection, New York; *p. 396,* Copyright © John Grossman, The John Grossman Collection of Antique Images; *p. 397, Harper's Weekly,* 1871; *p. 400,* Chicago Historical Society, ICHi-03808; *p. 402,* from the Collections of the Henry Ford Museum and Greenfield Village; *p. 405,* North Wind Picture Archives.

Chapter 20   *p. 412,* Frank and Marie-Therese Wood Print Collections, Alexandria, Virginia; *p. 415,* Chicago Historical Society, ICHi-29985; *p. 427,* National Museum of American History, Smithsonian Institution, Behring Center.

Chapter 21   *p. 435,* Picture Research Consultants and Archives; *p. 437,* Courtesy MetLife Archives; *p. 442,* Chicago Historical Society, G1959.217; *p. 448,* Library of Congress; *p. 454,* Library of Congress.

Chapter 22   *p. 461,* © Bettmann/Corbis; *p. 463,* U.S. Signal Corps Photo/National Archives; *p. 465,* The Granger Collection, New York; *p. 467,* (music sheet) Culver Pictures; (photo insert) © Bettmann/Corbis; *p. 473,* U.S. Army Military History Institute.

Chapter 23   *p. 484,* Chicago Historical Society, ICHi-06704; *p. 492,* Courtesy of the Strong Museum, Rochester, New York, copyright © 2005; *p. 494,* National Archives; *p. 501,* Library of Congress.

Chapter 24   *p. 507,* Library of Congress; *p. 512,* © Bettmann/Corbis; *p. 522,* Library of Congress; *p. 524,* Library of Congress; *p. 528,* Archives of Labor and Urban Affairs/Wayne State University.

Chapter 25   *p. 535,* W. Eugene Smith/Time-Life Pictures/Getty Images; *539,* Thomas McAvoy/Time-Life Pictures/Getty Images; *p. 552,* National Archives; *p. 557,* U.S. Army/Franklin D. Roosevelt Library; *559,* National Archives.

Chapter 26   *p. 562,* Edenhurst Gallery, Los Angeles, California; *p. 566,* © Bettmann/Corbis; *p. 572,* © Bettmann/Corbis; *p. 575,* Hy Peskin/Time-Life Pictures/Getty Images; *p. 578,* The Michael Barson Collection.

Chapter 27   *p. 583,* printed by permission of The Norman Rockwell Family Agency, Copyright © 1959 The Norman Rockwell Family Entities; *p. 587,* AP/Wide World Photos; *p. 593,* © 1992 Cindy Lewis: ALL RIGHTS RESERVED; *p. 598,* Chicago Historical Society, ICHi-00809.

Chapter 28   *p. 604,* Dan Budnick/Woodfin Camp and Associates; *p. 613,* AP/Wide World Photos; *p. 616,* © Bettmann/Corbis; *p. 618,* Photo Copyright © Prigoff/Dunitz, *Painting the Towns;* *p. 621,* © Bettmann/Corbis.

Chapter 29   *p. 625,* AP/Wide World Photos; *p. 629,* John Filo/Getty Images; *p. 637,* Wally McNamee/Woodfin Camp and Associates; *p. 639,* NASA/Johnson Space Center; *p. 642,* Cartoon News International.

Chapter 30   *p. 647,* Pat Sullivan/AP-Wide World Photos; *p. 657,* Sipa Press; *p. 666,* AP/Wide World Photos.

Chapter 31   *p. 669,* Seth Resnick/Stock, Boston; *p. 673,* Bruno Barbey/Magnum Photos; *p. 675,* © Bettmann/Corbis; *p. 683,* M. Almeida/The New York Times.

Chapter 32   *p. 688,* Steve Liss/Time-Life Pictures/Getty Images; *p. 700,* John Dominis/Time-Life Pictures/Getty Images; *p. 705,* Don Tellock/Gamma Presse USA, Inc.; *p. 710,* U.S. Department of Defense photo; *p. 713,* © Chip East/Reuters/Corbis.

Index

Mann, Horace, 408
Mann Act (1910), 444
Mann-Elkins Act (1910), 455
Man Nobody Knows, The (Barton), 487
Mansion, The (Faulkner), 596
Manson, Charles, 630
Manufacturers' associations, 488
Manufacturing, 367, 486, 683, 714; custom production, 373–374; factory system of, 378; mergers in (1895–1910), 371; prices in, 419; tariffs and, 418; vertical integration in, 370. *See also* Industry and industrialization
Mao Zedong, 571, 589, 620, 636
Marcos, Ferdinand, 637
Marianas, in World War II, 549
Marijuana, 630
Marines Battling for Seoul, 572 (photo)
Marketing, 374. *See also* Advertising
Marriage, 650; African-American, 332; gays and, 699–700; interracial, 334; Mormon polygyny, 356; New Woman and, 408, 437; 1930s, 526; 1950s domesticity and, 595; sexual revolution and, 631; World War II and, 553. *See also* Divorce
Marsh, George Perkins, 363
Marshall, George C., 568
Marshall, Robert, 521
Marshall, Thurgood, 611, 675
Marshall Islands, 571
Marshall Plan for Europe, 569
Martin, Bradley, 424
Marx, Karl, 385, 451
Marx Brothers, 530
Marxism, 472. *See also* Communism
Mashantucket Pequot Indians, 682
Massachusetts: gay marriage in, 699–700; Sacco-Vanzetti case in, 499–500
Mass culture, 697; entertainment, 492–493; in 1920s, 491–494. *See also* Popular culture
Masses magazine, 451
Mass media, 492–493, 494, 684; violence and, 681. *See also* Movies; Television; Radio
Mass production, 370, 371, 374, 486; World War I and, 470
Mayagüez incident, 655
Meat Inspection Act (1906), 453
Mechanization: of agriculture, 355; of manufacturing, 378
Media. *See* Mass media
Medicaid, 611, 651, 677
Medicare, 611, 677; reform of, 714–715
Medicine: education in, 396; patent nostrums, 453; 1920s, 498; work hazards and, 442; World War II, 546. *See also* Disease
Medicine Lodge Creek, Treaty of, 347
Meese, Edwin, 665
"Me Generation," 648

Mellon, Andrew, 488, 509
Memphis, race riot in, 329
Men: boxing and, 401–402; male chauvinism, 619; masculinity, 414. *See also* Gender
Mencken, H. L., 496
Menlo Park Laboratories (New Jersey), 372–373
Mennonites, 353
Menominee Indians, 600
Merchants: advertising by, 394; and sharecroppers, 336; in South, 376. *See also* Retailing
Meredith, James, 612
Mergers. *See* Consolidation and mergers
Metropolitan Life Insurance Company, 437
Meuse-Argonne campaign, 470 (map), 472
Meuse River, Battle at, 472
Mexican-Americans, 599; in California, 499; as cowboys, 360; culture of, 493; in Los Angeles, 392; in Southwest, 356–358, 600, 654; in urban *barrios,* 357, 529, 597, 600; World War II and, 555. *See also* Hispanics
Mexico, 490; *bracero* program, 555, 599; immigration from, 654, 714; NAFTA and, 677; oil nationalization in, 536; peso collapse in, 697; U.S. intervention in, 465–466; Zimmermann telegram and, 469
Michigan, welfare cuts in, 674
Middle class, 496, 674, 677, 678; diversity and, 686; feminism and, 619; higher education and, 395; as homesteaders, 354; poor and, 398–399; Progressivism and, 436, 438; reform and, 389, 404, 408; society and culture of, 393–396, 406; suburbs and, 393; tax credits for, 679; urban, 437; women, 393, 394–395, 407, 408, 436, 447; World War II and, 545
Middle East, 692–694; anti-communism and, 589–590; Arab-Israeli conflicts in, 637, 657, 662–663, 665–666, 692–694, 711–712; crisis (1980–2004), 693 (map); oil wealth of, 589, 663, 673; trusteeships in, 479. *See also specific country*
Midway, Battle of, 549, 550 (map)
Midwest (U.S.): New Deal and, 520; wheat in, 419. *See also* Great Plains
Migration: of African-Americans, 376, 423, 446, 476, 554; by free blacks, emancipation and, 321, 332, 341; rural-to-urban, 376, 390; suburban in 1950s, 594; World War II labor, 551. *See also* Immigrants and immigration
Militants and militancy: Black Panthers, 616; Islamic, 689, 706–707; Native American, 617, 653; Nixon and, 541
Military: Cold War buildup, 571–572, 574, 607, 663–664; and college programs,

553; gays and lesbians in, 555–556, 677; Iraq occupation and, 714; preparation for World War II, 539–540; universities and, 601, 627. *See also* Armed forces
Military districts, Reconstruction, 331 (map)
Military-industrial complex, 544, 590
Military tribunals, 707–708
Miller, Glen, 532
Milosevic, Slobodan, 692
Milwaukee, Germans in, 392
Milwaukee Leader, 475
Minimum wage, 523, 524, 525, 577
Mining and minerals: frontier, 358–359; mergers in (1895–1910), 371. *See also specific metals*
Minnesota, 354
Minorities: in California, 357. *See also* Ethnic groups; *specific minority*
Minor v. Happerset, 332
Miranda v. Arizona, 611
Missile crisis, in Cuba, 608
Missiles, 601, 636, 701
Mississippi, 340; black voters in, 421–422
Mississippi Freedom Democratic party (MFDP), 614
Mississippi Freedom Summer Project (1964), 614, 627
Mississippi River, flooding on, 489, 504, 530
Mitchell, John, 643
Mitchell, Margaret, 532
Mithelstadt, Jakob, and family, 391
Mobility: automobile and, 488; economic, 380–381. *See also* Migration
Mobilization: for World War I, 469–470; for World War II, 543–547
Mob violence, 422. *See also* Lynching; Vigilantism
Model T Ford (car), 485
Modernism, in art and architecture, 406
Modernization, 695
Molotov, V. M., 558
Mondale, Walter, 664
Monetary regulation, 415–416, 457, 641. *See also* Gold standard; Paper money
Monopolies, 369, 452. *See also* Consolidation and mergers; Trusts
Monroe Doctrine, 429, 464
Montgomery bus boycott, 598–599
Moon landing, 606–607, 638, 639
Morality, 393–394, 407, 409; business, 713; in cities, 443–444; middle-class, 398
Moral Majority, 652, 659
Moral-purity campaign, 399
Moran, Thomas, 363
Morgan, J. Pierpont, 369, 373, 399, 425, 427, 455; U.S. Steel and, 370, 440, 452
Morgenthau, Henry, Jr., 512
Mormons, 356
Morrison, Toni, 498
Morton, Jelly Roll, 497